Human rights and societies in transition

Human rights and societies in transition: Causes, consequences, responses

Edited by Shale Horowitz and Albrecht Schnabel

United Nations
University Press

TOKYO · NEW YORK · PARIS

© United Nations University, 2004

The views expressed in this publication are those of the authors and do not necessarily reflect the views of the United Nations University.

United Nations University Press
United Nations University, 53-70, Jingumae 5-chome,
Shibuya-ku, Tokyo, 150-8925, Japan
Tel: +81-3-3499-2811   Fax: +81-3-3406-7345
E-mail: sales@hq.unu.edu   general enquiries: press@hq.unu.edu
http://www.unu.edu

United Nations University Office at the United Nations, New York
2 United Nations Plaza, Room DC2-2062, New York, NY 10017, USA
Tel: +1-212-963-6387   Fax: +1-212-371-9454
E-mail: unuona@ony.unu.edu

United Nations University Press is the publishing division of the United Nations University.

Cover design by Sese-Paul Design

Printed in the United States of America

UNUP-1092
ISBN 92-808-1092-8

Library of Congress Cataloging-in-Publication Data

Human rights and societies in transition : causes, consequences, responses /
edited by Shale Horowitz and Albrecht Schnabel.
   p.   cm.
Includes bibliographical references and index.
ISBN 9280810928 (pbk.)
1. Human rights. 2. Human rights—Case studies. I. Horowitz, Shale Asher.
II. Schnabel, Albrecht.
JC571.H86   2004
323–dc22   2004004113

To our families

Contents

vii

Figures and tables

Note on measurements

In this volume:

1 billion	= one thousand million
1 trillion	= one million million
$1	= 1 US dollar

Acknowledgements

A number of individuals and organizations have provided invaluable assistance and support at various stages of this book project.

First of all, we are grateful to the Japanese government and the United Nations University for providing most of the funding for our work. We thank Patrice Petro and the Center for International Education, Richard Meadows and the College of Letters and Science, and Charles Kroncke and the School of Business Administration for additional funding and for hosting a most stimulating author meeting in early 2000 at the University of Wisconsin-Milwaukee. We deeply appreciate the logistical and administrative assistance offered for the entire duration of this project by Yoshie Sawada of the Peace and Governance Programme of the United Nations University. We are grateful to Monica Blagescu and Alina Meyer for logistical and editorial assistance in the preparation of the manuscript. We thank the UNU Press, particularly Gareth Johnston, for patiently supporting us in preparing and improving the manuscript for publication. We are grateful to two anonymous peer reviewers, whose comments allowed us to make important improvements to the initial draft manuscript; and we greatly appreciate the work of Heather Russell, who has copy-edited the volume, and of Sylvia Coates who has produced a most useful index. We would not have been in a position to work on this project for over three years, were it not for the support and encouragement of our families. It is to them that we dedicate this volume.

Finally, we thank our contributors for sharing their insights with us and the readers of this volume. We hope that, as a team, we have produced a useful examination of the challenges inherent in the advancement of human rights in societies faced with the difficulties inherent in political, economic, and socio-cultural transition. We hope that the discussions and findings presented in this volume will be of interest to both academics and practitioners involved in enhancing our conceptual understanding and in improving conditions on the ground.

Shale Horowitz
Albrecht Schnabel
August 2003

Introduction

1

Human rights and societies in transition: International context and sources of variation

Shale Horowitz and Albrecht Schnabel

Human rights violations are often particularly severe in transition societies that are undergoing significant political, social, and economic transformation.[1] Improving human rights practices in transition societies should therefore be a central goal for domestic reformers and the international community alike. This makes sense, not only because of the intrinsic value of improved human rights protection but also because of the indirect effects that such improvements have on democratization, economic development, and conflict resolution.

To address transitional human rights problems constructively it is necessary to understand both the international regime pushing for human rights improvements and the main sources of continuing violations. The international human rights regime consists of international and domestic norms and standards, on the one hand, and of practical promotion efforts by intergovernmental organizations (IGOs), non-governmental organizations (NGOs), and sovereign state policies, on the other. The main sources of continuing violations are hypothesized to be political regime type and political leadership, political cultures and national identities, economic structures and interests, and civil and international military conflict. Transitional human rights violations are common because the international and domestic factors favouring improved human rights are so often overwhelmed by international and domestic factors favouring continued violations. In future, more constructive efforts to promote transitional human rights should focus on building up the most promising favourable factors and targeting the most readily changed unfavourable ones.

This book represents a joint effort by 17 scholars from various parts of the world – specializing in political science, sociology, law, and diverse regional studies – to explore the contemporary international human rights regime, the factors predominantly responsible for human rights violations in transition societies, and the long-term consequences of such violations. The volume also tries to identify how NGOs, IGOs, and states can most constructively act to pre-empt or correct transition-related human rights violations and prevent the relapse of these societies into government failure, economic devastation, communal violence, and, eventually, war.

This introductory chapter begins by summarizing the main elements of the international human rights regime. It then sets out some basic hypotheses on important sources of transitional human rights practices. Next, it discusses some tentative findings concerning the sources of human rights practices, and explores some preliminary implications (a more detailed discussion of findings and recommendations is left to the concluding chapter). The final section describes the organization of the volume and summarizes the contents and findings of the individual chapters.

The international human rights regime

Today's international human rights regime consists of an accumulating body of internationally accepted norms and legal instruments, along with efforts by IGOs, NGOs, and national governments to promote improved human rights practices. The post-World War II foundation for the international human rights regime is the 1948 Universal Declaration of Human Rights (UDHR). The UDHR went beyond the traditional civil rights focus to embrace political rights and economic, social, and cultural rights. This set the precedent followed by a long stream of subsequent human rights conventions and resolutions. These provided more detailed statements of recognized civil, political, economic, social, and cultural rights and expanded human rights protection into new areas (such as various group rights).[2]

Unfortunately, the process of abstract standard setting has made more rapid progress than efforts to legitimize and enforce the standards in practice. Practical efforts by IGOs and governments have been limited by two main factors. First, the principle of non-intervention in the internal affairs of states is given great prominence in the UN Charter. Most states view this principle as the most important legal guarantee of their sovereignty against intrusions by other, more powerful states and the objectives and ideologies that animate them. A second, similar, constraint operates from the direction of states and societies that more strongly embrace human rights standards, both for themselves and for others. On the one hand, such states are more likely to link an ideological embrace of human rights with the complementary pragmatic view that expanding human rights protection is in their national security and economic interests. Moreover, such states are most likely to harbour well-organized and well-financed human rights NGOs. On the other hand, states' pursuit of their security and economic interests also tends to constrain their promotion of human rights, particularly *vis-à-vis* the most powerful and important human rights-violating regimes. Both non-intervention norms and limited interest in intervention explain the highly selective manner in which the relevant UN bodies recognize and condemn human rights violations.[3]

Human rights NGOs and their individual and organizational supporters are the final component of the international human rights regime. NGOs are largely unconstrained by national interests. Although they have their own ideological biases, competition among them produces a large and relatively objective stream of information about human rights practices around the world. Just as importantly, NGOs are engaged in ongoing efforts to popularize and advance the whole panoply of human rights causes around the world. These informational and advocacy functions can potentially have significant impacts on élite and public opinion, fertilizing and organizing local human rights traditions and movements to the point where they become prominent and influential in domestic culture and politics. This slow, decentralized process of building human rights awareness through local contacts is probably the international human rights regime's most powerful and consistent force for positive change.[4]

Yet human rights NGOs and their supporters are strongly constrained by local conditions. Most importantly, ruling regimes may impose strong restrictions against organized human rights advocacy, to the point of imposing arbitrary, draconian punishments on all those who try. There are also other types of barriers. On the basis of past national and local experiences, human rights NGOs may be associated with undesirable imposition of alien standards and policies; furthermore, even when the will is there, more pressing problems and threats – such as poverty, economic instability, and civil conflict – necessarily limit locally available audiences and resources.

Sources of transitional human rights practices

Our study focuses on four main factors that seem likely to influence human rights practices: political regime type and leadership; political culture and national identity; economic structure and interests; and civil and international conflict. These factors can have a significant impact both alone and in combination with one another. Apart from the direct effects of the factors operating separately, two types of interactive effects seem particularly likely: authoritarian political regimes are more likely to adopt informational and cultural policies, economic policies, and conflict-related policies that threaten human rights; second, civil and international conflict is likely to destabilize democracies and make authoritarianisms more repressive, which, as discussed, is likely to produce more unfavourable informational and cultural policies, economic policies, and conflict-related policies.

Let us now return in more detail to these four factors and their impact on human rights conditions. First, significant progress towards full democratization is usually associated with greater progress towards respect for human rights generally. In contrast, authoritarian regimes are more likely to employ various kinds of human rights abuses to forestall challenges to their political power.[5]

Full democratization necessarily involves free expression, freedom of the press, and freedom of association for political purposes and organizations, as well as free and fair elections to the positions of real political power. A free political process usually incorporates an array of legal and institutional human rights protections and facilitates mobilization for human rights improvements through the political process. More well-institutionalized and widely legitimate democratic processes are thus typically associated with stronger human rights protection. Of course, the association is far from perfect: extensive political freedom may exist alongside severe restriction of other human rights. For example, arbitrary and corrupt use of police and judicial powers might be significant, but not typically directed at political targets. There might be significant restriction of economic opportunities of individuals and groups, but these might affect people of all political persuasions more or less equally. Traditional forms of discrimination may flourish in the larger society, and political efforts to stop them and to remedy their effects may be intermittent and often ineffective.

However, the situation for other human rights is likely to be worse if political rights and freedoms are weak or non-existent. Authoritarian regimes and leaders typically use their discretionary power to attack and weaken their political opponents and to prevent new opposition from arising. This strategy usually goes beyond action against political freedoms proper: authoritarian regimes are more likely to try to monopolize control of the mass media and other "informational" institutions, particularly the educational system and religious institutions. This control will be used to shut out opposition voices, including human rights advocates. At the same time, the regime will argue that local traditions and historical experiences justify its own practices and that they are threatened by the supposedly "alien" demands of the opposition. Authoritarian regimes are also more likely to politicize economic subsidies and regulations in an effort to build bases of support through patronage networks. This results in more widespread discrimination and greater neglect in providing public goods. Last, authoritarian regimes may initiate or perpetuate civil and international conflicts, in order to divert public attention away from political and economic difficulties that undermine their legitimacy.[6] These likely interactions are shown in figure 1.1.

Second, norms and values associated with political cultures and national identities are likely to influence human rights practices in two ways: (1) they may lead political élites to adopt compatible objectives and to accept compatible constraints on their methods; (2) they make it possible to mobilize mass support for regimes and policies on grounds that go beyond calculations of individual self-interest. Political cultures and national identities are likely to contribute indirectly to stronger protection of human rights if political or other human rights are viewed as important means or ends in serving traditional values or fulfilling important national ideals. Similarly, political cultures and national identities are most likely to contribute indirectly to human rights violations where political and other rights are viewed as directly or indirectly inimical to traditional values or national ideals. There are many possibilities for greater or lesser ideological or practical compatibility between human rights norms and local political cultures and identities. Local political cultures and identities can also be invoked in disputes over regime type, economic policies, and civil and international conflicts. This can make it more (or less) difficult to adopt political institutions, economic policies, and conflict-related policies that affect human rights practices.[7]

Third, extreme poverty places intrinsic limits on public goods provision and leads élites and masses to place less emphasis on non-economic objectives (including non-economic human rights). Further, economic structure and the associated economic interest group cleavages over economic policies are an important determinant of what is at stake in the political process. Extreme political polarization, which often pre-empts or threatens protection of political and other rights, is sometimes due to disputes over economic policies.[8]

Fourth, war is a serious direct and indirect threat to human rights protection. Directly, human rights tend to be pushed aside as they interfere

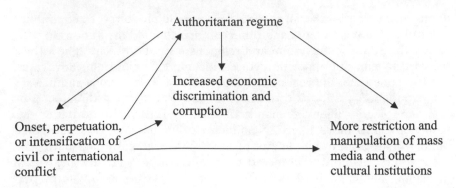

Figure 1.1 Interactive effects of regime type and other factors on human rights practices

with maximum mobilization amidst a national emergency. Even if human rights protection does not interfere with mobilization, national emergency is a convenient pretext for attacking human rights.

In a number of related ways, war is also an indirect threat. The ideological polarization unleashed by war makes regimes both more willing and more able to manipulate public opinion in a manner adverse to maintaining human rights protection. War undermines economic performance and involves a risk of military defeat. Both deteriorating economic performance and military defeat weaken the popular legitimacy of the existing regime, making it more susceptible to being overthrown through mass political processes or coups. Such developments are a serious threat to political regimes that uphold strong human rights protection. Such developments can also threaten political regimes that severely violate human rights practices. However, there is an important asymmetry between the two types: as "violator" regimes are more likely to move preemptively to forestall political threats, they are less vulnerable than "protector" regimes; in other words, war is a form of political "natural selection" that is more dangerous for regimes that respect human rights. War can be more safely used as a diversionary tactic by "violator" than by "protector" regimes[9] (see again fig. 1.1).

Tentative findings and basic implications

Although this volume's country and comparative case studies provide only a partial overview of the available evidence, they broadly support the previous section's hypotheses.[10] Consider, first, political regime type. In every country and region considered by the contributors, repressive authoritarian regimes are judged to bear the most direct responsibility for human rights abuses. This is true for the old military dictatorships of Argentina and South Korea, in Saddam Hussein's Iraq, in the authoritarian regimes of Iran and Pakistan, in Turkey's partially authoritarian regime, in post-communist authoritarian regimes such as the Federal Republic of Yugoslavia under Slobodan Milošević, in Somalia and apartheid-era South Africa, in most West African states, and in the People's Republic of China. Authoritarian regimes often attack or ignore non-political rights, but this is not always the case. For example, there were improvements in civil and (especially) economic rights after the South Korean military regime, and Deng Xiaoping's People's Republic of China (PRC) embarked on successful economic development programmes. On the other hand, democracies are in every case responsible for providing important human rights protection – although the extent to which political rights protection is also complemented by the pursuit of civil, economic, social, and cultural rights, varies considerably. This is true for newly democratized Argentina and South Korea, for the Republic of China (Taiwan) since democratization, and for India.

There is little evidence that political cultures and national identities directly lead human rights norms to be either strongly upheld or strongly defied. Authoritarian regimes consistently use their control of the mass media, the educational system, and religious and other social institutions to interpret political cultures and national identities in self-serving ways. However, there is no strong evidence that such manipulation generally has a significant effect on public opinion. It is more likely to do so if the regime's policies are producing economic improvements or if genuine "elective affinities" (relatively strong logical and practical compatibilities) exist between the regime's policies and what appears to the public to be implied by its traditions and collective goals. Similarly, in democracies, political culture or national identity is likely to favour improvements in non-political rights if "elective affinities" exist with the way the public understands its traditions and collective goals.

Consider the so-called "Asian values" debate. This largely concerns the priority to be attached to individual as opposed to collective rights and goals. To begin with, this is far from being a specifically "Asian" issue. After all, the PRC regime has a decidedly Western ideological lineage – a socialist rather than a liberal one. If correlations are examined, the strong current support for individual rights in South Korea and Taiwan, and among opposition voices in the PRC and Hong Kong, would not lead us to conclude that Confucian cultures are inimical to individual rights norms. The same is true for the relation between Hinduism and individual rights norms in India. These examples do, however, support the idea that limitation of individual political and civil rights may be more tolerable if the regime is delivering consistent economic growth and broadly improved economic opportunities and social services. However, they also indicate that such tolerance will fade if the limitations appear to be unnecessary or excessive, or if economic difficulties arise. In other words, popular support for an "Asian values" trade-off is likely to be conditional and thus temporary.

Similar points can be made about countries with Islamic cultures. Individual rights appear to have quite broad support in cases where regime policies allow some space for individual expression, such as in Turkey and in post-war Iran. Although some would argue that, in Turkey, these norms were inculcated specifically against traditional Islamic norms, such an argument can hardly be used in the case of Iran. There we see a familiar pattern: repressive policies justified with a particular interpretation of Islam received popular support, or at least tolerance, for as long as they appeared to serve important collective goals, such as overthrowing the Shah's regime and winning the war with Iraq. However, with these events in the past and with the Iranian economy stagnant, the Iranian populace and much of the Iranian élite have rallied strongly to the cause of individual rights. These rights are viewed both as intrinsically valuable and as a means towards restoring a more viable economic future and avoiding military conflicts.

A similar pattern appears to exist among the post-communist countries. Superficially, correlation here supports the religious culture argument: the Islamic post-communist countries have the worst human rights records, the Christian Orthodox countries the second-worst records, and the Catholic and Protestant countries the best records. However, the evidence is not as straightforward as it appears. It has traditionally been argued that, owing to its more hierarchical organization and top-down scriptural interpretation, Catholicism is less receptive to individual rights norms than Protestantism.[11] This is conveniently forgotten when Catholic "successes" in Eastern Europe are used to argue for the importance of religious cultures. More importantly, it appears that religion is only one aspect of post-communist political cultures and national identities. The most central ideological question was that of which policies would best serve the political birth (or rebirth) of countries emerging from Soviet or Yugoslav domination. Here, it seems that countries with experiences of greater pre-communist economic development and pre-communist political independence and power were most likely to embrace human rights norms along with democracy and market reform. This was due to the fact that these goals were associated with an alternative future that such countries sought – and believed that they would have possessed had their political systems and societies not been "hijacked" by a forcibly imposed, alien, communist system.

Religious identity was only one element affecting variation in such pre-communist experiences. This interpretation is supported by a closer look at the political processes of post-communist transformation. The countries with the best post-communist human rights practices featured reform movements and parties that most strongly emphasized the cause of national renaissance over that of political and economic "stability." These examples show that nationalist goals, which are inherently collective, are not necessarily damaging to individual rights. They can actually advance individual rights if these are widely perceived as being consistent with national identity and as advancing collective goals such as cultural rebirth, national independence and power, and economic development.

The African case studies also support these lines of argument. In West Africa, local cultures and identities do not appear to have been the main influence on post-colonial regime formation and policy-making: rather, the international ideological environment was one that emphasized state building and economic development over individual rights. This provided an influential ideological justification for the centralized authoritarian regimes that were consolidated throughout West Africa. Similarly, the end of the Cold War led to a collapse of legitimacy for these regimes. Both centralized authoritarianism and more liberal and democratic regimes could be justified by selective reference to local cultures and identities; in the long run, both are likely to be judged largely by the economic results they deliver. Similarly, in South Africa, the transition from apartheid was carried out after the end of the Cold War, in an ideological atmosphere that emphasized equal rights for individuals. This was important in making the transition one that attempted to broaden to all the rights previously enjoyed only by those of European descent, as opposed to a transition that would have sought to impose on those of European descent the restrictions hitherto endured by the African, Asian, and mixed-race populations.

Extreme poverty does, indeed, limit public goods provision and provide a reason and an excuse for neglecting non-economic rights. This is evident in many countries in West Africa, in Somalia, and in Pakistan. On the other hand, India shows that neglect for non-economic rights is not inevitable in the poorest countries. Middle-income countries are likely to have larger educated classes, which are needed to provide a reservoir of support for human rights norms and (where permitted) organizations. This can be seen in Argentina, in Iran and Turkey, in the post-communist countries, and in South Korea and Taiwan. On the other hand, *rentier* states, such as Iraq and Iran, are less dependent on popular mobilization to sustain their economies: their regimes can, therefore, afford to be less responsive to public and élite pressure to improve human rights practices. Rapid economic development sustained over a long period is almost invariably associated with broad provision of public goods and relatively broad diffusion of economic opportunities. It is also likely to lead to greater awareness of any restrictions on individual rights and greater pressure to relax these restrictions. This tendency can be seen in South Korea, Taiwan, and Hong Kong.

Civil and international conflict has, in all cases, led directly to severe or catastrophic human rights abuses. This is true in Argentina, Iraq, Iran, Pakistan, India, Turkey, the former Yugoslavia, a number of post-Soviet states, Somalia, and many West African states. In addition, such conflicts have indirectly facilitated greater state repression by both authoritarian and democratic regimes. Greater state intolerance and repression as a political by-product of conflict is evident in all cases: for instance, in Azerbaijan, a promising democratic movement briefly gained power but was unable to survive the effects of war. In the more democratic countries, the end or decline of conflict brought a revival of many freedoms – as in the post-Yugoslav states and in Armenia. War was also associated not only with direct economic costs but also with greater state intervention and cronyism in the economy. In democracies, peace generally brought a reversal of these interventionist and cronyist tendencies.

The most consistent forms of interaction between the four factors stem from the tendencies of authoritarian regimes. Authoritarian regimes not only tend to repress directly political and civil rights and to manipulate self-servingly the mass media and other cultural institutions but also tend to use state subsidies and regulations to build up supportive patron–client networks, thus neglecting public goods provision, discriminating against the mass of the population, and limiting economic growth opportunities. Furthermore, they tend to use civil and international conflicts as diversions from internal political, economic, social, and cultural issues that threaten their legitimacy. This tendency to perpetuate or cultivate civil and international conflicts produces a second round of interactions: conflicts directly lead to human rights abuses, but indirectly are associated with intensified authoritarianism, economic cronyism, and hardship. One or both of these types of interactions are evident in authoritarian-era Argentina; in Iraq, Iran, and Pakistan; in the post-Yugoslav states and in some post-Soviet states; and in Somalia and most of West Africa. All these tendencies, particularly that of diversionary military conflict, faced more resistance in democracies such as Turkey, India, post-apartheid South Africa, and post-authoritarian South Korea and Taiwan. At the same time, such interactions did not always occur in authoritarian regimes – particularly where (as in Deng and post-Deng China and authoritarian-era South Korea and Taiwan) authoritarian regimes linked their legitimacy to the cause of rapid economic development.

With this summary in mind, we can now return to the question of the probable impact of the international human rights regime. Our conclusion above was that creation of international human rights norms and decentralized propagation of such norms by NGOs would be expected to have a greater impact than actions taken by states – whether individually, through their own foreign policies, or collectively, through decisions of IGOs. We argued that this is because state policies reflect state interests and, even under the best circumstances, are predictably inconsistent and of limited scope.

These expectations are supported by the more detailed analyses of the international human rights regime and by the country and regional case studies. Although further discussion is given in the concluding chapter, it is useful to review the evidence briefly here. Human rights norms have become difficult for even the most repressive regimes to ignore. It is a victory for the human rights cause that such regimes feel compelled to concoct excuses for their abuses, thus implicitly admitting fault and accepting the need for remedial action. Wherever regimes allow sufficient freedom, international NGOs help to nourish the growth of local human rights organizations and cultures. As long as human rights norms can be plausibly presented as consistent with local traditions and widely held collective goals, they are liable to be embraced by wide segments of public opinion – including not only the opposition but also important elements traditionally allied with authoritarian rulers. In this way, human rights norms have been widely embraced in the post-communist countries, in many parts of post-Cold War Africa, in Argentina (and most of the rest of Latin America), in Turkey, in South Korea and Taiwan, and in India. Even in highly authoritarian countries such as Iran and the PRC, human rights norms have been widely accepted by the opposition, much of the population, and influential segments of the élite. In addition to political repression, the other primary barriers to widespread acceptance of human rights norms are extreme poverty and civil and international conflict. People in extremely poor countries are less literate, have less access to international information sources, and care less about non-economic goals. War facilitates regime efforts to stifle alternative voices, and creates personal and economic security risks that sideline most other concerns.

From a human rights perspective, then, cultural globalization is more important than economic globalization. However, international economic integration also has an important role to play. Most directly, sustained economic development efforts have involved international economic integration – particularly increased reliance on international trade. Such integration expands the economic opportunities available to the population and interacts favourably with improvement in the provision of civil rights and public goods. Such effects are evident in South Korea, Taiwan, Deng-era and post-Deng China, and more recently in much of the post-communist world, Turkey, and India. Of course, there are also significant risks and costs associated with international economic integration – particularly transitional economic downturns, periodic post-transitional losses of international investor confidence, and the associated economic hardship and political turmoil. These transitional and integration costs are more difficult to bear in extremely poor countries, such as those of West Africa. However, by the same token, the long-term gains are potentially much greater if transitions can be effectively implemented and sustained.

International economic integration probably has a more significant impact on human rights norms simply by increasing personal and cultural interaction with the rest of the world. This has all the beneficial effects already mentioned, and sustained international economic integration functions as a commitment to sustain such personal and cultural interaction. This tendency is evident, for example, in authoritarian-era South Korea and Taiwan and in the Deng-era and post-Deng PRC. Of course, this assumes that individual human rights norms continue to remain prominent in international culture and among NGOs. As the early post-colonial experience in West Africa attests, however, this can by no means be taken for granted.

Before summarizing the contents of the volume, two fundamental issues – one theoretical, the other historical – should be mentioned. First, this volume does not attempt to settle the issue of whether human rights are more important or fundamental than other values or goals:[12] here, it is simply assumed that human rights are an important and interesting object of empirical study and, hence, that examination of their causes and consequences is worth while. As already mentioned, however, many linkages between human rights and factors such as political institutions, economic structure and development, and cultures and national identities are discussed in detail. This provides important evidence for those interested in ethical or philosophical debates about the importance of human rights.

In the aftermath of the 11 September 2001 terrorist attacks in New York and Washington, some commentators have argued that human rights principles appear to be under siege.[13] On the one hand, the attacks themselves, along with the authoritarian institutional and ideological environments that often nourish terrorism, reflect a widespread rejection of human rights norms – not only in much of the Islamic world but also in East Asia and other parts of the developing world. On the other hand, the terrorist threat may lead many developed states of the West to compromise civil liberties – as has often been the case during periods of war and international tension. However, it can be argued that the September 11 attacks will also have a favourable impact on human rights practices. The attacks have produced a renewed conviction that human rights abuses can have dramatic negative consequences across borders. There is much disagreement about the priorities in fighting terrorism and about the means to be used in doing so. Nevertheless, improving human rights practices is probably the strongest common denominator among the rival points of view. Similarly, in countries with better records of human rights protection, it is almost universally accepted that anti-terrorism measures must be reconciled with the strongest possible protection of existing rights. In retrospect, we believe it is more likely that September 11 will be viewed not as the high point of global human rights protection but as a warning against ignoring the likely consequences of extreme human rights abuses in much of the world.

Contents of the volume

The volume begins, in chapters 2–8, by summarizing and analysing the most important elements and processes of the international human rights regime. Then, in chapters 9–17, it offers case studies of human rights development in a wide variety of countries and regions. For reasons of space, the case studies are not able to give equal attention to the four main factors influencing human rights practices; instead, they focus on the factor or factors of greatest importance. The concluding chapter summarizes local and regional tendencies and offers more detailed policy recommendations. Brief chapter summaries are provided here, so that readers can focus on issues of particular concern to them – for example, on particular aspects of the international human rights regime, on the development of human rights practices in particular countries or regions, or on particular causes of worsening or improving human rights practices.

In chapter 2, Johannes Morsink examines the influence of the UDHR, particularly its implications for transitional societies. Morsink describes how the UDHR became the central moral inspiration and practical reference point for the spread of human rights norms and laws around the world. He focuses on three elements of the UDHR as particularly relevant to formulating and implementing human rights in societies in transition: emphasizing protection of women and minorities from discrimination; including social, economic, and cultural rights; and including a right to democratic political participation.

In chapter 3, Richard Lewis Siegel examines universalist and relativist positions on, as well as conflicts and tensions between, various human rights. He favours an "expanding core" approach that integrates the most important insights of the universalist and relativist positions, and views increased intercultural and "intercivilizational" dialogues as important means towards consensual expansion of core rights. He argues that an "expanding core" approach is also most practical for states that are facing human rights-related transitional challenges.

Geneviève Souillac, in chapter 4, looks at how global norms foster local change. Human rights are viewed as "architectural norms" affecting the formation of states' political identities and political objectives. This is particularly relevant to transitional states, which are, by definition, going through a process of rapid political and economic change. Global human rights norms are most likely to have an impact through a gradual process, in which local structures and traditions are co-opted into the international human rights discourse as their political identities and priorities are being redefined domestically. International and local human rights networks can play a central role in this process, by engaging the local structures and traditions in a sustained dialogue aimed at reconciliation. In this way, international norms can be refitted for domestic use, so that it is less likely that they will be viewed as imposed from the outside.

W. Ofuatey-Kodjoe, in chapter 5, traces the United Nations' role in developing international human rights *standards* and *practices*. He argues that standards have been much more extensively developed than practices; however, despite significant progress, standards still often remain poorly defined. Practices involve "indirect protection" of human rights, in which UN bodies attempt to hold members to account for human rights violations, and "direct protection," in which the United Nations intervenes directly in states' internal affairs to protect human rights. Indirect protection has made significant progress but, for political reasons, remains selective. Direct protection is in its infancy and, in view of states' oft-perceived interests in avoiding unwanted intervention in their internal affairs, is likely to make only slow progress. Long-run improvements are likely to depend on "general acceptance of both human rights norms and the legitimacy of the protective activities of the international community."

In chapter 6, Paul J. Magnarella traces the development of international legal tribunals from Nuremberg (the International Military Tribunal) to Yugoslavia (the International Criminal Tribunal for the Former Yugoslavia) and Rwanda (the International Criminal Tribunal for Rwanda), to today's International Criminal Court. The evolution of the tribunals is traced in terms of definitions of crimes, jurisdiction, rules of procedure, proceedings, and other matters. He then analyses how the Nuremberg, Yugoslavia, and Rwanda tribunals have contributed to promoting and protecting human rights in the past, and how the International Criminal Court may do so in the future. He comes to the conclusion that international legal tribunals are most likely to fall short of their objectives when it comes to deterring future human rights violations.

Albrecht Schnabel, in chapter 7, examines the concept, legality, and practical record of international efforts to protect human rights in transition societies. He argues that the focus of international involvement should be at pre-conflict stages or, failing that, at post-conflict stages. His analysis of legal, political, and moral considerations leads him to conclude that international military interventions for humanitarian causes are likely to receive worldwide support and UN authorization only in cases of extreme, genocidal, violence. Military intervention in response to lower levels of violence – with or without the blessing of the United Nations and the wider international community – is likely only if there are particularly pressing political, strategic, or economic reasons. Therefore, international action to protect human rights in transition societies should emphasize pre-conflict support and assistance, enhanced by diplomatic pressure, to address the structural violence that usually accompanies transition processes. Schnabel shows that human rights conditions are extremely useful indicators of a state's capacity and performance in managing transition processes – indicators that should be better utilized by the international community to offer assistance in trouble-shooting deteriorating human rights conditions, thus preventing further violations and eventual escalation to armed violence and to state and society collapse.

In chapter 8, Barbara Ann J. Rieffer and David P. Forsythe examine how foreign policies of sovereign states can affect human rights practices in transitional societies. Focusing on the example of the US foreign policy, they find that foreign policies towards human rights are likely to be affected by national identity as well as by military and economic interests. The main US human rights-promotion efforts are made through bilateral diplomacy and aid programmes and through multilateral standard-setting regimes and aid programmes. The United States seeks to promote democracy and related civil rights abroad, in a manner consistent with the central place of US political institutions and civil rights norms in its national identity. Similarly, the relative US emphasis on civil and political rights compared with economic and social rights also reflects US traditions. However, human rights promotion is also widely viewed and justified as serving US military and economic interests. Military and economic interests are also evident in the way that diplomatic efforts and aid are targeted towards countries more important to the United States and in the way that political and civil rights standards are sometimes compromised to maintain good relations with such countries. Finally, Rieffer and

Forsythe argue that limited resources for promoting human rights – as well as variation in local cultures, limited economic development, and a variety of political factors – constrain the impact of states' human rights promotion efforts.

Jenab Tutunji, in chapter 9, describes the evolution of human rights practices in Iraq under the Ba'th regime, particularly under Saddam Hussein's rule. He argues that the economic and ideological nature of the political regime, which insulates it from social pressures and leads it to assume an exclusive legitimacy in the country's life, were at the root of severe human rights violations. Tutunji argues that Iraq's decolonizing context after World War II contributed more strongly to the formation of its *"rentier* ideocratic" character than did Islamic tradition. The resulting institutional potential for abuse was exacerbated by Saddam's personality and by his willingness to use virtually any means – including risky wars – to solidify and increase his power. These wars had further, massively negative effects on human rights practices in Iraq. Directly, they facilitated minority revolts and bloody repressions of such revolts and they laid waste Iraq's relatively developed economy. Indirectly, they undermined legitimacy derived from state provision of economic goods, leading the regime to substitute with increasing repression. Another indirect effect was international sanctions. Although the sanctions were not able to force Saddam Hussein to give up his programmes of weapons of mass destruction they exacerbated Iraq's economic collapse, with disastrous effects for the civilian population. Turning to consequences, Tutunji explains that increased human rights abuses, including political repression and economic cronyism, badly set back the prospects for democratization and economic development.

In chapter 10, Mahmood Monshipouri compares the human rights situations in Iran, Pakistan, and Turkey. He argues that authoritarian political institutions and leaderships are most responsible for human rights violations but that cultures and identities, civil and international conflicts, and economic structures and interest groups also play significant roles. In Pakistan, both military and civilian authorities have used Islam to try to hold their ethnically divided country together. This has contributed to the use of the Kashmir conflict with India to divert attention from internal problems and related legitimacy crises. In turn, this has led to intensified violence and repression both in Kashmir and in Pakistan itself. In Iran and Turkey, by contrast, strong historical memories of national greatness have focused élites more on advancing differently conceived missions of national development. In Turkey this has traditionally been defined against Islam, which in its more traditional forms has been viewed as a barrier to economic development and increased national prestige and military power. The Turkish military reserves the right to restrict human rights as necessary to protect and advance these modernizing methods and goals. The associated modernizing, national-assimilationist ideology has made it more difficult to settle the Kurdish conflict, which has resulted in severe human rights abuses. Since Iran's Islamic Revolution, the controlling religious élites have defined the national mission in terms of putting Iran in the vanguard of Islam. These ruling élites were able to consolidate their power during the war launched by Iraq's Saddam Hussein. However, since the end of the war, internal repression has produced a widespread backlash within society and among the moderate élites. These groups felt that Islam has been over-politicized, and they seemed determined to fuse local religious and national-historical traditions with modernist norms emphasizing human rights. In all three countries, the security forces have played central roles in imposing national objectives and policies. Over time, this has given the state a more dominant role in the economy, contributing to stagnation and crises. Both the military and private interest groups have developed significant stakes in the state-owned sector and in the state-subsidized private sector. This has made it more difficult to design and implement effective market reforms, particularly because the more economically vulnerable elements in society can be politically activated during post-reform recessions. Poverty and corruption are particularly severe in Pakistan, making significant economic progress difficult to achieve and leaving large parts of the population susceptible to political radicalism. This encourages civilian and military leaders to fall back on populist appeals, creating a more permissive environment for human rights violations. In all three countries, weak human rights protection threatens democratization and economic development efforts and makes it more difficult to settle civil and international conflicts.

Shale Horowitz, in chapter 11, examines the causes of variation in human rights practices in the post-communist world. He hypothesizes that political institutions, cultures and national identities, economic development, and ethnic conflict should have significant impacts. These hypotheses are tested statistically for the 28 post-communist countries at three different time intervals following the collapse of the old regimes. The results indicate that economic development has a relatively weak positive influence and war a relatively strong negative influence. Culture defined in terms of "frustrated" national identities has by far the strongest and most consistent impact. Cultures and national identities are here not analysed for their intrinsic value-content and traditional institutions; rather, they are distinguished in terms of their forward-looking tactical compatibility, in a specific historical context, with stronger human rights practices. Turning to consequences, stronger human rights practices appear to play an important role in advancing and conserving the democratization process and in facilitating further economic development. In contrast, human rights practices appear to have a more ambiguous and complex relationship to conflict resolution.

In chapter 12, Aleksandar Resanovic analyses the development of human rights practices in the Federal Republic of Yugoslavia (Serbia and Montenegro), Croatia, and Bosnia and Herzegovina. Resanovic argues that the more extreme human rights abuses were due to authoritarian leaders' use of war to take power and to pursue their objectives coercively. Historical grievances and mistrust among the Yugoslav peoples, along with tangled settlement patterns and rival territorial claims, made it extremely difficult to achieve a peaceful breakup of the Socialist Federal Republic of Yugoslavia. In this volatile situation, authoritarian-minded leaders used provocative rhetoric and unilateral actions to ride nationalist grievances to power; this made war unavoidable. Apart from the horrific human rights abuses committed against enemy peoples in the course of fighting, the war provided a pretext for consolidating authoritarian rule and committing a range of internal human rights abuses. Authoritarianism and war were also used to build crony networks that widely monopolized state resources and market opportunities. This worsened the already devastating economic effects of war. In the case of the Federal Republic of Yugoslavia, all of this was compounded by an international economic embargo and, later, a NATO bombing campaign. Human rights practices improved dramatically only after the wars in Croatia, Bosnia and Herzegovina, and Kosovo had ended. In peacetime, authoritarian leaders found it more difficult to maintain power. Eventually, newly aroused political oppositions and civil societies were able to establish democratic systems and end the worst human rights violations. While wars lasted, human rights abuses made it virtually impossible to make progress towards democratization and economic development; with the wars now over, continued human rights improvements will be essential to consolidate democracy, sustain economic recovery, and maintain the fragile peace.

In chapter 13, Wafula Okumu uses a "most different systems" approach, with a focus on Somalia and South Africa, to analyse human rights practices in transitional societies in Africa. Somalia's atrocious human rights record is rooted in corrupt colonial and post-colonial regimes. These regimes used state power to benefit politically connected groups and, not coincidentally, failed to provide basic public goods. Ethnically motivated wars of expansion further undermined public institutions and norms. All of this set the stage for a military take-over. State institutions became intensely personalized for the benefit of the dictator and his retainers, and military conflict erupted once more. This period ended with the collapse of central authority, civil war, and the emergence of local warlord regimes. By contrast, South Africa has made a successful transition from the apartheid regime to a rights-based democracy with a hopeful future. This was possible because human rights norms were an important part of the campaign against apartheid and because these norms were upheld by responsible leaders and supported by the public. This experience shows that African traditions are compatible with human rights norms. Okumu argues that the most important role for the international community is to inculcate human rights norms in transitional discourses, processes, and institutions. Looking to the future of transitional societies, human rights norms are also crucial in creating and preserving both democracy and peace.

In chapter 14, Eghosa E. Osaghae examines human rights in West African transitional societies. Authoritarian regimes, whether of military factions or ruling parties, have been the main source of human rights abuses. These regimes were able to take root so easily for a number of reasons. Economic backwardness and colonial rule weakened civil societies and exacerbated ethnic divisions. Ideologically, such regimes were legitimized by the post-colonial emphasis on collective peoples' rights over individual and group rights. The predominant emphasis on the anti-colonial struggle and on the post-colonial state-building and economic development missions rationalized the unaccountable centralization of state power. Authoritarian regimes abused human rights directly in their efforts to take and keep power. Other common characteristics had similar effects. State-led economic development strategies opened the way for extensive use of state subsidies and legal and regulatory preferences to build political support networks, commonly along ethnic lines. For the same reason, provision of public goods and services was neglected. This perpetuated poverty and exacerbated ethnic grievances. Corrupt (and often violent) authoritarian rule and heightened ethnic tensions fuelled civil conflicts, which usually raised human rights violations to new levels. The end of the Cold War brought paradoxical changes: on the one hand, the post-colonial ideology of state-led development largely collapsed, leading to a new emphasis on individual rights and ethnic minority rights; this was often associated with democratization and efforts to restructure state-dominated economies; however, high expectations were largely dashed by the difficulties of managing political and economic transitions consensually, given the heightened ethnic tensions, still-weak and poverty-stricken civil societies, and intense transitional economic downturns. Significantly, authoritarianism and widespread human rights abuses are no longer legitimate; however, under the prevailing difficult conditions they remain entrenched for lack of politically sustainable alternatives. Sustainable human rights improvements are themselves central to sustainable democratization, economic development, and conflict resolution. These goals remain in pressing need of international support, both ideologically and financially.

Man-To Leung, in chapter 15, examines the development of civil and political rights in the PRC, Hong Kong, and the Republic of China (ROC; Taiwan). In all three cases, the objectives of ruling political regimes are the key to progress. International human rights norms and cultural and economic integration have had an effect in all three cases. Internal economic reforms and long-term economic development have created increased internal pressures for reform, particularly in Hong Kong and the ROC. Although these international and internal changes favour further development of civil and political rights, the determining factor is likely to be whether authoritarian élites are willing to sacrifice their exclusive power to achieve other objectives. This has happened in recent years in the ROC, but it is unclear if it will happen at any time in the near future in the PRC and, by extension, in PRC-controlled Hong Kong.

In chapter 16, D.R. Kaarthikeyan looks at human rights practices in India. After giving a brief history of local human rights traditions and movements, Kaarthikeyan describes problems in a number of areas, namely children's and women's rights, caste and communal violence, political violence and terrorism, state violence, prisoners' rights, and environmental protection. He then discusses the roles of the Indian Constitution, the judiciary, government human rights commissions, and human rights NGOs in enforcing and enhancing human rights protection. Despite India's strong democracy and legal protection and an increasingly active civil society, there are numerous important causes of ongoing human rights violations. First, many *social* violations – relating to the status of women and children and to caste and communal divisions – are strongly rooted in historical traditions and social structures. Second, many *economic* violations are related to the social violations and other forms of discrimination, inadequate public goods provision and social services, and poverty per se. Third, political violence is also related to many of the same problems. Improvement depends largely on institutional reforms of the legal and political systems, more efficient provision of public goods and social services, and sustained economic growth.

In chapter 17, Terence Roehrig looks at the causes of human rights abuses under military regimes in Argentina and South Korea, and then examines how efforts to punish such abuses have affected subsequent transitions to democracy. Military leaders seized power and perpetrated human rights abuses in response to what they saw as fundamental internal and external threats to the nation. Military rule and its abuses ended once the perceived threats had subsided and large segments of civil society had mobilized against continued military rule. He argues that, although it is desirable to punish those chiefly responsible for human rights abuses, such punishment should not threaten transitions to democracy: punishment should target a small group of top military officers, to avoid the impression that the military as an institution is targeted; punishment should be delayed until the military has been reliably restored to civilian control; and punishment should not appear to unleash or re-create fundamental threats to the nation similar to those that prompted the military coups in the first place.

In the concluding chapter, Albrecht Schnabel and Shale Horowitz review regional variations. They also offer policy recommendations to NGOs, states, and IGOs involved in improving human rights practices in transition societies.

Notes

1. *Amnesty International Report 2002*, New York: Amnesty International USA, 2002; *Human Rights Watch World Report 2002: Events of 2001*, New York: Human Rights Watch, 2002. See also the Freedom House evaluations and rankings of countries at ⟨http://www.freedomhouse.org⟩.
2. See, for example, Ian Brownlie, ed., *Basic Documents on Human Rights*, New York: Oxford University Press, 1981; David Forsythe, *The Internationalization of Human Rights*, Lexington, MA: Lexington Books, 1991; Theodor Meron, *Human Rights Law-Making in the United Nations*, New York: Oxford University Press, 1986; Johannes Morsink, *The Universal Declaration of Human Rights. Origins, Drafting and Intent*, Philadelphia: University of Pennsylvania Press, 1999.
3. See, for example, Hayward R. Alker, Jr. and Bruce Russett, *World Politics in the General Assembly*, New Haven: Yale University Press, 1965; Stephen F. Burgess, *The United Nations under Boutros Boutros-Ghali, 1992–1997*, Lanham: Scarecrow Press, 2001; George J. Lankevich, *The United Nations under Javier Pérez de Cuéllar, 1982–1991*, Lanham: Scarecrow Press, 2001; Bruce Russett, ed., *The Once and Future Security Council*, New York: St. Martin's, 1997; Ramesh Thakur and Albrecht Schnabel, eds., *United Nations Peacekeeping Operations: Ad Hoc Missions, Permanent Engagement*, Tokyo: United Nations University Press, 2001.
4. See, for example, Lynda Bell, Andrew J. Nathan, and Ilan Peleg, eds, *Negotiating Culture and Human Rights*, New York: Columbia University Press, 2001; Jack Donnelly, *Universal Human Rights in Theory and Practice*, Ithaca: Cornell University Press, 1989; Thomas Risse, Stephen C. Ropp, and Kathryn Sikkink, eds, *The Power of Human Rights*, Cambridge: Cambridge University Press, 1999.
5. See, for example, Kenneth L. Cain, "The Rape of Dinah: Human Rights, Civil War in Liberia, and Evil Triumphant," *Human Rights Quarterly*, Vol. 21, May 1999, pp. 265–307; Jack Donnelly, "Human Rights, Democracy, and Development," *Human Rights Quarterly*, Vol. 21, August 1999, pp. 608–632; Rupert Emerson, "The Fate of Human Rights in the Third World," *World Politics*, Vol. 27, January 1975, pp. 201–226; Mark Gibney, "Prosecuting Human Rights Violations from a Previous Regime," *East Euro-*

pean Quarterly, Vol. 31, March 1997, pp. 93–110; Conway Henderson, "Conditions Affecting the Use of Political Repression," *Journal of Conflict Resolution*, Vol. 35, March 1991, pp. 120–142; Rhoda E. Howard and Jack Donnelly, "Human Dignity, Human Rights, and Political Regimes," *American Political Science Review*, Vol. 80, September 1986, 801–817; Sakah S. Mahmud, "The State and Human Rights in Africa in the 1990s: Perspectives and Prospects," *Human Rights Quarterly*, Vol. 15, August 1993, pp. 485–498; Neil J. Mitchell and James M. McCormick, "Economic and Political Explanations of Human Rights Violations," *World Politics*, Vol. 40, July 1988, pp. 476–498; Mike Oquaye, "Human Rights and the Transition to Democracy under the PNDC in Ghana," *Human Rights Quarterly*, Vol. 17, August 1995, pp. 556–573; Steven C. Poe and C. Neal Tate, "Repression of Human Rights to Personal Integrity in the 1980s: A Global Analysis," *American Political Science Review*, Vol. 88, December 1994, pp. 853–872. For more qualified views, see Akwasi Aidoo, "Africa: Democracy without Human Rights?" *Human Rights Quarterly*, Vol. 15, November 1993, pp. 703–715; Fareed Zakaria, "The Rise of Illiberal Democracy," *Foreign Affairs*, Vol. 76, November–December 1997, pp. 22–43; Amin Saikal and Albrecht Schnabel, eds, *Democratization in the Middle East: Experiences, Struggles, Challenges*, Tokyo: United Nations University Press, 2003.

6. Examples of relevant work in the "democratic peace" literature include Henry S. Farber and Joanne Gowa, "Common Interests or Common Polities? Reinterpreting the Democratic Peace," *Journal of Politics*, Vol. 59, May 1997, pp. 393–417; Scott Gates, Torbjørn L. Knutsen, and Jonathan W. Moses, "Democracy and Peace: A More Skeptical View," *Journal of Peace Research*, Vol. 33, January 1996, pp. 1–10; Zeev Maoz and Bruce Russett, "Normative and Structural Causes of Democratic Peace," *American Political Science Review*, Vol. 87, September 1993, pp. 624–638. For a discussion of diversionary theories of war, see Kurt Dassel, "Civilians, Soldiers, and Strife: Domestic Sources of International Aggression," *International Security*, Vol. 23, Summer 1998, pp. 107–140.

7. See, for example, Joanne Bauer and Daniel A. Bell, *The East Asian Challenge for Human Rights*, Cambridge: Cambridge University Press, 1999; Samuel Huntington, "The Clash of Civilizations?" *Foreign Affairs*, Vol. 72, Summer 1993, pp. 22–49; Bonny Ibhawoh, "Between Culture and Constitution: Evaluating the Cultural Legitimacy of Human Rights in the African State," *Human Rights Quarterly*, Vol. 22, August 2000, pp. 838–860; Douglass C. North, *Institutions, Institutional Change and Economic Performance*, Cambridge: Cambridge University Press, 1990; Lucien Pye and Sidney Verba, eds, *Political Culture and Political Development*, Princeton: Princeton University Press, 1965.

8. Alexander Gerschenkron, *Bread and Democracy in Germany*, Ithaca: Cornell University Press, 1989; Douglass C. North, *Structure and Change in Economic History*, New York: Norton, 1981; Amartya Sen, *Development as Freedom*, New York: Random House, 1999; United Nations, *Human Development Report 2002*, New York: Oxford University Press, 2002; World Bank, *World Development Report 2000/2001: Attacking Poverty*, New York: Oxford University Press, 2000.

9. See, for example, Rodney G. Allen, Martin Cherniack, and George J. Andreopoulos, "Refining War: Civil Wars and Humanitarian Controls," *Human Rights Quarterly*, Vol. 18, November 1996, pp. 747–781; Kenneth L. Cain, "The Rape of Dinah: Human Rights, Civil War in Liberia, and Evil Triumphant," *Human Rights Quarterly*, Vol. 21, May 1999, pp. 265–307; Rupert Emerson, "The Fate of Human Rights in the Third World," *World Politics*, Vol. 27, January 1975, pp. 201–226; Shale Horowitz, "War after Communism: Effects on Political and Economic Reform in the Former Soviet Union and Yugoslavia," *Journal of Peace Research*, Vol. 40, January 2003, pp. 25–48; Steven C. Poe and C. Neal Tate, "Repression of Human Rights to Personal Integrity in the

1980s: A Global Analysis," *American Political Science Review*, Vol. 88, December 1994, pp. 853–872; Karen Rasler, "War, Accomodation, and Violence in the United States, 1890–1970," *American Political Science Review*, Vol. 80, September 1986, pp. 921–945; Bruno Sinama and Andreas L. Paulus, "The Responsibility of Individuals for Human Rights Abuses in Internal Conflicts: A Positivist View," *American Journal of International Law*, Vol. 93, April 1999, pp. 302–316; Edward Newman and Albrecht Schnabel, eds, *Recovering from Civil Conflict: Reconciliation, Peace and Development*, London: Frank Cass, 2002.

10. See also the chapter summaries in the following section.

11. The original statement is in Max Weber, *The Protestant Ethic and the Spirit of Capitalism*, New York: Scribner, 1958.

12. For a recent survey, see Tim Dunne and Nicholas Wheeler, eds, *Human Rights in Global Politics*, New York: Cambridge University Press, 1999.

13. See, for example, Michael Ignatieff, "The Attack on Human Rights," *Foreign Affairs*, Vol. 80, November/December 2001, pp. 102–116.

Part One

Defining, delimiting, and understanding human rights in societies in transition

2

The Universal Declaration of Human Rights as a norm for societies in transition

Johannes Morsink[1]

A recent study of how international human rights norms cause domestic change identifies some of the most important mechanisms involved in this process. In their introductory essay, "[the] socialization of human rights norms into domestic practices," Thomas Risse and Kathryn Sikkink, two of the editors of the volume, identify three causal modes of interaction (adaptation, argumentation, and institutionalization) and five stages in which this causal work is done. I believe that these stages are recognizable as quite realistic and as applicable to most of the nations discussed in this volume. These stages are as follows: (1) repression and activation of the international network; (2) denial by the oppressing state; (3) tactical concession by the oppressor; (4) "prescriptive status," which occurs when the society involved starts to embrace the international norms in various ways, such as signing and ratifying treaties; and (5) rule-consistent behaviour.[2] This means that since the adoption of the Universal Declaration of Human Rights (UDHR) in 1948, in which these international norms were first delineated, the human rights movement has come a long way. We now have enough empirical data for scholars to develop causal models about how the human rights norms of the UDHR are brought to domestic audiences around the globe. That is a huge success story.

However, it is based upon the grand supposition that the norms of the UDHR are, indeed, valid moral (if not exactly legal at the time of adoption) norms that are worthy of implementation. In the concluding essay to the volume, Thomas Risse and Stephen C. Ropp (the third editor of the volume) point out that "[o]n the fiftieth anniversary of the UDHR we thought it appropriate to evaluate the processes by which human rights principles and norms found their way *from* the international *into* the domestic political arena."[3] This leaves open the question of the validity of these international or universal norms in the first place. Also, it does not explain how the norms of the UDHR are appropriate targets for societies in transition. The creation of these norms on the international level itself breaks down into several stages, and those of the UDHR are among the earliest ones.[4] For that reason, if we are interested in how these moral norms came to be internationally accepted (before they could be translated into various domestic settings), we would do well to study the adoption debates of a document like the Declaration.

The document itself was drafted and adopted when world society as a whole was reacting to the failures of the League of Nations and the horrors that were brought to light when the Nazi camps were liberated. The drafters tell us in their second recital that the "barbarous acts" of World War II gave them new insights into the dignity of every human being, which they then presented to the world as "a common standard of achievement for all peoples and all nations." I argue that the broad scope of these insights makes the Declaration a very helpful guide for societies in times of transition. First, I discuss drafting details that make the Declaration a moral norm that transcends any society. When societies come out of a crisis and are forced to make a transition to a more normal and stable state of affairs, they have both a need and an opportunity to make radical changes: the UDHR was written to meet this need. After I introduce the Declaration as the free-floating norm that it is, I make three more specific points that are particularly relevant to societies in transition. First, I point out that the Declaration expands on the short United Nations Charter list of non-discrimination items and (unlike the Charter) directly aims to protect members of minority groups. I then show how it came to embrace social, economic, and cultural human rights. Third, I argue that it sets up democracy as the mandatory form of government for any society that wants to respect the full range of human dignity. As I enumerate these four topics, I make occasional references to the work of theoreticians of human rights, which supports or conflicts with my reading of the Declaration.

The Declaration as a freely floating moral norm

Initially, the UDHR was envisioned as a legal document similar to the two international covenants that came into force in 1977; however, the tensions of the Cold War prevented this from happening. Distrust be-

tween the United States and the Soviet Union grew so intense in 1946 –
which is the year the preparations for the Commission that was to write
the Declaration started – that many believed that a third world war was
imminent. This holding back on enforcement questions was a great disappointment for many of the smaller nations.[5] On the positive side,
however, this distrust also suddenly set the drafters free to become moral
visionaries. As I see it, the Cold War's effect on the writing of the Declaration was a blessing in disguise: the necessity created by the Cold War
became the mother of moral invention and discovery. For as long as they
suspended questions of enforcement, the drafters agreed fairly easily on
the provisions to be included in the Declaration. Not being able to fight
about legal niceties and intricacies of implementation and so being
"forced" to look at the big, moral picture, they discovered that they had
far more in common than cultural, economic, and religious differences
would lead us to suspect.

   This view of the 1948 Declaration as being a type of document significantly different to the two later-adopted international covenants takes
exception to Jack Donnelly's "Universal Declaration (UD) model" of
international human rights.[6] In his model, Donnelly collapses the three
main texts of the International Bill of Rights (the Declaration and the
two covenants) into one unified model, and he quotes from them to make
general points about the model. As the two covenants are obviously addressed to states, Donnelly makes the mistake of treating the Declaration
in the same fashion. He describes his UD model of human rights as one
with a "state-centric conception."[7] No doubt Donnelly is correct when he
argues that "the modern state has emerged as both the principal threat to
the enjoyment of human rights and as the essential institution for their
effective implementation and enforcement."[8] However, he steps over the
line between possession and enjoyment with the assertion that what it
means for X to have a human right is that "[e]ach state has the authority
and responsibility to implement and protect the right to X within its territory."[9] The authority of states is, in my eyes (and in the eyes of most of
the drafters of the UD), not involved in this question of meaning. The
Declaration's first recital (with the ideas of inherent dignity and inalienable rights) and Article 1 (with the notion of being born free and equal)
give us the meaning of what it is to have a human right, while the two
covenants are among the most important practical measures of implementation. Donnelly's unified model blurs this division of labour.[10]

   One of the problems with Donnelly's unified model is that the UDHR
was not addressed to states. Toward the end of the drafting process the
Third Committee adopted (by a vote of 47 to none, with one abstention)
an Egyptian motion that formalized one of the rules that the drafters had
been following all along. This motion stated that, "[t]he Third Committee

decides that the declaration of human rights shall be limited to the formulation of principles relating to human rights which presuppose the existence of corresponding duties on the part of States and defers the formulation of principles relating to the duties of States for incorporation to an appropriate instrument."[11] It turned out to be two instruments instead of one – the International Covenant on Civil and Political Rights (ICCPR) and the International Covenant on Economic, Social and Cultural Rights (ICESC) – both of which came into force in 1977. This deferral did not take place simply because there had been no time to deal with the duties of states: it was also a conceptual question of keeping the statement of moral principles on the possession of human rights separate from the measures of implementation among which the duties of states would rank foremost.

As they were writing, the drafters came to realize that, if they were to write a standard that would improve the human condition (which, after the war, they all wanted to do), they would have to keep out all state references that might cripple the transcendent character of any of the rights they planned to include in their document. They did this very consistently, which is why there are only two references to the role of the state in the entire document – one in Article 16(3) (which indicates how intent they were about protecting the family) and one in Article 22 (which I mention below). For the rest, there is a resounding silence that speaks volumes about the transcendent (to, for instance, the power of sovereign states) moral character of the rights proclaimed. On a number of important occasions the USSR delegation submitted amendments that would have injected state references into the very conception of the right being considered. As Andrei Vyshinksky (who later was to be the prosecutor at Stalin's infamous conspiracy trials) put it, "Human rights could not be conceived outside the State; the very concept of right and law was connected with that of the State."[12] The great majority of drafters disagreed with this Benthamite, positivist interpretation of the rights to be listed. They rejected communist amendments that sought to inject state references into Articles 12, 15, 17, 18, and 29, where the USSR delegation proposed the phrase "democratic state" instead of "democratic society."[13] The Saudi Arabian delegation encountered a similar rebuff when it wanted to insert into the marriage rights of Article 16 the clauses "legal matrimonial age" and "as defined in the marriage laws of their country."[14] It is not a coincidence that both of these delegations abstained in the final vote on the Declaration. Since there were six communist delegations, the Saudi one makes for seven abstentions. The eighth abstention came from the Union of South Africa, which felt that many of the articles of the Declaration – in particular, the one on freedom of movement – conflicted with the prerogatives of what a state can and cannot do to its citizens.[15] However, the point of proclaiming the Declaration was precisely in order to take that unlimited prerogative away from the state.

The subservient role of the modern state pressed itself home on the drafters when they came to consider the human rights to movement across borders in Article 13, to asylum in Article 14, and to citizenship in Article 15.[16] State constitutions typically do not address themselves to these issues because they see themselves as setting out the rights of those who are already inside their legal domains, either as citizens or as aliens; they do not typically think of writing a list of rights that people have simply *as persons*. The three rights to movement across borders, to asylum, and to citizenship raise the question of which rights – our rights as citizens or our rights as human beings – take precedence. These Articles brought out into the open a latent feature of all human rights – namely, that they are possessed by persons first of all and that the states where these (citizen, alien, or refugee) persons happen to reside are nothing more than (although still the most important) part of the implementation machinery.

The pain of not yielding enough sovereignty is most clearly evident in Article 14, which gives everyone the right "*to seek and to enjoy* in other countries asylum from persecution." Unlike the unqualified right to a nationality in Article 15, Article 14 makes the enjoyment of the right to asylum dependent on its already having been granted. It does not state directly that (genuinely) persecuted people have, as persons, the human right to be *granted* asylum. The politics of what to do about the waves of refugees that were fleeing the newly created state of Israel interfered with the ability of some of the delegations to remain at the abstract level.[17] On the whole, however, it is remarkable how infrequently the politics of the real world interfered with the fundamental project of drafting a moral code that could (and therefore possibly would) serve "as a common standard of achievement for all peoples and all nations."

In addition to this glaring absence of state references in the document, the text of the Declaration also contains numerous positive indicators of this same moral transcendence. I mention some of the more obvious ones: the words "inherent" and "inalienable" in the first recital; the phrase "conscience of mankind" in the second recital; the "essential" connection between the right to rebellion and the rule of law in the third recital; the word "common" in the last recital and in the operative paragraph; the word "born" in Article 1; the words "arbitrary" in Articles 9, 12, 15, and 17; the word "degrading" in Article 5; the phrase "regardless of frontiers" in Article 19; the word "reasonable" in Article 24; the word "prior" in Article 26; and the phrase "just requirements" in Article 29.

Cassin, the French delegate who belonged to the core group of drafters, fought an uphill battle to have his colleagues recognize the fact that the United Nations was the key organization through which the transcendent moral rights of the Declaration could, in a first step, be brought down to earth. Following this, more regional regimes and national constitutions could finish the job.[18] He often lost; nevertheless, as the phrases "international cooperation" in Article 22 and "international order" in Article 28, as well as the reference in Article 29 to "the purposes and principles of the United Nations" indicate, they did recognize this viewpoint.[19] The two later-adopted international covenants were written and are being administered under UN auspices.

Protecting women and minorities through non-discrimination

With regard to discrimination based on sex, I should emphasize the remarkable "cleanliness" of the Declaration as a document.[20] In the late 1940s it was clearly ahead of its time, and it remains relevant for many parts of the world today. With the exception of clauses such as "his country" in Article 21 and "himself and his family" in Article 25, a strong women's rights lobby ensured that women were given a status very much equal to that of men. This fits with the stress on gender equality in the formation of UN structures, much of the early credit for which should go to the Commission on the Status of Women, which at that time was chaired by Bodil Begtrup from Denmark. When societies are caught in transitions of war, civil strife, poverty, or natural disasters, women and children almost always bear the greatest burden.[21] The causes of women's rights and of children's rights therefore weighed heavily on the drafters of the Declaration.[22] They spent a great deal of time in ensuring that these rights were acknowledged in the appropriate places throughout the text.

When it comes to the protection of members of minority groups, which frequently is a point of contention when societies are in transition, the UDHR presents us with a problem, for it does not contain a specific article devoted to the rights of members of these groups, such as that in Article 27 of the ICCPR. We therefore need to ask how the UDHR can be a good blueprint for societies in transition. If the document does not go out of its way to protect members of minority groups, how then can it help forestall the continued clash between cultural groups that has dominated the news in recent years? My answer is that the drafters of the UDHR *did* go out of their way to protect members of minority groups.

They did not do it by way of a special minority rights Article, as they well might have done (and almost did); however, they did make an effort by intentionally going far beyond the short ("race, sex, language, and religion") Charter list of non-discrimination items. To clarify this, and to combat the misconception that the UDHR does not protect members of minority groups very well, I enumerate below some of the pertinent drafting details.

It is important to do this because a growing number of communitarian thinkers are criticizing the liberal model of politics that we find in the UDHR as being woefully inadequate. The liberal model seeks to protect members of minority ethnic, linguistic, and religious groups solely by way of first setting up a list of rights for all citizens and then forbidding any kind of discrimination on the basis of standard characteristics such as those mentioned in the Charter list cited. Critics say that this simple (and, to them, simplistic) non-discrimination approach is not enough. They support Charles Taylor's thesis, "The Politics of Recognition," in the volume *Multiculturalism*, where he argues that liberal democracies must add overt measures of support for all minority groups because these groups and their members are at a disadvantage when majorities inevitably shape state policies to their own advantage.[23] Taylor and other communitarians (such as MacIntyre, Rorty, Kymlicka, and Brown)[24] do not believe that there is, or can be, a neutral state which treats all cultural traditions equally. To them, the absence of a minority rights article in the UDHR is a grave defect. I, myself, at one time also argued for an amendment to the document to correct this defect;[25] however, as I am reconsidering, I draw attention to the defence of minority rights that the document does provide. Even as it stands, members of minority groups receive a great deal of protection under this universal umbrella. This does not mean that the UDHR is fully conversant with the third generation of human rights, comprising the rights of peoples, for it is not; however, it does mean that the liberal model, as we find it expressed in the UDHR, is not nearly as defective as a rapid reading of the text might lead one to think.

The UN Charter contains seven references to "human rights and freedoms," but it does not give us a list of them: it simply states four times that these rights and freedoms are to be implemented without discrimination on the basis of "race, sex, language, or religion."[26] The UDHR was written to flesh out these inadequate Charter references. When they came to the question of non-discrimination, the drafters took their assignment as an opportunity for great expansion of this short Charter list. From the very beginning of the drafting process, the communist delegations (being led by the USSR) were very insistent that the UDHR should contain a clear and precise prohibition of discrimination. In the First Session of the Commission, Vladimir Koretsky, the delegate from the USSR, made the point "that one of the first principles to be adopted in the formulation of an International Bill of Rights must be the destruction of discrimination and inequality."[27] With one glaring exception, and with very significant assistance from the Indian delegation, the communists were largely successful in putting their non-discrimination stamp on the document.

The push to expand did not come from around the North Atlantic but, rather, from India and the communist delegations. Upon the recommendation of Minocheher Masani, the expert from India on the Sub-Commission on the Prevention of Discrimination and the Protection of Minorities, the item of *colour* was added to the non-discrimination list of Article 2.[28] His point was that, as there was no scientific definition of race, it was quite an open matter as to whether discrimination based on (skin) colour was included in the Charter's use of the word "race"; he wanted to ensure the addition of the term "colour" to the list: with the help of the French and Iranian experts, he had a note sent to the Commission on Human Rights suggesting that this should be done.[29] The item of *national origin* was added upon the recommendation of the Soviet Union. Because Mr Borisov, the Soviet expert on the Sub-Commission, did not want to use the term "ethnic," the Sub-Commission sent this item to the Commission on Human Rights with a gloss indicating that it wished "to make it clear that the words 'national origin' should be interpreted by taking this conception, not in the sense of citizen of a State, but in the sense of national characteristics."[30] The Human Rights Commission concurred with this reading by adopting the item as presented with this gloss.

Similar details explain the addition of the items "birth," and of "property or other status." There is no conflict between the occurrence of the word "born" in Article 1 and the expansion of the Charter list with the item of *birth* in the non-discrimination list of Article 2. The use in Article 1 fits with the metaphysics of inherent rights to which the phrases "inherent dignity" and "inalienable rights" of the first recital also point. The economic and sociological meaning of the item *birth* in Article 2 complements this idea of inherent dignity. Article 1 says that we are all born with these rights and Article 2 explains that they may therefore not be denied on the basis of any externally acquired (even if through one's own family) position or status.

A very interesting expansion of the short Charter list is the addition of the non-discrimination item of *political or other opinion*. This was initiated by the Canadian jurist John Peters Humphrey, who (as the first

Director of the Secretariat's Division of Human Rights) wrote the first draft of the UDHR. Charles Malik, the delegate from Lebanon, believed that "politics was one of the fundamental activities of man." He therefore urged his colleagues to decide "whether or not discrimination was allowable on the basis of political belief,"[31] which he felt was just as objectionable as any other kind of discrimination. Because of a desire not to go beyond the Charter list, many eyebrows were raised in the Sub-Commission about this item. Again, it was Masani, the Indian expert, who pressed for its retention. The item was adopted and kept in, over strong communist objections and their repeated manoeuvering to have it removed.[32] We can understand the worries of the communists for, if we combine this item with the right of Article 21 to "take part in the government of [one's] country" and to do so through "genuine elections … or by equivalent voting procedures," we come to the conclusion that the UDHR calls for multi-party democratic systems of government. I return to this point in the last section of this chapter.

Article 2 tells us that "[e]veryone is entitled to all the rights and freedoms set forth in this Declaration, without distinction of any kind, such as race, color, sex, language, religion, political or other opinion, national or social origin, property, birth, or other status." When combined with any of the other articles in the UDHR, this list of prohibitions provides enormous protection for members of all kinds of minority groups. The UDHR provides societies in transition with a moral warrant to create more inclusive societies with fairer, and therefore more stable, basic structures. The dual assignment indicated in the title of the Sub-Commission on the Prevention of Discrimination and the Protection of Minorities is significant, because it demonstrates that the founders of the United Nations were aware of the historical linkage between people being discriminated against for various reasons and their being members of minority groups. In our interpretations of the meaning and range of the items in Article 2, we need to keep this linkage in mind. The list of Article 2 provides a double protection for members of minority groups – first, because the list of Article 2 is so long and, second, because each item on the list can be applied in the context of "all the rights and freedoms set forth in this Declaration." As there are 30 Articles and therefore roughly 30 rights, and 12 items on this non-discrimination list, this yields 360 aspects of life that are being protected. For example, when we add the language item of Article 2 to the legal personality right of Article 6, we obtain the result that no one may be denied the right to "be a person before the law" based on the language he or she most naturally speaks. Apply this to the millions of refugees in the world and the radical character of the UDHR becomes immediately apparent.

The inclusion of social, economic, and cultural rights

Since the end of World War II, world society has moved on two parallel tracks. On the one hand (call it the moral track) it created human rights regimes that now cover most of the globe. From this normative point of view, all the nations in the world are in transit toward the goal of implementing the UDHR and they all have learned to speak the language of human rights in discussions about their developmental progress. Also in the late 1940s, world society established various economic institutions – the World Bank, the International Monetary Fund, and the General Agreement on Tariffs and Trade (GATT; which became the World Trade Organization). These organs were to help nations that lagged behind in development to catch up with the industrialized ones, to create stability in exchange rates between various national currencies, and to promote international trade; let us call this the economic track. For quite some time these two tracks did not communicate. This division of labour was induced by the Cold War when, in 1966, the United Nations adopted two international covenants instead of one – one for civil and political rights and one for social, economic, and cultural ones. This split in implementation instruments gives the incorrect impression that there are two kinds of human rights and that (depending on one's ideology) one kind is more important than the other: the communists stressed social and economic rights, and the North Atlantic nations and their allies emphasized civil and political rights.

Recently, however, these two tracks have started to "talk" to each other and a convergence is taking place that restores the UDHR to its pre-eminent place in international law and affairs. Unlike the two covenants to which it gave birth, the UDHR itself contains the entire scope of human rights; it can, therefore, better serve as the norm for the merger of the two tracks that is now taking place. Economists such as Amartya Sen have forsaken the strict language of the market-place and of economic man and have pulled the human rights track into the economic sphere.[33] From the other angle, human rights philosophers such as Alan Gewirth, Martha Nussbaum, and Thomas Pogge have started to take human development issues seriously in constructing their theories of human rights.[34] Sen and (especially) Nussbaum have developed a bridge theory (called the capabilities approach) that links human rights and human development questions. Recent publications by the United Nations Development Programme and by the World Bank also testify to the merger of these two tracks.[35] In this section I demonstrate how the document came to be so inclusive that it now can be the moral umbrella under which both tracks find philosophical justification.[36]

Transitions from crises to more cooperative frameworks last only if that cooperation is forged on fair terms. For that to be the case, societies need to acknowledge the full scope of human rights and not just the first half of the UDHR, which is devoted to civil and political rights. Some critics do not agree with this: they think that juridical complications and the cost of implementation justifiably relegate these liberal rights to second-class status.[37] Maurice Cranston, for instance, believes that social and economic rights are only "supposed" human rights and that their "utopian" flavour undercuts the moral authority of the "real" civil and political human rights.[38] Many libertarians still feel this way, even now that the two tracks have started to merge. Whatever the philosophical merits of Cranston's case,[39] the drafters of the UDHR let these liberal rights in from the very beginning. The great majority of them wanted to see these liberal rights included because they felt that these rights were comparable on moral grounds to the civil and political rights.[40]

John Peters Humphrey (who wrote the first draft) was a Canadian jurist and a socialist with a great interest in Latin American affairs. In the 1940s the great majority of Latin American nations had hit a democratic stretch, allowing them to speak with one voice when the United Nations was organized in 1945. They pushed for the inclusion of a Bill of International Rights in the UN Charter. When that failed, three Latin American nations (Cuba, Panama, and Chile) were the first to submit drafts of such a bill to the Commission of Human Rights. When that Commission turned to the Secretariat for help with a first rough draft, Humphrey (as he tells us in his memoirs) freely borrowed from these liberal Latin American proposals to help him to do that job. The Panamanian draft was prepared by the American Law Institute and the Chilean draft by the Inter-American Juridical Committee. The American Federation of Labor also submitted an early draft.

Humphrey's first draft had 48 articles, 14 of which were grouped in a chapter on "social rights." To write this social rights chapter, Humphrey borrowed more than 50 per cent of his text from his liberal or socialist Latin American sources. This is how the rights to health care (Art. 25), to education (Art. 26), to work and good working conditions and pay (Art. 23), to extra public assistance even when employed (Art. 23(3)), to social security in old age and bad times (not of one's own making) (Art. 25), to food and housing (Art. 25), to rest and leisure (Art. 24), and to participation in culture and the benefits of scientific research (Art. 27) entered the UDHR on the ground floor. Most of these rights were sponsored for inclusion in the document by Hernan Santa Cruz, the delegate from Chile. Since Rene Cassin, the delegate from France (who was asked to streamline the Humphrey text and shorten it), was himself a unionist, he trimmed Humphrey's suggestions slightly, but made almost no cuts.[41] Having survived the Drafting Sub-Committee, the text, with these liberal rights in it, was passed on to the full Commission. From that point on, the burden of proof was on any delegation to gather enough votes to have a certain unwanted right removed from the text – an action very difficult to achieve, as its existence on paper tends to be an indication of objectification and reification.

Most of the threats to remove these liberal rights came in the Third Session of the Commission, which met in May of 1948 and was ready to make drastic cuts in what had become a long list of human rights. The United Kingdom teamed up with the Indian delegation and presented a greatly shortened text. The new social and economic provisions provided a tempting area for cuts; however, voting as a block, the Latin American nations preserved the UDHR's commitment to these socialist values. Also, after World War II the world's unions engaged in a campaign to have the United Nations honour the contributions that workers had made to the war effort. One result was that the Economic and Social Council (ECOSOC, the parent body of the Commission that was writing the UDHR) gave the drafters a mandate to include union rights somewhere in the UDHR. The Commission obliged, and the result is to be found in Articles 23(4) and 20(2).[42] We can look at the right to join a trade union as a human right, or as a step to implement either the human right to fair working conditions or the human right to association. The Commission's minutes indicate its inclusion in the general right to association, but they also listed it specifically in 23(4). The drafters accepted a communist argument that the right to leisure time is meaningless if not paid for (Art. 24), but rejected a Swedish proposal to have the right to strike counted as an independent human right.[43]

If we place ourselves on the fence between stating a standard and implementing it, we can see how Article 25's rights "to food, clothing, housing and medical care and necessary social services" can be seen as a way of implementing Article 3's right to life. These rights can be viewed as raising questions of *public policy* or, alternatively, as raising the issue of what is to count as a constitutionally protected *right* of an individual.[44] The North Atlantic delegations had a mostly public policy perspective, whereas the communist and Latin American nations took the basic rights approach: they wanted to see these rights transferred from their own constitutions to the new international standard being written. For instance, when the delegations of the UK and India proposed cutting some rights from the above-cited clause of Article 25, many North Atlantic delegations were tempted to go along. Upon insistence by the Soviet delegation, and with crucial assistance from the International Labour Organization (ILO) representative to the proceedings, the items of *hous-*

ing and *medical care* were kept in the UDHR. It took an equally strong insistence by the Chinese delegation to keep the items of *food* and *clothing* in the UDHR: when he saw the threat to these two rights, Chung Chang pleaded with his colleagues in the crucial 71st meeting of the Third Session. He told them that he "did not see what possible objection there could be to that phrase when millions of people throughout the world were deprived of food and clothing." These rights were retained by 11 votes to 3. These liberal items are regular staples of what benevolent Confucian kings used to set before their people and what millions of persons living in societies in transition badly need. The UDHR makes the point that the world's poor have a *right* to have these and other such basic needs met. The other list in Article 25 pertains to "[social] security in the event of unemployment, sickness, disability, widowhood, old age, or other lack of livelihood in circumstances beyond his control." Because of the ECOSOC mandate to pay attention to union rights, and strong union delegations among the drafters, the particular items on this list were never questioned after Humphrey and Cassin had written them in.

When most of the social, economic, and cultural rights had been adopted, the drafters voted to give these "new" rights their own covering Article 22: "Everyone, *as a member of society*, has the right to social security and is entitled to realization, *through national effort and international cooperation and in accordance with the organization and resources of each State*, of the economic, social and cultural rights indispensable for his dignity and the free development of his personality." Critics of the liberalism in the second half of the UDHR are not correct when they seek to use the clauses italicized in the above citation as an indication that liberal rights have a lower status in the document. The motivation behind these clauses was not that the drafters doubted the authenticity of liberal rights as being genuine human rights; on the contrary, the Minutes of the meetings show that they inserted Article 22 with these clauses because these liberal rights were new or newly discovered, they usually require somewhat more material involvement on the part of the State, and they call for greater international cooperation.[45]

This greater need for material and international involvement was highlighted so that states would be aware of it and not shirk their correlative duties: it is for this reason that the drafters called upon them to set up frameworks of international cooperation. Article 22 was designed to make sure that these liberal rights would not starve for lack of resources. However, this special attention to social, economic, and cultural rights does not mean that civil and political rights do not require financial layouts and international cooperation: by the late 1940s the costs of these (old) rights had been borne for almost two centuries. The general necessity for international cooperation in this area was also underscored when the drafters adopted Article 28 without significant opposition: "Everyone is entitled to a social and international order in which the rights and freedoms set forth in this Declaration can be fully realized."[46]

The inclusion of a human right to democratic participation

It is remarkable how many of the points raised in present-day discussions about democracy were anticipated when the UDHR was being drafted. More than twenty international law scholars wrote lengthy contributions to a recently published volume entitled *Democratic Governance and International Law*.[47] These scholars agree that we are witnessing the birth of a new internationally recognized human right called democratic entitlement. They are not all equally sure of the content of this right or of the depth of its anchor in international law. However, none argue that no birth at all is taking place; they simply differ on how far the birthing process has developed. Space limitations allow me to mention only three of these essays.

Looking at the enormous election monitoring activities of the United Nations and the European and Latin American regional bodies, Thomas Franck concludes that "the opinions of mankind have begun in earnest to require that governments, as a prerequisite to membership in the community of nations derive their just powers from the consent of the governed."[48] Franck believes that, as a result of all this election aid and monitoring activity, "a global canon of legitimate rules and procedures" is developing and that, with this canon, we can judge "the democracy of nations." He also thinks that this canon "has trumped the principle of non-interference" enunciated in Article 7(2) of the UN Charter.

Gregory Fox investigated international legal texts and court decisions and came to the same conclusion as did Franck, namely, "that the right to political participation has established a firm grounding in both treaty law and international practice."[49] "The particulars of a human right to political participation," observes Fox, "once a flashpoint for grand ideological battles, now appear rather pedestrian. That receipt of an electoral mandate bestows legitimacy upon governments, that genuine choice in an election requires multiple political parties, that incumbent regimes cannot monopolize the mass media during a campaign, and that the other elements of fair elections must be provided, all seem to flow inevitably from treaties announcing commitment to representative government."[50] He wrote this after a thorough investigation of the text of Article 25 of the ICCPR and of decisions by the Human Rights Commission, the Human Rights Committee (of the ICCPR), the European Commission, the European Court, the Latin American System, the African System, and the Helsinki Accords of the Organization for Security and Cooperation in Europe (OSCE).

Both Franck and Fox mention Article 21 of the UDHR as the moral and legal anchor for these developments, but they do not give it nearly the attention it deserves. Franck mentions Article 21 of the UDHR only in passing, instead (briefly) mentioning the political implications of Articles 19 and 20. Fox begins his analysis of treaty law with a discussion of Article 25 of the ICCPR, making only a passing reference to discussions by the drafters of the UDHR as to whether "ballot secrecy was appropriate for States with a high percentage of illiterate voters, and the majority concluded that ballot secrecy was a fundamental aspect of a fair election and should be retained."[51] At this point, Fox put in a note observing that the UDHR does provide for "equivalent voting procedures," although this option was dropped from Article 25 of the ICCPR.

The presence of Article 21 in the UDHR is a clear sign that the outlook of the drafters differed from that of their predecessors in the eighteenth century. In the debates of the 1789 French Assembly, the right to political participation was grouped with the "rights of citizens" and not with the "rights of man." The 1948 Declaration makes no such distinction and calls all the rights that it lists – including the political ones in Articles 19 (of expression), 20 (of association), and 21 (of participation in government) – *human* rights. This suggests that people obtain these rights by birth (as Article 1 explicitly says they do) and that their implementation in the state in which they live is a secondary, although crucial, matter. However, if the form of government under which one lives makes no difference as to the possession (which is not the same thing as its enjoyment) of this right, then it cannot be the case that this right is given to people by the procedures or processes of democratic governments, however defined. Millions of people have always lived – and still live – under forms of government that exhibit none of the features described in Article 21. Yet these people are said to have the *human* right to "democratic entitlement." How can this be?

The UDHR was written in a shared mood of rebellion (metaphysical and otherwise) against the Nazi abuses of state power. Although we might be inclined to see the inclusion of Article 21's democratic entitlement to be a piece of Western ethnocentric thinking, the drafters themselves had no such compunctions. The only occasion on which they raised any kind of qualification was upon the addition of the clause "or by equivalent free voting procedures" at the end of 21(3). This was done upon the insistence of the Haitian delegation, which reminded the members of the Committee that they were drafting a declaration that was addressed not solely to the Western hemisphere but to the entire world and that (according to figures supplied by UNESCO) illiteracy was still very common, with 85 per cent of the world population remaining illiterate.[52] The drafters of ICCPR Article 25 (which was copied from UDHR 21) deleted the clause; nevertheless, in 1998 about one-quarter (24.8 per cent) of the world's adults (over 15) were still illiterate.[53]

We know, of course, that military and other dictatorial regimes can manipulate elections so that they appear free but, in reality, are not. The UN election-monitoring teams are sent to prevent these abuses from occurring. In the 1948 debates the Lebanese delegate also raised this point: the fact that elections would be held periodically and by secret ballot would not ensure that they would be free. The Nazi government could have subscribed to all those ideas and its elections would still not have been free, he argued. One factor that prevented Hitler's elections from being free was the intimidation and incarceration of opposition party figures, which indicates the reason why the communists wanted to keep the item "political opinion" from the list in UDHR Article 2.

When Article 21 was discussed in the First Drafting Session, Hernan Santa Cruz of Chile suggested that a provision concerning the right to form political parties be added to the article. At that point of time, UDHR Article 20 (on the right to association) included a list of legitimate reasons (which included political purposes) for which association should be allowed, resulting in the Chilean suggestion being viewed as unnecessary; unfortunately, that list was later deleted. When the Belgian delegate, Fernand Dehousse, brought up the same point later in the Third Committee, he ran into solid opposition from Mr Pavlov, the Soviet representative, who gave his colleagues a lecture on the benefits of one-party systems in peoples' democracies. When Dehousse withdrew his suggestion, Eduardo Plaza, the Venezuelan delegate, openly regretted this conciliatory Belgian gesture. I conclude that the weight of the evidence suggests that the kind of democracy called for by the UDHR is a multi-party one. This gives added sanction to recent pronouncements by various human rights judicial organs as to what a "genuine" election entails.

As I have previously stated, the communist delegations fought to have the item "political opinion" removed from the non-discrimination list in UDHR Article 2. They realized that, together with Article 21, this item implies that democratic multi-party forms of government are the only legitimate form of government. Any other type of government, whether a single-party system or a dictatorship, is a violation of the human rights of the people living under its jurisdiction. Related fights occurred when Articles 19 and 20 came up for adoption. The communist delegates wanted an exception built into these rights so that they could not be practised by Nazi and fascist-type groups or persons; they lost all of these drafting battles. The resulting Article 21 of the Declaration delineates a submerged (because it requires us to combine an item of Article 2 with UDHR 21) but otherwise unencumbered right to democratic participation.

Article 21 of the UDHR makes the following statements:

1. Everyone has the right to take part in the government of his country, directly or through freely chosen representatives.
2. Everyone has the right to equal access to public service in his country.
3. The will of the people shall be the basis of the authority of government; this will shall be expressed in periodic and genuine elections which shall be by universal and equal suffrage and shall be held by secret vote or by equivalent free voting procedures.

By locating the authority of government in the will of the people and then also spelling out how that will is to be determined, Article 21 conflicts with what, until recent years, was standard procedure in international law and practice: that practice was for nations not to judge how other nations came to have control over their people and territory. As long as governments were seen to have firm de facto control and could be relied on for treaty purposes, they were judged legitimate. UN membership is, for instance, (still) not based on the character of the government that asks to join the organization. Article 21 creates a vastly different picture: as Frank and Fox have shown, if Article 21 is to serve as a common standard for all nations, then the good standing of nations or peoples within the community of nations must, at least in part, be judged by whether they have an electoral democratic type of government; they must all be in transit to this goal. If this is not the case, Article 21 remains the most Western ethnocentric Article in the document. The broader rights stated in Articles 19 (to freedom of expression) and 20 (to freedom of association) also become heavily political when combined with Article 2. However, Article 21 is the only one that is explicitly political, even stipulating electoral democracy as the mandated form of government.

The third essay from the recent volume on democratic government in international law discussed is Fox and Nolte's piece, wherein the difference between procedural and substantive democracies is delineated. In procedural democracies there are no limitations on the rights to free speech and association that would prevent opposition figures and their parties from participating in elections, after which point they could then throw away the very ladder by which they climbed into office. They give as examples the Nazi quest for power in 1933 and the 1991 Algerian military coup that prevented a similar scenario from taking place. The question remains how far democracies are allowed to go to prevent themselves from being taken over by parties or dictators who, once they have secured power with much popular support, proceed to eliminate elections and the rest of UDHR Articles 19, 20, and 21. Can such democracies ban individual citizens – and even whole parties – from freely speaking out and standing for office? Fox and Nolte argue that they can and should be stopped. Democracies can legitimately put substantive requirements in their constitutions (or elsewhere in their legal systems) and, in that way, can safeguard their democracies from being overtaken from within. As examples of weak (which they call tolerant) substantive democracies, they discuss France, Canada, and India; they pick Germany, Israel, and Costa Rica as examples of strong (meaning militant) substantive democracies.[54] Their examples of procedural democracies are the United Kingdom, Botswana and Japan (weak), and the United States (which they see as a militantly procedural democracy). Without commenting on their choice of examples, I wish to point out that, given their classification scheme, we must rank the UDHR as calling for a substantive, not a procedural, democracy.

The story is a complicated one, as it appears initially as if the UDHR puts no limitations, other than those of Article 29, on the rights to free speech and free association, even for political purposes. The Soviet delegation repeatedly sought to have limitations added to Articles 19 and 20 that barred the use of these rights to Nazi groups; however, they failed in their attempts.[55] The idea was that, although the Nazis and other axis powers were not invited to help write the UDHR, once a democracy has been set up on the basis of respect for human rights, it should be quite tolerant of groups that are themselves known to be intolerant. Contemporary democracies differ on this issue. The procedural democracies examined by Fox and Nolte allow anti-democratic individuals and parties the same rights to free speech and association as other individuals and parties, whereas substantive democracies have constitutional and other safeguards to protect themselves against such citizens and their political parties. My reason for saying that the Declaration takes a substantive path is the much-overlooked last clause of the second sentence of Article 7. In the Second Session of the Commission, the communist delegations received an important assist from the Belgian delegation.[56] The result is the following sentence, the last clause of which I have italicized: "All are entitled to equal protection against any discrimination in violation of this Declaration *and against any incitement to such discrimination.*" The UDHR leaves open the question of how democratic governments are to provide this protection to their citizens, except that they did not want individual citizens' speech to be cut off at the start.[57]

We also need to call to mind Article 30 of the Declaration: "Nothing in this Declaration may be interpreted as implying for any State, group or person any right to engage in any activity or to perform any act aimed at the destruction of any of the rights and freedoms set forth herein." The adoption discussions for this Article are quite relevant to our own ongoing discussions of how democracies should deal with hate crimes and fanatical political parties. The drafters saw this issue as one of the spirit of the laws. A legal system can superficially appear thorough but in its spirit and application may flaunt human rights regularly, especially in cases where political opponents of the regime are involved. Eleanor Roosevelt, the American delegate, pointed out that "Nazi Germany had appeared to be legally fulfilling the duties and obligations of the state, but in practice had been destroying all human rights and liberties."[58] It was her opinion that no text could protect the spirit of the laws. Charles Malik, the Lebanese representative, countered that this was precisely the reason why such an article should be included in the UDHR. He received support from Pierre Ordonneau, the French representative to the Third Session of the Commission, who felt that it "was essential that the Declaration should at least recall the dangers of Nazism" and that "it was wrong to deny a possible recurrence of Nazism."[59] He saw the "danger against which Article [30] was aimed [as] a serious one."[60] When, in the later Third Committee meetings, the United States continued to object to Article 30, Pavlov, the Soviet Union's delegate, argued that this particular article "was the only one that could be used as a weapon against Nazism." Moreover, "[h]e appealed to the committee to consider its responsibilities before rejecting the article, which might in the future serve as a weapon against Nazism and fascism."[61]

Present-day discussions of what the democratic entitlement entails seem to suggest that Pavlov's future is here. The question that newly born (and, therefore, often fragile) democracies face is precisely that of how tolerant they should be of members of militant political groups, who abuse the freedoms of Articles 19 and 20 to come to power and then refuse to implement Article 21. To void this scenario, Pavlov was a strong supporter of a French amendment to insert the word "group" into the text of Article 30. The French proposed this amendment because "experience had shown that it was rarely States or individuals that engaged in activities aimed at the destruction of human rights; such activities in recent times had been pursued by groups sometimes acting on the instructions or with the connivance of states."[62] After Pavlov pointed out how the paths to power of both Hitler and Mussolini had been paved "by constant infiltration and propaganda," he added the example of the Klu Klux Klan in the United States. He wanted to answer the argument of those who belittled the influence of these kinds of hate groups because "their membership was very small and their activity of little consequence."[63] That rationale, he said, was exactly what had also been used in the early stages of Hitler's and Mussolini's political careers; "the disastrous consequences of such indifference were unfortunately all too well known."[64] Dehousse also agreed that the drafters should "prevent a repetition of the experiences of a number of countries in the years immediately preceding the war."[65] The word "group" was included in Article 30 unanimously by 42 votes, with just one abstention, as was the entire Article without any abstentions.[66]

I interpret these votes as an assertion that the drafters of the UDHR did not intend to let democracies be taken over from within, by military coups, by individuals, or by subversive groups (under which we may count political parties that have no intention to honour and respect human rights once they gain power by "legitimate" means such as the ballot box). This is the paradox of democracy: in the same manner that, in defence of personal liberty, political theorists of all persuasions argue that a person has no right to sell him/herself into slavery and, thereby, lose the very condition of liberty that allows him/her to perform this action, so, too, a democracy must protect itself against subversion from within and adopt measures and tactics that help it to accomplish this. That, I believe, is a strong, substantive kind of democracy – namely, the kind that cannot be undermined by its own procedures. It is the kind called for by the UDHR and supported by recent developments in international law.

Notes

1. This study is part of a larger project on the intellectual challenges posed by the Universal Declaration of Human Rights (UDHR).
2. Thomas Risse and Kathryn Sikkink, "The socialization of international human rights norms into domestic practices: Introduction" in *The Power of Human Rights International Norms and Domestic Change*, Thomas Risse, Stephen C. Ropp, and Kathryn Sikkink, eds, Cambridge: Cambridge University Press, 1999, pp. 22–35.
3. Ibid., p. 235 [emphasis added].
4. The Bogota Declaration adopted by the nations of Latin America in April of 1948 preceded the adoption of the Universal Declaration in December of that same year, but it is not really an international set of norms. For its influence on the drafting of the Declaration, see *Origins* (see note 5), chapters 4, 5, and 6, but especially sections 4.1 and 4.3.
5. For the effects of the Cold War on the drafting of the Declaration and the facts of this section, see Johannes Morsink, *The Universal Declaration of Human Rights: Origins, Drafting and Intent*, Philadelphia: The University of Pennsylvania Press, 1999, section 1.3. In the text and in the notes I refer to this volume as *Origins*, and then give the relevant section or sections.
6. He bases most of the second edition of this book (*Universal Human Rights in Theory and Practice*, Ithaca: Cornell University Press, 2003) on his analysis of this unified model.
7. Ibid., p. 34.
8. Ibid., p. 35.
9. Ibid., p. 34.

10. He does recognize the "paradox of possession" (p. 9), claiming that we have our human rights because of our human nature (e.g. pp. 10, 25 (note 4), and 90), but that nature is not connected to the basic human needs of which scientists speak; rather, it is a moral posit of societies reacting to the onslaughts of modern markets and states (section 1.3.B). I evaluate these more metaphysical and epistemological claims in a forthcoming volume on the intellectual challenges of the UDHR.
11. UN DOC (1948) A/C.3/94th Meeting, p. 81.
12. UN DOC (1948) A/C.3/94th Meeting, p. 924.
13. *Origins*, p. 342.
14. UN DOC A/C.3/240 and see *Origins*, section 1.4, for discussion of the proposal.
15. UN DOC A/C.3/240 and see *Origins*, section 1.4, for discussion of the proposal.
16. UN DOC A/C.3/240 and see *Origins*, section 1.4, for discussion of the proposal section 2.5.
17. Ibid.
18. In East and Central Europe alone, there were 25 new or revised constitutions written since the end of the Cold War. Since 1990, more than 20 new French African constitutions were published. Most of these contain bills of rights that were inspired by (and sometimes make explicit reference to) the UDHR. See the Comment in Henry J. Steiner and Philip Alston, eds, *International Human Rights in Context: Law, Politics, Morals*, Oxford: Oxford University Press, 2000, p. 990.
19. For drafting details see *Origins*, section 6.4.
20. For numerous details on the effects of the women's lobby summarized here, see *Origins*, section 3.5.
21. See Christine Chinkin's essay, "Gender Inequality and International Human Rights Law," in *Inequality, Globalization, and World Politics*, Oxford: Oxford University Press, 1999, pp. 95–122, as well as the statistics of the works cited in note 29.
22. For the protection of the rights of children in the Declaration, see *Origins*, section 7.2.
23. Charles Taylor, "The Politics of Recognition," in Amy Gutmann, ed., *Multiculturalism*, Princeton: Princeton University Press, 1994.
24. See Alasdair MacIntyre, *After Virtue*, Notre Dame, Indiana: Notre Dame University Press, 1984; Richard Rorty, *Contingency, Irony, and Solidarity*, Cambridge UK, Cambridge University Press, 1989; Will Kymlicka, *Liberalism, Community and Culture*, Oxford, UK: Clarendon Press, 1991; Chris Brown "Universal Human Rights: a critique," in *Human Rights in Global Politics*, Tim Dunne and Nicholas Wheeler, eds, Cambridge, UK: Cambridge University Press, 1999.
25. See Johannes Morsink, "Cultural Genocide, the Universal Declaration, and Minority Rights," *Human Rights Quarterly*, Vol. 21, No. 4, November 1999, pp. 1009–1061.
26. Article 1(3), Article 13(1b), Article 55(c), and Article 76(c).
27. UN DOC E/CN.4/AC.1/SR.5, p. 5.
28. For the adoption story of Article 2, see *Origins*, sections 3.3 and 3.4.
29. There his compatriot Hans Metha argued that, in the draft Covenant that was also being written, the item of "colour" did follow the item of "race," and that the same should therefore be done with the Declaration. With strong support from the Lebanese and Philippine delegations, this item was lifted from the note and put into the text of the Declaration.
30. UN DOC E/CN.4/AC.1/Sub.2/SR.21, p. 5.
31. UN DOC E/CN.4/AC.1/SR.12, p. 12.
32. *Origins*, section 3.4.
33. See Amartya Sen, *Inequality Reconsidered*, Cambridge, Massachusetts: Harvard University Press, 1992, as well as his more recent *Development as Freedom*, New York: Random House, Inc., 1999.

34. See Alan Gewirth, *The Community of Rights*, Chicago: University of Chicago Press, 1996; Martha Nussbaum, *Women and Human Development: A Capabilities Approach*, Cambridge, UK: Cambridge University Press, 2000; and Thomas Pogge, *World Poverty and Human Rights*, Oxford, UK: Blackwell Publishers Ltd, 2002.

35. United Nations Development Programme, *Human Development Report 2000*, New York: Oxford University Press, 2000; and The World Bank, *World Development Report 2000/2001: Attacking Poverty*, New York: Oxford University Press, 2000.

36. The reader will find supporting references for the drafting claims I make in this section in chapters 4, 5, and 6 of *Origins*.

37. There are always exceptions to general statements like this. See, for instance, Martin Golding, "The Primacy of Welfare Rights," in Ellen Frankel Paul et al., eds, *Human Rights*, Oxford: Basil Blackwell, 1984, pp. 119–137.

38. Maurice Cranston, "Human Rights, Real and Supposed," in Morton E. Winston, ed., *The Philosophy of Human Rights*, Belmont, California: Wadsworth Publishing Company, 1989, pp. 121–129.

39. I think that these have been laid to rest by Henry Shue's discussion of the distinction between positive and negative rights (which is what Cranston and others relied on) in his book *Basic Rights*, Princeton: Princeton University Press, 1980.

40. *Origins*, section 6.4.

41. The only outright cut he made was the right everyone has to (as Humphrey put it) "an equitable share of the national income as the need for his work and the increment it makes to the common welfare may justify" (UN DOC E/CN.4/AC.1/3/Art.39).

42. *Origins*, section 5.3.

43. *Origins*, section 5.4.

44. *Origins*, section 6.1.

45. *Origins*, section 6.4.

46. *Origins*, section 2.5.

47. Gregory H. Fox and Brad R. Roth, eds, *Democratic Governance and International Law*, Cambridge, UK: Cambridge University Press, 2000.

48. Thomas M. Franck, "Legitimacy and the Democratic Entitlement," in Fox and Roth, p. 26, note 42. His evidence is that "as of late 1997, approximately 130 national governments were legally committed to permit open, multiparty, secret ballot elections with universal franchise" (p. 27). He points out that just in the year "1996–97 elections were observed in Algeria, Ghana, Madagascar, Mali, and Yemen; further [that] electoral assistance was also provided to Bangladesh, the Comoros, Gambia, Guyana, Haiti, Liberia, Mali and Mexico" (p. 31). And he is of the opinion that a failure like the one in Angola is "balanced by successes in Namibia, Cambodia, Nicaragua and El Salvador" (p. 41). A lot of election monitoring was done in Eastern Europe with the post-1989 transition from communism. To facilitate the emergence of this right to democratic participation, the United Nations added an Electoral Assistance Division to its Secretariat in 1992.

49. Gregory H. Fox, "The right to political participation in international law," in Fox and Roth, p. 50, note 2.

50. Ibid., p. 89.

51. Ibid., p. 55.

52. See *Origins*, p. 60.

53. See United Nations, *Human Development Report 2000*, Oxford: Oxford University Press, p. 171.

54. Gregory H. Fox and Georg Nolte, "Intolerant Democracies," in Fox and Roth, p. 411, note 42.

55. See *Origins*, section 2.4.

56. See *Origins*, pp. 69–72.
57. See *Origins*, section 2.4, for further discussion of this topic.
58. UN DOC E/CN.4/AC.1/SR.28/p.4.
59. The Ordonneau and Pavlov citations are from UN DOC E/CN.4/SR.74/pp.7 and 8.
60. Ibid.
61. Ibid., p. 7.
62. The citations in this paragraph are from UN DOC GAOR, 1948, Third Session, Proceedings of the Third Committee, pp. 666–674.
63. Ibid., p. 671.
64. Ibid.
65. Ibid., p. 667.
66. Ibid., pp. 672–674.

3

Universalism and cultural relativism: Lessons for transitional states

Richard Lewis Siegel

Throughout the post-1945 era there have been disagreements among scholars, officials, and others concerning the universal applicability of all or some human rights. This chapter discusses these ongoing debates between advocates of universalism and cultural relativism. It also suggests how experience gained from complex global and national efforts to deal with such critical contemporary issues as human immunodeficiency virus/ acquired immunodeficiency syndrome (HIV/AIDS) and transitional justice can help to defuse the debate and broaden support for an expanding core of universally accepted human rights.

A search for common ground that advances the global implementation of fundamental human rights is of even greater importance to transitional societies and states than to established democracies. Transitional states tend to be highly dependent on foreign economic and political support during their often-prolonged emergence from authoritarian rule, war, regional hegemony, and highly regulated and protected economies.[1] This dependence tends to make such states and regimes highly susceptible to persuasion and pressure from powerful states and IGOs seeking to advance a universalist approach to human rights: their support for human rights may well be critical to their ability to gain material and political support from the international community. Further, some transitional states (e.g. South Africa and Poland) are in a position to play influential global and regional roles in support of human rights.[2]

Partisans of universalist positions usually argue that either the entire body of internationally recognized human rights or some core subset of such rights are applicable to all humans and to all states and societies. These rights are viewed as universally applicable standards that may legitimately challenge laws and practices that exist anywhere in the world, and any cultural or political contexts that reject, violate, or ignore those recognized norms and rules. The universalist position is rarely absolutist concerning how agreed rights are to be implemented. None the less, proponents of universalism nearly always reject efforts to justify norms and approaches deemed contrary to agreed elements of human rights on such grounds as tradition, religion, region, stage of economic development, and political culture.

The bases for acceptance of comprehensive universalist conceptions of human rights may be the recognition of the wide array of binding and non-binding prescriptive documents approved by authoritative organizations or forums, conceptions of natural or divine origins or rights, or recourse to perceived objective reason or morality.[3] While any such process produces conceptions of universal rights that evolve from century to century, there is an important distinction to be made between supporters of universalism who view their own or a consensus universalist position as already established and others who think of universalism in terms of a quest for future agreement. Peter Van Ness notes that the diverse views on Western and Asian perspectives on human rights in his book share "a notion of universalism as a continually changing, negotiated, and tentative definition of human rights."[4]

Such an evolving conception of universalism, however, does not seem to be the approach argued most often in political forums. Furthermore, whereas many scholars and officials are working to achieve common ground through dialogue, others would defend a universalist consensus with an array of strong political and other measures.[5] Although there are fundamental human rights that certainly deserve such strong support, how broad an array of rights should be defended by invoking financial, military, or political weapons?

The arguments presented at various global conferences concerning human rights, and in a host of scholarly contributions to this debate, reflect two overriding realities of the new century. First, the twentieth century is over, but its struggles relating to ideology, religion, and interests are far from fully resolved. Not even fascism and Marxism–Leninism are entirely dead; and the legacies of colonialism, racial apartheid, and military rule continue to have impacts together with such powerful forces as ethno-nationalism, militarism, and religious-based communalism. If the twentieth century involved a struggle to overcome "the age of extremes,"[6] there was only a very incomplete conquest of the forces that created and perpetuated war, genocide, and other forms of oppression, misery, and poverty. Modern universalist thinking about human rights gains political support from those seeking to challenge such surviving forces and conditions.

Shaped by, and seeking to interpret, these contemporary conditions are diverse conceptual and theoretical approaches to international relations and human rights. There is little doubt that international relations theory was slow to apply itself to international human rights, an issue area generally regarded as marginal by political realists and affirmed as self-evident by idealists. Nevertheless, by the 1990s, the academic and official commentators on the place of human rights in world affairs had achieved a critical mass and additional perspectives had emerged from identifiable realists (classical realists and neorealists), liberal internationalists, and proponents of various schools of critical theory.[7]

Generally, human rights scholarship has expanded in recent years from a locus in idealist and liberal internationalist approaches to a more comprehensive literature that increasingly also applies realist and critical theory. Andrew Hurrell, Tony Evans, David Forsythe, and Michael Ignatieff are among the human rights scholars who have addressed such explicitly realist dimensions of human rights as power, national interests, and polarity.[8] Although such a work as that by Risse, Ropp, and Sikkink is framed largely in terms of neoliberal internationalism, it also incorporates such valuable realist elements concerning human rights in transitional societies as the impacts of evolving power and polarity.[9] Furthermore, critical theories have been advanced in relation to the nexus of globalization and rights, as well as in critiques of American hegemony and empire:[10] such works have often linked feminist, neo-Marxist, and postmodernist approaches in order to reach conclusions concerning the illusions of discourse and the subtleties of social construction of rights.

The remainder of this chapter is written, explicitly and implicitly, to suggest the value of combining approaches to the study of universalism and pluralism generally and in relation to transitional societies. Some realist and critical approaches are invoked in order to denigrate much of the human rights enterprise.[11] However, it is argued here that many expressions of each of the approaches noted above are far more complementary than conflicting. As such, the study of universalism and pluralism in transitional societies clearly benefits from the incorporation of idealistic long-term goals, the mastery of the neoliberal internationalist terrain of international regimes, the deep-seated scepticism of contemporary globalism and human rights itself offered by critical theories, and the cautioning lessons of realists concerning power politics.

It is not only the remnants of twentieth-century adversaries of liberalism that challenge universalist claims for human rights in the present decade: even if evidence of an economic "race to the bottom" is contested, there is little doubt that economic globalization has had both negative and positive impacts on fundamental human rights.[12] In addition to its direct effects in particular countries and regions, globalization has provided opportunities for states and other international actors to utilize trade, diplomacy, and other instruments of policy both to support and to constrain efforts to implement universalist approaches to human rights.[13]

Resistance to universalist approaches contributed to the May 2001 vote in the UN Economic and Social Council (ECOSOC) that excluded the United States from its customary seat on the Commission on Human Rights. Although masked by secret balloting, this vote undoubtedly reflected, at least in part, secular and religious ideas, forces, and interests opposed to intrusive universalism. Although democracy has advanced through its "third wave" and beyond,[14] the current world is riddled with shallow or bogus national versions of democracy and constitutionalism that seek to mask the continuity of authoritarianism.[15]

Careful studies of many national political systems and the major world religions have failed to support simple linear theories concerning the global advance of human rights. The number of Islamic republics with strict interpretations of *Shar'ia* have increased in recent years, even as more moderate regimes in predominantly Muslim states face severe political challenges and make policy concessions that violate universalist conceptions of human rights.[16] Yet certain Muslim states are moving in progressive ways regarding such particular internationally recognized human rights as freedom of the mass media and free association, and the impacts on rights of the post-11 September 2001 US-led military interventions and occupations are too recent to be fully evaluated.[17]

Islam and Roman Catholicism, among other religions, offer alternative universalist perspectives on human rights and human dignity, even as some of their fundamental religious and political teachings are contested internally. The Catholic doctrines of Pope John Paul II have had potent effects on the current debates on the substance of fundamental human rights, with the Vatican seeking to move the consensus to the left on such issues as the death penalty and global poverty and to the right on such social and cultural matters as abortion, euthanasia, birth control, and gay and lesbian rights.

Although none of the forces and trends noted here are consistently inimical to human rights or their universal application, it is evident that the post-Cold War world lacks a universal vision concerning all human rights that is supported by a genuine global consensus. This is true despite numerous efforts of non-governmental and intergovernmental forums to proclaim such a universal consensus. In the next part of this chapter various political efforts to proclaim a universalist vision are reviewed.

The effort to declare universally applicable human rights standards

Despite continuing resistance to global agreement concerning universally recognized human rights standards, there is substantial documentation of apparent consensus on comprehensive universalism. Such evidence includes the huge scholarly literature supporting universalism, the contributors to which are spread around the world.[18] However, this support is primarily the product of great efforts by officials of national governments, NGOs, and IGOs to secure strongly worded endorsements of universalism at major international forums.

The scholarly justifications and the political efforts at international forums have endorsed either comprehensive or selective perspectives on the scope of human rights deemed universally applicable. Advocates of a comprehensive approach argue that all of the major globally adopted human rights instruments are interdependent and collectively applicable to the entire international community. They insist on the equality of economic, social, and cultural rights with civil and political ones and the inclusion of such collective rights as national self-determination and the right to development, together with traditional individual rights. Proponents of more selective approaches suggest, instead, that a core set of fundamental norms and principles are universally applicable. These are selected from comprehensive lists of rights on such bases as their non-derogable status, their designation by certain IGOs or international forums as fundamental as well as universally applicable, and their claimed designation as customary international law.

The origins of such efforts to proclaim universal standards included pre-1948 efforts to abolish the slave trade, object to massacres and atrocities of war, protect national minorities and colonized peoples, and establish minimum labour standards.[19] Charges of crimes against humanity made at Nuremburg and Tokyo, and claimed to be applicable universally, lacked a strong basis in international law before the 1948 Genocide Convention but had genuine historical antecedents.[20] Critical steps toward universalistic application of human rights norms included the acceptance of universal jurisdiction for such crimes as piracy and slave trading.[21]

The root of any universalist approach is the conviction that human rights "'inhere' universally in all human beings, throughout their lives, in virtue of their humanity alone."[22] Claims of universal applicability are generally pressed in order to legitimize and justify the progressive strengthening of the international human rights regime.

Amartya Sen is one of the many Asian scholars who insist that contemporary conceptions of rights have deep roots in non-Western as well as in Western societies. He notes in *Development as Freedom* that:

It will not have escaped the reader that this book is informed by a belief in the ability of different people from different cultures to share many common values and to agree on some common commitments. Indeed, the overriding value of freedom as the organizing principle of this work has the feature of a strong universalist presumption.[23]

Sen views human rights as a system of ethical reasoning that is the basis of political demands involving basic political liberties and civil rights in rich and poor countries alike. Although he focuses his argument on the universality of a wide array of civil and political rights and rarely invokes economic, social, and cultural human rights explicitly, he offers considerable substantive evidence on behalf of the latter set of rights.

Arguments for a comprehensive and interdependent universalism are rooted in natural rights doctrine, the overwhelming 1948 vote favouring the UDHR,[24] and international court rulings that this Declaration and certain other major and wide-ranging human rights instruments constitute parts of customary international law. Interdependence relates to the idea that civil–political and economic, social, and cultural rights, among other individual and collective rights, help to make each other viable and cannot be fully effective without all rights being respected.

The substantially increased intensity of global human rights supervision and enforcement in the last quarter of the twentieth century produced a backlash against the universal applicability of at least some parts of the "international bill of rights."[25] The ideological basis of this assault is reviewed below. In political terms, the multifaceted challenge to universalism constituted, by the early 1990s, a major perceived threat to universalist assumptions and expectations.

As a result, the 1993 Vienna Conference on Human Rights, the 1994 Cairo Conference on Population and Development, and the 1995 Beijing Women's Conference all involved efforts to articulate and reassert universalism definitively. The Vienna delegates declared "all human rights" universal, indivisible, interdependent, and interrelated, adding that "the universal nature of these rights and freedoms is beyond question."[26] The Vienna Declaration and Programme of Action amply incorporate third-generation rights as much as first-generation civil and political ones. Those rights given especially strong endorsement relate to national self-determination, development (with accompanying duties of international assistance), freedom from extreme poverty, and asylum from persecution. Although many key first-generation rights (e.g. freedom of expression and freedom of religion) are given rather little attention in the Vienna documents, the matter of which groups should benefit from the principle of equal protection and treatment is addressed broadly and with renewed intensity.[27] In comparison, the affirmation of comprehensive universalism in the United Nations Millennium Declaration, issued in September 2000 in the name of the heads of state and government of each member state, was rather perfunctory.[28]

Other concrete steps toward a comprehensive universalist approach have included the development by various global treaty-supervisory committees of "core minimum obligations," designed to give concrete meaning to many kinds of socio-economic as well as civil political rights.[29] Such efforts to make a wide array of adopted human rights more enforceable have been reinforced by rulings of national and regional courts, especially those that have referred explicitly to international human rights law in areas such as housing and gender discrimination.[30] Comprehensive approaches also can be found in the leading Inter-American and African human rights documents.[31]

Despite their participation in these global affirmations of universalism, various Western officials generally avoid stating or endorsing positions that link economic, social, and cultural rights with civil–political ones or combine the rights of individuals with collective rights. Their periodic endorsement of comprehensiveness has been the price paid for the affirmation by others of universalism concerning civil and political rights. None the less, the Charter of Fundamental Rights of the European Union, adopted at its Nice European Council meeting in December 2000, can be seen as a small step towards Western acceptance of a comprehensive universalist approach in a single document, an action that generated considerable controversy at that forum.[32]

Comprehensive universalism has certain flaws and limitations that weaken its global support. One source of concern is the politically motivated inconsistencies reflected in its formal endorsement at various meetings. At Vienna, several Western states, most notably the United States and the United Kingdom, agreed reluctantly to include the entire corpus of economic and social as well as collective rights as part of a comprehensive package of universal rights. Certain developing states acknowledged comprehensive universalism at that forum, despite their strong ongoing political campaigns to delegitimize the concept. They accepted compromise formulations that gave some standing to cultural relativism and avoided the negative political and economic consequences that might have resulted from the defiance of stronger states at that forum. Some of these developing states view the further recognition of such less well-established rights as that of development and self-determination to be worth the perceived negative impacts of global endorsement of comprehensive universalism.

Further, fully comprehensive approaches subject human rights norms, principles, and rules to a "weakest link" challenge. Those listed rights that arguably are least applicable to many poor developing states serve as lightning rods for broad attacks on the inclusive list.[33] These include references in the ICESCR to the rights to paid holidays and universal social insurance, as well as to the idea that some economic and social rights are immediately applicable in all ratifying states.

Comprehensive sets of rights also maximize difficulties relating to conflicts among rights.[34] This does not imply intrinsic contradictions between civil–political and socio-economic rights in general; rather, such conflicts primarily exist in relation to confluences of particular rights. For example, very serious conflicts occur when the protection of intellectual and other property rights confronts the rights to health and life. This is epitomized by the struggle to supply vitally needed pharmaceuticals and vaccines in the global context of HIV, tuberculosis, and other diseases that threaten the viability of entire nation-states as well as the lives of tens of millions of individuals. In such cases, deference to due process and other protections relating to intellectual and other property may threaten successful political and economic transitions as well as the right of millions to survive with dignity. This conflict illustrates the weakness of comprehensive universalist positions on human rights when certain interests of global capitalism and wealthy states confront the desperate needs of a growing number of developing and transitional states. Such trade-offs exist among economic rights as well as between socio-economic and other kinds of rights.

An inherent conflict very troubling to many advocates of universalism pertains to indigenous peoples' claims to self-determination and the maintenance of traditional approaches to justice, property, and religious practices that may be objectionable to the majority culture. Western and other supporters of universalism probably are much more sympathetic to such claims from indigenous peoples that may violate generally accepted standards of due process or other human rights than to similar demands from mainstream or majority groups. The basic issue is the extent to which every internationally prescribed human right can be reconciled with appropriate respect for the cultures and practices of indigenous and other protected subgroups.[35] This problem is, perhaps, more difficult for advanced democracies and transitional states than for authoritarian states that do not aspire to maintain strong respect for human rights for the larger society.

Such arguments point to a need for supporters of universalist positions to be open to some more flexible approaches to human rights that may diverge from some norms, principles, and rules championed as universally applicable. Such pragmatism commonly informs international courts and human rights supervisory committees and commissions and is reflected in the language of the ICESCR concerning the progressive realization of most of such rights. Advocates of universalism need to accept some pragmatic choices by transitional states, even as they legitimately challenge unjustified state efforts to excuse clear violations of core rights.

A core rights approach to universalism

The international community has combined its support of comprehensive universalism with endorsements of various sets of rights as core or fundamental, as well as universal. The political documents that articulate what Western states view to be core universally applicable human rights include such regional documents as the 1975 Helsinki Final Act and subsequent declarations of the member states of the OSCE. The European Convention on Human Rights and Fundamental Freedoms, the Charter of Fundamental Freedoms of the European Union, and the UN-adopted ICCPR also reflect the scope of their consensus. Nevertheless, it has long been clear that no set of core rights entirely or largely limited to civil and political rights will be accepted as the basis for global consensus.

The progress made towards defining the subject-matter jurisdiction of the proposed permanent International Criminal Court is only one piece of evidence that universalism is most effective and relevant when an expanding core set of fundamental rights are affirmed and implemented.[36] In July 1998, in Rome, some 120 countries adopted a statute for the proposed tribunal that included an expansive set of crimes against humanity and pointed towards universal jurisdiction and individual accountability for each such crime.[37] The Rome Statute built on such initiatives as the several Geneva Conventions on Crimes of War, the Genocide Convention of 1948, the 1987 Convention Against Torture, and the statutes and court decisions of the international tribunals for Rwanda and for the former Yugoslavia. It also incorporated and extended path-breaking efforts on behalf of the rights of women and against racial apartheid. Other concrete steps in support of a core rights approach to universalism have included bold rulings by national and regional courts in relation to Augusto Pinochet and other individual targets of transitional justice.[38]

Because of global political considerations and the varied nature of the most fundamental rights, it is essential that any core rights approach to universalism should incorporate fundamental aspects of second- and third-generation human rights as well as civil–political ones. As such, it was highly significant that the 1995 World Social Summit and the 1998 International Labour Conference (of the ILO) agreed on the same short list of universally applicable core labour or worker's rights. These fundamental rights relate to forced labour, freedom of association, collective bargaining, child labour, and non-discrimination in employment.[39]

However, which criteria should be applied when deciding on a core rights approach to universalism? It appears that both growing consensus and considerable remaining confusion mark efforts to decide which rights are most legitimate and appropriate for universal application. Various writers have focused on the non-derogable status of a particular right – the determination that no state can legally suspend (or justify the overriding of) a given right.[40] Others stress the recognition of core rights by one or more IGOs or by major international conferences addressing rights.[41] It is also pertinent to core designation that a given right has been the particular focus of binding international instruments (e.g. those concerning torture and apartheid), that special procedures have been created to implement certain rights (as in the ILO review process for freedom of association), and that certain legal instruments have been ratified by exceptionally large numbers of states or have been declared by courts or other authoritative bodies to constitute customary international law.[42]

Although such criteria incorporate standing as binding international law and the priorities of the member-states of particular international organizations, they do not guarantee that legitimacy and fundamental status will be decided objectively or rationally. A given right may well be excluded from an authoritative list of core human rights because it conflicts with interests, national or traditional law, religious or secular teachings, or practices in a small number of influential states. The actual decision-making processes primarily reflect the realities of national power and interests, the politics of international organizations, and the power of certain normative logics more than others.[43] None the less, criteria such as those noted above are the best evidence available of the nature and breadth of global consensus on important rights and standards.

It is a central contention of this chapter that an expanding core-rights approach to universalism offers the soundest strategy for maximizing effective global acceptance and implementation of human rights. The expanding core approach avoids most of the inherent weaknesses of comprehensive universalism: it builds upon areas of strong scholarly and political support and allows for the further development of the universalist consensus in terms of geographic breadth, binding authority, interpretation, and implementation.

The United States: Universalist or relativist?

Comprehensive universalism is also weakened when some of its strongest nominal state supporters – in particular, the United States – frequently act in ways inimical to its advancement. Such failures relate to civil and political rights as well as second- and third-generation ones. They involve refusals to ratify critical human rights instruments and actions that block major steps directed at effective universal enforcement of standards. It is not argued here that the United States consistently opposes the advancement of the international human rights regime: Kosovo stands out as an example of US leadership, and it is acknowledged that the loss by the United States of a seat on the Commission on Human Rights in 2001 was also related to America's assertiveness in regard to violations of human rights by particular authoritarian states. Also, the United States occasionally rejects or offers reservations to global civil–political rights instruments for arguably bona fide reasons of civil liberties. Nevertheless, even the record of the US delegation at various sessions of the Commission on Human Rights has been interpreted negatively in relation to universalist criteria.[44]

Several authors suggest that the formally universalist positions of the United States are, in many respects, culturally and politically relativist.[45] America and several allied states were largely responsible for the restrictive approach to the right to work that was incorporated into the ICESCR. The United States worked assiduously to avoid binding international obligations concerning the right to development in 1986 and opposed the Charter of Economic Rights and Duties of States passed by the General Assembly in 1975.[46] Washington has also refused to ratify most ILO labour rights conventions, as well as such global and regional instruments central to comprehensive (and even core) approaches to universalism, such as the ICESCR, the global conventions on the rights of the child and discrimination against women, and the American Convention on Human Rights. Other key human rights instruments have been ratified by the United States only after decades of political effort and with major (and, in some cases, arguably illegal) reservations and understandings. America holds to its own positions on hate speech, the death penalty (most egregiously in relation to youths under the age of 18 years),[47] and other issues on which it stands apart from most strong advocates of universalism. Recent US opposition to the global land-mine convention, age limits concerning child soldiers, and the International Criminal Court have reinforced perceptions of America's relativism and helped to clarify the idea that support for pluralism is not only a product of authoritarianism, religious fundamentalism, and tradition. The relativism of the United States and its rejection of intrusive universalism regarding the application and implementation of human rights to its nationals derives in part from the power of the military and the US Senate in Washington, politics, parochialism, disrespect for international law, federalism, and a legacy of racism. Some of the orientations and patterns that support this resistance to universalism are core aspects of American culture, democracy, and constitutionalism. Others are intrinsic to the US role as a global hegemon, particularly in the present era of pax Americana and its war on terrorism.

Cultural relativism's challenge to universalism

Opposition to universalism derives from many sources and takes many forms. Various opponents have rejected comprehensive and core versions of universalism, basing their arguments on the legitimacy of moral or cultural pluralism as well as on the need to adjust human rights standards to various stages of economic and political development. Such arguments are put forward by many Western commentators, as well as by many scholars and officials from Asia, Africa, and Latin America.[48]

Cultural relativists typically contend that many proclaimed human rights are inapplicable or of limited validity in many or most non-Western settings. They argue that particular rights are alien to certain values, practices, and purposes critical to human dignity. Various asserted rights, in the view of some relativists, reflect Western imperialism or hegemony and should be subordinated to religious authority and national or popular sovereignty. As noted by Donnelly, "[t]he doctrine of cultural relativism holds that at least some variation cannot be legitimately criticized by outsiders."[49]

Advocating respect for diverse customs and cultures, relativists also often allege that the "licence" promoted by the universal or Western consensus produces detrimental social effects. Many call for a rights agenda more compatible with community, sovereignty, order, and/or religious authority and claim that certain aspects of democracy and human rights are incompatible with the essence of various legitimate cultural and political traditions. Advocates of these positions frequently emphasize that the West's liberal consensus supporting human rights developed rather recently in broad historical terms and that the developing world's need for time to shape each societies' own synthesis of human rights and other cherished values must be respected.

Relativist positions focus on two primary human rights battlegrounds. One line of argument defends limitations on democracy and constitutional rights in the interest of economic development, order, political stability, and continuity. The other – which may well be combined with the first – stresses the need for and value of preserving traditional and religious approaches to issues of equality, family, gender, children, sexuality, and related matters. The former focus has been strongly challenged as an ideological mask of authoritarian regimes seeking to defend repression and hold onto power. Both perspectives are often widely shared by large proportions of citizens as well as by élites in various authoritarian and transitional states.[50]

Radical, strong, and weak versions of cultural relativism can be distinguished. Donnelly notes that the radical position holds that culture is the "sole source of the validity of a moral right or rule."[51] He suggests that the strong relativist position views culture as the principal basis of their validity and that weak relativism perceives culture as an "important source" of the validity of a moral or human right.[52] This American political theorist also offers this useful categorization of the possible relevance of cultural relativism to different aspects of human rights:

In a rough way, three hierarchical levels of variation can be established, involving cultural relativism in the *substance* of lists of human rights, in the *interpretation* of individual rights, and in the *form* in which particular rights are implemented.[53]

The latter formulation opens doors to the adaptation of core universally accepted rights in diverse cultural and political settings.

It is increasingly recognized that there are radical as well as more moderate versions of universalism, as well as relativism. According to Donnelly, the radical universalist stance reflects "the view that all values, including human rights, are entirely universal, in no way subject to modification in light of cultural or historical differences," and that "there is only one set of human rights that applies at all times and at all places."[54] To a considerable extent, Donnelly is offering conceptual straw men to be knocked down when he defines radical versions of both universalism and relativism.

The voice of relativism has been heard most loudly in the speeches and writings of such South-East Asian leaders as Lee Kuan Yew and Mahathir Bin Mohamad,[55] at preliminary regional forums of major international human rights conferences and at periodic gatherings of regional and global IGOs. The 1981 meeting of the Islamic Conference, the Asian Preparatory Meeting of the 1993 Vienna Conference, the 1994 meeting of the League of Arab States, and the Organization for African Unity's 1981 session consciously targeted aspects of universalism and supported key elements of moderate to strong cultural relativism.[56] Such other international forums as the 1994 Cairo Conference on Population and Development and the 2002 UN General Assembly Session on Children also demonstrated the absence of global consensus on some of the most vital human rights issues pertaining to personal autonomy and human dignity.

Relativism is not only expressed officially in minority or regional votes on key global instruments and initiatives: World Trade Organization (WTO) ministerial meetings have repeatedly rejected intrusive universalist responses to core labour and environmental standards, with large majorities equating the policing of minimal labour standards through the WTO with Western protectionism and hegemony. Most of the same states proceed to argue that their rejection of binding labour and environmental standards does not reflect opposition to those standards per se but, rather, rejection of their application to developing states that require more time and economic development to afford investment of the resources required. It should be noted, however, that not all such standards require investment of substantial resources by those states: equality of treatment of groups within the labour force and free association of workers are among the standards at issue.

Pluralist realities are reflected in the refusals of many governments to ratify certain human rights conventions and their additional optional protocols. They are strongly manifested in reservations and understandings on rights involving such subjects as discrimination against women, family law, and the rights of children. The relationships of human rights standards to *Shar'ia*, custom and tradition, national emergencies, stages of economic development, social harmony, and preferences for particular political systems are claimed bases for reservations offered and for resistance to implementation of certain rights.[57] Such policy positions and actions operate to lessen global consensus on human rights.

Transitional societies and intercultural dialogue

A more genuine universalism can best be shaped by building upon existing consensus in support of one or more sets of core human rights, agreement expressed through the broadest possible global endorsement, and explicit provision for meaningful scrutiny of violations and effective enforcement. As noted above, such consensus is strongest now in regard to a growing list of crimes against humanity, and can reasonably be claimed for the core labour standards identified in the 1990s. It also includes the non-derogable elements of the leading global human rights conventions.

In the view of this writer, a globally accepted core must reach beyond these agreed rights and standards, incorporating other key aspects of civil–political and economic, social, and cultural rights. Although the addition of other core rights can be logically derived from areas of agreement in the entire body of regional and national as well as global human rights instruments, further steps should be taken to legitimize an expanding core of rights that should be singled out for more effective global implementation. The hierarchy of rights implied in the enforcement work of the Human Rights Committee and the Committee on Economic, Social and Cultural Rights is a start to such a process.[58]

The broadening of these sets of core rights requires what has been termed "intercultural" or "intercivilizational" dialogue. This effort must be made, even if we accept pessimistic predictions concerning global order, peace, and stability in the decades ahead.[59] Such dialogues have been skilfully managed in recent decades at conferences and symposia organized by diverse sponsoring organizations.[60] Progress in understanding diverse perspectives and seeking ways to bridge gaps is evident in books and other publications, such as those edited by Berting (with others), Bauer and Bell, and Van Ness. The meetings that helped to generate the present book constitute another valuable effort at global dialogue. Vitally important communication occurs among NGO representatives and delegates before and during major human rights conferences – efforts that periodically contribute to the expansion of a core universalist consensus.[61] Needless to say, such dialogue also poses risks of hardened positions as outcomes, but this is a gamble worth taking when the meetings are well prepared and major participants on all sides have open minds and freedom to find common ground.

Various advocates of universalism who work actively in traditional Islamic and other societies have convinced this writer that the advancement of rights for women, children, religious minorities, and others depends on dialogue, persuasion, and compromise within particular states or on a pan-religious basis.[62] That is, the past and current demands made by proponents of *Shar'ia* and other religious or traditional doctrines and practices must be answered internally in order for progressive approaches to equality and tolerance to emerge and develop. There is a very real risk that external criticism of traditional societies will be counter-productive if it occurs while such internal dialogues and political efforts proceed. Yet, in the long run, the internal and international dialogues must proceed together and should be combined with global pressure when (as in Sudan, Myanmar, and Afghanistan) particularly severe approaches to inequality and intolerance are adopted.

Various transitional societies offer both great opportunities and major risks for internal and intersocietal dialogue relating to tradition and human rights. Respected quantitative research finds that transition status correlates positively with greater violence and "life-integrity violations."[63] Transitional states moving away from stable authoritarianism confront an exceptionally wide array of destabilizing forces and risks:

these include such seemingly intractable problems as exceptionally high rates of unemployment, civil and international war, foreign military occupation, corruption, the need for profound economic restructuring, AIDS and other devastating diseases, and vulnerability to (often unpredictable) manifestations of economic globalization and natural disasters.

Further, a substantial proportion of transitional societies continue to struggle with policy issues concerning transitional justice. Even states that ended military or other repressive regimes many years ago did not escape entirely the negative consequences of their choices concerning justice, truth, reconciliation, risks to the anticipated democratic transition, and other considerations.[64] States' choices to pursue such approaches as truth and reconciliation commissions, prosecutions, amnesties and other measures, or to refuse altogether to confront past grave violations of rights, significantly affect their subsequent responses to multilateral assertions of universalism as well as to global and regional, legal, and political initiatives concerning such issues as torture, war crimes, disappearances, and genocidal massacres. Decisions by particular states concerning transitional justice also affect their consideration of such cutting-edge norms as the prohibition of military coups designed to oust elected governments.

The confluence of such dangers and pressing issues make intersocietal and internal dialogue on human rights norms concerning equality, tolerance, justice, and other such values both more difficult and far more necessary. This is true in part because there are inherent limitations on the ability of outside forces to compel acceptance of such values and obligations.

Learning from experience with critical issues

The acceptance of advice from activists in Islamic and other countries concerning the need for domestic dialogue as well as legal and political efforts on behalf of human rights is but one example of necessary social learning. Various other insights can be discovered by studying the grass-roots struggles in transitional and other states concerning such issues as HIV/AIDS, transitional justice, war crimes, exploitation of women and children, and other critical issues.

One of the most important lessons learned from the HIV/AIDS pandemic is that there is no meaningful line separating the right to life from the right to health, gender equity, education, and development. Prevention and treatment are central to the control of this catastrophic disease, and these require individual and collective rights to both maximal national political efforts and increased international assistance.[65] For most of the post-1945 life of the contemporary global human rights regime there has been a struggle to take the right to life seriously in relation to genocide, war crimes, and other crimes against humanity;[66] however, infectious disease constitutes no less a threat to the right to life, and it is necessary to invoke effective approaches that are global, are multi-faceted, and that build upon an expanding conception of universally applicable human rights.

The HIV/AIDS pandemic also suggests the need for more astute approaches to certain traditional and religious ideas and practices that many see as impeding efforts to bring the disease under control. This crisis, particularly in various parts of Africa, has forced states and communities to utilize traditional medical practitioners, to engage in dialogues with religious authorities concerning the need to reinterpret traditional conceptions of morality and sexuality, and to study carefully the impacts of patriarchy on the pandemic. In some of the most successful highly affected countries, bearers of tradition are effectively mobilized and prevention campaigns are adjusted to gain the support of culturally diverse élites and others.[67] Unfortunately, there are more examples of failures to overcome such perceived barriers than to co-opt or transform them, and national leaders who fear the loss of certain benefits of economic globalization are often the leading voices of national denial concerning the pandemic. But admonitions concerning the need for inclusive strategies are being advanced by the Joint United Nations Programme on HIV/AIDS (UNAIDS) and its constituent organizations, even as national élites and others gradually abandon their various rationalizations for denial concerning the level of crisis and the solutions needed.

Lessons from the past two decades of experiments with transitional justice also suggest opportunities to embrace relativism on behalf of universalist conceptions of rights. South Africa has taught us how Christian and traditional religious ideas can contribute to the shaping of approaches to reconciliation.[68] Whether the South African effort to balance truth, amnesty, and prosecution has helped to entrench the rule of law will long be debated. It contributed to these larger goals by allowing the crimes of the victorious forces to be investigated and reported together with those of the apartheid state. According to Alex Boraine, Deputy Chairperson of South Africa's Truth and Reconciliation Commission, "Every attempt should be made to assist countries to find their own solutions provided that there is no blatant disregard of fundamental human rights."[69]

South Africa's (and some other states') experiences with amnesty and reconciliation have evoked mostly positive responses from the international community. International criminal tribunals in Tanzania and, especially, the Hague, offer models of transitional justice that mesh diverse legal procedures and traditions, avoid the death penalty, and assert as crimes against humanity such atrocities as systemic rape and sexual slavery.[70] Yet many transitional states have failed to respond meaningfully to grave violations of fundamental rights and have demonstrated an inability or unwillingness to provide appropriate procedural rights.[71] The unwillingness of such states as Cambodia, Nigeria, and Serbia–Montenegro to respond to grave violations results from many factors, including the continuance in power of participants in the prior regime, concern for the fragility of domestic peace and of the transition itself, and unwillingness to bow to external pressures for prosecutions and other measures.

The present writer has argued elsewhere that states have a duty to bring major individual perpetrators to justice in cases of grave violations of human rights.[72] Geoffrey Robertson and Diane F. Orentlicher also stress this point, citing as authority major international conventions and decisions of national and international courts.[73] There clearly have been abuses of amnesty, especially where departing leaders have negotiated their own immunity. None the less, the experiences of South Africa and many other states suggest that no single approach to justice and truth can, or should, be applied globally. The goals of transitional justice are varied, including the need to reject impunity for grave violations of human rights, the revelations of the scale and character of examples of those violations, and the furthering of national reconciliation and the rule of law. Each transitional society needs to shape a balanced approach consistent with its political culture, recent history, and power relations.

Many other lessons relating to cultural relativism and the expansion of core universally applicable rights can be learned from national, regional, and global efforts to deal with other critical contemporary issues. These include crises of religious tolerance; cultural and physical threats against indigenous peoples; denial of the fundamental rights of women and girls; and persistent forced labour, slavery, and exploitative child labour. These violations illustrate both the necessity of a universalist approach to an expanding core set of human rights and the enormous cultural and political challenges to their effective implementation.

Conclusions

This chapter has drawn attention to developments that have contributed to the recognition of an expanding core of universally accepted human rights. It argues for markedly expanded dialogue in pursuit of broad consensus on the scope of universally applicable rights and suggests that efforts to find additional common ground with religious and other traditional forces are needed in order to advance human rights and dignity in many transitional societies. Although there is a need to confront violators of core universally recognized rights through a wide array of national, regional, and global multilateral responses, coercive efforts should not be allowed to destroy opportunities to broaden and deepen the existing core universal consensus. For example, prosecutions undertaken after the fall of tyrannical regimes must respect the rule of law and demonstrate a fair and even-handed approach to violators on all sides of international and internal conflicts.

Any set of core human rights deserving universal consensus must transcend civil and political rights and extend to second- and third-generation standards. This is true because the several generations of rights are genuinely interdependent. As seen in the context of the HIV/AIDS pandemic, a particular socio-economic right such as health and a third-generation right to international assistance are both integral to a first-generation right to life.

It is not very productive to adopt universalist statements in major human rights documents when these are based on clumsy compromises. This occurs when support for universalism is combined in conference statements with references to relativism that can be read to justify a broad rejection of universalism. Although it is important to strengthen all the rights adopted in major multilateral instruments, an approach that demonstrates clear positive results on behalf of a core set of fundamental and universally accepted rights can do more to advance human rights in transitional and other societies than a comprehensive approach to universalism or a relativist position that rejects even a core universalist consensus. After all, the goal of the effort to expand respect for, and implementation of, human rights is to make concrete advances on the ground and to achieve progress in areas that are recognized as priorities by experts and ordinary citizens alike.

Numerous transitional states, from Africa to the Balkans and from the Ukraine to Central America, confront (or have recently faced) such threats to the human right to life as HIV and other infectious diseases, natural disasters, genocide, war crimes, and the collapse of state authority. Their critical needs necessitate generous levels of international assistance for development, at least minimal standards of justice and political participation, institutions that prevent exploitation of weaker groups, and the ability to remove corrupt and despotic governments. The expanding core approach to universalism helps to create and build upon agreement concerning such rights and obligations and increase the likelihood of successful transitions.

Notes

1. It can be argued that almost every society strongly affected by economic and cultural globalization is transitional. However, the consensus of the authors of this book is that the term should be employed more narrowly.

2. Andrew Moravcik presents evidence that "new democracies" were vital to the development of a strong European human rights regime that focused on civil–political rights both in the aftermath of World War II and in the 1990s. He argues that the insecurity of their situation as new democracies motivated their support of a strong regional human rights regime that would serve as "a bulwark against tyranny." Moravcik, "The Origins of Human Rights Regimes: Democratic Delegation in Postwar Europe," *International Organization*, Vol. 54, No. 2, Spring 2000, p. 237.

3. Michael Freeman, "The Philosophical Foundations of Human Rights," *Human Rights Quarterly*, Vol. 16, 1994, pp. 491–514.

4. Peter Van Ness, ed., *Debating Human Rights: Critical Essays from the United States and Asia*, London and New York: Routledge, 1999, p. 11.

5. Thomas M. Franck, "Are Human Rights Universal?", *Foreign Affairs*, Vol. 80, No. 1, January–February 2001, pp. 203–204.

6. Eric Hobsbawm, *The Age of Extremes: A History of the World, 1914–1991*, New York: Pantheon Books, 1994.

7. For a wide-ranging introduction to such schools or approaches see Scott Burchill and Andrew Linklater, *Theories of International Relations*, New York: St Martin's Press, 1996. For an excellent edited volume that applies several of these approaches to contemporary foreign policy, see C. John Ikenberry, ed., *America Unrivaled: The Future of the Balance of Power*, Ithaca, NY and London: Cornell University Press, 2002. The leading presentation of neorealism is Kenneth Waltz, *Theory of International Relations*, Reading, Mass.: Addison-Wesley, 1979. For liberal internationalism see M.W. Zacher and R.A. Mathew, "Liberal International Theory: Common Threads, Divergent Strands," in Charles W. Kegley Jr, ed., *Controversies in International Relations Theory*, New York, 1995, pp. 107–150. A leading and controversial recent work reflecting several schools of critical theory is Michael Hardt and Antonio Negri, *Empire*, Cambridge, Mass. and London: Harvard University Press, 2000.

8. Michael Ignatieff et al., *Human Rights as Politics and Idolatry*, Princeton: Princeton University Press, 2001, especially pp. 3–52; Andrew Hurrell, "Power, Principles and Prudence: Protecting Human Rights in a Deeply Divided World," in Tim Dunne and Nicholas J. Wheeler, eds, *Human Rights in Global Politics*, Cambridge and New York: Cambridge University Press, 1999, pp. 277–302; Tony Evans, "Introduction: Power, Hegemony and the Universalization of Human Rights," in Evans, ed., *Human Rights Fifty Years On: A Reappraisal*, Manchester and New York: Manchester University Press, 1998, pp. 2–23; and David Forsythe, ed., *Human Rights and Comparative Foreign Policy*, Tokyo: United Nations University Press, 2000.

9. Thomas Risse, Stephen C. Ropp, and Kathryn Sikkink, eds, *The Power of Human Rights: International Norms and Domestic Change*, Cambridge and New York: Cambridge University Press, 1999.

10. See Austin Sarat and Thomas R. Kearns, eds, *Human Rights: Concepts, Contests, Contingencies*, Ann Arbor: University of Michigan Press, 2001; Michael Ignatieff et al., *Human Rights as Politics and Idolatry*, pp. 53–98; Alison Brysk, ed., *Globalization and Human Rights*, Berkeley: University of California Press, 2002; and Upenda Baxi, "Voice of Suffering Fragmented Universality, and the Future of Human Rights" and Anne Oxford, "Contesting Globalization: A Feminist Perspective on the Future of Human Rights," in Burn H. Weston and Stephen P. Marks, eds, *The Future of Human Rights*, Ardsley, New York: Transnational Publishers, 1999, pp. 101–156, 157–186.

11. For such a realist version see Henry Kissinger, *White House Years*, Boston: Little, Brown & Company, 1979, especially pp. 54–70.

12. See Yash Ghai, "Rights, Social Justice, and Globalization in East Asia," in Joanne R. Bauer and Daniel A. Bell, eds, *The East Asian Challenge for Human Rights*, Cambridge and New York: Cambridge University Press, 1999, pp. 241–263.

13. See Ann Kent, *China and the United Nations, and Human Rights: The Limits of Compliance*, Philadelphia: University of Pennsylvania Press, 1999; Ming Wan, *Human Rights in Chinese Foreign Relations: Defining and Defending National Interests*, Philadelphia: University of Pennsylvania Press, 2001.

14. See Samuel Huntington, *The Third Wave: Democratization in the Late Twentieth Century*, Norman: University of Oklahoma Press, 1991.

15. For a view of this matter that is more positive than mine see Adrian Koratnycky, "A Century of Progress," *Journal of Democracy*, Vol. 11, No. 1, January 2000, pp. 187–2000; for more negative views see Renske Doorenspleet, "Reassessing the Three Waves of Democratization," *World Politics*, Vol. 52, April 2000, pp. 384–406, and Fareed Zakaria, *The Future of Freedom: Illiberal Democracy at Home and Abroad*, New York: W.W. Norton Publishers, 2003.

16. Numerous Muslim states have based reservations concerning ratified human rights conventions on the necessity of maintaining policies based on *Shari'a*. See Radhika Coomaraswamy, "Reinventing International Law: Women's Rights as Human Rights in the International Community," in Van Ness, ed., *Debating Human Rights*, pp. 167–168.

17. Abdullahi An-Na'im, "Human Rights in the Arab World: A Regional Perspective," *Human Rights Quarterly*, Vol. 23, No. 3, August 2001, pp. 701–732.

18. One major source of such scholarly arguments is Joanne R. Bauer and Daniel A. Bell, eds, *The East Asian Challenge for Human Rights*, Cambridge: Cambridge University Press, 1999. Their volume also includes opposing views.

19. Several of these historical efforts are reviewed in Paul Gordon Lauren, *Power and Prejudice: The Politics and Diplomacy of Racial Discrimination*, Boulder, CO and London: Westview Press, 1988. See also documentation in Henry J. Steiner and Philip Alston, eds, *International Human Rights in Context: Law, Politics, Morals*, 2nd edn. Oxford: Oxford University Press, pp. 56–125.

20. Louis Henkin et al. refer to the 1945 Nuremberg Charter as "the first formal assertion of an international law of human rights." They cite Adam Hochschild to the effect that the phrase "crimes against humanity" originated with a letter concerning the atrocities in the Congo from George Washington Williams to US Secretary of State Blaine dated 15 September 1890. Henkin et al., *Human Rights*, New York: Foundation Press, 1999, p. 73. See also Hochschild, *King Leopold's Ghost*, New York: Houghton Mifflin Co., 1998, pp. 111–112.

21. See Paul Gordon Lauren, *The Evolution of International Human Rights: Visions Seen*, Philadelphia: University of Pennsylvania Press, 1998, pp. 38–45; and M. Cherif Bassiouni, "Universal Jurisdiction for International Crimes: Historical Perspectives and Contemporary Practices," *Virginia Journal of International Law*, No. 42, Vol. 1, 2001, pp. 82–162.

22. Paul Sieghart, *International Law of Human Rights*, Oxford: Clarendon Press, 1983, p. 17.

23. Amartya Sen, *Development as Freedom*, New York: Alfred A. Knopf, 2000, p. 244.

24. Because most other human rights instruments adopted at the global level have been more narrowly focused, the UDHR is a rare example of wide-ranging first-, second- and third-generation rights in a single official document.

25. This term includes the UDHR and the international covenants on civil–political and economic, social, and cultural rights adopted by the General Assembly in 1966. Efforts to implement a more or less comprehensive universalist approach include the activation of several treaty-based UN human rights supervisory committees in the 1980s and 1990s. These committees help implement conventions on economic, social, and cultural rights and civil–political rights as well as conventions to overcome discrimination based on gender and race and to advance the rights of children, among others. Further, NGOs

such as Human Rights Watch utilize an increasingly comprehensive approach to their annual surveys. The effectiveness of such efforts grew with the increased participation of NGOs in some UN organs, the adoption of additional optional protocols allowing non-state complaints, and a broadening scope of inquiry (including such issues as AIDS and violence against women) on the part of the UN Commission of Human Rights and its Sub-Commission on the Promotion and Protection of Human Rights.

26. Vienna Declaration and Programme of Action, Adopted 25 June 1993, UN Doc. A/CONF. 157/23, para. 5.

27. For a review of the Vienna documents that includes the argument that religious tolerance was treated inadequately by the delegates see "Introduction," Special Issue of *The Review: International Commission of Jurists*, No. 50, 1993, p. 5. Notable attention is given to the rights of girls, the disabled, and linguistic minorities in the documents, and racial and gender discrimination are treated expansively.

28. "United Nations Millennium Declaration," adopted 8 September 2000, in *UN Chronicle*, No. 3, 2000, pp. 38–47.

29. For examples of such positions by supervisory committees see Gina Bekker, ed., *A Compilation of Essential Documents on Economic, Social and Cultural Rights*, Pretoria, South Africa: Centre for Human Rights, University of Pretoria, 1999. See also "The Maastricht Guidelines on Violations of Economic, Social, and Cultural Rights," in *Human Rights Quarterly*, Vol. 20, No. 3, August 1998, pp. 691–704, and Audrey Chapman and Sage Russell, eds, *Core Obligations: Building a Framework for Economic, Social and Cultural Rights*, Antwerp and Oxford: Intersentia Publishers, 2002.

30. Courts of the Council of Europe, the European Union, India, and South Africa have been among those that have made important rulings implementing economic, social, and cultural rights. See Henry J. Steiner and Philip Alston, *International Human Rights in Context: Law, Politics, Morals – Text and Materials*, 2nd edn. Oxford: Oxford University Press, 2000, pp. 158–315.

31. These include the 1948 American Declaration of the Rights and Duties of Man, the 1969 American Convention on Human Rights (with its additional 1988 protocol on economic, social, and cultural rights) and the 1981 African Charter on Human and People's Rights.

32. "Charter of Fundamental Rights of the European Union," 2000/C364/01, *Official Journal of the European Communities*, 18 December 2000; "The EU's Growing Pains," *Foreign Policy*, March–April 2001, pp. 76–77.

33. See Theodor Meron, "On a Hierarchy of International Human Rights," *American Journal of International Law*, Vol. 80, No. 1, January 1986, p. 21.

34. It is acknowledged that any set of prescribed constitutional or human rights engenders serious conflicts among those rights. This section emphasizes that a comprehensive and non-hierarchical approach to rights exacerbates the potential for, and scope of, such conflicts.

35. A strongly cultural relativist position on this question has long been strongly supported in the discipline of anthropology. This was reflected in the American Anthropological Association's 1947 Statement of Human Rights, which can be found in *American Anthropologist*, Vol. 49, No. 4, 1947, pp. 539–543.

36. As noted by Meron (see note 33), this involves "the quest for a hierarchy of international human rights." Meron, "On a Hierarchy of International Human Rights," p. 1.

37. See Michael P. Scharf, "Results of the Rome Conference for an International Criminal Court," *ASIL Insight*, August 1998.

38. See Geoffrey Robertson, *Crimes Against Humanity: The Struggle for Global Justice*, New York: The New Press, 1999, especially pp. 203–400; and Gary Jonathan Bass, *Stay the Hand of Vengeance: The Politics of War Crimes Tribunals*, Princeton and Oxford:

Princeton University Press, 2000. A limiting development is the 2001 decision of the International Court of Justice concerning immunity of an incumbent Minister of Foreign Affairs of the Congo from Belgium's claimed jurisdiction. Democratic Republic of the Congo v. Belgium, 14 February 2002.

39. See Organization for Economic Cooperation and Development, *Trade, Employment and Labor Standards*, Paris: OECD, 1996, pp. 10–28. These rights were justified in part on the basis that they provide "framework conditions" that make other labour standards possible.

40. Christina M. Cerna, "Universality of Human Rights and Cultural Diversity: Implementation in Different Socio-Cultural Contexts," *Human Rights Quarterly*, Vol. 16, 1994, p. 744.

41. Organization for Economic Cooperation and Development, *Trade, Employment and Labor Standards*, pp. 10, 26.

42. Cerna (see note 40), pp. 745–749; Meron (see note 33), "On a Hierarchy of International Human Rights."

43. On normative logics relative to human rights see Richard Falk, *Human Rights and State Sovereignty*, New York and London: Holmes and Meier Publishers, 1981, pp. 33–62.

44. See Human Rights Watch Press Release, "UN: Progress on Disappearances Pact Hailed," 26 April 2001, available at ⟨http://www.hrw.org/press/2001⟩.

45. See David P. Forsythe, "US Foreign Policy and Human Rights," pp. 27–38, and Daniel W. Wessner, "From Judge to Participant: The United States as Champion of Human Rights," in Peter Van Ness, ed., *Debating Human Rights: Critical Essays from the United States and Asia*, London and New York: Routledge, 1999, pp. 255–277.

46. Richard Lewis Siegel, *Employment and Human Rights: The International Dimension*, Philadelphia: University of Pennsylvania Press, 1994, pp. 65–71; Seyom Brown, *Human Rights in World Politics*, pp. 29–30. The vote on the Charter was 120 to 6 with 10 abstentions.

47. Although abolition of the death penalty has advanced significantly as an internationally recognized human rights standard, particularly in the past two decades, full abolition is not yet a universally accepted aspect of the right to life, or cruel and inhuman punishment. None the less, major inroads have been made. Abolition has been adopted as a binding regional norm in the growing domain of the Council of Europe and has progressed as a norm accepted in Latin America and Africa and in relation to the mentally ill and developmentally disabled, as well as those under the age of 18 years. See William A. Schabas, *The Abolition of the Death Penalty in International Law*, 3rd edn, Cambridge: Cambridge University Press, 2002.

48. For scholarly support for relativism see Jan Berting et al., eds, *Human Rights in a Plural World: Individuals and Collectivities*, Westport/London: Mechler Corporation, 1990; Richard A. Wilson, ed., *Human Rights, Culture and Context: Anthropological Perspectives*, London and Chicago: Pluto Press, 1997; and Adamantia Pollis and Peter Schwab, *Human Rights: Cultural and Ideological Perspectives*, New York: Praeger Publishers, 1980.

49. Jack Donnelly, *Universal Human Rights in Theory and Practice*, Ithaca and London: Cornell University Press, 1989, p. 109.

50. Abhullahi An Na'im states this point as a common feature of Arab States in *An Na'imm*, p. 722. For a somewhat more positive view of democratic prospects see Adrian Karatnycky, "The 2001 Freedom House Survey: Muslim Countries and the Democracy Gap," *Journal of Democracy*, Vol. 13, No. 1, January 2002, pp. 99–112.

51. Donnelly, *Universal Human Rights in Theory and Practice*, pp. 109–110.

52. Ibid., p. 110.

53. Ibid.

54. Jack Donnelly, *International Human Rights*, second edition, Boulder, CO: Westview Press, 1998, p. 33.
55. See Lee Kuan Yew, *The Singapore Story: Memoirs of Lee Kuan Yew*, New York: Prentice-Hall, 1999.
56. See Declan O'Sullivan, "The History of Human Rights Across the Regions: Universalism versus Cultural Relativism," *The International Journal of Human Rights*, Vol. 2, No. 3, Autumn 1998, pp. 31–34, 37–43 and Olusola Ojo, "Understanding Human Rights in Africa," in Jan Berting, et al., *Human Rights in a Pluralist World*, pp. 115–124.
57. See O'Sullivan, "The History of Human Rights Across the Regions," pp. 28–29.
58. This includes the effort to achieve consensus on core minimum obligations of states as well as to hold states parties to what the US Supreme Court would call "strict scrutiny" for designated elements of each multinational convention.
59. Pessimistic prognostications are presented in Samuel Huntington, *The Clash of Civilizations and the Remaking of World Order*, New York: Simon & Schuster, 1996 and Robert D. Kaplan, *The Coming Anarchy: Shattering the Dreams of the Post Cold War*, New York: Vintage Books, 2000.
60. These have included UNESCO, the UN Human Rights Centre, The Netherlands Commission for UNESCO, the Carnegie Council on Ethics and International Affairs, the Association for Asian Studies, and the Bulletin of Concerned Asian Scholars.
61. Examples of such progress have occurred recently in relation to child soldiers, exploitative child labour, violence against women, and a permanent international criminal court. Although not necessarily producing new core universally accepted rights, such developments clearly constitute steps in that direction.
62. See Norani Othman, "Grounding Human Rights Arguments in Non-Western Culture: Shari'a and the Citizenship Rights of Women in a Modern Islamic State," in Bauer and Bell, *The East Asian Challenge for Human Rights*, pp. 169–192.
63. See Helen Fein, "More Murder in the Middle: Life-Integrity Violations and Democracy in the World, 1987," *Human Rights Quarterly*, Vol. 17, 1995, pp. 170–191 and Steven C. Poe, C. Neal Tate, and Linda Camp Keith, "Repression of the Human Right to Personal Integrity Revisited: A Global Cross-National Study Covering the Years 1976–1993," *International Studies Quarterly*, Vol. 43, 1999, pp. 291–313.
64. For the most comprehensive set of essays and documents on the choices made see Neil J. Kritz, ed., *Transitional Justice: How Emerging Democracies Reckon with Former Regimes*, 3 volumes. Washington, D.C.: United States Institute of Peace Press, 1995; see also Robertson, *Crimes Against Humanity*.
65. I discuss these themes in Siegel, "AIDS and Human Rights," *Human Rights Quarterly*, Vol. 18, No. 3, August 1996, pp. 612–640; see also Helen Epstein, "Time of Indifference," *The New York Review of Books*, 12 April 2001, pp. 33–38.
66. See Samantha Power, *"A Problem from Hell": America and the Age of Genocide*, New York: Basic Books, 2002.
67. See Lawrence K. Altman, M.D., "In Africa, a Deadly Silence about AIDS Is Lifting," *New York Times*, 13 July 1999, p. D7.
68. See Alex Boraine, *A Country Unmasked: Inside South Africa's Truth and Reconciliation Commission*, Oxford: Oxford University Press, 2000, especially pp. 340–378; and Priscilla B. Hayner, *Unspeakable Truths: Confronting State Terror and Atrocity*, New York and London: Routledge, 2001.
69. Boraine, ibid., p. 433.
70. Robertson, *A Country Unmasked*, pp. 306–307; the rape cases include Prosecutor v. Akayesu, Trial Chamber, International Tribunal for Rwanda, 1998. Case No. ICTR-96-4-T, ⟨www.ictr.org/ENGLISH/judgements/AKAYESU/akay001.htm⟩, printed in part in Steiner and Alston, *International Human Rights in Context*, pp. 1178–1188.

71. This has characterized the approaches to transitional justice in some South American and African countries and the failure to this date to begin prosecutions in Cambodia.
72. Siegel, "Transitional Justice: A Decade of Debate and Experience," *Human Rights Quarterly*, 20, No. 2, May 1998, pp. 431–454.
73. See Robertson, *A Country Unmasked*, especially pp. 248–256, and Orentlicher, "Settling Accounts: The Duty to Prosecute Human Rights Violations of a Prior Regime," *Yale Law Journal*, Vol. 100, 1991, pp. 2537–2615.

4

From global norms to local change: Theoretical perspectives on the promotion of human rights in societies in transition

Geneviève Souillac

Behaviours by states and other groups are increasingly the object of scrutiny in our globalized world. Ever more, the legitimacy of state action depends on prior consultation, dialogue, and agreement with other states regarding the achievement of common goals. One of these common goals has become the respect and implementation of human rights, as the common ethical basis of political and social development activities. On a global, multilateral level, numerous ratifications by states testify to the increasing legitimacy of human rights norms. However, how human rights norms are domestically integrated into legal practices, political institutions, and social policies is unclear. In Western liberal democracies, human rights norms are typically implemented through the rule of law and cycles of challenges to, and reform of, social policies. Transitional communities with differing historical, political, social, and cultural backgrounds are a major challenge to the effective globalization of human rights norms. Whether because of local power and economic struggles, cultural and social challenges to human rights definitions, or competing strategies of implementation on the part of external agencies, clear communication on human rights issues seldom exists.

Implementation of human rights-related policies and projects include a complex heuristic process of definition, interpretation, and communication, involving consultation between different interest groups and consensus-building. This work occurs in the gap between the abstract, generalized nature of human rights norms, and the concrete, context-dependent level of institutionalization. The communication of human rights norms can be problematic to the point of antagonizing local populations. Vague claims to human rights on the part of Western parties are not conducive to sound, context-sensitive policy, and all too often reflect a lack of flexibility in the appeal to certain rights and not to others. This does not help the "ethical" cause of human rights (or even democracy) but, rather, serves as a reminder of the potential purpose of the promotion of human rights – the spread of the liberal socio-political cause. Clarification of the needs of different contexts; debate about which norms, institutional approaches, and persuasive strategies best suit different situations; these are necessary steps to the achievement of human rights goals in societies in transition. Formulating these issues at a micro-level reflects a more self-aware (and, even, possibly self-critical) approach to complex assistance by international organizations (IOs) and international non-governmental organizations (INGOs) in transitional societies.[1]

Although such empirical analyses help to elucidate the concrete problems and issues faced by international assistance, they also raise important theoretical questions. How can a highly abstract level of norms originating in a particular set of countries be communicated to societies that have not experienced those originating conditions? How does the internalization of human rights norms by local actors occur, and what implications does this have for the relationship between global norms and local change? Finally, how does this relationship relate to the goal of integrating states in a legitimate international order on the basis of transparency and accountability? These are the types of theoretical questions on human rights norms that are relevant to societies in transition. This chapter explores some of the theoretical implications of relating global human rights norms to transitional conditions. It does not propose "solutions" or concrete policy directions for the complex process of international cooperation in transitional societies; rather, it explores some theoretical points recently developed in the international relations and international organization literature and seeks to present them in a way that is relevant for the future study of transitional societies and transitional administrations.

There are two parts to the chapter. The first part looks at key points in recent efforts to theorize the nature and role of international norms and the resulting increase in the ideational dimension of globalization. Recognizing the specific character of human rights as "architectural" norms provides a constructive basis from which to understand the integrative power of human rights norms. Given the current historical context of a growing need for common ideational forms of political legitimacy, the second section assesses theoretical developments in the description of the ideational communicative processes. It examines the role of theories of communication and socialization in conceptualizing the influence of human rights norms on social and political change. Particularly in the context of transitional societies, an important issue is political identity formation in the production of a new state. Finally, I raise some points from recent debates in human rights theory regarding the need to keep a critical awareness of the essentially liberal ideology which Western actors transmit in transitional contexts, and the formalization of a universal/local dialogue about human rights ideas.

Human rights and global norms

Values on the good or right form of political organization are relative, and reaching a consensus on certain core universal values is a difficult process.[2] In the context of good governance, however, it is possible to develop an alternative reasoning regarding the nature and role of human rights as global norms. The drive for a cohesive international society regulated by global norms illuminates the functional role of human rights: the notion of human rights as abstract values recedes and their normative function is highlighted. Yet the notion of human rights as norms may unnecessarily emphasize their coercive function for the admittance of new states into the international community of states. The notion of human rights as architectural norms conveys their constructive function in the building of new and legitimate political institutions in transitional societies. This leaves more scope for local communities to renew their own political cultures within this "imported" framework and emphasizes the positive, reformist aspect of this process from the point of view of these communities. However, as discussed later, it is also imperative for various human rights actors to retain a critical perspective towards the communicational format of human rights norms.

Human rights as "architectural" norms

The language of human rights in the international public arena has sometimes taken the form of a discussion of the social and political values that they represent. The potential conflicts in values that they may generate as the liberal-democratic model of governance seeks to win universal appeal is typically a key point of discussion. From a historical point of view, human rights have emerged as a system of values making the human individual worthy of protection and flourishing. The classical argument in political philosophy, which made individual human rights a core principle for balancing absolutist power, has developed into a social and political theory of liberal democracy based on freedom and equality.[3] In liberal democracies, democratic representation, legislation, and domestic policies ensure that basic conditions for individual human safety and development are met. Furthermore, each new set of rights carries with it implications for a shared understanding of what constitutes a progressive and "civilized" international society. In this way, human rights communicate social and political purpose and will, and personal and universal relevance for policy-making. As Jürgen Habermas argues, "human rights institutionalize the communicative conditions for a reasonable political will-formation."[4] The result, ideally, is the management of plurality and potential conflict through a form of social and political equilibrium based on free communication and the existence of a consensus on standard operational political principles.

To add to this implicit understanding about human rights, there has recently been a noticeable shift towards a normative terminology in the analysis of international relations and international violations of human rights, emphasizing global justice and states' obligations,[5] in an effort to coordinate and integrate the international community. Essentially, global governance[6] is placing human rights principles even more firmly at the basis of a global architecture, as essential building blocks for a new international system of legitimacy and regulation of political behaviour. The institutions articulating global governance "govern" at an international rather than national level by expressing a new type of legitimacy centred around notions of equitable justice, accountability, and human security. Falk discusses how a social and political equilibrium is currently being sought at the global level, and reveals the tensions in the contemporary vision for a global justice system built on the basis of human rights. Human rights exist in a complex network of relationships involving entitlements and responsibilities. These include issues such as claims of economic equity versus economic growth, of present versus future generations, economic versus public interests, and public consensus versus the rights of minority groups.[7] Recent notions of human security based on the human right to life and integrity of the body may even override the principle of state sovereignty. On a global scale, the notion of global governance mobilizes collective human rights resources to render main actors accountable for their actions and to voice and coordinate a multiplicity of competing interests. Falk argues that his writing

... proceeds on the central assumption that achieving a human rights culture and realizing global justice are intertwined and mutually reinforcing goals. The overarching aim of normative commitment is to incorporate rights and justice into a framework of humane governance.[8]

Understanding the nature of human rights as architectural norms reinforces their functional, legal, and political meaning, whereas human rights as values are typically associated with personal and cultural frameworks. Whereas the role of values is to define, that of norms is to provide limits on political behaviour. Once destructive patterns of behaviour can be identified and generalized from empirical observation, norms can be generated to put brakes effectively on this behaviour. Another perspective is that provided by Ramesh Thakur: norms may be distinguished from the law but, as norms provide the underpinning of the law, both norms and laws end up being mutually reinforcing in the system of law.[9] Ideally, the aim of human rights as architectural norms is to make the international community more cohesive, thus playing a potential key role in structuring legitimate relations between states. In the case of transitional societies, the espousal of human rights principles through the establishment of appropriate forms of governance provides added structural legitimacy in the international community. To understand this process of integration into a broadly defined international community, it is necessary first to consider what is meant by the "power" of norms such as human rights, in the theoretical context of international norm dynamics.

International norm dynamics

Whereas international actors are talking of an international order, we find "disorder" at the level of norm definition, formation, consolidation, and implementation. Mireille Delmas-Marty, a French international lawyer, refers to a "normative disorder," whereby the law generated from humanitarian concerns is deemed "fuzzy law." This is reflected in the current system of global norms, as the quest for "higher" humanitarian norms reaches an ever-increasingly abstract level of legitimacy.[10] Delmas-Marty reminds us that the process of universalization and globalization we are witnessing today finds its roots in Enlightenment philosophy, namely in Kant's essay *On Perpetual Peace*. For Jürgen Habermas, globalization "has since a long time objectively unified the world to turn it into an involuntary community founded on the risks incurred by all."[11] This last distinction is important for the current discussion on the nature of global norms. Norms regulate behaviour, and justifications for them derive from various understandings of what constitutes a legitimate brake on certain behaviours. However, norms emerge against a backdrop of "non-norms," in a continuous process of identification of what constitutes non-legitimate behaviour.

Recent theoretical developments on the dynamics of norm dissemination explore the potential "might" of ethical claims against the power of "realist" claims related to territory, sovereignty, and state interest. In a now classic article, Alexander Wendt argues for the relevance of the agent–structure model to explain modifications in the system of international relations, especially regarding the alleged influence of certain wilful aspects of power and domination on the making of foreign policy.[12] The interpretative argument for state interest formation is helpful to reconceptualize state autonomy away from the notion of territorial integrity. Latitude for transformation may exist where a proper system is conceived: Finnemore and Sikkink point out the important distinction between regulative norms and "constitutive norms, which create new actors, interests, or categories of action."[13] This has implications for a historical interpretation of the development of international relations along different paradigms that are in constant evolution. In this interpretation, agency plays a role in the modification of structural constraints, rather than following a chaotic model of unequal power relations:

If we replace the premise of states' essential autonomy with the broader interpretive assumption that constitutive norms can exist at the level of systems, we allow for an explanation of the conditions under which states are relatively autonomous actors in a particular historical era.[14]

Human rights-related claims have played a crucial role in the challenge to neorealist claims. They further ensure the unique position of human rights values as architectural norms providing the basis and motivation for institutional construction and reinforcement. As Delmas-Marty writes, "it remains to transform this involuntary community into a true community, that is 'voluntary,' or at least desired – which brings us back to human rights."[15]

The acknowledgement of a political will to provide regulations is increasingly becoming a feature of theoretical interest. It expresses a "constructive dimension" to an otherwise "immutable" system of international relations articulated around relations of power, domination, and influence.[16] The constructive element in the progressive espousal of human rights-sensitive policies on the part of states is thus a crucial element in the development of ideational concerns in international politics. Theories of the "social construction" of the international order, derived from critical theory and the emphasis on the role of language in the "construction" of social reality, have recently strengthened the movement towards increased legitimacy of an ideational perspective versus a pragmatist or (neo)realist perspective.[17] The defining aspect of norms is their constraining nature and hence their problematic relationship with political will, when political will is classically understood as expressing the political interest of states in policy formation. However, it has also been argued that the type of political will associated with the emergence and consolidation of norms – especially internationally binding norms – cannot be explained as a progressive adaptation to risk and threat, nor solely in terms of self-interest but, rather, as following a complex and wilful process. This "life cycle" of norms, which determines their evolution and influence,[18] includes the emergence of norms; then a period of norm "cascade," involving various degrees of acceptance by states; and, finally, a third moment of internalization following a "tipping point," at which "a critical mass of relevant state actors adopt the norm," on the basis of a complex array of motivations. In the final stage of internalization, the norms in question are no longer the object of public debate and scrutiny as to their value, and work can continue for their ongoing implementation.[19]

These theoretical findings have implications for the transformative role of global human rights norms on foreign policy and on states' definitions of their identity and interests. This can be witnessed in the revival of interest in the relationship between ideas and politics, notably in studies of the impact of foreign policy on both domestic and international politics. Kathryn Sikkink argues for a more systematic understanding of the integration of human rights ideas into foreign policy in both the United States and Europe. According to Sikkink, understanding this process helps to shed light on the "impact" of human rights norms upon policy-making in general. As she convincingly argues, "[t]he emergence of human rights policy is not a simple victory of ideas over interests. Rather, it demonstrates the power of ideas to reshape understandings of national interest."[20] An architectural system of human rights norms influences policy in ways that are profoundly transformative of states' understandings of their own interest and location in the world system. As Sikkink argues:

A realist or neorealist explanation of foreign policy has trouble accounting for the adoption and implementation of human rights policies, except by dismissing them as insignificant.... But the essence of a multilateral human rights policy – acceptance of compulsory submission to the court's jurisdiction and of the right of individuals to petition regional and international organizations – involves acceptance of uncertainty about future outcomes, which does not coincide with a standard interpretation of furthering security interests.[21]

To a certain degree it also empowers individuals to international legal recognition of their humanity, in the face of potential abuse from governmental power. Human rights treaties are ethically efficient at least in that they impose obligations on states to their treatment of nationals. The nature of norms as a "dynamic" aspect of international relations becomes clear in this "constructivist" sense. According to Sikkink, "the doctrine of internationally protected human rights offers one of the most powerful critiques of sovereignty as the concept is currently understood."[22]

I would argue further, however, that there are problematic considerations that ensue from increased state identification with human rights values. As human rights agendas are placed in the international arena, increased identification with universal norms implies increased commitment to treaties that are globally binding and, in turn, a proliferation of multilateral relationships. Yet the "fuzziness" of human rights norms lies in the fact that, although they appeal to a "highest" or "irreducible" ethical principle of the value of human life and security, the definition and interpretation of human life remain only historically defined, in reaction to social, economic, and cultural circumstances and developments of various kinds. In other words, the terminology of norms may have helped tighten the perceived legitimacy of human rights values, but the element of value remains at the core of the definition of rightful behaviour. National interest may be enhanced by an association and identification with human rights norms. The connection between power and "legitimate social purpose"[23] confers an "enhancement" of the "image" of power, something central to foreign policy. However, as the intricate network of norms, interests, and identities is drawn tighter in an increasingly globalized international community, state interests as conceptualized from nationalistic, cultural, and other context-specific concerns may have trouble reconciling the whole gamut of human rights concerns within their own political and social cultures.

Thus, in any discussion about the communication of human rights norms, challenges to classical prioritization of human rights norms, as well as considerations about different types of political cultures associated with these rights priorities, must be acknowledged. Typically, as noted earlier, the implicit assumption is that the nature and function of the human rights concept justifies the evolution of human rights norms in a liberal socio-political framework, which accentuates the priority of individual rights to personal freedom and which claims the indivisibility of human rights under such a priority. For Jack Donnelly, for instance, the justification of the global emancipatory function of human rights requires a coherent theoretical account of human rights as a bounded and indivisible concept.[24] For Donnelly, the universal claim to human rights serves an emancipatory function within the global trend "toward political liberalization and democratization."[25]

Furthermore, in his conceptual distinction between right as rectitude and right as entitlement, the latter emerges as the key on which rests his later refutation of culturalist challenges to the Western concept of human rights.[26] In an article written with Rhoda Howard, entitled "Human

Dignity, Human Rights, and Political Regimes," the vindication of a liberal world-view appears even more clearly.[27] In the article, Howard and Donnelly contend that international human rights standards require "a particular type of 'liberal' regime, which may be institutionalized ... only within a relatively narrow range of variation."[28] As such it is *not* adaptable to a variety of social structures and political regimes, since "[c]onceptions of human dignity vary dramatically across societies, and most of these variations are incompatible with the values of equality and autonomy that underlie human rights."[29] This argument for the "necessary" connection between a liberal political culture and human rights typically expands on the priority of individual freedom and does not leave much room for dialogue regarding the prioritization and institutionalization of rights.

To conclude this section, it may be argued that human rights norms are architectural in providing the elements needed to build legitimate institutions on a common set of liberal-democratic political and social principles. Their transmission at a global level is now recognized as an integral source of a stronger ideational level in international politics and a weakening of classical realist anarchy. As such, their aim is far-reaching – namely, to bind states together at an ideational level. This architecture is, however, built upon several tensions. Human rights are principles that have a definite history but also make universal claims of suitability and sustainability. The postulate of the possibility of reconciliation of local and global levels at such a complex ideational level raises the question of the role of identification with global norms from a local perspective, in the process of integration into the international system. As discussed below, the link between local contexts and global norms can be articulated by considering how the communication between non-governmental actors and states helps to disseminate human rights norms, as well as the importance of the inclusion of a critical perspective on the substantive content of human rights norms.

A transitional process: Norms and identification

The last section proposed a sketch of the picture now generated by the growing influence of morally significant ideas and of a universal model of regulation of political behaviour. It delineates a framework whereby an ideally constituted international society is continuously attempting to communicate its norms. Human rights norms form an architectural model that burgeoning political societies are encouraged to follow. International organizations such as the United Nations and INGOs include such encouragement as part of their conditions for complex assistance. Yet, from the growing understanding of the constructive power of norms emerge two necessities: the first is to theorize the modalities of their communication; the second is to keep an awareness of the substantive nature of their content and of the need to engage in a constructive dialogue with local customs. There are two models that are helpful to consider the theoretical implications of the communication of ideational norms. First, constructivist theoretical perspectives help to draw attention to what is inevitably a long process of socialization and internalization of global norms within domestic frameworks. Second, the assumption of an ideal communicative situation must be problematized if we are to move away from a real or perceived imposition of international norms on local contexts.

Constructivism and identification

The impact of constructivism on norm theory highlights the role of ideas in generating policy-relevant relationships between the domestic and the international levels. This framework is helpful in understanding the "social construction" of multilateral relations based on the normative principles of human rights, within a group of states already engaged in cooperative activity. The process of integration of these states on a pattern of more or less resistance is fairly clear. Human rights are of functional relevance to the building of a global system based on some common ideas about good governance. What is less clear is the perception of an ideational international order, from the perspective of domestic structures that are historically, politically, or culturally more distant from a system of ideas emphasizing human rights. Although the analytic notion of transitional societies is distinct from that of domestic structures, they are comparable on such a scale of "integration" into the international order and the convergence to global norms. For these states, the reception of the "message" of human rights norms exists in a gradual process of "adaptation" of local patterns of governance and political behaviour, to conform to global standards. This can involve radical political and social change. Transitional societies typically experience powerful demands from the exterior regarding their self-definition. If anything, transitional societies are even more crucially aware of their process of self-definition than are relatively stable domestic structures, as they are grappling with a traumatic past and conflicting approaches to that past. Their people and representatives are defining both their internal social and political structures and their external boundaries. They are making crucial choices about the cluster of ideas that will govern the behaviour of their institutional actors.

Theoretical literature on the translation of ideas into international trends of meaning is helpful for thinking about these issues. A first way of identifying a process of "identification" with global norms lies in the theory of the impact of "external" normative ideas on domestic structures through transnational advocacy. The theoretical insights of recent scholarship on the nature and role of transnational advocacy formulates a flexible approach to the communication of norms. Transnational advocacy is now recognized as a unique form of norm entrepreneurship.[30] First, research into the causes of change in foreign policy preceded scholarship on transnational advocacy networks but gradually drew attention to the existence of "networks" of ideas. Thomas Risse-Kappen convincingly explores the idea that "ideas do not float freely," based on an empirical analysis of the changes in Soviet foreign policy.[31] In the past, transnational coalitions were ideological movements of ideas based on a philosophical framework. The most famous examples were the various interpretations of Marxism in different nationalist settings and struggles for emancipation, from Russia to China, Viet Nam, Laos, and many more. The ambition of these movements was often expansive, and their strategies resembled the religious model of conversion, as they aimed at transforming the consciousness of collectivities rather than altering the behaviour of states oppressing their own people. The political life of ideas, however, shifted in focus as states became both more emancipated from other (mostly Western) states' influence and, wishing to secure their interests *vis-à-vis* these states, more accountable to a growing international community. Such paradoxical interdependence has been illustrated by arguments that security interests may have been reconceptualized from the growing influence of the Western liberal internationalist community, which was formed into transnational networks and encouraged the emergence of "new thinkers" in the former Soviet Union.[32] This investigation of the relationship between a variety of agents, their ideas, and the development of these ideas into norms, bridges the framework of human rights as global norms and the studies of their promotion by state actors in foreign policy or through norm entrepreneurship.[33]

More recent theories examine the "power" of principled ideas to exert political pressure on human rights-abusing governments and to generate civic awakening through a process of political and social reconstruction in such societies. This identifies more precisely the ways in which nongovernmental parties interact with illegitimate governments to influence their policy and even provoke their collapse, if they do not abide by international standards and integrate into the international community. Margaret Keck and Kathryn Sikkink's groundbreaking book *Activists beyond Borders*[34] offers an even more convincing argument about the dependence of states on each other as the basic proposition or first condition from which other principles governing international relations may be derived. These authors note the insufficiency inherent in a "two-way street" concept "in which political entrepreneurs bring international influence to bear on domestic politics at the same time that domestic politics shapes their international position ... implying a limited access to the international system that no longer holds true in many issue areas."[35] They argue that the relationship between domestic interests and global structure is mediated by a different form of communication of norms through a third sector expressing more purely democratic interests – civil society and transnational advocacy. The emerging idea is to think of networks or coalitions advocating the same ideas, rather than a centralized ideology pursuing single-mindedly a pre-established ideal. This "network concept ... stresses fluid and open relations among committed and knowledgeable actors [who] plead the causes of others or defend a cause or proposition."[36]

Keck and Sikkink's work on transnational advocacy is important for reasons other than the wealth of empirical evidence that they provide in arguing for the impact of principled ideas of which transnational advocates are the vehicle: they are problematizing a vision of international politics that assumes pre-existing, bounded entities (state actors), where each state actor relates to a whole made up of similar actors. Second, the notion of "issue construction" provides a social constructivist perspective to international political change in its relationship with social change and, hence, local conditions. This is relevant for two reasons. First, in many cases, and by principle, transnational activism helps promote transition – if transition is understood as a more radical form of social and political change catalysed by traumatic events and collapsing structural conditions of power. Ultimately, transnational activism and its relationship with civil society is about transition. It is not surprising that scholarship on transnational activism is explicitly based on research on social movements.[37] The "third sector" of transnational advocacy, and the flow of ideas among civil society actors, strengthens the domestic–global interdependence of norms, independently of power relations based on state interest. Transnational coalitions, as Keck and Sikkink argue, "are organized to promote causes, principled ideas, and norms, and they often involve individuals advocating policy changes that cannot be easily linked to a rationalist understanding of their 'interests'."[38]

Second, Keck and Sikkink are drawing attention to a fundamental category in interest formation and its relationship with global norms – namely, identity. The notion of the impact of norms on policy change can be explained through the notion of issue construction, which articulates the basis for a new political and social identity. Transnational advocacy networks facilitate the careful exposure of facts through their public condemnation. Keck and Sikkink's extensive research into human rights-abusing regimes in Latin America demonstrates how transnational advocacy stimulates transition by exposing the illegitimacy of a dictatorial regime's behaviour. Identifying what claims and policies resonate in a particular, transitional stage of transmission of human rights norms is a first step in Keck and Sikkink's understanding of this process. Political identities are not only forever in the making but also closely interrelated with social identities and people's historically situated desires and interests in their own society. Transnational advocacy facilitates the emergence of these relationships. Moreover, "[h]ow the activists' messages carried and resonated with domestic concerns, culture, and ideology at the particular historical moment in which they campaigned was crucial." Keck and Sikkink "draw upon sociological traditions that focus on complex interactions among actors, on the intersubjective construction of frames of meaning, and on the negotiation and malleability of identities and interests," and emphasize social and psychological meanings in the mobilization of actors for the promotion of a political cause:[39]

Campaigns are processes of issue construction constrained by the action context in which they are to be carried out: activists identify a problem, specify a cause, and propose a solution, all with an eye toward producing procedural, substantive, and normative change in their area of concern.[40]

Norm communication and socialization

The "social construction" of the international order is also relevant from the perspective of those who do not actively generate global norms but who "import" them and must modify their political and social institutions and practices to reflect them better. The role of indigenous contexts of reception is especially relevant to understanding the reception of global human rights norms. How can one theorize about the appropriation of abstract human rights norms by societies in which these norms have not been formally developed? How is the role of global norms in so-called "good governance" perceived from the point of view of domestic structures that are renewing and reforming their institutional structures of governance? Transitional societies are particularly vulnerable to pressure to adhere to externally imposed norms and to integrate into the international community on the basis of a common political model. More often than not, they are emerging from destabilized political situations, struggles between warring parties, and, sometimes, open conflict.

The communication of human rights norms may provoke, encourage, or facilitate transition, but this path is always fraught with difficulties. The complex political and social ideals underpinning human rights norms, as well as the essence of their normative claims to the legitimate articulation of political and social power, complicate the process of their transmission. The theory of the communication of norms by INGOs sheds light on the phenomenon of political transition. The role of a "third sector" in the communication of human rights norms is one aspect of the dynamics of norm transmission that may explain the impact of norms on the transformation of local political identity. Keck and Sikkink, in their analysis of transnational networks, discuss the existence of such a "third sector" in terms of the "generative aspects of transnational networks," which "confirm the importance of attention to dynamic as well as static elements of domestic political opportunity structures."[41] The precondition of accountability for human rights-abusing governments is one of the first steps towards generating political transition and achieving norm consolidation. Exposure of human rights violations and shaming of governments, in collaboration with national and local NGOs, plays a vital role and is examined in its communicative dimension. The processes whereby international norms are communicated to various governments through the monitoring work of INGOs is an important aspect of the construction of a renewed social and political identity for these societies. INGOs generate, with increasing legitimacy, a public picture of the facts of human rights abuse in various locales, and the operational impact of advocacy networks lies in the potentially vast perimeter of their influence and infiltration. The socialization of norms into domestic practices can thus be identified in terms of a pressuring system following a sequence of communicative acts.[42] This is described in terms of moral consciousness-raising through collective mobilization, processes of instrumental adaptation and strategic bargaining, and processes of institutionalization and habitualization,[43] which may occur in different succession depending on local political and social contexts.

Local contexts are more likely to be receptive to the influence of international ideas if local advocacy networks have already been active. An example is Argentina, where NGOs first published information on human rights violations based on testimonies. This information was then backed up by findings by the Inter-American Commission on Human Rights.[44] However, socialization most often occurs in a context of conflicting ideas and evolves through a difficult process of bargaining, persuasion, and pressure. Various steps can be conceptualized whereby "repressive governments" gradually "cave in" as they face domestic and international scrutiny by an increasingly mobilized and cohesive domestic and transnational opposition.[45] The work of Audie Klotz on the relationship between norms and the apartheid regime in South Africa indicates to what extent the altering of state behaviour on the basis of new norms can be conceptualized in a variety of different ways, from coercion (through effective sanctions for instance), to incentives for government-instigated reforms, to international legitimation. For Klotz, these accounts stem from traditions in international relations theory, which reveal the predominance of the analytical categories of coercive power and material interests.[46] In her view, the case of the eventual South African elections with universal suffrage is evidence of the importance of international incentives and legitimation processes, yet analyses of such processes should also "include criteria that capture the role of norms."[47]

Audie Klotz uses the term "identity constraint" when she argues that the role of identity in international politics and the impact of international norms should be given more serious attention. In particular, her work on South Africa shows that the affirmation of a non-racist identity in this particular case of a society in transition revealed the origins of identity and its relationship to interests. From the starting point of the various aspects of South Africa's international identity, such as "global/Western, European/colonial, and African," various norms about race were negotiated between different local and international actors to lead South Africa finally away from its international isolation.[48] Similarly, Thomas Risse uses the examples of Kenya and Indonesia to point out the initial verbal resistance by these governments to international monitoring of their human rights records by such agents as Human Rights Watch, yet also the growing possibility of dialogue contained within this verbal resistance. Increasing pressure by growing national opposition groups and human rights organizations also has led these governments to begin a comparison between their own records and that of other states. An even more striking example given by Risse is that of Morocco, where King Hassan II was forced into a dialogue with national and transnational critics and eventually claimed that human rights were part of the Islamic tradition. As Risse points out, he "reconstructed the Moroccan identity as belonging to the (Western) community of civilized nations."[49]

Thomas Risse also attempts to move beyond both constructivism and its assumptions about norm-regulated behaviour, and rational choice arguments explaining strategic behaviour on the basis of material interests. He shows that we can observe a gradual process whereby communications move from purely instrumental rationality via rhetorical behaviour towards something resembling a dialogue. Risse proposes a series of concepts that reflect more faithfully a complex reality of communication involving both interest and identity redefinition. Risse's theory draws attention to Habermasian notions of "moral–practical learning" in social and political development, or, in words borrowed from Jon Elster's reading of Habermas, to the "civilizing effects" of public deliberation."[50] Risse notes how norm-violating governments move away from their role as international pariahs, to become valid (albeit argumentative) interlocutors with various transnational actors, thus generating a genuine dialogue. In particular, the role of argumentation over the validity of international norms by such resistant states reveals a significant shift, in Risse's view, from the mere use of rhetoric. This provides scope for actors' reconceptualization of their social and political identities, on the basis of argument and deliberation about ideational norms and negotiation of "shared definitions" of various situations, and towards a "common life world:"[51]

In each of the countries investigated that reached the final stage of sustained rule-consistent behavior, the improvement of the human rights record was accompanied by a profound change in state identity. States became eager to join the community of human rights-abiding "civilized nations."[52]

I would argue that communicative theory, which emphasizes the connection between moral learning and social development, is useful for both social scientific explanation and policy-making but is, nevertheless, problematic. In particular, the notion of a "common life world" presents difficulties for the global dialogue on human rights norms, especially in the areas of women's rights, second-generation rights, and minority rights, where differences abound in different cultures. Furthermore, repeated exposure by INGOs of the human rights abuses of past governments, humanitarian assistance in providing so-called "second-generation rights" to health and education, as well as capacity-building in the legal and political spheres, are crucial. But it is often argued that their accompanying discourse is lopsided, emphasizing typically "Western" rights such as civil and political rights enshrining individual freedoms, and disregarding other rights more classically associated with the building of social structures, such as social, economic, and cultural rights. As the attention is focused on resistant governments, the resistance of Western human rights discourses to shift their priorities may be overlooked.

On the other hand, the notion of socialization reflects the reality of a multi-layered local response to "norm impact" and helps to conceptualize the "gap" between the abstract level of global human rights norms and local conditions of political and social change. It especially helps to redraw the lines between what is perceived as belonging to the mere realm of interpretation, such as norms or values, and what derives from the material interests of states. Most importantly, conclusions drawn on the socialization of norms into domestic practices reveal an incremental process of identification. Rather than the unpredictable nature of causal relationships between norm perception and strategically motivated adaptation, the idea of socialization stresses the important role of "identity transformation," where norms initially adopted for instrumental reasons are later maintained for reasons of belief and identity in domestic structural transition. This approach reveals the necessarily incremental process of local identification with an abstract discourse of global norms communicated by a plethora of external agencies and allows for the possibility of indigenous appropriation of norms to be conceptualized and taken more seriously.

The myth of a global village, organized through the Internet and other forms of instant communication and reflected in international business, migration fluxes, diasporas, and ethnic diversity, avoids restating the need for physical and existential engagement with other cultures. It has traditionally been the task of ethnologists and anthropologists to systematize such epistemological pursuits into an academic discipline. These disciplines now encourage empirical cross-cultural research into the values that may validate human rights standards in specific cultural contexts. Alison Renteln was one of the first to suggest that "we should look not simply for rights cast in the Western mold but for the structural equivalents for human rights in other societies."[53] In combination, anthropological methodologies and critical theory have argued for the relevance of considering how local and transitional cultures (which are often highly politicized in contexts of ongoing political turmoil) appropriate concepts of human rights.[54] Richard Wilson has argued that culture should be examined in its proper dynamic under the influence of historical change and exterior cultural influences, rather than as a static entity. Empirical research into local discursive processes of human rights legitimation shows how discursive meanings of human rights are actually appropriated by local agents in the context of globalization. An example is what legal anthropologists call "legal pluralism" – that is, "overlapping local, national, and transnational legal codes." Wilson argues for the necessity of taking into account such sociological factors as local history and power struggles to describe local representations of agency accurately. The result is a balancing of theoretical accounts with the methodologies of discourse analysis and ethnography for the study of local events and meanings of justice.[55]

Context-sensitive approaches to the appropriation and reworking of the discourse on human rights offer an alternative idea of consensus-building through the notion of the cultural mediation of justificatory moral discourses. This considers a multiplicity of moral positions without excluding the possibility of at least minimal moral consensus. Local histories and knowledge provide the substance to an otherwise contextually meaningless international discourse on human rights, which must address competing power struggles such as those of cultural minorities and local political claims. This allows possibilities for thinking of both theoretically and practically constructive outcomes for the furthering of local implementation and developments of human rights regimes within differing political and social cultures. However, problems with practical issues of local cultural interpretation and resistances to liberal values also need to be addressed: this includes the potential transformation of their political and social values, whether locally or transnationally. One possibility is to locate, as discussed above, local interpretations of human rights, such as power struggles and local agendas, that inflict local processes of implementation of human rights norms, and to emphasize the grass-roots appropriation of human rights discourses to connect with local populations' vital interests.[56]

Most importantly, however, the distinction between outcome and different levels of justification suggests that the norms can stem from local social and political cultures. The unforced consensus approach comes to terms with a lack of agreement on the level of justification and substantive appeal to values. This approach claims that flexibility relates not to the question of the desirability of human rights norms but to the substantive justification of what constitutes vital human interests, including the frameworks through which these human interests are accounted for and legitimized.[57] In Charles Taylor's words, "[e]ach would have its own way of justifying this from out of its profound background conception. We would agree on the norms, while disagreeing on why they were the right norms. And we would be content to live in this consensus, undisturbed by the differences of profound underlying belief."[58] This does not advocate a consideration of locally legitimized regressive practices as a legitimate challenge to existing human rights norms. Rather, as Abdullahi An-Na'im proposes, it suggests the development of a "sensitivity to cultural integrity ... in arguing for the importance of universal cultural legitimacy for international human rights."[59] As Taylor evocatively writes:

Later, a process of mutual learning can follow, moving toward a "fusion of horizons" in Gadamer's term, where the moral universe of the other becomes less strange. And out of this will come further borrowings and the creation of new hybrid forms.[60]

Conclusions

In this chapter, I have suggested that there are benefits to a more precise theoretical consideration of the relationship between global norms and local change, in terms of the openings afforded by the emerging relevance of ethical communication in political identity formation. Theoretical developments emphasizing the role of constructivism in interest formation draw attention to more sociologically inspired categories of analysis in the adoption of norms, such as identity. Both notions of issue construction and of socialization are related to domestic structures in existing literature. The conceptual relationship between interest (understood in its classical sense) and identity (understood in the sociological or even anthropological sense) emerges as a key element of an attempt to formulate how transitional societies may relate to global human rights norms. Indeed, as I have shown in this chapter, these categories are applicable to societies in various stages of political transition, as they deal with a problematic past while constructing and projecting a new image of their political interests in the global arena. The way that these societies relate to global human rights norms, it has been shown, is one that is increasingly based on states' perception of their own identity and relationship with other transnational actors in the global arena. Furthermore, empirical and theoretical analysis of the impact of norm transmission, notably through INGOs and other transnational coalitions, suggests that the impact of human rights communication may be both in the promotion of transition and in the opening for ethical deliberation in the constitution of political identity.

Ultimately, from a more encompassing perspective, transition may thus be increasingly conceived of as a desirable state, precisely one in which potential for new conceptualizations of legitimacy emerge. States – whether in emergence from a complete lack of local authority and institutional structures (as is the case of Afghanistan since 9/11) or whether adapting their domestic policies and institutions to reflect human rights standards – can benefit from their dialogue with other state and non-state actors on the source of their legitimacy in the global arena. Options are revealed to begin altering their behaviour in a direction that reflects at least their willingness to cooperate with other actors and to comply with human rights standards. This may even allow these states to start to participate in a global public dialogue on human rights. All these discursive activities have an impact on states' conception of the source of their legitimacy, beyond the concept of sovereignty and towards a model of international cooperation on ideals and standards of international behaviour.

The above discussion shows that ideas and norms have increasing relevance to those states that wish to have a positive identity in the international arena. It also suggests the continued consolidation of a global public sphere of deliberation. However, these findings also reveal the different possible relationships between local conditions and abstract norms.[61] The notion of a "transitional society" is typically referred to as a political and social state from which structures emerge to fully "erect" a new type of society, based upon new legitimacy. It is important not to see this process as one of a "vacancy" concerning institutional protection of human rights, which may then be "filled" with appropriate institutions: a self-reflexive dimension on "both sides" remains a crucial component in a globally conceived dialogue. The role of indigenous interpretation and definition of norms is not sufficiently explored in current readings of norm dynamics: these need to be enriched by alternative perspectives present in more classical debates in the field of universal human rights theory. Explanations of norm diffusion further help to conceptualize the relationship of normative ideas with domestic transition and social and political change. The process of empowerment of local civil society should thus be made more explicit by IOs and INGOs intervening in social and political reconstruction. The goal of assistance in the development of a coherent local political culture should also be emphasized. A careful balance between the import of external structures and the analysis of local needs should be encouraged. This should be included as one of the goals of external transnational human rights promoters and should feature prominently in their discourse as a type of human rights promotion itself.

All these perspectives help to reinforce notions of local empowerment in political transition and counteract claims of an irreversible imposition of external norms on local communities. The example of the South African Truth and Reconciliation Commission is now a classical one but best illustrates this last point: the commission was a locally developed human rights institution for the purpose of transitional justice, aiding in South Africa's transition to a non-racist and fully democratic state. More recently, the cases of Afghanistan and Iraq illustrate the need to counteract formally a perceived American political imperialism in the field of human rights and democratization. Transitional societies are with us – and here to stay. The benefits of recognizing a process of socialization in local identification with global norms, and the reconciliation of indigenous patterns with externally imported models of political and social action, should not be underestimated in the ongoing process of coherent integration of local perspectives into a unified system of global values.

Notes

1. On the increasingly complex ethico-political issues surrounding IO and INGO assistance work, see the article by Alex de Waal, "The Moral Solipsism of Global Ethics Inc," *London Review of Books*, 23 August 2001, pp. 15–18. De Waal sums up the "business of assistance" well: "The philosophy of the specialist ethics business is overwhelmingly liberal: opposed to censorship, repression and corruption; in favor of tolerance, pluralism, respect for all. The relevant activities include training lawyers, monitoring elections, supporting citizens' organizations that ... are seen as laying the foundations for a strong civil society, sponsoring reconciliation between warring com-

munities and documenting violations of human rights. In some ways, this activity resembles that of a marketplace; in others, it puts you in mind of an intellectual production line for the liberal emporium – Global Ethics Inc."

2. See Joanne Bauer and Daniel A. Bell, *The East Asian Challenge for Human Rights*, Cambridge, Mass.: Cambridge University Press, 1999; Amy Gutmann, ed., *Human Rights as Politics and Idolatry*, Princeton: Princeton University Press, 2001; Lynda Bell, Andrew J. Nathan, and Ilan Peleg, eds, *Negotiating Culture and Human Rights*, New York: Columbia University Press, 2001.

3. Jack Donnelly's work on human rights epitomizes the view that human rights are necessarily accompanied by a liberal view of democracy. See Jack Donnelly, *Universal Human Rights in Theory and Practice*, New York: Cornell University Press, 1989. Another representative philosopher linking human rights theory with liberal theory is Alan Gewirth. See Alan Gewirth, "The Basis and Content of Human Rights," in J. Roland Pennock and John W. Chapman, eds, *Nomos XXIII: Human Rights*, New York: New York University Press, 1981. For a more recent volume discussing these debates, see Tim Dunne and Nicholas J. Wheeler, eds, *Human Rights in Global Politics*, Cambridge: Cambridge University Press, 1999.

4. Jürgen Habermas, "Remarks on legitimation through human rights," in Jürgen Habermas, *The Postnational Constellation. Political Essays*, translated and edited by Max Pensky, Cambridge: Polity Press, 2001, p. 117.

5. See Mervyn Frost, *Toward a Normative Theory of International Relations*, Cambridge: Cambridge University Press, 1986; Chris Brown, *International Relations Theory: New Normative Approaches*, Hemel Hempstead: Harvester-Wheatsheaf, 1992; Audie Klotz, *Norms in International Relations: The Struggle against Apartheid*, Ithaca and London: Cornell University Press, 1995; Simon Caney, David George, and Peter Jones, eds, *National Rights, International Obligations*, Boulder, Col.: Westview Press, 1996.

6. See Falk's definition of the distinction between government and governance: "... *governance* calls attention to various forms of institutional and collective efforts to organize human affairs on a global scale, encompassing the global institutions of the UN system, various regional actors, and transnational and local grassroots initiatives" (italics in the text). Richard Falk, *Human Rights Horizons: The Pursuit of Justice in a Globalizing World*, London: Routledge, 2000, p. 20.

7. Ibid., pp. 21–22.

8. Ibid., p. 10.

9. See Ramesh Thakur, "Global Norms and International Humanitarian law: An Asian Perspective," *International Review of the Red Cross*, No. 841, 2001, p. 25.

10. Mireille Delmas-Marty, *Trois défis pour un droit mondial*, Paris: Seuil, 1998, p. 77. Delmas-Marty compares this "fuzzy law" to the "soft law" currently regulating economic activities, which features the deployment of complex and opaque regulations under the "guise" of "deregulation."

11. Jürgen Habermas, *La paix perpétuelle, le bicentenaire d'une idée kantienne*, Paris: Cerf, 1996, p. 74 (personal translation), quoted in Mireille Delmas-Marty, *Trois défis pour un droit mondial*, p. 8. See also Hedley Bull, *An Anarchical Society*, London: Macmillan, 1977.

12. Alexander Wendt, "The Agent–Structure Problem in International Relations Theory," *International Organization*, Vol. 41, No. 3, Summer 1987, p. 41.

13. See Martha Finnemore and Kathryn Sikkink, "International Norm Dynamics and Political Change," *International Organization*, Vol. 52, No. 4, Autumn 1998, p. 893.

14. Audie Klotz, *Norms in International Relations*, p. 17. See especially the chapter "Norms in International Relations Theory," pp. 13–35.

15. Delmas-Marty, *Trois défis pour un droit mondial*.

16. On the critique of the "immutability" thesis that "political communities cannot escape the logic of power inherent in the condition of anarchy," see Andrew Linklater, "The Achievements of Critical Theory," in Steve Smith, Ken Booth, and Marysia Zalewski, eds, *International Theory: Positivism and Beyond*, Cambridge: Cambridge University Press, 1996, p. 282.
17. Kathryn Sikkink, "The Power of Principled Ideas: Human Rights Policies in the United States and Western Europe," in J. Goldstein and R.O. Keohane, eds, *Ideas and Foreign Policy*, Ithaca, NY: Cornell University Press, 1993, pp. 139–170.
18. See Martha Finnemore and Kathryn Sikkink, "International Norm Dynamics and Political Change," pp. 894–895.
19. Ibid., p. 895.
20. Sikkink, "The Power of Principled Ideas," p. 140.
21. Ibid., p. 157.
22. Ibid., p. 141.
23. See Finnemore and Sikkink, "International Norm Dynamics and Political Change," p. 887.
24. Jack Donnelly, *The Concept of Human Rights*, London: Croom Helm, 1985.
25. Jack Donnelly, "Post-Cold War Reflections on the Study of International Human Rights," *Ethics and International Affairs*, Vol. 11, 1997, p. 97.
26. Jack Donnelly, "Human Rights and Human Dignity: An Analytic Critique of Non-Western Conceptions of Human Rights," *American Political Science Review*, Vol. 76, 1982, pp. 303–316.
27. Rhoda E. Howard and Jack Donnelly, "Human Dignity, Human Rights, and Political Regimes," *American Political Science Review*, Vol. 80, 1986, pp. 801–817.
28. Ibid., p. 801.
29. Ibid., p. 802.
30. See William Korey, "Human Rights NGOs: The Power of Persuasion," *Ethics and International Affairs*, Vol. 13, 1999, pp. 151–174.
31. Thomas Risse-Kappen, "Ideas Do Not Float Freely: Transnational Coalitions, Domestic Structures, and the End of the Cold War," *International Organization*, Vol. 48, No. 2. Spring 1994, pp. 185–214.
32. Ibid.
33. See Finnemore and Sikkink, "International Norm Dynamics and Political Change," pp. 896–897: "Norms do not appear out of thin air; they are actively built by agents having strong notions about appropriate or desirable behavior in their community."
34. Margaret E. Keck and Kathryn Sikkink, *Activists beyond Borders. Advocacy Networks in International Politics*, Ithaca: Cornell University Press, 1998.
35. Ibid., p. 4.
36. Ibid., p. 8.
37. Ibid., p. 9: "Relationships among networks, both within and between issue areas, are similar to what scholars of social movements have found for domestic activism."
38. Ibid., pp. 8–9.
39. Ibid., p. 9. See reference to Myra Marx Feree and Frederick D. Miller, "Mobilization and Meaning: Toward an Integration of Social Psychological and Resource Perspectives on Social Movements," *Sociological Inquiry*, Vol. 55, 1985.
40. Ibid., p. 8.
41. Ibid., p. 72.
42. See a description of the "spiral model" of norm internalization by norm-violating governments, from repression, to denial, to tactical concessions, and finally to a response to global norms as possessing "prescriptive status," in Thomas Risse and Stephen C. Ropp, "International Human Rights Norms and Domestic Change: Conclusions," in

Thomas Risse, Stephen C. Ropp and Kathryn Sikkink, eds, *The Power of Human Rights: International Norms and Domestic Change*, Cambridge: Cambridge University Press, 1999, pp. 237–238.

43. See Thomas Risse and Kathryn Sikkink, "The Socialization of International Human Rights Norms into Domestic Practices: Introduction," in Risse, Ropp, and Sikkink, eds, *The Power of Human Rights*, p. 5.

44. See Keck and Sikkink, *Activists beyond Borders*, Preface, p. viii.

45. See Thomas Risse, "International Norms and Domestic Change: Arguing and Communicative Behavior in the Human Rights Area," *Politics and Society*, Vol. 27, No. 4, Dec. 1999, pp. 526–556.

46. See Klotz, pp. 152–164.

47. Ibid., p. 162.

48. See Klotz, pp. 169–170.

49. Thomas Risse, " 'Let's Argue!' Communicative Action in World Politics," *International Organization*, Vol. 54, No. 1, Winter 2000, p. 31.

50. Risse, "International Norms and Domestic Change," p. 551.

51. See Thomas Risse, " 'Let's Argue!' ", especially the section "International relations: a common life world?", pp. 14–16.

52. See Risse, "International Norms and Domestic Change," p. 550.

53. See Alison Dundes Renteln, *International Human Rights: Universalism Versus Relativism*, Newbury Park: Sage, 1990, p. 11.

54. Richard Wilson, "Human Rights, Culture and Context: An Introduction," in Richard Wilson, ed., *Human Rights, Culture and Context: Anthropological Perspectives*, London: Pluto Press, 1997, p. 11.

55. See also Richard Wilson's article on human rights reporting in Guatemala, "Representing Human Rights Violations: Social Contexts and Subjectivities," in Richard Wilson, ed., *Human Rights, Culture and Context*, pp. 134–160.

56. See for instance, Radhika Coomaraswamy, "To Bellow like a Cow: Women, Ethnicity, and the Discourse of Rights," in Rebecca J. Cook, ed., *Human Rights of Women: National and International Perspectives*, Philadelphia: University of Pennsylvania Press, 1994, pp. 39–57. See also Smitu Khotari and Harsch Sethi, eds, *Rethinking Human Rights: Challenges for Theory and Action*, Delhi: Lokayan, 1991.

57. Charles Taylor, "Conditions of an Unforced Consensus on Human Rights," in Joanne Bauer and Daniel A. Bell, eds, *The East Asian Challenge for Human Rights*, pp. 124–144; Taylor, "A World Consensus on Human Rights?", *Dissent*, Summer 1996, pp. 15–21.

58. Taylor, "Conditions of an Unforced Consensus on Human Rights," p. 124.

59. Abdullahi An-Na'im, ed., *Human Rights in Cross-Cultural Perspectives: A Quest for Consensus*, Philadelphia: University of Pennsylvania Press, 1992, p. 7.

60. Taylor, "A World Consensus on Human Rights?", p. 20.

61. Risse and Sikkink call this the "intersubjective nature of norms." See "The Socialization of Human Rights Norms," p. 8.

Part Two

Monitoring, promoting, and enforcing human rights

5

The United Nations and human rights

W. Ofuatey-Kodjoe

The relationship between transitional societies and the discourse and activities of human rights activities within these societies seems somewhat paradoxical. On the one hand, the revolutions and ideologies on the basis of which they gained their independence and statehood were framed in terms of the human rights of their inhabitants – and often of the right of the groups to self-determination. It is not altogether surprising, therefore, that many of these states have joined the emerging global consensus on respect for international human rights standards.[1] Many of them have expressed recognition of some legal obligation – or at least of some political pressure – to treat their citizens according to international standards of human rights. On the other hand, there are developments that seem to point towards an increase in human rights violations around the world. Although no region is exempt from these violations, some of the most egregious violations of human rights have been occurring in transitional societies.

In order to understand this apparent paradox, I attempt to present an account of the evolution of the principle of human rights in the contemporary world. In this effort, I pay particular attention to the role of the United Nations in the process of the internationalization and legitimation of human rights. This is because the United Nations has been the main arena within which the international politics of human rights have been played out. It is through the United Nations that the international norms regarding the human rights of individuals and groups were established, and it was through the United Nations that the institutions and mechanisms that give concrete expression to these norms were created.[2] Furthermore, as the United Nations moves into the new millennium, it is appropriate to analyse and evaluate its performance in the promotion of human rights, to review some of the new challenges which the world faces regarding the protection of individual and group rights, and to explore some of the ways in which the United Nations can continue to function more effectively in the face of these new challenges.

The UN Charter and human rights standards

The roots of the efforts of the United Nations in the promotion of individual and group rights are to be found in the UN Charter. According to the Charter, two of the purposes of the United Nations are "To develop friendly relations among nations based on respect for the principle of equal rights and self-determination of peoples" [Article 1(2)], and "To achieve international cooperation ... in promoting and encouraging respect for human rights and for fundamental freedoms for all without distinction as to race, sex, language, or religion" [Article 1(3)].

In order to achieve these objectives, the Charter enjoins the organization to "... promote universal respect for, and observance of, human rights ..." [Article 55]. Relating human rights specifically to the administration of colonial and trust territories, the Charter states that in accordance with the purposes outlined in Article 1, the basic objectives of the trusteeship system were to develop self-government or independence in these areas and to encourage respect for human rights.[3] Articles 13, 62, and 68 specifically authorize the General Assembly and the Economic and Social Council (ECOSOC) to undertake activities such as initiating studies, making recommendations, setting up commissions, and preparing draft conventions for the promotion of human rights.

In addition, the signatories of the UN Charter "pledge themselves to take joint and separate action in cooperation with the Organization for the achievement of the purposes set out in Article 55" [Article 56]. Thus, the Charter clearly established the legality of human rights and the right of peoples to self-determination. However, it left many definitional questions unresolved. In particular, it left ambiguous the exact meaning of human rights and self-determination, how they were to be applied, and the specific obligations (if any) the member states undertook with respect to the implementation of these rights.[4] It became the task of subsequent UN practice to refine and clarify these rights.

The development of human rights standards through UN practice

On the basis of the Charter provisions, the United Nations, especially in the General Assembly and the ECOSOC, began a series of activities, which, over the years, led to the clarification and elaboration of individual and group rights in international law. In 1946, the ECOSOC established the UN Human Rights Commission and gave it the responsibility for drafting an international bill of rights as its first priority. After considerable activity, the Commission, through ECOSOC, was able to present a draft to the General Assembly, which the latter adopted as the Universal Declaration of Human Rights (UDHR).[5] At the same time, the General Assembly began a concentrated effort to establish itself as the appropriate body with the authority and responsibility to determine which groups the principle of self-determination should be applied to and what the mode of application should be.

The process of clarification and refinement of individual and group rights began in earnest in 1952, with the initiation of a two-pronged action by the General Assembly. In one action, the General Assembly instructed the Human Rights Commission to incorporate the right of self-determination into the drafts of the Human Rights covenants which were already under preparation;[6] in a second action, it requested the Ad Hoc Committee on Decolonization to report on a study of "factors to be taken into consideration in establishing the obligations of administering powers under Article 73 of the UN Charter."[7] These two committees engaged in complementary streams of activities, which have resulted in the creation of a massive collection of instruments. The instruments have clarified and refined Charter principles on individual and group human rights and contributed significantly to their protection.[8]

International standards on human rights

In the clarification of the definition of human rights, the United Nations relied on a combination of standard-setting instruments – international conventions and UN declarations and resolutions – that derive their foundations from the UDHR, and the two Human Rights covenants. The covenants provided the first powerful treaty basis for individual human rights as well as the right of self-determination of peoples. They also defined the obligations of the signatory states regarding those rights and they provided for some judicial determination of the violations of those rights.

However, the covenants also left some important definitional questions unresolved. As a result, it became necessary for the United Nations to sponsor a series of conventions and to produce many declarations and resolutions, in order to define with some specificity the contents of the rights outlined in the covenants and the obligations they give rise to.

The outcome of these efforts is that, in the past 45 years, the United Nations has seen developments in the area of standard-setting of revolutionary proportions, involving the specification of rights of individuals and some groups. Thus, we are now at a point in the development of international law where it can be stated authoritatively that every individual is guaranteed a range of human rights – including the right to life, recognition as a legal person, due process, peaceful assembly, freedom of association and security of person. In addition, every individual is guaranteed freedom of thought and expression; of conscience and religion; the freedom of movement; and freedom from torture, summary execution, cruel and inhuman punishment, slavery, servitude, forced labour, imprisonment for non-fulfilment of contract, and subjection to retroactive laws.

International law also provides each individual with the right to work; the right to form trade unions and to strike; the right to social security, physical and mental health, and education. Some instruments also provide for the equality of all persons, regardless of the group to which they belong: thus, women, children, and minorities are accorded the same rights as other individuals, and there are prohibitions against discrimination based on sex, race, and religious beliefs, as well as injunctions against torture, cruel punishment, and slavery. Furthermore, there are specific rights which are relevant to groups of people – such as minorities, detainees, indigenous peoples, migrant workers, women, dependent peoples, children, stateless persons, aliens, and physically and mentally challenged persons.[9]

In general, the specification of group rights has not developed as quickly as that of individual rights. The Covenant on Civil and Political Rights dealt with the question of minority rights under Article 27, where it upheld their cultural, religious, and linguistic rights. However, subsequent attempts to define these rights faced the same type of definitional problems as had the right to self-determination of peoples. In August 1994, the Sub-Commission met in Geneva to consider a draft of an International Convention on the Protection of National or Ethnic Groups and Minorities. This preliminary draft contains sections on the right of self-determination and other forms of autonomy along the lines already developed by resolution 1514(XV), resolution 1541(V), human rights covenants, and the Declaration on Friendly Relations.

All indications from the *procès-verbaux* of the drafting conference show that the drafting committee rejected the notion that "peoples" could refer to scattered minorities, which were specifically covered by Article 27 of the Covenant on Political and Civil Rights. Furthermore, the notion that self-determination included the right of secession was emphatically rejected. Since the adoption of the covenants, the states have constantly maintained the position that self-determination is not the same as secession.[10]

The rights of indigenous peoples are also getting some well-deserved attention in the United Nations. On the basis of the recommendation of the Vienna Declaration, the General Assembly has declared 1994–2004 as the International Decade for the World's Indigenous People, and called on the Working Group of Indigenous People to complete its draft Declaration on the Rights of Indigenous People. Meanwhile, the Vienna Declaration endorsed the view that "states should take positive steps to ensure respect for the human rights and fundamental freedoms of indigenous people, on the basis of equality and non-discrimination...."[11]

The right to self-determination of peoples is the most highly developed aspect of group rights in the practice of the United Nations. The right to self-determination means that all people have a right freely to determine their political status and pursue their economic, social, and cultural development. In other words, self-determination means the attainment of self-government. In exercising this right, the group may choose one of three modes: the full integration into another state as equals, free and uncoerced; association with another state on the basis of equality; or achievement of independent statehood.[12] In practical terms, the option of independent statehood is not interpreted to imply a right secession, except in cases where something close to a political consensus exists.

In order to invoke the right to self-determination, a claimant group must be a territorially based, politically organized community and must be under alien subjugation. The right to self-determination is thus a right that all peoples possess; however, the exercise of the right can be claimed only under conditions of deprivation of sovereignty due to alien overrule. Furthermore, although the right is inherent in every group, it cannot be exercised unless the group has the capacity to do so. In the absence of this capacity, however, this right does not lapse: the exercise of the right is merely deferred until the group can acquire the necessary capacity. Under these circumstances, the group is given a period of time within which it may prepare itself and develop the capacity for self-government, before choosing the appropriate mode of self-government. Until such time that the people can develop the capacity to make this choice, it has the right to resist oppression[13] and the right to be protected by the United Nations.[14]

The right to self-determination imposes obligations on states. First, every state has the duty to promote, through joint and separate action, respect for the right to self-determination and the obligation to refrain from any forcible action that would deprive the people of their self-determination by subjugating them or violating the integrity of their territory.[15] The right to self-determination also imposes obligations on the United Nations: these include the obligation to determine the validity of the claim to the right to self-determination by ascertaining the qualification of the group (especially its territoriality and subject status), the obligation to provide interim protection for the group, and to provide assistance to that group in its quest for self-government.[16] Again, the validity of claims is inevitably determined in such a way as to protect the territorial integrity of the overwhelming majority of states.

Implementation mechanisms

The effort of the United Nations to protect the rights of individuals and groups may take the form of *direct* and *indirect* action. Direct action involves direct activity on the part of the United Nations to protect human rights; indirect action involves actions of the United Nations, designed to influence states to promote and protect human rights. Most of the UN efforts have been primarily indirect – that is, the United Nations has basically depended on the states to honour their obligations, incurred under the various standard-setting instruments, to protect the human rights of individuals and groups within their jurisdictions. In this process, the role of the United Nations has primarily been to cajole and shame the states into compliance.

Indirect protection

In the United Nations' activity of indirect protection, the principal organs on which the United Nations has depended have been the General Assembly and the ECOSOC, and a variety of mechanisms that they have created over the years. Among these are the Committee of Twenty-Four, the Commission on Human Rights and its Sub-Commissions, and the treaty committees, which monitor compliance with the human rights conventions.[17] The Commission on Human Rights is the primary institution for investigating the extent to which the human rights standards established by the United Nations are being adhered to by member countries. It performs these functions through working groups and special rapporteurs, which investigate country-specific human rights violations, and "thematic working groups" and rapporteurs, which study specific types of human rights violations wherever they may be found.

The "theme mechanisms" were established as working groups or rapporteurs with the responsibility for taking action with regard to severe human rights violations. These working groups and rapporteurs report directly to the Commission. More frequently, however, they report to its subsidiary, the Sub-Commission on the Prevention of Discrimination and the Protection of Minorities. By the end of 1993, the Sub-Commissions had ten working groups investigating a wide range of human rights issues, from gross violations of human rights to discrimination against persons infected with the HIV virus.[18]

In order to monitor compliance with the human rights conventions, treaty-monitoring bodies have been established. Among the most successful of these has been the Human Rights Committee, which was originally established as a subsidiary organ of the ECOSOC to monitor compliance with the International Covenant on Economic, Social and Cultural Rights (ICESCR). Since then, other bodies have been created to monitor compliance with other human rights conventions. Although technically independent of UN organs, they report to the General Assembly, and they depend on the United Nations for administrative support.

With regard to self-determination, the United Nations was also mainly engaged in indirect protection. In the main, the United Nations supervised, rather than actively engaged in, the decolonization process through which most of the colonies achieved independence. In the case of trusteeship, the United Nations had a more authoritative role, since it was signatory to the trusteeship agreements which the administering powers had signed and, therefore, had a more legally secure role as the protector of the peoples of those territories, as third-party beneficiaries of the treaties.[19] In this case, the Trusteeship Council was the major instrument through which the General Assembly supervised the administration of those territories and their eventual preparation for independence.[20]

In the case of the colonial territories, the General Assembly began with a more limited role. At the outset, the General Assembly was willing to accept the list of colonial territories prepared by the colonial powers themselves.[21] However, as time went on, the General Assembly began to develop criteria for the determination of just what was a non-self-governing territory on which the colonial powers were obliged to provide information to the United Nations, and what the modalities of the exercise of self-determination should be. In this process, the Committee of Twenty-Four was the major mechanism created by the General Assembly to monitor the activities of the colonial powers with regard to the movement of the colonial territories towards self-government.[22]

Direct protection

The United Nations has made some efforts to engage in the direct protection of human rights. However, in the main, these efforts have lagged behind the indirect protection activities. In general, direct protection involves taking action *within* states in order to protect the human rights of individuals or groups through preventive or corrective action. In some cases this intervention has been accomplished with the cooperation, and at the invitation, of the government concerned. However, sometimes it has taken the form of humanitarian intervention – the active (and sometimes forcible) intervention in the internal affairs of a state without the consent – or even despite active opposition – of the government.[23] Both of these types of direct protection have become more prominent aspects of the UN human rights activity, particularly since the end of the Cold War.

Technical assistance

The United Nations' direct protection of human rights with the consent of the government concerned involves the provision of technical assistance to help countries develop structures and procedures that can enhance support for human rights. Countries in need of technical assistance to comply with UN standards of human rights are considered by the Commission under the UN Advisory Services Programme. In the past few years, the United Nations has engaged in a number of such activities, involving the administration and monitoring of elections or the training of police and criminal-justice personnel, in countries such as Angola, Cambodia, El Salvador, Haiti, Namibia, Nicaragua, Mozambique, and Somalia.[24]

Humanitarian intervention

Humanitarian intervention brings the United Nations face to face with state sovereignty. Both the establishment of the legal basis for such intervention and development of the organization's capacity to undertake humanitarian intervention have been slow processes. Theoretically, the direct protection of human rights can be based on the right of the United Nations to intervene in states in which the government is unwilling, or unable, to safeguard the rights of individuals or groups at risk (as they are required to do by the various treaties they signed), or when states use force to deprive a group of its right to self-determination.[25] However, the United Nations has been very reluctant to use this justification. In one exceptional case the United Nations used this argument as a basis of its termination of the South African mandate over Namibia.[26] However, the United Nations was completely inactive in many situations of gross violations of human rights, as witnessed in the cases of Uganda, Cambodia, Sudan, Ethiopia, and Guatemala.[27]

Initially, in the very few cases when the United Nations has intervened, it has based the justification not directly on human rights violations but on the mandate given to the Security Council in Chapter VII of the UN Charter, to take whatever measures are necessary to maintain international peace and security. For instance, in the Security Council's imposition of economic sanctions on Rhodesia in 1966, there was no direct linkage with human rights violations. Similarly, in the case of the imposition of an arms embargo on South Africa in 1977, no reference was made to human rights violations.[28] It was only in the Rhodesia economic sanctions of 1968 that human rights violations were mentioned as a contributing factor to the threat to peace.[29]

By the 1990s, however, UN intervention for the direct protection of human rights was becoming a more important aspect of UN human rights activity. For the first time, the Security Council stated explicitly that there is a connection between human rights violation and threats to peace and security. In its Resolution 688 of 5 April 1992, the Security Council stated, inter alia, that "the repression of Iraqi civilian population in many parts of Iraq, including most recently in the Kurdish populated areas,... threaten international peace and security in the region." This resolution was followed by the establishment of an enclave for the protection of Iraqi Kurds.[30] The same reasoning was used to justify the need to provide security for the delivery of emergency assistance in Somalia, and to create a "no-fly zone"[31] and safe areas in Bosnia.[32]

Causes and consequences of human rights practices

There are several trends in contemporary international relations that have relevance for the causes and consequences of human rights practices. Some of these trends are especially related to conditions in transitional societies. On the one hand, there is a significant drive toward democratic government all over the world, including many transitional societies. The effect of this trend is the continuing emergence of a global consensus on respect for human rights. Most states now recognize some legal obligation, or at least some political pressure, to treat their citizens according to these international standards. Another effect of this process is that more and more people around the world are becoming aware of their rights, as human beings and as peoples, and they are becoming increasingly assertive in demanding that these rights be respected.

On the other hand, there are signs of rising levels of human rights violations around the world. Among others, they are the consequence of the

re-emergence of undemocratic, racist, and fascist ideologies that advocate the victimization of certain groups.[33] Partly as a reaction to such
ideologies, and partly owing to the breakdown of authority systems, there
continues to be a re-emergence of ethnic conflicts degenerating into
small-scale wars around the world.[34] Furthermore, the conditions of extreme economic crisis in third-world countries make it virtually impossible for their governments to meet the demands for economic, social, and
cultural rights to which they have officially committed themselves. Finally, in their attempts at economic recovery and development, some of
these states adopt unpopular economic policies. The result is that opposition to these policies, by the general population or counter-élites and
military elements that are trying to overthrow their governments, threatens the very existence of these regimes. Confronted with these situations,
many of these governments feel that they have to put concerns about
human rights "on the back burner" and adopt drastic measures to safeguard the security of their regimes.

The effect of these contradictory trends is that, whereas there are increasing demands by individuals, groups, and NGOs for more effective
enforcement of human rights, there is also an increased incidence of violations of human rights. This has all the ingredients of a collision that will
increase the chances of violent confrontations all over the world.

The United Nations and human rights: improving access and capacity

The key to implementation of human rights in the long run can be found
in the increasing general acceptance of both human rights norms and the
legitimacy of the protective activities of the international community. In
order to achieve this, NGOs, states, and the United Nations must be engaged in a creative "dance": NGOs must be relentless in their push for
the protection of human rights; states must increasingly recognize human
rights as issues of legitimate international concern, as opposed to issues
that are exclusively within the domestic jurisdiction of states; above all,
UN human rights bodies must establish their right in law – and their
ability in fact – to recognize individuals and sub-state groups (such as indigenous peoples, and minorities) and to provide them with legally recognized opportunities for presenting their cases to international bodies.[35]
The crux of the matter is that potential or actual victims of human rights
violations must have *access* to the United Nations (and other international bodies) and the United Nations, in turn, must improve its institutional and political *capacity* to deal effectively with acts of violation.

Access and capacity are crucial for both indirect and direct protection of both individual and group rights; they are also basic concerns in proposals concerning "humanitarian intervention."

Unless potential or actual victims of human rights violations have access to international political and judicial institutions, it will continue to be extremely difficult to protect them against oppressive or abusive governments.[36] In order to address the issue of access, the development of human rights law must be strengthened. Therefore, one of the tasks for the international community is to continue to refine the definitions of both individual and group rights. The development of individual rights seems to have made substantial progress in spite of all the setbacks in implementation. The area in which there has been some difficulty is in the development of group rights: this is due, in particular, to the reluctance of states to afford rights to sub-state groups, for fear that their integrity might be compromised by secessionist agitation.

However, it is precisely due to the problem of the assertion of sub-state groups that peaceful solutions need to be found. In the past, issues of ethnic or national self-assertion have been resolved by force. Typically, groups have demanded their cultural rights, local autonomy, or even secession; typically, the states have rejected these claims, and the issue has been settled on the battlefield. The whole development of group rights was due to the realization that these issues should be settled by right, not by force.

We are undoubtedly going to continue to see the assertion by sub-state groups of people of a whole range of demands for self-rule. If we are going to arrest the disintegration of international life into a series of mini-holocausts and ethnic cleansings, then we must continue the trend of seeking peaceful solutions based on law rather than on force. However, the development of the law alone is not going to resolve the problem: the law has to be unequivocally enforced. This requires the enhancement of institutional and political capacity.

Conclusions

From the perspective of human rights advocates, the United Nations' performance clearly needs to be improved. The need to improve the capacity of the United Nations in relation to human rights activities, particularly in crises, has also been recognized by the General Assembly itself in the following statement: "The United Nations system needs to be adapted and strengthened to meet present and future challenges in an effective and coherent manner. It should be provided with resources

commensurate with future requirements. The inadequacy of such resources has been one of the major constraints in the effective response of
the United Nations to emergencies."[37]

The following points summarize a few recommended practices of
NGOs, states, and the United Nations:

- NGOs should continue with the very significant role they have been
  playing in the promotion of human rights, including advocacy, promotion, and monitoring.
- States must increase their commitment to international human rights
  standards. Without abandoning their rights to sovereignty and territorial integrity, they must continue to limit the scope of what may
  be legitimately considered to be within the exclusive control of that
  sovereignty.
- The United Nations should continue to insist that human rights of individuals, minorities, and indigenous peoples are legitimate matters of
  international concern, and make strenuous efforts to increase its capacity to deal effectively with these issues.

However, if we take a longer view of the developments in the field of
human rights since 1945, compared with the previous history of the
world, the United Nations' achievements have been quite impressive.
This is particularly true of its standard-setting activities. Many observers
have noted the weaknesses of implementation and compliance. This
should not be surprising: the fact is, that the standards that have been set
by the United Nations with regard to human rights are futuristic. However, the reason for setting these standards is precisely because the current level of human rights performance is considered intolerable.

The numerous instruments and resolutions that have been adopted by
the United Nations have created a formidable legal basis for the rights of
individuals and have strengthened acceptance of the international legal
principles regarding the inviolability of the rights of individuals, minorities, and territorially based groups. At present, there is no doubt that
this process of the internationalization of human rights is irreversible:
more and more human rights issues are being accepted by states as legitimate subjects of international discussion and action; this trend will continue. To be sure, the states will continue to appeal to the principle of
state sovereignty but, eventually (as in the case of the decolonization
process), the states will be dragged along toward a fuller acceptance of
the need for (and legitimacy of) the international protection of human
rights. The result is that, whereas the commitment to human rights has
been expanding, the range of subjects that are considered by states to be
within their exclusive sovereign control has been contracting. In this situation, the most effective role for the United Nations to play might be to
encourage both aspects of this dialectical process – the expansion of the

commitment to human rights and the restriction of the scope of exclusive national sovereignty.

Meanwhile, the most important task for the United Nations is to enhance its own institutional capacities so that it can act decisively when the opportunities for action present themselves. There is little consolation in shrinking the scope of the states' exclusive jurisdiction of human rights issues, if the United Nations lacks the capacity to deal effectively with the issues that it is tasked to address. In this regard, it may be that the most significant role of the United Nations should be twofold: (1) increasing the "promotional aspects" of its human rights activities, in cooperation with human rights NGOs; (2) developing its capacity to handle truly "gross violations" of human rights, such as those witnessed in Cambodia and Rwanda.

Notes

1. David Forsythe, *The Internationalization of Human Rights*, Lexington, MA: Lexington Books, 1991.
2. David Forsythe, "The United Nations and Human Rights, 1945–1985," *Political Science Quarterly*, Vol. 100, No. 2, Summer 1985; W. Ofuatey-Kodjoe, "Recent Development and Evolving Trends in the Role of the United Nations in the Areas of Human Rights and Humanitarian Intervention," in Albert Legault, Craig Murphy, and W. Ofuatey-Kodjoe, eds, *The State of the United Nations*, Providence, RI: Academic Council on the United Nations System (ACUNS), 1992.
3. During the drafting of the Charter, it was explicitly stated that the principle of trusteeship enshrined in those two chapters was intended to be a specific application of the principle of self-determination, as indicated in Article 1(2), to a particular group of people. See W. Ofuatey-Kodjoe, *The Principle of Self-Determination in International Law*, New York: Nellen, 1977, pp. 106–107; see also United Nations Conference on International Organization (UNCIO) Documents, Vol. 10, p. 515.
4. For conflicting interpretations of UN Charter provisions on human rights and the right of self-determination, see Ofuatey-Kodjoe, *The Principle of Self-Determination in International Law*, pp. 39–66.
5. General Assembly Resolution 217(III) A, December 10, 1948. For a history of the drafting of the document, see Peter Meyer, "The International Bill: A Short History," in Paul Williams, ed., *The International Bill of Human Rights*, Encinitas, CA: Entwhistle Books, 1981; Ellen Glen and Louis Henkin, *The International Bill of Rights*, New York: Columbia University Press, 1981.
6. United Nations General Assembly Resolution 545(VI), 8 February 1952.
7. UNGA Res. 567(VI), 18 January 1952.
8. For a list of the most important of these instruments, see B. Lillich, *International Human Rights: Problems of Law, Policy and Practice*, 2nd edn, Boston: Little, Brown and Company, 1991; Ian Brownlie, ed., *Basic Documents on Human Rights*, New York: Oxford University Press, 1981; Roger S. Clark and Jay A. Sigler, *Human Rights Sourcebook*, New York: Paragon House Publishers, 1987.
9. Lillich, *International Human Rights*, pp. 187–189.
10. In spite of this, some commentators persist in this erroneous definition, and use that as a

basis for rejecting the legality of self-determination. See U.N. Doc. A/C.3/5R. 310 para. 33, 1955.

11. See Vienna Declaration and Programme of Action, UN Doc. A/CONF.157/23, 12 July 1993.

12. Ofuatey-Kodjoe, *The Principle of Self-Determination in International Law*, p. 122. For a discussion of the early attempts by the United Nations to develop rules regarding the rights of minorities, see Hurst Hannum, "Contemporary Developments in the International Protection of the Rights of Minorities," *Notre Dame Law Review*, Vol. 66, No. 5, 1991.

13. GA Res. 3103(XXVII), December 12, 1973; Antonio Cassese, "The Self-Determination of Peoples," in Louis Henkin, ed., *The International Bill of Rights*, New York: Columbia University Press, 1981, p. 427.

14. Ofuatey-Kodjoe, *The Principle of Self-Determination in International Law*, p. 177. The process of clarifying the meaning of self-determination began with General Assembly resolution 648(VII), December 10, 1952, which provisionally approved the idea that a territory may attain self-government in one of three ways, namely "the attainment of independence," "the attainment of other separate systems of government," and "free association of a territory with other component parts of the metropolitan or other country." The United Nations maintained this in a number of resolutions including Res. 742(VIII), Res. 1541(XV), the Human Rights Covenants, UNGA Res. 2200(XXX), 1966 and UNGA Res. 2200, 1966, and the Declaration on Friendly Relations, UNGA Res. 2625, 1971.

15. GA Res. 1314(XII), Res. 1541(V), Res. 2158(XXI); Res. 2625(XXVI); Res. 3201(S-VI); and Res. 3281(XXXIX).

16. Ofuatey-Kodjoe, *The Principle of Self-Determination in International Law*, pp. 160–177; J.J. Lador-Lederer, *International Group Protection*, Leyden: Sijthoff, 1968, p. 244; W. Ofuatey-Kodjoe, "Internal Peacekeeping in African Imbroglios: Problems and Prospects. The cases of Angola, Mozambique and Somalia," Paper presented to the 35th Annual Convention of the International Studies Association, Washington, D.C.: 28 March–1 April 1994; Aureliu Cristecu, *The Right to Self-Determination: Historical and Current Developments on the Basis of United Nations Instruments* (U.N. DocE/CN.4/Sub.2/404 Rev. 1, 1981). The right to protection by the United Nations is derived from the notion of trusteeship which was the basis of the UN trusteeship system, as well as the more general category of peoples described in Chapter XI of the Charter as "peoples of non-self-governing territories." Euphemistically characterized as "communities *not yet* able to stand on their own feet," they were considered politically unprepared, and therefore lacking the capacity to exercise their right of self-determination. However, the right of self-determination of such communities did not lapse: they were merely deferred until they could acquire that capacity. One of the duties which the administering powers undertook in the Charter was to prepare the peoples of such territories for eventual self-government. The United Nations became an agent of protection with the obligation to supervise the preparation of these peoples by the administering powers, to assist them in their development, and to protect them until they acquire the capacity to exercise their right of self-determination. The United Nations also had the duty to supervise the process by which these peoples would choose their mode of exercising their right of self-determination. Lador-Lederer, *International Group Protection*, p. 181.

17. Egon Schwelb and Philip Alston, "The Principal Institutions and Other Bodies Founded under the Charter," in Karel Vasak, ed., *The International Dimensions of Human Rights*, Vol. 1, Westport, Conn., 1982; Tom. J. Farer and Felice Gaer, "The UN and Human Rights: At the End of the Beginning," in Adam Roberts and Benedict

Kingsbury, eds, *United Nations, Divided World: The UN's Role in International Relations*, 2nd edn, Oxford: Clarendon Press, 1993.

18. Farer and Gaer, "The UN and Human Rights," p. 265. The first of the theme mechanisms to be created was the Working Group on Disappearances in 1980; it was followed by the Working Group on Arbitrary Executions (1982), the Special Rapporteur on Torture (1985), the Working Group on Religious Intolerance (1985), and the Working Group on Mercenaries (1987). More recently, other Working Groups have been created on Children (1990), Arbitrary Detention (1991), Internally Displaced Persons (1992), Racism and Xenophobia (1993), and Freedom of Expression (1993).

19. Lador-Lederer, *International Group Protection*, 181; Ofuatey-Kodjoe, *The Principle of Self-Determination in International Law*, p. 116. For a discussion of the trusteeship system of the United Nations, see Ernst Hass, "The Attempt to Terminate Colonialism: Acceptance of the U.N. Trusteeship System," *International Organization*, Vol. 7, 1965.

20. W. Ofuatey-Kodjoe, "The Role of the UN Secretary-General in the Decolonization of Namibia," in Benjamin Rivlin and Leon Gordenker, eds, *The Challenging Role of the UN Secretary-General*, Westport, Conn.: Praeger, 1993, pp. 133–151.

21. Ofuatey-Kodjoe, *The Principle of Self-Determination in International Law*, pp. 114, 226–227.

22. Usha Roy Sud, "Committee on Information from Non-Self-Governing Territories: Its Role in the Promotion of Self-Determination of Colonial Peoples," *International Studies* (Quarterly Journal of the Indian School of International Studies) Vol. vii, No. 2, October 1965; Ofuatey-Kodjoe, *The Principle of Self-Determination in International Law*, pp. 113–128; Benjamin Rivlin, "Self-Determination and Colonial Areas," *International Conciliation* No. 501, January 1955; Mohammed A. Shukri, *The Concept of Self-Determination in the United Nations*, Damascus: Al Jadidah Press, 1965.

23. Howard Adelman, "Humanitarian Intervention: The Case of the Kurds," *International Journal of Refugee Law*, Vol. 4, No. 1, 1992, pp. 4–38; Jack Donnelly, "Humanitarian Intervention: Law, Morality and Politics," *Journal of International Affairs*, Vol. 37, Winter 1984, pp. 311–328.

24. Ofuatey-Kodjoe, "The Role of the UN Secretary-General in the Decolonization of Namibia."

25. Howard Adelman and John Sorenson, eds, "Introduction," in *African Refugees*, Boulder: Westview Press, 1993, ix–xix; Ofuatey-Kodjoe, *The Principle of Self-Determination in International Law*; Surya P. Subedi, "The Concept of Safe Havens, Safe Areas, Enclaves and No-Fly Zones in International Law," Paper presented at the Annual Conference of the Academic Council on the United Nations, The Hague, Netherlands, June 1994; Donnelly, "Humanitarian Intervention." The use of chapter VII of the UN Charter to justify United Nations intervention in the internal affairs of a state to protect human rights has been the source of some controversy. See Lori Damrosch, ed., *Enforcing Restraint: Collective Intervention in Internal Conflicts*, New York: Council on Foreign Relations, 1993.

26. Ofuatey-Kodjoe, "Recent Development and Evolving Trends in the Role of the United Nations."

27. Donnelly, "Humanitarian Intervention."

28. U.N.Doc. S/Res/418 (1977).

29. S/Res/253 (May 29, 1968).

30. Graham E. Fuller, "The Fate of the Kurds," *Foreign Affairs*, Vol. 72, No. 2, Spring 1993, pp. 108–121; Jane E. Stromseth, "Iraq's Repression of Its Civilian Population," in Damrosch, ed., *Enforcing Restraint*.

31. Res. 781 (1992).

32. Res. 824 (1992); Subedi, "The Concept of Safe Havens, Safe Areas, Enclaves and No-Fly Zones in International Law."
33. Magnus Linklater, Isabel Hilton, and Neal Ascherson, eds, *The Nazi Legacy: Klaus Barbie and the International Fascist Connection*, New York: Holt, Rinehart, and Winston, 1985; Jerry Bornstein, *The Neo-Nazis: the Threat of the Hitler Cult*, New York: J. Messner, 1986; Dennis King, *Lyndon Larouche and the New American Fascism*, New York: Doubleday, 1989.
34. Hannum, "Contemporary Developments in the International Protection of the Rights of Minorities," p. 1446.
35. Ofuatey-Kodjoe, *The Principle of Self-Determination in International Law*, pp. 160–176; Ofuatey-Kodjoe, "Internal Peacekeeping in African Imbroglios"; Cristecu, *The Right to Self-Determination: Historical and Current Developments on the Basis of United Nations Instruments*, 1981. For a discussion of the role of NGOs in the protection of human rights, see David Weissbrodt, "The Contribution of International Non-Government Organizations to the Protection of Human Rights," in Theodor Meron, ed., *Human Rights in International Law: Legal and Policy Issues*, New York: Oxford University Press, 1984.
36. For a discussion of some recommendations for the enhancement of the effectiveness of the United Nations, see Theodor Meron, *Human Rights Law-Making in the United Nations*, New York: Oxford University Press, 1986.
37. A/Res/46/182, 19 December 1991.

6

The consequences of the war crimes tribunals and an international criminal court for human rights in transition societies

Paul J. Magnarella

The twentieth century witnessed two world wars and a number of brutal regional conflicts that resulted in massive killings. One response to some of these tragedies has been the imposition of war crimes tribunals on certain of the warring parties, by either the victors or the United Nations Security Council. More recently, the world community, through the United Nations, has embarked upon the venture of establishing a permanent international criminal court (ICC) with jurisdiction over humankind's most serious crimes.

This chapter deals with the background, legal structure, and consequences of war crimes tribunals and assesses the potential effects of an ICC on human rights in societies in transition. These tribunals and the ICC implement humanitarian law – that is, the customary human rights law that applies to situations of armed conflict as well as to crimes against humanity that may occur in the absence of armed conflict. Humanitarian law supplements and complements general human rights law. Some human rights conventions permit states to derogate from several of their human rights obligations during times of public emergency, such as war;[1] humanitarian law, in contrast, becomes operative during wartime and allows for no derogation. Consequently, humanitarian law offers people human rights protection just when states may be derogating from some of their conventional human rights obligations.

The post-World War II tribunals

In October 1943, the Allies began a series of meetings to plan the creation of a post-World War II tribunal to try major war criminals of the European Axis powers. Meeting in London in August 1945, American, British, French, and Soviet representatives reached an agreement establishing the International Military Tribunal (IMT) at Nuremberg. The resulting Nuremberg Charter established the principle that "crimes against international law are committed by men, not abstract entities, and only by punishing individuals who commit such crimes can the provisions of international law be enforced."[2]

Article 6 of the IMT Charter listed the following acts as crimes falling under the jurisdiction of the Tribunal and for which there would be individual responsibility:

(a) Crimes against peace: namely, planning, preparation, initiation or waging of a war of aggression, or a war in violation of international treaties, agreements, or assurances;

(b) War crimes: namely, violations of the laws and customs of war ... [including] murder, ill-treatment or deportation to slave labor or for any other purpose of civilian population of or in occupied territory, murder or ill treatment of prisoners of war or persons on the seas, killing of hostages, plunder of public or private property, wanton destruction of cities, towns, or villages, or devastation not justified by military necessity;

(c) Crimes against humanity: namely, murder, extermination, enslavement, deportation, and other inhumane acts committed against any civilian population, before or during the war, or persecutions on political, racial or religious grounds in execution of or in connection with any crime within the jurisdiction of the Tribunal, whether or not in violation of the domestic law of the country where perpetrated.[3]

The first two criminal categories concern international relations – specifically, wars between states. The third category – crimes against humanity – attacks the very heart of state sovereignty by defining gross human rights violations by governing powers against their own citizens as international crimes subject to universal jurisdiction: "crimes against humanity" covers atrocities committed by Germans against German citizens; this, of course, includes the Nazis' treatment of Jews, Gypsies, homosexuals, and other "undesirables" in concentration camps or factories. Prior to the IMT, a government's treatment of its own citizens, with few exceptions, was considered to be an internal affair not covered by international humanitarian law.

In the first and most famous of the IMT trials, 22 notorious Nazi figures – including Herman Wilhelm Göring – were prosecuted. Hundreds of other Germans were prosecuted by the Allied occupying powers under Control Council Law 10. American General Douglas MacArthur, the Supreme Allied Commander in Japan following the war, created the International Military Tribunal for the Far East (the "Tokyo Tribunal"), modelled after the IMT, to prosecute 28 high-ranking Japanese officials, including former premiers, war leaders, and former diplomats. The proceedings lasted from May 1946 to November 1948.[4]

The interim years

During the 50 years after Nuremberg, an estimated 250 armed conflicts occurred, causing approximately 170 million human casualties.[5] Although the UN General Assembly passed a resolution as early as 1947 calling for the preparation of a draft code of offences against peace and the security of humankind, and shortly thereafter directed the International Law Commission to begin work on a draft statute for an international criminal court, little progress was made on either task until the 1990s. Owing to the Cold War division, the Security Council failed to support efforts to create additional war crimes tribunals. Consequently, until the 1990s, political and military leaders responsible for war crimes, genocide, and crimes against humanity generally enjoyed impunity. Eventually, with the collapse of the Soviet Union and the spectre of atrocities on the doorstep of Western Europe, the Security Council acted creatively and in unison.

The International Criminal Tribunal for the former Yugoslavia

Most people were astonished by the brutality of the conflicts in the former Yugoslavia that erupted in June 1991 and intensified thereafter. As part of the UN response to the conflicts, the Secretary-General submitted a statute for an international criminal tribunal to the Security Council and recommended that it be established under Chapter VII of the United Nations Charter.[6] Given the urgency expressed by the Security Council, the Secretary-General did not involve the General Assembly in the drafting or review of the statute. At its meeting on 25 May 1993, the Security Council approved the Secretary-General's report and accepted the Statute of the International Criminal Tribunal for the former Yugoslavia (ICTY) without change.[7] Subsequently, the UN General Assembly, in its resolution 47/235 (14 September 1993), also expressed support for the tribunal.

One of the most innovative and expeditious recommendations in the

Secretary-General's report was that of establishing the tribunal through the exercise of the Security Council's powers under Chapter VII of the UN Charter. As the tribunal's first president, Antonio Cassese, later explained, "the traditional approach of establishing such a body by treaty was discarded as being too slow (possibly taking many years to reach full ratification) and insufficiently effective as Member States could not be forced to ratify such a treaty against their wishes."[8] By utilizing Chapter VII, the Security Council obliged all UN Member States to cooperate with the tribunal and to honour any lawful requests for assistance under its Statute.

Specifically, Articles 39 and 48 of Chapter VII of the UN Charter provide the legal basis for the Security Council's establishment of the tribunal. Article 39 states that the Security Council shall determine when threats to peace exist and shall determine what measures shall be taken to maintain or restore international peace and security. Article 48 obligates UN Member States to cooperate with the Security Council in the implementation of its chosen measures. Consequently, all UN Member States are obligated by the UN Charter to cooperate with the ICTY.

The ICTY differs from the post-World War II Nuremberg and Tokyo tribunals. First, unlike its predecessors, the ICTY does not have the authority to adjudicate crimes against peace: its jurisdiction covers war crimes, genocide, and crimes against humanity. Second, whereas its predecessors dealt only with crimes associated with an international armed conflict, the ICTY is empowered to adjudicate crimes committed in the course of either inter- or intra-state conflicts. Third, the ICTY is the organ not of a particular group of victor states but of the international community. It is the creation of the United Nations and consists of judges from many different states, regionally dispersed and representing different legal traditions.

Article 8 of the ICTY Statute extends its territorial jurisdiction "to the territory of the former Socialist Federal Republic of Yugoslavia, including its land surface, airspace and territorial waters." Its temporal jurisdiction extends from 1 January 1991 to a future date to be determined by the Security Council. This temporal and territorial scope authorizes the ICTY to consider any serious crimes, regardless of the ethnicity (e.g. Serb, Croat, or Bosniak) of their perpetrators or victims.

Because the Security Council is not a legislative body, it has no competency to enact substantive law for this tribunal. Instead, it authorizes the ICTY to apply "rules of international humanitarian law which are beyond any doubt part of customary law so that the problem of adherence of some but not all States to specific conventions does not arise."[9] Those portions of conventional international humanitarian law that were asserted to have unquestionably become part of international customary law are the laws applicable in situations of armed conflict as embodied in the following: (1) the four Geneva Conventions of 12 August 1949; (2) the Hague Convention (IV) Respecting the Laws and Customs of War on Land and the Regulations annexed thereto of 18 October 1907; (3) the Convention on the Prevention and Punishment of the Crime of Genocide of 9 December 1948; and (4) the Charter of the International Military Tribunal of 8 August 1945.[10]

Articles 2–5 of the ICTY Statute empower the tribunal to prosecute natural persons accused of ordering or committing grave breaches of the four Geneva Conventions, violating the laws or customs of war, committing genocide, or being responsible for crimes against humanity. Grave breaches include the following: wilful killing; torture or inhuman treatment, including biological experiments; wilfully causing great suffering or serious injury to body or health; extensive destruction and appropriation of property not justified by military necessity and carried out unlawfully and wantonly; compelling a prisoner of war or a civilian to serve in the forces of a hostile power; wilfully depriving a prisoner of war or a civilian of the rights of fair and regular trial; unlawful deportation or transfer or unlawful confinement of a civilian; and taking civilians as hostages.

Common Articles 49, 50, 129, and 146 of the First, Second, Third, and Fourth Geneva Conventions, respectively, obligate the High Contracting Parties to enact the legislation necessary to provide for penal sanctions for persons ordering or committing any of the grave breaches. They further obligate each High Contracting Party to search for alleged violators, regardless of nationality, and bring them before their own courts or hand them over for trial to another High Contracting Party. As of 1 January 1994, 185 States, including Yugoslavia, Slovenia, Croatia, and Bosnia–Herzegovina, had ratified the four Geneva Conventions.[11]

Statute Article 3, "Violations of the Laws and Customs of War," is based on the Annex to the 1907 Hague Convention, which was subsequently reaffirmed by Article 6(b) of the Nuremberg Charter. Its list of violations includes the employment of poisonous or other weapons calculated to cause unnecessary suffering; wanton destruction or devastation of cities, towns, and villages not justified by military necessity; attack on, or bombardment of, undefended towns, villages, dwellings, or buildings; seizure, destruction, or wilful damage of religious, charitable, scientific, art, or educational institutions or of historic monuments; and plunder of public or private property.

Article 4 of the ICTY Statute replicates Articles 2 and 3 of the Convention on the Prevention and Punishment of the Crime of Genocide (1948) and defines genocide as any of the following acts committed with intent to destroy, in whole or in part, a national, ethnic, racial, or religious group: killing group members; causing serious bodily or mental harm to group members; deliberately inflicting on the group conditions calculated to bring about its complete or partial physical destruction; imposing measures intended to prevent birth within the group; and forcibly transferring children to another group. Persons who commit genocide or who attempt, conspire, or incite others to commit genocide are punishable. Similar to the Geneva Conventions, the Genocide Convention obligates States Parties to enact the legislation necessary to provide effective penalties for persons guilty of genocide. Obligations under the Genocide Convention are not confined merely to the 107 or so states (including Yugoslavia, Croatia, Slovenia, and Bosnia–Herzegovina) that had ratified it. Because it has become part of international customary law, the International Court of Justice has noted that, "the principles underlying the Convention are principles which are recognized by civilized nations as binding on States, even without any conventional ratification."[12]

Statute Article 5, "Crimes against Humanity," follows the Nuremberg Charter. It empowers the tribunal to prosecute persons responsible for the following crimes against any civilian population committed during an international or internal armed conflict: murder; extermination; enslavement; deportation; imprisonment; torture; rape; persecutions on political, racial, and religious grounds; and other inhumane acts. The crimes constituting "ethnic cleansing," a term closely associated with the conflicts in the former Yugoslavia, are covered by Articles 2–5 but can also fall under genocide (Article 4).

Concurrent jurisdiction and tribunal primacy

Practically all European states, as parties to the Genocide and Geneva conventions, share convention-based competencies and obligations to arrest and prosecute those responsible for the kinds of crimes described in Articles 2 and 4 of the ICTY Statute. Furthermore, all states may exercise universal jurisdiction to prosecute persons responsible for the crimes listed in Articles 2–5. Given the magnitude of the crimes committed in the former Yugoslavia, the successful prosecution of those responsible would greatly exceed the resource capacity of the tribunal; therefore, the Secretary-General stated that national courts should be encouraged to exercise their jurisdiction with respect to such crimes.[13] Consequently, Statute Article 9(1) states that "[t]he International Tribunal and national courts shall have concurrent jurisdiction to prosecute persons for serious violations of international humanitarian law committed in the territory of the former Yugoslavia since 1 January 1991." However, the Statute goes on to state that the tribunal shall have primacy in this area, such that it may formally request national courts to defer to its competence at any stage of the procedure.

Rules of procedure

When constructing the rules of procedure, tribunal judges had little precedent to guide them. The procedural rules for the Nuremberg and Tokyo tribunals were rather rudimentary, numbering only 11 and 9 rules, respectively. After extensive debate and revision, with constructive inputs by NGOs, the Office of Legal Affairs of the UN Secretariat, and states, the judges adopted 125 procedural rules (hereinafter referred to as "Rules") at the end of their second session in February 1994.[14]

The Rules incorporate all the fundamental due process guarantees for a fair and speedy trial found in Article 14 of the International Covenant on Civil and Political Rights (ICCPR). With respect to suspects, articles 42–45 of the Rules even exceed the Covenant's requirements. According to these articles, a suspect has the right to counsel of his/her choice, free legal assistance if he/she is indigent, and free assistance of an interpreter and translator, if necessary. The Tribunal is not authorized to impose the death penalty, in deference to the Second Optional Protocol to the ICCPR of 1989.

The due process rights of the accused include the following: the right to the presumption of innocence; the right against self-incrimination; the right to counsel of choice or to free legal assistance if indigent; the right to inspect the prosecution's incriminating and exculpatory evidence; the right to privileged communication with counsel; the right to public proceedings; the right to challenge the prosecution's evidence and to present evidence in one's defence; and the right of appeal. There are no provisions for trials *in absentia*.

Outline of proceedings

Only the prosecutor or his/her duly delegated deputy may commence proceedings by submitting an indictment supported by evidence to a designated tribunal judge for confirmation. Neither victims, states, nor NGOs may initiate proceedings before the tribunal. The president of the tribunal assigns one judge each month to review indictments.

Once a judge confirms an indictment, he or she may issue arrest and search warrants. The tribunal's registrar transmits the arrest warrant to the national authorities of the state having jurisdiction over the accused, "together with instructions that at the time of the arrest the indictment and statement of the rights of the accused be read to him in a language he understands ..." (Rule 55). The arresting state authorities shall notify the registrar and arrange to transfer the accused to the seat of the tribunal, where the president will arrange for his detention. The detention unit is located within an existing Dutch prison, but it is under the control and supervision of the United Nations.

If the notified state has been unable to arrest the accused, and if the registrar has, at the prosecutor's request, published notices of the arrest warrant in widely circulated newspapers, a trial chamber may, after finding the prosecutor's evidence sufficient, issue an international arrest warrant that shall be transmitted to all states (Rule 61). The president of the tribunal has the authority to notify the Security Council of any state that refuses to honour the tribunal's arrest warrant or that impedes the execution of such a warrant. In practice, the Security Council has successfully placed pressure on Croatia and Serbia to hand over at least some of the indicted suspects that resided in their territories.

Judges who serve on the tribunal are elected by members of the United Nations from a list of candidates nominated by Member States and non-Member States maintaining permanent observer missions at UN Headquarters. According to article 13 of the ICTY statute, "the judges shall be persons of high moral character, impartiality and integrity who possess the qualifications required in their respective countries for appointment to the highest judicial offices." The standard of proof for a criminal conviction is guilt beyond a reasonable doubt.

The International Criminal Tribunal for Rwanda

In 1994, Rwanda erupted into one of the most appalling cases of genocide that the world had witnessed since World War II, as radical Hutu attempted to eliminate moderate Hutu and Rwanda's entire Tutsi population.[15] The UN Security Council, having just created an international criminal tribunal for humanitarian law violators in the European states of the former Yugoslavia, decided it could do no less for African Rwanda.

On 8 November 1994, the UN Secretary-General submitted to the Security Council a statute for the International Criminal Tribunal for Rwanda (hereafter referred to as ICTR), stating that he was "convinced" that "the prosecution of persons responsible for serious violations of international humanitarian law [in Rwanda] ... would contribute to the process of national reconciliation and to the restoration and maintenance of peace."[16] He recommended that this tribunal, like the ICTY, be established under Chapter VII of the United Nations Charter.

The Security Council adopted the Secretary-General's report and the resolution sponsored by the United States and New Zealand by a vote of 13 to 1, with China abstaining. Ironically, Rwanda, which was now led by a government dominated by Tutsi, was the only Security Council member to vote no.[17] Rwanda expressed three objections: it wanted the statute to contain a provision for capital punishment; it also preferred that the temporal jurisdiction of the tribunal extend back to 1990 to cover earlier crimes; and it wanted the ICTR to be based in Rwanda itself. The statute as accepted by the Security Council does not allow for capital punishment and limits its temporal jurisdiction only to the year 1994. Subsequently, the Security Council decided to locate the ICTR in Arusha, Tanzania. To avoid the charge that the ICTR would be a victors' court, the Security Council rejected Kigali's proposal that Rwandan judges sit on the tribunal. The UN General Assembly passed its own resolution welcoming the ICTR's establishment.[18]

The ICTR's jurisdiction

Article 1 of the tribunal's statute states that the ICTR "shall have the power to prosecute persons responsible for serious violations of international humanitarian law committed in the territory of Rwanda and Rwandan citizens responsible for such violations committed in the territory of neighboring states." Consequently, the statute gives the tribunal both personal and territorial jurisdiction in Rwanda as well as limited personal and territorial jurisdiction in surrounding states. By contrast, the statute of the ICTY grants tribunal jurisdiction "in the territory of the former Yugoslavia" only (Art. 1).

By granting the ICTR the competence to prosecute Rwandans who allegedly committed certain crimes abroad, the Security Council has added a new dimension to the humanitarian law of non-international armed conflict. Rwanda's neighbours must surrender some of their jurisdiction to the ICTR without choice. All states have the authority or competence to prosecute Rwandans for crimes committed on their territories. However, because the ICTR by its statute has primacy over the national courts of all states [Art. 8(2)], it may formally request that any neighbouring state's court defer certain cases to its competence. This request carries with it the threat of a penalty for non-compliance. Should any state notified of a deferral request not respond satisfactorily within 60 days, the ICTR's president may report the matter to the Security Council, which would presumably consider sanctions.

In 1995, for example, Kenyan president Daniel Arap Moi stated that not only would he not cooperate with the ICTR but also that he would prevent it from seeking out suspects in his country.[19] Immediately after Moi's remarks, ICTR Chief Prosecutor Richard Goldstone sent him a letter asking for clarification and warning that Kenya's refusal to cooperate with the tribunal would be regarded as a breach of Kenya's obligations under international law – a matter for the Security Council to consider.[20] President Moi soon retracted his statement and began to cooperate satisfactorily with the ICTR.

Subject-matter jurisdiction

The Security Council authorized the ICTR to apply existing international humanitarian law applicable to non-international armed conflict. The humanitarian law included in the tribunal's statute consists of crimes against humanity (as defined by the Nuremberg Charter), genocide, Article 3 Common to the Geneva Conventions, and Additional Protocol II (also ratified by Rwanda).

ICTR Statute Article 3, "Crimes against Humanity," is based on Article 6(c) of the Nuremberg Charter, but it eliminates the requirement that such crimes must have been committed "before or during the war." Consequently, crimes against humanity do not need a war nexus.

Article 4 of the statute empowers the ICTR to prosecute persons committing, or ordering to commit, serious violations of Article 3 common to the four Geneva Conventions of 1949 and of the Additional Protocol II thereto of 1977. These violations include the following: (a) violence to life, health, and physical or mental well-being of persons – in particular, murder, torture, or mutilation; (b) collective punishments; (c) taking of hostages; (d) acts of terrorism; (e) outrages upon personal dignity – in particular, humiliating and degrading treatment, rape, enforced prostitution, and any form of indecent assault; (f) pillage; (g) sentences or executions rendered extrajudicially or without due process; and (h) threats to commit any of the foregoing acts.

Neither Article 3 Common nor Protocol II applies to conflicts of an international nature. Rwanda's neighbours – Burundi, Tanzania, Uganda, and Zaire (but not Kenya) – had ratified both the Geneva Conventions and Protocol II. However, unlike the "grave breaches" sections of the Geneva Conventions, Article 3 Common and Protocol II do not require ratifying parties to criminalize the above acts or to prosecute or extradite alleged violators either to the state on whose territory their acts occurred or to a competent international tribunal. However, as each UN member state is obligated under Chapter VII of the UN Charter to cooperate with Security Council measures taken to maintain international peace, each must extradite suspects requested by the ICTR.

Concurrent jurisdiction and tribunal primacy

Given the magnitude of the crimes committed in Rwanda, the successful prosecution of all those responsible would greatly exceed the resource capacity of the ICTR. One scholar estimated that the number of Rwandans directly involved in the acts of killing amounted to between 75,000 and 150,000.[21] Statute Article 8(1) states that "[t]he International Tribunal for Rwanda and national courts shall have concurrent jurisdiction to prosecute persons for serious violations of international humanitarian law committed in the territory of Rwanda and Rwandan citizens for such violations committed in the territory of neighboring States ..." However, like the ICTY, the ICTR enjoys primacy over national courts of all states, such that it may formally request national courts to defer to its competence [Article 8(2)].

Rules of procedure

The ICTR's Rules of Procedure are based on those of the ICTY. They incorporate the fundamental due process guarantees to a fair trial found in Article 14 of the International Covenant on Civil and Political Rights (ICCPR). Judges for this tribunal are selected in the same manner as they are for the ICTY (see above), and the standard of proof for a criminal conviction is guilt beyond a reasonable doubt.

The International Criminal Court

On 16 July 1998, after 50 years of effort, the international community endorsed the creation of a permanent International Criminal Court (ICC) by a vote of 120 to 7 with 21 abstentions. This historic step took place in Rome at the end of a five-week UN diplomatic conference. Only Libya, Iraq, Qatar, Israel, Yemen, China, and the United States voted against the proposal (although in January 2001, both the United States and Israel signed the ICC Statute). On 6 May 2002, however, President George W. Bush formally withdrew the US's signature from the treaty, claiming that the ICC could be used for politically motivated prosecutions against American military personnel serving abroad. US allies and American human rights organizations expressed deep disappointment over Bush's decision: both claim that the ICC statute contains sufficient safeguards (see below) to prevent unfounded prosecutions.

The Court is designed to bring to justice those who commit the most serious crimes of concern to the international community, including genocide, war crimes, crimes against humanity, and aggression (to be defined later by a special law commission). In order for the ICC to come into existence, its statute, officially entitled the "Rome Statute of the International Criminal Court,"[22] required ratification by 60 states. The ICC received the requisite number of ratifications on 11 April 2002, when ten states presented their instruments of ratification at UN Headquarters, bringing the total number of ratifying countries to 66. The Court's statute entered into force on 1 July 2002.

The jurisdiction of the ICC will extend to war crimes committed in both international and internal armed conflicts. It offers the protections of the Geneva Conventions to combatants and prisoners of war, but also addresses the security needs of civilians of all ages, genders, and cultures. The Rome Statute criminalizes attacks on civilians, rape, and the recruitment of children under 16 years of age into militias; it also prohibits war crimes, genocide, and crimes against humanity.

The Statute permits a ratifying state to declare that it will not accept the jurisdiction of the Court for a period of seven years with respect to war crimes committed by its nationals or on its territory. Otherwise, the Statute permits no reservations. Ratifying states must accept it in its totality. Seven years after the ICC Statute comes into force, ratifying states can amend it and (it is hoped) improve the Court's ability to deal with changing times and crises.

Although the Court will not be fully independent of the Security Council, it will have a degree of autonomous jurisdiction. The Rome Statute offers a two-track system for triggering investigations and prosecutions. Under Track One, the UN Security Council, acting under Chapter VII of the UN Charter, can refer situations to the Court to be investigated. This track would involve situations that threaten or disrupt international peace. As the Court would be acting pursuant to Security Council Chapter VII authority, there would be binding obligations on all states to comply with court orders for evidence or the surrender of indicted persons. Court orders could be enforced by the Security Council in the form of imposed embargoes, the freezing of assets of leaders and their supporters, and the use of force. This track would most likely be utilized in the event of a future conflict similar to those in former Yugoslavia and Rwanda.

The second track constitutes situations referred to the Court by individual countries or the ICC Prosecutor. This track, which relies on the good-faith cooperation of the Parties to the Court's statute, has a number of restrictions attached to it, as outlined below.

First, the Court's jurisdiction under the second track would be based on a concept known as "complementarity," meaning the Court could act only when domestic authorities of the countries involved are unable or unwilling to prosecute. Second, the Rome Statute specifies that, as a precondition to the ICC's jurisdiction over a crime, either the state on whose territory the crime was committed or the state whose national allegedly committed the crime must be a party to the treaty or have granted its voluntary consent to the court's jurisdiction. Thus, the ICC can exercise jurisdiction over the nationals of non-state parties in cases where they have allegedly committed crimes in a country other than their own, if that country decides to turn the suspects over to the Court. Third, Article 16 of the Statute allows the Security Council to vote to postpone an investigation or case for up to twelve months, on a renewable basis. Thus, the Security Council can limit Court action, as long as no permanent member vetoes the resolution calling for postponement.

The ICC Statute evinces great care in the selection of highly qualified and impartial judges and prosecutors. Article 36 of the Statute spells out the rules for judicial nominations and elections. Any state party to the ICC Statute may nominate one candidate for judge to the Court. All nominated candidates must have demonstrated competence in criminal law or international law and extensive experience in a professional legal capacity. From the list of candidates, the State parties to the statute elect 18 full-time judges, who serve a term of nine years and are not eligible for re-election. No two judges may be from the same state. In their selection of judges, the state parties should take into account the need for fair representation of females and males, geographical diversity, and the principal legal systems of the world. ICC Statute Article 40 requires all judges to be independent in the performance of their functions: "A judge shall not participate in any case in which his or her impartiality might reasonably be doubted on any ground" (Art. 41). The standard of proof for a criminal conviction is guilt beyond a reasonable doubt.

ICC Statute Article 42 states that the prosecutor and deputy prosecutor shall be elected by the Assembly of States Parties for a nine-year term. Candidates must be of high moral character and legal competence. Prosecutors must be independent and shall not engage in any activity that is likely to interfere with their prosecutorial functions or affect confidence in their independence. A person being investigated or prosecuted may at any time request the disqualification of a prosecutor on reasonable grounds, such as partiality. The safeguards outlined in the above paragraphs should effectively prevent any unfounded, politically motivated prosecutions.

Tribunal contributions to the promotion of human rights

International war crimes and criminal tribunals can contribute to the promotion of human rights in a number of ways. These include the following:
1. Contributing to the cessation of humanitarian law violations by showing parties to any ongoing conflict that the international community is determined to arrest and punish those who violate the human rights protected by humanitarian law.
2. Achieving justice and retribution by actually prosecuting and punishing those responsible for humanitarian law violations.
3. Contributing to the reconciliation of the parties or opposed populations by creating an authoritative record of those responsible for

humanitarian law violations and, when possible through confessions, getting the responsible persons to acknowledge their crimes so that guilt may be removed from the innocent and the afflicted societies may heal and rebuild.

4. Deterring future humanitarian law violations by demonstrating that those responsible for such acts will be prosecuted and punished.
5. Securing indemnity/compensation for victims.
6. Promoting human rights through their own example by guaranteeing fair trials and respecting the due process rights of the accused, as contained in the ICCPR and other UN human rights conventions.[23]

An evaluation of IMT, ICTY, and ICTR with reference to these six functions follows next. The ICC is dealt with separately thereafter.

Contributing to the cessation of ongoing hostilities

Both the IMT and the ICTR came into existence after one side to the conflict had been defeated and a cease-fire had been declared. The ICTY, by contrast, began operations in 1994 at the height of the conflict in Bosnia and Herzegovina. The warring parties exhibited little fear of the tribunal: some rejected and mocked it.[24] In February 1994, Bosnian Serbs launched a mortar strike in a Sarajevo marketplace, killing 68 civilians and wounding 200. Bosnian Serbs also began shelling UN safe areas. In April, they took over the Gorazde safe area. In May, Bosnian Serbs attacked other UN safe areas and took UN peacekeepers hostage. In July 1995, under the direction of General Mladic, Bosnian Serbs captured Srebrenica and Zepa and massacred about 7,000 Muslim men and boys. Given events of this sort, it appears that the ICTY did little to contribute to the cessation of hostilities: it required NATO's intervention to end the war, not ICTY indictments and trials.

Achieving justice

Arguably, the IMT and the other post-World War II war crimes tribunals achieved significant (albeit one-sided) justice and retribution for victims of Germany and Japan by actually prosecuting and punishing many of those responsible for humanitarian law violations. The ICTY is on the road to achieving justice. On 29 June 2001, it took former Yugoslav President Slobodan Milošević into custody to try him for various humanitarian law violations allegedly committed in 1999 in Kosovo. In August 2001, the ICTY convicted Bosnian Serb General Radislav Krstic of genocide and crimes against humanity and took three indicted former Bosnian Muslim commanders (two generals and a colonel) into custody. As of 30 May 2003, the ICTY had issued over 90 indictments: it had 50 accused persons in custody and had tried 37; of those tried, 32 had been found guilty and 5 not guilty; 22 indictees were still at large.[25]

However, a number of persons alleged to be primarily responsible for genocide and crimes against humanity were among those at large. They included Radovan Karadžić, the former political leader of the Bosnian Serbs, and Ratko Mladic, the former commander of the Bosnian Serb forces. NATO commanders in Bosnia initially refused to arrest them, claiming such arrests were not part of NATO's mandate. NATO forces subsequently began arresting indictees and turning them over to the ICTY. Should the opportunity arise, it is expected that NATO forces will arrest Karadžić and Mladic as well.

The ICTR has also made significant progress. As of 26 May 2003, the ICTR had issued 75 indictments: of those indicted, 65 had been arrested and 10 were at large. The ICTR had completed 15 cases, in which all of the suspects either confessed or were found guilty; 18 trials were in progress and 31 indictees were in detention awaiting trial. Those arrested included cabinet ministers, high-ranking military leaders, key media figures, senior government administrators, and leaders of the murderous Interahamwe.[26] Interim Prime Minister Jean Kambanda's extensive confession concerning his government's intentional policy of genocide constitutes the fundamental fact upon which future ICTR prosecutions will rest. His confession clearly identifies the guilty and destroys the credibility (if it ever existed) of revisionist historians, who claim an intentional massacre or genocide never took place.[27]

Contributing to the reconciliation of the parties

Arguably, the IMT contributed to the reconciliation of the West European peoples by demonizing Nazism and creating an authoritative record of those responsible for World War II humanitarian law violations. Subsequently, Western Europe integrated itself into the Council of Europe and the European Community (EC) and Union (EU). More recently, countries from Central and Eastern Europe have joined both the Council and the EU. Undoubtedly, this peaceful integration was facilitated by the Marshall Plan and subsequent European economic success. Although neo-Nazism has recently reared its ugly head, especially among the unemployed in the newly united Germany, it is a minority movement that democratic Germans will hold in check.

By contrast, the ICTY has apparently contributed little to the reconciliation of the parties in states of the former Yugoslavia. The 1995 General Framework Agreement for Peace in Bosnia and Herzegovina (the Dayton Accords) created the independent state of Bosnia and Herzegovina (hereafter referred to as BH) consisting of two entities: these are the

Federation of BH (the Federation), made up of Croats and Muslims (Bosniaks), and the Republika Srpska (RS), made up of Serbs. However, despite the Dayton Accords and the presence of the Stabilization Force (SFOR), led by NATO, and the International Police Task Force, established by the United Nations, BH remains bitterly divided along ethnic lines. Serious ethnic and political rivalries continue to divide Croats and Bosniaks within the Federation, and all ethnic groups have intimidated minorities who try to re-establish homes in their sectors.[28] The situation is exacerbated by the country's poor economic conditions.

Officials of the RS distrust the ICTY and refuse to arrest indicted Serbs who reside there. Both Serbs and Croats have attacked SFOR and UN personnel operating in their areas. In short, BH continues to be a tinderbox of distrust and hatred that could easily ignite into another round of inter-ethnic violence, should SFOR withdraw.[29]

Inter-ethnic reconciliation has yet to occur in Rwanda. Former refugee Tutsi from Uganda dominate the Rwandan government, military, and police. For the past several years the police have been holding over 100,000 Hutu of all ages prisoner while they are investigated for possible participation in the 1994 mass killings. Human rights NGOs have accused both Hutu militants and the Rwandan army of serious human rights violations after 1994 in Rwanda and in the neighbouring Democratic Republic of the Congo.[30]

The situation in Rwanda is exacerbated by demographic and economic factors: Rwanda is the most densely populated country in Africa; it is cursed by extreme poverty, with a per capita income of only US$240; over 90 per cent of the population relies on agriculture for survival, yet there is insufficient land for many. Intense competition for land contributed to the 1994 genocide and continues to plague this poor country.[31]

Deterring future humanitarian law violations

The post-World War II tribunals had the limited purpose of prosecuting Axis war criminals; however, the IMT Charter's conceptualization of crimes against humanity eventually became part of customary international law and subject to universal jurisdiction. Consequently, it alerted political and military leaders everywhere to the fact that gross human rights violations against their own citizens were illegal and potentially punishable under international law. Western Europe has been free from such crimes since World War II. The absence of UN Security Council responses to humanitarian law violations around the world prior to 1990 can be blamed on the inability of Council members to act in unison, rather than on the legacy of the IMT.

As noted above, neither the ICTY nor the ICTR deterred humanitarian law violations in the territories over which they held jurisdiction. The important difference in the temporal jurisdictions of these two ad hoc tribunals needs to be reiterated. The ICTR has jurisdiction for certain crimes committed in the year 1994 only; hence, it has not been a threat to either Hutu or Tutsi who committed those crimes subsequently. By contrast, the ICTY's temporal jurisdiction continues until the UN Security Council pronounces a termination date; consequently, in 1999 it was able to indict former Serbian President Slobodan Milošević and others for alleged crimes against humanity in the province of Kosovo. Despite its continuing temporal jurisdiction, however, the ICTY failed to deter those responsible for post-1993 crimes in Bosnia–Herzegovina and Kosovo; it took NATO forces to accomplish this end.

Securing compensation for victims

Article 28 of the Nuremberg Charter gave the Tribunal "the right to deprive the convicted person of any stolen property and order its delivery to the Control Council for Germany." However, the Charter contained no provisions for securing indemnity for victims; this was dealt with by other means, including a West German reparations agreement with Israel.[32]

The ICTY and ICTR go beyond the IMT. Article 24(3) of the ICTY Statute and Article 23(3) of the ICTR Statute are identical. Both constitute a property return provision: "In addition to imprisonment, the Trial Chambers may order the return of any property and proceeds acquired by criminal conduct, including by means of duress, to their rightful owners." Neither statute, however, contains provisions to compensate victims for injuries, medical expenses, pain and suffering, destroyed property, or rehabilitation.

Promoting human rights by example

The most frequent criticisms levelled at the IMT concern its weak guarantees of fair trial and due process rights. According to its Charter, the IMT was not established to try all those mainly responsible for humanitarian law violations: it was established for "the just and prompt trial and punishment of the major war criminals of the European Axis" only (Art. 1); consequently, it ignored the war crimes committed by Allied forces.

The IMT is often called a "victors' tribunal" because its creators, judges, and prosecutors were from the four victorious Allied countries. Article 3 of the IMT Charter stipulated that, "neither the Tribunal, its members nor their alternates can be challenged by the prosecution, or by the defendants or their Counsel." According to Article 26, the judgements of the tribunal as to the guilt or innocence of any defendants were final and not subject to review.

Charter Article 12 allowed the IMT to conduct trials in absentia, and Article 19 freed the Tribunal from the necessity of observing the technical rules of evidence. This meant, among other things, that the defendants on occasion did not enjoy the right to confront witnesses against them: for example, the judges allowed the prosecution to introduce *ex parte* affidavits into evidence, without making the persons who made them available testify and be challenged by the defence.[33]

The IMT Charter did recognize some of the basic due process rights of defendants. Article 16 specified that a copy of the full indictment and all of its associated documents should be furnished to the defendant in a language he understood at a reasonable time before the trial. During any preliminary examination or trial, the defendant had the right to give any explanation relevant to the charges made against him. Article 16 also required the preliminary examination and trial to be conducted in, or translated into, a language that the defendant understood. It gave the defendant the right to conduct his own defence before the tribunal or to have the assistance of counsel, to present evidence at the trial in support of his defence, and to cross-examine any prosecution witness. Article 23 permitted a defendant to be represented by any counsel professionally qualified to conduct cases before the courts of his own country, or by any other person who might be specially authorized by the tribunal.

As a defence against IMT criticisms, one may argue that it preceded the UDHR and the ICCPR – two of the standards that the two recent UN tribunals have looked to for guidance. Also, trying suspected war criminals, even in less than ideal proceedings, was better than simply executing them by firing squad, as Winston Churchill and Josef Stalin had advocated. Despite its shortcomings, the IMT did find two of the defendants in the famous Nuremberg trial not guilty of the charges against them. In sum, however, the IMT is not a contemporary model of due process rights for the accused.

By contrast, UN authorities and ICTY/ICTR judges have shown great deference to the various UN human rights covenants and conventions when designing tribunal statutes and rules of procedure. In addition to respecting the UN ICCPR, they examined major US and European human rights due process cases. When drafting the rules of detention, ICTR judges looked to the 1977 United Nations Standard Minimum Rules for the Treatment of Prisoners, the 1988 Body of Principles for the Protection of All Persons under Any Form of Detention or Imprisonment, and the 1990 Basic Principles for the Treatment of Prisoners. They also took into account the higher standards recommended by the European Prison Rules, issued by the Council of Europe in 1987.

Consequently, both tribunals promote human rights, especially the due process rights of the accused, by their own example. Just recently, for example, the Supreme Court of Canada cited the statutes of the ICTY, ICTR, and ICC as evidence of a significant international movement towards the abolition of the death penalty.[34]

However, both the ICTY and the ICTR have been criticized for delaying or prolonging trials. Such problems, however, can be largely attributed to difficulties encountered in securing witnesses from unstable areas and other related obstacles.

The potential of the International Criminal Court

The ICC will have jurisdiction over the citizens of many more states than any of its predecessors. Consequently, its potential for contributing to the cessation of humanitarian law violations, achieving justice, contributing to the reconciliation of the parties, and deterring future humanitarian law violations is most probably greater. Despite the restrictions imposed on its ability to initiate prosecutions, the proposed ICC is a solid beginning to the deterrence of atrocities and to bringing offenders to justice. By March 2001, the nine African countries of Botswana, Gabon, Ghana, Lesotho, Mali, Senegal, Sierra Leone, South Africa, and Swaziland had already amended their constitutions to include the ICC Statute articles pertaining to crimes against humanity;[35] other African countries are expected to follow suit.

The Rome Statute is also designed to do more in the way of securing indemnity/compensation for victims. Article 79 directs the Assembly of States Parties to the Statute to create a trust fund for victims and their families; it also authorizes the ICC to order money and property collected through fines and forfeitures to be transferred to this fund. Article 75 directs the ICC to establish principles for determining the amount of restitution, compensation, and rehabilitation it may award victims and their families. The ICC may impose the cost of the above on convicted persons or it may authorize awards from the Trust Fund.

Like its predecessors (the ICTY and ICTR), the ICC is designed to guarantee the due process and other rights of victims and defendants as recommended in the most recent human rights conventions. Hence, it should be a model for national courts for the protection of human rights of victims and defendants.

Conclusions

Crimes against humanity and genocide generally occur in undemocratic countries that are afflicted with severe economic problems and intense competition for resources. In such countries, unscrupulous political or military leaders convince at least some of their followers that the solution to their plight is the persecution or elimination of some other religious, ethnic, racial, or political group(s). This was the case recently in the former Yugoslavia and Rwanda. Tribunals cannot create democracies or eliminate economic troubles, but they can contribute positively to the creation of more humane civic cultures by warning national leaders that crimes against humanity and genocide must not be part of their political strategies.

For such a warning to be effective, the world needs a permanent international court. The Security Council, after creating ad hoc tribunals for the former Yugoslavia and Rwanda, has reportedly reached the point of "tribunal fatigue" and cannot be relied on to establish additional courts to deal with future war crimes, genocides, and crimes against humanity. An effective permanent criminal tribunal, such as the ICC, would represent a warning and promise to all that widespread atrocities will not go unpunished. By posing an effective threat of prosecution, the ICC will encourage leaders to seek more humane solutions to their countries' economic and political problems. In this way, a permanent ICC will help to protect human rights around the world.

Notes

1. See, for example Article 4 of the International Covenant on Civil and Political Rights, which states in part that, "In times of public emergency ... States Parties to the present Covenant may take measures derogating from their obligations to the present Covenant ..."
2. *The Charter of the International Military Tribunal*, 8 August 1945, 59 Stat. 1544, 82 U.N.T.S. 279.
3. Ibid., article 6.
4. Richard May and Marieke Wierda, "Trends in International Criminal Evidence: Nuremberg, Tokyo, The Hague, and Arusha," *Columbia Journal of Transnational Law*, Vol. 37, 1999, pp. 725–765.
5. Dinah Shelton, "Introduction," in Dinah Shelton, ed., *The Role of the International Criminal Court*, Ardsley, NY: Transactional Publishers, 2000, p. ix.
6. UN Doc. S/25704, 1993.
7. ICTY Statute, UN Doc. S/RES/827, 1993.
8. Para. 7 of UN Doc. S/1994/1007, 29 August 1994. For a discussion of the establishment of the International Tribunal for the Former Yugoslavia, see M. Cherif Bassiouni, "Former Yugoslavia: Investigating Violations of International Humanitarian Law and Establishing an International Criminal Tribunal," *Fordham International Law Review*, Vol. 18, 1995, pp. 1191–1211. For a description and analysis of that Tribunal's legal structure, see Theodor Meron, "War Crimes in Yugoslavia and Development of International Law," *American Journal of International Law*, Vol. 88, 1994, pp. 78–87; Ruth Wedgwood, "War Crimes in the Former Yugoslavia: Comments on the International

War Crimes Tribunal," *Virginia Journal of International Law*, Vol. 34, 1994, pp. 267–275; John R. Jones, *The Practice of the International Criminal Tribunals for the Former Yugoslavia and Rwanda*, New York: Transnational Publishers, 1998; and Michael P. Scharf, *Balkan Justice: The Story Behind the First International War Crimes Tribunal Since Nuremberg*, Durham, NC: Carolina Academic Press, 1997.

9. Para. 34 UN Doc. S/25704, 1993.

10. Para. 35 of UN Doc. S/25704, 1993.

11. Jean-Bernard Marie, "International Instruments Relating to Human Rights," *Human Rights Journal*, Vol. 14, 1994, pp. 51–67.

12. "Advisory Opinion on Reservations to the Convention on the Prevention and Punishment of the Crime of Genocide," *International Court of Justice*, Vol. 15, 1951.

13. Para. 64 of UN Doc. S/25704, 1993.

14. *Rules of Procedure and Evidence*, IT/32/ Adopted on 11 Feb. 1994, subsequently amended.

15. Studies of the genocide include: Gerard Prunier, *The Rwanda Crisis: History of a Genocide*, London: Hurst, 1997; Philip Gourevitch, *We Wish to Inform You that Tomorrow We will Be Killed with Our Families*, New York: Farrar Straus and Giroux, 1998; Alison Des Forges, *Leave None to Tell the Story: Genocide in Rwanda*, London: Human Rights Watch, 1999; and Paul J. Magnarella, *Justice in Africa: Rwanda's Genocide, Its National Courts and the UN Criminal Tribunal*, Aldershot, England: Ashgate, 2000.

16. ICTR Statute, UN Doc. S/Res/955, 1994. For a description and analysis of the ICTR's legal structure and early functioning, see V.A. Morris and M.P. Scharf, *The International Criminal Tribunal for Rwanda*, Vols. 1 and 2, New York: Transnational Publishers, 1998; Magnarella, *Justice in Africa*.

17. Julia Preston, "Tribunal Set on Rwanda War Crimes; Kigali Votes No on UN Resolution," *Washington Post*, 9 November 1994, p. A44.

18. UN Doc. A/Res/49/206, 1994.

19. Donatella Lorch, "Kenya Refuses to Hand Over Suspects in Rwanda Slayings," *New York Times*, 6 October 1995, p. A3.

20. Richard Goldstone, "Statement by Justice Richard Goldstone," ICTR, 5 October 1995, The Hague.

21. Villia Jefremovas, "Acts of Human Kindness: Tutsi, Hutu and the Genocide," *Issue*, Vol. 23, 1995, pp. 28–30.

22. UN Doc. A/CONF.183/9, 17 July 1998.

23. Some of these functions have been delineated previously by other legal scholars, e.g. Antonio Cassese, "Reflections on International Criminal Justice," *Modern Law Review*, Vol. 61, 1998, pp. 3–6; Alinikisa Mafwenga, "The Contribution of the International Criminal Tribunal for Rwanda to Reconciliation in Rwanda," in Dinah Shelton, ed., *International Crimes, Peace, and Human Rights: The Role of the International Criminal Court*, Ardsley, NY: Transactional Publishers, 2000, pp. 11–17; Sandra Coliver, "The Contribution of the International Criminal Tribunal for the Former Yugoslavia to Reconciliation in Bosnia and Herzegovina," in Shelton, ed., *International Crimes, Peace, and Human Rights*, pp. 19–31.

24. See, for example Agence France Presse, "Serb Militant Rejects Legitimacy of the War Crimes Tribunal," *Lexis-Nexis News File*, 24 October 1994.

25. This and updated information are available at ⟨www.un.org/icty⟩.

26. Information available at ⟨www.ictr.org⟩.

27. Kambanda's confession is contained in Magnarella, *Justice in Africa*, pp. 85–93.

28. For the social, political, and human rights conditions in BH, see the annual U.S. Department of State reports on *Bosnia and Herzegovina Human Rights Practices*, 1995–2002, available at ⟨http://www.state.gov/g/drl/hr/⟩.

29. See "Serbian Analysts: Serbs a Long Way from Reconciliation with Their Past," *Balkan Report*, 22 February 2002, Vol. 6, No. 10. Available at: ⟨http://www.rferl.org/balkan-report/2002/02/10-220202.html⟩.

30. Des Forges, *Leave None to Tell the Story*.

31. Magnarella, *Justice in Africa*, pp. 1–27. See also U.S. Department of State Reports, *Rwanda: Human Rights Practices*, 1994–2002, available at ⟨http://www.state.gov/g/drl/hr/⟩.

32. For a discussion of reparations, see Benjamin Ferencz, "The Experience of Nuremberg," in Shelton, ed., *International Crimes, Peace, and Human Rights*, pp. 3–9.

33. For a first-hand description and critique of the IMT, see Telford Taylor, *The Anatomy of the Nuremberg Trials*, NY: Knopf, 1992.

34. *United States v Burns*, 2001 Supreme Court of Canada 7, File No. 26129, 15 February 2001.

35. "Africa News," 29 March 2001, *Lexis-Nexis News File*.

7

International efforts to protect human rights in transition societies: Right, duty, or politics?

Albrecht Schnabel

Faced with numerous human rights challenges, governments of transition societies are often neither able, nor willing, to end human rights violations or to address their economic, political, or cultural root causes.[1] Peaceful and, if necessary, violent actions then become necessary tools in redressing injustice, bringing about state compliance with international humanitarian human rights norms and laws and laying the foundations for lasting peace. Such actions may take various forms, ranging from economic assistance and non-violent diplomacy to massive military intervention; these actions may be supported and conducted by individuals, NGOs, or states, or by regional and global organizations on behalf of broader communities of concerned societies and states. Involvement may follow the consensual agreement of affected governments or it may be forced upon a government. Intervention in the internal affairs of a sovereign state to alleviate human rights violations, although potentially noble, is also risky and often self-serving.

Although all individuals should undoubtedly enjoy the same rights under international law, the defence of these rights is highly contextual. Political, economic, and (above all) geo-strategic contingencies determine the likelihood and extent of external intervention in defence of human rights standards. Intervention, whatever form it may take, is costly. Such costs are acceptable only if they yield a desirable return – whether ideological or practical. Thus, humanitarian intervention emerges as a highly contested activity grounded both in contemporary international law and morality and in power politics driven by national interest.

Much has been written about the general subject of humanitarian intervention, particularly since the end of the Cold War and the resurgence of international military intervention in internal conflicts. Many of these interventions were launched at least partly under the pretext of humanitarian protection. Often-cited and -studied cases range from America's intervention in Haiti in 1994 to the United Nations' intervention in Bosnia in 1992, to NATO's intervention in Kosovo in 1999. Past tragic failures of the international community to intervene effectively, along with the more recent debates on pre-emptive military strikes against rogue states (apparently) possessing weapons of mass destruction (WMD) have heightened interest in the broader concept of humanitarian intervention. There is little agreement on the legitimacy or duty of such humanitarian intervention: a review of the literature turns up arguments for operations that are more expanded or more limited, more proactive or more reactive, UN-authorized or not, and conducted with or without a host state's consent. It is not hard to make plausible arguments that a particular intervention was or was not (or would or would not be) legally, morally, politically, or economically sound.

Such uncertainty could be a blessing in disguise: flexibility in conceptualizing and applying human rights support and enforcement allows those who are willing and able to respond to do so. Yet this same flexibility leaves much room for abuse and it prevents or postpones the creation of permanent structures for principled responses to human rights violations. Thus, while some peoples' human security will be the international community's business, other peoples' lives and destinies will not.

The purpose of this chapter is to review and assess this ongoing and evolving debate and to suggest some ways to refine debates on the international community's rights and responsibilities to defend human rights in transition societies. The chapter argues that, despite all the shortcomings of the embryonic structures and principles of international solidarity, community, and citizenship, we have, in fact, come a long way towards breaking down the wall between the individual and the global community. This is leading to an erosion of institutionalized, structural injustice and the limits previously put on efforts to support and enforce universal principles of human decency. Although still in its infancy, and fraught with shortcomings and unintended consequences, the increased legitimacy of local, regional, and international human rights enforcement efforts may, in the long run, lead to a more just and secure global society.

The chapter is divided into five main parts. Following this introduction, I focus on the need to intervene in transition societies to protect human rights and thwart their violation. I then ask if there is, in fact, a right or a duty to intervene in the sovereign affairs of a state for humanitarian purposes. The chapter then calls for a greater focus on preventive involvement. Although preventing human rights violations may be a difficult undertaking, it can alleviate much suffering in transition societies and thus avert the need for more problematic military interventions later on. The chapter concludes with some suggestions for conceptually sound and practically feasible approaches to prevent and redress human rights violations in transition societies.

On the need for (and prospect of) external efforts to protect human rights in transition societies

As noted in the introduction to this volume, human rights violations frequently occur in societies undergoing political, social, and economic transformations. Structural violence, inequality, and inequity are the by-products of most political processes towards democratization, the introduction of a free market economy, or the reorganization of fragile relations between subnational, often ethnically defined, communities. Such transitions produce rearrangements of previous (often, deeply entrenched) political, economic, and social power relations. They forge new legal and authority structures, creating large and enduring grey areas of little or no authority and order.

Government incapacity and neglect

Governments in transition societies often do not provide for the most elementary security needs of their citizens. This may be due to lack of capacity: they may lack the necessary resources to provide basic needs, to ensure the physical security of individuals and groups, to distribute and redistribute national resources, to contain lawlessness and internal violence, to enforce basic human rights standards, and to monitor and punish their violations. In that case, rising levels of human rights violations are a direct result of weak state capacity and legitimacy. International assistance can improve such capacity while indigenous states are built and their political, social, and economic systems are consolidated. A responsible but weak government will ask for international assistance to ease the transition process and may thus avoid undesirable consequences for its human rights situation. If the support of both the government and large parts of society is guaranteed, the risks of involvement are low, and the chance of success is high, external actors will be more likely to help.

On the other hand, governments not only may be unable to protect citizens' human rights but also may be completely uninterested in doing so. This applies particularly to authoritarian, unaccountable governments that have risen to power without the legitimacy of open and fair elections. In such cases, international aid is either squandered or used to line the pockets of political officials and their cronies. Impoverishment, criminalization, and selective distribution of resources and opportunities are used to polarize society, to instrumentalize and politicize religious and ethnic identities, and to buy the allegiance of populations and local power holders. International involvement is not desired, as this would ultimately threaten the authority, position, and livelihood of the political leadership and its beneficiaries. In such cases, any external assistance has to be closely monitored to ensure that it is used for its intended purpose, and strong diplomatic pressure (rather than economic sanctions, which tend to hurt the people rather than its leaders[2]) must be applied in order to stop escalating human rights violations and their destabilizing long-term consequences.

If human rights violations are taken as indications of entrenched flaws in governance, economy, and social relations, these flaws must be addressed to alleviate existing violations of human rights and to prevent future violations. Transition societies are exposed to a wide variety of threats to human rights and, thus, to further degeneration of state legitimacy, inter-communal relations, order, justice, and stability. Similar to economic performance, levels of social service, education and employment levels, and other standard indicators of a society's development status, human rights conditions indicate how inadequate government performance and provision of state services contribute to inequalities, the state–society disconnect, and accompanying structural violence. Much can be done from outside to support the state in improving human rights conditions. Such improvements would then indicate enhanced state performance, economic development, and eased intra-societal relations. All these are necessary to put a transition society on the right track towards sustainable stability and development. Early recognition of human rights violations, and relevant diplomatic and economic responses by the international community, would be likely to ease transition pains and prevent subsequent armed conflict. For instance, if the international community would have reacted more firmly to anti-Albanian discriminatory practices following the annulment of Kosovo's autonomy status in 1989, much suffering, internal violence, the eventual military intervention from NATO, and the current reconstruction of Kosovo by the international community might have been avoided.[3]

International responses

At early stages of societal disintegration, particularly in cases where human rights violations are by-products of state inefficiency rather than of overt government-sponsored oppression and violence, there is a great deal of political and diplomatic room for external assistance and support. Governments will be more willing to accept external support. Provision of health expertise and supplies can ease pressure on the government to provide for basic medical care; energy and food supplies can alleviate pressure on strained state budgets; and political, legal, and technical advice can strengthen state capacity and legitimacy *vis-à-vis* its citizens. Such benevolent and non-violent involvement in a country's transition process defuses inevitable causes of human rights violations and tensions during times of political, economic, and social uncertainty.

Much heavier-handed support may be necessary in societies that are emerging from war, ravaged by near-total political, economic, and social breakdown: political and judicial institutions are weak and divided; infrastructure and economy are in shambles; communities are divided by a culture of violence and distrust; and the wartime security apparatus is ill-suited to meet the challenges of a fragile and dangerous post-war security environment. In such an environment, little progress towards durable peace can be expected unless the government, economy, and security sector are transformed and the population is able to meet its basic human needs – including food, shelter, and physical security. These tasks include all or some of the following: the provision of legislative, executive, and judicial authority; basic civilian and social administrative functions; coordination of elections and implementation of their results; coordination of humanitarian aid, disaster relief, and development assistance; reconstruction of key infrastructure; maintenance of civil law and order; protection of returning refugees and displaced persons; transformation of the security sector (including the disarmament, demobilization, and reintegration of former combatants).[4] Such comprehensive assistance in political, economic, and social reconstruction efforts is rare. The ongoing international involvement in Afghanistan, for instance, is qualitatively much weaker than international efforts to rebuild Bosnia, Kosovo, or East Timor. The depth of involvement generally depends not on need but on the magnitude of resources and political will available to launch effective post-conflict peacebuilding operations.

If a war had drawn international attention and was concluded with the assistance of an international military peace operation (by the United Nations or a regional alliance), wide-ranging and broad international support might be available to aid the society in its transition from war to reconciliation, peace, and economic development. Given the enormous task involved in rebuilding a society torn by war, significant international involvement is likely only as a continuation of ongoing international military involvement. In cases where little external interest could be mustered to stop a war, similar lack of interest will be likely to prevent substantial post-conflict involvement.

Particularly in post-conflict situations, it is difficult to differentiate between *support* and *enforcement* of human rights compliance. This depends largely on the level of consent secured during the original peace operation, launched during (or at the close of) a violent conflict. Much of the recent debate on humanitarian intervention has focused on the international community's right and duty to launch military operations to stop mass carnage. In this context, references are made in particular to the 1994 Rwanda massacres – massacres that were predicted but not prevented, monitored but not stopped. Is there a right, duty, or responsibility to intervene in such cases of grave human suffering?

Towards a principled approach?

At the UN Millennium Assembly in September 2000, the International Commission on Intervention and State Sovereignty (ICISS) was launched with the expectation of achieving three main goals: first, to promote a comprehensive debate on the issue of humanitarian intervention; second, to foster a new global political consensus on how to move forward; and third, to find new ways of reconciling the principles of intervention and sovereignty.[5] The Commission's final report, entitled "The Responsibility to Protect," was released in December 2001.[6] It argues that, where populations are suffering serious harm from man-made and natural disasters and the state cannot (or does not want to) halt or avert such harm, "the principle of non-intervention yields to the international responsibility to protect."[7]

The report argues that such a "responsibility to protect" is already inherent in the obligations that are part and parcel of the concept of state sovereignty: these include the responsibility of the UN Security Council to maintain international peace and security; existing legal obligations and human rights declarations, covenants, treaties, and international and domestic humanitarian law; and developing practice of states, regional organizations, and the United Nations.[8] The report specifies three main elements of the "responsibility to protect": these are, first, the responsibility to prevent violence, by addressing both direct and root causes of conflict; second, the responsibility to react to situations of grave human suffering; and third, the responsibility to rebuild after military intervention and to address and alleviate the causes that have led to violence in the very first place.[9]

The report stresses that preventive action should always be given priority and that less-intrusive and -coercive measures have to be exhausted before more coercive ones are applied. Military intervention should be considered as an exceptional and extraordinary measure – one that can be applied only in extreme cases of massive loss of life, such as genocide or large-scale ethnic cleansing.[10] The report sets the threshold for coercive intervention very high; short of such extreme cases, non-coercive measures should be applied.

The report insists that the UN Security Council should be the only acceptable authority to authorize military intervention for human protection purposes. It should do so quickly, and the permanent Five should refrain from using their veto power to prevent or stall quick and decisive action by the Security Council. Otherwise, alternative solutions should be considered, such as the General Assembly's "Uniting for Peace" procedure, or initiatives by regional and sub-regional organizations or by concerned and willing states (with or without Security Council approval).[11]

The report resembles a "wish list" – with very few truly new concepts or ideas. The report's focus on "responsibilities," not "rights" (or entitlements), and on a range of responsibilities – from prevention to intervention to reconstruction – is a convincing approach; although it has been around for a long time, it may now receive greater recognition in official circles. If this is the case, then the report will have played an important role as a bridge between academic debates and suggestions of the past decades, and their well-deserved recognition among official policy-making communities at state, non-state, and interstate levels.

However, given the depth and inherent dilemmas of the debate, it is neither surprising nor discouraging that none of the report's suggestions is particularly revolutionary. It would have been suspicious if the Commission had claimed to have come up with a politically feasible and legitimate recipe to overcome the moral dilemma between humanitarian protection, non-intervention, and the use of force. In general, the report's recommendations reflect reasonable demands that, however, still allow a high degree of flexibility and interpretation ... and, unfortunately, also plenty of room for inaction. As Jennifer Welsh asks, "[i]f September 11 had not occurred and the Taliban had survived, would its actions against its own citizens have crossed the threshold to 'shock the conscience of mankind'?"[12] The answer is probably a resounding "no."

This should not discourage those interested in more assertive human rights protection. As Linklater argues, "one of the fundamental responsibilities of the good international citizen is to strive to resolve the tension between legalism and progressivism in a new legal order that alters the relationship between order and justice, citizenship and humanity, and sovereignty and human rights."[13] This is a challenging task that should benefit from the thinking reflected in the ICISS Report.

We might, thus, find ourselves at the beginning of an emerging international consensus on the need to protect basic human rights and security from violations on a massive scale. Of course, it would be utterly unacceptable if another Rwanda was in the making, visible to the entire world, well known to the United Nations, and no action was taken. International consensus on strong and immediate reaction to such massive violence should be considered no more than the minimum responsibility of an international community committed to basic human decency. However noble it is to put structures in place to avert genocides, such international action takes place when much irreversible social, political, and economic destruction has already occurred. Such threshold criteria create response mechanisms for very exceptional cases – and for cases where the international community has failed to respond to a long and highly visible deterioration of a country's internal situation, accompanied by widespread violation of human rights.

Short of genocidal violence, military interventions may still be launched (for purely, primarily, or only partly humanitarian reasons) against small states where internal human rights violations threaten to destabilize regional security (through outpouring refugees, for example). To be sure, a truly principled response system would require responses wherever and whenever human rights violations occur that cannot be corrected through local efforts. All countries, irrespective of economic and political power status, would be subjected to such international scrutiny and response.

However, such a principled approach does not correspond to prevailing international realities. Short of a highly refined and established supranational world government, with the power, legitimacy, and resources to design and enforce globally accepted norms, rules, and principles (which would arguably be neither possible nor desirable), such a principled approach will not be possible. Regional and subregional organizations are in a better position to support and enforce such shared norms as human rights standards. The European Union (EU) – as well as the OSCE and NATO – can do this in Europe; the African Union (AU, formerly the Organization of African Unity; OAU) in Africa; the Organization of American States (OAS) in the Americas; and the Association of South-East Asian Nations (ASEAN) in East Asia. The United Nations' role is limited to promoting and monitoring human rights (and their defence) on a global scale and to serving as an agency of last resort when states and regional or subregional organizations are unable (or unwilling) to respond to truly outrageous violations. In these cases, the chances are higher that the Security Council will respond and that the necessary resources will be secured. Before we delve further into the limits and opportunities of international efforts to fight human rights violations in transition societies, however, we need to consider the legitimacy of such actions.

Is there a duty and right to intervene?

Is it legitimate to intervene in the affairs of a sovereign state to protect the human rights of its citizens? And is there a duty to do so? Before we return to these questions, we have to distinguish between different forms of, and justifications for, intervention. If we intervene in a state's sovereign affairs to redress violations of human rights and international humanitarian law, this can involve non-military and military actions, non-violent and violent actions, non-consensual enforcement or consensual assistance and support, and a great variety of state and non-state actors.

International involvement can take numerous forms, characterized by a number of key factors conditioning intervention. It may be characterized (1) according to different *types* of intervention – political, economic, and military; (2) according to the *method* of intervention – through relief and assistance, diplomacy, or the use of force; (3) according to the *timing* of intervention – from ongoing activities (including day-to-day diplomacy and operations of UN agencies and programmes, regional organizations and NGOs) to responses at pre-crisis, crisis/conflict/emergency, and post-conflict stages; (4) according to its *objectives*, including the protection of the population; defence of international norms, order, and security; or the prevention of armed violence and its spill-over; (5) according to the source and level of *legitimacy* accorded to an intervention – sponsored or authorized by the United Nations, by a (sub)regional organization, or by one or more states; (6) by the nature of *actors* conducting the intervention – including the United Nations, (sub)regional organizations, individual or ad hoc groups of states, NGOs, and individuals; and (7) according to the *visibility* of an intervention – ranging from silent to sensational, depending on the level of media coverage and on the combination of all of the above characteristics.

Assistance and support activities

Is there a duty to offer support and assistance to transition countries to prevent human rights violations? Most countries, as signatories to the UN Charter and numerous international treaties and conventions, are committed to protecting human rights, justice, and security. The UN Charter and the UDHR are probably the most explicit articulations of the international community's concern with human rights. Article 1 of the Charter calls upon all nations to "achieve international co-operation in solving international problems of an economic, social, cultural, or humanitarian character, and in promoting and encouraging respect for human rights and for fundamental freedoms for all without distinction as to race, sex, language, or religion." Article 55 calls for "universal respect for, and observance of, human rights and fundamental freedoms for all without distinction as to race, sex, language, or religion." According to Article 56, "[a]ll Members pledge themselves to take joint and separate action in co-operation with the Organization for the achievement of the purposes set forth in Article 55."

Lofty ambitions

So far, the international community has failed to live up to the principles enshrined in these international agreements. Many of these commitments appear to be no more than lofty ambitions: their realization depends on a wide range of highly contextual political and other factors; after all, the United Nations and its members are committed only to the "promotion" (Art. 55) of these goals, not to their enforcement. Principles of international solidarity and responsibility appear to be no more than rhetorical expressions, purposely devoid of enforcement provisions and dependent on ever-changing political, strategic, and moral contexts.

Nevertheless, the fact remains that most states have, at least on paper, committed themselves to the defence of many norms and practices that would, if enforced on a global basis, result in a vastly more just and secure world.[14] There are thus plenty of expressions of an ideal global order, although without reference to enforcement, as broad international agreement on these principles can be reached only in the abstract, not in reality. Yet, those abstract statements are first steps towards their realization, even if they express far-fetched hopes that clash with current realities.

The duty to assist

Having said that, commitments to international norms on human rights and justice do suggest a responsibility, if not a duty, to do the utmost possible to realize these norms. This commits states to promoting international peace, security, and justice, including the protection of human rights. States that cannot comply with these international standards must be – depending on the reasons for non-compliance – assisted, encouraged, or forced to fulfil their domestic responsibilities. In theory, the international community (preferably through the United Nations) has the legal (not only moral) duty to monitor and enforce state compliance with international standards. As mentioned above, very few transition societies are able to meet the challenges of transition and, at the same time, to provide for the most fundamental human needs of their citizens. Poor human rights conditions are the consequence and must be addressed through outside assistance.

Although the responsibility to maintain acceptable human rights standards exists, international law also prohibits intervention in the affairs of sovereign states without an explicit invitation to do so (Art. 2.7), unless international peace and security are threatened (chap. VII). The rules of international society are thus based on a cruel contradiction: the international citizen cannot fulfil the responsibility to protect basic security and justice for all without violating another key principle of this very society – the inviolability of state sovereignty.[15]

This dilemma may not necessarily be perceived as such. In fact, few political leaders would want to see this convenient contradiction and dilemma resolved. Fulfilling all of the noble goals expressed in international agreements would require the international community to overcome all political and economic inequalities, inequities, and injustices that currently ensure that a minority of the world's population is able to pursue a life of reasonable security and happiness, but at the expense of the majority. Establishing justice around the world would mean substantial sacrifices on the part of the rich and powerful. Such a transfer (and redistribution) of political and economic power is difficult enough to achieve within even the most advanced, wealthy, and participatory democracies; on a global scale, this would be a monumental task. Thus, the principle of non-intervention offers a welcome excuse to ignore a vast majority of international norms and principles. International solidarity, the international citizen, and the concept of a responsible international society are rhetorical expressions of a normative global condition that would be morally desirable.[16] Enlightened international citizens or leaders find it necessary to express a commitment to this ideal global condition, if only to counter the occasional guilt caused by the realization that much of their wealth and happiness – directly and indirectly – aggravates the continuation, if not permanence, of international injustice. Such commitment is, therefore, intentionally detached from its principled enforcement.

Current activities

Much of the assistance that would need to be granted to transition societies, or other fragile societies, is currently discussed in the context of development, human security, prevention, and peace-building debates.[17] Although sometimes presented as new and emerging debates, all of the key concepts and responsibilities discussed can easily be found in decades-old expressions of international legal commitments, starting with the Charter of the United Nations. It is laudable and important that these debates have resurfaced and are seriously examined in both academic and policy circles. Although the promotion and, sometimes, enforcement of international norms have long been treated as luxuries driven more by altruism than responsibility, the latter appears to be returning to academic and official debates. We may be very far removed from an international order in which global norms are advanced on a principled basis, because we have neither the resources nor the institutional structures to do so. However, the intention to do so – at least in part, sometimes, where politically and economically feasible and convenient – is a promising beginning.

There are many international and local actors that do their utmost to provide services and protection neglected by state authorities. For instance, much of the United Nations' work consists of continual efforts on the ground and at official levels to improve economic development, health, human rights, and basic security requirements where such basic needs are denied or neglected by government authorities. Such constant assistance is provided by the UN Development Programme (UNDP), the United Nations' Office of the Higher Commissioner for Human Rights (UNHCHR), the Office for the Coordination of Humanitarian Affairs (OCHA), the World Health Organization (WHO), the World Food Programme (WFP), and many other specialized agencies and programmes. Unfortunately, however, much of this work is mostly cosmetic, politically convenient, largely reactive (with responses in cases where violations and suffering have reached levels where international visibility and condemnation have generated the funds and goodwill to take meaningful action), and poorly coordinated with the activities of other international and non-state actors. Later in this chapter we revisit the current debates surrounding proactive activities to alleviate the root causes (among them human rights violations) of social destabilization and violence.

Of course, even symbolic expression of international citizenship and responsibility is better than their outright rejection. The current practice of military peace enforcement and humanitarian intervention is an expression of such symbolism – symbolism that may, in cases where exceptional threshold criteria are met, lead to principled action to enforce some selected basic human rights.

Enforcement operations

What can be said about the legitimacy of international efforts to *enforce* human rights? This debate receives widespread attention whenever humanitarian disasters shock the conscience of the informed international public, such as in response to the famine of war-stricken Somalia; the ethnic killings of Rwanda, Bosnia, or East Timor; or the Srebrenica massacre.[18] Political as well as academic and legal comments suggest that, whereas the legality of intervention for human rights protection and humanitarian purposes is questionable, international commitments to the promotion and protection of human rights seem to suggest a moral duty to enforce those rights.

History and legality

As Adam Roberts argues, "[m]ilitary action as a response to violations of human rights and humanitarian norms has a long history, well pre-dating the modern codifications of international law on the subject." He cites French and British naval support of Greece's independence from the

Ottoman Empire in 1827–1830, in response to reported Turkish atrocities, and the history of European colonialism as early interventions in which the defence of basic humanitarian norms has been cited to justify military action.[19] Further cases include Russia's intervention in Turkey (1877–1878); the Greek, Bulgarian, and Serb interventions in Macedonia in 1903;[20] France's intervention in Syria in 1860–1861; and the American Monroe Doctrine of 1823.[21] Certainly until the end of World War I and the Kellogg–Briand Pact of August 1928, renouncing war as an acceptable instrument of national policy, "[t]here was no general prohibition on the use of force, and indeed international law conceived of war as the ultimate and legitimate exercise of the attributes of state sovereignty." In the absence of formal international institutional frameworks, "[t]o protect themselves against aggression, states wove a complex web of treaties, pacts, and ententes, many of them secret, some accompanied by full-blown military alliances and duties to intervene if allies were attacked by a third party."[22]

Article 2 (4) of the Charter of the United Nations reaffirms the principles of the Kellogg–Briand Pact and prohibits the threat or use of force against states, while Article 2 (7) prohibits interventions into matters that are within the domestic jurisdiction of sovereign states. However, Chapter VII allows such intervention when international peace and security are threatened. During the Cold War, political expediency warranted the deployment of UN peacekeeping troops as a neutral third-party security presence to facilitate the resolution of international conflicts. However, those operations were launched under Chapter VI of the Charter, upon the invitation of conflicting parties, and without the use of force. Although, in theory, more forceful action by the United Nations would have been possible under Chapter VII, it was not feasible in the context of an ideologically divided Security Council (with the exception of the Korean War[23]).

The end of the Cold War, followed by the Gulf War of 1991, thawed suspicions and reduced divisions within the Security Council. Since then, the UN Security Council frequently referred to humanitarian issues, among other issues, when calling for or authorizing military interventions in response to threats to international peace and security.[24] This has been the case in Bosnia and Herzegovina (1992–1995),[25] Somalia (1992–1993),[26] Rwanda (1994),[27] Haiti (1994),[28] Albania (1997),[29] East Timor (1999),[30] and Sierra Leone (1999–2000).[31] The Security Council Resolution authorizing the UN Mission in Sierra Leone (UNAMSIL), for instance, called on all parties "to ensure safe and unhindered access of humanitarian assistance to those in need in Sierra Leone, to guarantee the safety and security of humanitarian personnel and to respect strictly the relevant provisions of international humanitarian and human rights law."[32] In two other prominent cases – Northern Iraq (1991) and Kosovo (1998–1999) – the Security Council cited concerns over violations of human rights and humanitarian norms but fell short of an explicit authorization of the use of force.[33] Nevertheless, in both cases the United States and its coalition partners (in the case of Kosovo, under the umbrella of NATO) decided to launch military actions encouraged by Security Council language but without its endorsement. They argued that the various Security Council Resolutions that condemned human rights violations and called for responses to humanitarian crises in fact constituted implied authorizations for interested and willing members of the international community to use force on behalf of threatened individuals and groups.

The dilemma of law and morality

Academic analyses and public discussions of these cases suggest "that the main problem of humanitarian intervention consists in the divergence of law and morality: while considerations of justice and human rights demand the recognition of a right to intervention, international law prevents this by anachronistically relying on order and state sovereignty."[34] Whereas law does not allow intervention, morality (as well as strategic, economic, or political considerations) calls for exceptions to the existing rule of non-intervention. As Kosovo has shown, regional alliances have decided when such exceptions apply.[35]

We are (as we have been for a very long time) struggling with some fundamental questions. What is the primary goal and purpose of international law – to protect states or to protect threatened individuals? Should sovereignty focus on the rights of states (and their governments) or the rights of their peoples? Recent debates focus on the fact that many states are abusing and neglecting their authority and responsibility and thus should be deprived of their own privileges, including that of full sovereignty.[36] Through the loss of empirical sovereignty[37] (i.e. the ability of the state to provide for its population), a failed state may, in fact, jeopardize its right to full sovereignty and thus to protection from international intervention. As Hugo Grotius already argued in the seventeenth century, "where [tyrants] provoke their own people to despair and resistance by unheard of cruelties, having themselves abandoned all the laws of nature, they lose the rights of independent sovereigns, and can no longer claim the privilege of the law of nations."[38] The current UN Secretary-General has been very outspoken on this subject. In 1999 he argued as follows:

State sovereignty, in its most basic sense, is being redefined – not least by the forces of globalization and international co-operation. States are now widely understood to be instruments at the service of their peoples, and not vice versa. At the same time individual sovereignty – by which I mean the fundamental freedom of each individual, enshrined in the Charter of the UN and subsequent international treaties – has been enhanced by a renewed and spreading consciousness of individual rights. When we read the Charter today, we are more than ever conscious that its aim is to protect individual human beings, not to protect those who abuse them.[39]

The absence of the nuclear threat after the Cold War has allowed human rights violations to move closer to the forefront of international attention. Slowly, the principle of non-intervention, a core principle of a state's national sovereignty (and security), seems to have become conditional on a state's ability to create an environment that protects minimum human rights standards promoted by international law. This is certainly a positive development.

The need for proactive reasoning and action

In the context of this volume, particularly given its focus on human rights protection in transition societies, a number of issues are striking. What is sometimes called "humanitarian intervention" takes place once the consequences of human rights violations, among others, begin to hurt communities beyond the borders of oppressed populations. Once political, cultural, and economic orders begin to crumble and social conflicts are the consequence, outside actors take notice. If trade is disrupted, or refugees or armed conflict threaten to spill over borders, they take even greater notice. In the latter case, sometimes this is considered a "threat to or breach of international peace and security." Chapter VII can be invoked, if the UN Security Council agrees on action. Of course, that presupposes that none of the permanent five members of the Security Council objects to such measures. Intervention in Chechnya is, therefore, impossible; UN intervention in Kosovo would not have been possible, either. If the threat is large enough to raise concern and trigger responses, action might be taken. If the threat is not large enough – in other words, if no significant outsider is significantly threatened – no action will be taken. If action is taken, it might be defined in humanitarian terms – the international community comes to the rescue of threatened populations. Of course, the story is often quite different: the international community in fact comes to the rescue of itself – namely, of those who may indirectly or directly suffer from civil or interstate strife in other parts of the world.

Reality shows that the international community is deeply rooted in a culture of reaction, not proaction, and that it reacts only if the interests of some major powers are significantly threatened. Is there a solution to these seemingly hopeless obstacles, one that would allow the international community to address meaningfully the violence so prevalent in failed and failing states? Given the difficulties inherent in humanitarian military interventions discussed so far in this chapter, proaction against structural violence and accompanying human rights violations is the most effective tool in preventing further destabilization of a society. Much scholarship would argue along the same lines. We need to promote and facilitate early humanitarian action, in the context of early warning and measures to prevent sustained structural violence and eventual breakdown of social, economic, and political order.[40]

Effective action by the international community to prevent or manage a conflict requires international legitimacy (ideally provided by the United Nations), regional resources (ideally by regional organizations), and local expertise (ideally by NGOs). However, in practice, non-state, state, and interstate actors pursue their own policies, activities, and development and security projects with little or no joint coordination. Each actor has its own goals and interests, driven by its own mandates and motivations. Competition and turf fights are very common.

Why is it so difficult for IGOs to prevent conflicts successfully? There are a number of reasons. First, their primary "clients" are their member states. The United Nations and regional organizations can do only as much as their member states want them to do. Second, only in rare cases and with great difficulty will international organizations be able to enforce their decisions beyond the use of moral power, economic sanctions, or political pressure. Third, most international organizations have been created to protect and defend, not to challenge and undermine, state sovereignty. Many states fear that preventive actions will be abused as an excuse for politically or ideologically motivated intervention by the strong into the affairs of the weak. The recent attempts by the US and UK governments to justify preventive strikes against Iraq are seen by many as strong confirmation of this fear.[41]

Finally, preventive action requires long-term commitment, a commodity that is difficult enough to secure when a conflict with all its visible and sensationally horrific consequences is in full swing. With no blood spilled and apparent peace and stability on the ground (as was the case, for instance, in post-1989 Kosovo), long-term commitment is even more difficult to achieve.[42]

Despite these difficulties, what steps can be taken to reduce the risk that human rights violations will destabilize society and eventually escalate into armed violence? Structural, long-term prevention of violent conflict can be achieved only if the following tasks are pursued in earnest by local, national, and international stakeholders:

- Poverty, unemployment, economic inequalities, and environmental degradation must be countered. This can be achieved through direct measures (such as technical and financial assistance) or indirect action (such as by opening up markets and discontinuing subsidies and other trade barriers).
- Coordinated, concerted, and sustained efforts must be taken to control and discourage the vast illegal trade in small arms, and malign interventions by other states in internal conflicts.
- It is crucial to invest in long-term preventive action and early warning and early response capacities, even in countries that appear momentarily stable, as well as in (sub)regional organizations.
- Conflict-management skills have to be taught and trained at all levels of society, inside and outside schools and universities.
- Activities by constructive civil-society actors and subregional and regional organizations need to be encouraged and supported.
- In post-conflict societies, territorial and political crises must be settled and resolved, and an entire range of remedial action must be geared toward the prevention of a recurrence of violence. This includes the education and reintegration of child soldiers and combatants, and targeted support of the weak in post-conflict situations, particularly women and children. It also requires, among many other challenges, the cultivation and sustained support of moderate local leaders as key figures in reshaping society's political life.[43]

Conclusions: Where do we go from here?

Addressing human rights violations in transition societies can avert major humanitarian disasters and the need for subsequent military intervention. If basic economic, social, and civil–political rights are assured (e.g. through conditionality in economic assistance schemes), much deterioration can potentially be averted.

Support and consensual assistance must come first; political and diplomatic pressure second; economic pressure third; and, finally, military pressure and intervention. At the first stage, interstate, state, and non-state actors have an important role to play. At the second and third stages, interstate and state actors are particularly important. The fourth stage, although rarely evoked, should (if at all possible) be conducted under the auspices of interstate organizations (and implemented by states or groups of willing states). Ideally, transition societies should be closely monitored by relevant regional organizations and the United Nations for human rights conditions and performance. Violations should be addressed by the international community on a principled basis: if done so systematically, the likelihood of massive human rights violations can be averted in many cases, along with corresponding negative effects on social cohesion, economic development, political stability, and violence.

While the reasons to address human rights violations may fall within the moral and ethical realms of international responsibility, the associated social, political, and economic repercussions of poor human rights performance have direct relevance for the stability of the country, its proneness to violent conflict, and subsequent negative and destabilizing consequences for neighbouring countries and the wider region. Thus, they relate directly to the regional and international community's interest in peace and security. Human rights conditions serve as useful indicators for the level of current and future peace and stability in a society. They also serve as a key entry point (possibly the most effective one) through which future instability, degeneration, and violent conflict can be averted. If human rights violations are detected early, and the causes of such violations are isolated and addressed, stability (even if fragile) can be preserved and further degeneration can be avoided.

The speed and diligence with which international actors move through the above-mentioned stages of response is highly contextual. It depends on the target country and its international status, its size and threat projection, its allies in the international system, its political system, its economic wealth, and its socio-cultural make-up.

Small, economically weak, and militarily powerless countries with little clout in international organizations and alliances may be the "easiest" targets for international efforts to enforce human rights protection. Little resistance may be expected from them, nor would significant negative political or economic repercussions for intervening parties be likely. If military interventions do become necessary and are undertaken, post-conflict reconstruction (increasingly viewed as an automatic responsibility of the intervener) is not an undoable task. Rebuilding Bosnia, Kosovo, or East Timor – already daunting tasks – are much more achievable goals than rebuilding Afghanistan, Angola, or other, much larger, countries.

Large and powerful countries may not be susceptible to diplomatic efforts of shaming the government into compliance with international human rights standards, or to economic sanctions or threats of military intervention. Nevertheless, they may fear the political isolation produced by their outright rejection of international norms, or they may be conscious of the dangers of societal "implosion" – the disintegrating effects of unattended human rights violations on the fabric and stability of their society. Moreover, they may depend on cooperative attitudes of other major powers in the pursuit of their own international interests. Such dependence also creates a greater willingness to cooperate and comply in other issue areas – as long as those issue areas are perceived to be high priorities for other major powers. It is, thus, important that economic and political partners do not shy away from discussing and criticizing human rights violations, even with their closest allies and trading partners.

Although it may be more difficult to find consensus to intervene in a country that enjoys the support of many regional allies, the latter also offer opportunities to assert indirect pressure on the government in question. Whereas rich countries may be less inclined to allow external influence in their internal affairs, their wealth tends to depend largely on their ability to do business with the wider regional and international community. Here, again, dependence on one issue (economy) may lead to compliance on other issues (human rights record). Finally, an ethnically diverse and charged society may be prone to inter-communal friction and accompanying human rights violations, especially when not all groups are equally represented in places of political and economic power. Nevertheless, the most powerful group's interests are not served well by international hesitance to invest in, and do business with, a fragile society with high potential for social upheaval and conflict. It thus remains the task of the international community to identify the most durable and promising entry points for early and effective support for a political, economic, and social environment that is conducive to the provision of basic human rights.

The challenges ahead

The real challenge in protecting human rights in transition societies does not lie in enforcement. By the time that public pressure and official circles discover and act upon their responsibility to intervene for the purpose of human protection (to use the language of the ICISS) – that is, when human suffering is easily visible and already represents a threat to the outside world and a shock to the conscience of mankind – we are much beyond transition pains. At that point we are faced with state failure and collapse, which – before and after armed violence – requires external and coercive intervention. The most effective – and, in the long run, beneficial – route to take is a preventive one. Assistance and support for transitional societies and their governments to increase their capacity to counter structural violence and, if necessary, diplomatic pressure (plus – if it does not further strain the human rights situation within the country – economic sanctions) should be the methods of choice. While an international consensus on coercive humanitarian intervention may be evolving, the much greater challenge will be to entice states to accept (and offer) international assistance to prevent human rights violations from becoming embedded in the transition process; this will, in turn, prevent human rights and humanitarian issues from slowing down (or completely derailing) the transition process. It is a core interest of the international community to see transition societies succeed in developing stable political, economic, and social systems. This not only will guarantee acceptable levels of human dignity and security for their populations but also will allow them to contribute more fully to the wider global community as productive partners, without posing a threat to wider regional and international stability.

Returning to the title of this chapter, international efforts to protect human rights in transition societies are thus characterized by the *right* of individuals to have their basic rights protected by the state or, if the state will not comply, by the international community at large. In turn, the latter has the *duty* (or, at least, responsibility) to live up to its commitments to human rights protection – under normal circumstances through non-violent means in the form of assistance and support; under exceptional circumstances of large-scale violence, through military intervention and reconstruction. Unfortunately, to a very large extent, both rights and corresponding responsibilities are subject to *political* scrutiny. Where does an individual go to charge the international community with gross negligence in the execution of its own laws, norms, and principles? Although, at the end of the day, politics and interests will usually prevail over the principled and automatic application of norms, politics and interests themselves are deeply grounded in normative perceptions of "oneself" and "the other." The debate on rights and on the responsibility to defend those very same rights if others are deprived of them, is bound to expand a sense of regional and international solidarity among peoples and states. This will be a slow process, one that will possibly span many lifetimes. Nevertheless, progress in that direction has the potential that, one day, the global community will manage to live according to the standards, norms, and principles that it has created for itself.

Notes

1. For further discussions of the particularities of human rights violations in transition societies, see the next section of this chapter, as well as chapter 1 and all chapters in part three of this volume.
2. See Tim Niblock, "Economic Sanctions and Human Rights," *Journal of Social Affairs*, Vol. 18, No. 71, Fall 2001, pp. 11–33.
3. For a comprehensive examination of the intervention in Kosovo, see Albrecht Schnabel and Ramesh Thakur, eds, *Kosovo and the Challenge of Humanitarian Intervention: Selective Indignation, Collective Action, and International Citizenship*, Tokyo: United Nations University Press, 2000.
4. See, for instance, Security Council Resolution 1244 of 10 June 1999 (establishing the UN Interim Administration Mission in Kosovo) and Security Council Resolution 1272

of 25 October 1999 (establishing the UN Transitional Administration in East Timor; UNTAET).

5. The Commission was established by the Canadian government, co-chaired by Gareth Evans and Mohamed Sahnoun, and modelled on the World Commission on Environment and Development (also known as the Brundtland Commission). For more information about the origins of the Commission, its members and activities, see ⟨http:// www.dfait-maeci.gc.ca/iciss-ciise/menu-en.asp⟩.

6. International Commission on Intervention and State Sovereignty (ICISS), *The Responsibility to Protect: Report of the International Commission on Intervention and State Sovereignty*, Ottawa: International Development Research Centre, December 2001. The Report was released in two parts: (1) the Report itself; (2) an impressive background document, with numerous papers written to inform the Commission; a massive bibliography capturing much of the international academic and public debate on prevention, intervention, peacebuilding, and related topics; and reports of various consultative meetings held by the Commission in different parts of the world. See ICISS, *The Responsibility to Protect: Research, Bibliography, Background, Supplementary Volume to the Report of the International Commission on Intervention and State Sovereignty*, Ottawa: International Development Research Centre, December 2001. For a review of the report in the context of the evolving debate on humanitarian intervention, see Jennifer M. Welsh, "From Right to Responsibility: Humanitarian Intervention and International Society," *Global Governance*, Vol. 8, No. 4, 2002, pp. 503–521.

7. Ibid.

8. Ibid.

9. Ibid.

10. Ibid., pp. XI–XII.

11. Ibid. The Report specifically calls upon the General Assembly to draft a declaratory resolution that confirms the basic tenets of "the responsibility to act," including the affirmation of the centrality of sovereignty; a commitment to prevention, reaction, and rebuilding; a definition of the threshold for military intervention; and an articulation of the precautionary principles that should guide military intervention (p. 74, para. 8.28). It calls upon the Security Council to agree on a set of guidelines for military action and it asks the Permanent Five to agree not to use their veto power to obstruct such intervention (para. 8.29). Finally, it calls upon the Secretary-General to promote the discussion and implementation of the Report in the General Assembly and the Security Council (para. 8.30).

12. Welsh, "From Right to Responsibility," p. 518.

13. Andrew Linklater, "The Good International Citizen and the Crisis in Kosovo," in Schnabel and Thakur, eds, *Kosovo and the Challenge of Humanitarian Intervention*, p. 493.

14. On these challenges, see Jean-Marc Coicaud, "Solidarity versus Geostrategy: Kosovo and the Dilemmas of International Democratic Culture," in Schnabel and Thakur, eds, *Kosovo and the Challenge of Humanitarian Intervention*, pp. 463–481.

15. However, if one distinguishes between juridical sovereignty (international law is the only authority to which states are subject) and empirical sovereignty (states have the right and capacity to control the people, territory, resources, and institutions within their borders), state sovereignty is dependent on state capacity – without such capacity there can be no sovereignty. This ties into the notion of "failed states." See Michael Barnett, "The New United Nations Politics of Peace: From Juridical Sovereignty to Empirical Sovereignty," *Global Governance*, Vol. 1, No. 1, 1995, pp. 79–97.

16. For an exploration of the role of the international citizen in the Kosovo crisis, see Andrew Linklater, "The Good International Citizen and the Crisis in Kosovo," in

Schnabel and Thakur, eds, *Kosovo and the Challenge of Humanitarian Intervention*, pp. 482–495.

17. For extensive bibliographies on these and related subjects, see ICISS, *The Responsibility to Protect: Research, Bibliography, Background*, pp. 223–336.

18. See *Report of the Secretary-General pursuant to General Assembly Resolution 53/35: The Fall of Srebrenica*, UN Doc. A/54/549, 15 November 1999. For an internal analysis of the failure of the United Nations and the international community in Rwanda, see *Report of the Independent Inquiry into the Actions of the United Nations during the 1994 Genocide in Rwanda*, UN Doc. S/1999/1257, 16 December 1999.

19. See Adam Roberts, "Humanitarian Issues and Agencies as Triggers for International Military Action," *International Review of the Red Cross*, No. 839, 2000, pp. 673–698.

20. John J. Merriam, "Kosovo and the Law of Humanitarian Intervention," *Case Western Reserve Journal of International Law*, Vol. 33, No. 1, Winter 2001, p. 119.

21. See William A. Schabas, "International Law and Response to Conflict," in Chester A. Crocker, Fen Osler Hampson, and Pamela Aall, eds, *Turbulent Peace: The Challenges of Managing International Conflict*, Washington, D.C.: USIP Press, 2001, p. 605.

22. Ibid., p. 604.

23. As Schabas notes, a deadlocked Security Council was bypassed in favour of the General Assembly, which utilized a Uniting for Peace Resolution to endorse a military intervention. However, "[f]orty years later ... the major powers had lost any enthusiasm for such a role being exercised by a General Assembly whose overwhelming majority now lay in the southern half of the planet." Ibid., p. 606.

24. The following information is based on Roberts, "Humanitarian Issues and Agencies as Triggers for International Military Action." For further details, see Roberts' discussion.

25. On measures to take military action in support of humanitarian assistance, see Res. 770 (13 August 1992). On the establishment of safe areas, see Res. 824 (6 May 1993) and Res. 836 (4 June 1993).

26. On the authorization of the Unified Task Force (UNITAF), an invasion led by the United States, see Res. 794 (3 December 1992). On the establishment of UNOSOM II, a UN-peacekeeping operation, see Res. 814 (26 March 1993).

27. On the pre-massacre attempt to expand the small UN Assistance Mission for Rwanda (UNAMIR) in early 1994, see Res. 918 (17 May 1994), part of which was adopted under Chapter VII. On the post-massacre authorization of France to address the humanitarian consequences of the massacre (which had already been referred to in Res. 925 of 8 June 1994), see Res. 929 (22 June 1994).

28. On the Security Council's call to remove the military leadership and the launch of the US-led Multinational Force in Haiti (MNF), see Res. 940 (31 July 1994). On the establishment of the UN Mission in Haiti (UNMIH), see Res. 975 (30 January 1995).

29. On the establishment of the Italian-led Multinational Protection Force (MPF), see Res. 1101 (28 March 1997).

30. On the establishment of the Australian-led UN Mission in East Timor (UNAMET), see Res. 1264 (15 September 1999). On the establishment of the UN Transitional Administration in East Timor (UNTAET), see Res. 1272 (25 October 1999).

31. On the establishment and subsequent strengthening of the UN Mission in Sierra Leone (UNAMSIL), see Res. 1270 (22 October 1999) and Res. 1289 (7 February 2000).

32. Security Council Res. 1270 (22 October 1999).

33. For Northern Iraq, see Res. 688 (5 April 1991); for Kosovo see Res. 1199 (23 September 1998) and Res. 1203 (24 October 1998).

34. Nico Kritsch, "Legality, Morality, and the Dilemma of Humanitarian Intervention after Kosovo," *European Journal of International Law*. Vol. 13, No. 1, 2002, pp. 323–337. Also see the following recent contributions to this debate, reviewed in detail in Kritsch's

essay: Simon Chesterman, *Just War or Just Peace? Humanitarian Intervention and International Law*, Oxford: Oxford University Press, 2001; Christine Gray, *International Law and the Use of Force*, Oxford: Oxford University Press, 2000; Nikolaos K. Tsagourias, *Jurisprudence of International Law: The Humanitarian Dimension*, Manchester: Manchester University Press, 2000; Nicolas J. Wheeler, *Saving Strangers: Humanitarian Intervention in International Society*, Oxford: Oxford University 2000; Reinhard Merkel, ed., *Der Kosovo-Krieg und das Völkerrecht*, Frankfurt: Suhrkamp, 2000. See also Oliver Ramsbotham and Tom Woodhouse, *Humanitarian Intervention in Contemporary Conflict*, Cambridge: Polity Press, 1996; Independent International Commission on Kosovo, *The Kosovo Report: Conflict, International Response, Lessons Learned*, Oxford: Oxford University Press, 2001; Schnabel and Thakur, eds, *Kosovo and the Challenge of Humanitarian Intervention*; and Albrecht Schnabel, *Ethnic Conflict, Sovereignty, and Humanitarian Intervention: Internationalization of Domestic Conflict and Systems Change in International Relations*, PhD Dissertation, Ann Arbor, Michigan: UMI Dissertation Services, 1995.

35. See Nicola Butler, "NATO: From Collective Defense to Peace Enforcement," in Schnabel and Thakur, eds, *Kosovo and the Challenge of Humanitarian Intervention*, pp. 273–290.

36. Some believe that the evolving – in fact, redefined – concept of sovereignty, while important, "pales in significance when compared to the basic moral imperative to protect human rights" and thus "allows for the international protection of human rights and thus avoids conflict between sovereignty and humanitarian intervention." See Merriam, "Kosovo and the Law of Humanitarian Intervention," p. 116.

37. See Michael Barnett, "The New United Nations Politics of Peace."

38. Quoted in Merriam, "Kosovo and the Law of Humanitarian Intervention," p. 118.

39. Kofi Annan, "Two Concepts of Sovereignty," *The Economist*, 18 September 1999. See also Annan's speech at the opening meeting of the General Assembly, UN Press Release SG/SM/7136, GA/9596, 20 September 1999.

40. For an extensive discussion of the conflict prevention debate, see David Carment and Albrecht Schnabel, eds, *Conflict Prevention: Grand Illusion or Path to Peace?* Tokyo: United Nations University Press, 2003; and, by the same editors, the forthcoming volumes *Conflict Prevention from Rhetoric to Reality: Organizations and Institutions*; and *Conflict Prevention from Rhetoric to Reality: Opportunities and Innovations*, Lanham: Lexington Books, 2004.

41. See, for example, the various contributions to *World Editorial and International Law*, Vol. 1, No. 1, 15 September 2002.

42. See Agon Demjaha, "The Kosovo Conflict: A Perspective from Inside," pp. 32–43, and Duska Anastasijevic, "The Closing of the Kosovo Cycle: Victimization versus Responsibility," pp. 44–63, both in Schnabel and Thakur, eds, *Kosovo and the Challenge of Humanitarian Intervention*.

43. For a more detailed analysis of post-conflict preventive challenges, see Albrecht Schnabel, "Post-Conflict Peacebuilding and Second-Generation Preventive Action," *International Peacekeeping*, Vol. 9, No. 2, Summer 2002, pp. 7–30; and, by the same author, "International Organizations and the Prevention of Intergroup Conflict: From Rhetoric to Policy to (Pro)Action," *Journal of Social Affairs*, Vol. 18, No. 72, Winter 2001, pp. 43–77.

8

Democratic transitions and foreign policy: The United States

Barbara Ann J. Rieffer and David P. Forsythe[1]

"The defense of freedom and the promotion of democracy around the world aren't merely a reflection of our deepest values. They are vital to our national interests."
Bill Clinton, Georgetown University, Washington, D.C., 12 December 1991

In the last 25 years, and especially after the Cold War, the international community has witnessed remarkable changes. More and more countries are turning away from their authoritarian past and moving towards liberal democracy. Since 1975, when there were approximately 30 liberal-democratic societies, there has been a vast increase in the number of such democracies in the world: now more than 120 countries arguably offer their citizens at least a liberal-democratic constitution.[2] These transitions toward liberal democracy have varied from country to country. Some countries such as the Czech Republic have been largely successful in achieving free and fair elections and in protecting a broad range of human rights (although, like all societies, the Czech Republic still violates some human rights). Other countries have made progress, but have a long way to go (e.g. South Africa), while some have not fared as well (e.g. Haiti). As countries have attempted to implement liberal democracy, many Western governments, including the United States, have developed democracy-assistance programmes as part of their larger foreign policy to promote liberal democracy.[3] These programmes encourage transition societies to promote democracy and to protect human rights.

Whereas some scholars offer a clearly optimistic account of the US role in these developments,[4] in this chapter we present a more guarded assessment of US democracy promotion and its affects on undertaking transitions. This is especially so after 11 September 2001, because the resulting US "war" against global terrorism caused Washington to reduce its interest in transitions to democracy as a realistic and primary goal in many countries.[5] Our focus is on the United States, the most powerful state in the world, although much of what we discuss is applicable to other Western states.

Types of rights

For many of the countries moving towards liberal democracy, the challenges they face revolve around three sets of human rights. First, there are democratization rights per se: participation rights combined with those civil rights necessary for meaningful participation in public policy issues.[6] This category refers to the right to vote in free and fair elections, combined with such civil rights as freedom of thought and opinion, and freedom of speech, organization, and assembly. The ability to organize and speak freely is deeply connected to the critical role played by civil society in a healthy democracy. Civil society is a vital aspect of democracy. NGOs often encourage tolerance and represent diverse and traditionally marginalized groups. Through this pluralistic activity, NGOs can keep the power of the state in check.[7] For these reasons, scholars have argued that a robust civil society is an essential characteristic of a healthy democracy.[8]

Second, there are liberalization rights that transform illiberal democracy into liberal democracy: these are the rights that restrain the majority from becoming tyrannical.[9] Illiberal democracies are popularly elected governments that violate the rights of minorities. To prevent illiberal democracy one finds various minority rights, including freedom from arbitrary arrest and detention, habeas corpus, and freedom of religion. Third, there are preservation rights; these are the socio-economic rights that establish a minimum threshold below which personal welfare should not be allowed to fall. Here, one finds the rights to adequate minimal standards of food, clothing, shelter, health care, and basic education. Preservation rights are required to consolidate liberal democracy. History has shown that, without social and economic security, political freedom is not entirely meaningful. Various governments emphasize different combinations of these rights, both at home and abroad; hence, it is useful to keep these sets of rights theoretically distinct.

Having said the above, we must hasten to add that, as with all categorizations, some ambiguity remains regarding our breakdown of human rights. The right to private property is seen by some as an economic/ preservation right; others see it as a civil right; still others say that private property is crucial to a genuine democratic process (if the state owns all property, it is said, there can be no room for real personal freedom). Likewise, the right to bargain collectively may be seen as a civil/ liberalization right, or an economic/preservation right essential to securing adequate material welfare. Despite these reasoned debates, we seek to highlight two points. First, there is an important difference between liberal and illiberal democracy, which hinges on the role of liberalization rights in informing democratization rights. Second, there is reason to believe that democracy per se is insufficient to protect human dignity; economic rights are also required.[10] Therefore, we attempt to show that the neglect of preservation rights can undermine democracy promotion. We show that it is significant that the United States often does not emphasize economic rights in its foreign policy.

Finally, we note that our approach is consistent with the content of the International Bill of Rights and with those many UN resolutions stating that all internationally recognized human rights are interdependent and of equal value.

Promoting human rights

Building liberal democracies that protect human rights, including preservation rights, is a complicated process. It is worth noting that all the stable, wealthy, liberal democracies of the Organization for Economic Co-operation and Development (OECD) not only promote individual responsibility and political competition but also provide varying welfare programmes to accommodate those who do not rise to the top in the competition. So the OECD states seek to advance both rugged individualism and social responsibility for the less fortunate. This is, however, not a simple process. Stable liberal democracy seems to require complicated and not entirely consistent factors: it requires a multitude of ideas, programmes, expenditures, leadership, and guidance. This involves not only money but also other forms of support, which sometimes involve only words but at other times involve various forms of coercion – as was clearly the case in Haiti when the United States deployed military personnel to force out military rulers and return the elected President Aristide to power.

Although our focus is on the United States – the one remaining superpower in the world – we note in passing that most of the OECD states, as well as other states, address democracy promotion in their foreign policies.[11] For example, the Netherlands gives great attention to liberal democracy in foreign policy and wrestles with questions such as whether foreign assistance should continue to be given to developing countries that are characterized by significant violations of civil and political rights. Thus, the Dutch have continued to debate and evaluate their foreign-policy practices towards Indonesia. That the latter is a former colony makes these decisions all the more difficult. Other states, such as Japan, although paying growing semantic attention to democracy in foreign policy, have yet to see that rhetorical concern greatly affecting foreign investment and foreign assistance. An example is Japan's decision to re-institute relations with China after the massacre in Tiananmen Square. Some democratic states, such as India, have opted to de-emphasize human rights in their foreign policy. Because India is less eager to incorporate human rights considerations into foreign policy, it has continued to deal with repressive regimes, such as the State Law and Order Restoration Council (SLORC) in Burma, in a "business as usual" fashion.

Space does not allow an extended discussion on democracy promotion, or the lack thereof, in other states beyond the United States of America. We do note, however, that all the OECD states give at least some attention to democracy promotion some of the time. This fact, combined with less-certain democracy promotion by other states, such as Russia, demonstrates that US democracy promotion does not exist in an intergovernmental vacuum. In fact, the great extent of democracy promotion efforts by the OECD states,[12] and their role in various intergovernmental organizations such as the United Nations, the Council of Europe, and the OSCE, makes the precise analysis of the US role in this regard exceedingly difficult. Thus, when viewing South Africa's progress towards liberal democracy since apartheid, one sees many actors offering assistance. In one year alone, South Africa received over $300 million (to assist Parliament, develop public administration, educate voters, and train political parties) from eight countries – excluding the United States – and the European Union. Hence, when one notes that South Africa has been largely successful in developing a liberal-democratic constitution and government, it remains difficult to pinpoint which, if any, of the donors were offering significant and meaningful assistance.[13]

The United States

To a great extent, a state's foreign policy with regard to human rights and democracy promotion is bound up with nationalism. How a society views itself affects its foreign-policy decisions. A nation's collective self-image sets the parameters for the policies that a country pursues with regard to human rights. Thus, to understand how the United States, as well as other liberal democracies, will assist countries undergoing transitions, we must understand how the citizens of the respective countries view themselves and their place in the world.

Americans generally believe that they are an exceptional people owing to the remarkable political system they have constructed. Americans of all classes and races endorse the democratic system and the civil and political rights enshrined in the Constitution and the Bill of Rights. The one tenet of American nationalism that is widely shared is a belief in American greatness, defined in terms of support for personal freedom, and the belief that American freedom should serve as a moral and political lesson to the rest of the world.[14] US foreign policy has echoed these sentiments over the twentieth century, and more actively since the end of the Cold War.[15]

Understanding US foreign policy

There are three standard theories for attempting an overview of US foreign policy and democracy promotion – liberalism, realism, and neo-Marxism. Liberalism would explain the place of democracy promotion in US foreign policy as the result of a moral and legal concern for the individual, regardless of citizenship. A liberal explanation emphasizes the pursuit of human welfare, regardless of nationality, and notes that this orientation seems precisely the content of modern international law, with its numerous and widely endorsed treaties requiring attention to human rights on an international basis. Liberals argue that history has demonstrated that democracies do not go to war with each other. The democratic peace theory, in its various forms, suggests that, if the global democratic community were enlarged, there would be a greater likelihood of peaceful interaction in international relations.[16]

A realist approach to our subject matter emphasizes democracy promotion as part of a US grand strategy for world order. In this view, US attention to democracy abroad reflects responsible leadership in pursuit of national interest, defined in terms of controlling power and encouraging free markets. It is said that, since liberal democracies are less likely to go to war with each other or to engage in destabilizing forced displacement, promoting democracy is beneficial to American interests at home and abroad. In addition, liberal democracies engage in capitalist free trade, which has a moderating affect on international relations. Thus, enlarging the global liberal-democratic community is more an example of hard-headed self-interest than of altruistic concern for others.

A neo-Marxist approach argues that all the lip service to personal rights and human welfare via democracy promotion is a discursive façade. The reality is that democracy is a fig-leaf for continued economic control and exploitation by the Western governments, which represent the dominant economic classes in Western nations. A neo-Marxist argues that, when the United States emphasizes the global enlargement of the number of market democracies, it is really interested in the markets, not the democracies. Weak markets allow penetration and control by global monopoly capitalism, as V.I. Lenin argued.

When examining the theoretical options for US foreign policy, one notices the tendency among administrations to adopt and justify policy decisions as indicated by the realist model. Even US Secretary of State Madeleine Albright, in the second Clinton Administration, took the realist approach to human rights in general, while mentioning "justice" in passing:

Promoting human rights is – and must remain – an integral part of US foreign policy. When governments respect human rights, they contribute to a more stable, just and peaceful world. When they do not, they often engender strife, for regimes that run roughshod over the rights of their own citizens may well show similar disregard for the rights of others. Such governments are also more likely to spark unrest by persecuting minorities, sheltering terrorists, running drugs or secretly building weapons of mass destruction. As a global power with global interests, our nation will be more secure, our armed forces less at risk, and our citizens safer and more prosperous in a world where international standards of human rights are increasingly observed.[17]

This statement is indicative of the Clinton administration's approach. Almost every major foreign-policy speech contended that the spread of democracy abroad advances US security and economic interests at home.[18]

It seems safe to argue that President Bush is not pursuing a foreign-policy approach that is considerably more liberal in orientation than that of his predecessor. In fact, given the trauma of 11 September 2001 and the resulting focus on global terrorism, the Bush administration focused on a realist exercise of hard power in places such as Iraq, despite the lack of approval by the UN Security Council. The administration's official national security strategy document did not hesitate to stress the notions of power and balance of power.[19] Without question, in countries such as Pakistan and Uzbekistan (among others), Washington's primary interest was in hunting down those alleged to be members of terrorist organizations, not in discussing free and fair elections and those human rights necessary for them. Despite the fact that most members of al-Qaeda and other alleged terrorist organizations came from non-democratic countries such as Algeria, Egypt, Pakistan, and Saudi Arabia, Washington largely suspended its interest in democratic transitions in such countries; the new emphasis was on support for US security policies defined in ways that excluded democracy promotion.

Although it is arguable that US foreign policy is motivated by a mixture of realism and liberalism, one clear pattern has been the development of democracy-promotion programmes. Various agencies spend over $700 million per annum in over 50 countries to promote the values of freedom and democracy. The United States has generally offered small amounts of funding to transition countries without much meaningful or long-term strategy.[20] This is the product of both the lack of agreement on the requisites of liberal democracy and the decentralized or fragmented nature of policy-making in Washington.

Scholars have long sought the necessary and sufficient conditions for the creation and consolidation of liberal democracy. After a lifetime of study, the noted political scientist Samuel Huntington has concluded that no one theory explains why liberal democracy arises and/or is eventually stabilized. In his view, shared by others, the causes of the successes and failures of liberal democracy are many and varied, and combine in different ways in different places.[21] This means, of course (if correct), that there is no single, successful model of liberal democracy for export.[22] Some suggest that democracy requires social capital such as an achievement orientation, social networks, shared liberal values (at least among the political élite), and/or feelings of trust.[23] Another school of thought stresses economic factors such as capitalism per se, or sometimes modern forms of capitalism, or a certain level of economic growth and/or development. Still other scholars stress other factors, such as a history of experience with pluralistic politics at some level in the nation, close association with other liberal democracies, and a well-developed civil society, along with high per capita income.[24]

Our purpose is not to catalogue the theories of democratic development but to indicate briefly that policy makers cannot rely on social science to provide a sure road map for how to assist countries attempting democratic transitions. Although there is no one statement or policy on how best to assist countries undergoing transitions, the United States generally engages in a few types of activities, including the following: electoral assistance to guarantee free and fair elections; support for state-institution building, including the military, judiciary, and legislative branches; and support for civil society and the tolerant private groups therein.[25]

Bilateral policy

Programmatic diplomacy

There is no clear, simple, long-term US programme to support liberal democracy abroad. General programmatic statements exist, but they fail to provide sure and specific guidance for US policy in concrete situations.[26] Despite the decentralized nature of US foreign policy, there are various agencies involved that can assist transition countries. The

Departments of Defense, Justice, and State; the Agency for International Development; the US Information Agency; and the National Security Council all participate in the US democracy-assistance programme. Moreover, Congress funds the National Endowment for Democracy (NED), the Asia Foundation, and the US Institute for Peace, all of which (particularly the NED with an annual budget near $30 million[27]) engage in activities related to democracy abroad. For the fiscal year 1999, the State Department reported that, together with the United States Agency for International Development (USAID) and the United States Information Agency (USIA), it was spending $622.9 million on democracy assistance.[28] This is a very small amount compared with US spending on all international affairs (about $22 billion), not including defence spending (about $350 billion). This suggests that building and assisting countries pursuing democracy is not, in reality, a high priority. During 1999, AID democracy and governance activities received only $137 million. Since USAID ran democracy and governance programmes in about 50 countries, its resources were obviously spread thin. For example, the United States apparently hoped to produce liberal democracy in rump Yugoslavia by spending $18 million in the fiscal year 1998,[29] a paltry sum in the context of public allocations. The above figures do not include Defense Department spending in support of a multifaceted (and at least anticipated) movement toward liberal democracy in such places as Bosnia, Haiti, and Kosovo: it has been reported that the Pentagon spent about $20 million per annum in Haiti between 1994 and 1999.[30]

Ad hoc (reactive) diplomacy

Democracy promotion is not just a matter of programmes and money but is also a matter of diplomacy, or the lack thereof. This diplomacy may at times be linked to coercion, as it was in both Haiti and Yugoslavia. One cannot be certain, but a reasonable argument can be made that, more than ever before, the United States had been paying only short-term attention to advancing liberal democracy – however, only until 11 September 2001. This argument is supported by the 2003 annual report of Amnesty International, which shows that, by that tragic date, the United States had greatly reduced its efforts on behalf of human rights and democratic transitions abroad.

Beyond efforts to reconstruct failed states (a separate subject altogether), it should come as no surprise that a sample of US ad hoc diplomacy indicates different short-term responses to events abroad. In Bosnia, for example, the United States was the principal mediator during 1995 in attempts to construct a liberal-democratic constitution and polity in that war-torn country. In Algeria, at approximately the same time, the United States deferred to the decision by Algerian military officials to suspend planned elections, lest a conservative Islamic party win them and possibly develop an illiberal democracy or an Islamist authoritarian regime. In Burma, failure of the SLORC junta to honour free and fair elections led to US economic and diplomatic sanctions. Although the Tiananmen massacre of 1989 did produce temporary sanctions for China, failure of the Communist party to allow open political dissent and organized opposition political parties, not to mention other violations of civil and political rights, led to a policy not of sanctions but of constructive engagement – and, ultimately, support for China's entrance into the WTO. When Russian troops committed offences in Chechnya in 1994, the United States muted its criticism of President Boris Yeltsin and other Russian leaders, fearing that the elected, moderate government in Moscow would be undermined. Washington continues to ignore serious human rights violations, including thousands of civilian deaths and the forced migration of over 120,000 people to neighbouring Ingushetia,[31] in order to keep relations on track with Moscow and to win support for the Bush administration's national defence system.[32]

Inconsistencies in US support for democratic transitions had become particularly dramatic by 2003. The US use of military force in Iraq was undertaken with the promise of transforming Iraq into a liberal democracy that would serve as a model for democratic transition in the rest of the Arab-Islamic world. However, in order to pursue its objectives in Iraq, Washington clearly turned a blind eye to the lack of democracy and numerous human rights violations in such countries as Egypt, Pakistan, and Uzbekistan. Under attack for its unilateralist tendencies, the Bush administration needed as broad a coalition as possible for its controversial Iraq policy: it therefore failed to press for democratic transitions in these countries at the highest level. In fact, in such countries as Egypt, it could be boldly stated that the United States did not have a democratic promotion policy at all.

Multilateral policy

IGO standards

As the most powerful state in international relations, the United States casts a great shadow over the decisions and activities of intergovernmental organizations. In some of these, such as the United Nations, US policy has been part of the growing attention accorded to the subject of democracy; in others, such as the World Bank, the attention to democracy has been very sporadic; in still others, such as the International Monetary Fund (IMF), there has been very little attention to democracy. The United States bears considerable responsibility for this record.

In contemporary US foreign policy, Washington has clearly endorsed democratic standards in the United Nations, OAS, OSCE, and other general or "political" IGOs. Since the Cold War, the United States has officially endorsed the view that the "only type of legitimate government is liberal democracy."[33] In this sense, the United States endorses the "end of history" thesis that argues liberal democracy is the ultimate way to legitimize the exercise of governing power.[34]

US leadership for democratic theory has been particularly pronounced in the OAS, especially in its support for the "Santiago Declaration," in which the presence or absence of democracy in hemispheric affairs was declared to be an international matter and not one of domestic jurisdiction.[35] This declaration was reaffirmed – and even expanded – at the Summit of the Americas in Quebec, in April 2001.[36]

US support for liberal democracy is much less certain in the international financial institutions. Only in the European Bank for Reconstruction and Development has the United States, like other donor members, endorsed the integration of democratic factors in that Bank's lending policies. In the World Bank, by contrast, there is evident confusion about the meaning of "good governance."[37] In some cases (e.g. Kenya, Malawi, Bosnia, Yugoslavia) the Bank has attached political conditions to its loans in order to press for liberal-democratic reform; however, in other cases (such as Indonesia, Nigeria, and China) it has not, and has made sizeable loans to clearly authoritarian governments. This record in the World Bank is largely the product of such important donor states as the United States and Germany, who have pressed political conditions on the Bank staff in a highly inconsistent way. Given recent trends, especially pertaining to Indonesia and Burma, the Bank appears to be strengthening its concern with repression that proves inimical to economic growth.

The IMF has, historically, been impervious to arguments that it should take democratic and human rights standards seriously, being much more adamant than the World Bank that most governance issues lie outside its proper domain. Yet even the IMF, following the US lead, suspended drawing rights after the Chinese regime massacred peaceful demonstrators in Tiananmen Square in 1989. During 1999, the IMF warned both Pakistan (under military rule) and Russia (when engaged in brutal policies in Chechnya) that they might forfeit IMF support. States such as Pakistan and Russia, however, are too important to the Western-state members of the IMF for democracy considerations to be the only factor controlling loans. Likewise, the evolution of democracy in these states is affected by many factors besides IMF loans.

IGO field operations

The United States has been supportive of IGOs undertaking programmes within countries to establish and consolidate liberal democracy. One of the striking developments, especially in the United Nations and OAS, but also in the OSCE, is the expansion of multilateral electoral assistance. In such places as El Salvador, Haiti, Nicaragua, Cambodia, and elsewhere, the United States supported important IGO roles in the conduct of free and fair elections. This multilateral diplomacy was in addition to bilateral US involvement and support for private activity (by NGOs).

In general, the United States has been supportive of complex peacekeeping by the UN and OAS. The deployment of a non-combat military force (with the consent of the parties), along with civilian personnel, is designed to secure not only narrow military objectives but also political ones, such as democratic and rights-protective national governance.[38] This can overlap with IGO electoral assistance. In places such as El Salvador, Namibia, Cambodia, Mozambique (and elsewhere), complex peacekeeping is directed at the construction of democratic order and a liberal-democratic state. El Salvador and Mozambique are clear, if relative and imperfect, success stories. Despite congressional reservations, the United States continues to pay for about one-third of UN peacekeeping, in addition to unilaterally covering the costs of US military forces deployed in the UN-approved Haitian field mission and the US share of NATO costs in Bosnia and Kosovo. All these field missions (whether officially under the aegis of the United Nations, or the OAS, or NATO) are linked to liberal democracy and would not have occurred had the United States objected.

The United States has supported UN, OAS, and OSCE programmes of technical assistance for such tasks as the reform of the judiciary, reconstruction of police forces, development of parliamentary procedures, protection of minority rights, and civilian superiority over the military. This technical assistance can be authorized through discrete projects or as part of complex peacekeeping. These and similar IGO programmes try to contribute to the construction and consolidation of liberal democracy. Congressional pressures to reduce IGO budgets, however, impair the ability of the organizations to respond to growing requests for democratic assistance. The UN Human Rights Centre still receives less than $20 million per annum for all of its human rights work, of which democracy-related efforts are only one part. By comparison, USAID alone was spending more than $35 million on its Rule of Law programmes abroad in 1999.[39]

Enforcing democracy

The United States has utilized IGOs to enforce democracy only in Haiti in 1994 and in Kosovo in 1999. Although there was no significant military combat in Haiti, it was clear that US military forces, given the green light by the UN Security Council, were prepared to use military force to restore Bertrand Aristide to power in keeping with the previous, internationally supervised election.

US policy toward Haiti, rather than being a principled commitment to liberal democracy, reflected mostly a response to unwanted Haitian migration to the south-eastern United States and a response to the power of the Congressional Black Caucus, whose support President Clinton needed for his domestic policy agenda. Nevertheless, unlike his predecessors, Clinton was finally prepared to deal with the root causes of Haitian migration, which lay in the authoritarian and exploitative nature of decades of Haitian rule. True, after the forced change of government in Port au Prince by the United States, Haiti remained far short of a stable, liberal democracy: its national history, poverty, and illiteracy were hardly conducive to an easy transition to successful democratic rule. Some observers found fault with US policy,[40] but it was difficult to see how human dignity – i.e. social justice – could improve in Haiti, or how improved relations with the United States would ensue, until the Duvalier dynasty and its military descendants had been ousted from the scene.

Where the United States might be fairly criticized was in the lack of long-term attention to Haitian economic growth and social security. Democracy-building is not very glamorous work; it does not lend itself to patriotic flag-waving by political leaders in Washington; and it takes much longer than the typical American attention span lasts.[41] Thus after five years the United States had removed most of its personnel from Haiti.

The United States has demonstrated that it finds funding for democratization and liberalization rights more acceptable than that for preservation rights (since the latter run counter to the country's emphasis on rugged individualism, self-reliance, and free markets). The subject, however, is complex. When the United States had just experienced the economic depression of the late 1920s and 1930s, President Franklin D. Roosevelt stressed that "freedom from want" was a legitimate freedom. He argued, with great resonance in an impoverished American society, that a person trapped in poverty and poor health was not a free person.[42] Thus, creative leadership such as FDR's could link the American concern with personal freedom to the need for preservation rights.[43] Despite the American antipathy to socialism and statism, the United States, like other OECD states, established social safety nets, even if Washington saw them not as entitlements underwritten by international law but rather as optional policies chosen by the federal and state governments.

Moreover, especially in the 1990s, US foreign policy joined the global semantic consensus in support of "sustainable human development," which stressed that the purpose of transnational economic growth was not simply national welfare but human welfare.[44] In agreeing to a reorientation by the World Bank (and other international financial institutions), Washington agreed that some forms of transnational capitalism could be injurious to certain sectors of society. Some US development assistance went to poor countries and the poorer sectors within those countries, and to countries wracked by various forms of upheaval, especially after the Cold War.[45] The US might not view human rights as entailing subsistence economic rights, and it might not like large bureaucracies to manage socio-economic policies, but at times it might (or might not) contribute to preservation rights through its foreign policy. For example, the Bush administration announced a new foreign-aid programme for poor countries, called the millennium account, as a companion move to its agreement that rich countries had an obligation to help poor countries if the latter would engage in significant economic and political reform. Moreover, the Bush administration also announced special funding to help fight HIV/AIDS in developing countries. These US policies were presented as voluntary acts of assistance, unrelated to welfare rights.

Factors affecting democracy promotion

Despite efforts by Washington to promote liberal democracies that respect a broad range of human rights, there are a variety of factors that impede this development worldwide. In some countries the political culture or strategic location may hinder US attempts to assist in the development of liberal democracy. In this section we discuss some of these "trumps" and barriers that prevent democracy-assistance programmes from implementation or, if implemented, from achieving success.

Political culture

Every society has its own dynamic political culture that defines its identity. The beliefs and history shared by a national people are an influential aspect of the goals and possible achievements of any given state. This is true of those countries promoting democracy, as well as of those countries attempting to develop liberal-democratic political systems. As already indicated in different terms, the political culture of the United States revolves around various democratic ideals. Individualism, liberty, political equality, and diversity within an assimilationist doctrine are all fundamental aspects of American political culture. This identity shapes the way the United States exercises its influence in the world.[46] One consequence of this identity is the tendency to neglect preservation rights (but see above). American belief in rugged individualism promotes the belief that individuals, and not the government, should provide for one's basic needs. Thus, the State Department will readily argue that the United States is committed to "international norms of respect for human dignity and freedom for all people," as long as this does not include preservation rights.

Political culture in the transition state is also critical to the promotion of liberal democracy. Countries with little or no experience of elections or of basic freedoms, and with an environment of intolerance are unlikely to move quickly towards consolidation of liberal democracy. Initial improvements may also be accompanied by backsliding. South Africa shows the ongoing difficulties with a transition to liberal democracy.

Until the 1990s, South Africa operated under apartheid and the government consistently violated the rights of non-Whites.[47] Growing economic difficulties and international pressure[48] eventually cajoled the South African government into holding multiracial elections, and in 1994 Nelson Mandela was elected President.[49] Under Mandela, major institutional changes were implemented, including the creation of a new constitution.[50] However, despite these democratic improvements, South Africa still faces many problems: political violence, although decreasing in level, still occurs; deaths in police custody remain a serious problem;[51] furthermore, the vast majority of Africans tend to vote for an African party (the African National Congress; ANC), whereas most Whites vote for a White party.[52] This suggests that the races and political parties remain politically segregated and have not yet obtained a working democratic system. Thus, despite the progress made – South Africa moved from a partly free country on the Freedom House survey from 1977 to 1994 to a free country from 1995 on – South Africa has not fully consolidated a liberal-democratic system.[53]

In addition, programmes that do not respect the local culture or that implement ideas and institutions contrary to the local culture are often ineffective and disregarded by the recipient country.[54] Furthermore, countries with "traditional cultures" that accept a paternalistic relationship between the individual and the state and incorporate some dominant religious tradition are often difficult to convert to a liberal-democratic political system. Russia demonstrates how a traditional political culture can be an obstacle to liberal democracy: the deeply entrenched beliefs in the need for a strong leader to deal with national problems, and the patriarchal values of the Russian Orthodox Church, promote public passivity,[55] which decreases the likelihood of popular democracy. These results are evident from public-opinion polls, which suggest that over 85 per cent of Russians believe that "the most important thing today is to elect a president who is capable of solving the nation's problems;" 75 per cent said they favoured a system of government *other* than democracy.[56]

Further evidence of the importance of a society's political culture is evident from a comparative glance at the Czech Republic and Haiti. In the 1990s, the Czechs could refer back to the post-World War II period to acquaint themselves with their quasi-liberal past.[57] Haiti had no similar history and therefore its citizens had no frame of reference or socialization to return to. The results show one reason why, when free elections were conducted in Haiti, many problems ensued. It was within this essentially illiberal political culture of Haiti that Father Aristide and his supporters continued to engage in policies that caused the international community to question the legitimacy of the elections held in November 2000.[58] In response, the George W. Bush administration elected not to send a representative to Aristide's inauguration. In addition, the United States, in tandem with other nations, chose to freeze over $500 million in aid.[59]

In the Czech Republic a rather different series of events have taken place. Recent authoritarian tendencies and the lack of full press freedoms at the end of 2000 were met by street demonstrations and strikes. In Haiti, worse authoritarian tendencies by the highest authorities and political violence in the streets were met by considerable apathy, if not outright support.

Economic realities

Economic factors are also relevant when understanding US foreign-policy objectives and the promotion of liberal democracy. US foreign policy almost always elevated economic concerns over human rights and democracy issues. Funding for market restructuring in favour of private enterprise was almost always much more substantial than funding for democracy assistance. Washington liked to talk of supporting democratic state capitalism. One observer regarded Clinton's enlargement doctrine as "econocentric" and based on the principle of "geo-economics"; if one promoted capitalistic economic growth, liberal democracy would follow.[60]

One example of this is US foreign policy toward the former Soviet Union. The Clinton administration achieved a 1999 Federal Budget that provided $925 million, a 20 per cent increase, to the newly independent states of the former Soviet Union through the "Freedom Support" initiative. This was designed "to jump start the political and economic transition to market democracies."[61] The real emphasis was market restructuring. The ratio of US dollars allocated for economic development versus democracy promotion was once as high as 8:1.[62] The 1999 budget includes clauses that prohibit the appropriation of funds if "the government is not making progress in implementing economic reforms based on market principles and private ownership." No similar clauses impede appropriation if authoritarian or illiberal policies develop.[63] The Clinton administration's decision, in 1994, to uncouple human rights from trade initiatives for China is another example of the elevation of economic interests over democracy and human rights issues.

There have been other periods of US history when the talk was not of democracy but the substance of US foreign policy focused on strategic and economic interests, especially in the Western hemisphere.[64] A leading observer of US democracy assistance concluded that the policy toward Eastern Europe and the former Soviet republics has emphasized economics and traditional security concerns, "while promoting democracy is an ancillary goal."[65]

Economic factors in the transition state are important for liberal democracy but defy simple analysis. A few lesser-developed countries have sustained democracy, and probably a weak form of liberal democracy, despite very low per capita income. India and Botswana come to mind, but also Sri Lanka – at least, from independence to the onset of its long-running civil war. In general, however, countries with higher per capita incomes, larger middle classes, and good rates of economic growth are more likely to create and consolidate liberal democracies than otherwise. This is why, despite South Africa's progress since apartheid, it still encounters difficulties in the consolidation of liberal democracy. Many of South Africa's problems arise from the fact that over 50 per cent of the population live in third-world conditions (22 million), while 13 per cent live in first-world conditions (5.4 million). This income inequality, the second highest in the world, remains a barrier to democratic progress despite the development of a new constitution.[66] Some believe the nature of modern, transnational capitalism, with its needs of open, unconstrained, and flexible decision-making, leads to a spill-over effect in politics;[67] whether this is true remains to be seen.

Political factors

Despite all the rhetoric concerning human rights and democracy as a pillar of US foreign policy, there was little change in some aspects of that overall policy. Through the Clinton administration the United States did not alter the percentage of aid given to Israel and Egypt – together they continued to receive over 50 per cent of US foreign assistance; thus, strategic interests trumped the promotion of liberal democracy in the Middle East. We have already noted how this tendency was accentuated by the Bush administration after 11 September 2001. On the other hand, after the Cold War the United States, in its development assistance to African states south of the Sahara, did provide more funds for democracy, human rights, and humanitarian concerns. In South Africa, the United States has given over $670 million since 1990; however, assistance given to South Africa is usually justified in government documents as essential to US national interests. South Africa is portrayed as a country with the potential for a large percentage of US exports. Another important aspect of South Africa is its potential to be the leading country on the continent, especially when dealing with humanitarian assistance to sub-Saharan Africa.[68]

In general, the more relaxed the international environment, the more one could logically expect the United States to accentuate human rights and other "liberal" concerns. The more international relations resembled a state of war – whether a war against terrorism or otherwise – the more one would expect "realist" concerns with security affairs and strategic concerns to predominate.

An additional obstacle to the development of liberal democracy is sometimes the perception of a disliked American hegemony. Some elements around the world (for example, in the former Soviet Union and in the Middle East) fear that more freedom will bring, for example, more pornography and outside religions. There is thus cultural opposition to personal freedom, as well as political opposition to extensive US influence.[69]

As for other political factors affecting the transition states, the "neighbourhood effect" clearly plays an important role in Europe, with the Council of Europe and the European Union proving to be magnets of democratic capitalism to transition states in Eastern Europe (as previously in southern Europe – e.g. Portugal, Spain, and Greece). In East Asia, some believe that economic growth in Taiwan and South Korea was accompanied by association with liberal-democratic states such as the United States, and by experience with political and socio-economic equality in local affairs prior to national developments. Corruption is often cited as a non-economic factor that can impede the health of the national economy, as in Indonesia and Russia in the waning years of the twentieth century. Corruption siphons off productive spending and investment, slowing the economic growth so necessary for people to believe that democracy works for them. Ultimately various political, economic, and cultural factors affect the impact of US democracy assistance on transition societies. Those societies with no history of democracy, little economic development, and few connections to democratic states present huge challenges for US democracy assistance.

Conclusions

Clearly, the United States could not have played a significant and direct role in all the events that have affected movements toward liberal democracy in the world over the past quarter of a century. Some countries, such as Slovenia, have proceeded much on their own, with perhaps some international factors of importance, but none necessarily stemming from Washington.[70] US funding is too meagre and too thinly spread to have a concentrated impact in most situations. US ad hoc diplomacy gives too much attention to strategic and self-interested economic pursuits to have a consistent impact per se on liberal democracy abroad. Furthermore, US democracy assistance has encountered major social barriers in such places as Bosnia and Kosovo, Rwanda and Burundi. Those countries with little democratic history, a dominant authoritarian culture, and contemporary ethnic hatreds are unlikely to make dramatic progress in the short run towards liberal democracy. In Russia, a long-term prognosis might be more optimistic.

Some countries have received much aid from the international community, making it difficult to isolate the impact of US policy alone. In a few countries such as El Salvador, Namibia, and Mozambique, the United States – along with other outsiders – has had considerable responsibility for the steps toward liberal democracy, however difficult it is to label precisely the overall situation at a given moment. However, even in these cases, other players beyond the United States were also important. In El Salvador, for example, the office of the UN Secretary-General, the states making up the Friends of the Secretary-General, and other states have all played important direct or indirect roles.

There is also no doubt that the United States could have done more to advance liberal democracy abroad, whether through ad hoc and programmatic bilateral policy, or through multilateral policy. A particular defect, in addition to the relatively low level of funding for this purpose, is the disinclination of Washington to put the question in a proper economic context. Not being a social democracy, the United States tends to see a simple correlation between capitalism and democracy. Along with authors such as Francis Fukuyama,[71] it tends to gloss over the fact that people want not only to have their freedom respected but also their social security protected. Thus, the United States was greatly surprised when (slightly) reformed communists improved their popularity in free and fair elections in several places in Eastern Europe – for example, Bulgaria. The reformed communists were opposed to markets with only meagre social safety nets.

There is considerable evidence that social security in the broad sense is necessary for the consolidation of liberal democracy. This can be achieved in several ways: through the US model, with very limited and optional safety nets; through the Scandinavian and other European models, with more extensive and better entrenched safety nets; through the Japanese model (currently being adjusted); or through others. Large

numbers of people in Chile (in the 1970s) and Peru (in the 1980s) supported governmental moves toward less freedom if promised more physical and social security. The United States should not have to be a social
democracy to understand that personal freedom without social security is
not a sure path to a stable liberal polity.[72] For this reason, one expert in
this field argues strongly for increased democracy assistance and greater
attention by the United States to issues of prosperity and social security,
for the sake of stabilizing the democratic gains that have been made.[73]
George Soros, the successful investor and philanthropist, argues that the
greatest threat to liberal democracy in areas of former European communism is unregulated capitalism: it is too harsh and threatens people's
sense of social security.[74]

One helpful step by the United States would be to move the World
Bank and other international financial institutions (IFIs) further along
the path of the European Bank, in that factors of liberal democracy and
welfare policies (if not social democracy) would be integrated with more
traditional economic factors. This would help to correct one of the problems evident in El Salvador, for example. At a time when the Salvadoran
government needed more money for land reform and the integration of
the former opposition forces into the economy and society, the World
Bank and the IMF were demanding structural readjustment programmes
that entailed a smaller, more austere role for the government in the
economy. The traditional IFI recipe for economic growth countermanded
the immediate requisites for the consolidation of moves toward liberal
democracy. Similarly, US foreign-policy rhetoric about democratic state
capitalism should be disaggregated to ensure that the democratic aspects
are not overwhelmed by the capitalist emphasis.

An additional recommended shift in democracy promotion concerning
economic factors centres on civil society. Democracy assistance with regard to civil society attempts to promote greater participation among the
population and tends to focus on human rights, NGOs, women's rights,
and environmental groups.

This is not surprising, given the US emphasis on civil and political
rights. However, the US orientation means that those NGOs with a socio-
economic focus – such as health clinics and other welfare organizations
– do not receive any democracy-assistance funds. Enhancing aid to a
variety of NGOs, including those supporting preservation rights, would
improve the prospects for consolidating democracy.

Ultimately, US support for democracy abroad may exist mostly to
allow Americans to maintain their self-image as an exceptionally good
people who stand for personal freedom. Still, it is on balance better
to have such an orientation than not, as long as this results in support

for liberal democracies and not the type of illiberal democracies that have existed in such places as Khomeini's Iran, Milošević's Yugoslavia, and Tudjman's Croatia. Washington could enhance its democratic programmes abroad if it communicated its goals to the American public. Explaining why and where American tax dollars are being allocated could gather public support for democracy-assistance programmes. Over time, US contributions to liberal democracy abroad, in conjunction with others, might make some difference at the margins and at least in some situations.

Conservatives who value order over moves toward liberal democracy do not make their case that US policy has been generally detrimental to the world. Even in Haiti, disappointing as results have been since 1994, the preferred policy is not a return to support for authoritarians but a longer-term commitment to liberal democracy with social security. Nor do radical leftists provide clear evidence that US democracy assistance comprises cultural imperialism. Washington does not insist on replication of the American political model, although it does favour as little statism as possible, which can be a problem – as already discussed.

US support for democracy abroad requires reduced expectations in the short term because of daunting social obstacles. Furthermore, funding with a more concentrated focus over time, less strategic and economic self-interest, and more integration between political and economic factors, would all seem to be required. Furthermore, since liberal democracy takes time, money, and nurturing, the United States must be patient, especially with regard to those countries that have no previous acquaintance with liberal democracy. None of these, however, are on the immediate horizon in Washington.

In fact, after 11 September 2001, owing to US foreign policy, the prospects for successful democratic transitions were significantly reduced in a number of countries, such as Pakistan. When the world's only hyperpower chooses to emphasize its traditional national security through an emphasis on fighting terrorism, such states as Pakistan will be free from US democracy promotion and pressures as long as they prove helpful to Washington in short-term security matters. It may be true that many Islamic "terrorists" arose out of repressive Islamic states; in the immediate aftermath of September 11, however, Washington did not respond with increased emphasis on democratic transitions in places such as Saudi Arabia or Algeria. Whether this pattern might change over time is a matter of great significance, certainly for the question of democracy but also, perhaps, for the question of national security in broader terms.

Notes

1. We would like to thank Patrice McMahon for her helpful comments on an earlier version of this chapter. Doug Bend also provided research assistance.
2. Press Briefing on the *Release of Country Reports on Human Rights Practices, 1999*, 25 February 2000.
3. Yuri Fedorov, "Democratization and Globalization: The Case of Russia," *Working Papers*, No. 13, Washington: Carnegie Endowment for International Peace, May 2000, p. 1.
4. Joshua Muravchik, *Exporting Democracy: Fulfilling America's Destiny*, Washington, D.C.: American Enterprise Institute Press, 1991. See also Gregory A Fossedal, *The Democratic Imperative: Exporting the American Revolution*, New York: Basic Books, 1989.
5. See further Michael Ignatieff, "Is the Human Rights Era Ending," *New York Times*, 5 February 2002, A25. Ignatieff correctly treats democracy as a subset of the larger concept of human rights.
6. For a classic approach to the subject see Robert Dahl, *Who Governs? Democracy and Power in an American City*, New Haven: Yale University Press, 1961.
7. Patrice McMahon, "What Have We Done? Evaluating International Involvement in Bosnia," paper presented at the annual conference of the International Studies Association, Chicago, 20–24 February 2001.
8. Robert Putnam, *Making Democracy Work*, Princeton: Princeton University Press, 1995.
9. Fareed Zakaria, "The Rise of Illiberal Democracy," *Foreign Affairs*, No. 76, Nov/Dec. 1997, pp. 22–43.
10. Scholars have convincingly argued for the need to emphasize more than simply civil and political rights. See Henry Shue, *Basic Rights*, Princeton: Princeton University Press, 1980; Rhoda Howard, *Human Rights and the Search for Community*, Boulder: Westview Press, 1995.
11. David P. Forsythe, ed., *Human Rights and Comparative Foreign Policy*, Tokyo: United Nations University Press, 2000.
12. It is worth noting that, for the first time, the Group of Eight countries committed themselves to coordinating their democratic assistance to countries in transition. See John Shattuck, "Diplomacy with a Cause: Human Rights in US Foreign Policy," in Samantha Power and Graham Allison, eds, *Realizing Human Rights*, New York: St Martin's Press, 2000, p. 282.
13. South Africa, for example, received $139 million in 1996 from the European Union, $16 million from Germany, and over $140 million from the United Kingdom. In addition, Canada, Australia, Sweden, Norway, Denmark, and the Netherlands all offered support for South Africa's transition to liberal democracy. See ⟨www.usaid.gov/democracy/afr/soafrica.html⟩.
14. Michael H. Hunt, *Ideology and US Foreign Policy*, New Haven: Yale University Press, 1987. The link between American national identity and democracy is also echoed in various documents from government agencies such as USAID. See ⟨www.usaid.gov/democracy/⟩.
15. Tony Smith has argued that democracy promotion has been the defining feature of American foreign policy for the greater part of the last hundred years. See Tony Smith, "US Democracy Promotion: Critical Questions," in Michael Cox, G. John Ikenberry, and Takashi Inoguchi, eds, *American Democracy Promotion*, Oxford: Oxford University Press, 2000, p. 63–84. See also Tony Smith, *America's Mission: The United States and the Worldwide Struggle for Democracy in the Twentieth Century*, Princeton: Princeton University Press, 1994.

16. The literature on the democratic peace thesis is abundant. For a good introduction see Michael Doyle, *The Ways of War and Peace*, New York: Norton, 1997. One of the more recent discussions comes from Bruce M. Russett and John R. Oneal, *Triangulating Peace: Democracy, Interdependence, and International Organizations*, New York: Norton, 2001.

17. Speech given on 25 February 2000. See ⟨www.state.gov/speeches⟩.

18. Thomas Carothers, "The Clinton Record on Democracy Promotion," *Working Papers*, No. 16, Washington: Carnegie Endowment for International Peace, September 2000.

19. *New York Times*, 20 September, 2002, ⟨www.nytimes.com/20002/09/20politics/20STEXT_FULL.html⟩.

20. See especially Thomas Carothers, "Aiding – and Defining – Democracy," *World Policy Journal*, Vol. 13, No. 1, Spring 1996, pp. 97–109.

21. Samuel Huntington, *The Third Wave: Democratization in the Late Twentieth Century*, Norman: University of Oklahoma Press, 1991. See also Greg Sorensen, *Democracy and Democratization*, Boulder: Westview, 1993; and Terry Lynn Karl and Philippe C. Schmitter, "Democratization around the Globe: Opportunities and Risks," in Michael T. Klare and Daniel C. Thomas, eds, *World Security: Challenges for a New Century*, New York: St Martin's Press, 1994.

22. See further Aung San Suu Kyi, "Freedom, Development, and Human Worth," *Journal of Democracy*, Vol. 6, No. 2, April 1995; and Jacques Barzun, "Is Democratic Theory for Export?," in Joel Rosenthal, ed., *Ethics and International Affairs*, Washington: Georgetown University Press, 1999, p. 57.

23. See, for example, Putnam, *Making Democracy Work*; Francis Fukuyama, "Social Capital and the Global Economy," *Foreign Affairs*, Vol. 74, No. 5, September/October, 1995, pp. 89–104; and Edgar Owens, *The Future of Freedom in the Developing World: Economic Development as Political Reform*, New York: Pergamon Press, 1987.

24. Thomas Carothers, *Aiding Democracy Abroad: The Learning Curve*, Washington D.C.: Carnegie Endowment for Peace, 1999.

25. See Carothers, "The Clinton Record on Democracy Promotion."

26. For an AID general statement, see "USAID's Strategies for Sustainable Development: Building Democracy," available at ⟨http://www.info.usaid.gov/democracy/strategy.htm⟩. See also Carothers, "Aiding – and Defining – Democracy."

27. Carothers, "Aiding – and Defining – Democracy."

28. Interhemispheric Resource Center and the Institute for Policy Studies, "In Focus: US Democratization Assistance," *Foreign Policy in Focus*, Vol. 4, No. 20, July 1999, available at ⟨www.foreignpolicy-infocus⟩.

29. "The Milosevic Regime Versus Serbian Democracy and Balkan Stability," Hearing Commission on Security and Cooperation in Europe, 105th Congress, 2nd session, 10 December 1998, Washington: GPO, 1999, p. 41.

30. *Washington Post*, 31 August 1999, p. 8.

31. See ⟨www.freedomhouse.org⟩.

32. *International Herald Tribune*, 12 June 2001, p. 9.

33. Thomas M. Frank, "The Emerging Right to Democratic Governance," *American Journal of International Law*, Vol. 86, No. 1, January 1992, pp. 46–91. However, for the argument that there are many sources of governmental legitimacy in fact, and for a review of the obvious fact that the United States has normal relations with numerous authoritarian governments, see David P. Forsythe, *Human Rights and Peace: International and National Dimensions*, Lincoln: University of Nebraska Press, 1993, chapter 3.

34. Francis Fukuyama, *The End of History and the Last Man*, New York: The Free Press, 1992.

35. See further Richard J. Bloomfield, "Making the Western Hemisphere Safe for Democ-

racy? The OAS Defense of Democracy Regime," *The Washington Quarterly*, Vol. 17, No. 2, Spring 1994, pp. 157–169.

36. To participate in hemispheric economic plans, a state had to be a democracy. See ⟨www.americascanada.org/eventsummit/declarations/declara-e.asp⟩.

37. See further David P. Forsythe, "The United Nations, Human Rights, and Development," *Human Rights Quarterly*, Vol. 19, No. 2, May 1997, pp. 334–349; David Gillies, "Human Rights, Governance, and Democracy: The World Bank's Problem Frontiers," *Netherlands Quarterly of Human Rights*, Vol. 1, No. 1, March, 1993, pp. 3–24.

38. David P. Forsythe, "Human Rights and International Security: United Nations Field Operations Redux," in Monique Castermans-Holleman et al., eds, *The Role of the Nation-State in the 21st Century*, The Hague: Kluwer, 1998, pp. 251–264.

39. USAID has created a new office – The Office of Transition Initiatives of the US Agency of International Development – which developed a Rule of Law programme that trains judges, court administrators, prosecutors, defence lawyers, etc. Available at ⟨www.state.gov/www/global/humanrights/hrsreportsmainhp.html⟩. See also Shattuck, "Diplomacy with a Cause: Human Rights in US Foreign Policy," p. 282.

40. Howard J. Wiarda, *Cracks in the Consensus: Debating the Democracy Agenda in US Foreign Policy*, Westport: Praeger, for the Center for Strategic and International Studies, Washington Papers #172, 1997.

41. Many agencies concerned with the public-opinion backlash of long-term, expensive programmes have imposed time limits on such programmes. For example, USAID plans to phase out an education programme by 2005 for this reason.

42. Frank Newman and David Weissbrodt, *International Human Rights: Law, Policy and Process*, Cincinnati: Anderson, 1990.

43. See further on this topic Amartya Sen, *Development as Freedom*, New York: Oxford University Press, 1999.

44. Jean-Philippe Therien, "Foreign Aid and Global Justice," Paper presented at ISA Conference, Chicago, 20–24 February 2001.

45. Nikolas Emmanuel, "The Determinants of US Foreign Assistance in the Post Cold War Era," Paper presented at ISA Conference, Chicago, 20–24 February 2001.

46. Cox, Ikenberry, and Inoguchi, eds, *American Democracy Promotion*.

47. Hermann Giliomee, "Democratization in South Africa," *Political Science Quarterly*, No. 110, Spring 1995, pp. 83–104.

48. One example of international pressure was the 1986 Comprehensive Anti-Apartheid Act adopted by the US Congress. Ibid., p. 88.

49. The US contributed $10 million to assist the 1994 election.

50. Under the Constitution various rights are articulated, including the right to freedom and security of person, which includes the right not to be deprived of freedom arbitrarily or without just cause; not to be detained without trial; to be free from all forms of violence from either public or private sources; not to be tortured in any way; and not to be treated or punished in a cruel, inhuman, or degrading way. In addition, everyone has the right to privacy, freedom of conscience, religion, thought, belief and opinion, freedom of expression, and freedom of association. Most of the rights established under the new constitution relate to those civil and political rights found in the ICCPR. Although South Africa's Constitution mentions some economic rights found in the ICESC Economic, Social and Cultural Rights, it does so in a passive manner: for example, Article 26 states that everyone has the right to have *access* to adequate housing; similarly, Article 27 states that everyone has the right to have *access* to health-care services, and sufficient food and water. However this amounts to a non-discrimination clause rather than a legitimate right to housing, food, water, and health care.

51. See ⟨www.amnesty.org⟩.

52. This is not surprising, as heavy ethnic party voting by ethnic groups is quite common in consolidated democracies.
53. See David Welsh, "The State of the Polity," in J.E. Spence, ed., *After Mandela: The 1999 South African Elections*, London: Chatham House, 1999; and also ⟨www.freedomhouse.org/ratings/index.htm⟩.
54. Sarah Mendelson and John Glenn, "Democracy Assistance and NGO Strategies in Post Communist Societies," *Working Papers*, No. 8, Washington: Carnegie Endowment for International Peace, February 2000.
55. Fedorov, "Democratization and Globalization."
56. Ibid, p. 2.
57. Bruce Garver, "Human Rights in Czech and Slovak History," in David P. Forsythe, ed., *Human Rights in the New Europe*, Lincoln: University of Nebraska Press, 1994, Chapter 4.
58. Ballot irregularities and disputed counting methods have led the opposition and the international community to question the election in 2000. See *New York Times*, 8 February 2001, A6. Recently, Aristide has offered to hold elections in 2002 because of the international pressure that he has received. His motive is partly financial: in return for holding elections next year, Aristide has requested that the OAS resume foreign aid to Haiti. *International Herald Tribune*, 5 June 2001.
59. *New York Times*, 5 March 2001, A23.
60. David Brinkley, "Democratic Enlargement: The Clinton Doctrine," *Foreign Policy*, Vol. 106, Spring 1997, pp. 111–127.
61. *Budget of the US Government, Fiscal Year 1999*, 105th Cong., 2nd session, H. Doc 105–177, Vol. 1, Washington: GPO, 1999.
62. Shattuck, "Diplomacy with a Cause." See also Mendelson and Glenn, who demonstrate that only 2.8 per cent of US assistance to Russia went to democratic activities from 1990 to 1999. Conversely, the European Union, while giving less assistance overall, gave a greater percentage of its aid – 19 per cent – for democracy assistance.
63. The Freedom Support initiative was in addition to the Support for Eastern European Democracies initiative. Both elevated economics over democracy in both theory and practice.
64. This is why many USAID statements argue that, through the promotion of democracy in Latin America, the United States was pursuing the national interest because doing so would reduce the region's poor from seeking refuge and better economic opportunities in the US. See further Smith, "US Democracy Promotion"; and Abraham F. Lowenthal, *Exporting Democracy: The United States and Latin America*, Baltimore: John Hopkins University Press, 1991.
65. Carothers, "Aiding – and Defining – Democracy."
66. ⟨www.usaid.gov/democracy/afr/soafrica.html⟩.
67. Max Singer and Aaron Wildavsky, *The Real World Order*, New York: Seven Bridges Press, 2001.
68. Secretary of State Albright stated that South Africa was "obviously the leading country on the continent." For Albright's speech, given in Pretoria on 9 December 2000, see ⟨http://secretary.state.gov/www/statements/2000⟩. For similar justifications of assistance to South Africa see ⟨www.usaid.gov/democracy/afr/soafrica.html⟩.
69. Fedorov, "Democratization and Globalization."
70. Slovenia desired to be accepted into the Council of Europe and eventually into the EU; the Council of Europe has become the ante-chamber for the EU, which makes both together a major pull factor for liberal democracy. See further David P. Forsythe, *Human Rights in International Relations*, Cambridge: Cambridge University Press, 2000, Chapter 5.

71. Fukuyama, *The End of History and the Last Man* and "Social Capital and the Global Economy."
72. Even realists such as Robert Gilpin accept the fact that the rough edge of capitalist democracy must be buffered by welfare/preservation rights. See *The Challenge of Global Capitalism*, Princeton: Princeton University Press, 2000, p. 4.
73. Larry Diamond, *Promoting Democracy in the 1990s*, New York: Carnegie Corporation, 1995.
74. George Soros, "The Capitalist Threat," *Atlantic Monthly*, Vol. 279, No. 2, February 1997, pp. 45–58.

Part Three

Sources of human rights violations and their impact on peace, democratization, and economic development

9

Sources and consequences of human rights violations in Iraq

Jenab Tutunji

The fall of the Ba'thist regime that had ruled Iraq since 1968 unleashed unpredictable social forces. Saddam Hussein, who rose from strongman to undisputed leader in 1979, and who ushered in an era of unprecedented human rights abuses in Iraq, was swept from power in April 2003 by the invading armies of the United States and the United Kingdom. Security Council resolution 1483 bestowed international legal standing on the occupation authority that was to govern Iraq and manage its oil resources until the formation of a new Iraqi government, which, at the time of writing, was not expected to happen for approximately another two years. One of the stated objectives of Washington and London was to transform the politics of Iraq and to institute a democratic regime that would be a model for the region as a whole. The future is uncertain, yet the best approach to predicting the future of human rights in Iraq is to revisit the past and identify the causes of the violation of those very rights.

In this chapter I attempt to identify structural and situational factors that have contributed to human rights violations in Iraq during the Ba'thist regime, which governed Iraq from 1968 to 2003. I focus on the role of institutions, while permitting recourse to cultural and other explanations to supplement the causal analysis. This enables light to be shed on important causal factors that are intangible but which, nevertheless, contributed to human rights violations.

The state of Iraq came into being after World War I, at which time it

191

came under British rule. A 1922 treaty with Britain transformed Iraq into a Mandate in all but name. The British established a constitutional monarchy and, in July 1924, an Organic Law (constitution) was adopted, which gave the country a limited parliamentary democracy. However, the British were not reluctant to subvert the authority of parliament – a lesson not lost on the Iraqis. Political groups and parties were established under the monarchy but not under conditions that would foster the conduct of healthy democratic life; nevertheless, a limited civil society existed at the time. In 1932, Iraq gained nominal independence. In 1936, General Bakr Sidqi mounted the Arab world's first coup, helping to undermine the prospects for democracy.

Iraq became a distinctly authoritarian state after the bloody revolution of 1958, in which the entire royal family was massacred and which brought a dictator, General Abdel Karim Qassem, to power. Qassem designated the cabinet as the supreme executive and legislative authority in the country. The Qassem regime was toppled in a second bloody coup by an alliance of the military and the Ba'th in February 1963. In November 1963, the first Ba'th regime was overthrown by Nasserist army officers, who remained in power until July 1968, when the second Ba'th regime was established. On 21 September 1968, a new provisional constitution vested full executive and legislative power in the Revolutionary Command Council (RCC) until the election of a national assembly. The actions of the president and the RCC were not subject to judicial challenge. This absence of the accountability of branches of government to each other, and of the government to the people, by virtue of the structure of the state allowed repression and chronic human rights violations to continue unchecked.

It will be argued that, between the Ba'th's return to power in 1968 and the early 1980s (a few years into the war with Iran), Iraq underwent a transition from an authoritarian to an ideocratic *rentier* state. A novel aspect of the regime that came to power in 1968 was single-party rule. The term "ideocratic" denotes the exclusive and ubiquitous hegemony of a doctrine, in this case Ba'thist ideology, in all aspects of life. The Ba'th Party gradually acquired a monopoly on political life and over the organizations of civil society found even in an authoritarian state, replacing them with Ba'th Party institutions. In the process, the state virtually swallowed up civil society. Being an ideocratic state also provided ample justification for repression, as differences with the government were perceived as heresy or treason.

In the second place, Iraq became a *rentier* state because of its dependence on economic rents from the sale of oil, which is the main source of government revenues. This granted the executive branch autonomy from the legislature, since the elected assembly no longer controlled the power of the purse and became a powerless body. Economic rents allowed the state to launch social and economic programmes for the benefit of the people, which established the dependence of society on the state. Being a *rentier* state diminishes accountability by the government and is inimical to participation by the people in government and contestation of state actions.

I have combined the terms "ideocratic" and *"rentier"* to highlight a particular type of government of which Iran and Saudi Arabia, as well as Iraq, are examples. The aspect of rentierism compounded the threat to political and civil liberties posed by the ideocratic nature of the state.

The third point has to do with Saddam Hussein and the changes he brought about. On 16 July 1979, Saddam Hussein (who had been the real power behind the scenes almost from the beginning) became President of Iraq. He also occupied the office of Prime Minister. Barely two weeks after he assumed power, there was a major purge of "all suspected elements" from the Ba'th party and its various organs, "including the army, the Popular Army, trade unions, student unions, professional and other associations, and departments.... For several weeks, a reign of unprecedented terror enveloped Iraq."[1] Twenty-two Ba'th leaders, including one-third of the Revolutionary Command Council, were executed, and about 500 senior party officials were arrested. Saddam had eliminated all internal opposition to his rule and gained uncontested control of the party.

In the mid-1980s, a few years into the war with Iran and primarily as a consequence of difficulties arising from the war, Saddam Hussein pushed through a transition that involved the partial de-institutionalization of state apparatuses, the relative marginalization of the Ba'th Party, and the ascendancy of the personal rule of Saddam Hussein, his family, and the clientelist networks loyal to them. He was willing to sacrifice tens of thousands of Iraqis in war in order to realize his ambitions for Iraq, and to execute an equal number of his countrymen to support his regime. Nevertheless, there is an entangled recursive relationship between Saddam's personality and the structural factors mentioned here.

The fourth point I establish in this chapter is that warfare has severely exacerbated human rights violations in Iraq, making an already bad situation even worse. It has led to rebellions that invited violent repression by the government and simultaneously provided the state with a justification for its actions. The most egregious example of human rights violations occurred in 1988 when the regime mounted the "Anfal" campaign to subdue Kurds in rural northern Iraq, who had rebelled against the state during the war with Iran. The combination of being an ideocratic *rentier* state and the fatality of warfare was poisonous for democracy and human rights.

The fifth point concerns Iraq's ethnic and sectarian make-up. The desire of the Kurds for a state of their own, for independence or at least meaningful autonomy, led to a series of rebellions on their part. These rebellions were met by brutal state repression dating back to the monarchy under British rule. In September 1961 the Kurds rose against the government, and the army launched the first major campaign against them. The Kurdish rebellion subsequently settled into chronic guerrilla warfare. This legacy has not been conducive to respect for human rights. The suppression of ethnic minorities was certainly not a successful policy when applied to the Kurds, breeding further rebellion and repression.

The conflict between religious Shi'ites, some of whom were influenced by the example of Iran, and the secular Ba'thist regime dominated by the Sunni minority, led to the suppression of manifestations of Shi'ite aspirations and even the banning of some Shi'ite religious rituals. Kurdish rebellions during the Iran–Iraq war, and Kurdish and Shi'ite uprising after Iraq's retreat from Kuwait, led to human rights violations on a massive scale, the victims of which are being uncovered today in mass graves. Here too, the combination of two powerful forces – the juxtaposition of ethnic conflict and warfare – proved to be another deadly combination, multiplying the effect of each other.

The sixth point is that the economic sanctions imposed by the UN Security Council, in addition to the destruction of Iraq's economic infrastructure during the 1991 war, have been responsible for egregious violations of human rights in Iraq on a massive scale. This includes the death of half a million children five years old or younger (not to mention older children and women) due to disease and malnutrition, according to a UNICEF study published in 1999.[2] Some traditionalists question whether the violation of such "third-generation" rights as the right to food or health should qualify as human rights violations; others maintain that the sanctions were responsible for crimes against humanity: surely, children have a right to life. Ironically, the victims of the economic sanctions outnumber the victims of repression by the Baghdad regime; this is particularly lamentable as the child victims covered in the UNICEF study had not been born at the time Iraq invaded Kuwait, an act for which the sanctions were imposed.

Lamentably, one has to conclude that human rights violations in Iraq are "overdetermined" in the sense that one can find more causes than one needs to explain them. When combined, these factors produced abuses that may not have resulted from any one of them alone.

Iraq as an ideocratic *rentier* state

The Arab-nationalist and socialist Ba'th regime in Iraq was guided by the mantra of unity, freedom, and socialism. These central objectives were rigorously pursued from the date of the assumption of power by the Ba'th regime until the early 1980s. A principal tenet of Ba'thist ideology was completing the liberation of the Arab world from colonialism and imperialism. Freedom referred not to individual liberties but to liberation from foreign domination and economic independence. The strategy for achieving the latter was based on the nationalization of the oil industry and a drive for import-substitution industrialization in an economically self-reliant framework. This was to be achieved by building a fully integrated, diversified, industrial base and through socialist transformation of the economy. Land redistribution, which began in 1958 but had stalled, was pushed forward by one of the first acts of the regime, partly to weaken the bourgeoisie and the political class of the "ancient regime" (whose interests were seen as tied to those of the former colonial rulers) but also because the measure was extremely popular. Land was given away to peasants; cooperatives were established and agricultural collectivization introduced.

However, in order to protect the achievements of the regime and to guard against an overthrow by its enemies, the regime had to consolidate its power and establish its ideological and functional legitimacy. Quite significantly, it is clear that an important rationale for turning Iraq into a one-party state, and the heavy reliance of the regime on intelligence services, was to defend against an army coup, such as the one that put an end to the first Ba'thist regime. This policy was quite successful in achieving its objective and goes a long way to explaining why Saddam Hussein managed to remain in power for so long. The transformation of Iraq into an ideocratic state was accompanied by the transfer of power from military officials to party bureaucrats and the transition to a one-party state. This process was evident in the changing membership of the RCC and the Regional (Iraqi) Command of the Ba'th Party. Baram notes that "[i]n 1968, the RCC consisted entirely of career officers, and their representation at the RL (Regional Leadership [or Command]) and in the government was fairly high, too. By 1986, career officers had all but disappeared and their place was taken, in all three bodies, chiefly by civilian party functionaries."[3] By early 1987 army officers represented only 11 per cent of the RCC and 13 per cent of the Regional Command.[4]

In what sense was the Ba'thist regime ideocratic? Ernest Gellner came to believe, in his later writings, that totalitarian regimes, notably communist ones, sought the fusion of truth, power, and society as the fulfilment of the human condition and the historic plan; that the government was the caretaker of absolute righteousness: political authority aimed at total virtue, and opposition to it constituted a vicious disturbance of the moral order.[5] Although the Ba'th is opposed to Marxism, it had its own version of a one-party quasi-totalitarian state, the doctrine of which embodied incontestable truth, and it did attempt such a fusion of truth and power. The mass media served as a mouthpiece for the regime and contributed in a significant way to the indoctrination of the public. Traditional means of socialization, including schools and the family, were recruited in the dissemination of the dominant ideology. Parents taught their children to love "Papa Saddam," lest those children should blurt out something in school that indicated that their parents were anti-regime.

To ensure loyalty to party ideology and the regime, Iraq became a police state. Kanan Makiya (writing under the pen name of Samir al-Khalil) elaborates on this theme in his book *Republic of Fear*. As he sees it, the state had instituted a culture in which true or real citizens were those who were loyal to the ideals of the Ba'th; those who were not loyal fell beyond the pale: they were dehumanized and excluded.[6] He argues that violence was pervasive and institutionalized, and fear and suspicion endemic. In addition, the Ba'th Party cadres were expected to report on their fellow citizens, and the party's mass organizations also functioned as surveillance organizations. The government's security apparatus included militias attached to the President, the Ba'th Party, and the Interior Ministry. Al-Khafaji speaks of "a network of intelligence apparatuses that pervaded all aspects of Iraqi society."[7] Some observers have even described the regime in Baghdad as Stalinist (Saddam Hussein was deeply impressed by Stalin, and studied him intensively).

In addition to its ideological hegemony, the regime sought to dominate the economy. The pursuit of the regime's economic articles of faith led it to nationalize the Iraq Petroleum Company in 1972. This had important consequences for the regime: by 1980, oil provided half of Iraq's national income and the lion's share of governmental revenues. This created a government that was autonomous of civil society, and a civil and economic society that was dependent on the government. However, the Ba'th regime believed that people had economic rights, even as it denied them political and civil rights. By 1978, the public sector had become dominant in the economy and a socialist agricultural sector was well established with about 80 collective farms, over 700 cooperatives, and eight giant state farms. The quasi-feudal landowning class of tribal leaders had been divested of most of its holdings.[8] During this period, the middle class doubled from one-third to two-thirds of the population. One may even argue that, at least for the first 10–15 years after 1968, Ba'th Party leaders thought they were carrying out the "general will" of the people and the nation. Egalitarian economic development was pursued, and many programmes were directed at the poor. Significant progress was achieved in the economic development effort. By 1982, the public sector accounted for 80 per cent of GNP.[9] This coincided with the apogee of the power of the Ba'th Party.

Owing to the overpowering significance of oil revenues, Iraq had become a *rentier* state (like Algeria and Iran), independent of tax collection for the lion's share of state revenues, and therefore less accountable to the public. In fact, it came to view itself as the benefactor of the public. It gained functional legitimacy as the provider of economic progress and development.

The term *"rentier* state" is used here to refer to developing economies in which the state is largely or primarily dependent on economic rents deriving from the exploitation of mineral resources, such as oil production and export.[10] Oil revenues in such countries tend to flow directly into the hands of a state élite. In the absence of the state's dependence on taxation, this undermines a principal traditional rationale for the demand for representative government. The consequence is that primarily those state institutions that perform a distributive function are fully developed; this is done at the expense of regulatory institutions; political and civil rights remain underdeveloped. In terms of societal norms, authoritative rather than market-oriented modes of allocation of resources become dominant. The state comes to provide certain functions on which segments of society become dependent: a welfare state is established. In times of hardship, as state revenues decline, the state is sorely tempted to resort to patron–client relationships in the allocation of limited resources, and to use those resources selectively to enhance its power base. This is what happened in Iraq, and there is some similarity in this regard between it and Algeria.[11]

The transition to sultanism

During the 1970s and early to mid-1980s, the regime's power was consolidated. For the first three years of the war with Iran, Iraq's government continued its welfare programmes by drawing down its foreign reserves and accumulating foreign debt, particularly to Kuwait and Saudi Arabia. However, the process of consolidation was halted and partially reversed as the war with Iran depleted state revenues. For a while the war went badly for Iraq, and the loyalty of the army to the regime could not be ensured. In 1984, the Republican Guard, consisting of troops loyal to the President, was hugely expanded, and the *amn khas* (intelligence service to protect the President) was formed, so that there were now four security services. Most damaging, perhaps, was the tendency to shift state power from the party to the family and clan of the President, laying the basis for sultanistic rule.[12] This was marked by despotic powers of the head of state, extreme glorification of the ruler, the undermining of the credibility of Ba'thist ideology and institutions, and the adulteration or

replacement of the instruments of party control of social life with patron–
client relationships and an increase in police coercion.

Two important transformations accompanied this. One was in the nature of the *rentier* state itself. As oil revenues fell as a result of world
market conditions in the mid-1980s, as oil installations were damaged in
the course of the war with Iran, and as military expenditures mounted,
reliance on economic rents diminished. Nevertheless, strategic rents in
the form of grants and loans from Kuwait and Saudi Arabia replenished
the state's coffers, as Iraq convinced its Arab neighbours that it was
fighting the war with Iran partly to protect them from the dominance and
depredations of a powerful Iranian state for which they themselves were
no match. The accumulation of debts to Kuwait would soon lead to another war. In addition, functional legitimacy (i.e. the sort of legitimacy
arising from the practical social services provided by the state) had declined with the fall in the government's oil revenues due to the war and
the international market. Ideological legitimacy was eroded by the privatization measures that undid land reform and restored the prerogatives
and property of tribal chiefs. These chiefs became essential elements in a
new clientelist network, which included clans from Saddam's hometown,
Tikrit.

Personal loyalty to Saddam came largely to replace party loyalty.
Zuhair al-Jazairi points out that the Iraqi variant of Ba'thism has gone
beyond the original ideology of Arab nationalism and socialism to
emphasize the role of the "historic leader" as hero and as a symbol, who
emerges to carry the nation forward towards its destiny. That hero, of
course, was Saddam Hussein.[13] Saddam became the "leader-symbol" of
the nation. The demoralization of the regime led to a slide into corruption by Saddam Hussein and his family (Saddam had initially been a
crusader against corruption in government),[14] and increased reliance on
violence to intimidate the population as a whole. Defaming or insulting
the President became an offence that was punishable by death. Later, the
cruel punishment of amputation of the tongue was introduced for such
offences.

Civil society

Democracy requires a vibrant civil society, freely formed civic associations, and solidarities.[15] The Ba'th regime and the sultanistic regime into
which it evolved swallowed up civil society, a crucial force for democratization. Civil society refers to organizations that mediate between citizens and the state, such as political parties and interest groups, labour
unions and employers' associations, women's organizations or NGOs,
autonomous of the state.

Under the 1968 constitution, only Ba'thists could be members of the RCC and the party retained exclusive control over the army. In an early experiment, a National Front was formed with the Communist Party and the Kurdish Democratic Party (KDP). The agreement with the KDP broke down in the summer of 1973. The agreement with the communists broke down when they tried to infiltrate the army. There was a crackdown on the communists in the spring of 1978, and the Ba'th went on to establish one-party rule.

The Provisional Constitution of 1968 stipulated that the Arab Ba'th Socialist Party governed Iraq through the RCC, which exercised both executive and legislative authority. The President could override the Provisional Constitution whenever he wished to do so. In addition, he was Secretary-General of the Regional (Iraqi) Command of the Ba'th Party. The Party constituted a sort of parallel government and was a power in its own right under the Leading Party Act No. 142 of 1974.

The Ba'th party spread its tentacles throughout state institutions. The Iraqi state usurped civil society. For example, there was one legal trade federation – the General Federation of Trade Unions, established in 1987 – which was associated with the Ba'th party and dominated by the government. Unions did not have the right to strike or to engage in collective bargaining. Moreover, it has been alleged that the General Federation of Iraqi Women was, in effect, part of the state security system.[16] The Federation enjoyed a monopoly: membership in any other women's organization was an offence punishable by a 15-year prison term. Student unions, peasants' associations, and unions of civil servants – even sports clubs – were taken over by the Ba'th party.

Al-Khafaji remarks:

... the mid-1980s witnessed the eclipse not only of the Revolution's Command Council and the Regional Command of the Ba'th Party, but also the organizations that the Ba'th had designed to mobilize supporters, such as the National Union of Students and Youth and the Federation of Peasants' Associations. The Federation of Labor Unions was abolished altogether, and workers in the state sector, comprising a majority of wage earners, were henceforth banned from joining unions.[17]

Ba'thist institutions did not disappear, of course, but they were often sidelined and their ideological foundations were undermined. Alternatively, they were used as an extension of the clientelist networks loyal to Saddam.

At the end of the Iran–Iraq war, political liberalization measures were contemplated and elections for the National Assembly were announced for April 1989. The regime spoke of allowing the formation and licensing of political parties other than the Ba'th. One cannot tell what these plans for political liberalization would have amounted to; at any rate, they were cut short by the second Gulf War.

In theory, according to a 1991 law, non-Ba'thist parties could exist. However, the regime did not recognize the political associations formed by Kurds, Assyrians, Turkomans, and Shi'ites. Although elections for the National Assembly were held in March 2000, the candidates either belonged to the Ba'th Party (which won 165 seats), or ran as unaffiliated but pro-government candidates (these won 55 seats), or were appointed by the President (30 seats). No candidates ran as representatives of parties other than the Ba'th. Dissent within the party, the bureaucracy, or the army was not tolerated – this was, in fact, almost invariably lethal to the dissenters. Opposition was severely repressed – not only were opposition parties illegal but also membership of some of them was punishable by death.

Real opposition was to be found only outside Iraq, or in areas of the north beyond the control of Baghdad since the early nineties. Independent trade unions did not exist. In the Kurdish area outside the government's control, a regional parliament was elected in 1992; however, because of infighting between the Kurdish Democratic Party (KDP) and the Patriotic Union of Kurds (PUK), it has not met since 1995.

However, it became apparent after the fall of the Ba'th regime that one element of civil society had not been crushed. The mosque is a centre where people continued to meet and socialize and Islamic groups and solidarities in Iraq tended to survive, despite the repression and the attempt by the state to intimidate, co-opt, and patronize the religious establishment. Prominent clerics have networks of disciples and lay emulators, and a share of religious taxes. Despite the former regime's best efforts to suppress and co-opt Shi'ism, we have witnessed the sudden proliferation of Shi'ite groups.

Political, civil, and human rights violations by the regime

It is possible to categorize the Iraqi regime's main human rights violations under two main headings: (1) war crimes; (2) the violation of individual civil and political rights, as well as the right to life and security of citizens from torture.

On 24 February 2000, the UN General Assembly passed resolution A/RES/54/178, which stated that the Assembly strongly condemns:

(a) The systematic, widespread and extremely grave violations of human rights and of international humanitarian law by the Government of Iraq, resulting in an all-pervasive repression and oppression sustained by broad-based discrimination and widespread terror;

(b) The suppression of freedom of thought, expression, information, association, assembly and movement through fear of arrest, imprisonment, executions and other sanctions;

(c) The widespread use of the death penalty in disregard of the provisions of the International Covenant on Civil and Political Rights and the United Nations safeguards;

(d) Summary and arbitrary executions, including political killings and the continued, so-called clean-out of prisons, as well as enforced or involuntary disappearances, routinely practiced arbitrary arrests and detention, and consistent and routine failure to respect due process and the rule of law, for example, in the execution of delinquents for minor property offenses and customs violations;

(e) Widespread, systematic torture and the enactment and implementation of decrees prescribing cruel and inhuman punishment as a penalty for offenses.[18]

Amnesty International (AI) has been reporting for years on such violations.[19] In its 2001 annual report, AI reported that in the year 2000, "[t]orture and ill-treatment were widespread, and new punishments, including beheading and the amputation of the tongue, were reportedly introduced. Non-Arabs, mostly Kurds, continued to be forcibly expelled from their homes in the Kirkuk area to Kurdistan."[20] Also in 2001, AI issued several appeals, among them one entitled, "Iraq: Relentless executions must end." AI called for an immediate moratorium on executions, commenting that "[t]he high rate of executions in Iraq shows a continuing disregard for human life."[21] On 15 August, it issued a report saying that, "[t]orture is used systematically against political detainees in Iraqi prisons and detention centers. The scale and severity of torture in Iraq can only result from the acceptance of its use at the highest level," noting that this is in violation of the ICCPR, which Iraq ratified in 1971.[22]

According to Max van der Stoel, who served as Special Rapporteur of the Commission on Human Rights on the situation of human rights in Iraq from 1992 to 1999, there were an estimated 16,496 outstanding cases of missing persons in Iraq during that period, the vast majority of them Kurds who disappeared during the Anfal Campaign[23] (discussed at length below). This rendered Iraq the country with the highest number of disappearances reported to the Working Group established by the Commission on Human Rights.

Some human rights groups have placed the number of missing persons over the past 35 years as high as 300,000, most of them presumed dead. After the fall of the regime, Iraqis started digging up suspected mass-grave sites, looking for missing family members. According to Sandra L. Hodgkinson, a State Department official who had been documenting some of the sites for the American occupation forces in Iraq,

[t]he truly frightening part is that the number of suspected mass graves is so un-fathomable (...) They are everywhere. Literally every neighborhood and town is reporting possible grave sites, and from all different periods of time. I think we're going to find them everywhere.[24]

The Ba'thist regime has also forcibly displaced hundreds of thousands of ethnic minorities opposed to the government; however, there is no reliable figure on internal displacement in Iraq. Several waves of internal displacement have occurred to and within northern Iraq. The number of internally displaced persons in Iraq tends to fluctuate widely with time.

The impact of war and ethnic conflict on human rights violations

War is a social and political process that has had a profound impact on the organization of state–society relations in Iraq. Al-Khafaji speaks of "the normalization of war as a social condition and system of governance, the construction of a war-driven political economy."[25] The development of hyper-nationalism in various forms and Iraq's self-appointed role as defender of the Arab nation may well have shaped Iraqi political identity and been used to valorize its military prowess, as al-Khafaji suggests. There is little reason to doubt that the Iraqi regime sought to carve out a niche for itself as a regional power and to derive strategic rents from its role as the defender of other Arab states, notably small ones in the Gulf. The regime cultivated militaristic attitudes and values and resorted to war all too readily; it adapted itself to chronic conflict and was inventive in using warfare to buttress its position.

The economic causes and consequences of warfare

War has had a devastating effect on the economy of Iraq, on civil and human rights, and on political rights as well. The Iran–Iraq war (or the first Gulf War) lasted from 1980 to 1988 and had the most severe consequences for both participants. The second Gulf War, precipitated by the invasion of Kuwait in 1990, completed the devastation, practically knocking Iraq back into the pre-industrial age. The subsequent economic sanctions, which are still in place at the time of writing, have perpetuated malnutrition, disease, death, and suffering. The invasion of Kuwait, which brought down the regime of Saddam Hussein, has so far left the county in chaos.

Economic difficulties arising from the war with Iran were a major causal factor in the invasion of Kuwait. The government responded to the public sector's difficulties amid war's crushing economic burden with a strategy of privatization. Privatization policies began in July 1982 and further intensified in February 1987. They gave birth to an opportunistic and state-dependent private sector, leading to higher inflation and economic stagnation in Iraq, as well as increased social injustice and economic inequality. The state became not only the main investor in the economy but also the principal customer of private capital, nurturing a private sector that is dependent on the state (not unlike Syria, another Ba'thist state).[26] Yet this was done at the expense of egalitarianism, particularly in the agricultural sector. Tighter governmental controls on the public became necessary.

As economic stagnation intensified, the Iraqi regime became desperate. The Kuwaiti government refused to cancel the debts the Iraqi government had incurred in the course of the war with Iran (perceived at the time as a war that was fought partly in defence of Kuwait). When Kuwait went on to exceed its production quota in the Organization of Petroleum-Exporting Countries (OPEC) and entered into a dispute with Iraq over drilling rights, the regime announced that Kuwait had declared economic war on Iraq, and attempted to annex Kuwait.[27] This only multiplied Baghdad's difficulties.

Kamran Mofid calculates the cost of the Iran–Iraq war for Baghdad to be $452.6 billion. This amounts to 435 per cent of Iraq's oil revenues during the eight-year conflict or 112 per cent of its Gross National Product (GNP) for each year of that war.[28] Al-Nasrawi gives the figure of $519 billion for the economic cost of the second Gulf War.[29] This is equal to 53 times Iraq's Gross Domestic Product (GDP) in 1993. The cost of the two wars verged on one trillion dollars.

Another illuminating perspective is offered by tracing the change in Iraq's per capita GDP in 1980 prices: it rose from $1,745 in 1970 to $4,083 at the beginning of the Iran war in 1980, but then fell to $1,756 in 1988 at the end of the war with Iran and to $627 at the end of the second Gulf War in 1991.[30] Iraq's per capita GDP in 1991 in real terms was actually less than in 1950, when per capita GDP (in 1980 prices) stood at $654 and the population was only 5.2 million. By 1993, per capita GDP had fallen from the 1991 figure of $627 to $485, although the population had increased by only one million. The above figures of the costs of the two wars tell their own story. It is hard to imagine that the regime's functional legitimacy could have survived – although, after the economic sanctions started to bite, its ability to distribute desperately needed food rations must have restored some of that loss. The regime had no way to substitute for the loss of functional legitimacy, except to resort to repression; with the carrot gone, one has to rely on the stick more heavily.

According to Workman, "[w]arfare ... often tips the balance of social forces in favor of dominant social groups. Warfare more often than not reinforces existing asymmetries of social power; that is, it tends to the maintenance of socially oppressive relations."[31] In a nutshell, the cost of the wars in which Iraq has been involved since 1980 has been borne by the general population, ethnic minorities, labour, and women, while the regime succeeded in enhancing its position – except in the 2003 war, naturally.

The Shi'ites

Shi'ite unrest broke out in February 1977. By the end of the decade, as many as 200,000 Shi'ites may have been stripped of their nationality and forcibly deported to Iran.[32] Selective repression of Shi'ites resumed in the aftermath of the Iranian revolution and the advent of Khomeini to power. Khomeini's overt enmity to the Ba'thist regime and his exhortations to the Shi'ites of Iraq to religious rebellion were followed by assassinations of scores of government officials by the Islamic Da'wa Party (which had been founded in the late 1950s to combat atheism and communism). Later, in April 1980, an attempt was made to assassinate Deputy Prime Minister Tareq Aziz. Subsequently, there was an attack on the funeral of those killed in the assassination attempt. Membership in the Da'wa Party was made a capital offence and hundreds were executed. Imam Muhammad Baqer al-Sadr, the guiding light of the party, and his widely venerated sister, Bint al-Huda, were arrested, tortured, and killed. Riots broke out in the south and many were killed; however, the vast majority of Iraq's Shi'ites remained loyal to their country throughout the Iran–Iraq war.

It is clear that the government's fear of Iran's ability to foment discontent among the Shi'ite population, segments of which could be mobilized by Iraqi clerics, was a precipitant of the Iran–Iraq war.[33]

In the aftermath of the invasion of Kuwait, some retreating soldiers mounted a rebellion and took refuge among Shi'ite opponents of the regime. The rebels, who numbered as many as 50,000, carried out bloody massacres, and their repression by the regime was particularly brutal. The insurgency spread to the cities of Najaf and Karbala', holy to the Shi'ites. The rebels mounted a fierce resistance to government forces and took refuge in a number of holy shrines, which were shelled by the Republican Guards in putting down the rebellion. A large number of people (including civilians), estimated at the time at anywhere between 600 and 6,000, were killed; another 3,000–6,000 were taken prisoner.[34] Ever since the fall of the Ba'th regime, mass graves, each containing scores of bodies, have been discovered in many places in the south. On 14 May 2003 the *New York Times* reported the discovery of a mass grave in Mahawil, 50 miles south of Baghdad, where an estimated 3,000 bodies were unearthed from the salt marshes.[35] A preliminary estimate, albeit unreliable, extrapolated that the general area, which used to be a military camp, may contain as many as 11,000 bodies. They are all presumed to be Shi'ites executed in different stages as a result of the rebellion of 1991.

Many of the rebels fled to the predominantly Kurdish north and to the Mesopotamian marshlands of the Tigris–Euphrates Delta in the south. Government forces then burnt and shelled villages in the south, and the regime ordered the construction of dams to divert water from the marshes. This enabled government forces to penetrate into formerly inaccessible areas, where their Shi'ite opponents had found refuge.[36]

According to AI, there were many clashes in March 1999 between Iraqi security forces and armed Islamist opposition groups in southern Iraq, especially in Basra. These were sparked off by the killing of Ayatollah Muhammad Sadeq al-Sadr, a prominent Shi'ite religious leader, the previous February. This reportedly led to dozens of deaths on both sides and was followed by arbitrary mass arrests and summary executions.[37] There were reports later in 1999 of deliberate artillery attacks by government forces against Shi'ite civilians and large-scale burning operations in the southern marshes. In 2001, government forces were reported to have attacked villages in the marshes.[38]

In the first two years after the second Gulf War, the US and Britain imposed "no-fly zones" over northern and southern Iraq to deter aerial attacks against the marsh Arabs and the Kurds of northern Iraq.

The Kurds

Iraqi Kurdistan covers about 17 per cent of the area of Iraq, constituting the northern part of the country, including the oil-producing region of Mosul and Kirkuk. After World War I, Britain attached the former Ottoman *vilayet* of Mosul to the former *vilayet*s of Baghdad and Basra to form the state of Iraq, over Kurdish objections. The Kurds have sought independence and, in the pursuit of that objective, have been used, at times wittingly or unwittingly, as pawns by the enemies of Iraq. There were Kurdish rebellions in 1922 and 1930 stretching through 1931 and 1932. The first Barzani tribe rebellion in Iraq began in 1931. Mullah Mustafa Barzani formed the KDP. During 1961–1963 the Iraqi army and air force waged a campaign against Mullah Barzani's forces – the *pesh merga* (those who face death) – who numbered as many as 20,000 at the time (and were to reach 50,000 in 1975).

In March 1970, the second Ba'thist regime struck an agreement with the Kurds that granted them linguistic, educational, cultural, economic, and political rights, including the appointment of a Kurdish vice-president and a demographically proportionate share of seats in the legislature.[39] If anything, the Ba'th regime made a more viable attempt than its predecessors to recognize Kurdish rights. Iraq thus became the only one among the four countries sharing parts of the area of Kurdistan to recognize the cultural rights of the Kurds. In 1974, the Baghdad regime amended the March agreement by introducing the Autonomy Law (which, in fact, curtailed the earlier agreement). During the 1974–1975 clashes with Iran, the Kurds received support from Iran, Israel, and the United States; however, the fighting ended in March 1975 and Mustafa Barzani was forced into exile.

In 1976 the KDP split into two, under the leadership of Idris and Masud Barzani, respectively, and the PUK began to take shape, being formed by 1978 under the leadership of Jalal Talabani. After the outbreak of the Iran–Iraq war, the KDP negotiated a cease-fire with the Ba'th regime, but this fell apart slowly.

Halabja

The attack on civilians in the Kurdish town of Halabja is one of the most notorious examples of the atrocities attributed to the reign of Saddam Hussein, an incident which was behind President George Bush's repeated references to the Iraqi regime gassing its own people. On 16 March 1988, the town of Halabja was bombed with poison gas (killing about 5,000 Kurds). This reportedly occurred during a counter-attack by the Iraqis, who had been driven out of the town by the PUK fighting alongside the Iranians.[40] Immediately after the battle the United States Defense Intelligence Agency investigated, and produced a classified report that maintained that the Kurds had died from Iranian, not Iraqi, chemical weapons. As the report was classified, it is hard to explain its conclusions as part of an effort to support Iraq.

Stephen Pelletiere was the senior political analyst on Iraq for the Central Intelligence Agency (CIA) during the war with Iran and led an US Army investigation in 1991, which went into great detail about Halabja. He wrote in an op-ed piece in the New York Times:

This much about the gassing at Halabja we undoubtedly know: it came about in the course of a battle between Iraqis and Iranians. Iraq used chemical weapons to try to kill Iranians who had seized the town, which is in northern Iraq not far from the Iranian border. The Kurdish civilians who died had the misfortune to be caught up in that exchange. But they were not Iraq's main target (...) The agency did find that each side used gas against the other in the battle around Halabja. The condition of the dead Kurds' bodies, however, indicated they had been killed with a blood agent – that is, a cyanide-based gas – which Iran was known to use. The Iraqis, who are thought to have used mustard gas in the battle, are not known to have possessed blood agents at the time.[41]

The Anfal campaign

The Ba'th regime made a systematic attempt to eliminate the Kurdish rebels, whom it viewed as collaborators with Iran during the 1980–1988 war. This took the form of the Anfal campaign during 1988 – the most egregious case of human rights violations in Iraq. Over a period of months, almost 4,500 Kurdish villages along the Turkish and Iranian frontiers were destroyed. One estimate is that the Anfal campaign resulted in the killing of between 50,000 and 200,000 Kurds and the deportation of about 500,000 others to new "collective settlements" and to detention camps.[42]

The Anfal campaign was an attempt by the Iraqi government to wipe out the rebels (or *pesh mergas*) once and for all. The regime felt that they constituted a "fifth column" that had been exploited by Iran during Iraq's hour of need, when it was on the defensive in the war, and that they could be so exploited again. The PUK had consummated an alliance with Iran in October 1986. In the eyes of the Baghdad regime the Kurdish rebels were guilty of aiding and abetting the enemy, and they are referred to in government documents as "*mukharribeen*" or "saboteurs." Members of the PUK are referred to in government documents as "agents of Iran," while KDP members are referred to as "the offspring of treason."[43]

The campaign began once Iraq could free sufficient divisions from the Iranian front near the end of the war. It was meant as a final solution to the problem of Kurdish rebellion and was not merely a punitive campaign. The target was the rural Kurdish population in northern Iraq between the southernmost Kurdish zones and the Turkish border. The intention was first to identify and then to eliminate all Kurdish men who had fought against the state, and to arrest men of fighting age to determine whether they posed a threat. The plan was also to prevent Kurds from returning to a large number of villages. For this purpose, the Iraqi army started by bombarding Kurdish villages in the southern zones with conventional (and, in some cases, perhaps, chemical) munitions in order to start an exodus towards the Turkish border. The villagers fled and were then caught in a giant "pincer" movement as the Iraqi army simultaneously drove north and south from the Turkish border. The Kurds had no option but to surrender. Middle East Watch, a branch of Human Rights Watch, argues[44] that there is strong reason to believe that a pattern of government action could be discerned. Those who were carrying guns were lined up and shot on the orders of the Northern Bureau of the Ba'th Party under the command of Ali Hassan al-Majid, a cousin of Saddam Hussein. Many of those arrested were never released, and some were executed. Boys below the age of puberty, women, and old men were displaced and held in camps for a long time without adequate food supplies or medical care. Villages were razed and surviving villagers were prohibited from rebuilding, or returning to, their villages.

The Kurdish population of the cities was not targeted in the Anfal campaign. Prior to Anfal, Kurds who voluntarily moved from rebel areas ("prohibited areas" in the government's jargon) to areas under government control were resettled in housing complexes or "modern villages" or "new cities," and were referred to in government documents as "returnees to the national ranks." Those remaining in the prohibited areas were subject to execution.

The 1991 and 1996 rebellions

Three years later, the Shi'ite rebellion in the wake of the expulsion of Iraqi forces from Kuwait ignited a wide Kurdish rebellion, in which the insurgents gained control of most of northern Iraq. On 6 March 1991, Kurds in the town of Rania mounted a rebellion against the Baghdad regime. All major Kurdish towns, including Kirkuk, rose up against Baghdad. Government forces attacked, precipitating an exodus of between 1 million and 1.5 million Kurds. The uprising was crushed within three weeks, but the United States, Britain, and France intervened and set up a safe haven for the Kurds in the Dohuk governorate. Iraq withdrew its troops from the Kurdish areas (except for Kirkuk) by October 1991, and a Kurdish regional government was established following elections in May 1992.

In August 1996, following internecine fighting between the KDP and the PUK, Baghdad intervened in the Kurdish area at the request of the KDP. Baghdad withdrew its forces following a US bombardment.

Impact on women

Between the period that the Ba'th came to power for a second time and the first few years of the Iran–Iraq war, women benefited considerably from the educational and professional opportunities created by the Iraqi government and came to occupy high professional positions. They enjoyed the same rights of citizenship as men, and were expected to contribute their share to the development of Iraq. In 1980, 27 of the 250 members of the National Assembly were women. The General Federation of Iraqi Women was a nationwide institution that represented the interests of women. The government subverted clan control over women through its policies and legislation, such as the 1978 personal status laws, which undermined patriarchal domination over women. That was to change: during the war, as conditions deteriorated and the regime started courting the tribes, women's liberation suffered a set-back to please the conservative elements in society.

The charge has also been made that the government has used the new laws against prostitution to eliminate some of its female critics. According to AI:

In October [2000] dozens of women accused of prostitution were beheaded without any judicial process in Baghdad and other cities. Men suspected of procurement were also beheaded. The killings were reportedly carried out in the presence of representatives of the Ba'ath Party and the Iraqi Women's General Union. Members of Feda'iyye Saddam, a militia created in 1994 by 'Uday Saddam Hussein, used swords to execute the victims in front of their homes. Some victims were reportedly killed for political reasons.[45]

Unfortunately, the economic sanctions against Iraq since the invasion of Kuwait have particularly victimized children and Iraqi mothers: Iraqi women have borne the brunt of the traumas of warfare. Furthermore, as the regime sought to consolidate its position (which had been undermined by economic losses and political menaces), it turned to the traditional support networks, consisting of Bedouin tribes and clans – notably, Arab Sunni tribes. Both modernization and women's emancipation were sacrificed in the process.

UN sanctions

During the six-week Gulf War, which began on 16 January 1991, more bombs rained down on Iraq than had been dropped in all of World War II. The relentless air campaign destroyed food processing and pharmaceutical plants, power plants, sewage pumping stations, roads, and bridges.

Security Council Resolution 661, of 16 August 1990, had already established a blanket embargo on all of Iraq's imports and exports, with the exception of "supplies intended strictly for medical purposes, and, in humanitarian circumstances, foodstuffs," according to paragraph 6c of the resolution. Yet the exception was meaningless, as Iraq could not sell oil to buy food or medicines. Death from starvation and disease, particularly the dramatic rise in infant mortality, as a result of the targeting of the country's industrial infrastructure during the war and the economic sanctions imposed since, should be viewed as a violation of human rights and, in fact, qualifies as a crime against humanity.

It has been said many times that sanctions are blunt instruments. The political target of the economic sanctions was the Iraqi regime but the most profound effect of the sanctions has been on the most vulnerable elements of the population – children, the aged, and the poor in general.

The mechanism by which sanctions may cause civilian hardship is relatively well understood: all non-essential supplies are prohibited, resulting in shortages of many civilian-related items. Meanwhile, restricted access to foreign markets contributes to economic depression – including soaring unemployment, rising inflation, and a higher cost of living. These problems may translate, at the level of the family, into stress, extreme poverty, malnutrition, and poor health, which can be particularly devastating to children.[46]

Sanctions affect food and agriculture, medicines and medical services. Vaccination programmes for children in Iraq were impaired. Infectious diseases spread because of the deterioration of the water supply and sanitation facilities. There has been a steep increase in unemployment, inflation, and family debt. By September 1991, less than a year after the war, 48 per cent of households in Iraq had incurred heavy sanctions-related debt.[47]

The impairment of Iraq's water and sewerage systems as a result of the sanctions has had profound public health consequences for the population. Prior to the sanctions, potable water networks distributed over four million cubic metres (MCM) of treated water to 93 per cent of the urban and 70 per cent of the rural population. Before the 2003 war, water-treatment plants were operating at about 50 per cent capacity and most sewage-treatment plants had stopped chemical treatment altogether. Pipe networks had many breaks, resulting in sewage overflows and dangerous cross-connections between water and sewage lines. Untreated sewage was pumped directly into the Tigris and Euphrates rivers, along which two-thirds of Iraq's population lives.[48]

The Food and Agriculture Organization of the United Nations (FAO) reported in 1995 over a million deaths in Iraq, of which 570,000 were among children. It described 4 million people as starving. UNICEF's 1999 Iraq Child and Maternal Mortality survey measured the difference between mortality rates for children in Iraq for the 25 years from March 1974 to March 1999; a sufficiently long period was chosen before and after the war to permit the emergence of trends. UNICEF collected its own data, using interviews and questionnaires, and did not rely on Iraqi government data. Separate surveys were conducted for the Kurdish region in the north under UN control and the 15 southern governorates controlled by the Baghdad government. The survey of the southern regions found that the under-five mortality rate had increased from 56 deaths per 1,000 live births in 1984–1989, to 92 deaths per 1,000 live births in 1989–1994, to 131 deaths per 1,000 live births in 1994–1999.[49] Projecting trends that preceded the war and comparing that with the existing situation permitted the deduction that half a million more children under the age of five years had died since the end of the war than would have been the case if the war had not occurred and the sanctions had not been imposed.[50] The survey also found that, although the maternal mortality rate was not high, maternal deaths were, nevertheless, a leading cause of deaths among women, accounting for 31 per cent of adult female deaths.[51]

A study commissioned by the United Nations Children's Fund (UNICEF) recommends that a Child Impact Assessment be prepared prior to the imposition of sanctions, and that the application of sanctions should be subject to close monitoring to assess its impact on human rights.[52]

Denis Halliday, the former United Nations Humanitarian Coordinator in Iraq (and Assistant Secretary-General for Human Resources Management), who resigned his post in autumn 1998 in protest against what he witnessed in Iraq, points out that the oil-for-food programme "was designed to prevent further deterioration, not more than that."[53] Halliday has written that the economic sanctions constitute a crime against humanity. He has also pointed out that the economic sanctions are undermining family life and the previously strong family values in Iraq, which is certainly not a situation that is conducive to the emergence of democracy or the cessation of human rights violations. The US State Department places the blame for the situation squarely on Saddam Hussein for not taking up the oil-for-food programme immediately when it was offered, and also blames him for delays in food distribution; Halliday dismisses this attitude as simplistic and dishonest. The oil-for-food programme may have prevented massive starvation, but it did not allow for the rebuilding of Iraq's infrastructure devastated by war, and economic recovery is essential if the country's public health system is to be rebuilt.

The primary rationale for clinging on to the economic sanctions after all those years was that they were to be kept in place until Iraq got rid of its weapons of mass destruction. However, the sanctions themselves have probably been responsible for the deaths of more people in Iraq than all those killed by all weapons of mass destruction throughout history.[54]

Sadly, even if one accepts the high figure of 300,000 for the victims of state repression, and if one adds another 200,000 to represent the victims of the Anfal campaign (although there is certainly strong overlap between the two categories, so that the numbers cannot simply be added as, in fact, the second group may simply be a subset of the first), the awful truth is that the UN sanctions claimed more victims than did governmental repression.

The sanctions regime was eased. Iraq was eventually allowed to sell as much oil as it could, bearing in mind that the infrastructure of its oil industry had not been fully repaired. Nevertheless, the economic situation and the plight of ordinary Iraqis improved. According to the *CIA World Factbook*, Iraq's GDP grew at the rate of 15 per cent in 2000, and per capita income had risen to $2,500 a year.[55] In mid-May 2002, the Security Council adopted Resolution 1409, effectively allowing Iraq to buy whatever it wants (except for a 332-page checklist for so-called "dual use" items).

Conclusions

What would a solution to Iraq's problems look like? Wars change history in unforeseen ways. Any recommendations made here are subject to the proviso that the occupation authority will, in fact, do what is necessary to install a democratic regime in Iraq. Democracy is a normative and "constructed" aspiration, not the normal condition of human societies or a form of society and polity that somehow emerges by default. The 2003 war has deposed the Ba'thist regime but has left behind a chaotic situation: law and order have to be established; an efficient bureaucracy has to be rebuilt. We are reminded by Abbas Alnasrawi that, despite Iraq's oil wealth, we have been witnesses to "the destruction of development."[56] Economic reconstruction is needed.

This chapter has identified seven main sources of human rights violations in Iraq. The war has eliminated a number of these; others remain to be dealt with.

First, it was argued that Iraq was an ideocratic *rentier* state as a source of human rights violations. Not only has the Ba'thist regime gone, but so have its repressive institutions; what remains to be seen is whether a liberal democracy will take its place. A new constitution is needed: Iraq must become a country of laws. A parliamentary (rather than a presidential) system of government, with an independent judiciary, would be the best place to start. State institutions must be rebuilt.

A prominent threat to democratic government in Iraq would be the emergence of an Islamic state, along the lines of the Islamic Republic of Iran, where the country is led by a religious authority under the principle of *velayat-e faqih* (rule of the jurisprudent), particularly if the principle of popular sovereignty is trumped by the veto of a council of guardians whenever the council feels that legislation passed by parliament is inconsistent with divine law or the *Shari'ah*. In particular, one should ask if the dominant Shi'ite factions in Iraq support the idea of *velayat-e faqih*. Iraq's Shi'ites do not have a united position and it is not clear, at the time of writing, which group will be dominant. The Supreme Council of the Islamic Revolution in Iraq, or SCIRI, has favoured the idea of *velayat-e faqih*, but this position is weakening. Al-Da'wa al-Islamiyah, another major group, was founded in the 1950s by Muhsin al-Hakim, who outlined a system of Islamic government in which an elected assembly could substitute for the imam; this goes against the idea of *velayat-e faqih*. Another major group is led by Muqtada al-Sadr, a young firebrand with a large number of followers, who has adopted an anti-US position. Muqtada al-Sadr is a religious follower of Kathem al-Ha'iri, who resides in Qom in Iran and believes in *velayat-e faqih* – whereas Muqtada himself does not and seems to be rather secular in many ways. Finally, there is the traditional Shi'ite establishment, which survived the rule of Saddam, led by Ayatollah Ali Sistani. He is opposed to the politicization of religion but is challenged by the more radical Shi'ites. In principle, it should be possible for an Islamic Democratic Party to arise.

It can be concluded from the above that there will be a struggle for supremacy among these factions. However, one ought to remember that the Shi'ites in Iraq have been part of a secular tradition for eight decades. The upsurge in Shi'ite self-affirmation may largely be the result of a sudden-found liberty after a quarter-century of oppression by Saddam and the Ba'th.

Second, Iraq should cease to be a *rentier* state. However, denationalizing Iraq's oil industry after 12 years of economic sanctions runs the risk of foreign ownership or control of the country's natural resources. To eliminate the risk to democracy posed by oil revenues accruing to the state, it is not necessary to denationalize Iraq's oil: it will be sufficient to place oil revenues under the control of parliament rather than of the executive. The fiscal autonomy of the state from society should end, the state should be made dependent on tax revenues, and parliament should wield the power of the purse. An efficient and honest tax-collection system is required. If parliament controls the power of the purse, it will have real and effective power. Aside from the oil sector, economic privatization plans should be pursued.

Third, while the US and British military intervention in Iraq has put an end to the sultanistic state, war cannot, unfortunately, erase the legacy of that state. One result of this legacy is that civil society has been emptied of content. Civil society – a set of organizations (such as political parties, labour unions, employers' associations, NGOs, civil rights organizations, and parent–teacher associations) that act as intermediaries between the people and the state – will have to be created. At the moment, Iraq does not represent fertile ground for the emergence of a effective civil society. It will take many months – probably years – to inculcate the norms, attitudes, and political culture needed, to create the necessary organizations and institutions, and to institute checks and balances.

There were political parties in Iraq under the monarchy from 1921 to 1948, which functioned within a parliamentary system. Opposition parties were tolerated, and debate and contestation of state policies was permitted. Parliament did exercise influence over state policy, although the executive enjoyed a great deal of power. There were over 23 independent newspapers published in Iraq. Can Iraq simply return to that kind of society overnight? Regrettably, this is unlikely: it takes time to form political parties, as they need time to develop platforms and to mature; unions and associations do not spring up overnight, particularly given the lack of trust and social cohesion.

Fourth, the Ba'th regime sought to maintain a stranglehold on power, in part because of its fear of a military coup. This fear is legitimate and could re-emerge in the future, constituting a threat to democracy and human rights. One way to get the army to stay in its barracks is through socialization and the creation of a political culture that acknowledges that politicians, not the military, should rule. Institutional measures can also be taken – such as creating a balance between the army and the national guard. The army could be kept relatively small and sizeable national guard units could be made truly professional and battle ready, to be called up only and exclusively at times of war.

Fifth, to end the problem of warfare, Iraq should be demilitarized for 25 years (emulating post-World War II arrangements with Germany and Japan), which should allow the state to focus on development. The military embargo has not been lifted; perhaps it should be kept in place for a generation, as long as Iraq's security is guaranteed by the United States or the United Nations.

Sixth, the ethnic conflict problem has not been eradicated. The solution to this difficulty may lie in the choice of a consociational model of democracy – as in the Netherlands, Belgium, Switzerland, Lebanon, or Malaysia – where different communities share power and there are guarantees against the dominance of any one community over the others. This may be done first through constitutional guarantees that Kurds, Sunni Arabs, and Shi'ites will be able to practise their religion, customs, and traditions. In addition, these three communities must share power: seats in parliament and positions in government can be allocated in a manner proportional to the demographic ratio of each community in the population; the three communities would also be represented in a fair way in the bureaucracy and the army.

On 4 October 1992 the Kurdish legislative assembly, established in the Kurdish no-fly zone in northern Iraq, unanimously adopted a law espousing federalism as a solution for the Kurdish problem in Iraq. This action was supported by the KDP, the PUK, and other Kurdish groups. Although the law is not specific on the nature of federalism, in 2002 the KDP submitted its own proposal concerning the nature of federalism in Iraq: it recommends renaming the country as the Federal Republic of

Iraq, and that Iraq should be a federation consisting of an Arab region and a Kurdish region, with a democratic government and pluralist civil society, guaranteeing the legitimate rights of all minorities. In addition, demographically the federation would consist of two nationalities, Arab and Kurd; Arabic will be the official language of the Arab region, and Kurdish that of the Kurdish region.[57]

Seventh, UN Security Council Resolution 1483 ended the ill-considered regime of economic sanctions that had been imposed by the Security Council following Iraq's invasion of Kuwait in 1990, and which itself contributed to human rights violations in Iraq. It is to be hoped that that source of human rights violations has gone for good.

Notes

1. Said Aburish, *Saddam Hussein: The Politics of Revenge*, New York: Bloomsbury, 2000, p. 172.
2. UNICEF, Eric Hoskins, Consultant, Office of Emergency Programs, "The Impact of Sanctions: A Study of UNICEF's Perspective," 1999, available at ⟨http://www.unicef.org/emerg/Sanctions.htm⟩.
3. Amazia Baram, "The Ruling Political Elite in Ba'thi Iraq, 1968–1986: The Changing Features of a Collective Profile," *International Journal of Middle East Studies*, Vol. 21, No. 4, 1989, p. 447.
4. Ibid., p. 467.
5. Ernest Gellner, *Conditions of Liberty*, New York: Penguin Press, 1994, p. 137.
6. Samir Al-Khalil (Kanan Makiya), *Republic of Fear: The Inside Story of Saddam's Iraq*, New York: Pantheon Books, 1998, p. 128.
7. According to Makiya (*Republic of Fear*, p. 20), these include five agencies with over-lapping duties: *Jihaz a-Himaya al-Khas* (the President's Special Protection Apparatus); *Jihaz al-Mukhabarat al-'Ammah* (General Intelligence Apparatus); *Al-Istikhbarat al-'Askariyah* (Military Intelligence); *Mudiriyat al-Amn al-'Ammah* (General Security Directorate); and *Maktab al-Amn al-Qawmi* (Bureau of National Security).
8. Tareq Y. Ismael and Jacqueline S. Ismael, "Iraq's Interrupted Revolution," *Current History*, Vol. 84, No. 498, January 1985, p. 30.
9. Phebe Marr, *The Modern History of Iraq*, Boulder: Westview, 1985, p. 242.
10. Economic rent may be defined as the difference between the market price of a good or factor of production and its opportunity cost. Such states enjoy a strategic position that allows them to set oil prices well above the opportunity cost for the oil they are providing.
11. Dirk Vandewalle, "Islam in Algeria: Religion, Culture, and Opposition in a Rentier State," in John L. Esposito, ed., *Political Islam: Revolution, Radicalism or Reform?* Boulder: Lynne Rienner, 1997.
12. Juan Linz and Alfred Stepan, *Problems of Democratic Transitions and Consolidation*, Baltimore: Johns Hopkins University Press, 1996, pp. 51–54.
13. Zuhair al-Jaza'iri, "Ba'thist Ideology and Practice," in Fran Hazelton, ed., *Iraq since the Gulf War*, London: Zed, 1994, pp. 30–51.
14. Said K. Aburish, *Saddam Hussein: The Politics of Revenge*, London: Bloomsbury, 2000.
15. See Juan Linz and Alfred Stepan, particularly chapter 1.

16. Ibid., p. 61.
17. Isam Al-Khafaji, "War as a Vehicle for the Rise and Demise of a State-Controlled Society: The Case of Ba'thist Iraq," in Steven Heydemann, ed., *War, Institutions, and Social Change in the Middle East*, Berkeley: University of California Press, 2000, p. 281.
18. UN General Assembly Resolution A/RES/54/178 of 24 February 2000.
19. Amnesty International, *Country Report. Iraq: Victims of Systematic Repression*, AI-index: MDE 14/010/99.
20. Amnesty International, *Report 2001*, New York: Amnesty International, 2001, p. 131.
21. Amnesty International, "Iraq: Relentless Executions Must End," AI-index: MDE 14/004/2001, 05/04/2001.
22. "Iraq: Systematic Torture of Political Prisoners," AI-index: MDE 14/008/2001, 15/08/2001.
23. UN General Assembly, A/54/466, 14 October 1999, "Situation of Human Rights in Iraq," relating to the interim report by the Special Rapporteur of the Commission on Human Rights on the situation of human rights in Iraq.
24. Susan Sachs, "A Grim Graveyard Window on Hussein's Iraq," *New York Times*, Internet edition, 1 June 2003.
25. Al-Khafaji, "War as a Vehicle for the Rise and Demise of a State-Controlled Society: The Case of Ba'thist Iraq," in Steven Heydemann, ed., *War, Institutions and Social Change in the Middle East*, Berkeley: University of California Press, 2000, p. 259.
26. Marion Farouk Sluglett and Peter Sluglett, *Iraq since 1958*, New York: I.B. Tauris, 1990.
27. Ibid., pp. 74–76.
28. See Abbas Alnasrawi, "Economic Devastation, Underdevelopment and Outlook," in Fran Hazelton, ed., *Iraq Since the Gulf War*, London: Zed, 1994, pp. 73–74.
29. Abbas Alnasrawi, *The Economy of Iraq: Oil, Wars, Destruction of Development and Prospects 1950–2010*, Westport: Greenwood Press, 1994, pp. 152–153.
30. Alnasrawi, *The Economy of Iraq*, p. 152.
31. W. Thom Workman, *The Social Origins of the Iran–Iraq War*, Boulder: Lynne Rienner, 1994, p. 16.
32. Al-Khalil (Makiya), p. xxx.
33. Majid Khadduri, *The Gulf War: The Origins and Implications of the Iraq–Iran Conflict*, New York: Oxford University Press, 1988.
34. Majid Khadduri and Edmund Ghareeb, *War in the Gulf 1990–1991: The Iraq–Kuwait Conflict and Its Implications*, Oxford University Press, 1997, p. 194.
35. Patrick Tyler, "An Open Secret is Laid Bare at Mass Grave in Iraqi Marsh," *New York Times*, Internet edition, 14 May 2003.
36. US Committee for Refugees (USCR), *2001, Country Report: Iraq* [Internet] and US Department of State (US DOS), 25 February 2000, *1999 Country Report on Human Rights Practices: Iraq* [Internet].
37. Amnesty International (AI), "Introduction," 24 November 1999.
38. Ibid, and Iraqi National Congress, 20 May 2001.
39. See Edmund Ghareeb, *The Kurdish Question in Iraq*, Syracuse: Syracuse University Press, 1981.
40. Khadduri and Ghareeb, pp. 200–201.
41. Stephen C. Pelletiere, "A War Crime or an Act of War?", *New York Times*, Internet edition, 31 January 1991.
42. US Committee for Refugees (USCR), *World Refugee Survey 2000*, "Country Report: Iraq," Washington, DC, 2000, p. 187; and Chris Dammers, "Iraq," in Janie Hampton, ed., *Internally Displaced People: A Global Survey*, London: Earthscan, 1998, pp. 180–185.
43. See *Bureaucracy of Repression: The Iraqi Government in Its Own Words*, New York: Middle East Watch, 1994, pp. 17–19.

44. See *The Anfal Campaign in Iraqi Kurdistan: The Destruction of Koreme*, New York: Middle East Watch and Physicians for Human Rights, 1993.
45. Amnesty International, *Report 2001*, p. 132.
46. UNICEF, "The Impact of Sanctions."
47. Ibid., 7.
48. Roger Normand, "Iraqi Sanctions, Human Rights and Humanitarian Law," Middle East Report (Merip), Summer 1997, p. 2, also available online at ⟨http://www.merip.org/mer/mer200/normand.htm⟩.
49. UNICEF, *South Center Mortality Survey – Full Report*; Chapter 8: "Infant and Child Mortality," 11/08/01, p. 5, also available online at ⟨http://www.unicef.org/iraq/library/sou-ful/chapt8.pdf⟩.
50. UNICEF, *Iraq: Under-five Mortality*, 05/29/01, also available online at ⟨http://www.unicef.org/receval/iraqr.html⟩.
51. UNICEF, *Results of the 1999 Iraq Child and Maternal Mortality Surveys*, "Survey of the 15 Southern Governorates," pp. 15–16, also available online at ⟨http://www.unicef.org/reseval/irqr.html⟩.
52. UNICEF, "The Impact of Sanctions," p. 4.
53. Denis Halliday, "Economic Sanctions on the People of Iraq: First Degree Murder or Manslaughter?" *AAUG Monitor*, Vol. 15, No. 1, Spring 2000.
54. John Mueller and Karl Mueller, "The Methodology of Mass Destruction: Assessing Threats in the New World Order," *Journal of Strategic Studies*, Vol. 23, No. 1, March 2000, pp. 163–187.
55. As cited in Howard Schneider, "Little by Little, Iraq Shows Signs of Economic Life," *Washington Post*, 17 May 2002, p. A01.
56. Abbas Alnasrawi, *The Economy of Iraq: Oil, Wars, Destruction of Development and Prospects, 1950–2010*, Westport: Greenwood Press, 1994.
57. See Edmund Gharib, "The Kurdish Issue," in Shams Inati, ed., *Iraq: Its History, People, and Politics*, New York: Humanity Books, 2003.

10

Exploring the dynamics of human rights and reform: Iran, Pakistan, and Turkey

Mahmood Monshipouri[1]

The establishment of institutional infrastructure and some semblance of the rule of law are necessary prerequisites to creating a market economy and to initiating economic reform more generally. On the other hand, the protection and promotion of human rights, as well as the building of a civil society, are highly relevant to generating political and social capital. Finding the right balance, however, poses a special challenge to transitional societies and their leaders. These premises raise several fundamental questions. How do these economic and political dynamics interact? Under what circumstances does one set of priorities override the other? Who benefits or suffers from reforms? And what strategy and pace of reform is most effective in each setting? To frame and address these questions properly, we have to contextualize the prospects of reform and human rights in each country or region by examining political institutions, economic structures and interests, cultural identities, and civil and regional conflicts.

As in all transitional countries, economic and political reforms – or their absence – have created a variety of modern tensions and dilemmas for the Middle Eastern region. Iran, Pakistan, and Turkey, which represent the region's non-Arab Muslim countries, have marked similarities but also notable differences. The selection of these cases is justified by minimizing the ethnic factor (Arabism) while focusing on the parameters that closely relate to the state of human rights and the dynamics of reform. Iran is a *rentier* state; Pakistan is a poor country, with heavy de-

218

pendence on raw materials such as crude oil; and Turkey is a fully fledged newly industrialized country.

The progress toward full democratization in these countries has been hampered by historical and contemporary forces, with many concerns regarding state–society relations hanging in the balance. All three countries have struggled to maintain an equilibrium between Islamic and modernizing pressures. The contest between secularists and Islamists (as in Pakistan and Turkey) and the divisions among Islamists themselves (as in Iran) over the inclusion of Western principles of law and political practice in Islamic society have complicated political processes in these countries.[2] While searching for an Islamic identity, these Muslim societies have been undergoing transformation. Furthermore, the difficulties of economic reform are widespread in all three countries. The rise of political Islam owes much to the painful process of economic restructuring, as well as to the lack of a social safety net for the poor, who have been adversely affected by neoliberal economic reforms. Socio-economic and ethnic disparities have further complicated the effective operation of political reform. In all three cases, non-governmental organizations (NGOs) have had limited success in addressing human rights concerns. Caught between Islamic and secular forces, NGOs have been unable to take the initiatives necessary to improve human rights conditions.

In this chapter, I first describe dominant political institutions in Iran, Pakistan, and Turkey, in an attempt to explain how such institutions influence human rights practices. Iran is a modern theocracy with an elected president; Pakistan is ruled by a military government; and Turkey is a secular parliamentary democracy. The key political actors in all three countries either have close connections with the military or themselves control instruments of violent coercion. In Iran, the supreme leader – not the president – is the most important political player. In Pakistan, the chief executive (who currently represents the military) and the president are the main players on the political scene. In Turkey's political structure, the prime minister, the president, and the military are the key political actors.

I then examine the impact of economic structure and interest groups on the dynamics of reform or the lack thereof. Economic reform has come to be synonymous with an increased emphasis on private investment and an opening to international markets. Policy makers in Iran, Pakistan, and Turkey have found economic reform a daunting task – one that involves serious political challenges, especially when the public sector continues to carry a heavy weight in the economy.[3] All three countries face the challenge of implementing economic liberalization in the face of political fragmentation and cultural politics, ethnic politics, interest group resistance, and endemic corruption.

Examination of cultural identity and its impact on the practice of human rights reveals complexities of different kinds involved in the dynamics of reform. Middle Eastern people, like people anywhere, have become increasingly preoccupied with the issue of identity and encounter many diverse problems in their relations with their states.[4] In their struggle against authoritarian forces, these societies have reached a new level of participation and emphasis on using their own specific cultural and identity issues.[5] In all three countries, cultural identity has assumed the prominence of a new *Zeitgeist*.

Finally, I investigate the impact of local and regional conflicts on the notion of justice and order in these societies. The internal and external conflicts in these countries have left lasting imprints on these societies and their transition toward democracy. In some (such as Iran and Turkey), ethnic strife around the Kurdish issue and the subsequent conflicts have had a devastating impact on minority rights. The Iran–Iraq War (1980–1988) fuelled revolutionary fervour in many fundamental ways and was a key reason why the realization of an open society, economy, and polity was delayed for as long as it was. Pakistan's internal strife, combined with the regional insecurity and dispute with India over Kashmir, has over the years complicated the prospects of democratization there, while paving the way for the perpetuation of the interests of feudal and tribal élite groups, for the slow growth of civil society, and for burgeoning military–bureaucratic rule.

The chapter concludes that human rights abuses in these countries are, in great measure, the result of the absence of institutionalized means and processes of democratization, a lack of accountable political order, inter-élite and cultural cleavages, unbalanced state–society relations, and poor liberalization strategies. The role of religion remains unclear: Islam is not as institutionalized in the politics of Pakistan and Turkey as it is in Iranian politics; it is not clear whether Islam hinders or advances the prospects for democratization. The Kurdish issue has provoked state repression in both Iran and Turkey. Cooperation on the Kashmir question eludes not only Pakistani and Indian leaders but also Kashmir's own people, despite the fact that the conflict holds potentially dangerous implications for the region. The link between economic and political reform remains somewhat unpredictable in all three countries. Personalistic politics continue to override constitutional politics at some level. The absence of an independent judiciary and the continuing military intervention in politics present major obstacles to democratization in these countries.

In all three countries, human rights violations can be explained largely by leaders' employment of the instruments of violent coercion. The availability to political élites of coercive powers and institutions – the military, paramilitary, and police – and the absence of accountability to any higher institution correlate strongly with existing repressive policies. Subcultural cleavages, economic conditions and policies, identity politics, and local and regional conflicts, although listed among principal constraints on the respect for human rights, can be dealt with effectively if proper political institutions are in place. This is not to discredit the significance of such factors as ethnic diversity or local and regional conflicts in these coun-tries; it is only to argue that democratization and observance of human rights are, to a large degree, the function of calculated acts of political élites. I end the chapter by analysing the consequences of variation in human rights practices and advancing policy recommendations.

Human rights practices

A comparative examination of human rights conditions in Iran, Pakistan, and Turkey reveals both similarities and differences. All three countries hold regular elections and display other signs of democracy. In Iran, de-spite fair and free elections in recent years, the unelected supreme leader controls the levers of power, including the military, the intelligence ser-vices, and the judiciary. The supreme leader can override parliamentary majorities in the name of the country's national interests, as conceived by the conservative clerical establishment. This, in effect, can neutralize any institutionalized gains for the legal protection of human rights.[6] The re-cent waves of assault on the free press, followed by jailings of reformist journalists (sometimes called "apostate") and closures of reformist news-papers and magazines (referred to as "traitors") on charges of defaming the security forces and threatening national security, have shown the in-herent flaws in Iran's theocratic state.

Although the constitution of the Islamic Republic guarantees women equality both legally and politically, patriarchal social relations account for de facto inequalities throughout the society. Extrajudicial executions of dissidents and the mistreatment of human rights lawyers are rampant. The Kurds, the largest ethnic minority, suffer discrimination and the Baha'is, the most victimized religious minority, remain subject to harass-ment and unfair prosecution.

The prospects for improvement of human rights are even bleaker in Pakistan, a poor country with shallow roots as a nation-state, great ethnic diversity, and strong feudal traditions. The armed forces have con-sistently shaped the nation's political landscape through direct or behind-the-scenes intervention in domestic and foreign affairs. A combination of religious intolerance, poverty, and many local and regional alliances forged by feudals, generals, and bureaucrats has blocked any improvements in the country's human rights conditions. De facto inequality and low literacy rates have also stymied political and legal progress of women's human rights. Government officials continue to demonstrate a bias against women by failing to investigate egregious human rights violations, including "honour killings" of several hundred girls and women and the trafficking of women.[7]

Respect for civil and political rights has deteriorated in the years following the military coup on 12 October 1999, which deposed Prime Minister Nawaz Sharif and brought General Pervez Musharraf to power. Musharraf's administration moved to neutralize political parties through the application of laws governing terrorism, sedition, and public order, and through the establishment of a powerful extraconstitutional "accountability" bureau.[8] The US campaign against terrorism in the post-September 11 era has reinforced Prime Minister Musharraf's tenure of office. The disputed region of Jammu and Kashmir, the only Muslim-majority state in India, has turned into an element of struggle for power between state and central government élites.[9]

Turkey's human rights situation is no better than those of Iran and Pakistan. The military – the most dominating force in the country's politics – continues to be a factor in forestalling reform, especially as it relates to freedom of expression. The army has reasserted its power in the selection of presidential candidates, justifying its intrusion on the grounds that it is a guardian of the republic against separatism and religious extremism.[10] The army's opposition to religious extremism has led to the campaign to restrict the wearing of headscarves for religious reasons in educational settings. This campaign, waged in the name of secularism, has deprived many Muslim women of having access to education, both temporarily and permanently. Others have been suspended or discharged from employment in teaching or health care.[11]

Evaluating the human rights conditions of women in Turkey is difficult. Women have had the right to vote and the right to run for elective office since the 1920s. Their literacy and professional employment rates are higher than those of most Middle Eastern countries. In rural areas, however, a different situation prevails: female literacy rates are low and fertility rates are high. The practice of contractual religious marriage is widespread.[12]

The most flagrant human rights violations in Turkey also relate to extrajudicial killings, disappearance, indefinite detention, death in custody, and torture – particularly under emergency laws or the Anti-Terrorism Law. The Kurds, the largest ethnic minority in Turkey, have endured the most severe socio-economic privation and official discrimination. The European Court of Human Rights has repeatedly found Turkey responsible for such violations. Moreover, the European Union (EU) has predicated its economic aid to Turkey on progress on Kurdish cultural rights and the economy in the south-east, where many Kurds reside.[13] Human rights groups in the United States have protested against the pending sale of 145 attack helicopters to Turkey, on the grounds that this class of equipment has been widely used to commit human rights violations such as "disappearance" and arbitrary killings.[14] In what follows, I examine the impacts on the practice of human rights of political institutions, economic structures and interests, cultural identity, and local and regional conflicts in Iran, Pakistan, and Turkey.

Iran

As a modern theocracy, Iran's key political institutions have been built around the supreme leader Ayatollah Sayed Ali Khamenei, a selected head of the nation, and President Mohammad Khatemi, an elected head of the government. The dual system of governing has enlarged the chasm dividing the country's political factions. Under the Iranian constitution, the ultimate authority rests with the supreme leader, who effectively controls the country's police and security forces – the military, the national police, the Ministry of Intelligence, the Basij Paramilitary, the Ministry of Information, and the Revolutionary Guards. Additionally, the supreme leader controls the judiciary and national broadcasting, including state radio and television, and selects the key members of the Council of Guardians, a watchdog body capable of blocking legislation it deems unfit for the Islamic Republic. This division of authority has become known as the mixed system of Islamism and republicanism – that is, a mixture of theocracy and electoral democracy. The Islamic Republic's contradictions have stemmed largely from the lack of clarity as to who actually directs the state and who controls the levers of power.

The first decade of revolution witnessed a reign of terror backed by Islamic tribunals that executed thousands of people – including the ex-Shah's army officers, and intellectuals and political leaders, civilian as well as military. The outbreak of war with Iraq, however, overshadowed the existence of wide-ranging internal conflicts between different political factions. The Iran–Iraq War (1980–1988) proved to be, in the words of one expert, one of the most intense and costly wars of the twentieth century in terms of casualties, destruction, expense, and duration.[15] By the mid-1980s, the war had degenerated into a campaign of massive Iranian human-wave attacks on Iraqi targets. With US military support and intelligence assistance, Iraq managed to resist Iranian attacks – hence, the prolongation of the war. Predictably, the continuation of the conflict without any definitive winner made Iran war-weary.[16] The war underscored the Islamic Republic's desperate need to put its economic and institutional house in order. Rafsanjani's presidency (1989–1997) marked a new era, one in which the policy priority was given to the reconstruction of the economy after eight years of war. This direction required the adoption of several liberalizing measures and constitutional reforms. Rafsanjani's cabinet was dominated by technocrats who sought to revive the private sector and attract foreign direct investment.[17] The failure of economic reforms paved the way for the 1997 landslide electoral victory of Mohammad Khatami and his agenda for political reform.

Internally, Iranian political life has been dominated by hyperpoliti-cization and deep ambiguity. The seemingly muddled nature of Iranian politics, Jon B. Alterman argues, is accentuated by the absence of formal party politics and structures. Instead, Alterman continues, "fronts," "as-sociations," and "societies" seem to conduct political campaigns for can-didates and mobilize popular support.[18] The hyperpolitical nature of Iranian society notwithstanding, political machines are poorly organized. No strong and direct connection exists between voters and elected offi-cials. Furthermore, conservatives and reformists seem to have achieved an uneasy *modus vivendi* to share power, compete, and cooperate where common ground can be found. This tacit agreement, although unsat-isfactory, remains superior to any apparent alternative.[19] Under these circumstances, the combination of intense competition and pragmatic cooperation prevents a political system from falling into rancour and division.[20]

Elections, parliamentary and presidential, have been regular features of post-revolutionary Iran. Although subject to political and religious manipulations, elections have still taken place, and a restricted democ-racy (or, more accurately, an electoral illiberal democracy) has pre-vailed.[21] Put differently, pluralism and dissidence are noticeably lacking. The concept of Islamic government under the rule of the supreme leader (*velayat-e faqih*, guardianship of the jurisconsult), along with the power of the Council of Guardians to veto any politicians, has more often than not led to clerical repression.[22]

Many clerics and laymen have questioned the way religion has been turned into a political ideology.[23] Ayatollah Hossein Ali Montazeri, a high-ranking political and religious cleric, has argued that, according to the constitution of the Islamic Republic, "the basis of government at all levels is the votes of the people, and the ruling authorities, even the *vali-e faqih*, are elected by the people."[24] Likewise, Montazeri draws attention to Article 6 of the constitution: "In the Islamic Republic of Iran, the af-fairs of the country must be conducted with reliance on the votes of the public and through elections...."[25]

Intra-élite cleavages over whether clerics should govern the political system and, if so, to what extent, are becoming pronounced. Contrary to the widely held perception that the Iranian clerics constitute a unified and homogeneous social stratum and that they are universally inimical to the separation of Church and State, they are deeply divided. In fact, a small faction of the clerics now dominates the state apparatus, indicating obvious divisions within the clerical hierarchy.[26]

The clerics have been extremely careful to initiate economic liberalization without political reforms. Even so, the theocracy's collective leadership has created a regime more tolerant in some ways than that of the late Shah. For instance, Iran's parliament today is "a far cry from the rubber stamp that existed during the rule of the Shah."[27] Although Iran's political institutions provide a setting for managing factional rivalries peacefully, the fact remains that the institutions have themselves been manipulated and in some instances subverted by the ruling élites.[28]

In the first decade since revolution, the ratios of real government expenditures to the real GDP decreased to a low of 9 per cent in 1988 and then rose to a high of 24 per cent in 1993. Ratios of government revenues to real GDP followed the same trend during the period. This decline was caused largely by the decrease in oil revenues, which in turn resulted from the ravages of the eight years of the Iran–Iraq War (1980–1988) and the national policy of economic independence and self-sufficiency.[29] The government's system of subsidy, including subsidies for basic commodities and hidden subsidies for gasoline (petrol), proved insufficient. The recent proposal to start direct subsidies to low-income families has been comparatively effective. This system, however, runs into inefficiencies and corruption in government circles.[30]

Income inequalities and poverty intensified during Iran's Second Development Plan (1995–2000). Published records, according to one expert, indicate that 20 per cent of the people own 80 per cent of the country's wealth; the share of the bottom 10 per cent is 1.5 per cent. Approximately 20 per cent of the Iranian people go hungry; 15 per cent of five-year-old children are shorter than normal, and 11 per cent are underweight as a result of malnutrition.[31] Throughout the Second Plan, the public sector expanded well beyond the previous period. The recipients of government subsidies and rent-seeking beneficiaries of state largess have resisted the public sector's downsizing. Several dozen parastatal *bonyads* (Islamic charitable foundations), which pay virtually no taxes but have access to public perks and often are not subject to government regulation, continue to exert control over the economy through their connections with the country's clerical *nomenklatura*.[32]

Meanwhile, the economy's dependence on oil and gas has intensified. Because of continued public investment in oil and gas exploration and in refining, petrochemicals, steel, and aluminium, the state reinforced its assets rather than selling them via a consistent privatization programme.

Similarly, the total national budget increased at an average annual rate of 37.2 per cent. The public sector absorbed more than half of the banking-sector credits. The unemployment rate worsened from the official 9.4 per cent rate prevailing in 1995 to 16.5 per cent in 2000, the highest since 1949.[33]

Despite assigning a high priority to political liberalization, the Khatami administration lacked a coherent and effective economic blueprint in its first term (1997–2001). During this time, both the process of liberalization and its implementation lacked transparency and consistency. Fiscal, trade, and exchange policies were fluid, and annual resource allocation was regularly influenced by rent-seeking elements.[34] Furthermore, two interest groups have opposed economic reforms – namely, radical *mullahs*, who are in charge of both the Basiji (mobilization) corps and the Islamic *anjomans* (associations), who have infiltrated the high ranks of the bureaucracy, and the "conservatives" with strong financial and blood ties to the *bazzar*, who have traditionally represented the interests of landlords and the urban bourgeoisie.[35]

In Iran, the difficulty associated with the issue of national identity is endemic in a modern theocratic state that lacks a viable way of dealing with emerging demands for a new social contract with its citizens. A generation of those born and raised under the Islamic revolutionary regime now contests the theocratic establishment by supporting the reform-minded politicians, journalists, parliamentary deputies, academics, and intellectuals. According to some experts, because of a combination of a revolution against tyranny, the eight-year war with Iraq, and the subsequent massive politicization, Iranian political culture has become secularized. The youth's demands for political freedoms and the women's push for the relaxation of social restrictions are supported by both reform-oriented clerics and laymen who point to a more enlightened and modern application of Islamic laws. That is to say, an unstoppable process of secularization of religion has occurred, pushing social debates, individuals, and their rights to the forefront.

Not surprisingly, the burgeoning respect for the rule of law has compelled the conservatives, who control the instruments of violent coercion, to resort to the judicial process to punish their reformist opponents.[36] The economic and cultural liberalization of the post-Khomeini era (1989 –present) has led to both an increasing gap between rich and poor and the emergence of a youth subculture and way of thinking that have "flouted the ascetic norms of the regime."[37]

Perhaps nothing has illustrated such disenchantment better than the framing of grievances and demands via student unrest. The 1999 student unrest took the clerical establishment by surprise. The language of the students was the language of rights, citizenship, the rule of law, and international human rights.[38] Instead of adopting tactics to adjust to the modernizing demands of students, the theocratic state chose to repress the movement, rendering it impossible to mobilize mass support for its objectives in the future. Ever since, a climate of fear and repression, reminiscent of the pre-Khatami era, has cast its shadow over the whole country.

Despite these political and legal set-backs, as well as a poor economy, the landslide re-election of Khatami for a second term (2001–2005), on 8 June 2001, proved to be a referendum on the nature of the Islamic Republic. The re-election of Khatami, who won 77 per cent of votes, demonstrated that the public has not grown apathetic since the previous election and has, in fact, embraced the principles of Khatami's reform.[39] Khatami's popularity has decreased dramatically as the reform process has stalled. During November 2002, student groups in Hamedan and Tehran protested against the blasphemy sentences on reformist professor Hashem Aghajari (who, in a speech in August 2002, had challenged the rule of hard-line clerics). Using this occasion, the students expressed their deep frustration with the slow pace of reform pledged by President Khatami, whose broad mandate has been consistently ignored by the conservative establishment.

Pakistan

Since the partition of the British raj into India and Pakistan and the creation of the latter as a Muslim country in 1947, Pakistan has undergone a turbulent process of nation building, seeking to create consensus and institutions sufficient for stability. The struggle to establish parliamentary democracy in a federal setting has been hampered by inter-ethnic strife, fragmented élites, praetorian rule, and regional and global influences. Four times since 1947 (in 1958, 1969, 1977, and 1999), military officers have administered governments through either martial law or caretaker mechanisms, seeking to gain legitimacy en route to nation building. In the latest military take-over, the parliamentary government of Nawaz Sharif was suspended on 12 October 1999; two days later, General Pervez Musharraf declared a state of emergency and issued the Provisional Constitutional Order (PCO).

Instead of promoting the tradition of civilian supremacy bequeathed by Great Britain, civilian rulers have often relied on the military to preserve power. The military, which is dominated by Punjabis and represents landed and industrial interests, regards its dominance of Pakistan politics as vital to any attempt to safeguard the country's territorial integrity in the face of perplexing ethnic, linguistic, and regional diversity. Military and non-military governments have appealed to Islam to maintain their legitimacy and uphold different political, economic, and class interests.[40]

The economic situation in Pakistan was overwhelmed by the country's debt crisis. Pakistan has a foreign debt of $38 billion, and its domestic economy is in deep recession.[41] Investors have closely followed the controversy created by Religious Minister Mahmood Ghazi in January 2001, when he said that the government would fix interest (*riba*) by 1 July 2001, in accordance with a Supreme Court ruling on Islamicizing the economy. Thus far, General Pervez Musharraf has placated militant Islamic fundamentalist parties, who are keen on the creation of an Islamic system.[42]

Other studies have shown that Pakistan spends 67 per cent of its budget to service interest repayment on its massive external debt.[43] Many aspects of the economy at the end of 1999 showed no sign of economic progress. Aside from exports, Pakistan's two other sources of foreign exchange – foreign investment and remittances from overseas Pakistani workers – have also shown a drastic decline. The poor performance of Sharif's government led to the 12 October 1999 military coup. The country's ruling élites owed $4 billion in non-performing and defaulted loans to state-owned banks at the time of the coup.[44] The military's own huge budget raises serious questions about the prospects of reviving the economy. Preoccupied with a fully fledged nuclear weapons programme, the military cannot afford to cut its budget unless there is peace with India – a prospect that remains unrealistic for the foreseeable future. Meanwhile, these dire economic straits have fuelled Islamic militancy.[45]

To these difficulties could be added other formidable economic problems. During 2000, the country remained vulnerable to regular price hikes with all the features of an uneven economy. International monetary institutions contributed, however indirectly, to this unevenness by their insistence on the withdrawal of price subsidies. Corruption was also pervasive; and the problems of governance, a growing population, and low literacy rate stunted the country's economic growth. Before the end of the year, the IMF and other IFIs allowed new loans to Pakistan, which prevented a complete economic breakdown while encouraging the military regime to contemplate an ambitious privatization programme.[46]

In Pakistan, the identity problem has reached crisis proportions. Because Pakistan came into being as a separate political identity to provide an independent homeland for Muslims on the Indian subcontinent, the religious identity of the community and the political legitimacy of the state have become inextricably intertwined. Ever since its creation, Islam has been a common thread holding diverse groups together. It continues to bind the country: in the face of economic adversities, Islam has been dominant in bridging ethnic differences and neutralizing subnationalistic proclivities. The future of Pakistan seems inseparably linked to a re-assertion of its Islamic government and society.[47]

The emphasis on the Islamic state serves both ideological and nation-alistic purposes; therefore, it empowers the government to stabilize socio-economic conditions, distribute scarce resources equitably, and generate a nationalistic passion for the country – even if that passion is filtered through a spiritual devotion that surpasses the nation-state.[48] Yet Paki-stani leaders have never systematically laid down the legal basis for an Islamic state, and Pakistanis have always struggled with the meaning of their Islamic identity. The chasm between what the Pakistani people de-sire and what their leaders have in mind has been unbridgeable: whereas religious conservatives advocate an Islamic state based on Islamic law (*Shari'a*), Pakistani leaders generally have adopted the British parlia-mentary model of political development. Such an ambiguity illustrates the nature of the ideological quandary that has been present throughout Pakistan's history.[49] Islam and democracy have often existed more in form than in substance, more influenced by than influencing the country's socio-political realities.

The Indo-Pakistan conflict over the sovereignty of Kashmir for more than half a century has resulted in serious human rights abuses. The ac-cession of the princely states to India or Pakistan at the time of parti-tion was not resolved entirely in 1947. Although Muslims in the princely state of Jammu and Kashmir (generally referred to as Kashmir) have constituted a majority of the state's population, Kashmir has been ad-ministered by Hindu rulers. The subsequent Indo-Pakistan war of 1947–1948 over Kashmir ended with a cease-fire brokered by the United Na-tions. Kashmir was divided by a UN line (also known as "the Line of Control"), and a 1949 UN Security Council resolution provided for a plebiscite to be held under UN auspices to decide the issue of accession. However, India has rejected the idea of plebiscite and tensions have re-sumed. In 1965, India and Pakistan fought another war over Kashmir, without finding any political solution to the problem. The third Indo-Pakistan war (1971), although fought mainly over East Pakistan (Ban-gladesh ever since), was also concentrated along the Kashmir cease-fire line.

Following the end of this war, under the Simla Agreement of 1972 both parties agreed not to use force in Kashmir;[50] however, this agreement disguised a much more complex and variegated picture. At times, the dispute appeared to have faded away; nevertheless, after an anti-Indian uprising in 1989 and the nuclear tests of 1998, the dispute became more volatile and potentially explosive.[51] Today, extreme atrocities, collusion with terrorists, and drug smuggling constitute routine police action in

Kashmir. The police themselves have become heavily involved in collud-
ing with criminals; committing human rights abuses such as beating, torture, and rape in police stations; and attacking and looting villages.[52]

Increasingly, Pakistanis themselves have become disenchanted with the
military. Members of the *mohajir* community of Sindh Province – who
have repeatedly been the subject of army attack, terror, and persecution
– have questioned the integrity of the Pakistani military. Contrasting
their plight with that of the Kashmiri Muslims, they have voiced a major
concern.[53] For both Pakistan and India, the issue of Kashmir is inexora-
bly connected to their sense of strengths, sovereignty, and security.[54]
Because of the threat of war over Kashmir, both Indian and Pakistani
leaders have relied on nuclear deterrence. Moreover, Musharraf's close
cooperation with the Bush administration, in an attempt to hunt down al-
Qaeda terrorists and to dismantle the Taliban regime, weakened civilian
institutions and resulted in growing military interference in national politics. As a result, substantial institutional resources have been placed in
the hands of the executive branch.

Turkey

The present government of Turkey is described as a republican parliamentary democracy. The executive branch's responsibilities are divided
between the chief of state, President Ahmed Necdet Sezer (since 16 May
2000), and the head of government, Prime Minister Abdullah Gul (since
3 November 2002). Prime Minister Gul, the leader of the Justice and
Development Party (AKP), won a landslide victory. The AKP received
an outright majority, with 363 of 550 seats in parliament. Gul has pledged
changes in laws to expand freedom of religion and expression, to promote a more transparent government, and to expedite liberalization programmes.

Turkey remains a divided country on religious matters, a problem
largely attributable to Ataturk's secular legacy (1923–1938). After the
creation of the modern Turkish Republic, Ataturk abolished the caliph-
ate and gave women the right to vote in parliamentary elections and to
become members of parliament.[55] His westernizing reforms split Turkey
between those who advocated secular values and those who desired a
return to Islamic principles and institutions. Beneath the surface and
apparent stability, Turkey remains a troubled country.[56] As a major
beneficiary of multi-party politics since 1946, Islamic parties are regular
participants in Turkey's political process. The Islamic-oriented National
Salvation party, which later formed the Welfare Party (the *Refah*) and
forged a coalition government to rule Turkey for the period 1996–1998,
was declared illegal and banned on 16 January 1998. Its deputies joined

the newly formed Virtue Party (the *Fazilet*). Before being banned, Refah took part in three coalition governments between 1973 and 1980. From 1991 to 1995, however, a coalition of the centre-right True Path Party and the leftist Social Democratic Populist Party ruled Turkey. During that period, tensions caused by the economy and the Kurdish crisis in the south-east increased Islam's political voice and revitalized Islamic movements.[57]

In the late 1995 parliamentary elections, the Refah Party won with 21.3 per cent of the vote; by June 1996 it had become the senior partner of the governing bloc in parliament. After the formation of the coalition government, media pundits routinely speculated on the military's role in the country's stability and order. Under heavy pressure from the military (which exerted considerable influence over the political transformation), Prime Minister Necmettin Erbakan resigned on 18 June 1997, after eleven turbulent months in office. Then-President Demirel granted Motherland Party leader Mesut Yilmaz approval to form a new government on 30 June 1997. Yilmaz was the prime minister until his government was subjected to a vote of no confidence on 25 November 1998. In June of 1999, a coalition government led by Prime Minister Bulent Ecevit of the Democratic Left (DSP), which included the far-right National Action Party (MHP), won a vote of confidence. As mentioned above, in the national election of 3 November 2003, Abdullah Gul became the country's new prime minister.

The deep roots of military intervention in politics (1960, 1971, and 1980) and the military's regular behind-the-scenes powers continue to render precarious the realization of human rights in Turkey. During the military rule of the early 1980s, all civil and political rights were suspended. Restrictions were gradually lifted in 1983, when multi-party parliamentary elections were held. Since 1987, Turkey has become a party to various international human rights conventions, including the European Convention of Human Rights, the European Convention Against Torture, and the UN Convention Against Torture.

Turkey has also recognized the compulsory jurisdiction of the European Court of Human Rights; has signed the UN Convention on the Rights of the Child, the revised European Social Code, and the Paris Charter; and has accepted the Ninth Additional Protocol to the European Convention on Human Rights. Nevertheless, many cases of torture and ill-treatment (which are reported in annual reports of Human Rights Watch) illustrate the widespread nature of human rights abuses in Turkey. The military, still an overriding force in the country's politics, continues to be a factor in restricting civil rights, such as freedom of expression. Many abuses are reported by detainees accused of theft and other common criminal offences, as well as by those interrogated under the Anti-

Terror Law.[58] During the year 2000, the European Court of Human Rights found Turkey responsible for "disappearance, extra-judicial execution, death in custody, torture, and suppression of freedom of expression in numerous new decisions."[59]

On balance, as Middle East observers argue, the military has been more instrumental in building state apparatuses than in creating strong economies. By strengthening the state apparatus and the public sector, military rulers have structured the political arena along corporatist models: "Order has taken precedence over mobilization, organic unity over pluralism, discipline over spontaneity."[60] The combination of war and military rule has been the major barrier to the genesis of more liberal political practices, if not to democracy itself. Further, the region's lingering and unresolved conflicts keep the military in the thick of the political fray and enable it to exert claims to substantial resources.[61]

Turkey's economic liberalization policies were accompanied by little or no political democratization. Income distribution became less equitable as a result of years of liberalization. Despite a preference throughout the 1980s for restructuring of the metropolitan municipalities, the Turkish political system remained largely centralist.[62] The greater emphasis on the private sector notwithstanding, by the mid-1990s the public enterprises produced about one-third of the total output in the manufacturing industry.[63] During the 1980s and early 1990s, foreign and domestic debt rose sharply, the public deficit increased, high rates of inflation became chronic, and privatization proved problematic. These difficulties became even more pronounced under the True Path Party–Socialist Democratic Populist Party coalition government that ensued, forcing Turkey once again to adopt strict stabilization programmes in the spring of 1994.[64] The economic crises of late 2000 and early 2001 demonstrated that the austerity programmes, rising unemployment, and an increase in the number of companies going bankrupt have led to loss of faith in the liberalizing measures.[65]

More recently, Turkey has announced a package of austerity measures aimed at winning between $10 billion and $12 billion in new foreign loans and restoring confidence in the country's battered economy.[66] To this end, the government will cut spending by 9 per cent and freeze hiring by the state's bloated bureaucracy. This means that the lira, the country's currency, will continue to float and the government will not protect the currency. Many people in Turkey have protested against such an approach, fearing that it will lead to the doubling of prices and hundreds of thousands of lay-offs.[67]

Since the late 1990s, Turkey has intensified its lucrative commercial and financial ties with Europe and is now regarded as one of the world's ten most promising emerging markets by the US government. Turkey, however, has yet to display full compliance with the Copenhagen rules (which are guidelines established in 1993 requiring EU applicants to build Western-style democratic institutions in an effort to guarantee the rule of law, individual rights, and protection of minorities).[68]

The military's economic power base figures prominently in the country's economic configuration. The powerful, activist, officer corps holds a firm grip on certain aspects of the economy. Eric Rouleau describes this situation as "mercantile militarism." Rouleau writes: "[I]t is the chief of staff, not the prime minister, the cabinet, or the parliament, who oversees arms production and procurement (which do not figure in the state budget). It is also the general staff that draws up the annual budget of the armed forces (even though it absorbs more than a third of state revenues)."[69] Additionally, the military controls several industries, including the most lucrative one, OYAK, which is a vast conglomerate comprising some 30 enterprises in sectors as diverse as automobile manufacturing, cement works, food processing, pesticides, petroleum, tourism, insurance, banking, real estate, supermarkets, and high technology.

Despite its leaders' claims that secularism and democracy are the two fundamental concepts that bind the people together, the contradictions of the Turkish political system are obvious. The military is so powerful and ethnic diversity so little respected that some experts have called our attention to Turkey as "the great laboratory of Westernization in the world of Islam, and the epic battleground of resistance to it."[70] Others have argued that Turkey – at first glance, and better than any other country – dramatizes the paradox of Westernization. Yet a closer examination reveals that the real cultural clash is not between modernity and tradition but between contrasting visions of modernity. It is in such a context that the emergence in Turkey of multiple identities – such as Kurdish identity, Islamism, Kemalism, or pan-Turkism – must be seen.[71] Turkey appears to be the solution to preserving the right to cultural and ethnic diversity. Some observers, however, have warned that such diversity cannot come at the expense of Turkey's territorial integrity.[72]

Without a democratic framework in place, these multiple identities and cultural traits are becoming more explicit and harder to reconcile.[73] The Turkish state shows few signs of admitting the presence of alternative national identities.[74] Arguably, major economic progress and increased democratization in south-east Turkey are likely to alleviate some symptoms of the crisis. Ultimately, however, there is a consensus among experts that only a solution that underscores the ethnic character of the problem will be a lasting solution: "at a minimum that means a clear recognition of the existence of the Kurds as a culturally distinct identity, and recognition of the rights of Kurds to express their culture fully under a system of cultural autonomy."[75] Thus far, the state's repressive methods of coping with the quest for recognition by the Kurds (by far the country's largest non-Turkish-speaking group) have complicated and prolonged the Kurdish security problem, with no solution in sight in the immediate future.[76]

In south-eastern Turkey, many human rights violations have been directly linked to the Kurdish question. Since 1984, the war between the Turkish government and the Kurdish Workers' Party (Partiya Karkeren Kurdistan; PKK) has claimed over 30,000 lives.[77] The Kurdish question has become one of the most formidable challenges facing the Turkish Republic since its establishment (1923) and is certainly the key obstacle to its aspiration to full integration with the EU.[78] The Kurds have become increasingly disenchanted with the PKK: only a minority of the Kurds see the PKK as their main representative organ, and the majority do not desire a separate Kurdish state. A significant number of Kurdish people have integrated into Turkish society.[79] With the PKK militarily vanquished and its leader, Abdullah Ocalan, arrested, Turkey is expected to accelerate the process of democratization as well as the process of granting cultural rights to the Kurds. "In its relations with the European Union and international human rights bodies," experts concur, "Turkey's very defeat of the PKK rebellion makes it increasingly difficult to justify restrictions on cultural rights."[80]

The Turkish government has, to date, refused to sign either the (European) Framework Convention on Minorities or the European Charter for Regional or Minority Language. Recently, it signed the International Covenant on Civil and Political Rights, which addresses the issue of national minorities, but it is unclear whether the government will make a reservation to the document.[81] Europeanized secular élite groups, and religious elements who defend an "Eastern" way of life, constitute the opposite poles of a renewed cultural struggle to determine the country's future course. Opening up to the EU in order to gain recognition as a partner has failed to bring about reconciliation between the two sides.

Consequences of variation in human rights practices

The practice of human rights is far more difficult in poverty-stricken Pakistan than in Iran and Turkey. The efforts of the Pakistani government to promote the economic rights of its citizens are substantially hampered by the poverty level there. Yet, the prevailing climate of violence – as evidenced by widespread reports of terror, torture, and ill-treatment[82] in all three countries – proves that the protection of the rights of the integrity of the person is *not* necessarily related to the level of economic development. On the other hand, because of rampant poverty and corruption in their country, Pakistanis appear to have developed more tolerant attitudes toward the military coup.

There is less enthusiasm in Turkey and Iran for such an eventuality, despite the fact that both governments are subject to the overriding influence of the security forces. Regardless, policy makers in all three countries widely share the view of the problematic nature of democratization, questioning the value of democracy in resolving intrastate and communal conflicts.[83] Middle East experts have maintained that, as long as challenges to the state and the regime are defined within a security–military framework (as is the case in Turkey), they are certain to reinforce the dominant role of the military as an institution in the political process.[84] This so-called "securitization" of politics accounts for why the military plays such an autonomous role in policy-making and why democratic consolidation too often is undermined in Turkey.[85]

Iran is also in the midst of a legitimacy crisis, for the conservative clerics have tried to undermine the democratization efforts of the reformers by calling the voices of change "threats" to the nation's security and to the ideals of the Islamic Republic. The unwillingness to pursue democratic solutions has boded ill for the rights of all, including ethnic minorities such as the Kurds and religious minorities such as the Baha'is.

Neoliberal economic reforms have presented dilemmas for policy makers, as attempts to balance economic growth, social order, and political stability have had constraining impacts on the longevity of the democratic process. The complex interplay between economic and political reform has rendered it impossible to predict with certainty which process will be consistently more important. In Iran, President Khatami took a different tack during his first term: *political development first; economic development later*. The conservative clerics have strongly opposed such an approach, fearing the gradual erosion of their power bases and resources. As a result, not much has been achieved in the way of reform under President Khatami's first term (1997–2001). Now in his second term, Khatami has pledged to achieve three main goals: to reform the administrative structure, to reform the economy, and to establish a civil society.[86]

Similarly, the current leadership in Turkey is bent on stressing both economic and political liberalization. The fear of the Kurdish secessionist movement in post-war Iraq looms large in the minds of the country's military leaders, who have until now been preoccupied with the "Islamic threat." Although the resolution of the Kurdish crisis could have a stabilizing impact on the region, its unresolved status has serious consequences for Turkey. This is so because the current Kurdish problem in Turkey may well jeopardize the country's relations with the EU, if not with America, and may limit its role as a stabilizing force in the region.

Likewise, stability and peace in Afghanistan and Iraq, as well as the refugee situation resulting from two recent wars in these countries, require closer cooperation between Turkey, Iran, and Pakistan. While Pakistan and Iran have played an active role in the reconstruction of Afghanistan, Turkey and Iran have turned their attention to the post-conflict difficulties facing Iraq. The resolution of ethnic and regional conflicts there will surely have considerable ramifications for these countries. The complex political dynamics and a lack of political will on the part of the ruling élites, rather than Islamic ideologies or cultural traditions, best illustrate the difficulties of improving the human rights performance of these countries. A much greater long-term capacity for élite-led innovation or reform-from-above in both Iran and Turkey than in Pakistan demonstrates stronger expectations for national development. These expectations are arguably rooted in memories of national historical greatness in two of the region's oldest nation-states.

Conclusions

Iran, Pakistan, and Turkey are places of stern opposition to authoritarianism and of continuing human rights violations. It is possible to discern certain similarities amid the differences among these countries: human rights violations in these countries are due largely to the absence of sustainable democratic processes, the lack of accountable political order, inter-élite fragmentation, imbalanced state–society relations, ethnic tensions, and badly flawed liberalization strategies.[87]

The long-standing role played by the military in this region has had constraining impacts on any consistent and enduring transition toward democracy. As the guardian of nationalistic ideals and sentiments, the force behind nation building, and the most powerful economic enclave, the armed forces have a history of intrusion into politics in the Middle East, as they do elsewhere in the developing world. This, we should also note, has complicated the process of democratization in the Middle Eastern region, making the civilianization of their political systems very slow.[88] In all three countries, egregious violations of human rights have had less to do with economic conditions and national wealth than with the lack of democratic institutions in place.

The realization of ethnic and religious minority rights – as well as women's rights, labour rights, and curbing the trafficking of refugees – will stabilize the political climate of each country. Political stability in each country demands legitimate outside attention and cooperation in the form of foreign direct investment and technological assistance. IFIs, such as the IMF and the World Bank, can play a major role in nudging along these countries' economic liberalization by expanding economic contacts with them. The IFIs' macroeconomic medicine and austerity measures have thus far been especially painful for the poorest segments of these countries and have failed to address their pressing socio-economic needs. IFIs can, and should, play a constructive role in reducing trade barriers by helping these countries gain better access to Northern markets.

National governments are, indeed, the key players in the human rights drama: without their political commitment, human rights conditions are unlikely to improve. Factors responsible for human rights abuses in this region are primarily internal: these include, among others, poor leadership, personalistic politics, constitutional predicaments and flaws, gender-based violence, the slow pace of development of civil society, the absence of judicial independence, and the lingering military–bureaucratic rule. It is in these governments' interest to prevent domestic crises and promote regional cooperation.

More specifically, the empowerment of the president *vis-à-vis* the supreme leader will shore up Iran's civic institutions and society, provide political openings, and strengthen the move toward integration with the international community. Increasingly, experts argue that the United States' unilateral sanctions on Iran are likely to ignore the Iranian people's clear call for reform, as evidenced by the second landslide victory of Khatami.[89] President George W. Bush's 2002 State of the Union address – which lumped together Iran, Iraq, and North Korea in an "axis of evil" – could undermine the progress made in enhancing the democratic movement in Iran. It is unfortunate that Iran, going through fragile ideological conflicts and the fledgling liberalization struggles it currently faces, is getting no consideration or rhetorical support from the Bush administration. Iran's constructive role in the war on the Taliban and the war in Iraq, as well as its willingness to participate actively in Afghanistan's post-war reconstruction, as well as in establishing permanent peace there, point to the positive role it has thus far played in stabilizing the region.

The Kurdish problem cries out for a political solution. Military solutions pursued in south-eastern Turkey have thus far undermined the effort to seek a sustainable political solution. Some observers have argued that the best hope for ethnic peace is to divorce ethnic identity from political access and to stress transethnic identities such as Islam.[90] The resolution of the Kashmir dispute lies at the heart of Pakistan's bitter conflict with India. An end to this dispute would significantly curtail human rights abuses against the Kashmiris and (by weakening the militarization of politics), indirectly, the Pakistanis as a whole.

In such a country as Pakistan, cooperation with the UN special representative, the UN Commission on Human Rights, the IMF's Poverty Relief and Growth Facility (PRGF), and regional organizations such as the EU and the Commonwealth of Nations, is critical to political viability and international legitimacy.[91] The regional organizations must balance their commercial and strategic interests, such as trade and investment contracts, with human rights concerns. The EU's two-track approach toward Iran – that is, condemning human rights violations in Iran while supporting the reformist policies of President Khatami – is a proper strategy.[92]

These countries' dilemmas in dealing with liberalization programmes represent a microcosm of the problems facing the developing world, where adjustment programmes have come at uncertain costs. Political will and right planning will properly address the questions of equity and transparency. If bloodshed, uprisings, or any other form of instability are to be avoided in these countries, their leaders must opt for a viable reform strategy that combines economic liberalization and the expansion of civil society. Equally crucial will be the pressure of the international community in demanding close adherence to international human rights laws and conventions.

Notes

1. Some of the discussions here have been further elaborated in the author's *Islamism, Secularism, and Human Rights in the Middle East*, Boulder, CO: Lynne Rienner Publishers, 1998.
2. William Spencer, "The Middle East: Cradle of Islam," in William Spencer, ed., *Global Studies: The Middle East*, 8th edition, Guilford: Dushkin/McGraw Hill, 2000, p. 12.
3. Alan Richards and John Waterbury, *A Political Economy of the Middle East*, 2nd edition, Boulder: Westview, 1996, p. 222.
4. Roundtable, "Civil Society in Iran and the Middle East," *Discourse: An Iranian Quarterly*, Vol. 2, No. 2, Winter 2001, p. 5.
5. Ibid., pp. 6–7.
6. *Human Rights Watch World Report 2001*, New York: Human Rights Watch, 2000, p. 378.
7. For more on this, see Amnesty International at ⟨www.amnesty.org⟩.
8. *Human Rights Watch World Report 2001*, New York: Human Rights Watch, 2000, p. 213.
9. Sten Widmalm, "The Rise and Fall of Democracy in Jammu and Kashmir," *Asian Survey*, Vol. 37, No. 11, November 1997, pp. 1005–1030.
10. *Human Rights Watch World Report 2001*, p. 325.
11. Ibid., p. 327.
12. Mahmood Monshipouri, *Islamism, Secularism, and Human Rights in the Middle East*, p. 224.
13. *Human Rights Watch World Report 2001*, p. 329.
14. Ibid., p. 329.
15. James A. Bill and Robert Springborg, *Politics in the Middle East*, 5th edition, New York: Longman, 2000, p. 171.
16. Ervand Abrahamian, "Iran," in Mark Kesselman, Joel Krieger, and William A. Joseph, eds, *Introduction to Comparative Politics: Political Challenges and Changing Agendas*, Boston: Houghton Mifflin, 2000, pp. 607–654.

17. Daniel Brumberg, *Reinventing Khomeini: The Struggle for Reform in Iran*, Chicago: University of Chicago Press, 2001, pp. 127, 151.
18. Jon B. Alterman, "Iran: Came the Revolution," *Current History*, Vol. 100, No. 642, January 2001, p. 29.
19. Ibid., p. 29.
20. Ibid., p. 32.
21. Mahmood Monshipouri, "Civil Society, Democracy, and *Velayat-e Faqih*," *Journal of Iranian Research and Analysis*, Vol. 15, No. 2, November 1999, pp. 106–107.
22. John L. Esposito and John O. Voll, *Islam and Democracy*, Oxford: Oxford University Press, 1996, p. 70.
23. See, for example, the writings and declarations of the Islamic philosopher Abdulkarim Soroush, in which he rejects any official interpretation of Islam and warns against turning religion into an ideology. Hojatoleslam Mohsen Kadivar, a prominent cleric, has also publicly espoused similar views. For a particularly informative analysis on this subject, see Dariush Zahedi, *The Iranian Revolution, Then and Now: Indicators of Regime Instability*, Boulder: Westview, 2000, pp. 40–92.
24. See Geneive Abdo, "Re-Thinking the Islamic Republic: A Conversation with Ayatollah Hossein Ali Montazeri," *The Middle East Journal*, Vol. 25, No. 1, Winter 2001, p. 14.
25. Ibid.
26. See Zahedi, *The Iranian Revolution, Then and Now*, pp. 67–84.
27. Ahmad Ghoreishi and Dariush Zahedi, "Prospects for Regime Change in Iran," *Middle East Policy*, Vol. 5, No. 1, January 1997, p. 98.
28. H.E. Chehabi, "Eighteen Years Later: Assessing the Islamic Republic of Iran," in William Spencer, ed., *Global Studies: The Middle East*, 7th edition, Guilford: Dushkin/McGraw-Hill, 1998, pp. 199–202.
29. Hamid Zangeneh, "The Post-Revolutionary Iranian Economy: A Policy Appraisal," *Middle East Policy*, Vol. VI, No. 2, October 1998, pp. 118–119.
30. Kamran M. Dadkhah and Hamid Zangeneh, "The Straw that Could Break the Camel's Back: An Economic Analysis of Subsidies in the Iranian Economy," *Journal of Iranian Research and Analysis*, Vol. 16, No. 1, April 2000, pp. 123–134.
31. Jahangir Amuzegar, "Iran's Post-Revolutionary Planning: The Second Try," *Middle East Policy*, Vol. VIII, No. 1, March 2001, p. 36.
32. Ibid.
33. Ibid., p. 37.
34. Ibid., p. 40.
35. Alan Richards and John Waterbury, *A Political Economy of the Middle East*, p. 244.
36. A. Reza Sheikholeslami, "The Transformation of Iran's Political Culture," *Critique: Journal for Critical Studies of the Middle East*, No. 17, Fall 2000, p. 133.
37. H.E. Chehabi, "Eighteen Years Later," p. 201.
38. Val Moghadam, "The Student Protests and the Social Movement for Reform in Iran: Sociological Reflections," *Journal of Iranian Research and Analysis*, Vol. 15, No. 2, November 1999, p. 103.
39. *International Iran Times*, June 15, 2001, p. 1.
40. Esposito and Voll, *Islam and Democracy*, pp. 102–123.
41. Ahmed Rashid, "Pakistan: Balancing Act," *Far Eastern Economic Review*, 1 February 2001, pp. 60–61.
42. Ibid.
43. Ahmed Rashid, "Pakistan's Coup: Planting the Seeds of Democracy," *Current History*, Vol. 98, No. 632, December 1999, p. 414.
44. Ibid.
45. Ibid.

46. Iftikhar H. Malik, "Pakistan in 2000: Starting Anew or Stalemate?," *Asian Survey*, Vol. XLI, No. 1, January/February 2001, pp. 110–111.
47. Mahmood Monshipouri, "Backlash to the Destruction at Ayodhya," *Asian Survey*, Vol. 33, No. 7, July 1993, p. 715.
48. Lawrence Ziring, *Pakistan: The Enigma of Political Development*, Boulder: Westview, 1980, pp. 41–57.
49. John L. Esposito, "Islam: Ideology and Politics in Pakistan," in Ali Banuazizi and Myron Weiner, eds, *The State, Religion, and Ethnic Politics: Afghanistan, Iran, and Pakistan*, Syracuse: Syracuse University Press, 1986, see p. 333.
50. Mary Louise Becker, "India: Government and Politics," in Peter R. Blood, ed., *Pakistan: A Country Study*, Lanham: Berman, 1995, pp. 244–245.
51. Stephen P. Cohen, "Old Issues and New Opportunities," *The Brookings Review*, Vol. 18, No. 4, Fall 2000, p. 33.
52. Paul R. Brass, "India: Democratic Progress and Problems," in Selig S. Harrison, Paul H. Kreisberg, and Dennis Kux, eds, *India and Pakistan: The First Fifty Years*, Cambridge: Cambridge University Press, 1999, pp. 33–34.
53. Lawrence Ziring, *Pakistan in the Twentieth Century: A Political History*, Oxford: Oxford University Press, 1997, p. 560.
54. Paula R. Newberg, *Double Betrayal: Repression and Insurgency in Kashmir*, Carnegie Endowment for International Peace, Washington, D.C., 1995, pp. 73–74.
55. James A. Bill and Robert Springborg, *Politics in the Middle East*, pp. 134–138.
56. Arthur Goldschmidt, Jr, *A Concise History of the Middle East*, 6th edition, Boulder: Westview, 1999, p. 200.
57. Jenny B. White, "Islam and Democracy: The Turkish Experience," *Current History*, Vol. 94, No. 558, January 1995, p. 8.
58. *Human Rights Watch World Report 2001: Events of 2000*, New York: Human Rights Watch, 2000, p. 327.
59. Ibid., p. 329.
60. Alan Richards and John Waterbury, *A Political Economy of the Middle East*, p. 345.
61. Ibid.
62. Ersin Kalaycioglu, "Decentralization of Government," in Metin Heper and Ahmet Evin, eds, *Politics in the Third Turkish Republic*, Boulder: Westview, 1994, pp. 87–100.
63. Ergun Ozbudun, "Turkey: Crises, Interruptions, and Reequilibrations," in Larry Diamond, Juan J. Linz, and Seymour Martin Lipset, eds, 2nd edition, *Politics in the Developing Countries: Comparing Experiences with Democracy*, Boulder: Lynne Rienner, 1995, p. 250.
64. Ibid., p. 258.
65. *Middle East International*, No. 644, February 23, 2001, pp. 17–18.
66. Douglas Frantz, "Needing Cash, Turkey Plans More Sacrifice," *New York Times*, Sunday, 15 April 2001, p. 14.
67. Ibid.
68. Eric Rouleau, "Turkey's Dream of Democracy," *Foreign Affairs*, Vol. 79, No. 6, November/December 2000, p. 101; see also Aslan Gunduz, "Human Rights and Turkey's Future in Europe," *Orbis*, Vol. 45, No. 1, Winter 2001, p. 17.
69. Rouleau, "Turkey's Dream of Democracy," p. 109.
70. Ian McGillis, "A View of Turkey Beyond Stereotypes," *The Gazette* (Montreal), 22 January 2000, available at ⟨www.lexis-nexus⟩.
71. Dov Waxman, *Turkey's Identity Crises: Domestic Discord and Foreign Policy*, Conflict Studies #311, Research Institute for the Study of Conflict and Terrorism, Leamington Spa, Warwickshire, 1998, p. 6.

72. Kemal Kirisci and Gareth M. Winrow, *The Turkish Question and Turkey: An Example of a Trans-State Ethnic Conflict*, London: Frank Cass, 1997, pp. 212–213. See also Nader Entessar, *Kurdish Ethnonationalism*, Boulder: Lynne Rienner, 1992, pp. 9–10.
73. Paul Kubicek, "Turkish–European Relations: At a New Crossroads?" *Middle East Policy*, Vol. VI, No. 4, June 1999, p. 161.
74. Henri J. Barkey and Graham E. Fuller, *Turkey's Kurdish Question*, Lanham: Rowman and Littlefield, 1998, p. 133.
75. Ibid., p. 180.
76. Heinz Kramer, "Turkey: Toward 2000: In Search of National Consensus and a New Political Center," in William Spencer, ed., *Global Studies: The Middle East*, pp. 232–233.
77. Svante E. Cornell, "The Kurdish Question in Turkish Politics," *Orbis*, Vol. 45, No. 1, Winter 2001, p. 31.
78. Ibid.
79. Ibid., p. 43.
80. Ibid., p. 44.
81. Aslan Gunduz, "Human Rights and Turkey's Future in Europe," *Orbis*, Vol. 45, No. 1, Winter 2001, p. 26.
82. *Amnesty International Report 1999*, New York: Amnesty International USA, 1998, pp. 198, 265, 336.
83. See Mahmood Monshipouri, "The Fate of Human Rights in the Middle East and North Africa," in Manochehr Dorraj, ed., *Middle East at the Crossroads: The Changing Political Dynamics and the Foreign Policy Challenges*, Lanham: University Press of America, 1999, pp. 75–76.
84. Philippos K. Savvides, "Legitimation Crisis and Securitization in Modern Turkey," *Critique: Journal for Critical Studies of the Middle East*, No. 16, Spring 2000, p. 62.
85. Ibid., pp. 69–71.
86. *New York Times*, 10 June 2001, p. 4K.
87. This should not obscure the fact there are many difficulties inherent to economic liberalization programmes, regardless of the ways in which such reforms are implemented. Good governance alone cannot provide the answer for the human and political costs of economic reforms, including ending price controls, cutting government spending and subsidies, and adopting other painful market-related measures.
88. Alan Richards and John Waterbury, *A Political Economy of the Middle East*, p. 345.
89. See Lee H. Hamilton and James Schlesinger, "Turning a Friendlier Face to Iran," *New York Times*, 16 June 2001, p. A15.
90. M. Hakan Yavuz and Michael M. Gunter, "The Kurdish Nation," *Current History*, Vol. 100, No. 642, January 2001, p. 36.
91. *Human Rights Watch 2001*, pp. 216–217.
92. Ibid., p. 383.

11

Causes and consequences of variation in post-communist human rights practices

Shale Horowitz

The post-communist world offers a fascinating setting in which to examine the development of human rights practices. With the liberalization and then collapse of the Soviet, Yugoslav, and Albanian communist regimes, 28 new or transformed political entities emerged across Eastern Europe and Soviet Eurasia. Despite broadly similar conditions of political rule under the old regimes, the new regimes have adopted widely varying human rights practices. What are the most important causes of this variation? What are the consequences of variation in human rights practices for economic development, democratization, and conflict resolution?

Consider first causes. Political institutions appear to be the primary proximate cause of human rights practices. But are there more fundamental causes, which affect both political institutions and human rights practices? Promising candidates include culture and national identity, economic development, and ethnic conflict. Are cultures and national identities inherently favourable or unfavourable to formation of strong human rights practices, or do they have more complex and changing "implications"? Do different levels and patterns of economic development lead to more intense political conflict over economic policy, as a result threatening human rights protection? Does large-scale military conflict – in the post-communist context, typically ethnic in character – precipitate more frequent and intense human rights violation and erode existing human rights protection?

Interestingly, reform in the post-communist world tended to be correlated across a number of important areas. Significantly improved human rights practices tended to develop along with more complete democratization and more rapid and thorough market reform. Similarly, continued human rights violations were associated with continued authoritarianism and heavy state intervention in the economy. Such synchronization has not always been the most obvious pattern in other parts of the world. For example, in Latin America in the 1970s and early 1980s, better human rights practices and democracy were often associated with greater state intervention in the economy. Similarly, in East Asia, more market-oriented economic policies have often been associated with authoritarian regimes – in some cases, quite repressive authoritarian regimes.

It will be argued here that the specific properties of the communist systems, combined with the historical timing of their rise and fall, explain the synchronized patterns of reform or non-reform to be observed in the post-communist states. Both stronger human rights practices and greater democratization are hypothesized to have three fundamental causes: (1) national identities that contributed to a desire to break decisively with the communist past; (2) more advanced economic structures that facilitated transition to a market economy; and (3) peace.

It is argued that national identities did not have their greatest impact through being *intrinsically* more compatible with modern conceptions of human rights. Rather, they were most influential in discrediting more repressive human rights practices and authoritarian political rule, which were perceived as having set back national development during the communist period. In other words, it was sometimes widely felt that communist-type methods did not work, relative to what the pre-communist period had led people to expect. In such cases, and in the historical setting of the late twentieth century, stronger human rights protections and democracy appeared as components of the most promising alternative developmental model. This logic implies that these "frustrated" national ideals might have had different implications under different historical circumstances – as appears to have been the case, for example, in Eastern Europe between the two world wars.

Consider now the consequences of variation in human rights practices. Stronger human rights protections are likely to advance democratization and economic development, but not necessarily conflict resolution. Human rights protections are likely to make both ideological and institutional contributions to the democratization and economic development processes. However, the size of the effects is difficult to estimate because of the wide variety of other conditions that are relevant and even necessary. The relation of human rights practices to conflict resolution is likely to be even weaker, because greater freedoms can intensify as well as pacify various sources of internal and international conflicts.

The following sections begin by building hypotheses about the causes of variation in post-communist human rights practices. These hypotheses are then operationalized and tested statistically. The tests find that war is a relatively important source of human rights violations, and economic underdevelopment a relatively unimportant source. The tests also show that cultural factors are by far the most important influence. Frustrated national ideals have an impact comparable to that of religious tradition. This suggests that rational and instrumental ways of interpreting the influence of culture may be a promising addition to existing approaches, which emphasize non-rational, habitual effects of culture. A briefer treatment of the consequences of variation in human rights practices follows. The concluding section summarizes the findings. It also discusses how the rational, instrumental approach to culture might be used to explain variation in human rights practices in other regions and time periods.

Causes of variation in human rights practices in the post-communist world

Theory and hypotheses

Movement towards full democratization is usually associated with significant progress towards respect for human rights generally. In evaluating this relationship, there are important issues of definition and potential overlap. Full democratization necessarily involves not only free and fair elections to positions of real political power but also freedom of expression, freedom of the press, and freedom of association for political purposes and organizations. Suppose human rights are defined narrowly in terms of civil liberties. It is conceivable that all the political freedoms relevant to democratization might exist alongside severe restrictions of other human rights. For example, arbitrary and corrupt use of police and judicial powers might be significant, but not directed at political targets. There might be significant restrictions of economic opportunities of individuals and groups, but these might affect people of all political persuasions more or less equally. However, such a separation between political and other freedoms is relatively rare. Arbitrary exercise of police and judicial powers and restrictions of economic opportunities often involve discretionary political power on a large scale. Those in positions of authority almost invariably use such discretionary power for political as well as other ends.[1]

This is the basis for the argument that democratization should tend to increase protection of civil liberties. This will be true by definition for civil liberties in their directly political dimensions. Furthermore, the political consensus and institutional protections favouring political freedoms will tend to extend to other types of freedoms. After all, political freedoms are highly sensitive, because they provide access to political power that can affect all other types of activities. If it is possible to tolerate and enforce political freedoms, then the same climate of opinion and institutional procedures should be similarly accommodating to enhanced cultural and economic freedoms and to more neutral police and judicial institutions.

The potential problem with an explanation based on political regime type is that it verges on being practically tautological. The point here is not the definitional one – that there is inevitably some overlap between free and fair elections along with political freedoms on the one hand and civil liberties more broadly on the other. It is still possible for there to be significant differences between the two outcomes taken in the aggregate, since protection of non-political civil liberties may differ significantly from political civil liberties. The problem is that, as discussed, the capacity for political toleration is one of the most sensitive types of freedom, so that it is relatively obvious that this capacity, once improved, will be more likely to extend to other freedoms. From a theoretical point of view, the more interesting question is why the capacity to tolerate and enforce both political and other freedoms has developed. In this sense, it may be more accurate to see democracy as an often-important intervening variable that commonly mediates the relationship between more fundamental factors and non-political civil liberties.

The decline and fall of the Soviet, Yugoslav, and Albanian regimes meant the break-up of specific types of authoritarian political orders and heavily interventionist economic systems. Most juridically independent Eastern European countries regained real political autonomy, which had been lost to the Soviet Union during and immediately after World War II. The break-up of the Soviet Union and Yugoslavia also meant the break-up of older territorial orders – which had been internally reconstructed using the Soviet system of ethnically defined provinces ("Republics") administered by ethnically defined sub-parties of the central communist parties.

Politically, there were three important dimensions of the Soviet and Yugoslav collapses. First, they provided an opportunity for individuals to acquire greater political freedoms and civil liberties, both for their own sake and as a means of pursuing other goals. Second, with the exceptions of Albania and, arguably, Russia, the successor states gained real political independence from their former Soviet or Yugoslav overlords. To the extent that these successor states incorporated traditions of political, economic, and cultural development that were set back or blocked by Soviet or Yugoslav rule, genuine political independence provided an opportunity to revive and pursue such national developmental goals.

Third, many of the successor units incorporated large, territorially concentrated, ethnic minorities with their own autonomy or independence aspirations. Such aspirations were amplified by often-legitimate fears of discrimination, for minorities were typically confronted by new regimes oriented towards political, economic, and cultural revival of the dominant ethnic group. Such situations often erupted into violent ethnic conflicts, and these conflicts were often intensified when other states intervened. If Russia's conflict in tiny Chechnya is excluded, eight of the 28 post-communist states became embroiled in large-scale, ethnically based warfare.[2]

Economically, the collapse of planned or socialized economies meant that a broad redistribution of opportunities and resources became possible. Apart from the privileges enjoyed by those directly employed in high party and state positions, planned and (in the Yugoslav case) socialized economies directed large subsidies in typical patterns. As a general rule, capital-intensive industry and agriculture were subsidized by the mostly urban service sector. These subsidies were taken in the form of overpriced or unavailable consumer goods and compressed incomes. They were distributed to industry and agriculture through open-ended soft credits to cover enterprise debts and artificially cheap inputs (particularly energy and energy-intensive inputs). The debate over transition to a market economy predictably pitted the mostly urban service sector against heavy industry and agriculture, for a transition to a market economy would mean subjecting industry and agriculture to greater competition (particularly from abroad) and eliminating most credit and input subsidies. These resources would flow back to the service sector in the form of higher retained incomes and cheaper, higher-quality, consumer goods.[3]

A more advanced economy has a larger service sector and smaller industrial and agricultural sectors. Moreover, in more advanced economies, a higher percentage of communist-era industry is likely to be economically viable after transition to a market economy. Among other things, democracy and improved human rights were typically used as means of pursuing market reforms. So, more advanced economies should have larger economic interest groups favouring market reform, democratization, and improved human rights practices, and smaller economic interest groups opposing them. A readily available measure of economic development is the agricultural share of the workforce.[4]

During the late Soviet and post-Soviet periods, movements for national independence and revival of national identities were an important source of political reform. What are here termed "frustrated national ideals" are widely held beliefs that the communist system frustrated pre-communist national potential, particularly in the areas of political autonomy and greatness, economic development, and cultural autonomy and expression. Such widely held beliefs should be reflected in better-organized, more politically aggressive, nationalist opposition movements and in local communist parties more sympathetic to the agenda of national revival. Such opposition movements and reformist communist parties did, in fact, have central roles in the cases where communist regimes were replaced by more democratic governments. More democratic governments typically showed greater respect for human rights and imposed more radical market reforms.

There is no inherent reason why nationalist movements should pursue democracy, human rights, and market reform. However, there was a good reason for this in the specific post-communist context. The communist system was typically viewed as something imposed by alien rulers; democracy, human rights, and market reforms were the most obvious means of destroying the alien system and replacing it with one more compatible with national developmental objectives. Methods that were less democratic, more repressive, and more economically interventionist were discredited as all-too-Soviet or all-too-Yugoslav. On the other hand, the combination of democracy, human rights, and market economies was politically ascendant in other parts of the world and was politically and economically compatible with pursuing national-revival goals.

Measurement of the extent of frustrated national ideals is a more difficult undertaking. The measure proposed here starts with pre-communist political and economic achievements. Where these achievements were greater, there should be greater hostility to the communist system as one that set back national developmental potential. Greater pre-communist achievements might also be expected to amplify resentment at communist-era repression and at threats to demographic and territorial integrity associated with communist rule. A quantitative index designed to predict stronger frustrated national ideals is offered below. The index is based on country classifications given in table 11.1 and explained in more detail in the Appendix (pages 260–263).

The predictive power of frustrated national ideals can be compared with that of predominant religions. It is relatively obvious that predominantly Islamic post-communist countries have had the worst human rights practices, and that predominantly Orthodox Christian countries have had worse human rights practices than predominantly Catholic or Protestant countries. One can devise intrinsic reasons why this should be so, but such reasons have a strongly *ex post facto* character. To take the most obvious example, efforts to explain outcomes such as economic development, democratization, and human rights practices in Western Europe and Latin America have typically classified Catholicism as a relatively authoritarian tradition. Similarly, if, in the post-communist world, the Orthodox Christian countries had seen outcomes such as those in the Catholic and Protestant countries, it would be easy to rationalize a simple dichotomy between Christianity and Islam.

Large-scale military conflicts are threats to human rights and democratization. Directly, apart from combat-related casualties per se, war is commonly associated with a situation of national political emergency. Human rights tend to be pushed aside to the extent that they are perceived to interfere with the conduct of military operations or with the achievement of maximum mobilization and solidarity. Such perceptions also serve as a convenient pretext for using repression to consolidate more exclusive political control. War also has important indirect effects by causing economic deterioration and military setbacks. These developments make democratic regimes (which are typically more respectful of human rights) more vulnerable to electoral defeat or military coups. On the other hand, authoritarian regimes (which are likely to have inferior human rights records) are less vulnerable to such threats. The longer large-scale military conflicts last, the greater should be the damage to human rights practices.

This discussion is the basis for the following hypotheses:
1. The main proximate cause of improved human rights practices should be greater democratization.
2. The most important sources of both greater democratization and improvement in human rights practices should be stronger "frustrated national ideals," a more advanced economy, and absence or brevity of large-scale military conflict.

Method, measurement, and data sources

The variables to be considered in the statistical hypothesis tests are human rights practices, democratization, frustrated national ideals, agriculture's share of the workforce, and share of time at war. The 28 post-communist countries are Albania, Armenia, Azerbaijan, Belarus, Bosnia–Herzegovina, Bulgaria, Croatia, the Czech Republic, Estonia, Georgia, Hungary, Kazakhstan, Kyrgyzstan, Latvia, Lithuania, Macedonia, Moldova, Mongolia, Poland, Romania, Russia, Slovakia, Slovenia, Tajikistan, Turkmenistan, Ukraine, Uzbekistan, and the Federal Republic of Yugoslavia (Serbia and Montenegro). All models of interrelations among the variables are estimated using ordinary least-squares regression.

Human rights outcomes are measured at three intervals: approximately two years following the onset of the new regime (two years after the founding election in Eastern Europe and Mongolia, and two years after the collapse of the Soviet Union for the Soviet successor states); four years following the end of the first interval; and approximately eight years following the end of the first interval. Since the new regimes came to power over the three years 1989–1991, the first interval ends in one of the years 1991–1993, the second in 1995–1997, and the third in 1999–2001, depending upon the country. As data were not gathered beyond the end of 1999, the third interval is truncated to less than four years for a number of countries.

Variables are measured as follows:

Human rights practices

Human rights practices are measured using Freedom House's Civil Liberties Index (CLI). This includes four major categories of freedoms or rights: freedoms of expression and belief (including freedoms of the press and religion); freedoms of association and organization; a neutral rule of law and an independent, professional judiciary; economic freedoms and opportunities, and protection of property and contractual rights. Rankings on these indices are then averaged to produce an overall ranking on a scale of one to seven, with *one* indicating most complete protection of human rights.

Democratization

Democratization is measured using Freedom House's Political Rights Index (PRI). There are direct and indirect dimensions. Directly, there must be elections in which all parties can compete equally, in which votes are accurately counted, and in which the victors take political power. Indirectly, the ability of parties to compete equally is affected by the ability of individuals to express themselves politically, through both free association and organization for political purposes, and open competition of political views in the mass media. Again, rankings on these indices are then averaged to produce an overall ranking on a scale of one to seven, with *one* indicating most complete protection of human rights.[5] In two areas there is limited but unavoidable overlap between the CLI and PRI: individual expression and association, particularly through the mass media and formal organizations, are general human rights. In specifically political forms, they are also necessary conditions of free political competition. All the other components of the two indices – the overwhelming majority – are, in principle, distinct. As discussed, there is reason to expect a much greater overlap for practical political reasons.

Frustrated national ideals

This is an index of pre-communist political and economic achievement, along with a weighted component picking up communist-era repression and threats to national cultural and territorial integrity. It is designed to predict the extent to which the communist era is viewed as a serious setback to national development, and thus to predict the extent to which the most plausible alternative systems will be embraced as a means of achieving a political, economic, and cultural renaissance of the nation. The index is operationalized as follows:

$$[(Pol_i + Econ_i)/2] * [1 + (Pol_i + Econ_i/10)(Repress_i + ImmigTerr_i)],$$

where Pol_i is pre-communist political achievement of country i, $Econ_i$ is pre-communist economic achievement, $Repress_i$ is severity of communist-era repression, and $ImmigTerr_i$ measures significant threats to national integrity in traditional homelands. Past political and economic achievements are ranked on a scale of one to five, with *five* indicating highest achievement. Note that the middle term $(Pol_i + Econ_i/10)$ makes the impact of repression and anti-national policies or situations conditional on the level of national expectations deriving from pre-communist achievements. Repression and threat to ethnic identity each receive weights over a five-level spectrum from 0 to 0.25 (at intervals of 0.0625). Their sum is then weighted on a scale from 0.2 to 1 (at intervals of 0.1) based on scores for frustrated economic and political potential. This composite term added to one – with a maximum of 1.5 – is then multiplied by the average of the political and economic weights. The maximum is 7.5. The overall score is then divided by 1.5 to bring the maximum back down to 5. Classifications of countries along the different component dimensions of the index are given in table 11.1, and explained in more detail in Appendix A.[6]

Predominant religion

Two dummy variables are used. For the first, a country is coded as a one (where the most widely observed religion is Islam) and otherwise as a zero. For the second, a country is coded as a one (where the most widely observed religion is Orthodox Christianity) and otherwise as a zero.[7]

Agriculture's share of workforce

This is the percentage of the workforce directly employed in agriculture, fishing, and forestry.[8]

Share of time at war

The total amount of "independent political time" starts with the first post-communist election for Eastern Europe and Mongolia and from

Table 11.1 Sources of frustrated national ideals in the post-communist context

	Index of past economic achievement	Index of past political achievement	Threat to national integrity (demographic dilution or territorial loss)	Repression
Very strong	Czech Republic[a], Hungary, Slovenia	Baltic States, Hungary, Mongolia, Poland	Bosnia–Herzegovina, Kazakhstan, Kyrgyzstan, Latvia	Mongolia, Soviet Republics
Strong	Croatia, Estonia, Latvia, Poland, Slovakia	Bulgaria, Croatia, Czech Republic, Serbia–Montenegro, Slovenia	Estonia, Macedonia, Moldova, Tajikistan	Albania, Poland, Romania
Moderate	Albania, Armenia, Azerbaijan, Bosnia–Herzegovina, Bulgaria, Georgia, Lithuania, Macedonia, Romania, Russia, Serbia–Montenegro	Armenia, Georgia, Romania, Slovakia	Azerbaijan, Belarus, Croatia, Georgia, Lithuania, Serbia–Montenegro, Turkmenistan, Ukraine, Uzbekistan	Croatia, Hungary
Weak	Belarus, Moldova, Tajikistan, Ukraine, Uzbekistan	Albania, Moldova, Russia, Tajikistan, Ukraine, Uzbekistan	Armenia, Poland, Romania, Slovakia	Bulgaria, Czech Republic, Serbia–Montenegro, Slovenia, Slovakia
Very weak	Kazakhstan, Kyrgyzstan, Mongolia, Turkmenistan	Azerbaijar, Belarus, Bosnia–Herzegovina, Kazakhstan, Kyrgyzstan, Macedonia, Turkmenistan	Albania, Bulgaria, Czech Republic, Hungary, Mongolia, Slovenia, Russia	Bosnia–Herzegovina, Macedonia

a. For the early period in which a unified Czechoslovakia still existed, its rankings are the same as for its dominant Czech part.

August 1991 for the Soviet successor states. It ends at the points at which human rights practices and democratization are being examined (1991/ 92/93, 1995/96/97, and 1999). The share of time at war is the proportion of the time during which the country has been engaged in large-scale military hostilities. The countries embroiled in such hostilities for extended periods of time were Armenia, Azerbaijan, Bosnia–Herzegovina, Croatia, Georgia, Moldova, Tajikistan, and the Federal Republic of Yugoslavia.[9]

Model results and discussion

Models 1A–3B of table 11.2 show the relationship between democratization, frustrated national ideals, agricultural share of the workforce, and share of time at war on the one hand, and human rights practices on the other. Democratization has extremely strong predictive power, accounting for almost all of the variation in human rights practices. As can be seen by comparing the "A" and "B" versions, the other independent variables add virtually no predictive power. Frustrated national ideals and agricultural share of the workforce have the predicted relationships, but are not statistically significant. Share of time at war usually has the opposite of the predicted relationship. As is shown hereafter, this indicates not that the variables other than democratization are not important but only that most of their explanatory effect is picked up through their indirect influence on the more directly important democratization variable.

Models 4A–6B of table 11.3 show the estimated impact of agriculture's share of the workforce, share of time at war, and cultural factors – either frustrated national ideals or predominant religion – on human rights practices. Models 7A–9B of table 11.4 show the estimated impact of these same variables on democratization. Recall that high CLIs and PRIs indicate poorer human rights practices and weaker democratization, so that all the variables are estimated to have an effect in the expected direction. The impact of the three variables on human rights practices and democratization is generally similar. The cultural variables – either frustrated national ideals, or Islam and Orthodox Christianity – and share of time at war are almost uniformly statistically significant. Frustrated national ideals or Islam have the most consistent impact and account for the largest share of explained variation. Agricultural share of the workforce has some impact on human rights practices, but is not generally statistically significant. Share of time at war has a dramatic effect, although somewhat more so on democratization than on human rights practices.

Table 11.2 Democratization and other factors as predictors of human rights practices

	Model 1A 1991/92/93	Model 1B 1991/92/93	Model 2A 1995/96/97	Model 2B 1995/96/97	Model 3A 1999	Model 3B 1999
Political rights index	0.635***	0.759***	0.558***	0.655***	0.599***	0.700***
	(0.134)	(0.088)	(0.111)	(0.054)	(0.099)	(0.052)
Frustrated national ideals	-0.148		-0.214		-0.240	
	(0.220)		(0.197)		(0.185)	
Agriculture's share of the workforce	0.015		0.044		0.017	
	(0.044)		(0.032)		(0.031)	
Share of time at war	0.853		-0.123		-0.040	
	(0.513)		(0.597)		(0.700)	
Intercept	1.617*	0.994**	2.352***	1.552***	2.309***	1.446***
	(0.922)	(0.385)	(0.759)	(0.217)	(0.697)	(0.204)
R^2	0.780	0.748	0.864	0.849	0.884	0.874
Adjusted R^2	0.740	0.738	0.840	0.843	0.863	0.869
N	27[a]	27[a]	28	28	28	28

*** $p < .01$, ** $p < .05$, * $p < .10$

a. Models 1A and 1B include a unified Czechoslovakia, so there is one less data point.

253

Table 11.3 Cultural, economic, and conflict-related sources of human rights practices

	Model 4A 1991/92/93	Model 4B 1991/92/93	Model 5A 1995/96/97	Model 5B 1995/96/97	Model 6A 1999	Model 6B 1999
Frustrated national ideals	-0.879*** (0.217)		-1.038*** (0.155)		-1.152*** (0.168)	
Islam		2.475*** (0.561)		2.296*** (0.509)		2.780*** (0.505)
Christian Orthodoxy		0.923** (0.531)		1.106** (0.471)		1.293*** (0.468)
Agriculture's share of workforce	0.068 (0.059)	0.053 (0.058)	0.093** (0.043)	0.066 (0.056)	0.041 (0.049)	0.013 (0.057)
Share of time at war	1.752** (0.663)	1.743** (0.656)	1.430* (0.725)	1.480 (0.912)	1.769* (0.994)	1.773 (1.148)
Intercept	5.539*** (0.563)	2.583*** (0.366)	5.884*** (0.405)	2.571*** (0.326)	6.156*** (0.438)	2.406*** (0.324)
R^2	0.556	0.597	0.715	0.569	0.700	0.618
Adjusted R^2	0.498	0.524	0.679	0.494	0.662	0.551
N	27[a]	27[a]	28	28	28	28

*** $p < .01$, ** $p < .05$, * $p < .10$
a. Models 4A and 4B include a unified Czechoslovakia, so they have one less data point.

254

Table 11.4 Cultural, economic, and conflict-related sources of democratization

	Model 7A 1991/92/93	Model 7B 1991/92/93	Model 8A 1995/96/97	Model 8B 1995/96/97	Model 9A 1999	Model 9B 1999
Frustrated national ideals	−1.153*** (0.243)		−1.477*** (0.201)		−1.521*** (0.219)	
Islam		2.878*** (0.688)		3.685*** (0.586)		3.958*** (0.588)
Christian Orthodoxy		0.842 (0.651)		1.527*** (0.543)		1.414** (0.544)
Agriculture's share of workforce	0.083 (0.066)	0.069 (0.071)	0.088 (0.056)	0.057 (0.064)	0.040 (0.064)	0.016 (0.067)
Share of time at war	1.415* (0.742)	1.493* (0.805)	2.786*** (0.940)	2.774** (1.051)	3.020** (1.298)	2.966** (1.335)
Intercept	6.178*** (0.630)	2.510*** (0.449)	6.333*** (0.526)	1.536*** (0.376)	6.422*** (0.572)	1.494*** (0.377)
R^2	0.572	0.533	0.758	0.710	0.716	0.712
Adjusted R^2	0.516	0.448	0.728	0.660	0.680	0.662
N	27[a]	27[a]	28	28	28	28

*** $p < .01$, ** $p < .05$, * $p < .10$
a. Models 7A and 7B include a unified Czechoslovakia, so they have one less data point.

It is notable that the instrumental and intrinsic cultural factors – frustrated national ideals on the one hand and predominant religion on the other – have virtually identical explanatory power across all the models. However, although the predominant religion variable cannot be dismissed as totally irrelevant, the frustrated national ideals variable seems to have significant logical and empirical advantages. First, in the post-communist historical context, frustrated national ideals have intelligible policy implications. They provide a rationale for why masses and élites would support improved human rights practices and democratization as means to achieving widely held collective goals. It is less clear that traditional Islamic or Christian Orthodox religious values and institutions would be better served by having weaker human rights practices or less democracy. If the influence of traditional religious values and institutions is supposed to be a habitual one, it is not clear why the secularized, literate, urban élites that led both establishment and opposition political formations should have been strongly influenced by such habits.[10]

Second, if one looks at the political discourse of both opposition and establishment parties in the post-communist countries that chose improved human rights practices and greater democracy, one finds a discourse of reform nationalism. Similarly, in the countries with weaker human rights practices and more authoritarian regimes, one also finds a nationalist discourse – although one that emphasizes the need for political and economic stability. The latter is of course much more self-serving for the power and economic interests of incumbent élites. In both cases, though, it is national development rather than religion that is at the ideological centre of political life.

For some examples, consider the majority Islamic countries of Albania, Azerbaijan, Kazakhstan, Kyrgyzstan, Tajikistan, Turkmenistan, and Uzbekistan. Among all these countries, there is only one example of a prominent late Soviet or post-Soviet movement or party that prioritized religious revival per se – the Islamic Renaissance Party (IRP) of Tajikistan. Apart from having a relatively narrow, regionally specific, popular base, the IRP was also internally divided over whether respect for human rights and democratization would best serve the cause of Islamic revival. IRP leaders more inclined towards authoritarianism and repressive methods appear to have come to the fore later, as a consequence of the bloody post-Soviet civil war.[11] Reform nationalist opposition parties in the Islamic countries, which favoured revival of Islam as part of a broader rebirth of national cultural traditions, also favoured improved human rights practices and democratization. This was in marked contrast to the communist successor parties, which outside of Albania have been authoritarian and usually quite repressive.[12]

Consequences of human rights variation in the post-communist world

Theoretically, stronger human rights protection favours democratization. Regimes able and willing to provide stronger human rights protection are less likely to view democratization as a political or personal threat and are less likely to be ideologically opposed to democratic norms. On the other hand, there can be significant protection of human rights outside the political sphere per se, without free elections or extensive political freedoms. Although this situation often produces pressure for greater democratization, authoritarian regimes are often able to resist such pressures – particularly when the economy performs well.

Human rights protection in the legal and economic spheres is necessary to provide broad equality of economic opportunity. Nevertheless, such opportunities, although necessary for sustained economic growth, are not sufficient. Moreover, broad human rights protection in the legal and economic spheres can coexist with extensive restrictions on the rights of various minorities, as well as with significant selective restrictions on the rights of the broader population.

Last, in the presence of significant internal or international conflicts, one would not expect human rights practices to have a strong relation with conflict resolution. This is because stronger human rights protection can intensify as well as pacify sources of conflict.

The effects of human rights practices on democracy, economic development, and conflict resolution are not easily subject to statistical testing. This is because, as already discussed, human rights practices are likely in the first instance to be largely caused by these other variables, and then to have secondary, feedback impacts on them. There is no space here to attempt a thorough discussion of this difficult subject. Only a briefer, suggestive treatment of the apparent feedback impact of human rights practices in the post-communist world is offered.

Human rights and democracy

A large democratization literature emphasizes the importance of democratic norms and culture for the consolidation of democratic political institutions. Arguably, human rights practices should play a central role in establishing and sustaining such norms. The evidence and discussion above suggest some supplementary points. Democracy and strong human rights practices often have an instrumental as well as an intrinsic position in the pursuit of national ideals. If this instrumental position is not strongly positive, both popular and élite support for democracy and human rights practices will more easily flag in the presence of military, political, and economic instability. Although human rights practices may play an important role in sustaining democracy, in the face of war and political and economic polarization such "traditions of civility"[13] may prove unreliable where they have not been ideologically incorporated as conditions of fulfilling the national collective's potential.

Human rights and economic development

Human rights practices, to the extent that they have contributed to maximum equality of economic opportunity, appear to have made an important contribution to the more successful post-communist transition economies. The dismantling of the planned economies invariably produced a large-scale collapse of capital-intensive industries and an associated economic downturn and unemployment surge. In all the economies that experienced rapid recoveries and sustained post-recovery growth, a crucial role was played by new, small-scale enterprises. This was, of course, made possible by permissive and stabilizing economic policies and supplemented by a range of other factors. Among these other factors, great importance is attributed to rule-of-law conditions.[14] These conditions are easily recognized as the basic human rights protections of equality under the law, along with neutral and efficient enforcement and adjudication.

Human rights and conflict resolution

In the former Soviet Union and Yugoslavia, enhanced human rights were often associated with increased conflict. This was because underlying ethnic conflicts over political and cultural autonomy, territory, and economic resources were controlled under the old regime – largely through the credible threat to use overwhelming force. When the "enforcer" disappeared, the disputes had to be resolved somehow. In particular, when it came to disputes over collective ethnic "rights" to territorial autonomy, it was often quite difficult to come to a mutually acceptable accommodation. Such disputes were at the root of all the severe post-communist ethnic conflicts.

Improvements in human rights practices were often associated with nationalist mobilizations and uncontrolled local and regional inter-ethnic hostilities – for example, in Croatia, Bosnia–Herzegovina, Serbia, Moldova, Azerbaijan, Georgia, and Tajikistan. Of course, often this did not happen – for example, in Ukraine, Latvia, and Estonia. On the other hand, communist parties retaining authoritarian powers were typically careful to avoid provoking inter-ethnic strife – for example, in Kazakhstan and Uzbekistan.

When it was in their interest to do so, authoritarian regimes were able to end ethnic fighting through timely concessions. For example, this was done by Heidar Aliev's regime in Azerbaijan and by Imomali Rakhmonov's in Tajikistan. However, these settlements are likely to last for only as long as "cold peace" is in the rulers' survival interests. It is typically in the interest of such rulers to maintain the rhetorical diversion of an unresolved conflict, as well as the option of a "hot" diversion should this prove desirable.

Democracies, even after learning that their maximal national goals may be unattainable, will not thereby automatically make whatever concessions are necessary to achieve a lasting peace agreement – even if this is possible, given the nature of their adversaries. Even after Slobodan Milošević, Serbians are not about to ratify an independent Kosovo Albanian state. Under Alija Izetbegović and his successors, Bosnian Muslims do not accept a partition in which the Serbs and Croats adhere to their mother nations. Ethnic Moldovans do not accept independent Gagauz and Transnitrian Slavic states. Under Eduard Shevardnadze, Georgians do not agree to an independent Abkhazian state or to the transfer of South Ossetia to form a "greater" Ossetia within the Russian Federation.[15] However, in all these cases, catastrophic military losses have convinced both masses and élites that they need to offer stronger political and cultural autonomy than they could comfortably contemplate in pre-war days. This is not to say either that conflict could have been avoided, had these concessions come at the outset, or that such concessions are sufficient to reach a long-term settlement at any later stage of the conflict. All sides must usually be willing to make significant compromises for a long-term settlement to be possible. Where reciprocal concessions were forthcoming, from a more popularly legitimate and moderate Gagauz leadership in Moldova, a long-term settlement was, indeed, reached.

Conclusions

All the hypothesized causes of variation in post-communist human rights practices appear to have had impacts in the predicted direction. However, frustrated national ideals and war had much stronger and more consistent effects than did level of economic development. Partly, this may be because pre-communist economic development remains somewhat correlated with post-communist economic development, so that the more powerful national identity variable picks up some of the impact of post-communist economic development; nevertheless, the influence of economic development remains surprisingly weak.

Stronger human rights protection is likely to have beneficial consequences for democratization and economic development; however, these beneficial effects are likely to be limited unless an array of other conditions are also favourable. The effects of improved human rights protection on conflict resolution are more difficult to predict.

The discussion of causes of human rights practices supports a way of examining cultures and national identities that is somewhat at variance with the norm. Rather than trying to assess whether religious, political, and other traditions are intrinsically more or less hospitable to modern conceptions of human rights, it is possible to assess whether those upholding such traditions are likely to view modern conceptions of human rights as advancing their cultural and national causes in a specific historical context.

Future research on causes of human rights practices might attempt to apply this rational and instrumental approach to culture in other regions and time periods. Very briefly, it may be helpful to suggest some possibilities. Natural comparisons to the post-communist states are offered by Latin America, the Middle East, Africa, and South and East Asia following decolonization. Within and across all of these regions, there was significant variation in the outcomes. The present approach would imply that two factors should be investigated in looking for cultural explanations of this variation: one factor is the pre-colonial history of political and economic development; another is the most powerful alternative model or models of national development existing at the historical moment of decolonization. The hypothesis is that regions and peoples with memories of greater pre-colonial political and economic development should be more likely to choose the most powerful contemporary alternative models of national development – those not tainted by association with the colonial regime. In turn, these post-colonial choices of development models should have systematic implications for human rights practices.[16] Needless to say, such implications might be negative as well as positive.

Appendix: Country rankings on predictors of frustrated national ideals

This appendix offers a brief explanation of the country rankings in table 11.1, which are used to construct the predictive index of frustrated national ideals. The idea behind the first, economic ranking is that countries with greater pre-communist economic achievements will look much more unfavourably on the consequences of planned (Soviet) or socialized (Yugoslav) economic regimes. The best available quantitative index of development is share of the workforce employed in agriculture. Particularly in the former Soviet Union, the titular ethnic group's share was often markedly higher than the total share, owing to the predominance of ethnic Russians in the big cities. The units fall into six distinguishable groups: (1) Czechoslovakia is at the bottom, with 34.6 per cent; (2) Hungary and Slovenia have around 50 per cent; (3) Croatia, Estonia, Latvia, and Poland have around 60 per cent; (4) Albania, Armenia, Azerbaijan, Bosnia–Herzegovina, Bulgaria, Georgia, Lithuania, Macedonia, Romania, Russia, and Serbia–Montenegro have 70–85 per cent; Ukraine, Belarus, Uzbekistan, and Tajikistan have 85–95 per cent; and Kazakhstan, Kyrgyzstan, Turkmenistan, and Mongolia have 95–100 per cent.[17]

The second ranking refers to past political achievement for states having independent juridical and administrative status under communism, and to past independence and political achievement for states not having such independence under communism.[18] Thus, Russia, Mongolia, Poland, and (somewhat more ambiguously) Hungary were all once centres of greater empires. However, this standard would not have been violated during the communist period for Russians, the dominant ethnic group of the former USSR. Czechoslovakia, Bulgaria, and Romania were once truly independent states that were reduced to satellite status after World War II. Under Nicolae Ceausescu, Romania was able to carve out a limited autonomy from Soviet control; hence, Romanians would not be expected to feel the same level of resentment towards the communist political order per se. Newly independent Slovaks, emerging from the shadow of the more numerous and economically advanced Czechs, would not be expected to feel the same level of political hostility towards the period of communist rule. Albania was able to maintain an independent national communism, while Russia, again, provided the ethnic core of the USSR.

Among states that did not have separate juridical status under communism, the Baltic States (Estonia, Latvia, and Lithuania) had the most recent and most popularly legitimate period of independence. Here, the Soviet political yoke was felt most strongly. The Caucasian States had a few brief years of independence after the end of World War I, but only in Armenia and Georgia did this involve an influential mass mobilization process aimed at securing a self-consciously held national identity. Nor is this surprising, given that Armenia and Georgia both had broken (but consistently recovered) histories of political independence and regional prominence going back over a millennium. Given the dominant role of Serbia within the interwar Yugoslavia, and the preceding decades of Serbian independence following the collapse of Ottoman power in Europe, the Federal Republic of Yugoslavia could be plausibly placed in between the Baltic and Caucasian states. Although Serbs were numerically preponderant in the Yugoslav state and army, they increasingly viewed Josep Broz Tito's federal system as artificially marginalizing them relative to the smaller ethnic groups. Slovenia and, to a somewhat lesser extent, Croatia had strong traditions of regional political autonomy within larger territorial units. Both would have preferred independence after World War I, but felt compelled to unify with Serbia in order to protect themselves from Italian and Hungarian territorial ambitions. They, too, viewed Tito's system as one that marginalized them. Ukrainian political independence developed in the ninth through the eleventh centuries, but the region was then partitioned among different empires until its consolidation under Soviet rule after World War II. Over the centuries, a large part of the Ukrainian population came to identify closely with the Russian nation. In Moldova there was a distinct pre-communist national identity, as in the Baltic States violated in more recent memory; however, this identity was as part of the Romanian nation. The Persian-speaking Tajiks and Turkic-speaking Uzbeks were jointly at the core of a number of medieval Islamic empires and civilizations centred on Bukhara and Samarkand. But their distinct national identities developed only during the Soviet period and, to this day, there is dispute over which people has the "correct" claim to Bukhara, Samarkand, and their historical legacies. None of the other Soviet successor states had a prior independent political existence. The same can be said for Bosnia–Herzegovina. Macedonian Slavs are ethnically closest to Bulgarians, and were subjected to intense Serbianization during the interwar period. A sharply distinct Macedonian political identity did not develop until the Yugoslav period.

These political rankings can, of course, be debated at the margins. For example, compared with Bulgaria, the Czech Republic arguably achieved more and had greater popular legitimacy during the interwar period of independence. Arguably, Croatia and Slovenia had somewhat weaker traditions of political independence than Serbia. However, making limited adjustments, such as moving the Czech Republic up one level and/or moving Croatia and Slovenia down one level, do not significantly affect the overall rankings.

Threat to national integrity (the third ranking) refers to extent of large-scale presence and immigration of other ethnic groups – often under Soviet auspices – and, to a lesser extent, to Soviet territorial annexations. Upon the collapse of the old regimes, Kazakhstan, Kyrgyzstan, and Latvia all had huge minority populations (46 per cent or more of the total), while Bosnia–Herzegovina had no ethnic majority. The minority populations of Macedonia, Estonia, Moldova, and Tajikistan were also quite large (35–38 per cent). Croatia, Belarus, Lithuania, Ukraine, Azerbaijan, Georgia, Uzbekistan, Serbia–Montenegro, and Turkmenistan had sizeable but not so threateningly large minority populations (20–30 per cent). Romania (despite its 9 per cent Hungarian minority) and particularly Poland were more homogeneous, but suffered significant territorial losses at the hands of Russia and the Soviet Union in the recent past. Armenia was also relatively homogeneous, but her claims to Nagorno-Karabakh must be factored in.[19]

Repression under communism (the fourth ranking) was most severe within the Soviet Union itself and in Mongolia. Collectivization and mass purges and deportations under Stalin took the greatest human tolls, although repression and casualties on a comparable scale often occurred during the period of civil war following the Bolshevik Revolution. In Eastern Europe, all countries experienced severe purges of non-communist élites during and/or after World War II. Of the latter, Poland and (somewhat less so) Hungary suffered most in the Soviet sphere, and Croatia and (to a lesser extent) Serbia–Montenegro and Slovenia most in the Yugoslav sphere. National communist regimes in Albania and Romania maintained high levels of repression until just before their collapse.[20]

Notes

1. To clarify, two issues are being argued. There is some definitional overlap between human rights and necessary elements of democratic political processes. For practical reasons, protection of political rights is more likely to be associated with protection of non-political rights, and violation of political rights with violation of non-political rights.
2. For overviews, see the relevant chapters in Ian Bremmer and Ray Taras, *New States, New Politics: Building the Post-Soviet Nations*, Cambridge: Cambridge University Press, 1997, and Bogdan Szajkowski, ed., *Political Parties of Eastern Europe, Russia and the Successor States*, London: Longman, 1994.
3. See Janos Kornai, *The Socialist System: The Political Economy of Communism*, Princeton: Princeton University Press, 1992; Marie Lavigne, *The Economics of Transition: From Socialist Economy to Market Economy*, London: Macmillan, 1995; and World Bank, *From Plan to Market: World Development Report 1996*, Washington, DC: Oxford University Press, 1996.
4. Another measure, which is highly correlated with agricultural share of the workforce, is gross domestic product at purchasing power parity. However, the latter measure is not available for many poorer post-communist countries.
5. The CLI and PRI indices are given in Freedom House, *Annual Survey of Freedom Country Scores, 1972–1973 to 1999–2000*, Washington, DC: Freedom House, 2001. Along with a more detailed discussion of the ranking criteria, they are also available at the Freedom House website, ⟨http://www.freedomhouse.org⟩.
6. Alternatively, simpler indices could be constructed by using the average or the maximum of the rankings of pre-communist political and economic achievement. Since the

correlations between these alternative indices and the one in the text exceed 90 per cent, the alternative indices have a virtually identical impact. Results for the two alternative indices are available upon request.

7. Except in Bosnia–Herzegovina, the plurality religion is everywhere the majority religion.

8. For data on agricultural share of the workforce and GDP per capita at purchasing power parity, see World Bank, *From Plan to Market*, pp. 188–189 and pp. 194–195; World Bank, *The State in a Changing World: World Development Report 1997*, Washington, DC: Oxford University Press, 1997, pp. 214–215 and pp. 220–221; Socialist Federal Republic of Yugoslavia, "The Non-Agricultural Population," *Yugoslav Survey*, No. 28, 1987, pp. 3–24.

9. Information on the incidence and duration of warfare can be found in Szajkowski, *Political Parties*; Karen Dawisha and Bruce Parrott, eds, *Conflict, Cleavage, and Change in Central Asia and the Caucasus*, Cambridge: Cambridge University Press, 1997; Karen Dawisha and Bruce Parrott, *Democratic Changes and Authoritarian Reactions in Russia, Ukraine, Belarus, and Moldova*, Cambridge: Cambridge University Press, 1997; and Karen Dawisha and Bruce Parrott, eds, *Politics, Power, and the Struggle for Democracy in South-East Europe*, Cambridge: Cambridge University Press, 1997.

10. The virtually all-pervasive institutions of the communist system itself would appear far more relevant for this sort of habitual impact. Yet these institutions should have affected all post-communist countries more or less equally. Duration of time under communist rule is also a weak predictor: it cannot explain the significant variation both across the former Soviet Union and Mongolia and across Eastern and South-eastern Europe.

11. A similar story holds for the relatively less important Islamic Renaissance Party of Uzbekistan.

12. See the summaries of party platforms in Szajkowski, *Political Parties*, and in the 1997 Cambridge University Press series edited by Dawisha and Parrott: *Conflict, Cleavage, and Change in Central Asia and the Caucasus*; *The Consolidation of Democracy in East-Central Europe*; *Democratic Changes and Authoritarian Reactions in Russia, Ukraine, Belarus, and Moldova*; and *Politics, Power, and the Struggle for Democracy in South-East Europe*. For Tajikistan, see also Shahram Akbarzadeh, "Why Did Nationalism Fail in Tajikistan?" *Europe–Asia Studies*, Vol. 48, July 1996, pp. 1105–1129; Allen Hetmanek, "Islamic Revolution and Jihad Come to the Former Soviet Central Asia: The Case of Tajikistan," *Central Asian Survey*, Vol. 12, Summer 1993, pp. 365–378; and Habibollah Abolhassan Shirazi, "Political Forces and Their Structures in Tajikistan." *Central Asian Survey*, Vol. 16, Fall 1999, pp. 611–622.

13. This phrase is used by the British political theorist, Ernest Barker.

14. Anders Åslund, *How Russia Became a Market Economy*, Washington, DC: Brookings Institution, 1995; EBRD [European Bank for Reconstruction and Development], *Transition Report*, London: EBRD, 1994–1999; World Bank, *From Plan to Market: World Development Report 1996*, Washington, DC: Oxford University Press, 1997.

15. For treatments of these conflicts, see Bruno Coppieters, *Contested Borders in the Caucasus*, Brussels: VUBPRESS, 1996, available at http://poli.vub.ac.be/publi/ContBorders/eng/info.htm; Michael Croissant, *The Armenian–Azerbaijani Conflict: Causes and Implications*, Westport, CT: Praeger, 1998; the series edited by Dawisha and Parrott; Laura Silber and Allan Little, *The Death of Yugoslavia*, London: Penguin, 1996; and Szajkowski, *Political Parties*.

16. For examples of studies that contain elements of such an approach, see Jill Crystal, "The Human Rights Movement in the Arab World," *Human Rights Quarterly*, Vol. 16, August 1994, pp. 435–454; and Bonny Ibhawoh, "Between Culture and Constitution:

Evaluating the Cultural Legitimacy of Human Rights in the African State," *Human Rights Quarterly*, Vol. 22, August 2000, pp. 838–860.

17. Czechoslovakia is grouped with Hungary and Slovenia in order to use five-level rankings across all four dimensions. Allowing a sixth level for past economic achievement has no significant effect on the results. Data are from Ralph Scott Clem, *The Changing Geography of Soviet Nationalities and its Socioeconomic Correlates, 1926–1970*, PhD Diss., Columbia University, 1976, p. 278; B.R. Mitchell, *European Historical Statistics, 1750–1975*, New York: Facts on File, 1980, series C1; Dijana Plestina, *Regional Development in Communist Yugoslavia: Success, Failure, and Consequences*, Boulder, CO: Westview, 1992, 22; Joseph Rothschild, *East Central Europe between the Two World Wars*, Seattle, WA: University of Washington Press, 1974, pp. 37, 39, 91, 167, 204, 285, 359, 367, 369; Socialist Federal Republic of Yugoslavia, "The Non-Agricultural Population"; Jozo Tomasevich, *Peasants, Politics and Economic Change in Yugoslavia*, Stanford, CA: Stanford University Press, 1955, pp. 239, 304.

18. Bremmer and Taras, eds, *New States, New Politics: Building the Post-Soviet Nations*; D.A. Dyker and I. Vejvoda, eds, *Yugoslavia and After: A Study in Fragmentation, Despair and Rebirth*, London: Longman, 1996; Zev Katz, ed., *Handbook of Major Soviet Nationalities*, New York: Free Press, 1975; Rothschild, *East Central Europe between the Two World Wars*; Tomasevich, *Peasants, Politics and Economic Change in Yugoslavia*.

19. Bremmer and Taras, eds, *New States, New Politics: Building the Post-Soviet Nations*; Adrian Karatnycky, Alexander Motyl, and Boris Shor, *Nations in Transit 1997: Civil Society, Democracy and Markets in East Central Europe and the Newly Independent States*, New Brunswick, NJ: Transaction, 1997; Szajkowski, *Political Parties*.

20. Stéphane Courtois, Nicholas Werth, Jean-Louis Panné, Andrzej Paczkowski, Karel Bartosek, and Jean-Louis Margolin, *The Black Book of Communism: Crimes, Terrors, Repression*, trans. by Jonathan Murphy and Mark Kramer, Cambridge, MA: Harvard University Press, 1999; see also Nora Beloff, *Tito's Flawed Legacy: Yugoslavia and the West, 1939–1984*, London: Gollancz, 1985, pp. 115–128; Sabrina P. Ramet, *Nationalism and Federalism in Yugoslavia, 1962–1991*, Bloomington, IN: Indiana University Press, 1992, p. 255; Peter Vodopivech, "Seven Decades of Unconfronted Incongruities: The Slovenes and Yugoslavia," in Jill Benderly and Evan Kraft, eds, *Independent Slovenia: Origins, Movements, Prospects*, Boulder, CO: Westview Press, 1994, pp. 34–35.

12

Human rights and conflict in the former Yugoslavia[1]

Aleksandar Resanovic

Overview of human rights and freedoms in the political context

The former Yugoslavia was, and has remained, a politically tectonic region. Human rights and freedoms as political issues were insufficiently known to the general public, and were pushed aside to be addressed in future – hopefully better – times. The price of this policy turned out to be high, particularly in the Federal Republic of Yugoslavia (FRY; since 4 February 2003, Serbia and Montenegro), Croatia, and Bosnia and Herzegovina.

The relations between Serbia and Croatia, often embittered by war and crisis, should be the basis of peacemaking and integration processes in the Balkans. The case of Serbia and Montenegro is interesting for a number of reasons: the fate of this two-member union is still unknown, because disputed relations between Serbia and Montenegro, and the status of Kosovo, are all awaiting a final resolution. Finally, Bosnia and Herzegovina, a very complex national and confessional community, has since time immemorial been the object of aspirations and territorial claims by Belgrade and Zagreb. Bosnia and Herzegovina's Dayton structure (see later) is very fragile and therefore remains in need of international support.

The Communist regime that was in power during the post-World War II period came to an end following the break-up of the former Socialist

266

Federal Republic of Yugoslavia (former Yugoslavia) in 1991. Instead of addressing the numerous political, economic, and other problems, the regime used repression to suppress them. Following the death of former President Tito in 1980, the problems, accumulated over decades, were not appropriately addressed; they were, instead, put "on the back burner." The challenges of post-1980 former Yugoslavia were exacerbated by the country's demographic and socio-cultural make-up, comprising several ethno-nationalities, with different religions, mentalities, histories, and levels of development. In both the distant and more recent past, these peoples had waged numerous conflicts, including wars with tremendous human costs and other destruction. Continuous conflicts created a culture of violence, not of rights and freedoms. Similar problems between former Yugoslavia and its neighbours – and within the region – further aggravated the situation in Serbia and Montenegro.

Inter-ethnic, inter-religious conflicts between states and peoples of the former Yugoslavia still exist. Both historically and currently, these conflicts have been worst between Serbs and Albanians. The subject of dispute is the territory of Kosovo, which formally still belongs to Serbia, with the status of an autonomous province; however, for decades the Albanians have been the majority population. The present situation regarding the status of Kosovo is well known: in compliance with UN Security Council Resolution 1244, Kosovo has been placed under international rule, whereas Serbia exercises virtually no authority over the area. Human rights violations have been commonplace in Kosovo for a very long time, particularly during times of armed confrontations. They are directed against Albanians and, nowadays, also against Serbs. This has slowed (and sometimes prevented) democratization, establishment of the rule of law, and economic development.

In order to understand the human rights situation in the various states of the former Yugoslavia, it is important to reassess the events that unsettled this region during the past decades. Our focus is on the last decade of the twentieth century, in which we witnessed the break-up of the state, tragic wars, various forms of state violence against citizens, an international bombing campaign against one of the states (FRY), and violations of human rights and freedoms in all the states under review.

The accumulated problems in the territory of former Yugoslavia escalated drastically in 1991. The war on the territories of Croatia and Bosnia and Herzegovina lasted almost four years and ended with the signing of the Dayton Peace Accords in 1995. The most conspicuous consequences of the war were its many victims – including large numbers of brutally killed civilians – and extensive infrastructure damage. This war was waged contrary to all standards of international law and ethics. The most drastic examples include the killing of some 8,000 Muslim civilians, including women and children, by Bosnian Serb forces in the summer of 1995 in Srebrenica; extremely inhumane treatment of prisoners of war (e.g. the Omarska camp); the removal of traces of the killing of members of the opposite side by throwing dead bodies into pits and torching them; and the rape of women of other nationalities for the purpose of humiliating their ethnic community. These acts, committed by all sides to the conflict on many occasions, represent gross violations of international humanitarian law. After the ratification of the Peace Accords, inter-governmental relations between these former Yugoslav republics were slowed down considerably by the "baggage" and memory of years of conflict. The consequences are evident to this day.

Although the 1990s were marked by major violations of human rights and freedoms, these were not exclusively caused by the war. The "war of arms" had been preceded by a "war of words" or, more precisely, by the language of hatred, as apparent in all state-owned media in all of the mentioned states. This language of hatred drove and accompanied the separation and independence movements that took place from 1991 in Croatia, Slovenia, Bosnia and Herzegovina, and Macedonia.

Hate speech was used in the electronic media more than in the print media. Special TV and radio stations were established in particular areas, often close to the border, to put pressure on the population. This was not ordinary propaganda: it was incitement of hatred toward persons belonging to other ethnic groups and religions, and a call to join new or continuing armed conflicts. In particular, there were appeals to lynch individuals and groups, or such morbid proposals that every good "master of the house" should kill at least one neighbour of another ethnic group or religion. Such "hate speech" was broadcast on state television in Serbia and Croatia almost daily from autumn 1991 (battles for Vukovar) until the Croatian Army's operations forced several hundred thousand Serbs to leave Croatia and flee to Serbia (1991–1995). Almost all print media were also strictly government controlled. They, too, incited hatred, antagonism, and violence through hate speech, albeit not as intensively as electronic media.

The states experienced largely interwoven and mutually interdependent historical, economic, and cultural development but they differed, nevertheless. In the historical perspective, the accumulated problems from our distant past surfaced especially during World War II, when a large number of Serbs and Croats perished in brutal conflicts. Since previous Yugoslavia was formed in 1918, the nationality question has not been solved. The complexity of these overarching problems indicates that former Yugoslavia, formed for the most part following the diktat of Western allies after World War I, did not have good prospects for developing into a common, multinational, and multi-confessional state. The emphasis in former Yugoslavia throughout her life was on national, religious, and other differences, rather than on similarities that could have been used as the basis of a common state or, at least, its peaceful demise by agreement.

Most inhabitants of Serbia and Montenegro share the Orthodox faith. Most scholars believe that Serbs and Montenegrins represent one people, with particularities that have of late become more pronounced. These two peoples managed to preserve their identity even during 500 years of Turkish rule; however, they acquired characteristics from the Ottoman Turks, including a tradition of disrespect for human rights. This is most evident from the fact that the Balkan peoples are mostly intolerant of persons belonging to other nations and religions and especially of women, whom they view as second-class citizens. Other minority groups are similarly discriminated against on racial, sexual, professional, political, and other grounds. Various human rights violations result from such national and cultural characteristics.

At the same time, Croatia came under considerable German influence, as part of the Austro-Hungarian monarchy until its demise. The territory of Croatia was, and remains, mostly inhabited by the Croats, a people of Roman Catholic faith.

Bosnia and Herzegovina is characterized by an extremely complex national and religious society. In certain stages of its development, this was felt to be the national wealth and, hence, an advantage; in the later stages, however, it was viewed as an insurmountable, aggravating circumstance, which was one of the main reasons for the outbreak of war and the cruel inter-ethnic killings of the early 1990s.

In such historic circumstances, with very different religious and cultural influences exerted by powerful states, the issue of human rights was a purely academic one. The basic human right to life was, for the most part, jeopardized, and the enjoyment of other human rights and freedoms was made impossible.

Even if the best intentions had existed to overcome all the problems – or, at least, to mitigate them – it would not have been easy to come to terms with such a diverse historical legacy. However, there were no such good intentions; rather, the political élite in former Yugoslavia (which was, at the same time, the financial élite) wanted to gain state and legal independence. Each élite in its own state became the only authority and power. The successor states of the former Yugoslavia were governed by these same élites, displaying the same disregard for human rights. This made it extremely difficult for the process of separation, which was initiated in 1990, to end peacefully. It soon became clear that the republican leaders did not intend to give up their positions on the future political relations between the republics. Their initiatives for a peaceful division of the former Yugoslavia were dishonest, and armed conflicts broke out in the following year of 1991. It even seems that they wanted the break-up of the common state to be brutal and violent, so that subsequent difficulties could always be externalized, and blamed on another ethnic group. Borne on the waves of nationalism, inter-ethnic intolerance, and hatred, they set out to acquire and maintain political leadership and financial power.

The methods employed by Slobodan Milošević in Yugoslavia/Serbia were the same as (or very similar to) those used by Franjo Tudjman in Croatia, or by Alija Izetbegović in Bosnia and Herzegovina. The rise of nationalism on one side caused a corresponding phenomenon on the other side – the strengthening (and hardening) of the position of one national leader had the same effect on the other national leaders. The absence of the desire and capacity for peaceful negotiations and dispute settlements destroyed the prospects for peaceful inter-republic relations. This dynamic resulted in the isolation of the FRY from the rest of the world, impoverished it, and pushed it several decades into the past.

In all three of these states, authoritarian leaders imposed strict control over legislative, executive, and judicial powers. All government institutions functioned under their strict orders, in defence of the "national interest." They also controlled the media, universities, banks and other financial institutions, insurance companies, business firms, phantom political parties, NGOs (that they, themselves, had established), and other vital institutions. In cooperation with loyal, like-minded followers, they therefore controlled all spheres of life. This situation was most pronounced in Serbia. Milošević was a classical dictator and managed to stay in power longer than any of the other post-Yugoslav leaders. The country's international isolation facilitated his work.

Causes and consequences of human rights violations in the FRY (Serbia and Montenegro), Croatia, and Bosnia and Herzegovina

The Federal Republic of Yugoslavia – Serbia and Montenegro

For two reasons, the FRY deserves greater attention in this chapter than Croatia and Bosnia and Herzegovina: first, massive political changes have occurred only recently (some ten years later than in other former Yugoslav Republics); second, widespread disrespect for human rights was most pronounced in this republic. Human rights violations were marked by certain particularities that require additional explanation.

The FRY's constitution and human rights

Of a total of 144 articles in FRY's constitution, one-thir
rights and freedoms (Section 2, Articles 19–68).[2] This is not s.
Milošević's regime always formally advocated respect for human ,
and freedoms – while, of course, in reality treating them quite differently.
However, the constitutional arrangements are not sufficiently harmonized with contemporary international legal standards and domestic laws.

Between 1992 and 2000, the FRY was expelled from numerous international organizations or had its membership "frozen." It could not
accede to a single instrument of these organizations. Yugoslavia's full
membership in most of those organizations was restored after the fall of
the Milošević regime.

Serbia and Montenegro has been admitted to the Council of Europe
on 3 April 2003. As far as discrepancies of the internal legal system
are concerned, it should be noted that both Serbia's and Montenegro's
Republican Constitutions[3] depart significantly from that of the FRY;
however, as major constitutional changes are on the horizon, these differences do not have to be rectified now.

As for the lack of coordination between laws and the FRY Constitution, it should be noted that the Constitutional Law for the implementation of the FRY Constitution[4] contains a list of 37 important laws that
were supposed to be harmonized with the FRY Constitution by 31 December 1992. Nevertheless, in 2001–2002, almost all of these laws have
been brought into line with the FRY Constitution.

The Constitutional Chapter of the union of Serbia and Montenegro[5]
transferred numerous hitherto former federal jurisdictions to the two republics. Provisions for human rights are, however, one of the few items
that are within the competency of the union, regulated in the Chapter of
human and minority rights and civil freedoms.[6] Both chapters have been
harmonized with international standards. The few positive legal developments that have taken place over the past ten years were rarely implemented in practice.

The Serbian Premier Zoran Djindjić was assassinated on 12 March
2003, at the point when he was preparing for a showdown with the organized crime and mafia that have obstructed the cooperation with the
Hague Tribunal and the reform process. According to the Law on Measures to be Taken in the Case of a State of Emergency, "certain" citizens'
rights and freedoms guaranteed in the Constitution of Serbia were restricted. The Interior Ministry was entitled to arrest a person who was
jeopardizing the safety of other citizens and to retain him/her in 60-day
custody, without the right to an attorney or visits by relatives. During the
state of emergency (six weeks) the Interior Ministry arrested over 18,000

persons suspected of being, in one way or another, connected with Premier Djindjić's assassination, tied up with organized crime, or in possession of information crucial for tracing down suspects. Over 4,500 people were brought into – and retained in – custody.

The Milošević regime

The malevolent nature of the situation in Yugoslavia came to full expression with Milošević's ascent to power. He established a dictatorship and surrounded himself with obedient and corrupt followers. He quickly asserted total control over the entire political and economic system of the country. The State Security Service (which was part of the Serbian Police) excelled in putting Milošević's ideas into practice and, in the process, showed brutal disrespect for human rights and freedoms. Milošević utilized the (until then, mostly contained) national and patriotic feelings of the Serb people to promote the idea that all Serbs should live together in one state, which would have to be carved out at the expense of the territories of Croatia and Bosnia–Herzegovina. Similar nationalist rhetoric and behaviour by Croatia's dictator Franjo Tudjman played into his hands.

Milošević played a significant role in creating public support for an eventual war in the territories of Croatia and Bosnia and Herzegovina. In the course of 1991 the media constantly carried information about meetings between Milošević and Tudjman, who were negotiating how to carve up and divide Bosnia and Herzegovina between Serbia and Croatia. Failed negotiations on this issue were one of the reasons for the outbreak of open armed conflict between Serbia and Croatia in the autumn of 1991.[7] At the same time, and because of the dangerous policy pursued by the Milošević regime, the international community imposed a political and economic blockade on the FRY. The UN Security Council introduced economic sanctions on 2 June 1992, suspended them in late 1995, and finally lifted them in 1996. After 1996, the so-called "outer wall" of sanctions remained in place; it was abolished after the changes of October 2000 in Serbia. These sanctions contributed in part to the conclusion of the Dayton Peace Accords in November 1995, but at the same time left a strong – and negative – imprint on the entire society and economy of the country.

The economic situation

The intensity of sanctions varied over the years. The economic situation was disastrous: in 1993 the registered annual inflation rate was more than 20 million per cent, a world record. In those days, monthly salaries of highly educated professionals equalled roughly US$10; if not exchanged for US dollars or another hard currency on the very day of receipt, it was almost completely worthless a day later.

Factories were entirely deserted, with production halted. Miraculously, life went on in the streets. Hundreds of thousands of people became jobless and were forced to resort to smuggling and selling of goods that were in short supply on the street, and to committing other petty criminal offences.

Minority relations

Milošević's authoritarian regime had no adequate answer to address the challenges posed by the country's national and religious minorities, who make up more than 30 per cent of Serbia and Montenegro's population. The overall complexity of these problems can best be seen in Kosovo. Over a long period, Albanian separatists have been advocating an ethnically pure and independent state of Kosovo. In pursuing this goal, they have committed drastic acts of violence against the non-Albanian population and Albanians loyal to Yugoslavia;[8] this has resulted in a steady reduction in the number of Serbs and other non-Albanians in Kosovo. According to a 1981 census, with participation of almost the entire population of Kosovo, Albanians accounted for 77 per cent and the Serbs for 13 per cent of a total population of 1,585,000. Judging by still preliminary and unprocessed data from the population census carried out in Yugoslavia in April 2002 (and in which only the Serbian population, which lives in enclaves, participated), Serbs now account for less than 4 per cent of Kosovo's total population.

However, these developments do not by any means justify a whole range of violent political and military actions carried out over the years by the authorities in Belgrade, that greatly diminished any chance for peaceful cohabitation of Albanians, Serbs, and others. The atrocities carried out by Serb forces in 1998 – not only against Albanian separatists but also against the civilian population at large – are well known. In early 1998 the Serbian police and Yugoslav army began to shell mostly Albanian settlements in Kosovo, forcing the Albanian civilian population to move into areas that were not under control of the Kosovo Liberation Army (KLA). In the process, a large number of Albanians were forced to abandon their homes.

According to a report from December 1998, about 300,000 persons, mostly Albanians and representing about 15 per cent of Kosovo's population, were displaced within the province during the first ten months of 1998. The United Nations reacted to such actions by "condemning the excessive use of force by Serbian police forces against civilians and peaceful protestors in Kosovo,"[9] and introduced an embargo on arms exports to the FRY. Six months later, the United Nations noted "the deterioration of the situation in Kosovo and the FRY" and therefore demanded all sides to "cease all hostilities and the Serbian side to withdraw security forces used for repression against civilians."[10] These and similar efforts resulted in the signing of an Agreement on the OSCE Verification Mission for Kosovo.[11] Regrettably, all these efforts did not alter the situation on the ground in Kosovo, and from 1 January until 24 March 1999 many lives were lost in continuing outbursts of violence. According to FRY government sources, the casualties included 102 Albanians, 26 Serbs, and 4 persons of other nationalities.[12] In contrast, according to the Kosova Information Centre, during the first 40 days of 1999 alone, Serb forces had killed 171 Albanians.[13] Particularly during 1998 and 1999, such significant differences in the number of casualties became a standard feature of reports from Kosovo, which is characteristic of the lack of impartiality and level of politicization in data collection and interpretation. Much information, from all sources, should be taken with a grain of salt.

Albanian citizens were detained for no reason and subsequently subjected to various acts of physical and mental torture. The Humanitarian Law Fund in Belgrade registered the commission of 500 torture cases during 1998 in Yugoslavia, of which over 400 were registered in Kosovo alone.[14] To this day an estimated 2,000 cases of torture have remained unaccounted for.[15] The killing of 45 Albanian civilians in the village of Štimlje on 15 January 1999 served as a direct pretext for NATO to launch air strikes on the FRY and Kosovo, lasting from 23 March to 7 June 1999. The precise number of civilian victims of the bombing campaign is unknown. As the level of violence rose during the campaign, around 600,000 Albanians fled Kosovo; about 2,000 of them have remained unaccounted for to this day. According to unconfirmed NGO reports, over 800,000 people, mostly Albanians, were forced out or voluntarily abandoned their homes. Following the suspension of the NATO intervention, the Albanian forces also engaged in unbridled violence against Serbs and other non-Albanian civilians: according to UNHCR data, an estimated 240,000 of these civilians were forced to flee Kosovo.

NATO's bombing campaign

NATO bombing operations were suspended with the passing of UN Security Council Resolution 1244.[16] The Resolution envisaged a political solution for the Kosovo crisis, including the immediate end to all armed hostilities, urgent withdrawal of the Yugoslav Army and Serbian police forces, as well as the deployment of representatives of international civil institutions and security forces under UN auspices. On 20 June 1999, all Yugoslav and Serbian forces pulled out of Kosovo.[17] As a result of the international military and civilian presence, a shaky peace has been maintained in Kosovo; without such presence, inter-ethnic war would probably reignite.

A similar scenario has also begun to unfold in southern Serbia. At the end of 2000, groups of Albanian militants carried out open armed attacks and incursions into the territory of southern Serbia. Following military threats and attacks, several thousand inhabitants fled these multinational municipalities. A peace agreement was concluded in May 2001, signed by Nebojša Čović, Vice-Premier of the Serbian Government and Šefćet Musliu, representative of the local Albanians. In addition to the cessation of all armed operations, the most important provision of this agreement was the disbanding of the Liberation Army of Preševo, Bujanovac, and Medvedja, previously commanded by Musliu. After signing the agreement, the Serbian government invested significant funds in this region: it attempted to raise the living standards of the population and thereby partially offset the prevailing dissatisfaction with government authorities. The Serbian government and many NGOs have been developing projects that address, among others, respect for human rights (especially those of minority groups), cohabitation of persons belonging to different ethnic communities, development of democratic institutions, establishment of the rule of law, and women's rights.

Civic unrest and the fall of Milošević

Particularly from 1998 to 2000, the Milošević regime's pressure on the media and universities intensified. The regime recognized the seriousness of an unfolding process of civic activism on the part of democratic opposition parties, various NGOs, Otpor (Resistance), the free media, intellectuals, and all those who openly raised their voices against the regime. Milošević began to apply drastic force to suppress the very few human rights and freedoms that remained. Struggling for these human rights and freedoms, the citizens of Serbia spent months in the streets of Serbian towns protesting against Milošević's dictatorship. Country-wide public protests in response to the regime's refusal to recognize the outcome of the November 1996 elections had already generated peaceful marches and rallies three months long, attended by several million Serbs between November 1996 and January 1997. Similar accusations sparked ten days of protests between 25 September and 5 October 2000.

The long-awaited end of this dictatorial regime came on 5 October 2000. A peaceful, democratic revolution asked for the implementation of the will of the people, as expressed at the elections held two weeks previously. After his attempts to rig the elections, and the subsequent open opposition of a vast majority of citizens, Milošević's regime was forced to acknowledge electoral defeat. About 71.5 per cent of the electorate had turned out for the presidential elections on 24 September 2000:[18] 50.2

per cent of the electorate voted for Koštunica and 37.2 per cent for Milošević. The remaining votes were evenly distributed among three more candidates. Elections for the Federal Assembly were held at the same time, with a turnout of 74.4 per cent: the Association of Opposition Parties (Democratic Opposition of Serbia; DOS) won 53.7 per cent of the seats, Milošević's Socialist Party of Serbia (SPS) 40.7 per cent, and Šešelj's Serb Radical Party (SRS) 5.6 per cent. In the republican parliamentary elections in Serbia, held on 23 December 2000, 74.4 per cent of the voters took part:[19] in these elections, DOS won 70.4 per cent of the seats, SPS 14.8 per cent, and SSJ (Party of Serb Unity; the party of the late Željko Ražnatović Arkan) 5.6 per cent.

The newly elected authorities at the Yugoslav and, subsequently, at the Serbian level faced the extremely difficult task of democratizing the society, promoting respect for human rights, and – in a nutshell – bringing all regulations and practices in Yugoslavia into line with relevant international standards.

The most daunting challenge for the new democratic authorities in Serbia is the need either to improve relations between Serbia and Montenegro or to separate peacefully by agreement.[20] Furthermore, in co-operation with the international community, they must settle the issue of Kosovo. Kosovo is only formally a part of Serbia, with actual power being exercised by international civil and military bodies. The Serbian authorities must regulate relations with their neighbouring states, particularly Croatia and Bosnia–Herzegovina, and integrate more than 800,000 refugees from Croatia, Bosnia and Herzegovina, and Kosovo into Serbian society.

The authorities must pursue full inclusion in the international community and membership in international organizations, and cooperate fully with the Hague Tribunal (including the surrender of persons charged by this Court with war crimes). They must implement the transition to a democratic society, despite a ten-year lag behind other former communist countries of Eastern and Central Europe. Together with the other countries that have been formed from the ruins of former Yugoslavia, they must address the issue of succession (i.e. property rights and liabilities of the former Yugoslavia).[21] They must establish an ombudsperson, as Serbia and Montenegro is one of the few countries in the world that still has not established this institution for the protection of human rights.

The new democratic authorities of Serbia were installed after all democratic opposition forces united. This anti-Milošević coalition, composed of 18 parties with very different orientations, inherited a number of problems and obligations that date from the time of the Milošević regime. Moreover, they take different positions on a variety of issues, differences that have become increasingly pronounced over time. Although the burden of the past has been alleviated to a great extent, in both political and economic respects, the rift between the two largest parties of the DOS coalition – the Democratic Party (the late Zoran Djindjić) and the Democratic Party of Serbia (Koštunica) – is threatening to jeopardize the gains made in the 2000 elections and the subsequent October revolution.

Republic of Croatia

Croatia's constitutional arrangements are similar to those of Yugoslavia. Approximately one-third of Croatia's Constitution is devoted to human rights issues.[22]

Laws are much better harmonized with the Constitution than in the case of the FRY. In the first few years following the formation of the independent state of Croatia, under wartime conditions (1991–1995), great disrespect was shown for human rights. The broad powers of President Tudjman were virtually limitless: he surrounded himself with loyal, corrupt, and incompetent persons and assumed full control of all political and economic institutions. For several years, public embrace of nationalism was encouraged: pent-up nationalist emotions, both cause and effect of Croatia's independence in 1991, were instrumentalized by the leadership. Intolerance of, and even hatred against, the Serb people developed, particularly in the aftermath of Serb operations in Slavonia and Krajina and the 2–3 May 1995 Serb shelling of Zagreb.[23]

Notwithstanding his authoritarian rule, Tudjman nevertheless initiated a process of transformation from communism to democracy – in terms of both actual changes and skilful presentations of changes that had little to do with genuine democratization. In any case, the international community acknowledged his "efforts" and offered him their support. On that basis, Croatia secured for herself much more favourable relations with the international community than did Yugoslavia (or Serbia), although human rights and freedoms were oppressed in a similar fashion: for example, during two successive local elections for the Mayor of Zagreb, President Tudjman simply did not allow the election results to be recognized; freedom of the press existed only to the extent that the media supported the Tudjman regime. On occasion, the people took to the streets to raise their voice against these restrictions of their rights and freedoms.[24]

Military actions against the Serb population – in Operations Flash and Storm – led to the emigration of more than 200,000 Serb civilians from their ancestral homes in Krajina and Eastern Croatia. During Operation Storm alone (4–7 August 1995), 267 Serb civilians were killed.[25]

The situation improved in many respects following the death of President Tudjman and the January 2000 elections. The authoritarian leader's departure from the political scene contributed significantly to the democratization of Croatian society. The newly elected democratic authorities delegated the wide powers of the former president, his family members, and followers to the Parliament and to other political and economic institutions. The electoral victory of the coalition of six democratic parties, which won close to two-thirds of the seats in Parliament, allowed Croatia in November 2000 to adopt constitutional amendments that switched from its specific semi-presidential system to a parliamentary one.

Nevertheless, the official attitude towards Serbia and the Serbs did not change significantly. This can be seen from the behaviour of the new authorities towards Serb refugees. The new authorities prevented their return by persistently creating new and difficult conditions. A large number of their burnt-down or destroyed homes, as well as other properties, have not been restored. Only 15,000 refugees have so far been able to return to the region of Kninska Krajina and only some 3,000 to the region of Eastern Slavonia. At the same time, the process of quiet emigration of Serbs from these areas continues. This can be confirmed by preliminary and unofficial data of the population censuses carried out in Croatia in 1991[26] (when Croatia was still part of the former SFRY) and in 2001.[27] According to the 1991 census results, there were 580,000 Serbs in Croatia; the 2001 census counted 180,000 Serbs, although the voters' lists for elections held in 2000 contained the names of 280,000 Serbs. In other words, in the 1991–2000 period, the number of Serbs fell from 580,000 to 280,000. From 2000 to 2001 – in just one year – it declined further from 280,000 to 180,000. In this connection, Milorad Pupovac, President of the Serbian National Council (of Croatia) stated that this was the result of "the ethnic cleansing of the Serb people."[28] In contrast, Siniša Tatalović, a Croatian expert on national minorities, explained this phenomenon with the claim that 100,000 Serbs asked to be deleted from the national minority voting rolls.[29]

The most daunting challenges for the new democratic authorities in Croatia are the following:

- to achieve genuine reconciliation between the Tudjman-era, hard-line, nationalist party (HDZ), which still enjoys strong support of the people, and the new democratic policies championed by President Mesić and Prime Minister Račan;
- to opt truly, both in words and in deeds, for democracy and for the rule of law;
- to ensure the speedy repatriation, under a simple procedure, of all refugees who wish to return;

- to integrate refugees effectively from specific parts of Croatia and of Bosnia and Herzegovina into the post-war society;
- to regulate relations with the neighbouring countries, particularly with Yugoslavia, Bosnia and Herzegovina, and Slovenia;
- to engage in full cooperation with the Hague Tribunal, including the surrender of persons indicted for war crimes;
- to eliminate the effects of war operations – in particular, to clean up an estimated one million anti-personnel mines;
- to continue and to speed up Croatia's substantive transformation into a democratic society; and
- to raise the low living standard of the population.

Bosnia and Herzegovina

The Constitution of Bosnia and Herzegovina (BiH) guarantees a broad range of human rights and freedoms. These are also in the constitutions of the two entities of BiH – the Republic of Srpska and the Muslim–Croatian Federation. Nevertheless, reality is quite another issue.

The tragic war in BiH left hundreds of thousands of people dead, wounded, or as refugees;[30] enormous infrastructure damage; a territory covered with some 1.5 million anti-personnel mines;[31] and inter-ethnic hatred. According to the 1991 population census, the total population of BiH[32] numbered 4,378,000 inhabitants – including 1.9 million Muslims, 1,365,000 Serbs, and 760,000 Croats – together accounting for some 92 per cent of the total population. According to estimates, some 220,000–290,000 people went missing or were killed[33] in the 1991–1995 war; 1.2 million people fled from BiH; and around 1 million inhabitants were forcibly displaced within BiH.[34]

The seemingly senseless war caused large-scale resettlements of the Bosnian peoples and their eventual separation into two ethnic communities. Naturally, this horrible task has not been fully completed – enclaves of national and religious minorities still exist. According to estimates by the BiH state authorities,[35] at the end of 2001 around 600,000 refugees were still living outside BiH and 550,000 persons remained displaced within BiH's borders. According to the same estimates, the population of BiH at that time was 3.5 million; that figure would have been about 4.5 million had it not been for the war.

After the war, the international community supported the creation of a Muslim–Croatian Federation, the dominant entity in BiH, under its leader Alija Izetbegović. In the first years after the war, Izetbegović's authoritarian regime attempted to force its will upon all of BiH's citizens. However, the Serbian and Croatian communities resisted such efforts.

The Serbian population was, and has remained, strongly nationalistic. The Serbian Democratic Party (the party of the former President of the Republic of Srpska, Radovan Karadžić) has won all parliamentary elections held so far in the Republic of Srpska. Likewise, the Croatian Democratic Union (HDZ) in the BiH Federation remained very homogeneous and resentful of attempts to move towards a more civil and democratic society.

Substantial changes were initiated upon Izetbegović's departure from the political scene. Political authority has returned to government institutions, and the international community, in the form of the UN High Representative, is now in charge of supervising and administering overall political affairs. The High Representative's authority to change or rescind decisions of the parliaments, governments, and other authorities, to override the will of the people expressed at elections, and to adopt laws with retroactive effects, represents a wide-ranging influence on the political life of BiH, reminiscent of the powers of governors in Commonwealth colonies in the early nineteenth century. Nevertheless, the fact remains that the common state of BiH has managed to survive only because of the presence of the international community. It is generally believed that, without this presence, an inter-ethnic conflict would break out immediately, escalating very soon to a full-blown war. Clearly, the lesser of two evils – international involvement or more war – has been chosen.

The old wounds of the long inter-ethnic conflict have not yet healed. It will probably take at least two generations before internal inter-ethnic understanding and reconciliation can be achieved. The presence of representatives of the international community is likely to be indispensable for decades to come (the situation in Cyprus is a case in point).

With the latest elections in BiH, new, democratic, and pro-Bosnian authorities were brought to office, composed of the Alliance for Change and a dozen other civic and democratic-minded parties. The electoral results have, de facto, created conditions for the dissolution of the Croation Union as a para-state within BiH and thus have eliminated efforts to create a third, Croatian, entity. In the Republic of Srpska the authorities have been divided. As a precondition set by the EU and United States for granting financial assistance, an expert government was formed.

The Commission for Human Rights, established under the Dayton Peace Agreement, holds an important place. It consists of the ombudsman's office and the Council for Human Rights, and the work of both has so far been very successful. Most importantly, citizens are actually utilizing these offices, rather than shunning them. Official authorities acknowledge their positions, statements, and findings – despite the fact that they have no legal status.

The future development of BiH depends on its ability to evolve into an integrated and authentic state and social community. This involves accomplishing a number of important – and difficult – tasks for the democratic authorities of BiH:

- to establish genuine unity of state and society, given that nationalist and separatist feelings are still very much alive;
- to adopt a single constitutional document for the entire BiH, which would aggregate all three existing constitutions – the BiH Constitution, the Constitution of the BiH Federation, and the Constitution of the Republic of Srpska;
- to integrate BiH itself, as a precursor to join the processes of regional and European integration legitimately and responsibly;
- to join, along with other states of the region, European integration processes and relevant organizations, especially the Stability Pact for South-East Europe;
- to promote and realize equality, inter-ethnic reconciliation, and the return of all interested refugees;
- to promote good-neighbourly relations with Yugoslavia and Croatia;
- to cooperate with the Hague Tribunal, including the surrender of persons accused of war crimes;
- to eliminate the consequences of war operations, particularly in respect of some 1.5 million remaining anti-personnel mines;
- to continue genuine transformation of the state of BiH into a civil, democratic society; and
- to raise the living standards of the population.

Differences in the exercise of individual human rights and freedoms in FRY (Serbia and Montenegro), Croatia, and Bosnia and Herzegovina

The most crucial development of human rights and freedoms in all three countries has been the departure of the authoritarian leaders Milošević, Tudjman, and Izetbegović. Subsequent strides towards democratization of all three societies have led to an expansion of human rights and freedoms. However, there is a continuation of nationalist feelings and accompanying separatist tendencies among parts of the population in each country. The nationalist-separatist ideas promoted by the former leaders still have strong appeal, particularly in Kosovo, Montenegro, and both entities of BiH. This represents one of the greatest problems and challenges of transition – to transform societies that harbour such feelings of intolerance towards members of other nations and religions into democratic, civil societies.

Death penalty, prohibition of torture, inhumane or degrading treatment, and punishment

The death penalty has been abolished in Croatia, BiH, and Yugoslavia.[36] Other improvements have been sanctioned by legislation in all three states. In practice as well, the situation is improving in all three states. There are still instances of torture in police detention but their occurrence is substantially lower than in previous years, owing to improved training of the police and harsh penalties for offenders.

Right to personal freedom and safety

Rights to personal freedom and safety have been addressed in the legislation of all three states. An important legal inconsistency existed in Yugoslavia for more than ten years: the Constitution specified that only a competent court can order detention, whereas the Law on Criminal Proceedings extended that right to the police as well. Relevant amendments to criminal legislation, mentioned earlier in this chapter, have rectified this inconsistency.

Treatment of persons deprived of liberty

Unfortunately, in all three states, poor prison conditions – primarily health care, hygiene and food, harassment, abuse and blackmail by prison guards, and, in some cases, inadequate treatment of women and adolescents – are the result of a widely held belief that "the guilty ones should suffer for what they have done." As a consequence, in all three states, conditions are well below contemporary international standards.

The right to a fair trial

The human right to a fair trial has been continually violated by authoritarian regimes in all three states. Courts and judges were (made) dependent on the regime. For as long as Milošević, Tudjman, and Izetbegović were in power, the practice of appointing only obedient and incompetent party cadres as judges degraded the principle of an independent judiciary: the right to a fair trial was greatly compromised. After the departure of the authoritarian leaders, the situation improved significantly in Croatia and BiH; however, because the judges that were appointed by Milošević's regime are still in office, there has been no improvement in the courts of Serbia. Very complicated recall procedures allow them to stay in office and continue to follow the demands of their party chiefs, thus hampering just trials. Eventually, the Law on Lustration (Sunshine

Law, banning former Communist operatives from public office) was adopted in Serbia on 30 May 2003.

The right to privacy

In all three states, special services (primarily intelligence services) ruthlessly endangered numerous rights and freedoms of citizens, especially the right to privacy (including access to personal data, sexual preferences, protection of homes/apartments, correspondence, and honour and reputation). Improvements have been noticeable since the departure of the former authoritarian leaders. In Serbia, those improvements have been slow, as the same secret service has been in place for decades, with only minimal personnel changes. However, procedures are currently under way for the adoption of a number of laws (on the reform of police, on the separation of secret police from the regular police force into a special agency, and on the opening of secret police files) that would call for significant personnel changes, particularly in the secret service.

Freedom of expression, i.e. freedom of the work of the media

In all three states a strictly government-controlled media had been put in the service of the regime to spread regime propaganda and ethnic hatred among the population. Owners and editors-in-chief of the small number of organizations that opposed such control (such as the *Dnevni Telegraf* [*Daily Telegraph*], *Danas*, *Anem*, and the radio station B92) became victims of assassinations: for example, Slavko Ćuruvija, the owner of the *Daily Telegraph*, was killed in Belgrade in 1999; the paper's editor-in-chief, Zeljko Kopanja, lost both legs after a bomb was planted under his car in Banjaluka in 1998; numerous newspapers, magazines, or radio stations were prohibited and heavily fined; conditions in Serbia were particularly appalling. With the departure of the authoritarian leaders, the situation improved radically.

The right to peaceful assembly

The right to peaceful assembly has been violated in all three states – most blatantly, in Serbia. The authorities banned all gatherings that appeared to threaten the regime. Public gatherings were immediately ordered to disperse. The largest number of rallies was registered in Serbia. With all political institutions and the media completely under the regime's control, this was the only way for citizens to express their views. The Milošević regime did shy away from using violence to put down protests (this was particularly true during protests by students and Otpor against electoral theft from November 1996 to January 1997 and against the government's rigging of the September–October 2000 elections).

The right to unhindered use of property

The right to unhindered use of property was widely violated in all states. The destruction, burning, seizure, or forcible acquisition of property of refugees and internally displaced persons was used to further the nationalist policies of authoritarian leaders. The situation in Croatia and BiH is still poor, as the return of Serbs and other refugees is still largely being prevented. The situation is similar in Kosovo. The lion's share of responsibility lies with the international community, which is not enforcing conditions under which Serbs and other non-Albanians can return and repossess their property without hindrance.

Minority rights

Minority rights have been disregarded in all three states. Irrespective of existing legislation on minority issues in all three countries, their actual behaviour towards persons from national and religious minorities has changed only slightly since the departure of the authoritarian regimes: persons belonging to other ethnic groups and religions are still widely considered and treated as enemies. Their property was destroyed or forcibly taken when they were forced to abandon their homes before or during the war, all with the intent to prevent their eventual return. Worst of all, the prevailing public attitude still holds that members of other ethnic or religious communities should be driven out of the state or, in some cases, should be assimilated. For instance, the Serb population of Croatia has dropped by one-third, in the capital of Zagreb even to one-sixth of its pre-war population. On the other hand, the number of Croats in Yugoslavia, more precisely in the province of Vojvodina, has fallen to one-eighth of its pre-war level.[37]

Clearly, a long and difficult road lies ahead for all three states in their efforts to achieve inter-ethnic reconciliation and the creation of societies that fully respect the rights of their ethno-national minorities.

The right to free elections

The right to free elections was also violated severely by all three states. It was commonly assumed that those authorities that call elections are also the ones that win them. This perception was the result of the regimes' total control over the entire electoral process – from the adoption of relevant election laws, to the elections, and to vote counting. Unfortunately, this perception proved to be correct while these authoritarian regimes were in power; nevertheless, elections did bring about political changes, most recently in Yugoslavia during the elections of October 2002. However, events in Belgrade have shown that this was achieved with much more difficulty in Yugoslavia than in Zagreb and Sarajevo. Well-organized elections benefited the post-electoral protests that defended the actual election results, which, in turn, led to Milošević's subsequent fall from power. A number of international organizations played an extremely important role in these developments: in particular, the observer missions of the OSCE and the Council of Europe significantly contributed to the democratic organization and monitoring of elections.

Special protection of women and children

Special protection of women and children has not been adequately implemented in any of the former Yugoslav states. Particularly in Montenegro and BiH, women are traditionally disparaged, and it is commonly believed that women and children should be beaten, as "the stick is the surest peacemaker." Since none of these states provide either full practical or legal protection, numerous NGOs have dedicated their efforts to educating the population and providing protection, including emergency telephone lines for victims of violence, women's autonomous centres, and children's rights centres.

Freedom of association

The constitutional freedom of association is guaranteed in all three states. However, there are limits to the formation of political or trade unions if their purpose is to undermine the Constitution.

Economic and social rights

Economic and social rights have been significantly jeopardized in all three states, with the worst violations in Serbia. Ineffective economic policies, the tragic legacy of the past, destroyed and plundered companies, and the grey economy are all problems that seem insurmountable at the moment. Citizens are driven to smuggling, street peddling, and other petty criminal offences. In all states, economic improvement can be achieved only with efficient financial assistance. Usually, this comes with political strings attached, further complicating a difficult situation. The international community's political demands on Yugoslavia (Serbia and Montenegro) include close cooperation with the Hague Tribunal (including the hand-over of all indictees and access to all state archives), a domestic settlement of the relations between Serbia and Montenegro, and an adequate political solution for Kosovo.

Certain contemporary human rights and freedoms (such as the protection of consumers and the right to a healthy environment) have not yet become the subject of major research, as citizens of all three states are still concerned with some of the more vital rights. The considerable financial resources and civic–cultural level required of citizens for their implementation are remote prospects: after all, it has been only a few years since the war in Croatia and BiH ended and Yugoslavia witnessed NATO bombing and the end of a dictatorial regime. In all three states the first priority is to resolve the most burning problems of state regulation, development of democratic institutions, and respect for basic human rights and freedoms, before third- and fourth-generation rights can be addressed.

Concluding remarks

In the FRY (Serbia and Montenegro), Croatia, and Bosnia and Herzegovina, the authoritarian regimes and their leaders (Milošević, Tudjman, and Izetbegović) were the main sources of human rights violations. They skilfully utilized the rise of nationalism within the population, which resulted from 50 years of communist dictatorship and numerous unresolved national questions throughout the former Yugoslavia, in an attempt to fulfil their own separatist aspirations and to emerge as undisputed rulers of their newly formed states.

Nationalism and hatred of other peoples and religions were promoted (and virtually institutionalized) as a precondition for the brutal break-up of the former Yugoslavia. Ethnonationalism was, and has largely remained, widely and deeply entrenched among the three constituent ethnic groups. So far, nationalism is not on the retreat, and nationalists have not renounced the support they had given to their former leaders. Nationalists have redirected their support to new leaders who have now donned "democratic suits," by skilfully declaring themselves as either democrats or nationalists, depending on the political circumstances.

In all these states, political, economic, and judicial institutions, as well as the media and other civic organizations, were tightly controlled by the authoritarian leaders: their main function was to protect the regime. None the less, movement towards democratization and establishment of the rule of law has been initiated and the first results are visible. In large part owing to the work of NGOs, the media, and academic experts, a culture of human rights is taking root: numerous professional panels and

workshops are being organized, professional lit
and relevant international documents are being

It is the general impression of citizens, intern
tional NGOs, as well as local and foreign media
improved their human rights record. This is not
inely strengthened commitment to the culture of
doms; rather, governments know that both the in
and their own citizens are not willing to tolerate t
vious excesses.

Against this backdrop, the chances are slim of ....tions in
which all contemporary human rights are respected and protected. In the
past, none of the three states had substantive human rights protection
policies in place: constitutional provisions were restricted or conditioned
by various legal provisions. This was particularly pronounced and commonplace in Yugoslavia, during the Milošević period.

In the three states, disrespect for human rights was exacerbated by
inter-communal conflict and war. Improvements took place after the wars
ended, in the wake of democratization, the strengthening of democratic
institutions, the establishment of the rule of law, and economic progress.

Consistent protection of human rights would be one of the wisest investments in these countries: respect for a wide gamut of human rights
would create a culture of tolerance that would help to prevent future violence. Sustained reconciliation and education are key components of
this process, along with the resolution of ongoing conflicts (Kosovo and
Macedonia); cooperation between the countries of the Balkan region;
their integration into the wider regional and international community
(EU, Stability Pact, Central-European Initiative, Council of Europe); and
internal and external professional, technological, and financial assistance
in strengthening democratic institutions, fostering economic development, and thus significantly raising people's social and economic security.

The three countries' national governments play a key role in this process: they must renounce all forms of violence; they must speak out
against nationalist parties and their programmes; and they must create,
through education, a climate that is conducive to the development of a
civil, democratic society committed to sustained and genuine reconciliation. As long as the criminals are divided into "ours" and "theirs;" as
long as ethnic discrimination is not replaced with moral and professional
criteria; as long as already initiated democratic processes do not take
roots; there will be little chance of reconciliation, economic development,
and respect for human rights and freedoms.

An important first step in this direction would be to implement the
already formally completed national commissions for truth and reconciliation. For instance, the Truth and Reconciliation Commission in Yugo-

...stablished by President Koštunica in March 2001,[38] but until ...as held only one public meeting.[39] Such commissions are based, ...n revanchism and revenge but on the need for each nation to look ...ward, to recognize its mistakes, and to remedy them; otherwise, what happened in the past might happen again in the future. Further, the national governments should take all steps necessary to allow full integration with the wider international community. This will require full cooperation with the Hague Tribunal and, as such, the surrender of all persons indicted for war crimes. The Hague Tribunal is expected to act professionally and impartially and to take actions also against Albanians who have committed crimes against humanity in Kosovo.

The national governments should further strongly commit themselves to the process of internal national reconciliation, to the development of civil society, and to respect for the rights and freedoms of all citizens – regardless of their national origin, religious affiliation, or any other such defining characteristics.

Successful completion of internal integration should be the prerequisite for further regional or European integration. After concluding the difficult process of domestic integration within each individual state, a "small Europe" should be created in the Balkans (perhaps within the framework of the Southeast European Cooperative Initiative; SECI), to prepare the region for entering the institutions and regional arrangements of the larger Europe. In particular, the various IFIs should render strong support to democratic institutions and – through investments, credits, and other financial arrangements – assist the development of the economy.

Human rights must be promoted by citizens organized in NGOs and in professional and other associations, as well as by experts and the media. Although NGOs were suppressed under the former dictatorial regimes, citizens now realize that NGOs represent a popular voice, a corrective of state rule, a place where citizens can actively join and work for their ideas and objectives. Several hundred such organizations are already operating in all three states, promoting a human rights culture and extending professional and humanitarian aid.

The media continue to play an important role in shaping public opinion. Media outlets in all states have recently begun to popularize human rights by reporting on cases of human rights abuse. For instance, the daily *Today* (*Danas*), which is published in Belgrade, regularly reports on cases of state violence against citizens. The case of the disappearance (murder) of Ivan Stambolić, who was President of Serbia from 1984 to 1987, has been covered on a daily basis during the period of August 2000 until April 2003.

These conclusions might create the impression that all these processes and activities of the national governments and relevant international organizations have already been initiated. Unfortunately, as a result of persistent nationalist feelings, including intolerance and hatred for other nations and religious communities, these processes have not registered much progress. Tolerance and reconciliation are the most urgently needed factors that will drive all subsequent improvements. Unless all relevant actors address these with the greatest possible care and expertise, the modest results achieved to date will be jeopardized.

Notes

1. The chapter covers the FRY, Croatia, and Bosnia and Herzegovina. It does not cover the former Yugoslav republics of Slovenia and Macedonia.
2. *The Official Gazette of FRY*, No. 1, 1992.
3. Constitution of the Republic of Serbia, *The Official Gazette of the Republic of Serbia*, No. 1, 1990, and Constitution of the Republic of Montenegro, *The Official Gazette of the Republic of Montenegro*, No. 48, 1992.
4. *The Official Gazette of FRY*, Article 15, No. 1, 1992.
5. *The Official Gazette of Serbia and Montenegro*, No. 1, 2003.
6. *The Official Gazette of Serbia and Montenegro*, No. 6, 2003.
7. For this activity, an indictment was rendered against Milošević before the Hague Tribunal on 24 May 1999 and amended on 16 October 2001. Milošević was in Central Prison in Belgrade from 31 March until 28 June 2001.
8. This included murders, expulsions from land or evictions from homes under the threat of murder, below-value buy-outs of land or houses, rape, and various other forms of abuse.
9. UN Security Council Resolution 1160 (1998).
10. UN Security Council Resolution 1199 (1998).
11. The Agreements were signed on 16 October 1998 by the FRY on the one hand and the UN and OSCE on the other.
12. Report of the FRY Government of March 1999.
13. Report of the Kosovo Information Centre, February 1999.
14. "Under Scrutiny," Report on Human Rights in the FRY in 1998, *Humanitarian Law Fund*, No. 28, 1998, p. 3. There are definite indications that, of 400 cases of torture in Kosovo committed during 1998, seven resulted in the death of persons tortured while in detention (six Albanians and one Serb).
15. *Humanitarian Law Fund*, Report, July 1999.
16. UN Security Council Resolution 1244 (1999).
17. Kosovo Force (KFOR)'s Report, July 1999.
18. Report of the Federal Election Commission, 2000.
19. Report of the Federal Election Commission, 2000.
20. In April 2001 elections, over 50 per cent of Montenegro's citizens voted, for the first time, for a coalition that favoured Montenegro's separation from Serbia.
21. Accordingly, an international commission was established. After years of blockade, the Commission produced its first results after the political changes in Yugoslavia in 2000.
22. *The National Gazette (Narodne novine)*, No. 124, 2000.
23. In numerous appearances in various media in 1989–1991, Tudjman and other Croatian national leaders portrayed the Serbs as plain "evil."

24. In the case of Radio 101, 100,000 citizens of Zagreb publicly protested against the closing of the station in March 1998. However, unlike in Serbia, where police violence against Serb citizens was commonplace, police violence against Croatian citizens was comparatively limited.

25. The Croatian Helsinki Committee for Human Rights Report, 1996. The regime had informal links with notorious World War II war criminals, who had been hiding for decades in Latin America and elsewhere in the world. This was an insult to the feelings of all victims and honest citizens in Croatia.

26. *Republic of Croatia Statistical Yearbook 1992*, Zagreb, Central Bureau of Statistics, 1993, p. 64.

27. The population census was carried out on 1–15 April 2001 on the basis of the Law on the Census of the Population, Households and Flats. *The National Gazette* No. 64, 2001.

28. *Voice* (*Glas*), 25 May 2002, p. 8.

29. Siniša Tatalović, "The Position of National Minorities in Croatia," in *Democracy and National Minorities*, Centre for Ethnic Studies, Belgrade 2002, p. 275.

30. UNHCR Report BiH, 1996.

31. Jody Williams, coordinator of the International Campaign Against Landmines, Speech at ICBL Meeting, Oslo, September 1997.

32. Statistical Bulletin of the Statistical Office of BiH, No. 223, Sarajevo 1993.

33. See Ante F. Markotić, *Bosnia Will Lose all Its Witnesses*, Mostar: Croatian Homeland Society (Matica Hrvatska), 1998, p. 253.

34. National Report on the Human Development of BiH–2001, Economic Institute of Sarajevo and UNDP Sarajevo, 2001.

35. Ministry of Human Rights and Refugees of BiH, Information on the Implementation of Annex VII of the General Framework Agreement for Peace in BiH, Sarajevo 2001.

36. Law on Amendments to the Criminal Code of FRY, *The Official Gazette of FRY*, No. 61, 2001.

37. Based on a comparison of the 1991 population census in the former Yugoslavia and preliminary results of the 2001 population census in Croatia and the one carried out in FRY in 2002.

38. Decision on the Establishment of the Truth and Reconciliation Commission, *The Official Gazette*, No. 15, 2001.

39. The meeting took place on 28 May 2002 in Belgrade.

13

Human rights in transition societies: The cases of Somalia and South Africa[1]

F. Wafula Okumu

The restoration, protection, and promotion of a human rights culture is one of the toughest challenges facing societies in transition. This is particularly so when the transitional process, institutions, and practices are non-existent, inadequate, or warped to serve the interests of the oppressive old regime. More than any other region of the world, Africa has societies that are constantly in transition; in Africa, too, there is an urgent and immediate need for protection and promotion of a human rights culture. Using Somalia and South Africa as case studies, this chapter is an effort to show the difficulties in, and prospects for, protecting and promoting human rights in transitional societies. The transition in South Africa has been a difficult one, owing to the persistence of institutions and practices that were established by the apartheid state. It has been a nightmare in Somalia, as state institutions have been destroyed by a raging civil war. Whereas South African state institutions are being transformed to guarantee and protect human rights fully, those in Somalia are being rebuilt from scratch. Why have human rights practices deteriorated in Somalia and significantly improved in South Africa? How and why did human rights lose protection in Somalia? What has the international community done to restore a culture of human rights in Somalia? How did South Africa go through a successful transition that has prompted us to view it as an international model? What can other societies in transition learn from the South African experience? These are some of the questions that this chapter seeks to answer.

The people of South Africa and Somalia, who suffered misfortunes at the hands of brutal regimes, have taken different transition paths towards installation of democratic societies that are just and respectful of human rights. After establishing that the Somalis have no state institutions that can protect their right to life, political participation, property ownership, and other basic rights prescribed in international human rights conventions, this study gets to the roots of these human rights violations. It then explains why and how the Somalis are still grovelling under the rule of warlords, who have gained international infamy for grossly violating fundamental human rights and freedoms. Somalia lacks governmental institutions that can protect human rights, and the orgies of violence seem to be unending.

Although the breakaway Republic of Somaliland has adopted a constitution that highlights what rights and freedoms are to be protected, this constitution does not fully protect human rights. Among the rights and freedoms guaranteed under the new Somaliland constitution are the right to participate in political, economic, social, and cultural affairs; the right to life; security of the person; the right to liberty; the right to own private property; the right to have one's dignity, reputation, and private life respected; freedom of movement and association; and freedom of communication. It also prohibits human rights crimes such as torture, extrajudicial killings, mutilation, and similar acts. Furthermore, it calls on the state to guarantee and provide conditions for all the citizens to enjoy and practise their rights. However, despite the constitutional claims that human rights are upheld, political activities have been banned in Somaliland.

Finally, South Africa is used to provide an example of a transition that has overcome an oppressive regime and installed a government that is democratic and respectful of human rights. Since the demise of apartheid, South Africa, having learned from its history, has taken giant steps in promoting and protecting human rights. It has a vibrant human rights community with independent organizations. It has one of the world's best-written constitutions, which places emphasis on human rights and establishes state institutions that strengthen constitutional democracy. South Africa also went through a national catharsis, in which an attempt was made to heal the old wounds of apartheid through a "Truth and Reconciliation Commission."

The premise of this chapter is that transitions from autocratic or conflict societies, regardless of where they are taking place, require enabling environments. Such environments include an appropriate political atmosphere and culture, political leadership, a constitution that adequately protects human rights, and political will of the general population. Whereas South Africa had all these elements, Somalia lacks some or all of them. The case of South Africa shows that it is not enough for human rights to be recognized in a constitution: a political culture that creates conditions for a genuine and lasting peace is a prerequisite for the persistence of a human rights culture.

Analytical framework

Individuals form states for the main purpose of distributing and redistributing goods and services, including public safety, and the creation of an environment that allows them to meet their basic needs. Unfortunately, most states in Africa have been unable, to use the words of H.J. Kotze, "to deliver public goods to all citizens, irrespective of ascriptive identity, communal affiliation, or partisan loyalty." The failure of the state to live up to this challenge leads to schisms, in which partisan interests seek to control and use the state as "an instrument of discrimination and domination, favoring certain communities in the provision of public goods."[2] Eventually, when the state comes under total control of one social group, as it did in apartheid South Africa and in Siad Barre's Somalia, it becomes an epitome of a ruling clique and its institutions are transformed to serve that clique's exclusive interests.

H.J. Kotze contends that, "in a truly democratic state, citizens must have equal opportunity to gain access to public goods. In addition to voting rights, these include the provision of social services such as schools, welfare, and economic infrastructure, as well as less tangible symbolic goods including official languages, flags, and national anthems."[3] Conflicts and wars in Africa occur when small, rapacious, and praetorian coteries of politically well-connected individuals misuse and deny access to public goods. It is a violation of one's rights to be denied the benefits or access to public goods that one has paid for or is entitled to. These rights are further violated when one is stripped of basic freedoms to demand access to those goods and services, or when an environment is created in which these goods and services cannot be acquired. Although wars have captured headlines of African-related events, the world has rarely been told that human rights violations are one of the causes of these wars. In the case of Somalia, the flagrant abuse of basic rights left Somalis so paralysed by hopelessness that many are now virtually unable to take care of themselves and have to rely on international humanitarian assistance. Prior to the total collapse of their state in 1992, the Somalis were already living in a state of fear and insecurity – they were fearful of arbitrary arrest, seizure or destruction of their properties, and loss of life. The violation of human rights, I point out later in this chapter, is central to the failure of the Somali state.

In his declaration of "the human right to peace" in 1997, the then Director-General of UNESCO, Federico Mayor, pointed out that "lasting peace is a prerequisite for the exercise of all human rights and duties."[4] He added that peace, development, and democracy mutually reinforce each other and that none is sustainable without the other. Patrick Hayden argues that "both democracy and human rights are at risk unless each includes the other."[5] He adds that democracy and human rights need a context in which they can be promoted. Hence, for there to be "democratic governments and sustainable human rights," there has to be "stable peace."[6] In other words, stable peace in a nation-state is made all the more possible by state institutions constituting a democratic government committed to human rights for all. Hayden calls on democratic nations to "encourage and support transitions" from non-democratic to democratic ones.[7] "Such transitions will require enhancing the democratic commitment to norms of peaceful conflict resolution," that normally characterize mature and stable democracies. In this regard, contends Hayden, a society that is undergoing a democratic transition has not only to repudiate war but also to "embrace the ideals of social justice and nonviolence." Hayden's argument is based on the Kantian notion of cosmopolitan right that seeks to create "basic social conditions, institutions, and practices through which all human beings can actually realize themselves as free and equal in nonviolent and peaceful" societies.[8] These benchmarks are hard not only to meet but also to maintain, as the following analysis of human rights practices in Somalia and South Africa shows.

Human rights practices in Somalia

The civil war and factional fighting that have overwhelmed Somalia since 1988 have caused up to 500,000 deaths.[9] The conditions in Somalia worsened during 1991–1992, when violence and massive population displacement produced famine, sending an estimated 800,000 Somali refugees to neighbouring countries and internally displacing as many as two million people. Before getting to this stage, people's rights in Somalia had been recognized only on paper as, in practice, constitutional guarantees had been routinely violated. Political rights and freedoms were virtually non-existent. The government of General Muhammed Siad Barre was a military dictatorship that showed no respect for the constitution and its rights. Mock elections were held from time to time to give the Barre regime a veneer of "democracy," and the right to peaceful assembly was restricted to officially sanctioned rallies showing undying loyalty to the leadership.

At any one time the Barre government is known to have "held several thousand prisoners entirely outside the framework of the law."[10] Somalia under Barre was a state in which ...

long prison sentences awaited individuals who stepped out of line; any hint of independence was proof of links to sinister "dissident movements." Women activists were especially cruelly treated – held in prison and subjected to sexual abuse and rape as forms of torture. A climate of fear made the exchange of free opinion virtually impossible.[11]

As anarchy still prevails in Somalia, economic and social progress has been stalled. Somalia has lost its most talented people, who have been either killed or forced to flee. Arbitrary actions by warlords have endangered a sustainable way of life. Somalia has been systematically destroyed: this is true not only of its delicate set of communal values and structures that allowed survival of its people for generations but also of its fragile ecosystems. Somalia is filled with the suffering that follows when rights are denied or violated – it is a picture of the agony of self-destruction:

... harsh *Shari'a* punishments, including public whippings, amputations, and stoning; harsh prison conditions; the judicial system's reliance in most regions on some combination of traditional and customary justice, Islamic (*Shari'a*) law, and the pre-1991 penal code; infringement on citizens' privacy rights; some limits on religious freedom; restrictions on freedom of movement; and the abuse of women and children, including the nearly universal practice of female genital mutilation (FGM).[12]

Other violations include "abuse and discrimination against ethnic minorities in the various clan regions," lack of protection of worker's rights, and isolated cases of forced labour.

In more specific terms, there is total lack of respect for the integrity of the person. This has been manifested in several forms. In the political and other extrajudicial killings that have taken place since the revolt against Siad Barre started in January 1991, political violence and banditry have claimed tens of thousands of Somalis, mostly non-combatants. There has also been an escalation of kidnappings and disappearances that appears to be politically motivated. Torture and other cruel, inhumane, and degrading treatment or punishment is also widely practised.

In the absence of constitutional or other legal protections, arbitrary arrests and detentions without trial are prevalent in Somalia. Somali factions and armed bandits continue to engage in arbitrary detention, including the kidnapping of humanitarian workers that prompted the Red Cross to pull its aid workers out of the country. In 1997 in Somaliland, a special security unit ordered approximately 100 individuals to be arrested without warrants and then sentenced without trial. Among those arbitrarily arrested and sentenced in a kangaroo court was businessman Ahmed Farah Jire, who "came under suspicion when he brought his clansmen together for a road construction project ... (that) did not pose a threat to the authorities."[13]

Owing to the legal system's lack of uniformity, in most regions the judiciary applies either traditional and customary law, Islamic *Shari'a* law, or the penal code of the pre-1991 Siad Barre government, or a combination of the three. For instance, whereas Bardera courts apply a combination of Islamic *Shari'a* law and the former penal code, those in north Mogadishu, a segment of south Mogadishu, the Middle Shabelle, and parts of the Gedo and Hiran regions, base their decisions solely on *Shari'a* law. In areas where Islamic culture is particularly entrenched, such as in Gedo and Hiran, those convicted of certain offences might receive harsh punishments ranging from public whippings to amputations and stoning.[14]

The Constitution of the Republic of Somaliland, which was endorsed by clan elders in 1991, contains guarantees for human rights. However, this constitution also contains inherent contradictions that compromise some of the human rights. For instance, it places limitations on religious freedom by making Islam the official and only religion. Christians are not allowed to proselytize, although they can deliver relief aid and keep their beliefs privately. It also guarantees the rights of women, but only as "specifically ordained in Islamic *Shari'a*."[15] This constitution only "encourages" the government to "legislate for the right of women to be free of practices which are contrary to *Shari'a* and which are injurious to their person and dignity."[16] It also gives women "the right to own, manage, oversee, trade in, or pass on property in accordance with the law," as well as "the right to have extended to them education in home economics."[17]

The administration of justice is hampered by a shortage of qualified judges and defence attorneys in Somaliland. In those areas where traditional and customary judicial practices or *Shari'a* law are applied, the right to representation by an attorney and the right to appeal do not exist. In some cases the *Shari'a* courts have also contravened the norms of *Shari'a* law by denying basic rights, including defendants' rights to face witnesses during trial. Although the Hargesa administration has not lived up to the letter and spirit of the document, Somaliland has taken the positive step of stipulating human rights protection in its constitution. The other breakaway parts of former Somalia neither possess constitutions nor practise the rule of law.

For democracy to thrive and peace to prevail in a society there must be adherence to the rule of law. This law must also "be universally heeded, that is, obeyed and complied with."[18] The rule of law, according to I. Mohammed, implies the following:

- the law is sovereign over all authority, including the government;
- the law must be clear and certain in its content and accessible and predictable for the subject;
- the law must be general in its application;
- the judiciary must be independent and accessible to every aggrieved citizen;
- the law must have procedural and ethical content.[19]

All these components are lacking in Somalia; instead, the rule of law in Somalia is guided by particularism – that is, it is based "on either experience or on substitution of some sort of moral judgment for legality."[20] But more so, the Somali warlords have gained notoriety for their antipathy to the rule of law. This is understandable, since power in Somalia is arbitrary, personal, and unpredictable.

In the period following the fall of Barre, Somalis did not know how to relate to the state or how the state ought to treat them, as none existed. The collapse of the state coupled with the particularity of the rule of law meant that renegade warlords and the people could take whatever laws they deemed beneficial to their interests into their own hands. Gibson and Gouws caution that "although rule of law is ... necessary for democratic government, it is certainly not sufficient." It must have "meaning as an attribute of institutions, cultures, and the belief systems of ordinary citizens."[21] To help us better understand the present state of Somalia so that we can propose viable solutions, we trace, in the next section, the historical roots of the present lack of human rights guarantees and the collapsed state.

What went wrong in Somalia?

In order to gain a better understanding of the present state of human rights and the difficulties encountered in introducing a human rights culture, we need to put it in a historical perspective. In pre-colonial times, Somalis had developed into a pastoral population that "despised settled agricultural cultivation, the formal cooperation this required, and the hierarchy, authority and governmental organization that resulted."[22] Over the years, and before the colonialists arrived, Somalis had fragmented nomadic social organizations that were based on families. Although there were inequalities between families, sub-clans, and clans, and "appetites for the strong or the weak ... to feed on this inequality, there is no reason to suggest (that) Somalis" had a history of "perpetual and internecine violence of the kind that characterized 1991."[23] Chopra also notes that

Somalis had a code of conduct called *xeer* that established rules and norms that promoted security and social justice among themselves. Furthermore, Chopra adds, "clans and families could not muster enough resources and were not sufficiently centralized to exploit inequalities. The communitarian nature of Somali society prevented classes from being stratified according to wealth."[24] Abdi Ismail Samatar points out that, acting as a social contract, the *xeer* regulated conflicts "in the absence of centralized coercive machinery" by ensuring that people relied and lived on their "labor/livestock rather than exploiting others."[25]

Leadership in pre-colonial Somalia was based on merit and conferred upon proof of effective management of one's household. Leaders were "elected by majority votes of informal councils or assemblies known as *Shir*, composed of any member of a particular lineage. A *Shir* also made most political and judicial decisions, hence limiting the exercise of leadership powers. Committees of elders appointed for a specific purpose by the elected leaders implemented decisions. In this manner, the ideal of decentralization was guaranteed and checks and balances against exploitation were safeguarded."[26]

When the British, French, and Italians arrived and claimed territories (in 1886, 1888, and 1905, respectively) they established states that were convenient for colonial rule – that is, centralized and with hierarchical power structures. In the process of claiming supreme authority, the colonial state had to ignore or undermine the existing traditional sources of authority. Beside the colonial state that was designed in Europe, the colonialists also introduced a form of capitalism that diminished the role of pastoralism in economic production and the communitarian social order. Colonialism also introduced into society an alien class of western-educated Somalis that was ferocious in its accumulation of material goods introduced by the Europeans. Henceforth, all Somali social institutions and practices were either completely destroyed or weakened and subjugated to serve the colonial interests.

The implantation of conflict in Somali society took form when Somalis started resisting colonial domination and had to muster resources to do so. This, Chopra claims, entailed competing for control of resources that the colonialists were also seeking. The outcome of this was a complicity in destruction of their own pastoral nomadic culture and creation of tools to fight each other. By destroying the "*xeer* glue that regulated conflicts and held Somali society together," seeds for future chaos were planted. This partly explains why the Somali conflict has become intractable.[27]

The situation was exacerbated by the failure of the colonial states to govern effectively and justly. Instead of protecting and promoting human rights, the British, French, and Italians established administrations that made their violations a *modus operandi*. To make matters even worse, the departing colonialists handed over power to their preferred leadership, that of Aden Abdullah Osman Daar. This leadership not only assumed powers similar to those wielded by the colonialists but also accumulated more and more, ad infinitum. The new ruling élite's obsession for power was matched only by its drive to control all Somali-inhabited territories in the region. As a result, Somalia went to war with Ethiopia in 1961, 1964, and 1977–1978, and with Kenya in 1963–1967.

In the absence of the *xeer* system to check the exercise of power, the post-colonial leaders not only abused their authority but also misused public goods and offices for personal gains. Not only were the new leaders inexperienced in running the affairs of a colonial state, they also had no knowledge of democratic practices and culture, which never existed during the colonial period. The civil society necessary to support democracy and human rights was too weak and was soon destroyed. The incompetence of those running the state was also manifested in the mismanagement of the economy, as a result of intense competition among the élite to accumulate national resources at the expense of each other and of the people. Samatar points out that "it was the competition among the élite for these resources that ultimately led to the degeneration of the major political parties and the demise of parliamentary governance."[28]

After politicians had weakened the Somali State through unbridled corruption, it was not a surprise when, in 1969, Major-General Muhammed Siad Barre seized power. Barre dismissed parliament, suspended the constitution, banned political parties, proclaimed "scientific socialism" as the new national ideology, and named the country the "Somali Democratic Republic." In 1976 he established the Somali Revolutionary Socialist Party and named himself its Secretary-General. As he entrenched his dictatorship, Barre also created a kleptocracy that ushered in a new competition for power, but this time through violent means. In response to a coup attempt in 1978, Barre's rule became more repressive and personal: he increasingly used force to silence his opponents; he relied on sycophants, who were allowed to loot national resources, to carry out his unpopular and arbitrary decisions. Besides institutionalizing violence, Barre also nurtured nepotism by promoting the members and interests of his sub-clan (Marehan) and clan (Darod) over those of the nation. By personalizing the state, Barre helped to ensure its demise when he was finally forced out of power in 1991.

However, Barre did not bring about the demise of the Somali state single-handedly: he had foreign accomplices, mainly the Soviet Union and the United States, who during the Cold War period endlessly supplied him with arms in exchange for access to Somalia's strategic port facilities. Since these superpowers were driven by global geo-strategic goals, they never held Barre accountable for his abysmal human rights and bad governance record and practices.

When Barre was hurriedly spirited out of the country he left behind a monumental mess that has turned out to be most difficult to clean up. His tyranny was replaced by violent factional disorder that has now completely shredded the Somali social fabric and state. Instead of the various warlords seeking to establish a democratic state, they have been vying to re-create Barre's Somalia. Their preferred means of doing this is violence. Since the warlords have institutionalized violence as the best means for survival, democracy, peace, and human rights have become major casualties. Although there are no full-scale armed hostilities at the time of writing, the warlords have remained obstacles to the creation of a new government.

Somalia's Transitional National Government (TNG) that was installed in August 2000 never got off the mark. Owing to the obstinacy of Hussein Mohammed Aideed (son and successor of the late General Mohammed Farah Aideed), Osman Ali Atto, and Musa Sudi Yalahow, among others, it was not able to establish peace or authority in Mogadishu, let alone in the whole country.[29] These three men, who belong to the same Hawiye clan, continue to make life intolerable in the capital for the young transitional government. Another infamous warlord, General Mohammed "Morgan" Hersi, who used to control Kismayu (Somalia's second port), now operates from Baidoa, a town that, in the early 1990s, served as the centre for international humanitarian assistance. Besides the 15 warlords who are slinging shots at each other are Abdullahi Yusuf, who is in charge of the predominantly Mejerteen-dominated Puntland, and President Dahir Riyale Kahin,[30] who is heading the Isaak clan's self-declared Republic of Somaliland. None of these self-declared nations has been recognized internationally. Both Yusuf and Mohammed Igal, before his replacement by Kahin, are usually placed in a separate category from the warlords, since they do not hold or defend their positions by force; Yusuf was "elected by the leaders" of his clan, and Kahin was elected in a close poll in April 2003, in which he won by an extremely tight margin of only 80 votes.

Among the daunting tasks that the Somalia transitional government faced, and in which they failed miserably, were those of building both national and international legitimacy, setting up means of communications (the two main radio stations in Mogadishu are controlled by Aideed and Osman Atto), establishing basic services, coming to terms with the warlords, and demobilizing the "technicals" (the freelance gunmen who enforced the warlords' versions of law and order). In order for the Somalis to return to normal life there must be peace, which will usher in stability and encourage economic activity. Somalia's neighbours, particularly Kenya, also have stakes in its peace: the Kenya government is anxious to resolve the burdensome problem of refugees from Somalia and to curb the inflow of illegal firearms, which Kenyan security personnel blame on the porous border with Somalia.[31]

International response to human rights practices in Somalia

The international community has responded in different ways to the human rights tragedy in Somalia. Despite the various attempts to restore peace in the war-torn country, the international community has yet to come up with a workable approach. In South Africa, the international community used sanctions to lend "positive legitimacy" to the ideals of pluralism, tolerance, and democratic government;[32] the same means cannot be used to introduce these ideals in Somalia, which has no functional government to be targeted.[33] After hastily withdrawing in 1995, the international community has undertaken only half-hearted and disjointed actions to restore peace and a culture of human rights in Somalia.

However, rebuilding Somalia into a peaceful and democratic nation where human rights are respected will require a much more concerted effort than the feeble one currently being carried out by the United Nations, the African Union, and the Intergovernmental Authority on Development (IGAD). The United Nations might have good intentions, as illustrated by its high-sounding policy documents and the rhetorical statements of its top-ranking officials,[34] but Somalia will need more than these to complete its transition from anarchy to a democratic state that provides for the human security of the Somalis. The high hopes that many had in the AU–IGAD-led talks, which have been taking place in Kenya since October 2002, have now fizzled out. The talks are on the verge of collapse for various reasons, ranging from clan rivalry to poor management of the peace process.

Somalis are unlucky in that their country does not have South Africa's economic importance, which saw international governments jump on the anti-apartheid bandwagon for reasons of national interest. For instance, whereas third world and Soviet bloc governments opposed apartheid on the "principle of anti-racism or the ideological priority of socialism," Western governments did so "to protect their economic and strategic interests."[35] The Somalis are suffering partly because of the Cold War and its end: the Cold War led the superpowers to support the oppressive Barre regime; the end of the Cold War has meant that Somalia has lost its geo-strategic value and has virtually disappeared from the radar screens of most Western foreign-affairs offices.[36] The 1993 debacles that ended in the death of 25 Pakistani UN peacekeepers and 18 US Army Rangers, and the abandonment of the international effort to enforce peace and feed the starving Somalis, is still fresh in the international community's psyche and will be there for a long time to come.

Despite the international pullout in 1993–1995, there have been continuing efforts by the United Nations to build peace and the Somali state. The UN Coordination Unit (UNCU)'s "operational plan to support governance and peace building in Somalia" is premised on the fact that "formulation of a post-conflict transitional programme" will be contingent on "peace and security" as one of the fundamental prerequisites.[37] Hence a call for "commencement of post-conflict intervention aimed at supporting peace, good governance and protection of human rights." UN Somalia, a consortium of 13 UN agencies working in Somalia, has committed UN agencies to continue supporting "on-going community efforts to encourage respect for principles of good governance, human rights, the equitable treatment of women and minorities, and social integration of marginalized groups."[38] Specifically, the Office of the High Commissioner for Human Rights, in close cooperation with UNDP, will continue its support of civil-society organizations that helped to establish the Somalia National Peace Conference.[39] UNIFEM will support women's rights and the elimination of all forms of violence against women, as well as providing further capacity-building support to women's organizations and women living in displaced communities. UNICEF programmes in this sector will continue working towards the eradication of FGM, supporting women's organizations to increase their empowerment in the community, and furthering child protection.[40]

However, for these efforts to succeed, the United Nations must learn from its past mistakes. In his candid criticism of the international community's failure, particularly those of the United Nations and the United States, to restore peace in Somalia, Martin Ganzglass points out that a golden opportunity was lost when no concerted effort was made to assist "in restoration of governmental functions, particularly the police and judiciary."[41] In highlighting the haphazard nature of United Task Force (UNITAF) and United Nations Operation in Somalia (UNOSOM) missions, Ganzglass specifically states that, instead of hunting down General Muhammed Aidid (a notorious warlord), the mission should have concentrated on implementing "a full scale civil affairs programme" that focused on rebuilding institutions. Ganzglass notes that UNISOM I was doomed to fail when it was first launched as a humanitarian relief effort that was to last six weeks. This became more apparent when the six weeks were up, when the humanitarian mission confusedly started "recreating a central government" by committing "resources primarily for military purposes," building *new* national political institutions, and reconciling warring clans.[42] In a nutshell, UNOSOM failed to restore peace in war-ravaged Somalia because it did not have the mandate to "disarm the factions of all weapons" and to *rebuild* institutions that were "capable of preventing Somalia from descending into the chaos of civil war."[43]

Ameer Jan advises that any international effort to bring about peace in Somalia must "first of all,... understand the local social and political context." This will involve "recognizing the fact that the country (is) deeply divided along clan lines and that it would take a lengthy, internally generated process to heal those divisions."[44] The role of the international community in promoting peace in Somalia should first focus on "clan political reconciliation" and then support the Somalis to determine their own political institutions and leadership. On top of this there must be adequate international funding for rebuilding institutions and training a new cadre of Somalis to run them. The rule of law must be promptly established in Somalia as part of restoring a level of peace that allows human rights to be protected and promoted, as happened in South Africa. Indeed, South Africa offers numerous lessons for Somalia.

Lessons from South Africa

Afro-pessimists predicted that the transition from an apartheid system to a democratic society would be bloody, chaotic, and (perhaps) a failure. Nevertheless, South Africa has evolved not only into a democracy but also into a society respecting human rights. David Black contends that there is considerable truth in the perception that "South Africa's transition from racial authoritarianism of the apartheid era to the non-racial democratic institutions and entrenched constitutional rights of the post-1994 period is ... one of the great human rights triumphs of the post-Second World War era."[45] Despite a few bumps in its transition to a democratic society, South Africa now boasts one of the best-written constitutions in the world (as mentioned in the first section of this chapter), which guarantees and promotes human rights and sustains democracy. However, the reconstruction of a new South Africa will take time, as the old apartheid system was deeply entrenched and will require years to uproot completely.

When racial segregation was codified into law in 1948, it essentially legalized the hardship endured by the majority non-White populations. However, it was not long before massive resistance to apartheid emerged, with the African National Congress (ANC) and the Pan Africanist Congress (PAC) as trail-blazers for a just and democratic South Africa. The deeper the system of apartheid entrenched itself by excluding and marginalizing Blacks, the more instability it created in South Africa: for instance, it forced the ANC and the PAC to become more militant and violent, transformed the Black townships into cauldrons of political mayhem, and led the international community to isolate South Africa. By the 1980s, political violence had become a common means of communication between the government and its oppressed populations. By the beginning of the 1990s, it had become obvious to the apartheid stalwarts that the system was doomed. As the burdens of apartheid became too heavy to bear, the government of F.W. de Klerk made concessions: it legalized nationalist movements, released Nelson Mandela and other jailed leaders, and embarked on a path of "liberalizing" South Africa.

Human rights violations in South Africa attracted international attention, opprobrium, and action because they were specifically directed at non-White racial groups. From 1948 to the early 1990s, the apartheid regime – built on intolerance, violence, and disrespect for life – "was responsible for a multitude of increasingly systematic human rights violations in the course of initiating, elaborating, and defending" the system of racial discrimination.[46] Among these violations were "arbitrary arrests and detentions without trial; the denial of basic civil and political rights to more than three-quarters of its people; systematic press censorship; denial of equal social and economic rights and opportunities to its people; and torture and extra-judicial executions."[47]

Apartheid was constructed as a scheme to deny non-Whites access to public goods. By giving Whites exclusive access and maximum benefits, the Whites came to enjoy "unprecedented rates of economic growth" in the second half of the 1960s and first half of the 1970s.[48] However, towards the end of the 1970s, South Africa had become internationally despised for its flagrant violations of human rights. As domestic opposition and international pressure mounted, the government was forced to make piecemeal reforms. These were rejected, since they merely sought to protect the privileges and extend the control of the Whites. The apartheid government responded to these pressures by adopting draconian measures, including a partial state of emergency, strict media censorship, brutal suppression of protestors, and extensive powers of arrest and detention of state opponents. Using legislation, arbitrary executive orders, and unregulated powers of executive officers such as the Minister of Law and Order, the apartheid government flagrantly infringed the universalism of the rule of law.[49] By allowing the police and security forces to run the state unrestrained and unfettered by the rule of law, South Africa was essentially a police state.

Because apartheid was anti-human rights, it became very easy to sell the anti-apartheid struggle to the international community as a human rights struggle. This, in turn, greatly contributed to the success of protection of human rights in the post-apartheid society, as the anti-apartheid movement and organizations that later formed the transitional government have been an important socializing force. Human rights were one of the main issues that both the domestic and international oppositions to the apartheid state were seeking to advance. The anti-apartheid activists carried out a struggle that sought a radical transformation of South Africa to embody universally accepted human rights norms and practices. Because apartheid was a system that denied access to public goods, the anti-apartheid opponents' agenda went beyond promotion of basic civil and political human rights norms and aimed at instituting new human rights that would guarantee all South Africans the right to social and economic well-being.

In a chequered transition that dumbfounded many sceptics, the South Africans entered into a number of pacts establishing rules for negotiated agreements between the major players in the political system, embarked on serious discussions on creating a new South Africa, and established foundations for a negotiated settlement. With the embrace of constitutionalism and acceptance of a new Interim Constitution in late 1993, the birth of a new country was almost guaranteed. However, this transition would not have reached this point without the nature of the political leaders that South Africa possessed at that time. The various political groups also deserve credit for the way they "negotiated together in a multiparty forum, the Convention for a Democratic South Africa (Codesa)."[50]

The Constitutional Assembly took two years to write the final Constitution that was adopted in 1996 and came into effect during February 1997. This constitution guarantees political rights, press freedom, a multiparty political system, and proportional representation in the electoral system. It also contains a Bill of Rights that protects fundamental rights, and establishes an ombudsman and a judicial review process that enhances checks and balances in the political process.

A number of notable trends could be detected during the transition: one of these was the popular support of the new processes, pacts, and leaders; a second was the cooperation that took place in power transfer and sharing between the former oppressed and the oppressors; lastly, there was a realization by all parties that they had more to lose by not playing a positive-sum game. Of course, there were exceptions, as some parties (such as the Inkatha Freedom Party) chose to continue utilizing violence to achieve their aims. Such violence manifested itself in "massacres, political assassinations, intimidation, and forced mobilization for mass demonstrations, revenge attacks, attacks on rail commuters and minibus taxi wars."[51]

As power transfer was taking place, the new South Africa had to grapple with two main challenges – namely, how to transform the apartheid state into a democratic one, and how to reconcile and build a new nation. The transformation of the apartheid state started with redistribution of political power. A new parliament was created, consisting of two chambers – the National Assembly with 400 members and the Council of Provinces with 90 members. Half of the members of the National Assembly were elected from national constituencies, the other half being elected proportionally from the provincial lists. After peaceful elections in 1994, a "Government of National Unity" was formed and given a five-year lease of life to establish a firm foundation for a new South Africa. In the new cabinet that was formed, the 27 positions were distributed among all the parties that received more than 5 per cent of the vote. When Mandela was elected President, he picked former President F.W. de Klerk (a former adversary and leader of the White National Party) and Thabo Mbeki (of the ANC) as his deputies.

Although the final shape of the transition was not determined in advance, there is no doubt that the transition was driven by liberal international human rights norms. Indeed, of the five minimum conditions that the apartheid government was required to meet before the international community could lift international restrictions, four were related to human rights: these were (1) repealing the state of emergency, (2) releasing all political prisoners, (3) legalizing the ANC and other political parties, and (4) eliminating apartheid laws.[52] However, this international emphasis on political rather than on social and economic rights meant that the transformation was not radical enough to restructure the economy and "redress South Africa's deep historic inequalities."[53] By promoting "the more narrow goals of political democratization, particularly universal suffrage," instead of the socio-economic transformation of apartheid South Africa, the international community may have planted seeds for future unrest.

Whereas Whites in post-apartheid South Africa have sought to protect the gains they made during the apartheid era, the Black majority population, who had been disadvantaged and deprived of economic opportunities and decent living standards, are demanding more than legal, political, and civil rights:[54] unless "South Africa's deep, racially structured, inequities" are "addressed in some form," the transition will be not only stalled but possibly even reversed.[55] This transition, of which Western states were, basically, the midwives, has turned out to be a promotion of Western liberal democracy and capitalism.[56] Nevertheless, the most important thing is that "the post-apartheid government, through its socially progressive, constitutionally entrenched bill of rights, has demonstrated its intent to entrench the prescriptive status of liberal human rights norms, and to adhere to rule-consistent behavior."[57] Among the indicators that South Africa's new government is committed to fostering a human rights culture are the abolition of the death penalty and the establishment of the Truth and Reconciliation Commission to help heal the wounds of the apartheid era.[58]

The final act of restructuring the state involves democratizing its instruments, which had been designed to oppress, suppress, and exploit the majority of people. This is more important, since these instruments are also needed to implement new policies of reconciliation and reconstruction of the nation, and redistribution of public goods and services. Nevertheless, this task has not been easy: for example, the constitution provides for a policy of affirmative action, with the intention of redistributing positions to Blacks previously denied public-service appointments in the apartheid state; however, the implementation of such policies in core state agencies (such as the military, police, and the courts) has run into problems, particularly from the Whites, who have accused the state of reverse discrimination. Great care is being taken because these state apparatuses are crucial to the survival of the state, the rule of law, and maintenance of civil order.

There was an urgency to create and promote a human rights culture in South Africa after the fall of the apartheid state.[59] Although human rights are no longer at the top of the post-apartheid government agenda, the country remains on the path toward a human rights-based constitutional democracy. So far, all human rights institutions provided for in both the interim[60] and final[61] constitutions have been established and the legislature has enacted important human rights laws. South Africa has also shown its commitment to human rights by signing the International Covenant on Economic, Social and Cultural Rights, the International Covenant on Civil and Political Rights, and the Convention on the Elimination of All Forms of Racial Discrimination. By 1996, it had ratified the Convention on the Rights of the Child, the Convention on the Elimination of All Forms of Discrimination Against Women, the Protocols to the Geneva Convention, and the African Charter on Human and People's Rights. The South African Parliament has also played a leading role in promoting human rights by passing laws that have "significant implications for the establishment of a human rights based democracy"[62] and setting up of human rights institutions.[63] To ensure that all laws and executive acts did not undermine the human rights standards established in the Bill of Rights, a Constitutional Court was inaugurated in February 1995. So far, this court has handed down judgements abolishing the death penalty, outlawing civil imprisonment for civil debt, and taking other decisions related to equality, privacy, freedom of expression, and access to information.[64]

South Africa took a major step towards the promotion of human rights by establishing a Human Rights Commission. This Commission promotes human rights by educating the people and the communities about their rights, making recommendations to Parliament, reviewing human rights-related legislation, and "investigating alleged violations of fundamental rights and assisting those affected to secure redress."[65] Another commission that has played a crucial role in South Africa's transition to a democratic society was established to help the country come to terms with its past. The Truth and Reconciliation Commission (TRC) was given the primary role in developing a complete picture of the causes, nature, and extent of the gross human rights violations committed from 1 March 1960 to 10 May 1994. Additional tasks included facilitating the grant of amnesty to those who owned up to their political crimes, establishing the fate or whereabouts of victims, restoring the human and civil dignity of the survivors of abuse, and recommending measures to repair past human rights violations and prevent them in the future.[66]

South Africa has also identified the need to ensure that public goods are not misused or abused by individuals, by establishing the office of the Public Proctor. The Public Proctor has the duties of investigating any conduct in state affairs that is alleged or suspected to be improper, to report that conduct, and to take remedial actions. According to Jeremy Sarkin, the Public Proctor is also ...

empowered to investigate, report, and take remedial action in relation to improper prejudice, maladministration, dishonesty or improper dealings with respect to public money, improper enrichment, and receipt of improper advantage. The office is concerned not only with ensuring the honesty of those working for the state but also with ensuring that they treat people with respect.[67]

Among the obstacles facing this transition are continuing violence in KwaZulu-Natal and the taxi industry, high rates of crime, government corruption, and widespread poverty among the majority Black populations. The human rights institutions established by the constitution are still "functioning with different levels of energy and efficiency and some have yet to demonstrate their capacity for achieving the objectives for which they were established."[68] As pointed out earlier, South Africa also faces the challenge of restructuring the state instruments that had been designed specifically to oppress, suppress, and exploit the majority of the people. There is a great need for this transformation to take place rapidly, not only because most of the population hold these instruments in contempt, but also because they have roles to play in the new society. These instruments are needed to implement new policies of reconstruction, redistribution, reconciliation, and nation-building. One such instrument is the police force, which, despite having become more transparent and having embarked on an effort to build a human rights culture, still faces enormous problems. These include "ever-increasing numbers of deaths in custody," widespread corruption, and brutal tactics including torture.[69] On top of this, a balance has to be struck between curbing arbitrary or excessive police powers and curbing spiralling levels of crime.

A significant achievement in South Africa's transition to a democratic society has been the de-escalation of political violence since the democratic elections of 1994. Not only have the levels of deaths and injuries from political violence decreased significantly but also the country seems to be witnessing a climate of peace. This significant decrease in the "levels of political violence may be seen as a sign of progress towards a culture of human rights."[70] However, it can also be argued that "continuing deaths relating to political feuds and other indices of violence, such as conflict in the taxi industry and at educational institutions, indicate that a human rights culture is yet to permeate the fabric of South African society in a meaningful way."[71]

The above analysis of South Africa's transition to a democratic society offers a number of useful lessons for restoring human rights. The first lesson is that Somalia will need respected national leaders to put human rights on top of the agenda for post-conflict reconstruction of the war-torn nation. The second lesson is that there must be an environment that enables human rights to be incorporated into the new national political culture. Nation-building in a transitional society requires the depoliticizing of ethnic and cultural groups, the creation of an enabling environment for peace to be restored, the establishment of a human rights culture, and the prevalence of democracy. The third lesson is that the international community can play only a complementary role in supporting the restoration of human rights, the most important aspect of such a role falling to the international human rights community, which can be influential in establishing a human rights culture.

Another important lesson is that, in a transitional society, there is a need to balance the human need for justice and punishment with nation-building, reconstruction, and reconciliation.[72] South Africa was able to do this by offering a full amnesty for full disclosure of political crimes committed over a period of 34 years. However, Walter Wink, who lists "rules of thumb" that transitional societies should follow when dealing with "issues of reconciliation," argues that "leading architects of the policy of disappearances, murder, and torture, should be prosecuted."[73] Whereas South Africa has pursued the goal of reconciliation that was based on the African notion of *ubuntu*,[74] which explicitly excludes retribution and favours restorative justice, the Somali notion of *aar goosi* seeks vengeance and revenge. Somalia will continue to be a wounded nation with elusive justice and peace unless its notion of retributive punishment is dispensed with and replaced by one that will contribute to reconciliation and reconstruction of the conflict-battered nation. Besides fostering a culture of human rights, the transitional period in Somalia must also focus on reconciliation, which must take place in order to overcome the trauma of the past undemocratic society and the civil war.

Conclusions

Violations of human rights, impoverishment of the population, and state collapse are major indicators of emerging national conflicts in Africa. The human rights situation in Africa is grave and deteriorating, despite 2000 having been touted as the beginning of the Millennium of Human Rights. State collapses in Somalia and former Zaire were accompanied by massive and egregious violations of human rights. The continuing decay of African states is an ominous sign for the future of human rights in Africa. The collapsing states are now employing a wide array of measures, including state terrorism and informal repression, to clamp down on civil-society movements reacting against state violations of human rights.

Human rights abuses that result in civil wars have had the most far-reaching effects, as wars have contributed to loss of lives, destruction of the property and infrastructure that supports economic life, displacement of populations, and untold psychological and physical suffering. Corruption, a breakdown in the rule of law, impunity for terrible abuses, and the disenfranchisement of whole swathes of society, have created a breeding ground for the likes of Muhammed Aidid, Ali Mahdi, Charles Taylor, and Foday Sankoh. Finally, after the collapse of states (as was the case with Somalia), the effective construction of new societies is impossible without a culture of human rights as a cornerstone.

During South Africa's transition period, "strategies for addressing human rights abuses concentrated on formulating treaties, adopting standards, and implementing procedures to remedy such human rights abuses as torture and arbitrary detention." Whereas the international community, when promoting human rights, can use political pressure and economic sanctions in pursuit of this goal, "these strategies, however, are of limited value where political order has broken down and a government, if it exists, can no longer conform its conduct to acceptable international standards."[75]

With the establishment of the African Union, which will have the mandate to intervene in collapsing states and to stem violations of human rights, Africa now possesses a mechanism to enforce its human rights treaties and standards. However, because it will be some time before this mechanism can be used to protect human rights in countries such as Somalia and the Democratic Republic of the Congo, the international community, particularly the United Nations, must continue to play a crucial role in establishing a human rights culture and seeking justice. Somalia, in particular, needs both bilateral and multilateral assistance programmes to help her to strengthen the institutions of accountability, reconstruct the judicial and law enforcement systems, ensure civilian control of the military, build the capacity of democratic institutions, provide political education for the population, and train political leadership.

Notes

1. The views expressed in this chapter are personal and do not necessarily reflect those of the African Union.
2. H.J. Kotze, "The State and Social Change in South Africa," *International Social Science Journal*, No. 163, March 2000, p. 79.
3. Ibid.
4. Federico Mayor, *The Human Right to Peace – Declaration by the Director-General*, Paris: UNESCO, 1997, p. 5.
5. Patrick Hayden, "From Laws of the Peoples to Perpetual Peace," *International Journal on World Peace*, Vol. 13, No. 2, June 2000, p. 48.
6. Ibid.
7. Ibid., p. 60.
8. Ibid., p. 58.
9. See US Committee for Refugees, *Country Report – Somalia, 2002.* ⟨http://www.refugees.org/world/countryrpt/africa/somalia.htm⟩.
10. Paulos Tesfagiorgis, "Democratic Elbow Room," *New Internationalist*, No. 238, December 1992.
11. Ibid.
12. US Department of State, *Somalia: Country Report on Human Rights Practices for 1998.* Available at ⟨http://www.state.gov/www/global/human_rights/1998_hrp_report/somalia. html⟩. This list suggests that some traditional values still exist in Somalia and can be used as foundations for reconstruction of a new human rights culture. See also the Report of the Special Rapporteur on the "Situation of Human Rights in Somalia," submitted to the United Nations Commission on Human Rights on 26 January 2000. Document number E/CN.4/2000/110.
13. Ibid.
14. See the Report of the Special Rapporteur on the "Situation of Human Rights in Somalia," submitted to the United Nations Commission on Human Rights on 26 January 2000. Document number E/CN.4/2000/110.
15. See Article 36 of the Revised Constitution of the Republic of Somaliland, adopted on 31 May 2001.
16. Ibid.
17. Ibid.
18. James Gibson and Amanda Gouws, "Support for the Rule of Law in the Emerging South African Democracy," *International Social Science Journal*, No. 152, June 1997, p. 174.
19. I. Mohammed, "Preventive Detention and the Rule of Law," *South African Law Journal*, Vol. 106, 1989, pp. 547–549.

20. Gibson and Gouws, "Support for the Rule of Law," p. 175.
21. Ibid.
22. Jarat Chopra, *Peace-Maintenance: The Evolution of International Political Authority*, New York: Routledge, 1999, p. 133.
23. Ibid., p. 134.
24. Ibid.
25. Abdi Ismail Samatar, "Destruction of State and Society in Somalia: Beyond the Tribal Convention," *The Journal of Modern African Studies*, Vol. 3, No. 4, December 1992, pp. 632–633.
26. Chopra, *Peace-Maintenance*, p. 134.
27. Ibid., p. 135.
28. Samatar, "Destruction of State and Society in Somalia," p. 633.
29. An AU–IGAD fact-finding mission to Somalia in June 2003 found that the TNG had control over only four buildings in Mogadishu, while Hussein Aidid controlled less than 200 square metres of the capital city.
30. Dahir Riyale Kahin replaced Mohammed Igal, who died on 2 May 2002.
31. Gitau Warigi, "Why Warlords Mission in Kenya Came Unstuck," *Sunday Nation*, 18 March 2001.
32. David Black, "The Long and Winding Road: International Norms and Domestic Political Change in South Africa," in Thomas Risse, Stephen C. Ropp, and Kathryn Sikkink, *The Power of Human Rights – International Norms and Domestic Change*, Cambridge: Cambridge University Press, 1999, p. 102.
33. The TNG, embroiled in scandals over embezzlement of donor funds, has so far failed to disarm and demobilize armed militias and to reunite Somaliland or Puntland with the unstable regions in the south.
34. See Security Council Resolutions 733 (of 23 January 1992), 746 (of 17 March 1992), 751 (of 24 April 1992), 767 (of 27 July 1992), 775 (of 28 August 1992), 794 (of 3 December 1992), 814 (of 26 March 1993), 837 (of 6 June 1993), 865 (of 22 September 1993), 879 (of 29 October 1993), 885 (of 16 November 1993), 886 (of 18 November 1993), 897 (of 4 February 1994) and press statements of the President of the Security Council on 16 October 1992, 14 June 1993, and 18 June 1993.
35. Ibid., p. 106.
36. Somalia flickered on the screens after the 11 September 2001 terrorist attacks in the United States, when it was suspected to have provided havens for some of the terrorists and was targeted for retaliation. As a failed state, Somalia is regarded as a breeding ground for al-Qaeda terrorists targeting Western and Israeli interests in the region.
37. See ⟨http://www.unsomalia.org/UNCU/index.htm⟩.
38. See ⟨http://www.unsomalia.org/unsomalia/unagencies.htm⟩.
39. Somalia National Peace Conference (SNPC) took place in Djibouti from 2 May to 13 June and led the creation of the Transitional National Assembly. On 25 August 2000, it elected Mr Abdiqassin Salad Hassan as President of Somalia. For more details, see ⟨http://www.un.org/peace/africa/pdf/SOMALIA.pdf⟩.
40. See ⟨http://www.unsomalia.org/⟩.
41. Martin R. Ganzglass, "Restoration of the Somali Justice System," *International Peacekeeping*, Vol. 3, No. 1; Spring 1996, p. 117.
42. Ameen Jan, "Somalia: Building Sovereignty or Restoring Peace?" in Chetan Kumar and Elizabeth Cousins, *Peacebuilding as Politics: Cultivating Peace in Fragile Societies*, Boulder: Lynne Rienner, 2001, p. 76.
43. Ganzglass, "Restoration of the Somali Justice System," pp. 125–126.
44. Jan, "Somalia," p. 76.
45. Black, "The Long and Winding Road," p. 78.

46. Ibid., p. 80.
47. Ibid.
48. Ibid., p. 87.
49. Gibson and Gouws, "Support for the Rule of Law," p. 175.
50. Kotze, "The State and Social Change in South Africa," p. 81.
51. Ibid., p. 82.
52. The fifth condition was initiating negotiations that would lead to a new South Africa. See Black, "The Long and Winding Road," p. 98.
53. Ibid., p. 103.
54. Thomas Ohlson and Stephen John Stedman, *The New is Not Yet Born – Conflict Resolution in Southern Africa*, Washington, The Brookings Institution, 1994, p. 148.
55. Black, "The Long and Winding Road," p. 103. Black notes that in the negotiation process with the National Party to write a new constitution, the ANC had to compromise some of its principles, the exclusion of most second-generation social and economic rights being among these.
56. Ibid., p. 103.
57. Ibid., p. 105.
58. Ibid., p. 106.
59. Jeremy Sarkin, "The Development of a Human Rights Culture in South Africa," *Human Rights Quarterly*, Vol. 20, 1998, p. 629.
60. The Interim Constitution included a chapter on fundamental rights (or the Bill of Rights, as it was commonly referred to), guaranteed citizens protection against state abuses, and established human rights institutions such as the Human Rights Commission, the Commission on Gender Equality, the Commission on the Restitution of Land Rights, and the Public Protector. See Chapter 8, Sections 110–123 of the South Africa Interim Constitution of 1993.
61. It contains a Bill of Rights that also establishes socio-economic rights. See Chapter 2, Sections 24–29 of the Final Constitution of 1997. This constitution also includes provisions on equality, just administrative action, children's rights, and the right to freedom and security of the person (that includes reproductive autonomy).
62. For instance, in 1996 the Parliament enacted legislation that transformed the police service. Because of its central role in the protection of the Apartheid State, this institution was one of the most despised.
63. These were the Human Rights Commission, the Truth and Reconciliation Commission, the Land Restitution Commission, the Public Protector, and the Pan South Africa Language Board. See Sarkin, "The Development of a Human Rights Culture in South Africa," pp. 639–640.
64. Sarkin, "The Development of a Human Rights Culture in South Africa," pp. 642–643.
65. Ibid., p. 649.
66. For an analysis of the TRC see Aletta Norval, "Truth and Reconciliation: The Birth of the Present and the Reworking of History," *Journal of Southern African Studies*, Vol. 25, No. 3, September 1999.
67. Sarkin, "The Development of a Human Rights Culture in South Africa," p. 653. However, Sarkin feels that, owing to "South Africa's history of human rights abuse and the difficult challenges involved in the current transformation and the building of a human rights culture, the Constitution ought to have offered maximum protection to human rights." See ibid., p. 634.
68. Ibid., p. 630.
69. Ibid., p. 645.
70. Ibid., p. 649.
71. Ibid.

72. David Little, "A Different Kind of Justice: Dealing with Human Rights Violations in Transitional Societies," *Ethics and International Affairs*, Vol. 13, 1999, p. 65.
73. Walter Wink, *When the Powers Fall: Reconciliation in the Healing of Nations*, Minneapolis: Fortress Press, 1998, p. 53.
74. For a detailed analysis of *ubuntu*, see Michael Battle, "The Theology of Community: The Ubuntu Theology of Desmond Tutu," *Interpretation*, Vol. 54, No. 2, April 2000.
75. Peter Manikas and Krishna Kumar, "Protecting Human Rights in Rwanda," in Krishna Kumar, ed., *Rebuilding Societies After Civil War*, Boulder: Lynne Rienner, 1997, p. 63.

14

Human rights and trans. societies in Western Africa

Eghosa E. Osaghae

Context and challenges of transition in West Africa

In spite of differences of colonial legacy, post-colonial affiliations, and the resulting patterns of political organization, countries of the West African geo-political region have enough in common to make the region a meaningful unit of analysis.[1] The commonalities, which are germane to the concerns of this chapter, include the longer years of political independence of West African countries relative to countries in other regions of Africa, a high degree of ethnic division and conflict, pervasive military intervention and rule, political violence and civil war, prolonged economic decline, informal commercial flows and migration, and the fact that West Africa has been a breeding ground for regional integration and collective security, which are currently built around the Economic Community of West African States (ECOWAS).

West Africa has also been a hotbed of human rights violations. Unfair trial, suppression of freedom of the press and of opposition, torture, detention without trial, murder, disappearances, rape, and war-situation abuses are common in the region. Interventions by the international community against repressive regimes, ostensibly on account of human rights abuses and other excesses, can also be taken as evidence of the despicable state of human rights in the region. The interventions have ranged from denial (or threat of denial) of aid and sanctions, to suspension or expulsion from membership in international organizations. In

or instance, Gambia was suspended from the Commonwealth after
a Jammeh overthrew President Dauda Jawara in a coup and un-
hed a reign of terror on the country. Sanctions were similarly im-
sed on Nigeria's repressive military governments, especially after the
nnulment of the 1993 elections and the execution of Ogoni minority
rights activists, led by Ken Saro-Wiwa, by the government of General
Sani Abacha in 1995. They were also imposed on Liberia's President
Charles Taylor in May 2001 because of his involvement in the illegal
trade in diamonds and his support for rebels in Sierra Leone, which were
critical factors in the wars in Sierra Leone and Liberia.

The poor human rights situation in West Africa is a major factor in the
persistent domestic and external pressures for reforms, following which
West Africa has emerged as a centre of some of the most engaging
transitions in Africa. National conferences convened by self-asserting
civil-society organizations and previously excluded opposition elements
(of which the 1990 Benin conference became prototypical), represents
one face of these transitions. Military-managed transitions – which have
tended to produce relatively fragile but growing forms of democracy, as
in Nigeria, Ghana, Liberia, Sierra Leone, Guinea, and Niger – represent
another face of transition. There have also been less orderly and conflict-
aggravating transitions, such as those forced upon countries by civil war
and warlords.

It is against the backdrop of the transition ferment, and on the assumption that human rights are critical instruments of conflict management and state reconstitution, that this chapter analyses the trajectories
of human rights in West Africa. The remainder of the chapter is divided
into three sections. The next section presents a broad overview of human
rights in West Africa and searches for the sources of human rights abuses
across the region. Then the transformation of the human rights regime
under democratization is examined. The final section grapples with the
question of why recent transitions in West Africa, which held the promise
of the much-touted "second liberation" in Africa, failed to transform the
human rights regime.

Sources of human rights violations in West Africa

Although notions of human rights are embedded in traditional African
thought and institutions,[2] human rights of the so-called Western genre
are a recent phenomenon in West Africa. They emerged as elements
of decolonization, when nationalist movements invoked the provisions
of human rights charters and covenants that affirmed the right of self-
determination to all peoples to legitimize their demands for indepen-

dence. What is of interest in this beginning is that rights were conceived of as belonging to the state for which independence was sought and its (collective) "peoples." In the hierarchy of rights that subsequently developed, this rendered the rights of the state superior to those of individuals and groups.

This was the background to the poor human rights regime of the post-independence period. To be sure, the constitutions of many countries were "decorated" with bills of rights modelled on the Universal Declaration of Human Rights (to which many countries have now added the African Charter on Human and Peoples' Rights). In addition, francophone countries imported and grafted portions of the French Declaration of the Rights of Men and Citizens. For example, the Preamble to the independence constitution (1960) of Côte d'Ivoire stipulated that: "The people of Côte d'Ivoire proclaim their attachment to the principles of Democracy and Human Rights, such as they have been defined by the Declaration of Human and Citizens Rights of 1789, by the Universal Declaration of 1948, and such as are guaranteed in this constitution." Diabate's commentary that, "[t]he explicit reference to the vested interests of the French Revolution and to the Declaration of 1948 leaves not a shadow of doubt as to the meaning of the words 'democracy' and 'human rights,'"[3] summarizes the hollowness and mere formality of human rights provisions.

Thus, although the bills of rights provide for a wide range of civil or democratic rights (of access and participation), political or liberalization rights, and socio-economic or preservation rights that empower individual capacity for survival and sustainability (food, shelter, employment, social security, etc.), they have all had little success in the region. Socio-economic or third-generation rights, which are usually considered prerequisites for the enjoyment of other rights, have fared worst of all. In fact, there are no explicit socio-economic rights in West Africa other than those that can be inferred from declarations of social, economic, and political objectives (or intentions) in the preambles or statements of objectives and principles of the various constitutions. The 1999 Nigerian constitution, for example, provides that the state shall direct its policy towards ensuring that "all citizens without discrimination on any ground whatsoever have the opportunity for securing adequate means of livelihood as well as adequate opportunities to secure suitable employment." Similar provisions are made with regard to adequate health care, the protection of children against exploitation, equal pay for equal work, etc. But the enjoyment of these "rights" is tied to the solvency and capability of the state, which calls their justiciability into question.[4]

Let us now turn to a more detailed examination of the major sources of human rights violations in West Africa.

Political institutions

The state in West Africa typifies the post-colonial African state, and therefore suffers from the pathologies that are associated with that state. Foremost of these is an endemic legitimacy crisis that is embedded in the imposed origins of the state under colonial rule. The crisis manifests itself in different ways, such as low level and sectional support for government, lack of transparency and accountability in the public domain, and contested and disorderly succession to power, including a vicious cycle of inconclusive elections and military interventions. Civilian control of the military is problematic and frequently breached. There is also neo-patrimonial rule, in which state power is privatized and over-centralized, support is secured through patron–client linkages and pay-offs, and government positions are made instruments of accumulation by predatory office holders.[5]

The cumulative effect of the foregoing factors is that constitutionalism and governmental institutions are underdeveloped, weak, and fragile, leading in many cases to arbitrary and ineffective governance. Typically, civil society is emasculated by what Bayart calls the totalizing tendency of the state,[6] which includes attempts at mobilizing popular support through state-directed schemes such as the "June 4 movement" in Ghana and the "movement for economic recovery, self-reliance and social justice" in Nigeria. Furthermore, separation of powers exists mostly in the formal sense, as the legislature and judiciary function more or less as elongations of the executive, which is built around a powerful ruler and a single or dominant party (the military variety had supreme councils with unchallengeable powers).

The political scene in West Africa has witnessed some of the most extreme forms of these pathologies. By 1989, on the eve of the end of the Cold War, virtually every country in the region was under one form of authoritarian rule or another. The regime of authoritarianism had two demonstrable effects: first, it raised the stakes of politics and made the struggle for state power grim, zero-sum, and violent. Second, the constant threats to the survival of incumbent rulers led to an emphasis on the security and stability of the ruler at the expense of the well-being of citizens. In many states, state security services, secret police, terrorist units, and so-called élite forces were probably the most developed agencies of the state and attracted disproportionately large budgetary allocations. Demands and struggles by aggrieved elements for access, participation, redress, and equitable allocation of resources were suppressed through instruments such as preventive detention, emergency power, and state security acts.[7]

The fractional nature of élite organization and competition is another major factor in explaining the adverse political situation in West Africa. As far back as the period of the independence struggles, the political élite have mobilized support on the basis of ethnic, religious, and regional cleavages. In the ensuing zero-sum politics, domination of government by members of one or a few ethnic groups (Americo-Liberians in pre-1980 Liberia and members of Samuel Doe's Krahn ethnic group after 1980, or Hausa–Fulani in Nigeria) was all the displaced, marginalized, or excluded élite needed to engage in counter-mobilization through military coups, warlord politics, and bitter opposition.

The persistence of élite division and acrimony may be taken as an indication of the underdevelopment of what Horowitz has termed "multiethnic democracy,"[8] that is the arrangement of state power relations in a manner that guarantees a reasonable level playing field for competing ethnic interests, including access to resources and privileges. For a long time, Nigeria (and Ghana to a lesser extent) seemed to be the exception in the region in this regard. Spurred by a federal arrangement, the countries' leaders built an impressive system of multi-ethnic democracy that thrived even under the military. The main instrument was guaranteed power sharing, which was built around the principle of federal character, creation of states and local governments, and a flexible system of resource allocation.[9] Although these instruments helped to keep the divided country together in the period after the civil war (1967–1970), their efficacy was seriously weakened by the de-federalizing policies of prolonged military rule.[10]

Let us now briefly consider civil society, the active non-governmental segment of the public sphere. Civil society has been weak, in part because it has been difficult for it to withstand the totalizing onslaught of the post-colonial state. Another reason is that many civil-society constituents – labour, professional associations, youth organizations, the press, independent churches, farmers' associations, women's groups, and voluntary ethnic associations – were part of the nationalist coalitions that won independence; hence, they were easily co-opted into government. Those who stayed out (and probably joined ranks with the opposition) became "enemies" of the state. For reasons of its fragility, contested legitimacy, and instability, the state was highly suspicious and intolerant of autonomous spaces in the public domain.

Autonomous civil-society constituents were routinely proscribed, while the leaders of "enemy" organizations were detained and imprisoned. The legal requirement that NGOs had to be formally registered by the state to operate was exploited to the fullest. Under such suffocating conditions, the efficacy of civil society was greatly constrained. Part of the problem was the privileging of the state, which, at least in the African situation, conferred superior and overarching claims on it. The other problem was that civil-society constituents were not in a position to confront the state in any realistic way without some form of support from forces stronger than the state itself. It was only when human rights became an issue of global politics, to which world powers and international organizations were committed, that such support came.

In sum, it can be said that human rights were not an important part of the state agenda for a long time. The best that was on offer consisted of declarations and formalistic bills of rights. Worse still, the institutions for promoting and protecting or safeguarding rights were either absent or poorly developed and ineffective. The independence of the judiciary was compromised by the non-separation of powers and the expectation that judicial interventions should be consistent with state interests, as determined by the executive and ruling party. There were instances when judgements not favourable to state power holders were set aside (as in the case of *Lakanmi and Anor* v. *Attorney-General (West)* and others in Nigeria), or when judges were sacked for giving independent judgements (as happened to Chief Justice Sir Arku Korsah in Ghana under Nkrumah).

Where rights-protecting institutions existed – such as the ombudsman in Ghana and the Public Complaints Commission in Nigeria – their subordination to the whims and caprices of the rulers also rendered them ineffective. Overall, the notion that the state had to survive and be stable, cohesive, and developed, made human rights issues of secondary importance. The only right that was to be jealously guarded was the right of the state to self-determination and of its power holders to the loyalty and support of the citizenry. In this scheme, opposition was demonized, eliminated, and suppressed.

Economic institutions

The basic formations and tendencies of the economies of West African countries, the roots of which date back to the integration of African economies into the global capitalist system and which have implications for human rights violations, can be briefly outlined as follows. First, the dominant economic configuration is centralized planning, an inevitable concomitant of political centralization and state-led development. Second, on the basis of quality-of-life and development-capacity indexes (gross national product, income per capita, literacy, industrialization, health-care delivery, etc.), West Africa has some of the poorest countries in Africa and in the world, including Burkina Faso, Niger, Sierra Leone, and Nigeria.[11] The economies are basically agrarian, with an average of 70 per cent of the population of each country engaged in subsistence agriculture in rural areas. This makes land a very important production factor, explaining why contestation over land is one of the main sources of communal and ethnic conflicts. In addition, a significant proportion of ordinary people, especially in the urban areas, are engaged in the vibrant informal sector that runs parallel to the formal sector. The informal sector helps to absorb large portions of the population that would otherwise be unemployed or live below the poverty line. It also houses such illegal practices as smuggling, moonlighting, piracy, currency counterfeiting, drug trafficking, prostitution, child labour, and foreign-exchange "black markets" that are subversive of government economic policies. Accordingly, they usually attract punitive measures – crackdowns, mass arrests, demolition of illegal structures, etc. – from the state.

Third, virtually all the states in the region are monocultural, dependent on the export of one main agricultural or mineral commodity: crude oil accounts for over 90 per cent of Nigeria's total revenue; cocoa is the mainstay of the Ivorian economy; gold and cocoa for Ghana; rubber for Liberia; diamonds for Sierra Leone; and so on. Largely because the states have no control over the prices of their export commodities, their economies are susceptible to, and have been adversely affected by, unstable commodity prices and other shocks and depressions that the global economy suffers from time to time. One direct effect of this has been the accumulation of foreign debts. The volume of debts owed by West African countries (estimated at $77.3 billion by 1996) is not unduly large, compared with the rest of the third world (Nigeria and Côte d'Ivoire, with estimated debts of $32 billion and $19.8 billion respectively, are the exceptions). However, when the volume of total debt service is considered, such debts are quite a burden on poor and fragile economies. It is as such that foreign debts have diminished the developmental capacity of the states and left them with no option but to swallow the bitter pill of International Monetary Fund and World Bank-authored economic reforms built around structural adjustment programmes (SAPs).

Fourth, although most states have been active in the economy since independence and have tried to live up to their titles of developmental states, they have depended on rents and royalties paid by multinationals that dominate the productive sector of mining and agriculture. The government's greatest showing is in the bloated public service and enterprises sector, which is not only the largest employer of labour in the formal sector but also the recipient of the bulk of revenues, with as much as 90 per cent of total revenue going to recurrent expenditures (salaries and overheads) in many countries. The industrial and manufacturing (assembly) sectors are miniscule (most countries in the region recorded negative real growth rates in these sectors in the 1980s and 1990s). Fifth, going back to the foundations laid during colonial rule, the economies are dominated by foreign concerns – multinationals and hosts of Asian and

Middle-Eastern business people (Lebanese, Syrians, Indians, Koreans, and Chinese) who control the organized private sector. A large number of the multinationals are found in the trading sector; however, they also constitute the major players in the mining and manufacturing sectors.

The rise to prominence of issues of environmental preservation, local self-determination, and good governance, at the same time that the developmental capacities of states have declined, has opened multinationals to the demands and vagaries of local politics. Although they might be exceptions to the rule, the cases of Shell, Chevron, Elf, Mobil, and other oil companies in Nigeria are instructive. As resource allocation from the state declined, oil-bearing minorities of the Niger Delta region increasingly vented their anger and frustrations against the state on the oil companies, which were forced to become involved in state security arrangements. Shell, for instance, was reported to have supplied arms to the Nigerian police and security agencies for protection of strategic oil installations. To pacify the angry communities, the oil majors were forced to expand their involvement in the development of their host communities.

Sixth, the economies of West Africa remain closely tied to those of the West and the erstwhile colonizers. This is especially true of the francophone countries, whose fiscal and monetary policies were literally controlled from France, and whose currency (the Communauté Financière Africaine; CFA) was tied to the French franc until the mid-1990s. Although the Cold War afforded a few "socialist" countries such as Benin and Togo the opportunity to diversify foreign economic relations, the pattern of trade and investment inflows was highly skewed in favour of the West and former colonial masters. This pattern of dependence was a crucial facilitator when it came to exerting external pressure on the countries to embrace economic and political reforms. As indicated earlier, SAPs were the mainstay of economic reforms. The programmes basically involved sets of macroeconomic reform policies (liberalization of trade; the financial sector; foreign exchange; prices of goods and services; and retrenchment of the public sector through privatization, rationalization, and downsizing), the aim of which was drastically to reduce so-called "unproductive" state control of the economy and to entrench market forces.

Although Ghana was touted as a successful case of adjustment, the demonstrable effect of adjustment programmes in almost all cases was aggravation of poverty and a reduction of the quality of life of citizens to levels far below those of the years immediately following independence. There were huge job cuts and retrenchments in the formal sector, devaluations of currency, whittled-down incomes and purchasing power, and increased costs of such basic services as water, electricity, transport, education, and health care to beyond the reach of most ordinary people. The state itself was also a major casualty: with the decline in resources and revenues that prefaced SAP and the increased dependence on foreign aid, governments found it increasingly difficult to satisfy the minimum imperatives of statehood, including provision of such basic goods and services as the regular payments of salaries to public officers, the security of lives and property, the running of public schools and hospitals, and the maintenance of infrastructure. Increased poverty is a major factor in the upsurge in violent crimes, prostitution, child labour, emigration, the spread of HIV/AIDS, and the resurgence of the slave trade and such killer diseases as malaria and cholera.

It did not come as a surprise, therefore, that, after a review of initial failures, the World Bank became a major proponent of poverty allevia-tion. However, this could not stem the tide of massive opposition by labour, youth, academics, professional associations, women's associa-tions, and the urban poor, nor of the phenomenal increase in anti/counter-state conflicts. The massive opposition led the state to higher levels of authoritarianism and repression, without which SAPs could not be implemented – indeed, the real success cases were those implemented by more authoritarian rulers – such as General Babangida of Nigeria (who passed a decree forbidding discussion of alternatives to SAP) and J.J. Rawlings of Ghana.

Cultures and identities

All countries in West Africa are multi-ethnic, although the difficulties and state-threatening problems posed by this make-up have differed from country to country. Nigeria – with over 300 ethno-linguistic groups (the divisions of which are reinforced by a complex mix of regional and reli-gious cleavages) and with a long history of separatist agitations and ethnic, regional, religious, and communal conflicts – is clearly the worst case. Another country that has failed in ethnic terms is Liberia, the oldest republic in the region. Although the country has only 16 major ethnic groups, it has suffered bitter ethnic feuds that ultimately resulted in civil war in 1989. Ghana's post-independence history has witnessed con-tinuous wrangling between the Asante and the Ewe, the largest of the country's (over 90) ethnic groups, for control of the state, and a fairly large number of localized ethnic and communal conflicts (involving the Kokomba and Nanumba, Nawuri and Gonja, etc.), which have been on the increase since the 1990s.

In general, ethnicity has been more politically salient and troubling in anglophone countries (notably Nigeria, Ghana, and Sierra Leone) than it has been in such francophone countries as Côte d'Ivoire, Benin, and

Burkina Faso. This can be largely attributed to differences in colonial legacy: whereas the British pursued a policy of indirect rule that nurtured and strengthened ethnic identities and loyalties, and operated a relatively open system that permitted ethnic political mobilization and participation, the French system was much more centralized and closed.

After independence, the francophone countries moved along the one-party–centralist–assimilationist trajectory, whereas the anglophone countries were relatively more open, pluralistic, competitive, and decentralized. However, this semblance of tranquility and cohesion did not prevent the francophones from also tasting the bitter pill of ethnic politics, mostly in their struggle for state power. Thus, state power holders in Niger and Senegal have respectively had to contend with Tuareg and Casamance separatists. Côte d'Ivoire, which had enjoyed relative peace and stability under Felix Houphouet-Boigny, has had more than its fair share of ethnic troubles, including separatist agitations by the Sanwi and Guebie and the rash of ethnic and religious tensions over control of state power in the post-Boigny years.[12]

The point that emerges fairly clearly from what has been said so far is that ethnicity and ethnic conflicts have been instigated by competition, in most cases for scarce resources and control of state power. The élite (and political parties), who are at the forefront of the struggle for power, are at the pivot of ethnic mobilization. The élites manipulate members' fears, which arise from conflicts carried over from the past, colonial legacies of favoured ethnic groups and races, uneven development, and partisan actions of state power holders. In the process, personal ambitions, successes, and failures become tied to those of the group, and inter-élite competition becomes inter-group conflict. What is of greater concern to us, however, is the state's response to ethnicity and ethnic conflicts – especially to those that directly threaten its existence, such as demands for equitable power and resource sharing, claims to self-determination, and warlord politics.

The response has basically been twofold. On the one hand, as was consistent with the state-privileged hegemonic approach that dominated national cohesion discourse in Africa for a long time, ethnic claims were seen as a threat that had to be eradicated (or reduced to the barest minimum). This approach has been highly unsuccessful, to the extent that the suppression of ethnic nationalism served only to justify claims to ethnic rights and entitlements and strengthened the case of "marginalized," "displaced," "excluded," and "oppressed" élites and groups.

On the other hand, expediency and good politics have frequently led even such avowed enemies of ethnicity as Kwame Nkrumah of Ghana and Sekou Toure of Guinea to embrace ethnic-balancing formulas and other reconciliatory measures. Attempts to build supra-ethnic national cultures through the adoption of a lingua franca, and cultural symbols (such as President Tubman's integration of the Poro society into Liberia's national culture), also belong to the reconciliatory trajectory. However, the advent of warlord politics and the centrality of ethnic grievances to civil wars and separatist agitations suggest that power sharing has to be taken more seriously.

Civil and international conflict

As in most other parts of the world, in West Africa the post-Cold War political scene witnessed an upsurge in civil conflict and war. There have been protracted civil wars in Liberia, Sierra Leone, Niger, Guinea, and Guinea Bissau, the effects of which have resonated all over the region. Furthermore, virtually every country in the region has experienced one form or another of devastating ethnic, regional, religious, and communal conflict. Counter-state mobilization, including separatist agitation, has risen phenomenally since the late 1980s. Examples include Casamance separatism in Senegal, Tuareg separatism in Niger, the Niger Delta uprising in Nigeria, and "rebel" activities in Liberia, Sierra Leone, Guinea-Bissau, Guinea, and Côte d'Ivoire. In a word, West Africa has become something of a theatre of war, as attested to by the presence of warlords, refugees, displaced persons, exile communities, child soldiers, and so on.

The scenario may be regarded as one of the inevitable consequences of Cold War manipulations and tensions, especially the arms build-up and support lent to authoritarian regimes and ethnic adversaries while the war lasted. A host of other factors, however, served to accentuate the state of instability and war in the region. Foremost among these is the combination of desperate economic crises and state collapse, which afforded the opportunity, finally, for previously marginalized and oppressed groups, ambitious politicians, and warlords to demand reconstruction of the state.[13] Second, there has been a paradigm shift in the discourse on national cohesion. The collapse of the Soviet Union, Czechoslovakia, and Yugoslavia seemed to have brought the old conventional wisdom – which privileged the state and justified the hegemonic projects of post-independence ruling élites in Africa – to an end. Ethnic claims were no longer illegitimate, after all; in fact, the rights of minorities, indigenous peoples, and oppressed groups became the new privilege, and various groups in the region were on line to make the most of the opportunities created by that new privilege.

The political reforms prescribed (some would say imposed) by the hegemony-seeking global powers, whose hallmark was political liberalization – pluralism, multi-partyism, and human rights – further boosted the new-found voice for ethnic claimants. Indeed, there was something of a direct link between developments in the international arena and the upsurge of ethnic restiveness and claims in Africa, which were integral parts of the democratization in the continent. For example, the Ogoni uprising in Nigeria, one of the notable examples of new-style minority assertiveness, benefited a great deal from the support of international environmental and minority activists, as well as from the facilitative declarations of the United Nations and other international organizations on the rights of indigenous peoples, minorities, and other oppressed peoples.[14]

What has been the impact of war and violence on human rights practices in West Africa? The first general point that needs to be made is that situations of war and violence elicit different human rights practices and challenges from situations of peace and stability, with the medley of refugees, displaced persons, child soldiers, and war crimes and the collapse of normal law and rights enforcing institutions in war situations. War situations also legitimize and justify violence and the denial of fundamental human rights. Worse still, the atrocities are usually concealed and beyond public scrutiny. Rebel forces, in particular, are secretive and distrustful of outside interference: women are raped, unarmed civilians are tortured and killed in the most bizarre ways, children are abducted and forcibly conscripted into fighting armies, and soldiers are treated as people without rights of any kind – all in the name of propagating and winning the war. These situations raise a different set of questions. What rules and rights apply, and who would monitor and enforce them? Who would be held responsible for war crimes, considering the lack of accountability on the part of the leadership?

The inability of subsisting governments – or what is left of them – to enforce rights makes foreign backers of rebel groups, peacekeeping forces, the United Nations, and other international bodies (including humanitarian agencies and NGOs) critical actors in the wartime human rights discourse. Foreign backers wield a great deal of influence and can, for example, make compliance with war laws a condition for assistance. Nevertheless, they failed to do so in Liberia and Sierra Leone, where the illegal diamond and timber trade (which was facilitated by war) was the main attraction. It took the intervention of the United Nations for Charles Taylor of Liberia finally to be charged with war crimes. In both Liberia and Sierra Leone, indiscipline and corruption among the ECOWAS Military Observer Group (ECOMOG) peacekeepers, upon whom a lot depended, further worsened the human rights situation. The human rights unit of the UN Observer Mission in Sierra Leone (UNOMSIL) and its follow-up mission – the UN Mission in Sierra Leone (UNAMSIL) – reported gross human rights abuses on the part of ECOMOG in 1999.[15]

Another human rights problem associated with war, which certainly arose from the wars in Liberia and Sierra Leone, is that of the status and rights of refugees and displaced persons. Host states have all kinds of problems with refugees, not the least of which is the security risk they pose. Indeed, refugees from Liberia were a source of tension in neighbouring Côte d'Ivoire, Sierra Leone, and Guinea, and were believed to be conduits in the outbreak of war in these countries. However, even more urgent problems arose over the welfare of refugees. Being poor and unstable themselves, the host countries were not in a position to provide adequate food, shelter, and security for them. In some cases, refugees were forced to seek employment – mostly menial jobs for men and prostitution for women – which exposed them to the danger of xenophobia from members of the host communities.

Civil wars were only the more extreme situations of conflict in West Africa: other localized conflicts afforded the state the opportunity to deprive individuals and groups of their rights. Conflicts that were perceived as a threat to the stability, cohesion, and survival of the state were met with the full might of state terrorism, and the rights of the "offending" groups were brazenly violated. This point is illustrated by the virtual war declared by the Nigerian federal government on the country's oil-rich Niger Delta region to "crush" the rebellion of aggrieved equity-seeking minorities.

Transition consequences

Democratization and the transformation of human rights

Human rights were pivotal to the wave of democratization that swept through Africa from the late 1980s onwards. However, although the impulses for democratic change were generated internally by the malcontents and failings of the state, the process was strengthened by a number of supportive external factors that emerged in the aftermath of the Cold War.[16] Chief among these were the stipulation of pluralism/multi-party politics, human rights, and good governance as conditionalities for aid by the international donor community; the effort to build up civil society as an alternative engine room of development to the state; and the material and moral support given to pro-democracy and other civil-society constituents in the struggle against the state.

There were also the less hegemony-seeking factors of globalization. These ranged from the demonstration effect of dramatic events in previously authoritarian parts of the world such as the former USSR and Poland, to the key roles played by citizens of the democratizing countries in the diaspora, who helped to expose the atrocities and human rights violations of the repressive regimes in their countries and, with the support of sympathetic "host" states, played an active part in the diplomatic offensives to oust dictators. What is of importance, however, is not the mechanics of democratization per se, but the pivotal role of human rights in the process. In a real sense, the struggle was for liberation – for the rights and freedom of the people, as opposed to the state, which, as the repository and recipient of rights at independence failed to actualize the expected gains of decolonization. It was the failure of the state, as it were, that made a second liberation struggle necessary – this time, from internal colonialists and despots.[17]

The concept of a second liberation, which I consider the most original contribution by African scholars to democratization scholarship, helps to place the transformation of the human rights agenda in the context of transition in perspective. This involves a shift in conception from that of rights as state property to that of rights as the property of individuals and groups, and from that of rights as duties to the state to that of rights as rights from and against the state. To elaborate, we use the insights offered by Ekeh, who has made the most remarkable attempt so far to interrogate the analytical power of the concept of second liberation in relation to human rights.[18] For him, liberation as freedom is at the core of democratization, and the main difference between the first and second liberations lies in the differing conceptions of freedom that informed the movements. In the first liberation, freedom was approached as the collective right of peoples and states. This, as we have already indicated, not only submerged individual rights but also made it possible to deny individual rights, if doing so was perceived to be in the interest of the state. By contrast, the freedom of the individual was the object of the second liberation.[19]

The lesson from the failure of the first liberation was that any struggle for freedom from the all-powerful state would be hollow if steps were not taken to safeguard the autonomy of individuals and groups and to prevent a relapse to state monopoly of the public sphere. This meant that practical ways of checking the totalizing tendency of the state had to be found, making its power holders responsive and accountable, and protecting human rights. From the common steps taken throughout the region, there was something of a consensus that constitutional reform and constitutionalism held the best promise.

However, the resulting constitutions were no longer to be clones of erstwhile colonial authorities with elegant but hollow bills of rights. A major objective in the struggle was, therefore, to have constitutions that reflected the balance of social and political forces, were people-centred and, above all, were not imposed from above (that is, by incumbent governments). Thus, civil-society leaders were critical of the 1999 Nigerian constitution: on the grounds that it was written and fraudulently passed by the military administration of General Abdulsalami Abubakar without popular consultation, they campaigned for its repeal. They also criticized the constitutional review process initiated by the successor civilian administration of General Olusegun Obasanjo because, as they argued, government control limited the extent to which the constitutional process could have been democratic and sovereign.

Other measures that were deemed capable of preventing a relapse to authoritarianism were embraced by constitutional reforms. The 1992 Ghanaian constitution, for example, forbids parliament from establishing a one-party state and declares as unlawful any activity "which suppresses or seeks to suppress a lawful political activity." The reformers were particularly mindful of the need to prevent violent and unlawful overthrow or abrogation of the constitution by the military, which was a major source of human rights abuse in the past. The constitution saddles citizens of Ghana with the responsibility and duty, at all times, to resist any person or group of persons seeking to overthrow the constitution, and stipulates the death sentence for those who aid and abet such overthrow. Such provisions can do very little to stop ambitious military officers from seizing power, as Nigerians learnt when, in spite of similar provisions in the 1979 constitution, the military still struck in 1983. Nevertheless, Ihonvbere thinks that such provisions are still significant, because they represent a feeling "that such illegal seizures of power ought to be resisted and discouraged."[20]

Another area that has received the attention of constitutional reforms is the promotion and protection of rights enshrined in the constitution. The constitutions of Nigeria (1999) and Ghana (1992) provide for the establishment of Human Rights Commissions (Commission on Human Rights and Administrative Justice in Ghana), which are mandated to investigate and deal with cases of human rights violations. The Benin constitution provides for a constitutional court to deal with similar issues. The Ghanaian constitution also provides for a National Commission for Civic Education, and assigns it functions that include creating and sustaining awareness of the principles and objectives of the constitution, and educating and encouraging the public to defend the constitution at all times, against all forms of abuse and violation. The commission is further mandated to formulate programmes intended to inculcate in the citizens of Ghana awareness of their civic responsibilities and an appreciation of their rights and obligations as free people.

However, it goes without saying that constitutions, by themselves, cannot keep the state in check or affect people's rights. In any case, the Nigerian and Ghanaian constitutions retain emergency powers provisions and other detestable laws that can potentially make nonsense of whatever gains were made in the democratization struggles. Considering how crucial are the organization and distribution of state power to the enjoyment of rights, the real test of the success of democratic transitions would include the following:

- Is there greater freedom now for opposition, and how realistic are the opposition's chances of securing power?
- Have electoral machineries and processes become more independent and open, and are elections now more free and fair?
- Are political institutions now stronger?
- Have separation of power and independence of the judiciary become meaningful?
- Does the system now ensure greater access and safeguards to competing groups, or is the state still dominated or controlled exclusively by people from one or a few ethnic, religious, or regional groups?
- Is the state now more accountable, transparent, and responsive?

Answers to these questions suggest that West African democracies have not yet arrived: this conclusion is based on the persistence of tendencies toward one party (dominant) rule; the deprivations (such as state subsidy and access to official media) and harassments from which opposition parties still suffer; and the continued organizational weaknesses, tight control of electoral commissions by incumbent power holders, and the generally violent and inconclusive nature of elections. However, the 2000 elections in Ghana and Senegal (which saw rare defeats of incumbents) give hope that things may be changing in the region. By vigorously contesting control of the public sphere with the state, civil society has also been actively involved in the struggle to entrench pluralism, multi-party politics, good governance, and human rights. In Nigeria, for example, a number of NGOs (with the support of foreign donors) have set up teams to monitor and assess the state of democracy and human rights records and to publicize cases of violation and abuse. One of these teams, Media Watch, publishes weekly reports in newspapers, which expose and discuss state wrongdoings and excesses. Human rights awareness campaigns, voter and civic education programmes, and provision of free legal aid to the poor, complete the efforts that civil-society organizations have made to promote a human rights culture and defend the people against the excesses of the state.

Economic development

Two points are crucial to analysing the human rights implications of the economic transition that occurred in West Africa from the late 1980s. The first is the precipitate decline in the developmental capacities of states and their ability to discharge the basic functions of statehood effectively. The decline is more visible in countries such as Sierra Leone and Liberia, where NGOs, humanitarian agencies, international organizations, and foreign donors have taken over many of the functions that traditionally belonged to the state. However, the situation is not much better in the relatively more peaceful states: long periods of neglect and lack of maintenance have ruined basic infrastructure and public establishments. Capital expenditures have declined, especially in the social sector. Salaries of public servants go unpaid for months. The withdrawal of so-called subsidies on essential public goods has increased social costs. Privatization of government enterprises has accentuated the steady disappearance of the state.

The only way to appreciate fully the implication of this decline is to remember the central role played by the state in the economy and to see that its decline has not changed that role in popular perception. This largely accounts for the massive social unrest – protracted workers' strikes, urban riots, and demonstrations – that has greeted state decline. On the other hand, the exigencies of meeting the challenges of survival and development have forced more people to rely increasingly on the shadow state functions performed by the traditional self-help (voluntary ethnic, hometown, religious) organizations that dot the social landscape. The ranks of the informal sector have also been swollen by an increase in the number of people entering "self-employment" and small-scale enterprises. Interestingly, these relocations have received encouragement from governments. The advent of poverty alleviation programmes, in particular, led to a stepping-up of the efforts to encourage people to look away from the state and meet their basic needs themselves.

The implications of these developments for human rights, especially socio-economic rights, should be fairly obvious: responsibility for the well-being of citizens is removed from the state and placed on the shoulders of the citizens themselves, which negates the norm of reciprocity that governs the rights–duties intercourse in citizenship. It might be argued that a freeing of socio-economic relations from the stranglehold of the state is a necessary condition for liberalization and, therefore, that a retrenchment of the state is positive rather than negative. However, this overlooks the fact that the state still has responsibility for important areas of the capital-intensive development sector (run-down universities, dilapidated roads and transport systems, hospitals); that the poor will continue to need the support of the state; and that state intervention is still necessary to ensure that, as much as possible, there is a level playing field in the competition for scarce resources. With regard to the last point, the need for the "correction factor" to ensure that members of weak and disadvantaged groups are in a position to compete with others cannot be overemphasized. In Nigeria, where privatization of government enterprises provoked ethnic sentiments and tensions, the Bureau for Public Enterprises (the state agency saddled with the exercise) was forced to advance loans to members of poor communities to ensure that the exercise was not turned into an opportunity for members of more affluent communities to take over the economy. The overall point, I think, is that political democracy has to be matched with economic and social democracy to make human rights meaningful.

The second point relates to the fact that economic reforms embodied in SAPs were undertaken alongside political reforms. Several studies have pointed to the contradictory pulls elicited by a twinning of the two processes:[21] whereas political liberalization is participatory and supportive of democracy, the packaging and implementation of economic reforms encourages authoritarian tendencies. This often sets governments on collision courses with the more discerning elements of civil society – notably labour, students, and academics – and reinforced authoritarian tendencies.

However, the major problem remains that the reforms so far undertaken have not led to significant transformations in economic structures and recovery. The economies remain monocultural and as vulnerable as ever to external shocks; trade liberalization and privatization have not yielded the expected dividends, whether in terms of foreign investment or increased local and global competitiveness; the public sector, with all its inefficiency, remains at the core of the economy; the commanding heights of the economies are still controlled by multinationals and other foreign interests; poverty levels appear to be on the increase in spite of the popularity of poverty-alleviation programmes; foreign debts are still a major burden and have left the countries at the mercy of the World Bank and the IMF; and the social sector has remained in the doldrums.

Explanations for the apparent failure of adjustment programmes have ranged from the lack of will and managerial ability on the part of the state (whose efficiency, contrary to expectation, was not enhanced by its trimming), to cultural inertia, the point being that African cultures are generally impervious to change. Although these explanations are partly valid, the missing link is still the state. The only realistic path to economic recovery would be to invest more in its dwindling credibility and legitimacy by strengthening its capacity for just and equitable distribution of resources. This is an area that needs urgent attention because of the primacy of economic development to democratization, conflict resolution, and the creation of a culture of rights. The point cannot be overemphasized that the continued poverty of African states poses a threat not just to the stability of the states but to the peace and security of the global system as a whole.

Conflict resolution

The fact that democratization processes were taking place in West Africa while several parts of the region were embroiled in civil war and violent conflicts, had direct consequences for conflict resolution in individual countries and the region as a whole. One of these was the realization that, as Dahl has argued, peace, resolution of conflict, and stability are necessary for democracy and development.[22] This realization saw the emergence of new attitudes towards conflicts and adversaries, as in the reconciliatory meetings organized by the government of Côte d'Ivoire in 2001, and the workings of the Oputa panel in Nigeria, whose sessions were similar to those of the Truth and Reconciliation Commission in South Africa. It also underlay the rapid growth of the conflict-resolution industry, involving both governmental and non-governmental agencies. Another was the realization that the democratization and development of any state were closely tied to the peace and stability of the entire sub-region. A key variable in this regard is de-militarization, an absolutely necessary condition for peace, civility, and human rights. This regional dimension increased the importance of the bold initiatives of ECOWAS, the regional organization, in the areas of collective security (through ECOMOG), a regional culture of peace (through arms-proliferation control), and regional development (through establishment of a regional parliament, a high court, and a common currency).

Three other developments combined to raise the challenge and urgency of conflict resolution. First was the increase in the number and size of conflicting parties (as a result of the opening up of previously closed systems), which afforded groups that had been suppressed or excluded, the opportunity to join first-order competition, leading to an expansion of grievances and competitors. The problem was not, however, the expansion of competitors per se, but the fact that some transitions involved the loss of state power and that this engendered counter-revolutionary action on the part of "losers." These losers – such as the conservative Hausa–Fulani of northern Nigeria – swelled the ranks of the aggrieved. In South Africa, the short-term compensations conceded to the White Afrikaners who were displaced from power contributed immensely to the smooth passage of transition. In Nigeria, there was no such compensation or reassurance; instead, there appeared to be an attempt literally to vanquish the losers – to punish them for the excesses of past military governments. Such actions increased the tension and bitterness of transition.

The second development was that, unlike the past, when the state enjoyed the privilege of dealing with demands that were deemed "illegitimate," the new discourse of pluralism and liberalization privileged rival groups, whose claims and demands on the state were accordingly legitimized. To be able to cope with this new challenge and enhance its legitimacy, it was obvious that the state had to devise new forms of political accommodation in place of the old authoritarian and hegemonic structures. The third development was the (near) breakdown of law and order in many countries, which was a concomitant of state collapse. The breakdown, which manifested itself in different ways, including an increase in crime and criminal violence and the rise of ethnic militias, demonstrably made the task of conflict resolution more difficult.

So how did the various states cope with the new challenges? This takes us back to the major source of conflicts discussed in the previous section: the fact that the state lacked relative autonomy (or "neutrality") and was not insulated from exclusionary personal or ethnic capture. The opening up of political systems means that one of the structural requirements for a turnaround has been met; however, the question is how this can be translated into greater accountability, responsiveness, and guaranteed access to competing groups, especially those in opposition. Constitutional safeguards may be helpful, to the extent that they reduce the fluid and volatile character of power contestation and provide a reference point for seeking redress; however, a lot more needs to be done in the realm of political action to make political institutions and processes effective. This is where the role of civil society, as the ultimate watchdog over state actions, becomes very useful.

Not yet *Uhuru*

Although some significant changes have taken place, the overall state of affairs in the region suggests that no fundamental change has occurred. It is, therefore, not surprising that, in his classification of regimes at the end of 1997 (based on the average Freedom House score on political and civil liberties), Diamond listed only Benin in the lower rung of the category of "free" states, while Mali was an "outside" entry at the very bottom of the category.[24] Most of the countries in the region were listed under the categories of "(Non-liberal) Electoral Democracies" and "Pseudo-Democracies," while Nigeria and Sierra Leone fell in the category of the countries with the least freedom (authoritarian regimes). Changes in some countries since 1997 would give them better – or worse – ratings: Nigeria, for example, has come closer to being an electoral democracy since the inauguration of civilian government there in 1999; Ghana post-Rawlings would probably be ahead of Benin; and Guinea, Liberia, and Côte d'Ivoire would have descended to the category of least freedom. Nevertheless, the overall picture remains as Diamond found it in 1997.

Specifically, the level of human rights violation and abuse remains high despite the constitutional reforms and democracy/human rights-protection initiatives of civil society discussed in the last section. Disappearance, torture, and suppression of opponents remain common; freedoms of speech, of political association, and of assembly are still highly circumscribed; and the superior will of the state remains the prism from which human rights are approached. Social and economic rights continue to be injusticiable, for the ostensible reason of state incapacity. Why have the excitement and hope generated by the second liberation not translated into the emergence of a culture of rights as expected? The reasons are not hard to discern.

The first is that rights still remain abstract and meaningless to people who have still not found any viable alternative to the omnipotent state. Civil society has come on strongly, but is not strong enough to seriously counter the state or take its place. The other problem is the extent to which the rights granted in the constitution can be redeemed. Given the high costs of litigation and the corruption of law courts in Nigeria, for example, legal redress remains unattractive, despite the efforts of various civil society organizations at providing legal aid. As for social and economic rights, these remain tied to state solvency, as indicated earlier. Perhaps the only rights that have made tremendous progress in places like Nigeria, where they have been used as weapons and objects of struggle (especially by minorities), are group rights. The growing significance of group rights, which is at issue in most of the civil wars in the region, suggests that the second liberation may have been more about expanding political space to enable non-governing élites previously excluded and in opposition to renegotiate access to, and participation in, government, than about defending the rights of the individual.

Second, the authoritarian instruments of the state remain strong. In at least two cases (Eyadema's Togo and Kerekou's Benin) the authoritarian one-party state remains virtually intact. This is largely because the logic of over-centralization and strong state power remains firmly entrenched. The liberalization policies of adjustment have been too half-hearted and opportunistic (some governments merely pretended to liberalize and decentralize just to satisfy donor conditionalities) to change this logic. Furthermore, the brutality and impunity of the military, police, and other security forces that are yet to be "born again," including their self-bestowed "immunity" from scrutiny and accountability, have not changed. The same applies to the judiciary, which lost its independence in most countries and was a key agent of authoritarianism in the past. In addition, the draconian legislation that sustained past authoritarian regimes, including provisions for preventive detention and detention without trial, remain in force and have encouraged anti-democratic tendencies. For example, shortly after coming to power, the Obasanjo administration in Nigeria invoked the emergency powers of the 1999 Constitution to crush groups protesting against government high-handedness in the Niger Delta in Odi village. The Nigerian state has also used the land use decree, which vests the state with ownership of land in the country, to deny property rights and compensation in the case of government take-overs.

Third, and finally, a combination of continuing – or worsening – economic crisis and foreign debt, repression-inducing adjustment pro-grammes, fear of military intervention, and the potentially destabilizing spill-over effects of the civil wars and political turmoil in most parts of the region, have provided state power holders with the justification they need to continue to violate human rights. All in all, it seems that the more things have changed, the more they have remained the same – or even worsened. Hence, there is no liberation yet for oppressed and deprived individual citizens. Even so, the gains of democratization that have been discussed in this chapter should not be underplayed. Without a doubt, more and more people have become aware of their rights and the need to defend them. Also, even though we have been critical of the over-whelming concern with group rights and entitlements, there is no doubt that the struggles for these rights have restored dignity and have been empowering for minorities and other marginal groups. Members of these groups can be expected to use this as a launching pad in coming struggles for individual self-actualization.

The growing importance of, and familiarity with, human rights issues has also enabled people to draw the line between the state realm, which is to be kept in check, and the private autonomous realm, which is to be defended at all costs. Human rights awareness has been advanced through the activities of the human rights commissions and panels, such as that headed by Justice Oputa in Nigeria, which investigated past human rights violations. In such places as Ghana and Nigeria, where the links between military rule and human rights abuses have become part of the popular consciousness, it is unlikely that future military interventions will be welcome. The popular resistance to military take-over in Mali and Côte d'Ivoire may, in fact, be prototypical of future trends. Over and above all this is a nascent culture of constitutionalism. This culture's chances appear bright, given the determination of civil society to ensure that accountability becomes a key feature of governance. These are a few of the modest gains of democratization that will, it is hoped, make the next struggle – the third liberation, perhaps – for individual rights and dignity more meaningful. Finally, of course, the processes of de-militarization and economic recovery have to be accelerated. Here, the support of the donor community and international organizations, in terms of funds and monitoring skills, cannot be overemphasized.

Notes

1. The states in the region belonging to ECOWAS are Benin, Burkina Faso, Cape Verde, Côte d'Ivoire, Gambia, Ghana, Guinea, Guinea-Bissau, Liberia, Mali, Niger, Nigeria, Sierra Leone, Senegal, and Togo.
2. Joy Mukubwa Hendrickson, "Rights in Traditional African Societies," in John A.A. Ayoade and Adigun A.B. Agbaje, eds, *African Traditional Political Thought and Institutions*, Lagos: Centre for Black and African Arts and Civilization, 1989, pp. 19–43.
3. H. Diabate, "The Process of Nation and Constitution-Building in Côte d'Ivoire," in I.G. Shivji, ed., *State and Constitutionalism: An African Debate on Democracy*, Harare: SAPES, 1991, p. 170.
4. O.C. Eze, *Human Rights in Africa: Some Selected Problems*, Lagos: Nigerian Institute of International Affairs (NIIA) and Macmillan, 1984, p. 27.
5. P. Chabal and J. Daloz, *Africa Works: Disorder as Political Instrument*, Oxford: James Currey, 1999; P. Englebert, *State Legitimacy and Development in Africa*, Boulder: Lynne Rienner, 2000.
6. J.-F. Bayart, "Civil Society in Africa: Reflections on the Limits of Power," in P. Chabal, ed., *Political Domination in Africa*, Cambridge: Cambridge University Press, 1986, pp. 106–125.
7. In Nigeria, the instruments multiplied under military rule, but the main one was the State Security (Detention of Persons) Decree no. 3 of 1966, which was amended as deemed fit by successive military governments. In Ghana, it was the Executive Instrument: 151 Preventive Custody (no. 54) Order of 1977 that was used to legalize the detention without trial of opponents of the government.
8. D.L. Horowitz, "Democracy in Divided Societies," in L. Diamond and M.F. Plattner, eds, *Nationalism, Ethnic Conflict and Democracy*, Baltimore: Johns Hopkins University Press, 1994, pp. 35–55.
9. P.P. Ekeh and E.E. Osaghae, eds, *Federal Character and Federalism in Nigeria*, Ibadan: Heinemann, 1989, pp. 1–10; E.E. Osaghae, "Human Rights and Ethnic Conflict Management: The Case of Nigeria," *Journal of Peace Research*, Vol. 33, No. 2, 1996, pp. 171–188.
10. R. Suberu, "The Travails of Federalism in Nigeria," in Diamond and Plattner, eds, *Nationalism, Ethnic Conflict, and Democracy*, pp. 56–70; K. Amuwo, A.A.B. Agbaje, R. Suberu, and G. Herault, eds, *Federalism and Political Restructuring in Nigeria*, Ibadan: Spectrum, 1998.
11. African Development Bank (ADB), *African Development Report 1998: Human Capital Development*, Oxford: Oxford University Press for ADB, 1998.
12. G. Gonnin, "Ethnicity, Politics and National Awareness in Côte d'Ivoire," in O. Nnoli, ed., *Ethnic Conflicts in Africa*, Dakar: CODESRIA Books, 1998, pp. 159–182.
13. R. Joseph, ed., *State, Conflict, and Democracy in Africa*, Boulder: Lynne Rienner, 1999.
14. E.E. Osaghae, "The Ogoni Uprising: Oil Politics, Minority Nationalism, and the Future of the Nigerian State," *African Affairs*, Vol. 94, No. 376, 1995, pp. 325–344.
15. W.G. O'Neill, "Gaining Compliance without Force: Human Rights Field Operations," in Simon Chesterman, ed., *Civilians in War*, Boulder: Lynne Rienner, 2001, pp. 93–122.

16. While the focus here is on supportive external forces, it should be noted that, by the very nature of the contradictions that attend relations between African states and the global capitalist system, the external factors also had democracy-weakening aspects. A case in point is the adjustment programmes that African states were compelled to implement.

17. G. Nzongola-Ntalaja, "The State and Democracy in Africa," in G. Nzongola-Ntalaja and M.C. Lee, eds, *The State and Democracy in Africa*, Harare: AAPS Books, 1997, pp. 9–24; P.P. Ekeh, "The Concept of Second Liberation and the Prospects of Democracy in Africa: A Nigerian Context," in P. Beckett and C. Young, eds, *Dilemmas of Democratization in Nigeria*, Rochester: University of Rochester Press, 1997, pp. 91–106; E.E. Osaghae, "The 'Second Liberation' and African Development," in Myriam Gervais, ed., *Development: The Need for Reflection*, Montreal: Centre for Developing Areas Studies, 2000, pp. 22–29.

18. Ekeh, "The Concept of Second Liberation and the Prospects of Democracy in Africa," p. 96.

19. Ekeh, "The Concept of Second Liberation and the Prospects of Democracy in Africa," pp. 96–97.

20. J. Ihonvbere, *Towards a New Constitutionalism in Africa*, Centre for Democracy and Development Occasional Paper Series No. 4, London: CDD, 2000.

21. Various contributions in P. Gibbon, Y. Bangura and A. Ofstad, eds, *Authoritarianism, Democracy and Adjustment: The Politics of Economic Reform in Africa*, Uppsala: Nordiska Afrikainstitutet, 1992.

22. R. Dahl, "Democracy and Human Rights under Different Conditions of Development," in O. Savic, ed., *The Politics of Human Rights*, London: Verso, 1999, p. 172.

23. *Uhuru* is Kiswahili (the commonest language for most of East, Central, and Southern Africa) for "freedom".

24. L. Diamond, *Developing Democracy: Toward Consolidation*, Baltimore: Johns Hopkins University Press, 1999, pp. 279–280.

15

Political development and democratic rights in Greater China

Man-To Leung[1]

Human rights issues are among the most disputable issues in international discourse. After World War II, various countries, especially the European countries, felt an urgent need to have some kind of consensus on the importance of respecting human rights. This led to an agreement on a Universal Declaration of Human Rights (UDHR), the International Covenant on Civil and Political Rights (ICCPR), the International Covenant on Economic, Social and Cultural Rights (ICESCR), and dozens of other international covenants and conventions.

Both the ICCPR and the ICESCR conventions came into force in 1976. Countries ratifying these two covenants have to submit reports to the Human Rights Committee and can be criticized for violating human rights. For those countries that have not ratified the conventions, the force of international pressure comes indirectly through diplomacy and the influence of international human rights NGOs. The three regions in Greater China – the Mainland, Taiwan, and Hong Kong – have been under pressure from various sources to improve their human rights record.

Apart from international pressures, internal forces also affect human rights implementation. The Republic of China (Taiwan) (ROC) was effectively governed by the Kuomintong (KMT) before the founding of the Democratic Progressive Party (DPP). After the lifting of the martial law in July 1987, the process of democratization sped up in Taiwan. It took 15 years for the DPP to take control of the government. Significant improvements in Taiwan's socio-economic conditions now provide a solid base for improving the implementation of political and civil rights.

The PRC is led by a Leninist party, the Chinese Communist Party (CCP). The political system is the so-called "democratic centralism." Since the adoption of the open door policy, the PRC has emerged as a great economic power. The economic system has changed from a command economy to state capitalism and is on the road to private capitalism. It is not clear whether this gradual change will induce democratization. Hong Kong has been transferred from the colonial authoritarian government to the local government of the PRC. The future of democracy in the Hong Kong Special Autonomous Region (HKSAR) depends largely on the political development in the PRC.

The Republic of China

Immediately after World War II, the Republic of China played an important role in the drafting process of the UDHR. With regard to the Charter of the United Nations, China (represented by the ROC) made substantive contributions to the provisions on international cooperation in the solution of economic, social, cultural, and other humanitarian problems. At the end of the 183rd Meeting of the General Assembly, the ROC voted in favour of the UDHR. Dr P.C. Chang, the ROC representative on the Commission on Human Rights, declared that the objectives of the Declaration were to set up a universal moral standard.[2]

The ROC signed the ICCPR and the ICESCR in 1967, but did not ratify them under the KMT government, although that government ratified 16 other covenants.[3] As a result, the ROC was not held formally accountable to the international community. This is one reason why the implementation of civil rights and political rights in the ROC was defective through the 1960s. After being expelled from the United Nations in 1971, the ROC has not been subject to international pressure with respect to the implementation of these two covenants. Nevertheless, the ROC government, under the leadership of the DPP, showing its determination to protect human rights better, ratified the two covenants in April 2001. However, as the ROC is no longer recognized by the United Nations as an independent sovereign country, the government in Taiwan does not have to submit human rights reports to the United Nations, and this has proved to be an important set-back to monitoring the human rights situation in Taiwan.

In the past, despite the fact that the KMT government committed itself to the drafting process of the UDHR and other covenants, the KMT had been criticized as an authoritarian government suppressing human rights.

Taiwan had been a Japanese colony for several decades before its restoration to Chinese control in 1945. The mainlanders, appointed by the KMT, imposed authoritarian rule over the local Taiwanese, who are mostly ancestors of migrants from the mainland to the island before Japan's occupation. The 28 February incident of 1947 was the first case of massive human rights suppression. Later, the KMT and its followers fled to Taiwan. Chiang Kai-shek imposed martial law on Taiwan in 1949, suspending the Constitution and subjecting hundreds of individuals to unlawful arrests, inhumane torture, long-term imprisonment, and extrajudicial executions. In 1954, the National Assembly extended the Temporary Provisions, which allowed the KMT to issue a Garrison Command that placed people under martial law, thereby curtailing peoples' democratic rights.

From its arrival in Taiwan in 1950 until 1986, the KMT was intolerant of political opposition. Under the leadership of Chiang Kai-shek, internal reform was slow. The KMT government introduced electoral competition at the local level in the early 1950s. Direct elections were later extended to cover the Provincial Assembly. Since the 1977 local election, the political opposition (Tangwai) has participated in local elections;[4] however, supplementary elections for the Legislative Yuan and the National Assembly were tightly controlled by the KMT. Together with activists and intellectuals of both local and mainland origin, Lei Chen (the founder and editor of the liberal journal *Free China Fortnightly*) attempted to form the China Democratic Party in 1960. When this attempt failed and Lei Chen was arrested, the development of political rights was severely hindered.

More importantly, freedom of the press was not respected before the lifting of martial law. Censorship by the government was vigorous during the 1950s and 1960s. Violators of martial law faced long-term imprisonment. Despite improvements in the 1970s and the early 1980s, there was widespread confiscation of underground magazines and newspapers: the number of journals and newspapers banned from publishing continued to increase in the 1980s.

Freedoms of demonstration and association were not respected, either. The so-called Kaohsiung incident or Formosa incident of 10 December 1979 is perhaps the most significant human rights issue in Taiwan. A massive demonstration organized by the Formosa (*Mei-li Tao*, the coalition of dissidents) was held to celebrate International Human Rights Day and to protest against alleged government violations of human rights; however, the police brutally suppressed this demonstration and arrested more than 100 members of the political opposition.

The seeds of democratization in Taiwan were sown during the process of "Taiwanization" of the KMT in the 1970s.[5] Under the leadership of Chiang Ching-kuo, the percentage of local Taiwanese elected to the KMT Central Committee increased from 6.1 per cent in 1969–1976, to 19.3 per cent in 1976–1981.[6] As the local presence within the KMT matured, the original authoritarian system could not be maintained without great cost. The political system under which mainlanders (who followed Chiang's family) had ruled Taiwan for several decades, gradually changed. Martial law was imposed in the hope of retrieving the Mainland from the CCP; as this hope proved illusory, martial law was lifted in July 1987, during the final stage of Chiang Ching-kuo's leadership. Subsequently, the presence of ageing parliamentarians in the National Assembly and the Legislative Yuan, who had not faced competitive elections since the late 1940s, could no longer be justified.

Before the lifting of martial law, human rights activists fought for basic civil and political rights through campaigns calling for the release of political prisoners; an end to the practice of blacklisting; and demands for freedoms of speech, association, and assembly. The political opposition, Tangwai, formed the DPP on 28 September 1986, a milestone event in the democratization process of Taiwan.

After martial law was lifted in 1987, human rights movements pushed Taiwan further towards democracy. Open elections for public offices were held; the rights to free expression, assembly, and association were gradually introduced. Human rights activists focused on the revision of undemocratic laws and administrative regulations – such as the National Security Law, the Parade and Assembly Law, the Civic Organizations Law, and restrictions on radio broadcasting – all of which deprived people of basic civil rights.

The democratic and human rights movement relied a great deal on the student movement that emerged in the early 1970s. The KMT tried to take control of the movement: for instance, by feeding "political students" into universities, the KMT ensured that students would not participate in anti-government campaigns or join political opposition groups. In the early 1970s, however, some university students were actively involved in protesting against the KMT's weakness in the international community after Taiwan's withdrawal from the United Nations. This nationalist movement soon developed into a campaign for political and social reforms; however, the students' enthusiasm was quickly channelled into non-political social service campaigns.[7] Student movements in the 1980s mainly focused on universities' internal affairs,[8] but some individual student activists joined the political opposition.

Towards the end of the 1980s, students were active in promoting democracy. Stimulated by the 4 June Tiananmen Square incident on the Mainland and the democratic movements in Eastern Europe, Taiwan's students demonstrated, at the Chiang Kai-shek Memorial Hall in March

1990, in favour of direct popular election of the president. President Lee agreed to call for a National Affairs Conference from 28 June to 3 July 1990: this was the first step in the reform of the presidential system. On 1 May 1991, Lee Teng-hui went further, to announce the termination of the Period of Communist Rebellion. In a White Paper published on 5 July 1994, the KMT government announced that the ROC would no longer compete with Beijing for the right to represent China in the international arena. This symbolic move was important in paving the way for direct presidential elections. In fact, on 28 July 1994, the reformed National Assembly voted to amend the constitution to allow for direct presidential elections at the end of Lee Teng-hui's presidential term in 1996. The underlying message was that the directly elected future president would represent the people living in Taiwan, not those living on the Mainland.

The cumulative effort of the political opposition paid off in March 2000, when Chen Shui-bian won the presidential election. This was the most significant event on Taiwan's path towards democratization, as it was the first transfer of political authority from the KMT to the political opposition; however, the KMT still controlled the Legislative Yuan. As Taiwan suffered a serious recession in 2001, many observers were surprised that the DPP won even more seats in the December 2001 election, becoming the largest political party in the Legislative Yuan. Chen's strategy was to accuse the opposition – the KMT and the People First Party – of irresponsible obstruction in the Legislative Yuan.

Democratization in Taiwan is a result of the social movements led by local élites and of the democratic movements led by political leaders. Human rights NGOs played an important part in promoting human rights in Taiwan; however, because the two main local human rights NGOs – the Chinese Association for Human Rights (CAHR) and the Taiwan Association for Human Rights (TAHR) – have different political backgrounds, it is difficult to predict whether sincere collaboration between them will result in human rights initiatives.

With the support of the KMT, the CAHR was founded in 1979 after the Formosa incident; however, it was criticized as a conservative organization used by the KMT to defend the deplorable human rights situation in Taiwan under martial law. In 1984, despite the existence of martial law, the political opposition decided to set up its own organization, the TAHR. This organization was under great pressure from the KMT government and could not be officially registered until 1995. Despite the fact that the CAHR was formed much earlier than the TAHR, the latter claims to be "the oldest independent human rights organization in Taiwan."[9] The implication is that the CAHR is not independent and thus is biased. As the DPP now controls the government, it now seems that the TAHR is not an independent organization: the CAHR has thus become more and more critical of the current government. Ironically, despite the apparent improvement in human rights implementation, the CAHR published human rights indexes in 2001 and 2002 suggesting that the human rights situation in Taiwan has deteriorated under Chen's presidency.[10]

Apart from the two main human rights NGOs, organized activities of so-called disadvantaged groups developed into various types of human rights movements – the environmental movement, labour movement, women's movement, the Hakka Rights movement, the Non-homeowners' "Shell-less Snail" movement, the Indigenous People's Rights movement. This resulted in a gradual expansion of Taiwan's civil society.[11] Nevertheless, the impact of these movements is restricted because of their limited financial support. Most local foundations are government-funded or party-funded, and many NGOs depend on the government for financial support. The ROC remains a country with a strong state and a weak civil society: the state controls cultural groups; state-owned enterprises have a major presence in the economy. The development of an independent third sector was hindered by the lack of funding from sources other than the government. Despite the fact that President Lee Teng-hui has reallocated resources to civil society, prospects for a healthy development of civil society remain limited.[12]

The main determinant of human rights standards in the ROC has been the nature of the political regime. As long as the KMT regime felt itself under siege and maintained that it was the legitimate government of all China, mainlander élites would not begin the process of transferring political rights and powers to the Taiwanese majority. However, as rapid economic growth provided a new source of legitimacy and fuelled the rise of a middle class, KMT leaders increasingly took advantage of the opportunity to pursue mass legitimacy for the regime. Although this did not make a full transition to democracy inevitable, it made it easier for more enlightened KMT leaders to pursue this goal without jeopardizing the social and economic positions of the hitherto dominant mainlanders.

Towards the end of the 1990s, the KMT government led by President Lee began to acknowledge past human rights violations. On 10 December 1999, Lee's government established a human rights monument on Green Island, where political prisoners had been imprisoned. The KMT apologized to the victims of "White Terror" under martial law: such victims might now seek compensation from the government through legal means. The DPP is determined to end the era of "White Terror": recently, the DPP government announced that the prison on Green Island would be shut down before the end of 2002;[13] this is a symbolic action to demonstrate that there will never be political prisoners again.

Before the March 2000 presidential election, 22 NGOs formed a coalition in December 1999 to exert pressure on candidates. They campaigned for the establishment of the National Human Rights Commission and forced the three chief presidential candidates – Chen Sui-bian, Lien Chan, and James Soong – to address human rights issues. In his inaugural address on May 2001, Chen declared his intention to strengthen human rights implementation in Taiwan. In response to the demand of local human rights NGOs, the new president promised to work for the adoption of international standards of human rights as domestic law.

In October 2000, President Chen established a President's Advisory Group on Human Rights, headed by Vice-President Annette Lu. This group consists of 21 individuals, who are human rights activists, leaders of human rights NGOs, and representative scholars. The group members are responsible for promoting human rights education, raising human rights consciousness among Taiwanese, advising the president on human rights issues, reviewing existing legislation, and investigating human rights abuses. In the long run, the group works for the establishment of an independent National Human Rights Commission.

The most acute problem in Taiwan under the KMT regime is the rule of law. This is reflected in the problem of vote-buying and corruption. In past elections, candidates have alleged that there has been large-scale vote-buying; this is also evident in the recent election of mayors and members of the Legislative Yuan. The new government of President Chen is determined to eliminate political corruption. In addition, the legal system should be better instituted so that the rule of law is respected more fully. Given the situation of strong-state/weak-society in the ROC, the lack of respect for the rule of law is detrimental to the implementation of human rights. Although many student activists under the "White Terror" are now politicians or bureaucrats, as Taiwan is in the initial stages of democratic consolidation it is not clear, at the moment, how far they can facilitate democratic reform within their government.

According to the Corruption Perception Index provided by Transparency International, Taiwan was ranked 25th out of 41, with a score of 5.08 (10 is the full mark) in 1995, before the introduction of the direct presidential election.[14] The score increased to 5.9 in 2001, but then fell to 5.7 in 2002 (the rank is 29th out of 102). Democratization and, hence, the better implementation of democratic rights seem to have contributed to a reduction in corruption.

On the international level, the transition was also facilitated by close military ties with the United States and international cultural and economic integration. Again, these factors did not make a full transition to democracy inevitable; rather, they provided sustained exposure to democratic norms and models that were increasingly compatible with the

ROC's internal development. This helped to convert the ruling main-lander élites to the democratic norms championed by an increasingly self-conscious and vocal Taiwanese civil society.

The People's Republic of China

Although the PRC had not yet been established at the time of the draft-ing process of the Universal Declaration, the representative of the CCP (Dong Biwu) took part in the process. Nevertheless, owing to its isolation policy, the PRC had not paid much attention to the development of the international human rights regime since the early 1950s.[15] The Cultural Revolution – which, ironically, emerged in the year (1966) that the two international covenants of human rights (ICCPR and ICESCR) were pro-posed, and which ended in the year (1976) that the two covenants came into force – was disastrous for human rights protection. Whereas, since the adoption of the Open Door Policy, liberalization in the economic sphere has become unstoppable, in the early stages of the economic re-form human rights were still regarded as a bourgeois slogan.[16]

In the process of liberalization, the PRC faces a dilemma. If it opens itself up to the world, it subjects itself further to international norms and standards; this would curtail its sovereignty. From the PRC's perspective, human rights are used as a propaganda weapon by particular Western countries to spread their political system and values all over the world. Although Deng Xiaoping seldom talked about human rights directly, nevertheless (under pressure from the West) he once made an infamous comment: "What are human rights? Are human rights for the majority or for the minority, or for the people of the whole country? So-called 'human rights' as understood in the Western World and human rights we talk about are two different things. There are different viewpoints re-garding this matter."[17] Deng's comments on the difference between the Western interpretation of human rights and the PRC's interpretation are regularly quoted by Chinese officials and human rights scholars.

The Tiananmen Square incident marks an important turning point in the attitude of the CCP toward human rights issues. The suppression of the student anti-corruption movement to a certain extent undermined the legitimacy of CCP rule. The CCP was forced to deal with the issue of human rights. Before the Tiananmen Square incident, the notion of hu-man rights was understood as a weapon used by the West to overthrow the CCP: the initial response from the PRC was a "hard-line" policy founded on the concept of national sovereignty, suggesting that the PRC had the right to resist foreign intervention.[18]

After the suppression of the student movement in Tiananmen Square in June 1989 in the PRC, Western countries imposed various types of sanctions on the PRC.[19] The PRC's official response to the West was reactionary: when dealing with international pressure, the CCP attempted to launch a series of propaganda events to show that the PRC had always guaranteed human rights.[20] From the perspective of the Chinese government, an extensive study of human rights theory and practice in the PRC was seen as indispensable to the development of a positive response to the West. The early 1990s have thus seen a tide of human rights studies in the PRC. This was triggered by an important change in official attitudes towards the issue of human rights.[21] Moreover, Chinese human rights scholars attempted to develop a socialist theory of human rights to back up official propaganda.[22]

Unlike previous attempts to deny the validity of human rights norms in the late 1980s, CCP officials maintained in the 1990s that the human rights situation in the PRC deserves examination. The White Paper on Human Rights of 1991 was the first official document that dealt with the human rights situation in the PRC. The Paper acknowledges that it is "a long-term historical task for the Chinese people and government to continue to promote human rights and strive for the noble goal of full implementation of human rights as required by the PRC's socialism."[23] Other official reports summarized the human rights situation in the PRC.[24] These reports are intended to show that human rights have been sufficiently implemented in the PRC. The publication of these reports does not imply that human rights implementation in the PRC is as adequate as is depicted in the documents, or that it will necessarily improve: these documents are largely the result of an attempt to take human rights seriously among scholars and officials. Nevertheless, from the viewpoint of the West, these reports are merely cover-ups of gross violations of political and civil rights, and the validity of these reports was denied. To be fair, just as no one can deny that the PRC has tried to improve its legal system in order to protect human rights, equally no one can plausibly declare that there are only a few defects in the protection of human rights in the PRC.[25]

The PRC's concessions to human rights norms are partly a result of pressure from the international community. The pressure from international human rights NGOs is of crucial importance. The CCP government has been severely criticized by international NGOs, such as Amnesty International, Human Rights Watch, Freedom House, and Human Rights in China. These NGOs criticize not only the PRC but also all other countries that violate human rights norms. The claim that human rights promotion is a political weapon of particular countries in attempting to overthrow the CCP government does not hold up in the face of these criticisms. Freedom House ranks the record of political rights and the protection of civil liberties in the PRC at the same level as that of Cameroon, Congo, and Rwanda.[26]

As a response to persistent and harsh attacks from international NGOs, the PRC appeals to relativism. While agreeing with the universality of the human rights concept, PRC officials and human rights scholars claim that the implementation of human rights should be subject to variations of cultural contexts in different countries. In arguing for their views on human rights, the PRC leaders also appeal to developmentalism,[27] according to which political and civil rights may be curtailed for the sake of social and economic development.

Western countries, especially the United States, are unhappy with the deplorable human rights situation in China. The United States and the European Union have published reports on the human rights situation in the PRC. In the last decade, attempts were made through the Human Rights Commission of the United Nations to censure the PRC for its allegedly appalling human rights record. The PRC used a procedural rule to block a vote on the merits of the Commission's motion, which expressed deep concerns about the reports of violations of various civil rights.[28]

Despite its reluctance to adopt the so-called Western perspective, the Beijing government signed both the ICCPR and the ICESCR covenants in 1998 in order to demonstrate the CCP's commitment to human rights protection. Other factors, including the bid for the 2008 Olympic Games and efforts to gain World Trade Organization (WTO) membership, are all part of Beijing's increased effort to show this commitment in recent years. The People's Congress ratified the ICESCR in March 2001; the PRC has ratified over thirty other conventions,[29] and it is possible that the People's Congress will ratify the ICCPR in the near future.

As long as the CCP is in power, the United States and other Western countries will continue to use "human rights" in international political bargaining. Human rights will still remain a "structural weakness for the PRC's diplomacy" and an important part of many countries' foreign policies towards the PRC.[30] However, as the PRC now enters the WTO, the PRC's economic concerns will have much less influence on human rights issues. It is not clear how far the international community may affect human rights implementation in the PRC in the future. What is important for the development of the international human rights regime is sincerely to respect human dignity and protect individual and group interests. The role of international NGOs may prove to be even more important in the implementation of human rights norms in the PRC in the future.

The PRC leadership's gradual change in its attitude towards human rights norms is not only a result of international pressure but also a product of domestic pressure for democratization. The Democratic Wall

Movement, led by the dissident Wei Jing-Sheng, is well known in its significance as a grass-roots demand for political democratization. It originated in the discontent with the government's failure to redress the grievances of those who suffered in the Cultural Revolution;[31] however, as soon as CCP élites felt that their political monopoly was challenged, the movement was suppressed.

Similar democratic movements occurred some 11 years later in 1989, when the Chinese people were discontented with the corruption and authoritarianism of the government. From the perspective of dissidents, political democratization was seen as the only remedy for misgovernment. Wei Jingsheng, Hu Ping, and Yan Jiaqi all appealed to the idea of human rights.[32] However, because the political monopoly of the CCP was directly challenged, the demand for democratization was brutally repressed. Large-scale political movements have changed into bold small-scale attempts to organize political parties. These attempts have failed, and organizers have been imprisoned or subjected to unlawful long-term detention.

It should be noted that, whereas political reform at the national level has been avoided, local political reforms have carried on since 1987, when the Standing Committee of the National People's Congress adopted the Organic Law of Village Committees.[33] The focus of political reform is placed on village democracy. It looks promising but it poses serious difficulties for the CCP, because many elected representatives at the village levels are not CCP members.

Although the human rights situation before Deng's death is well documented, it is useful to look at recent developments. First, people on the Mainland cannot freely express ideas that differ from those of the CCP political élites without fear of severe punishment. Freedom of expression of those who oppose the CCP rule and policy has been reduced to a minimum. In the summer of 2000, four right-wing scholars of the Chinese Academy of Social Sciences, who openly urged the CCP fully to liberalize the economy or who criticized President Jiang were expelled from the institute. In the summer of 2001, leftists criticized President Jiang for allowing "red capitalists" to enter the CCP, in a piece of "ten-thousand words" circulated on the Internet. Subsequently, two journals that are controlled by the leftists and supported by government funding were banned. Democratic change in China is possible only if there is better political and civil rights implementation. Freedoms of speech and expression are essential for democratization. Without a marketplace of ideas, there will not be a "common democratic consciousness" that will promote political reform.[34] It is reasonable to believe that the political control of free speech has become even tighter after the transition of political power from the old generation to the new generation of CCP leaders in late 2002: this is because, to ensure the legitimacy of the new leadership and political stability, voices from opposition on the right and the left need to be suppressed.

Second, religious freedom and freedom of association are still suppressed.[35] Political monopoly by the CCP is possible only if religions are marginalized in (if not totally swept out from) the PRC. In Marx's dictum, religion is the "opium of the people." Since 1999, Falun Gong members have not been allowed to propagate their views and practise their qigong in public.[36] For many who practise qigong, it is incomprehensible that they would find themselves accused of committing a political crime. Of course what Li Hongzhi, the founder of Falun Gong, has in his mind is not known. It may be possible that Li Hongzhi intends to subvert communist rule or, at least, to harass CCP leaders. But what seems clear is that he is able to capture people's dissatisfactions with the government. The number of Falun Gong practitioners, estimated to be more than 100 million all over the world, even exceeds the number of CCP members, which is about 60 million. Many CCP members and even government officials are Falun Gong practitioners. More importantly, Falun Gong's mobilization power is even greater than that of the CCP. On 25 April 1999, 10,000 members of Falun Gong surrounded Zhongnanhai, the Beijing compound housing the CCP leaders. This not only embarrassed the CCP leaders but also posed a threat to the political leadership of the CCP. This was followed by the repression of Falun Gong, and large-scale persecution of qigong associations, religious groups, and family churches.

The message from the PRC leadership is very clear: no matter what their background or class, intelligentsia, social élites, economic tycoons, and religious leaders who support CCP rule are in good standing; those who disagree with the CCP leadership, even if they are proletarians, will be suppressed.

In contrast to the élites in civil society, the public is more concerned about freedom of information. Freedom of information has been a key human rights issue in the PRC. It seems that, in the foreseeable future, this freedom will be even further restrained. The Beijing government blocked domestic access to thousands of Internet websites early in January 2002.[37] There are three reasons for the Beijing government having done so: first, there is information on the Internet that is considered politically sensitive and believed to convey messages that damage the image of the government and its policies; second, the flow of information inevitably introduces public space for free discussion, which, in turn, fuels calls for democratization; third, cyberspace supersedes the territories of nation-states. In cyberspace there is no supreme sovereignty, and there is no central government. In the PRC's efforts to resist international pressure for democratization and better implementation of human rights, national sovereignty is of the utmost importance.

In order to maintain national sovereignty, the Beijing government lays a heavy hand on the Internet. Observers are quick to point out that virtual censorship is nothing but a defensive policy to prevent China's domestic cyberspace from being merged with foreign cyberspaces.[38] However, it should be noted that high technology is also used to interfere with exchange of information and opinions within the PRC. As reported by Human Rights Watch, "the Ministry of State Security has installed monitoring devices on Internet service providers capable of tracking individual e-mail accounts."[39]

Apart from the Internet, the influence of foreign media on the people exceeds the limit set by the CCP. The Beijing government has tightened control over the media: there are new regulations that dictate who is allowed to view overseas cable and satellite television broadcasts; from December 2001 onwards, all universities, government institutions, hotels, and residences have to re-apply for the right to view foreign television programmes. This move calls for an 80 per cent reduction of foreign television programmes in Beijing via cable and satellite. The "Provisions on the Management of Satellite TV" clearly state that the move is concerned with curbing the negative influence that, in the opinion of the Beijing government, is exerted by foreign broadcasts.

Apparently, there is a sign of positive development: as revealed in President Jiang's speech of 1 July 2001, entrepreneurs who consent to CCP rule are genuine red capitalists and may be able to join the CCP.[40] It is obvious that the nature of the CCP will be changed if red capitalists are allowed to enter the party: this move will result in a crisis of the formal legitimacy of its rule. If the nature of the CCP has changed, its political legitimacy will be undermined and there is no a priori reason why other groups of people cannot, and should not, form new political parties and compete for political authority. If capitalists are able to grasp real power, it will become more and more difficult to stop the rising middle class from searching for political power in the future. Allowing red capitalists to become members of the CCP induces more diverse voices within the party but, ironically, this may result in further suppression of dissidents. It is not at all clear whether or when this political reform will end the CCP's political monopoly.

The rise of red capitalists brings to the forefront the acute issue of corruption. The problem of corruption in the PRC is worse than that in the ROC: according to the Corruption Perception Index (CPI), the PRC was ranked 40 (the second worst) with a score of 2.16 in 1995.[41] Although the score increased to 3.5 in 1998, from 1998 to 2002 there has been no improvement on a CPI score of 3.5. One possible reason for the stagnation is that, without democratization, the coalition between red capitalists and government officials has remained strong; hence the problem of political corruption shows little improvement.

Economic liberalization led to greatly increased economic opportunities, as well as ongoing legal reform efforts to build a more neutral rule of law. However, the CCP's desire to retain power has led it to slam the brakes on civil and political rights whenever and wherever these appear to create new political threats. Although international economic and cultural integration and political pressure by Western governments and NGOs have led the CCP to address human rights issues, so far this appears to be merely part of an effort to justify CCP policies designed to maintain its political monopoly.

Hong Kong

Under British colonial rule, Hong Kong has had an undemocratic system since the cession of sovereignty to the British in the unequal treaty in 1842. The system was undemocratic in two senses. The first concerns Hong Kong's constitution, which was founded on the Letters Patent issued by the Crown: according to these Letters Patent, the British government had unrestrained power to invalidate any ordinances enacted by the Hong Kong Legislative Council. The second sense concerns the way in which legislators were elected: before 1991, legislators were appointed by the Governor; It was not until 1991 that Hong Kong had directly elected members in the Legislative Council.

The British persistently used force to suppress political dissent in Hong Kong. The first large-scale use of force by the British can be traced back to the 1920s, after strikes by the Seamen's Union. The suppression of freedom of speech can be traced back to 1925, when a local critical newspaper, *San Man Po*, was ordered to be closed because of its anti-British stance. Despite the fact that the British have boasted about their achievements in Hong Kong, the human rights record under their rule was poor before (and even after) World War II.[42]

Although Britain is a signatory to the ICCPR and ICESCR, the people of Hong Kong hardly enjoyed their benefits, even in the 1970s and 1980s. The Letters Patent did not contain any guarantee of civil liberties and human rights, and the British attached some reservations to the ICCPR that restrained Hong Kong people from political participation.[43] The British justified their reservations with the claim that Hong Kong was not ready for self-governance;[44] this is a typical nineteenth-century justification for maintaining British rule in its colonies.

The attitude of the British changed (or was forced to change) when the

British and Beijing governments signed the Sino-British Joint Declaration in 1984, according to which there would be a transfer of sovereignty from Great Britain to China. The agreement declared the establishment of "one country, two systems," with the emphasis on the protection of human rights and the maintenance of the rule of law. Since the time of Governor Grantham, Britain has expressed its commitment to ensure the rule of law in Hong Kong.[45]

Although the colonial government did not promote democracy in Hong Kong, it had attempted to establish a legal system as reliable as any other liberal democracy since the 1970s. The anti-corruption campaign since the early 1970s has been successful: to a certain extent, the success of the Independent Commission Against Corruption (ICAC) safeguards the maintenance of the rule of law, even after 1997.

In a Green Paper and a White Paper proposed in 1984, and believing in its benevolence, Britain attempted to grant Hong Kong people the right to elect directly members to the Legislative Council and the Municipal Councils in 1988.[46] This suggested either that Hong Kong people were now ready for self-governance or that Hong Kong people, governing themselves under a system designed by the British, would be better than the CCP governing Hong Kong directly. In any case, the direct elections were postponed under pressure from Beijing; it was not until 1991 that the Legislative Council would be chosen in direct elections.

A further restraint on democratization in Hong Kong was the alleged political apathy of its people. Yet, during the Tiananmen Square incident, millions of Hong Kong people marched in the streets supporting the anti-corruption student movement in Beijing. The CCP leaders feared that Hong Kong might be turned into a base of subversion. Since the arrival of Governor Chris Patten in mid-1992, the British had not ceased to attempt to speed up the democratization process in Hong Kong. However, from the perspective of the PRC leaders, stepping up the democratization process in Hong Kong was a Western anti-China conspiracy; PRC officials even complained that the British tried to politicize Hong Kong.

The 1990s witnessed important changes in the implementation of democratic rights. The human rights movement pushed Hong Kong towards democracy. Pro-democracy activists founded the Hong Kong Human Rights Commission (HKHRC) in March 1988, to promote political and civil rights. The HKHRC is a coalition of 11 NGOs, including religious, community, women's and students' groups.[47] In the early 1990s the HKHRC remained inactive, apart from issuing occasional statements; however, since 1997 the HKHRC has become much more active, led by Mr Ho Hei-wah, the Director of the Society for Community Organization, an active grass-roots organization.

In April 1995, another human rights NGO, the Hong Kong Human Rights Monitor (HKHRM), was established by professionals and academics and sponsored by democrats.[48] It focuses mainly on promoting democratic rights. The organization publishes shadow reports on human rights, supplementing the government's reports. By submitting these shadow reports to the UN Human Rights Commission, the organization attempts to present a critical perspective from civil society alongside the official viewpoint of the government.

After the suppression of the student movement in June 1989 in Beijing, Hong Kong people feared that the Chinese government would not fulfil its promise to maintain "one country, two systems." In response, Beijing allowed the endorsement of two basic international covenants of human rights in the Basic Laws for post-1997 Hong Kong. However, before the People's Congress passed the Basic Law in 1990, the colonial government had planned to grant Hong Kong a Bill of Rights. In November 1989, the former Governor of Hong Kong, Sir David Wilson, had revealed the intention of the government to adopt a Bill of Rights for the people of Hong Kong. In 1991 the Legislative Council passed the Bill of Rights,[49] and the Letters Patent were amended to guarantee the ICCPR supremacy over future ordinances.[50]

The Bill of Rights served two purposes. First, it tried to relieve the confidence crisis in Hong Kong (as evidenced by another tide of emigration) after the Tiananmen Square incident. Second, the British believed that they were obligated to make sure that Hong Kong would not be turned into a totalitarian society ruled by the CCP; the Bill of Rights was used to demonstrate the benevolence of the British. As the British had granted a Bill of Rights in the Falkland Islands and other dependent territories by the end of the 1980s, there seemed to be no reason why there could not be one in Hong Kong, especially when the British government was very uncertain about whether Hong Kong peoples' rights would be respected by Beijing after 1997.

As a cosmopolitan city, Hong Kong always tried to comply with international norms and standards. Before the take-over of Hong Kong by the PRC, the Bill of Rights Ordinance assumed supreme constitutional status. Section 4 of the Ordinance dictates that all legislation enacted on or after the commencement date of the Ordinance shall be construed so as to be consistent with the ICCPR as applied to Hong Kong. In February 1997, the Standing Committee considered that this section and two other sections (2(3) and (3)) of the Bill of Rights Ordinance had an overriding effect over other laws, including the Basic Law. Thus, the Committee decided that they contravened the Basic Law and could not be adopted after the take-over of Hong Kong by Mainland China.[51] This move hindered implementation of political and civil rights. For the pro-China local élite, there is no need to implement the Bill of Rights, as the Basic Law already protects Hong Kong people's basic rights and freedoms.[52]

Regarding the election in Hong Kong, in the first election under PRC sovereignty, on 24 May 1998, pro-democracy candidates won more than 60 per cent of the directly elected seats in the Legislative Council. In September 2000, elections for the Legislative Council were held for the second time since 1997. It is noteworthy that only half of the seats in the legislative body will be directly elected in 2003. The pace of democratization is severely restrained under the provisions of the Basic Laws.

In the early 1990s, PRC senior officials kept reminding Hong Kong people and Western countries of the PRC's commitment to guarantee freedom of the press in Hong Kong.[53] In 1994, however, reporter Xi Yang was sentenced to 12 years in prison for allegedly stealing state secrets. The PRC's action was a warning to Hong Kong reporters that they should exercise greater self-restraint. During a trip to the United States in March 1995, Lu Ping, the top official on Hong Kong Affairs, declared that freedoms of the press and speech are guaranteed in Hong Kong; however, in June 1996, he suggested that the freedom of the press in Hong Kong could not remain unbridled.[54] He warned that advocacy of Hong Kong and Taiwanese independence would not be allowed after the take-over.[55] The Xi Yang incident definitely fostered self-censorship among reporters and editors working in the local media. One way for the PRC to restrict freedom of press in Hong Kong is to refuse visas to blacklisted journalists.[56] Following the reversion of Hong Kong to PRC sovereignty, there has been no obvious evidence of direct interference by the Beijing government, although it is likely that there is severe self-censorship by members of the media themselves.[57]

Before and after the take-over, political power in Hong Kong was vested in the hands of the entrepreneurs and pro-Beijing élite. In the transition, both the first Chief Executive (Tung Chee-Hwa) and the Provisional Legislature were chosen by a 400-member Selection Committee, consisting mainly of entrepreneurs. The election of the new chief executive in 2002 was also by a selection committee, now consisting of 800 people. Even before the nomination period started, President Jiang, Premier Zhu, and Vice-Premier Qian Qichen openly announced their support for Tung. Although President Jiang Zhemin claimed that Tung was widely supported in the HKSAR,[58] this is not in accordance with the facts: popular support for Tung has remained weak since the take-over. Given the blessing of the Beijing leaders, the élite cohesion inevitably guaranteed that Tung was re-elected. The pace of democratization in HKSAR is exceptionally slow.

The take-over of Hong Kong posed a challenge for the PRC. The CCP leaders sincerely hoped that the success of Hong Kong would continue.

In spite of the fact that the PRC intends to grant autonomy to Hong Kong, the CCP leaders have to ensure that the HKSAR will not become out of control; they hope to prove that "one country, two systems" is also a suitable model for the reintegration of Taiwan and the Mainland. However, no significant improvement in the implementation of human rights has been made. Two incidents merit a brief discussion – namely, Falun Gong and the right of abode.

Falun Gong poses a challenge to the HKSAR government. In order to maintain the autonomy of the special administrative region, the government allows Falun Gong practitioners in the HKSAR to demonstrate and to organize public meetings. The local leftists and pro-China élite have been urging the government to enact laws to prohibit acts of subversion against the central government. The laws in the PRC forbidding treason, secession, sedition, and subversion against the government are not applicable to the HKSAR, as, according to Article 23 of the Basic Law, the region has to enact its own laws. Nevertheless, as it is an extremely sensitive issue, the region has not enacted its own laws to punish treason, secession, sedition, and subversion against the government. Since the Falun Gong practitioners do not violate the laws of the HKSAR, they are allowed to promote their beliefs and practise their qigong publicly.

Another major human rights issue after 1997 is that of the right of abode. Because of lack of resources and the allegedly heavy economic burden on public expenses, the HKSAR Government decided to exert strict control over the quota of immigrants from the Mainland, thereby failing to assist those who have the right to come to HKSAR for the purpose of family reunion.[59] On 10 July 1997, the Provisional Legislative Council, whose members are pro-Beijing, enacted two ordinances to prohibit the originally qualified immigrants from entering HKSAR without prior application.

Human rights activists objected on the grounds that the government was violating a basic human right to have a family reunion. The defenders of the mainlanders who have the right of abode argued that the restrictions breached the Basic Law, and the mainlanders submitted a legal appeal; subsequently, on 29 January 1999, the Court of Final Appeal declared the two ordinances unconstitutional. In June 1999 a major debate arose over whether the HKSAR Government should seek the judgement of the Standing Committee of the National People's Congress (NPCSC) in Beijing for interpretation of the Basic Law on Right of Abode. However, critics argued that it was inappropriate for the HKSAR government to seek an NPCSC interpretation because this would infringe the autonomy of the HKSAR. The government decided to seek an interpretation from the NPCSC, which subsequently declared that the HKSAR government's immigration ordinances are constitutional and that the verdict of the Court of Appeal was inconsistent with the basic intent of the Basic Law. Accordingly, the rights of abode of qualified immigrants were curtailed.

Since the take-over, the PRC intends to demonstrate that the human rights of HKSAR are well protected. Although the PRC, the sovereign authority in HKSAR, has yet to ratify the ICCPR, the Central People's Government has made special arrangements for HKSAR to submit the reports to the treaty-monitoring body and to attend this hearing. How far these reports reflect the real situation is, however, debatable.

It should be noted that, as in the case of Taiwan, democratization and the improved implementation of democratic rights has reduced the level of corruption in Hong Kong: from 1995 to 1997, the CPI score was between 7.01 and 7.28; it increased to around 7.7–8.2 in the period from 1998 to 2002.[60] Thus, despite HKSAR's difficulties in coping with the Asian economic crisis, the prevalence of corrupt practices seems to have decreased.

To sum up, human rights violations in the ROC and PRC are driven by policies that suppress freedom of association, of speech, and of expression. Despite the protection promised by the laws, the political system in Hong Kong remains largely undemocratic after the take-over by the PRC. Government officials are held accountable to the Chief Executive of HKSAR rather than to the people. Thus, it is the PRC-backed regime and its larger power-conserving objectives that stand in the way of further progress relating to civil and political rights in HKSAR.

Prospects for human rights implementation in Greater China

The international human rights movement is faced with the difficulty that not all sovereign states have ratified the international covenant, thereby accepting their provisions as binding. From this perspective, regional instruments have proved to be indispensable in enabling the protection of human rights.[61] Regional commissions on human rights – such as the African, the Inter-American, and the European commissions – provide viable instruments for human rights protection in their respective regions.[62] The Asian Human Rights Commission (AHRC) was founded in 1986 by a prominent group of jurists and human rights activists in Asia;[63] however, unlike other regional commissions, the establishment of the AHRC was not endorsed by Asian governments. The AHRC is only a non-governmental body seeking to promote greater awareness and better implementation of human rights in the Asian region. For cultural and political reasons, there is no intergovernmental regional instrument for Asia as a whole: the countries of that continent embrace a wide range of cultures with a great diversity of religious and cultural traditions. Unfortunately, conflicts between the constituent nations persist at the subregional level.

Without an intergovernmental regional instrument, it is difficult to monitor the human rights situation in Greater China at the regional level. Since there is no intergovernmental human rights organization in Asia, the role of NGOs is of crucial importance, Amnesty International and Human Rights Watch Asia being the most influential NGOs in this region. The PRC, the ROC, and Hong Kong should cooperate with the international NGOs and endeavour to achieve the objectives stated in the Asian Charter.

In Taiwan, the KMT government was protected by Taiwan's diplomatic isolation from international pressure; however (ironically), Taiwan's isolation now constitutes an obstacle to the promotion of human rights. The ROC is moving forward as human rights activists are working towards the establishment of a National Human Rights Commission. To go further, the DPP government should promote exchanges with the international human rights community. In Hong Kong, the implementation of democratic rights depends on the provisions of the Basic Law. The HKSAR government should submit reports to the UN Human Rights Commission that truly reflect HKSAR's human rights situation. International pressure and the effort of local NGOs can be effective in pressing for improved human rights provisions in Greater China.

When we compare the situation in the PRC, Hong Kong, and the ROC, one has to ask if the rule of law should have higher priority than democracy in the course of political development, or vice versa. Taiwan and Hong Kong have taken two different routes towards political development: Taiwan is more democratic than Hong Kong in the sense that, in Taiwan, there are more open competitions for most of its political offices; however, Hong Kong has a better legal system, as the rule of law is respected to a greater degree. The PRC's performance is the worst in terms of both democracy and the rule of law; however, it is not certain that a sudden transition from democratic centralism to a multi-party system would be a useful path to take. Arguably, it would be more promising to follow the Taiwan and Hong Kong precedents and focus first on the rule of law and economic prosperity. Once China has attained economic development and a rule of law comparable to those of Hong Kong or Taiwan, there will be greater internal pressure for enhanced political rights. The CCP regime will have an easier pathway towards political liberalization, as did the KMT before it in Taiwan. However, it is difficult to predict whether the CCP would take the democratic route.

Greater China remains deficient in three main areas – rule of law, independence of the judiciary, and accountability of the police and military authorities. Discrimination in all its forms remains pervasive. Human rights consciousness among the people is relatively low. Although government leaders are familiar with international human rights norms and mechanisms, they seldom take these provisions seriously. Local NGOs in Taiwan and Hong Kong and international NGOs should launch more joint campaigns to protect basic civil and political rights, safeguard due process of law, secure fair trials, and eliminate all types of discrimination.

Notes

1. This chapter is based on research conducted within a broader project on "The Theory and Practice of Human Rights in mainland China, Hong Kong, and Taiwan: A Comparative Study" (Grant No.: HKU 7129/98H), which is financially funded by the Hong Kong Research Grant Council. The author would like to thank Dr Joseph C. W. Chan, as well as the editors and referees of this book, for valuable suggestions in the preparation of this chapter.
2. See Kuen-Chen Fu, "Application of International Human Rights Law within the Legal Framework of the Republic of China," *Journal of Social Sciences (Taiwan)*, No. 37, 1988, pp. 488–489.
3. See ⟨http://www.tahr.org.tw/internaliz/nu.html⟩ (in Chinese), accessed on 12 November 2001.
4. For the development of the Tangwai into the DPP see Alexander Ya-Li Lu, "Political Opposition in Taiwan: The Development of the Democratic Progressive Party," in Tun-jen Cheng and Stephan Haggard, eds, *Political Change in Taiwan*, Boulder: Lynne Rienner Publishers, 1992, pp. 121–145.
5. Hung-mao Tieb, "Transformation of an Authoritarian Party State: Taiwan's Development Experience," *Political Change in Taiwan*, pp. 40 43.
6. Yun-han Chu, "Taiwan's Unique Challenges," *Journal of Democracy*, No. 7, 1996, p. 73.
7. Hsin-huang Michael Hsiao, "The Rise of Social Movements and Civil Protests," in *Political Change in Taiwan*, p. 62.
8. Jaushieh Joseph Wu, *Taiwan's Democratization*, New York: Oxford University Press, 1995, pp. 66–67.
9. See ⟨http://www.tahr.org.tw/english/engintro1.html⟩.
10. See ⟨http://www.cahr.org.tw/human.htm⟩.
11. Hsin-huang Michael Hsiao, "The Rise of Social Movements and Civil Protests," in *Political Change in Taiwan*, pp. 63–69.
12. For an overstatement see Chyuan-jeng Shiau, "Civil Society and Democratization," in S. Tsang and Hung-mao Tien, eds, *Democratization in Taiwan*, London: Macmillan, 1999, p. 114.
13. *China Post*, 1 January 2002.
14. See ⟨http://www.gwdg.de/~uwvw/⟩.
15. R. Cohen, "People's Republic of China: The Human Rights Exception," *Human Rights Quarterly*, No. 9, 1987, pp. 447–549.
16. Xiao Weiyun, Luo Haocai, Wu Xieying, "Makesi zhuyi zenmayang kan 'renquan' wenti" ("How Marxism Views the Question of Human Rights"), *Hongqi ("Red Flag")* No. 5, 1979.

17. See ⟨http://english.peopledaily.com.cn/dengxp/⟩.
18. John F. Cooper, "Peking's Post-Tiananmen Foreign Policy: The Human Rights Factor," *Issues and Studies*, 1994, pp. 49–73.
19. For a discussion with regard to the MFN status see R.F. Drinan, S.J. and T.T. Kuo, "The 1991 Battle for Human Rights in China," *Human Rights Quarterly*, Vol. 14, 1992, pp. 19–42.
20. For an insightful treatment of China's response see Rosemary Foot, *Rights Beyond Borders: The Global Community and the Struggle over Human Rights in China*, Oxford: Oxford University Press, 2000.
21. Zhou Wei, "The Study of Human Rights in the People's Republic of China," in J.T.H. Tang, ed., *Human Rights and International Relations in the Asia Pacific*, London: Pinter, 1995, p. 83.
22. For a list of selected Chinese human rights literature see Zhu Guobin, "Research on Human Rights in China: A General Survey and an Annotated Bibliography of Selected Chinese-Language Publications," *China Law Reporter*, Vol. VIII, 1999, pp. 157–185.
23. Information Office of the State Council, *Human Rights in China*, Beijing: Foreign Languages Press, 1991, p. III.
24. All these documents and other official reports, such as reports on human rights in Tibet and women's rights, are collected in Dong Weizhen, *Zhongguo Renquan Baipishu Zonglan (A Collection of White Papers on Human Rights in China)*, Sichuan: Sichuan Renmin Chubanshe, 1998.
25. In fact, the legal system of China has been under severe criticism from the human rights perspective. See, for example, Guo Luoji, "A Human Rights Critique of the Chinese Legal System," *Harvard Human Rights Journal*, No. 9, 1996, pp. 1–14.
26. The scores of China are 7 and 6, respectively, with 7 referring to the least free category. See ⟨http://216.119.117.183/research/freeworld/2001/table1.htm⟩. The score of China has stayed roughly the same over the last decade.
27. Michael J. Sullivan, "Development and Political Repression," *Bulletin of Concerned Asian Scholars*, No. 27, 1995, pp. 24–39.
28. See R. Foot, *Rights Beyond Borders: The Global Community and the Struggle over Human Rights in China*, New York: Oxford University Press, 2000, chapter 7; Ann Kent, *China, the United Nations, and Human Rights: The Limits of Compliance*, Philadelphia: Pennsylvania Press, 1999, chapter 7.
29. For a list of these conventions in Chinese, see Li Yunlong, *Renquan Wenti Gailun (A Comprehensive Study of Human Rights Issues)*, Sichuan: Sichuan Renmin Chubanshe, 1998, pp. 138–142.
30. Cf. A. Nathan, "Human Rights in Chinese Foreign Policy", *China Quarterly*, 139, 1994, p. 643; R. Foot, *Rights Beyond Borders*, p. 165.
31. Hua Sheng, "Big Character Posters in China: A Historical Survey," *Journal of Chinese Law*, No. 4, 1990, p. 245–251.
32. See Baogang He, *The Democratization of China*, London: Routledge, 1996, chapter 4.
33. D. Kelliher, "The Chinese Debate over Village Self-Government," *The China Journal*, No. 37, 1997, pp. 63–86; Tianjian Shi, "Village Committee Elections in China: Institutionalist Tactics for Democracy," *World Politics*, No. 51, 1999, pp. 385–412.
34. Peter Lin, "Between Theory and Practice: The Possibility of a Right to Free Speech in the People's Republic of China," *Journal of Chinese Law*, No. 4, 1990, p. 268.
35. For a discussion of religious rights in China see E. Kolodner, "Religious Rights in China: A Comparison of International Human Rights Law and Chinese Domestic Legislation," *Human Rights Quarterly*, No. 16, 1994, pp. 455–490.
36. Danny Schechter, *Falun Gong's Challenge to China: Spiritual Practice or "Evil Cult"?*, New York: Akashic Book, 2000.

37. "China Issues Internet Controls," 18 January 2002, Associated Press, ⟨http://www.washingtonpost.com/wp-dyn/articles/A2124-2002Jan18.html⟩.
38. Jack Linchuan Qiu, "Virtual Censorship in China: Keeping the Gate between the Cyberspaces," *International Journal of Communication Law and Policy*, No. 4 1999/2000, p. 3.
39. "China and Tibet," *Human Rights Watch World Report 2000*, available at ⟨http://www.hrw.org/wr2k/Asia-03.htm#⟩.
40. Jiang Zemin's Speech at the Meeting Celebrating the 80th Anniversary of the Founding of the Communist Party of China, Section III. Available at ⟨http://www.china.org.cn/e-speech/a.htm⟩.
41. See ⟨http://www.transparency.org⟩.
42. For an excellent account see Richard Klein, "The Empire Strikes Back: Britain's Use of the Law to Suppress Political Dissent in Hong Kong," *Boston University International Law Journal*, No. 15, 1997, pp. 1–70.
43. Nihal Jayawickrama, "Hong Kong and the International Protection of Human Rights," in R. Wacks, ed., *Human Rights in Hong Kong*, Hong Kong: Oxford University Press, 1992, pp. 129–131.
44. Linda Butenhoff, "East meets West: Human Rights in Hong Kong," in Peter Van Hess, ed., *Debating Human Rights*, London: Routledge, 1998, pp. 107–109.
45. Shiu-hing Lo, *The Politics of Democratization in Hong Kong*, London: Macmillan, 1997, p. 49.
46. See Hong Kong Government, *The Further Development of Representative Government in Hong Kong*, Green Paper, July 1984; Hong Kong Government, *The Further Development of Representative Government in Hong Kong*, White Paper, 1984.
47. See ⟨http://www.hkhrc.org.hk/⟩.
48. See ⟨http://www.hkhrm.org.hk/⟩.
49. For a detailed discussion of the Bill of Rights see Raymond Wacks, ed., *Hong Kong's Bill of Rights*, Hong Kong: Faculty of Law, University of Hong Kong, 1990; Johannes Chan and Yash Ghai, eds, *The Hong Kong Bill of Rights: A Comparative Approach*, Singapore: Butterworth Asia, 1993.
50. A.Y. Chen, "The Interpretation of the Basic Law," *Hong Kong Law Journal*, No. 30, 2000, p. 418.
51. See Peter Wesley-Smith, "Maintenance of the Bill of Rights," *Hong Kong Law Journal*, No. 27, 1997, pp. 15–16, and Yash Ghai, "The Continuity of Laws and Legal Rights and Obligations in the SAR," *Hong Kong Law Journal*, No. 27, 1997, pp. 141ff.
52. Article 4 of the Basic Law reads, "The Hong Kong Special Administrative Region shall safeguard the rights and freedoms of the residents of the Hong Kong Special Administrative Region and of other persons in the Region in accordance with law."
53. See, for example, "Assurance on Freedom for Journalists," *South China Morning Post*, 10 April 1995.
54. D.C. Turack, "The Projected Hong Kong Special Administrative Region Human Rights Record in the Post-British Era," *Akron Law Review*, No. 31, 1997, pp. 96–97.
55. See Frances H. Foster, "The Illusory Promise: Freedom of the Press in Hong Kong, China," *Indiana Law Journal*, No. 73, 1998, pp. 765–796.
56. James E. Sciutto, "China's Muffling of the Hong Kong Media," *Annals of the American Academy of Political and Social Science*, No. 547, 1996, p. 136.
57. W.H. Overholt, "Hong Kong: the Perils of Semidemocracy," *Journal of Democracy*, No. 12, 2001, p. 7.
58. *Ming Pao*, 20 December 2001.
59. J.M.M. Chan, H.L. Fu, and Y. Ghai, eds, *Hong Kong's Constitutional Debate*, Hong Kong: Hong Kong University Press, 2000.

60. See ⟨http://www.transparency.org⟩.
61. For a discussion of the role of regional instruments in human rights protection see T. Meron, *Human Rights Law-Making in the United Nations: A Critique of Instruments and Process*, Oxford: Clarendon Press, 1986, pp. 165ff, 229ff.
62. See ⟨http://www.hg.org/cgi-bin/redir.cgi⟩ and ⟨http://www.umn.edu/humanrts/africa/index.html⟩.
63. See ⟨http://www.ahrchk.net/index.html⟩.

16

Human rights in India

D.R. Kaarthikeyan

"Om Sarvey bhavantu Sukhinaha
Sarvey Santu Niraamayaha
Sarvey Bhadraani pashyantu
Ma kashchit dukhbhaak bhavet"[1]

[Om, May all be happy
May all be healthy
May all see auspiciousness
May none suffer.
Om, Peace be!! Peace be!!! Peace be!!!]

From *"Vasudaiva Kutumbakam"* – an ancient scripture of India in Sanskrit language

The human rights movement in India is an offshoot of the social and cultural renaissance that began in nineteenth-century British India. The establishment of British rule united the subcontinent. The pioneering work of orientalists such as Sir William Jones, James Prinsep, Charles Wilkin, and Max Muller established and promoted intellectual unity.

However, the ideals of modern-day human rights can be seen in various classic religious and secular sources, such as the *Vedas*, *Puranas*, and epics. Although human rights in the ancient Indian literature did not form a coherent unified structure, they were widely referred to. The *Rig Veda* talks about three civil liberties – *Tana* (body), *Skridhi* (dwelling house), and *Jibazi* (life). *Mahabaratha*, the great Indian epic, describes civil liberty of the individual in a political state.[2] The *Aitareya Brahmana* states that kings were required to act according to "whatever law there is and whatever is dictated by ethics and not opposed to politics."[3] The *Arthasastra*, the greatest political treatise of ancient India, written by Kautilya, provides for detailed civil and legal rights. It states that "the king shall provide the orphan, the aged, the infirm, the afflicted and helpless with maintenance. He shall also provide subsistence to the helpless expectant mothers and also to the children they give birth to."[4] The *Manusmriti*, *Mahabaratha*, and *Arthasastra* also focus on the conduct of war – when a war should and should not be fought, as it was one major cause of human rights violations in ancient India. Furthermore, the underlying principle of *vasudaiva kudumbakam* propounded the concept of universal equality.[5]

In modern history, Raja Ram Mohan Roy can be considered as the father of India's human rights movement. He was the first to oppose all discriminations and evil practices against women. He pursued his efforts against polygamy and *sati* (widow burning) at two levels: first, he approached the British rulers directly to legally ban such practices; second, he mobilized the masses in favour of such a ban. He published *Modern Encroachments on the Ancient Rights of Females according to the Hindu Law of Inheritance* in 1822 and established *Brahmo Samaj* in 1828. The *Brahmo Samaj* deplored sacrifice and emphasized love of mankind, irrespective of colour, race, or creed. As a result of Raja Ram's efforts, Lord William Bentinck, then Governor-General, passed Regulation XVII in December 1829, which declared *sati* illegal and punishable. Thus began the human rights movement in India in the 1820s.

The formation of *Brahmo Samaj* led to the growth of an organized social movement, which gave importance to many modern-day human rights ideals. Keshav Chandra Sen,[6] following Raja Ram, took up issues such as women's education and intercaste marriage, and began a campaign against child marriage. Sen started a fortnightly journal called the *Indian Mirror* (which later became the first Indian daily in India) to propagate these ideals. Jyotiba Phule[7] took up the "untouchable" issue and began an organized crusade against untouchability. He formed *Satya Shodak Samaj* in 1873 to liberate the oppressed castes and to create awareness among them. The Theosophical Society was established in the 1870s and preached universal brotherhood of men, irrespective of caste, creed, and race.

The efforts of these various nineteenth-century movements were reflected in the Indian National Congress in the twentieth century. The Congress fought both against the British and the social evils within India. Long before Indian independence, Jawaharlal Nehru, Mahatma Gandhi, and other Congress leaders created awareness on various human rights issues. The Indian National Congress, to an extent, could be considered as one of the largest human rights movements. The Motilal Nehru Committee, appointed in 1928, made recommendations that include the following:

- personal liberty and inviolability of dwelling place and property;
- freedom of conscience and of profession and practice of religion;
- right of free expression of opinion;
- right to free elementary education;
- equality for all citizens before law.

When India became independent, these ideals were reflected in its new constitution, especially in the Fundamental Rights and the Directive Principles of State Policy.

However, promulgation of a new constitution incorporating various human rights provisions did not automatically do away with violations. The age-old traditions and evil practices, coupled with problems facing a newly independent country, proved to be an effective stumbling-block in achieving the human rights objectives. Even today, problems of nation-building and society-building haunt the country. As a result, human rights violations still persist, despite the efforts made over the last 53 years.

The change-over and transition did not come overnight: the process has been spread over centuries. India's freedom movement led by Mahatma Gandhi brought about considerable diminution and reduction in age-old inequalities in social, economic, and political spheres. The deliberations that took place during the formation of the United Nations and those discussions in the UN General Assembly, which ultimately led to the Universal Declaration of Human Rights, had a great impact on the Constituent Assembly of India and the founding fathers of the Indian Constitution.

This chapter analyses forms of human rights violations; their causes; provisions in the constitution; and the role of the government, the judiciary, and governmental and non-governmental organizations in fighting human rights violations.

Violence against children: Child labour and abuse

According to the 1991 census estimates, some 11.3 million children of 200 million aged between 5 and 14 years are engaged in child labour.[8] These children work in various spheres, from agriculture to mining. Although the practice continues (despite a ban and a series of court verdicts), encouragingly, child labour is in decline. According to the National Sample Survey, there were 16.3 million child labourers in 1981 and 11.3 million in 1991.

There are at least three types of child labour. First, there is non-monetary domestic labour: in this case, girls do most of the domestic work. Second, there is monetary labour, which is non-domestic: here, children are employed as wage labourers in organized and unorganized sectors, both in rural and urban areas. Third, there is bonded labour, where children are pledged by their parents.

Most of the child labourers are employed primarily in the agricultural sector as workers. They also work in industries including leather factories, hosiery units, carpet factories, glass factories, textile units, and plastics factories. Some work as servants in private homes. Worse, some work as bonded labourers and sex workers. According to a *UNDP Position Paper on Child Labor*, India accounts for the largest number of child workers in the world.[9] According to a UNICEF study, there are more than 100,000 child labourers in the Mirzapur carpet industries, 50,000 in the Firozabad glass industries, 30,000 in the Moradabad brass industries, and 10,000 in the Aligarh lock industries (which manufacture various articles – such as locks, scales, letter boxes, badges, knives, and scissors – for supply to the postal department country-wide).[10]

The government and child labour

The Indian government has passed several laws prohibiting child labour, the most important being the Child Labour (Prohibition and Regulation) Act of 1986, which prohibits employment of children below 14 years of age in specified hazardous occupations and processes. The Juvenile Justice Act (1986) superseded all existing legislation related to children in

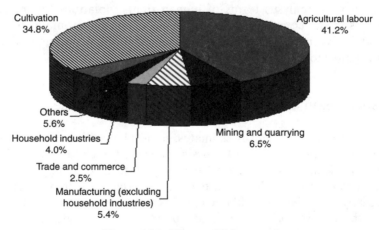

Figure 16.1 Where children work

different states and Union territories. The Act provides for the creation of Advisory Boards and the establishment of State Children Funds, the objective of which is to protect children and to provide educational, training, and rehabilitation facilities for neglected children. In 1993, the Union government set up a National Authority to eliminate child labour. It provided rupees 850 crore (Rs8.5 billion; US$185 million), which aimed to benefit two million child labourers by undertaking measures on education, poverty reduction, and awareness creation.

The Constitution, Supreme Court, and child labour

The following articles of the Indian Constitution prohibit child labour: according to Article 23, "traffic in human beings and beggar and other similar forms of forced labour are prohibited and any contravention of this provision shall be an offence punishable in accordance with law." Article 39 (f) states that "children are given opportunities and facilities to develop in a healthy manner and in conditions of freedom and dignity and that childhood and youth are protected against exploitation and against moral and material abandonment."

The Supreme Court of India, in December 1999, directed the withdrawal of children from hazardous occupations. It has also constituted a welfare fund for children and has regulated working conditions in non-hazardous occupations. Earlier, in *M.C. Mehta* v. *State of Tamil Nadu* (known as the Child Labour Abolition Case), the Supreme Court ruled that children less than 14 years of age cannot be employed in any hazardous industrial, mining, or other employment.[11] In addition, the Court also directed the government to set up a Children Labour Rehabilitation Welfare Fund, and ordered the offending employers to pay each child Rs20,000 (US$435) as compensation. In non-hazardous jobs, children should not work for more than four to six hours and the employer should provide education for them.

The implementation of these judicial decisions varies from place to place, depending on the level of awareness and political commitment of the states. The increasing influence of NGOs, the media, and a proactive judiciary has, to a great extent, made it possible for these regulations to be adhered to.

Violence against women

Violence against women in India mainly relates to dowry deaths, female infanticide and foeticide, *sati* (widow burning), and rape. Other forms of violence against women include sexual abuse, wife beating, eve teasing,[12]

Table 16.1 Crimes against women in India, 1990–2000

Crime	1990	1999	2000
Rape	9,518	15,468	16,496
Kidnapping and abduction	11,699	15,962	15,023
Dowry deaths	4,836	6,699	6,995
Torture	13,450	43,823	45,778
Molestation	20,194	32,311	32,940
Sexual harassment	8,620	8,858	11,024

Source: National Crime Records Bureau.

and the refusal to allow women to inherit. The Indian National Crime Records Bureau (NCRB) provides statistics of crimes against women in the last decade (table 16.1). The increase in crimes is mainly due to an increased willingness to report them, driven in part by a growing awareness of women's rights, pressure on law enforcement agencies, and the work of voluntary organizations.

According to the statistics shown in table 16.2, the states of Rajasthan, Madhya Pradesh, and Delhi record the highest levels of crimes against women, whereas states such as Nagaland, Meghalaya, and Punjab have reported lower levels.[13] As table 16.3 reveals, lower-class women have most crimes committed against them.

Dowry

Dowry is a major issue in crimes against women. Dowry is defined as any property or valuable security given, or agreed to be given, directly or indirectly, by one party to the marriage, or by parents of either party to the marriage, or by any person to either party to the marriage, or to any other person at (or before, or at any time after) the marriage, in connection with the marriage of the said parties.[14]

Dowry has been one of the most significant factors in violence against women: it results in harassment, beating, and (in many cases) murder. According to the NCRB, in 2000 alone there were 6,995 dowry deaths. Dowry deaths per year have increased significantly since the beginning of the 1990s, mainly because of increased reporting of occurrences.

Dowry-related violence against women, in which a woman has been subjected to harassment by her husband and his family, has also been increasing. In 2000, 45,778 cases were registered. It should also be noted that the NCRB figures may not be accurate, as many dowry-related violence goes unreported. Lack of awareness, fear of retaliation, distrust of legal instruments, or inability to take legal measures prevent families

Table 16.2 Crime rate against women in Indian states and Union Territories

States/Union Territories	No. of crimes per million persons
Daman and Diu	17.5
Nagaland	25.3
Meghalaya	29.9
Pondycherry	31.9
Punjab	35.8
Bihar	39.0
Manipur	44.6
Goa	50.5
Tamil Nadu	72.0
Karnataka	74.5
Andaman and Nicobar	75.2
Uttar Pradesh	77.4
West Bengal	86.8
Gujarat	89.3
Arunachal Pradesh	91.8
Chandigarh	92.2
Kerala	95.8
Tripura	99.1
Jammu and Kashmir	101.0
Orissa	110.4
Dadri and Nagar Haveli	111.0
Sikkim	114.6
Assam	118.8
Haryana	119.4
Andhra Pradesh	122.0
Mizoram	127.9
Himachal Pradesh	139.4
Maharashtra	173.8
Delhi	197.1
Madhya Pradesh	207.0
Rajasthan	208.2

Source: *Economic and Political Weekly*, 27 October 2001, p. 4072.

Table 16.3 Composition of crimes against women by social status (values are percentages)[a]

Social status	Rape	Kidnap/ Abduction	Dowry death	Molestation	Sexual harassment	Cruelty at home
Low	34.0	25.0	12.2	11.7	1.3	15.8
Lower-Middle	11.2	17.3	7.7	23.0	5.7	35.0
Upper-Middle	16.7	19.5	2.5	33.8	3.9	23.7
High	14.3	14.5	5.3	28.1	5.3	32.6

Source: *Economic and Political Weekly*, 27 October 2001, p. 4072.
a. Some percentages do not total 100 because of rounding errors.

from reporting dowry-related violence to the police. To counterbalance this, the increased figures could be the result of increased awareness, led by the various women's movements in all parts of India.[15]

Most of the victims of dowry death belong to the middle class and are of the age group 21–24 years. Dowry deaths are found more among the middle and upper castes than the in lower caste. Dowry deaths are more prevalent in urban and semi-urban areas than in rural areas. One of the main reasons for dowry deaths has been lack of economic self-sufficiency among victims.

Rape

The above-mentioned statistics show that rape as a crime against women has been increasing. Most of the victims belong to the age group of 16–30 years and are from all classes of society.

Female infanticide and foeticide

Female infanticide and foeticide is yet another form of crime against women in India. Female infanticide, in most cases, takes place with the consent of the parents after the baby is born. The main reason for female infanticide in India is the cost of raising a girl child[16] in a patriarchal society. Female foeticide involves aborting the female foetus, once its sex has been determined, the reasons being the same as those for female infanticide. Female infanticide is more prevalent among the lower classes, whereas foeticide is prevalent among the middle and upper classes.

According to the 2001 Census in India, though the overall sex ratio has increased from 927 females per 1,000 males in 1991 to 933 females per 1,000 in 2001, there is a decline in sex ratio of the population in the age group of 0–6 years. An analysis of the last 40 years would reveal a steady decline in the F:M sex ratio in India (table 16.4). Although the sex ratio has increased in such states as Bihar, Jharkhand, Rajasthan, and Tamil Nadu, there has been a decline in Haryana, Himachal Pradesh, Punjab, and Chandigarh (table 16.5).

The child sex ratio – especially in two states (Haryana and Punjab) with sex ratios (of males per 1,000 births) of 122.8 and 123.3, respectively – shows the "rampant practice of female foeticide along with a certain amount of infanticide in these two states."[17]

The IPC and crimes against women

The Indian Penal Code (IPC) is the basic criminal law, prescribing deterrent punishments. Cases under the IPC are investigated and tried in

Table 16.4 Sex ratio in India, 1901–2001

Census year	Sex ratio (females per 1,000 males)
1901	972
1951	946
1961	941
1971	930
1981	934
1991	927
2001	933

Source: *Census of India*, New Delhi: Office of the Registrar-General, India, 2001.

higher courts of law. The IPC covers issues related to crimes against women – rape (Section 376), kidnapping and abduction (Sections 363–373), dowry killings (Sections 302 and 304B), molestation (Section 354), eve teasing and sexual harassment (Section 509), and importation of girls (Section 366 B).

Political violence: Terrorism

To a large extent, political violence in India affects human rights. It is manifested mainly in terrorist violence against the state and affects the

Table 16.5 Sex ratio and child population in the 0–6-year age group in selected states of India in 1991 and 2001

States and Union Territories	Total population (1991)	Total population (2001)	Child population (0–6 years)	
			(1991)	(2001)
Himachal Pradesh	976	970	951	897
Punjab	882	874	875	793
Chandigarh	790	773	899	845
Uttaranchal	936	964	948	906
Haryana	865	861	879	820
Delhi	827	821	915	865
Rajasthan	910	922	916	909
Uttar Pradesh	876	898	927	916
Bihar	907	921	953	938
Gujarat	934	921	928	878
Daman and Diu	969	709	958	925
Dadra and Nagar Haveli	952	811	1,013	973
Maharashtra	934	922	946	917

Source: *Census of India*, New Delhi, Office of the Registrar-General, India, 2001.

Table 16.6 Loss of life in Jammu and Kashmir since 1988

Year	No. of incidents	Lives lost by		Security forces	Total lives lost
		Terrorists	Civilians		
1988	390	1	29	1	31
1989	2,154	0	79	13	92
1990	3,905	183	862	132	1,177
1991	3,122	614	594	185	1,393
1992	4,971	873	859	177	1,909
1993	4,457	1,328	1,023	216	2,567
1994	4,484	1,651	1,012	236	2,899
1995	4,479	1,338	1,161	297	2,796
1996	4,224	1,194	1,333	376	2,903
1997	3,004	1,177	840	355	2,372
1998	2,993	1,045	877	339	2,261
1999	2,938	1,184	799	555	2,538
2000	2,835	1,808	842	638	3,288
2001 (up to June)	1,628	760	503	278	1,541
Total	45,584	13,156	10,813	3,798	27,767

Source: South Asia Intelligence Review (SAIR), Weekly Assessments & Briefings ⟨www.satp.org⟩

common population. Terrorism results in the destruction of all human rights of large segments of the population. India, at present, is facing terrorist violence in two areas – (1) Jammu and Kashmir and (2) the North East.

In Jammu and Kashmir, there has been armed and organized violence against the state and the people since 1989. Three major terrorist groups are operating in Jammu and Kashmir – Hizbul Mujahideen, Lashkar-e-Toiba, and Jaish-e-Mohammad – along with a number of minor groups. Inspection of the human and material casualties (table 16.6) reveals the violations of human rights by these terrorist groups.

Of the seven states in India's North East, the four most affected in terms of militancy are Assam, Manipur, Nagaland, and Tripura. Assam has been witnessing militancy for the last two decades, ever since the start of large-scale migration from Bangladesh (previously East Pakistan). There are more than 30 militant groups in Assam today, including the United Liberation Front of Asom (ULFA), the National Democratic Front of Bodoland (NDFB), the Kamatapur Liberation Organization (KLO), the Bodo Liberation Tiger Force (BLTF); the Dima Halim Daogah (DHD), and the Karbi National Volunteers (KNV). These militant groups have been fighting in various parts of India against the security

Table 16.7 Civilians killed by various terrorist groups in Assam

Terrorist group	1992	1993	1994	1995	1996	1997	1998	1999	2000[a]
ULFA	35	48	49	16	59	68	97	55	35
NDFB	37	25	108	132	176	137	305	107	52
BLT&BTF	0	0	0	8	53	52	126	22	1
NSCN/DHD	8	1	16	14	14	28	3	30	5
UPDS	0	0	0	0	0	0	0	0	33

Source: South Asia Intelligence Review (SAIR), Weekly Assessments & Briefings ⟨http://www.satp.org/08aprilinternet/graph/Assam/Data-Civilians.htm⟩
a. Data up to 28 June 2000.
BLT&BTF: Bodo Liberation Tiger & Bhindranwale Tigers Force.
NDFB: National Democratic Front of Bodoland.
NSCN/DHD: National Socialist Council of Nagaland/Dima Halong Daga.
ULFA: United Liberation Front of Asom.
UPDS: United People's Democratic Solidarity.

forces of India and also among themselves. For example, in India's heavily tribal north-eastern states, most militant organizations are organized on a tribal basis. These intratribal and tribe–state conflicts give rise to a wide range of human rights violations (tables 16.7, 16.8).

Manipur is yet another north-eastern state facing both inter- and intra-ethnic tribal conflict, with more than 30 tribes in the state, the Meiteis, Nagas, and Kukis being among the most prominent. More than 30 militant groups operate in this small state, including the United National Liberation Front (UNLF), the People's Liberation Army (PLA), the People's Revolutionary Party of Kangleipak (PREPAK), the Kangleipak Communist Party (KCP), the National Socialist Council of Nagaland–Isak-Muivah (NSCN–IM), the Kuki National Front (KNF), and the Kuki National Army (KNA) (tables 16.9, 16.10).

Table 16.8 Security force personnel killed by various terrorist groups in Assam

Terrorist group[a]	1992	1993	1994	1995	1996	1997	1998	1999	2000[b]
ULFA	10	15	7	14	48	50	42	29	28
NDFB	10	6	22	16	25	25	22	14	6
BLT&BTF	0	0	0	1	6	1	5	8	0
NSCN/DHD	14	3	6	42	8	9	3	26	6
UPDS	–	–	–	–	–	–	0	2	0
Total	34	24	35	73	87	85	72	79	40

Source: South Asia Intelligence Review (SAIR), Weekly Assessments & Briefings ⟨http://www.satp.org/08aprilinternet/graph/Assam/Data-SF%20killed.htm⟩
a. Abbreviations as in Table 16.7.
b. Data up to 28 June 2000.

Table 16.9 Civilians killed by various terrorist groups in Manipur

Terrorist group[a]	1992	1993	1994	1995	1996	1997	1998	1999	2000[b]
NSCN	27	80	104	30	21	27	20	6	0
Meitei	43	119	79	139	90	62	57	75	26
Kuki	14	67	6	14	6	144	10	8	1

Source: South Asia Intelligence Review (SAIR), Weekly Assessments & Briefings ⟨http://www.satp.org/08aprilinternet/graph/Manipur/Data-Civilians.htm⟩
a. NSCN, National Socialist Council of Nagaland.
b. Data up to 28 June 2000.

Table 16.10 Security force personnel killed by various militant groups in Manipur

Terrorist group[a]	1992	1993	1994	1995	1996	1997	1998	1999	2000[b]
NSCN	8	46	67	20	8	5	2	1	2
Meitei	22	41	21	38	52	67	57	63	24
Kuki	0	4	10	6	5	39	3	0	0

Source: South Asia Intelligence Review (SAIR), Weekly Assessments & Briefings ⟨http://www.satp.org/08aprilinternet/graph/Manipur/Data-SF.htm⟩
a. NSCN, National Socialist Council of Nagaland.
b. Data up to 28 June 2000.

NSCN, the major militant group operating in Nagaland, is divided into two factions – Isak-Muivah and Khaplang. As well as their fight against the Indian security forces, the conflict between the two factions is very intense (table 16.11).

Caste violence

Caste conflict is yet another source of human rights violation in India. Caste violence is predominant in such states as Bihar, Uttar Pradesh,

Table 16.11 Insurgency-related killings in Nagaland

Lives lost by	1992	1993	1994	1995	1996	1997	1998	1999	2000[a]
Civilians	34	62	110	80	144	104	26	26	5
Security Force	33	43	26	25	48	38	14	4	4
Militants	29	68	56	108	112	218	72	118	52

Source: South Asia Intelligence Review (SAIR), Weekly Assessments & Briefings ⟨http://www.satp.org/08aprilinternet/graph/Nagaland/Data-Insurgency.htm⟩
a. Data up to 28 June 2000.

Table 16.12 *Senas* (caste militias) of Bihar

Name of *Sena*	Caste affiliation	Year of formation	Operational districts
Kuer Sena	Rajput	1979	Bhojpur, Rohtas
Kisan Suraksha Samiti	Kurmi	1979	Patna, Jehanabad, Gaya
Bhoomi Sena	Kurmi	1983	Patna, Nawada, Nalanda, Jehanabad
Lorik Sena	Yadav	1983	Patna, Jehanabad, Nalanda
Brahmarshi Sena	Bhumihar	1984	Bhojpur, Patna, Jehanabad, Aurangabad
Kisan Sangh	Rajput Brahmin	1984	Palamu
Kisan Sewak Samaj	Rajput	1985	Palamu, Aurangabad
Sunlight Sena	Pathans Rajput	1989	Palamu, Gaya, Garwah, Aurangabad
Swarna Liberation Front	Bhumihar	1990	Gaya, Jehanabad
Kisan Sangh	Bhumihar	1990	Patna, Bhojpur
Kisan Morcha	Rajputs	1989–90	Bhojpur
Ganga Sena	Bhumihar	1990	Bhojpur
Ranvir Sena	Rajput and Bhumihar	1994	Bhojpur, Patna, Jehanabad, Rohtas, Gaya, Aurangabad

Source: *Economic and Political Weekly*, 24 June 2000.

Tamil Nadu, and Andhra Pradesh. The main reasons for increased caste violence in these states have been the feudal nature of society, the concentration of land in the hands of a select few, suppression of the lower castes by land-owning upper castes, and the reluctance of the upper castes to provide equal social status to the lower castes. The following section focuses especially on caste violence in Bihar, where it is more organized. States such as Bihar and Uttar Pradesh are characterized as highly feudal societies, where caste lines are clearly drawn between the upper and lower castes. These caste groups have well-funded and organized armed militias, known as *Senas*. Every caste group has its own *Sena*, as shown in table 16.12. Of these caste militias, *Ranvir Sena* is the most powerful. It has been involved in more massacres than any other militia: since its formation it has been involved in more than 25 massacres, in which more than 250 people have been killed.

Minorities and human rights

India is a multireligious society composed of Hindus (82 per cent), Muslims (12 per cent), Christians (2 per cent), Sikhs (2 per cent), and other small communities (each less than 1 per cent).[18]

Especially during the past three years, India has witnessed increased attacks on minority communities, especially on Muslims and Christians. More than 600 incidents took place in 1998; in December 1998, churches and other Christian establishments were attacked in Gujarat in Dangs district; on 22–23 January 1999, an Australian missionary, Graham Staines, and his two sons were burnt alive; on 13 January 1999, a church in Dangs district was burnt and a Muslim Dargah was razed to the ground in the Surendranagar district of Gujarat. In April 1999, sectarian violence between Shias and Sunnis resulted in the killing of two people; in the same month, two more were killed in the Rai Bareli district of Uttar Pradesh in a communal clash, and a priest of the Roman Catholic Church was killed in the Koenjar district. Seven people were killed in Surat, Gujarat, in September 1999, in a communal clash during a Lord Ganesh procession.

Communal violence has been the result of religious conversions from one faith to another, or of rival claims to property or land. These sensitive and emotional issues are being handled carefully by various authorities: for example, a procession by a Hindu community through a street where a mosque is located is handled with extreme care and caution by senior officers of the state; although the right of a community to take part in a procession needs to be maintained, this action should not offend the religious sentiments of another community. Tact and diplomacy in handling the situation is essential to ensure that the procession does not involve loud music and drum beats while crossing select streets or places.

State violence

It is not only non-state entities that are involved in violence: the state, at times, is also involved in violence against its citizens. Such state violence takes place at four levels: first, it occurs in an insurgency situation where the armed forces are involved in tackling terrorist groups; there are a number of complaints against Indian armed forces deployed in Jammu and Kashmir, and in the various north-eastern states; second, the police used force to control organized political uprisings of armed groups, especially that of the Naxalites[19] and caste militias; third, during political crises – especially in situations such as bandhs (strikes) and processions – the state has, in the past, used force to bring disorderly situations under control; fourth, under even normal political conditions police atrocities occur. The police force in India was set up by the British to serve their colonial interests: even after independence, the police have not been able to transform their mind-set to serve in a free and democratic society; even then, the laws of procedure remained unchanged and, as such, were not in the best interests of the police. The enactment of a large number of laws places a great burden on a police force that is inadequate and not appropriately equipped to discharge their responsibilities effectively. The police force is one of the most visible arms of the government and frequently confronts a public that is disenchanted with the government's failure to fulfil election promises. The increasing politicization of the law-and-order machinery has been undermining the neutrality, credibility, acceptability, and effectiveness of the police force. The birth and spread of organized crime, terrorism, insurgency, and extremism also puts enormous pressure on the police. Unable to bear such pressure of rising expectations of both the government and the public, the police lose their equilibrium and balance: to prove themselves to be effective, at times they resort to excesses. However, with the public becoming increasingly aware of their rights, and with human rights organizations growing more active, efforts are being made to bring about legal reforms. The situation seems to be changing for the better.

Police atrocities are considered a major area of human rights violations falling under the category of state violence. This includes torture and death in police custody, "encounter" death,[20] and atrocities against women including rape and illegal detention.

The government has also been accused of systematically violating international law by using lethal force against peaceful demonstrators and engaging in widespread and arbitrary arrest of persons suspected of sympathizing with the militants, detaining them for extended periods without charge or trial.

Conditions in Indian prisons, rights of prisoners, and duration of trials

While addressing the issues of prison conditions in India, it is important to draw attention to the rights of prisoners, including that of a speedy trial.

To begin with, prisons in India are overcrowded. According to a recent survey, there were around 9,000 prisoners against a capacity of a mere 2,500 in Tihar jail in New Delhi, and 3,000 against a capacity of 650 in Meerut. Invariably, the conditions are very similar all over India. The reasons for such overcrowded facilities are mainly an administrative failure to provide adequate jails and the slow process of investigations and trials. These overcrowded prisons "do not have space, facility and resources to provide prisoners their normal work, training and other educational opportunities."[21]

Second, the medical facilities in jails in India are very poor. The National Human Rights Commission (NHRC) received reports of 308 cases of deaths in 1995–1996, and 700 deaths in 1996–1997. One of the reasons for the high incidence of death in jail custody is the complete inadequacy of treatment facilities in jails.[22]

The judiciary of India has played a leading role in prison reforms and the rights of the prisoners and their conditions. In *Sunil Batra* v. *Delhi Administration*, the Court expressed the opinion that:

> To fetter prisoners in irons is an inhumanity unjustified save where safe custody is otherwise impossible. The routine resort to handcuffs and irons bespeaks a barbarity hostile to our goal of human dignity and social justice.[23]

In yet another judgement in *Kishore Singh* v. *State of Rajasthan*, it was observed that,

> ... the State must reeducate the constabulary out of their sadistic acts and inculcate a respect for human person – a process which must begin more by example than precept if the lower rungs are really to emulate ... Nothing is more cowardly and unconscionable than a person in police custody being beaten up and nothing inflicts a deeper wound on our constitutional culture than a state official running berserk regardless of human rights.[24]

Third, the cases pending trial, the slow process of prosecution (both deliberately and by chance), and the attitude of the administration (both State and Centre), need to be discussed. Confinement without trial for a long period is against the spirit and principles of the Indian Constitution and its commitment to the 1948 Universal Declaration of Human Rights. As Sharma argues,

> The distributive justice demands that the criminal justice should be swift and sure, that the guilty should be punished while the events are still fresh in public mind and that the innocent should be absolved as early as is consistent with a fair and impartial trial. A criminal trial, which drags on for an unreasonably long time, is not a fair trial. Sometimes, the offences with which the accused charged are so trivial that even if proved, would not warrant punishment for more than few months, but the accused has to suffer detention because of the protracted nature of the trial.[25]

According to Article 9(3) of the International Covenant on Civil and Political Rights, 1966, to which India is a party, "[a]nyone arrested or detained on a criminal charge shall be brought promptly before a judge or other officer authorized by law to exercise judicial power and shall be entitled to a trial within a reasonable time or to release." The Covenant also mentions that "[i]n the determination of any criminal charge against him, every one shall be entitled ... (c) to be tried without undue delays" (Article 14(3)(c)).

Although the judiciary in India has repeatedly condemned the delay in trials, nothing much has happened in actual terms. Justice Krishna Iyer in *Babu Singh* v. *State of UP* points to the following problem:

Our justice system, even in grave cases, suffers from slow motion syndrome, which is lethal to fair trial whatever the ultimate decision. Speedy justice is a component of social justice, since the community as a whole is concerned in the criminal being condignly and finally punished within a reasonable time and the innocent being absolved from the inordinate ordeal of criminal proceedings.[26]

In another case, *Nimeon Sangma* v. *Home Secretary, Govt of Meghalaya*, it was observed that "[i]t is unfortunate, indeed pathetic, that there should have been such considerable delay in investigation by the police in utter disregard of the fact that a citizen has been deprived of his freedom on the ground that he is accused of an offence."[27] Upendra Baxi argues that, "[i]f I am locked up in 'protective custody' without even a charge against me or if I am not produced before the magistrate periodically, I could remain under trial for an indefinite period of time. The state is under no duty to render me legal assistance; nor is it under any liability to pay me compensation for illegal or wrongful confinement."[28]

Environmental issues and human rights

Major environmental problems in India include air and water pollution, as well as deforestation, discharge of hazardous wastes by industries, and land degradation. These problems result in respiratory diseases, lung cancer, and related illnesses. According to data compiled by Greenpeace, up to September 2000 more than 100,800 tons of hazardous wastes have entered the country illegally. According to Greenpeace,

Wastes such as zinc ash, residues and skimmings; lead waste and scrap; used batteries; and waste and scrap of metals such as cadmium, chromium, cobalt, antimony, hafnium and thallium have been exported to India from countries including OECD nations such as Germany, USA, Australia, Denmark, the Netherlands, UK, Belgium and Norway. These imports have occurred without any authorization or the knowledge of the Indian Ministry of Environment. Some of these waste items are also illegal under the laws of European Union nations and Australia, both of which have banned the exports of hazardous wastes to non-OECD countries.[29]

Such issues as protection of the environment and access to pure water and air have been viewed in India as a part of human rights, especially since the 1990s. Although the government and the people in general are yet to become aware of this issue, it has been championed by the judiciary and NGOs.

The rights of people to unpolluted air and water have been seen as a part of Article 21 of the Indian Constitution, which states that "[n]o person shall be deprived of his life or personal liberty except according to the procedure established by law." In one of its verdicts, the High Court of Andhra Pradesh argued that

The enjoyment of life and its attainment and fulfillment guaranteed by Article 21 of the Constitution embraces the protection and preservation of nature's gifts ... The slow poisoning by polluted atmosphere caused by environmental pollution and spoliation should be regarded as amounting to violation of Article 21 of the Constitution.[30]

In another judgement, the court gave the verdict that ensuring enjoyment of pollution-free water and air should be considered as a part of Article 21.[31]

Human rights and the Indian Constitution

Parts III and IV of the Indian Constitution focus on many aspects of human rights: in fact, it is widely considered as a social document.[32] Article 14 states that "[t]he State shall not deny to any person equality before the law and equal protection of the laws within the territory of India." Article 15 states, "(1) The State shall not discriminate against any citizen on grounds only of religion, race, caste, sex, place of birth or any of them. (2) No citizen shall on grounds only of religion, race, caste, sex, place of birth or any of them be subject to any disability, liability, restriction or condition with regard to (a) access to shops, public restaurants, hotels and places of public entertainment." Article 16 states "(1) there shall be equality of opportunity for all citizens in matters relating to employment or appointment to any office under the State." Article 19 states that all citizens shall have the right to freedom of speech and expression; to assemble peacefully and without arms; to form associations or unions; to move freely throughout the territory of India; to reside and settle in any part of the territory of India; and to practise any profession or to carry on any occupation, trade or business."

Article 20 states that "[n]o person shall be convicted of any offence except for violation of a law in force at the time of the commission of the act charged as an offence, nor be subjected to a penalty greater than that which might have been inflicted under the law in force at the time of the commission of the offence." Article 21, the most important article of all in the Fundamental Rights section, states that "[n]o person shall be deprived of his life or personal liberty except according to the procedure established by law."

All of the above-mentioned Articles of the Indian Constitution come under the Fundamental Rights guaranteed by the State. Article 32 provides that, if any of the above Fundamental Rights are violated, one has the right to call on the Supreme Court directly. Thus the above-mentioned articles form the bedrock of human rights, guaranteed by the Indian Constitution.

In addition, a number of other rights come under the "Directive Principles of the State Policy." Although these rights (unlike the Fundamental Rights) are not enforceable, they provide guidelines for the states to follow in legislating and implementing laws. These rights focus on the following:

- Providing adequate means of livelihood (Article 39 (a));
- Equal pay for equal work for both men and women. (Article 39 (d));
- Adequate protection of the health and strength of workers, men and women (Article 39 (e));
- Equal justice and free legal aid (Article 39A);
- Living wage, conditions of work ensuring a decent standard of life and full enjoyment of leisure and social and cultural opportunities (Article 43);
- Free and compulsory education for children (Article 45);
- Increasing the level of nutrition, the standard of living and improving public health (Article 47);
- Prohibiting the slaughter of cows and calves and other milk and draught cattle (Article 48).

Judiciary and human rights in India

In India, the judiciary plays a leading role in protecting and enhancing human rights. Broadly speaking, the judiciary performs the following major functions in protecting human rights. First, it ensures that human rights are not legally violated. Article 32 of the Indian Constitution confers the enforcement of fundamental rights on the Supreme Court. Under Article 32, every citizen has a right to request the Supreme Court directly to enforce the Fundamental Rights. The Supreme Court has the power to issue orders or writs in the nature of habeas corpus, mandamus, prohibition, and certiorari, whichever may be appropriate.[33] This power to issue writs has been used extensively by both the Supreme Court and the High Courts.

Second, the judiciary has interpreted the Constitution in various cases, expanding the scope of human rights in India. Some of the cases and their judgements are worth mentioning. In *Francis Coralic Mullin* v. *Administrator, Union Territory of Delhi* (1981), the Supreme Court of India observed that,

The right to life includes the right to live with human dignity and all that goes along with it, namely the bare necessaries of life such as adequate nutrition, clothing and shelter and facilities for reading, writing and expressing oneself in diverse forms, freely moving about and mixing and commingling with fellow human beings.[34]

In *Bandhara Mukti Morcha* v. *Union of India* (1984), the Supreme Court expressed the opinion that,

... Right to live with human dignity ... must include protection of the health and strength of workers, men and women, and of the tender age of children against abuse, opportunities and facilities for children to develop in a healthy manner and in conditions of freedom and dignity, educational facilities, just and humane conditions of work and maternity relief. These are the minimum requirements which must exist in order to enable a person to live with human dignity and no state – neither the Central Government nor any State government – has the right to take any action which will deprive a person of the enjoyment of basic essentials.

That governments do face problems in achieving these ideals is due to the social and economic backwardness of the nation and its huge population. The state is attempting to reach these ideals and, of course (as in any society), there are always shortfalls that need to be taken into consideration.

In another judgement in *Consumer Education and Research Centre* v. *Union of India*, the Supreme Court held that,

'Right to life' in Article 21 includes protection of the health and the strength of the worker. The expression 'life' in Article 21 does not connote mere animal existence. It has a much wider meaning, which includes right to livelihood, better standard of life, hygienic conditions in workplace and leisure.[35]

Fighting human rights violations in India

Human rights violations, whether perpetrated by state actors or by non-state entities, are being countered by three major agencies – namely, the

National Human Rights Commission and the State Human Rights Commissions (all funded by the State), NGOs, and the judiciary.

The National Human Rights Commission (NHRC)

The National Human Rights Commission (NHRC) was established by legislation – the Protection of Human Rights Act 1993. The main objective of the NHRC is to protect human rights by inquiring into specific complaints of human rights violations and to provide human rights education. Although the NHRC is instituted by the government, its autonomy has been ensured through the following provisions. First, the Chairperson and the members of the NHRC are appointed by the President of India from a list of individuals recommended by a committee, which consists of the Prime Minister, Speaker of the House of the People, Leader of the Opposition in the Lower and Upper Houses, Minister of Home Affairs, and the Deputy Chairman of the Council of States. Second, the members of the NHRC can be removed only by the order of the President of India on the grounds of proved misbehaviour or incapacity. Third, the members have a fixed tenure – they are elected for a period of five years.

The main functions of the NHRC include the following:

- Inquiring *suo moto* or on petition presented to it by a victim or any person on behalf of victims on complaints of human rights violations;
- Reviewing factors that curtail the enjoyment of human rights acts such as terrorism, and giving recommendations;
- Reviewing the provisions in the Indian constitution that protect human rights;
- Studying international treaties and documents and ensuring their effective implementation;
- Undertaking research to promote human rights in India;
- Promoting human rights awareness.

In the last eight years of its existence, the NHRC has issued a number of directives and guidelines to the government, especially in the following areas:

- Misuse of police power, especially arbitrary arrests;
- Elimination of child labour;
- Compulsory education;
- Setting up human rights cells in state and city police headquarters;
- Prison reforms;
- Caste and communal violence.

One of the major limitations of the NHRC has been that its scope of investigation does not include human rights violations by the Armed Forces. The success of the government in applying the recommendations made by the NHRC is varying, owing to the economic and social factors discussed earlier in this chapter.

State human rights commissions

The Protection of Human Rights Act 1993 also provides for the establishment of State Human Rights Commissions (SHRC). An SHRC is to consist of a Chairperson, who has been a Chief Justice of a High Court, one member who is/has been a High Court Judge, one member who is/has been a District Judge in that State, and two members who are persons having knowledge of human rights.

As in the case of the NHRC, the members of the SHRCs are appointed by a committee consisting of the Chief Minister of the State, Speaker of the Legislative Assembly, Minister of Department of Home, Leaders of the Opposition in the Legislative Council and Assembly, and the Chairman of the Legislative Council. The Governor appoints the members for a fixed period of five years. Members can be removed by the Governor only on the grounds of misbehaviour or incapacity; this strengthens the autonomy of the SHRCs. The effectiveness of the SHRC depends on its structure, its chairman, and its members. The responsibilities of the Chief Minister, who heads the State government, also play a crucial part in making the SHRC effective. Moreover, the success of an SHRC depends on public awareness and the role of society, led by the media and voluntary organizations. At present only 12 of 28 states in India have established SHRCs.

Other human rights commissions

Besides the NHRC and the SHRCs, there are other commissions, whose functions involve protecting human rights in India.

National Commission for Women (NCW)

The National Commission for Women was established in January 1992 under the National Commission for Women Act (1990). The Commission consists of a chairperson and five other members. The main functions of the NCW are as follows:

- To examine issues relating to the safeguards provided for women under the Constitution and other laws;
- To provide reports to the Central Government on safeguards provided for women under the Constitution;
- To recommend measures to implement the safeguards effectively by the Union or any state;
- To take up cases of violations of constitutional provisions and of other laws related to women's issues with the appropriate authorities;

- To analyse and address complaints related to the deprivation of women's rights; the failure to implement laws aimed at protecting women; the failure to implement laws aimed at gender equality and development; and the failure to comply with policy decisions, guidelines, or instructions aimed at mitigating hardship and ensuring the welfare of women.

National Commission for Minorities (NCM)

The National Commission for Minorities was established in 1992 under the National Commission for Minorities Act. The objectives of the NCM include:

- Evaluating the progress of the development of minorities issues in India;
- Monitoring constitutional and legal safeguards for minorities, as enacted by the National Parliament and the State Legislatures;
- Recommending effective implementation of safeguards for the protection of minority interests by the Central Government or the State Governments;
- Focusing on specific complaints regarding the deprivation of rights and safeguards of minorities;
- Suggesting appropriate measures to be undertaken by the Central Government or the State Governments.

National Commission for Scheduled Castes and Scheduled Tribes

The National Commission for Scheduled Castes and Scheduled Tribes (SC/STs) was originally formed as the Commission for Scheduled Castes and Scheduled Tribes in 1978. Its functions include the following:

- Monitoring issues related to constitutional safeguards provided for SC/STs;
- Enquiring into specific complaints with respect to the deprivation of rights and safeguards of SC/STs;
- Reporting to the President regarding the functioning of these safeguards;
- Recommending measures that should be taken by the Union or any state for the effective implementation of these safeguards and other measures for the protection, welfare, and socio-economic development of SC/STs.

Non-governmental organizations

Besides commissions established by the government at the Union and State levels, a number of NGOs function at the national and regional levels to protect human rights and protest against their violations. There are at least three major NGOs – the People's Union for Civil Liberties

(PUCL), the People's Union for Democratic Rights (PUDR), and Citizens for Democracy.

The PUCL was originally founded as the People's Union for Civil Liberties and Democratic Rights (PUCLDR) in 1976 by Jayaprakash Narayanan. The objective was for PUCLDR to be free from political ideologies, so that people of different groups and parties would come together to fight for civil liberties and human rights. PUCL was established in its present form after a conference held in November 1980, at which a new Constitution was drafted and adopted. This made the PUCL a membership-based organization, with branches all over the country.

The PUCL had set up units in various states (for example in Delhi, Bombay, Bihar, Madhya Pradesh, and Allahabad) and efforts are being made to establish units in other states. The PUCL is actively involved in fighting human rights violations, whether by the state or non-state actors. It has set up a number of fact-finding missions to investigate human rights violations, and has published many reports, which are mostly based on the results of those missions.

The PUDR is another offshoot of the PUCLDR. Like the PUCL, the PUDR has also been involved in a number of fact-finding missions and reports related to social, economic, and political issues. In particular, the PUDR focuses on police atrocities and "encounter" deaths.

Conclusions

The main categories of human rights abuses – such as untouchability, dowry, and atrocities against women – are social. Although the Hindu religion, at its inception, had no such discrimination or distinction, over a period of time these distortions crept in, in a physically and economically male-dominated society.

The second category is economic – child labour, bonded labour, and violence related to economic factors, such as Naxalite violence. These categories result from the economic subjugation and exploitation of the weaker sections of society by dominant classes. The third major category is political – denial and/or abrogation of fundamental rights. These rights are denied by the state and the politically dominant sections for a variety of reasons, such as inadequate resources and a desire to perpetuate privileges inconsistent with the fundamental rights.

All these and related abuses can be remedied to various degrees in different parts of the country by the enactment of laws, by revision of existing laws to make the procedures simpler, by enhancing the punishments, by speeding up investigations and trials, by granting financial relief to the victims, and by creating social awareness of human rights violations.

The colonial mind-set of the past still exists in certain sections of bureaucracy, in law enforcement agencies, and even among the civil society. Loopholes exist in law and procedure. Powerful elements exploit the existing ineffective investigation and undue delay in judicial trials. Political power and wealth sometimes impede the course of investigation and dispensation of justice. Poverty and ignorance on the part of victims very often prevents them from seeking relief. Poor, ignorant, and vulnerable sections of the society need to be empowered to seek and to obtain remedy and justice.

India must accomplish a number of key tasks before major – and sustainable – advancements in human rights protection can be achieved. These include an increase in literacy; reduction of poverty, particularly in rural areas of the country; and revision of laws and investigative procedures concerning human rights violations. Other key tasks are decentralization of political and economic powers from the national government to state governments, from states to districts, and from the latter to the village level. Such advancements will create a more secure and just environment, conducive to economic growth, political stability, and social justice ensuring "All Human Rights for All."

Notes

1. *Vasudaiva Kutumbakam* is a concept that believes all human beings are one family and that we are part of each other.
2. Subhash Kashyap, *Human Rights and Parliament*, New Delhi: Metropolitan Publishers, 1978, p. 19.
3. *Aitaraya Brahmana*, I, 14 cited in Subhash Kashyap, *Human Rights and Parliament*. *Brahmanas* are explanations of the *Vedas*; *Aitaraya Brahmana* is appended to the *Rig Veda*.
4. Ibid., p. 20.
5. M. Sundara Raj, "Awakening of Human Rights," in C.J. Nirmal, ed., *Human Rights in India*, New Delhi: Oxford University Press, 1999, p. 2.
6. Keshav Chandra Sen joined the *Brahmo Samaj* in 1857 and established *Sangat Sabha* in 1859. He focused especially on humanitarian activities and provided help during famines and epidemics.
7. Jyotiba Phule played a significant role in the nineteenth-century fight against untouchability. He fought for the rights of all non-Brahmins, as they were considered untouchable.
8. The census in India takes place every ten years. The latest census was taken in 2001, but until now there has been no official report on this issue. Children in the 5–14 age group constitute roughly 23 per cent of the population. Ram Ahuja, *Social Problems in India*, New Delhi: Rawat Publications, 1997, p. 218.
9. ⟨http://us.cry.org/child_issues/unicef.html⟩.
10. Ram Ahuja, *Social Problems in India*, New Delhi: Rawat Publications, 1997, p. 218. Mirzapur, Firozabad, Moradabad and Aligarh are leading industrial towns in Uttar Pradesh State.
11. AIR 1997 SC 699.

12. "Eve teasing" is a form of harassment, especially of young girls in public places.

13. Lower levels of crime against women correspond to higher levels of literacy – female literacy in particular.

14. N. Jayapalan, *Human Rights*, New Delhi: Atlantic Publishers, 2000, p. 118.

15. These include, for example, the Self Employed Women's Association (SEWA), the Forum against Oppression of Women, Maitri, Sakshi, and the Women's Rights Initiative.

16. Dowry is one major factor that is considered to be a major burden in raising a girl. However, dowry is not a one-time affair that is given at the time of marriage: even after marriage, the girl's family (not only the parents of the girl, but also her brothers) is expected to offer "gifts" on various occasions, especially during religious festivals. In addition, there are certain rituals and practices (although not uniform all over India) in which, during ceremonies conducted for the children, the mother's family side is expected to offer huge sums as gifts.

17. Mahendra K. Premi, "The Missing Girl Child," *Economic and Political Weekly*, 26 May 2001, p. 1880.

18. These (approximate) figures are based on 1995 data.

19. Naxalites are armed groups that follow the teachings of Karl Marx and other Communist thinkers and leaders. They believe in armed conflict with the state and the élite sectors of society to achieve their goals. At present there are a number of Naxalite groups in the states of Bihar, Jharkhand, Andhra Pradesh, and Madhya Pradesh.

20. "Encounter" deaths refer to those deaths that occur in clashes with the police. Whereas the police claim that all such deaths are due to self-defence, in many cases NGOs claim that such deaths are "false encounters," meaning that innocent, unarmed persons were killed unjustifiably by the police. Very often a judicial or administrative inquiry is ordered by the government to establish whether the death is due to a "genuine encounter" justified under the law.

21. Sankar Sen, "Indian Prisons: A Survey," in K.P. Saxena, ed., *Human Rights: Fifty Years of Indian Independence*, New Delhi: Gyan Publishing House, 1998.

22. Ibid., p. 102.

23. AIR 1980 SC 1675.

24. AIR 1981 SC 625.

25. See Sudesh Kumar Sharma, "Realization of Speedy Justice: An Overview of Human Rights in Criminal Proceedings," in B.P. Singh Seghal, ed., *Human Rights in India*, New Delhi: Deep and Deep, 1995, p. 318.

26. AIR 1978, SC 527.

27. AIR 1979, SC 1518.

28. Upendra Baxi quoted in Sudesh Kumar Sharma, "Realisation of Speedy Justice: An Overview of Human Rights in Criminal Proceedings," p. 325.

29. Greenpeace, "India Remains a Favored Dumping Ground for Global Toxic Wastes," 11 September 2000. ⟨http://zope.greenpeace.org/z/gpindia/pressdetails?pressid=9⟩.

30. *Damaodar Rao* v. *Muncipal Corporation, Hyderabad*, AIR 1987, AP 171.

31. *Subhas Kumar* v. *State of Bihar*, AIR 1991, SC 420.

32. Granville Austin, *The Indian Constitution: Cornerstone of a Nation*, Bombay: Oxford University Press, 1991, p. 50.

33. J.N. Pandey, *Constitutional Law of India*, Allahabad: Central Law Agency, 1997, p. 405.

34. AIR 1978 SC 597.

35. (1995) 3 SCC 42.

17

Human rights, the military, and the transition to democracy in Argentina and South Korea

Terence Roehrig

During the 1960s, numerous countries around the world experienced the tragedy of military-led *coups d'état* and the imposition of rule by the armed forces. Over time, these regimes accumulated long lists of human rights abuses, including kidnapping, torture, and execution. Two such cases were Argentina and South Korea: in both instances, these regimes were responsible for serious human rights violations carried out by military and security forces, although with differences in the scope and methods of the violations. The abuses also largely resulted from perceived political and economic threats to these countries – threats emanating from both internal and external sources. Finally, the legacy of human rights abuses complicated the transition to democracy, which both countries began in the 1980s as part of what Samuel Huntington called the "Third Wave" transitions.[1] Specifically, these governments faced two important questions: (1) should members of the previous military regime be prosecuted for past human rights abuses, and (2) can these trials occur without disrupting the transition to democracy? Although in both cases the new civilian governments attempted to prosecute their former military leaders, each case had different results and different consequences for the protection of human rights.

Two important conclusions seem evident from an analysis of these two cases: first, the human rights violations in Argentina and South Korea were based primarily on political divisions, as opposed to more deeply rooted racial, ethnic, and/or religious differences; second, these two cases offer lessons on how states can hold perpetrators of human rights abuses accountable without derailing the transition to democracy. Both countries tried to prosecute their former leaders for human rights violations; however, the results differed and may offer lessons for others involved in democratic transitions.

This chapter is divided into four sections. The first section briefly reviews the history of these two military regimes and their transitions to democracy. The next sections examine the causes of human rights violations in each case and the consequences that these violations had for the transition to democracy. The final section concludes with some lessons that these two cases provide concerning human rights and countries in transition.

Military rule and the transition to democracy

Argentina

Argentina's most recent experience with military rule occurred during two relatively contiguous periods, from 1966 to 1973 and then again from 1976 to 1983. Military intervention has long been a part of Argentine politics. However, on most previous occasions (for example, the coups of 1930 and 1943), the armed forces intervened to replace civilian leaders, bring order to a political system in disarray, and install a more acceptable civilian regime before returning relatively promptly to the barracks. When the military intervened in 1966, they were determined to do it differently: now, the military leadership remained in power and led the country (as, they believed, only they could). In their view, as opposed to previous democratic governments that were ineffective and locked in partisan bickering, the military could impose needed solutions to Argentina's political and economic problems. Furthermore, military leaders believed that they had acquired the necessary expertise through new curricula taught in many of the service academies in Latin America: these included studies in management, politics, economics, and business. The first years of military rule produced some important economic gains, including decreased inflation and industrial growth. However, by 1969, the economy had again begun to tumble, prompting the working class (upset by its exclusion from politics and the economic downturn) to take to the streets.[2]

Opposition to military rule also escalated from leftist guerrilla groups. The junta responded with harsh measures in an effort to defeat the internal threat of communist subversion. The left answered with even greater counter-attacks that included the kidnapping of business executives, attacks on military institutions, and (in May 1970) the abduction and eventual murder of former President and General Pedro Eugenio Aramburu.

By 1973, it was becoming clear that the military junta had failed to achieve a broad consensus for their rule and had difficulty in maintaining public support for its policies. After achieving some initial success, their economic policies began to fail. Increased opposition from labour, and bombings and kidnappings by leftist guerrillas, added to the discontent with military rule. Even the junta was divided over what to do, as evidenced by the several changes made within the junta's leadership during the early 1970s.[3] By 1972, it was evident that the junta was in trouble and the country was falling apart, with little hope for peace and stability in the near future. At this time, the head of the junta, General Alejandro Agustín Lanusse, started a dialogue with Juan Domingo Perón, the one man most thought could bring order to the country and unite the people.

For years, Perón had been a powerful force in Argentine politics, having risen to fame as the Secretary of Labour and champion of the working class. In 1946, he was elected to the presidency with over 60 per cent of the vote. However, in 1955, opponents removed Perón in a coup and he was exiled to Spain. Perón remained outside Argentina until military authorities contacted him for a possible return to help bring peace and stability to the troubled country. Perón returned in 1972 but declined to run for office himself, insisting that Dr Héctor José Cámpora run in his stead, while he remained behind the scenes.[4] It was not long before Cámpora angered military leaders and conservatives by failing to control leftist violence and giving numerous pardons to imprisoned guerrillas. After only a few months, Cámpora was forced to resign and new elections brought Perón himself to power in October 1973.

Unfortunately, Perón's rule was short-lived, as he died of heart problems after less than a year in office.[5] His Vice-President and third wife, Isabel Martínez de Perón, was now thrust into leading a country whose economy was unravelling yet again and was being pressed by ever more aggressive guerrilla actions. Isabel Perón struggled in her new role, having little political experience and often being subject to manipulation by subordinates.[6] As the economy worsened and the political violence escalated, the military intervened in 1976 to remove Isabel Perón from office.

Once more, the armed forces seized control of the government, determined to remain in power; however, this time, the officers believed that they would do a better job in bringing order and prosperity to Argentine society. As Gary Wynia noted, the military was convinced that "Argentines needed discipline not liberty and now they would have it."[7] To that end, military and security forces conducted a massive campaign to eliminate the "terrorist subversives" of the left, especially the Montoneros and ERP (*Ejército Revolucionario del Pueblo* – Revolutionary Army of the People) guerrillas. The junta also terrorized the population at large, in order to deny the guerrillas a base of operation. The campaign would be conducted in secret and, according to Iain Guest, "[t]he generals were determined not to make the same mistakes that Pinochet had made in Chile. They would not round up thousands of people in the football stadium and haul them away to be tortured in front of television cameras."[8] In the course of the conflict (often referred to as the "dirty war," human rights groups estimate that approximately 30,000 people were abducted, tortured, and killed. Close to one-third of those who disappeared (*desaparecidos*) were affiliated in various ways with the guerrilla groups, but many of those who were seized had done little or nothing to warrant their fates.[9] Guest maintains that, "if someone's face appeared on a wanted poster they pulled in his tailor, his barber, anyone remotely connected to the wanted man."[10] Friends, relatives, neighbours, co-workers, and former classmates were often guilty by association. According to a report released after an investigation of the dirty war, "it was enough to appear in somebody's address book to instantly become a target...."[11] Other horrors of the regime included drugging detainees and dropping them, while still alive, into the Atlantic Ocean[12] and selling the children of victims seized or born in captivity to police or military families for adoption. It is estimated that authorities distributed close to 400 children for adoption in this manner.[13]

By the close of 1976, the military had largely defeated the guerrillas and succeeded in winning this "Third World War." General Leopoldo Fortunato Galtieri, a hard-liner in the junta, declared in a *La Prensa* article in 1981: "The First World War was a confrontation between armies, the Second was between nations, and the Third is between ideologies. The United States and Argentina must stand together because of their common concerns and aspirations."[14] Despite the victory, repression continued as military leaders maintained that the danger was ever present and required constant vigilance.

The military's economic policies had shown some initial success but soon became ineffective. Discontent with the junta was growing as inflation increased and protests from business and labour mounted. In an effort to boost sagging support for the regime, the junta launched a daring gambit in April 1982 to seize the Malvinas/Falkland Islands from Britain. However, military leaders gravely miscalculated Prime Minister Margaret Thatcher's determination and a British expeditionary force soundly defeated the Argentine military.

Defeat at the hands of the British was the last straw, and public support for the regime crumbled. The junta soon broke apart and beat a hasty retreat back to the barracks. In 1983, the country held elections and, to the surprise of many, the people chose Radical Party candidate Raúl Alfonsín as president and leader for the transition to democracy. Following the Malvinas War there was deep contempt for the military: according to David Pion-Berlin, "a profound gulf separated the armed forces from society. Military incompetence, self-aggrandizement, and repression in office contributed to an unprecedented repudiation of the profession at the hands of civil society. The military found itself discredited by and ostracized from the larger Argentine community to a degree not previously experienced."[15] Nevertheless, the military remained adamant that it had done nothing wrong. During the election campaign, Alfonsín had pledged to prosecute the armed forces for the past and, once in office, he began a limited effort to go after high-level officers that had actually been part of the junta. He hoped that, by steering this more moderate course between no trials and extensive prosecutions deep into the ranks, some measure of the military regime could be held accountable without provoking a backlash that would disrupt the transition to democracy. In addition, Alfonsín simultaneously undertook several efforts to reassert civilian control of the military, including restructuring the Ministry of Defence, drastically cutting the military budget, and confining the armed forces to an external security mission – thus excluding them from involvement in domestic surveillance. In the end, Alfonsín was unable to control the judicial proceedings and avoid the military backlash he feared.

Alfonsín resigned in 1989, five months before his term expired – not because of the trial but, rather, because of the continuing economic malaise. In early elections in 1989, Carlos Saúl Menem won the presidency and chose a different route from his predecessor. Although continuing to push the democratic transition forward, Menem moved to end the trials. In the election, he received a significant share of the votes of military personnel and, according to Wynia, "Menem neither feared nor loathed the armed forces as Alfonsín did. He knew that he could not allow officers to claim any more authority than Alfonsín had allowed them, but he also believed that direct assaults on the military had to stop."[16] Between October 1989 and December 1990, Menem issued pardons for all those who had been convicted or were still under indictment. The pardons were very controversial and angered many, but Menem argued that they were necessary to restore the military's faith in constitutional government.[17] In 2001, lower courts ruled that earlier measures enacted to protect the military were unconstitutional. The matter is awaiting a final ruling from Argentina's Supreme Court. If the Supreme Court affirms the lower court rulings, another round of prosecutions may follow.

South Korea

The military's involvement in South Korean politics has been relatively recent compared with that of Argentina, but Korea has had a long history of authoritarian rule. From 1392 to 1910, Korea was governed by a series of monarchs where power was centralized in Seoul and administered by a strong bureaucracy. From 1910 to 1945, Korea was subjected to a harsh occupation under the Japanese empire until its liberation after World War II. Neither dynastic rule nor Japanese occupation did much to prepare Korea for a democratic system of government.

Liberation in 1945 was bitter-sweet for Koreans. Although they were freed from imperialism, US and Soviet authorities divided the peninsula at the 38th parallel to take the Japanese surrender. The subsequent Cold War made the reunification of North and South Korea extremely difficult. After a brief period of US occupation that ended in 1948, South Korea held elections and began a tumultuous period of supposedly democratic civilian rule under its first President, Syngman Rhee. However, Rhee ruled much more like a monarch of old than a democratically elected president.[18]

In 1960, Rhee was driven from power by massive demonstrations following a particularly fraudulent election. After a short-lived attempt at democracy, Major General Park Chung Hee led a coup in 1961 to bring order to an increasingly chaotic political situation. In two years, Park resigned his commission and won a series of elections (although by small margins) to remain in power until 1979. Park ruled most of the time as a civilian, but there was little doubt that the military was the power behind his authority. After his election in 1963, and until 1971, the authoritarian character of Park's rule subsided to a certain extent: opposition parties and the press operated with little hindrance and, according to Bruce Cumings, it was a "fairly stable, if often raucous, form of limited pluralism...."[19] However, following the 1971 election, the regime became exceedingly authoritarian. In October 1972, Park dissolved the National Assembly, declared martial law, banned political parties, and shut down all colleges and universities. The following month, Park rammed through a new constitution that granted him sweeping power and essentially made him President for life.

Several reasons lay behind Park's shift to a harsher version of authoritarian rule. First, the opposition was growing in strength under the leadership of such men as Kim Dae Jung and Kim Young Sam, both of whom would later become presidents.[20] Park was becoming less tolerant of the opposition and wanted more power to shape political outcomes. Second, Park intended to shift South Korean economic policy in new directions and believed that he needed the increased political power to accomplish his goals. Finally, in the wake of the Viet Nam War and a US commitment that seemed to be waning, Park believed that firm rule was necessary to unify and strengthen South Korea for the possible decrease in American support that seemed on the horizon.[21]

During his tenure, Park instituted economic policies that surpassed the dismal performance of the Rhee era. However, Park ruled with an iron fist: he showed little tolerance for the opposition, and extensive human rights abuses occurred owing to his efforts to suppress political opponents. Thousands were arrested for criticizing the government or on suspicion of being communists, an accusation that could be used against nearly any political opponent. Repression, especially during the latter years of Park's rule, included "arbitrary arrests, prolonged detentions, forced confessions under torture, and sham trials followed by imprisonment or execution...."[22] Emergency Measure Number 9 even made it a criminal offence to criticize the President. Usually, the repression was carried out by the Korean Central Intelligence Agency (KCIA), which was given wide latitude in ferreting out opponents of Park's rule.

In 1979, the Park era came to an abrupt end: in a heated argument over the proper response to increasing political unrest, the head of the KCIA shot and killed Park at a dinner meeting. Many thought that South Korea might at last begin a transition to democracy; yet, once again, after a brief period of democratic rule, Major General Chun Doo Hwan orchestrated a "multistage coup" in 1979–1980 that returned the military to power.[23] As Park had done, Chun resigned his commission and won a series of elections under a system that gave his ruling party decisive advantages. Chun continued the Park legacy of economic growth accompanied by suppression of the opposition and human rights abuses. Particularly galling to South Koreans was an event that occurred in May 1980 in the city of Kwangju: Chun sent in crack troops from the South Korean army to crush demonstrations that had been building in response to his seizure of power and years of economic neglect by the central government. Although the government placed the number killed at 200, other groups have maintained that the number was closer to 2,000. The government announced that they had thwarted a communist plot; however, for South Koreans, Kwangju left a bitter memory. The violence at Kwangju made it nearly impossible for Chun to establish any legitimacy for his rule.

Throughout his term (which was to end in 1988), Chun maintained that he would step down and comply with the constitutional restriction of one seven-year term. However, under the electoral system of that time – an indirect electoral college process that heavily favoured the ruling party – it was virtually assured that whoever ran under Chun's government party label would become the next president. By 1986, pressure to reform the political system (especially to institute a direct presidential election) was mounting. When talks with the opposition stalled, Chun abruptly announced that he was suspending further discussions until a later date. Furthermore, he nominated Roh Tae Woo (a former General and Korean Military Academy classmate who was involved in the coup and the Kwangju massacre) to be his successor as the next ruling-party candidate. Demonstrations against the government skyrocketed, as it appeared that South Korea would once more have a General leading the country. In the face of this determined opposition and Roh's surprise announcement in June 1987 of an Eight-Point Plan that supported many of the opposition's demands, Chun relented and allowed the reform process to go forward. In December 1987, South Korea held a direct, popular election for the presidency to begin its transition to democracy.

Why did Chun decide that he was now willing to compromise with the opposition? Several reasons seemed to be at play. First, South Korea had won the right to host the 1988 Olympic Games and even Chun did not want to jeopardize this chance to show off the economic progress that the country had made in the past 20 years. Given the level of political violence, there was even a possibility that the Games would be cancelled or moved to an alternative site. Second, the United States placed tremendous pressure on Chun to reach a compromise with the opposition, rather than to use force to crush it. Third, public support for reform was now more broad based and included other segments of South Korean society, especially the growing middle class that had mushroomed during the country's economic take-off. Finally, there is some speculation that Chun and Roh gambled on the possibility that the two chief opposition leaders – Kim Young Sam and Kim Dae Jung – would have difficulty in uniting their camps to form a solid front against Roh Tae Woo, the Government Party candidate.

The gambit worked, as neither Kim would step aside to let the other unite the opposition: instead, they split the opposition vote, allowing Roh to win the presidency.[24] Thus, although South Korea began its transition to democracy, it was an uncertain beginning that left many South Koreans disillusioned with politics.

Once again, South Korea would have a president with ties to the military. Was Roh Tae Woo eager to proceed with a true transition to democracy? Would he be willing to hold the previous regime accountable for human rights abuses? Roh did lead South Korea forward in its transition to democracy, supporting greater freedom for the press, more tolerance of opposition, and a vastly improved respect for human rights. He also instituted several measures to return the military to civilian control by removing generals appointed for political purposes and replacing them with officers committed to staying out of politics. He also prohibited the Agency for National Security Planning, the former KCIA, from domestic surveillance activities. Furthermore, Roh announced that the ruling party's next presidential nominee would not be a military man. As Roh noted, "for the sake of the nation and its political development, I should be the last president to come from the army."[25] However, some vestiges of the old regime remained, especially the National Security Law[26] and the government's rough treatment of labour.

Despite tremendous pressure from the opposition, Roh and Chun were able to escape prosecution. After all, Roh had as much incentive as Chun to avoid any judicial action, given his own involvement in the coup and the Kwangju massacre. Thus, this task would be left to the next President, Kim Young Sam, who assumed the office after the 1992 election.

President Kim continued South Korea's transition but was also uninterested in pursuing an accounting of past abuses, preferring to leave these events up to "the judgement of history." As Kim noted, "we should not forget the atrocities but let's forgive them to achieve national reconciliation."[27] In large part, this was due to a surprising coalition formed by his opposition party and Roh's ruling party two years prior to the 1992 election. The merger gave Kim the inside track on the presidency; however, this meant that, if elected, he would have been going after members of his own party.

However, President Kim also added fuel to prosecution efforts by describing the Kwangju incident as a "pro-democracy movement," not a rebellion, as Chun had maintained. He also said that the 12 December incident was "a development tantamount to a *coup d'état* in which lower ranking officers disobeyed the orders of superior officers."[28] His comments encouraged numerous individuals to initiate lawsuits in 1993 and 1994 against Chun and Roh. However, for a variety of reasons, the Seoul prosecutor's office chose not to indict them, possibly taking their cue from President Kim's preference to let the matter rest. Ultimately, an unexpected revelation that Chun and Roh had accumulated huge campaign slush funds re-energized efforts to prosecute them. Public pressure rose to the point where the process could not be stopped. Owing to this ground swell, Kim Young Sam reluctantly supported the prosecution of Chun and Roh.

Causes

In both Argentina and South Korea, military leaders seized the reins of government because they believed that there were serious threats to the survival of the nation. In turn, the human rights abuses that followed flowed largely from efforts to quell the threats and quash opposition to their rule. These threats were political and economic in nature. The absence of deep-seated racial, ethnic, or religious divides within Argentina and South Korea meant that the transition to democracy was likely to have one less complication: societies that are severely fractured along racial, ethnic, and/or religious lines have greater problems with power sharing and establishing the necessary political institutions for an effective democracy. Let us now consider each case.

Argentina

When the military intervened in 1966 and again in 1976, they felt that they were reacting to several threats that endangered the country. First, despite efforts by the civilian government, the economy struggled during the 1960s: inflation rates rose, agricultural production declined, and investor confidence waned. Numerous strikes and factory take-overs organized by the General Confederation of Labour (*La Confederación General del Trabajo*; CGT) accompanied these woes, leading to a perception that the government was in chaos and the country was spinning out of control. In the military's view, something had to be done to save Argentina from the impending economic collapse.

In addition to the fears of economic breakdown, military leaders saw communist subversion as a second threat that would prey upon the country's rapidly deteriorating economy. During much of the 1960s, guerrilla groups supporting Marxist ideologies utilized unconventional violence, including kidnapping and murder, to achieve their goal of bringing societal change. These groups were interspersed within the population, making their detection by the government unlikely. In the junta's view, these subversive elements were dangerous enemies bent on destroying the state and, therefore, harsh measures were required to eliminate the threats. As José Zalaquett noted, military leaders saw "Marxist penetration and insurgency as an all-pervading presence of a new type of enemy fighting a new type of war," and "since the war on Marxism is an insidious one, unorthodox methods are called for, including torture and extermination of irredeemable political activists."[29] According to General Jorge Rafael Videla, army commander-in-chief and leader of the junta in 1976, "we will combat, without respite, subversive delinquency in all of its forms until its total annihilation."[30] Subsequently, the government cracked down hard on these guerrilla groups, arresting suspected leaders, many of whom were tortured and executed.

When the military returned to power in 1976 after a three-year respite, they were even more determined to end the threat of "left-wing subversives." According to General Videla, "[a]ll those persons necessary will die in order to achieve the security of the country."[31] As junta leaders saw it, Argentina was being attacked from within by a cancerous disease that, if left unchecked, would eat away at a society weakened by an inept democratic system of government. Democracy had tried and failed; now it was time for the military to bring order and structure to society, a task at which they excelled. The remedy was radical surgery to remove the infected parts, since it was unlikely that subversives could be reformed. Also, given the high stakes for the country, any methods were acceptable. According to Admiral Cesar Guzetti, the first Foreign Minister of the junta in 1976, "subversion or terrorism of the right – there is no such thing. The social body of the country is contaminated with a disease that corrodes its entrails and forms antibodies. These antibodies cannot be considered in the same way that one considers the microbe."[32]

Can these actions taken against the left be considered as human rights violations? In 1980, General Leopoldo Galtieri stated emphatically:

... in this country there was not, and could not have been any violation of human rights. There was a war, an absurd war, unleashed by a treacherous and criminal barbarism, a war which in spite of the fact that it was directed not only against the people but also against a way of life which is supported by a large number of nations of the world, had to be confronted and resolved by Argentines alone.[33]

The military argued vehemently that their actions were part of a war to save the country. Rather than be accused of human rights abuses, they instead should be congratulated for performing their patriotic duty in rescuing the country from the scourge of communism. As the military saw it, the disappeared (*desaparecidos*) were not the victims; instead, they were the perpetrators and the military was protecting Argentine society from their sickness.

Military leaders also saw the threat in terms of the National Security Doctrine (NSD), an ideology of sorts developed in France and the United States and taught at the time throughout many service academies in Latin America. According to NSD, the most pressing threats to national security were not external but, rather, internal threats from subversive elements, especially the spread of communism. These threats were ongoing and difficult to detect, requiring constant vigilance and a vigorous response with whatever means were necessary to ensure the safety of the nation.[34] Yet, despite the fact that the military succeeded in eliminating the threat of these "subversive elements" during their first year in power in 1976, the repression and horror continued, victimizing many who had little or no connection with the left. As long as the "threat" remained a possibility, military authorities believed that they were justified in continuing to rule and impose their harsh measures.

South Korea

In South Korea, human rights abuses also flowed from the military's perception of serious threats to the country. However, whereas the threat in Argentina was primarily an internal one, for South Korea the threat had a much larger external component – namely, the danger of a grave security threat from a hostile North Korea. In the face of growing political unrest and economic turmoil, military officers stepped into power, determined to impose order and bring economic development to the country, while showing little tolerance for opposition to their political rule or economic plans.

Early in the morning on 16 May 1961, the military seized power from the civilian government in Seoul. One year earlier, South Korea had undergone a major political shake-up with the ousting of Syngman Rhee, President of South Korea since its inception in 1948. A fledgling democracy followed Rhee's tenure, but the coup led by a group of colonels and lieutenant-colonels interrupted this brief period of democratic rule. The junior officers had several reasons for intervening. First, the democratic political system had great difficulty in functioning. The ruling Democratic Party held a solid majority in the National Assembly but was badly fractured, making it difficult to develop and execute policy.[35] As a result, serious problems (especially a stagnant economy debilitated by high inflation rates) were left unattended. The political climate was so polarized that accomplishing anything was a difficult task and, increasingly, this government appeared feeble and ineffective.[36]

Second, students, who had been an important force in ousting Rhee, continued large-scale demonstrations after his departure. The students felt so energized by their power that they considered themselves to be the "fourth" branch of government.[37] On several occasions, students marched into the National Assembly to lecture politicians on the proper course of action in legislative matters. Even worse, these student groups called for meetings with fellow students in the North and pushed for peaceful reunification of the two Koreas.[38] North Korea exploited these developments by stepping up propaganda and infiltration activity.

Finally, the South Korean economy continued to struggle, showing few signs of growth and suffering from spiralling inflation. Rhee had little knowledge of (and almost no interest in) managing economic affairs: during his 12 years of rule, Rhee never implemented a comprehensive economic plan.[39] Corruption was rampant and, despite large doses of US economic aid, the South Korean economy made little progress. Following Rhee's rule, the administration under Chang Myon attempted to implement a major economic initiative, but the plan did not have sufficient time to work. The lack of economic development threatened not only the livelihood of the people but also the South's ability to defend itself. As military leaders saw it, economic growth had to occur soon to ensure that the country had sufficient resources to maintain a robust defence capability in its struggle with the North.

For Park Chung Hee and other military leaders, these were dangerous threats to the regime, and the civilian government seemed incapable of addressing them. It was now their turn to bring order to the political system and to implement an effective plan for economic development. According to Park, the country would now "have to resort to undemocratic and extraordinary measures in order to improve the living conditions of the masses ... one cannot deny that people are more frightened of poverty and hunger than totalitarianism...."[40] A vigorous economy and stable political order would end the threat of internal political and economic disintegration and also build the country's strength to confront the external threat from the North.

As Park's rule progressed, he tolerated little opposition to his economic plans or political leadership. Thousands were arrested for criticizing the government or on suspicion of being communists. As noted earlier, his regime became particularly harsh in the later years of his rule. To implement his draconian measures, Park utilized the KCIA. Many were arrested, detained for long periods of time, tortured, and, after hasty trials, imprisoned or executed.[41]

After Park's assassination in 1979, Chun Doo Hwan continued the legacy of authoritarian rule. His violent crackdown at Kwangju, followed by further repressive rule, placed a cloud over the legitimacy of Chun's regime. Yet, as Chun and others maintained, given the threat from the North, South Korea could not afford democracy: they believed that South Korea had to be united politically and to grow economically in order to confront the communist threat; thus, the internal and external threats were linked. The danger of political unrest and economic chaos had a direct bearing on South Korea's ability to maintain the necessary defence posture to deter Pyongyang.

Authoritarianism and the consequent human rights abuses in South Korea and other Asian societies have some roots in Confucianism. As a political philosophy and code of social order, Confucianism stresses the importance of hierarchy and obedience to those above on the social and political ladder: good citizens must be loyal and obedient to the central authority, accepting of its dictates for the greater good of the entire country; in return, leaders are expected to rule justly and provide for their people. When things go wrong, leaders lose the "mandate of heaven" and subjects have the right to overthrow those who are apparently acting unjustly. Both Park and Chun utilized Confucianism to reinforce their authority, emphasizing loyalty and obedience to the state and to justify measures taken to halt opposition to their rule. In this manner, they grounded their authoritarianism in traditional values and an ideology familiar to all in an effort to legitimize their rule. During Park's tenure, phenomenal levels of economic growth helped to produce the success that maintained the mandate for his rule. However, even continued prosperity under Chun could not overcome the lack of legitimacy created by the Kwangju massacre and a growing desire for greater political participation. Later, when Chun and Roh were accused of corruption in addition to the charges of mutiny stemming from the coup and the events at Kwangju, it would become clear that the citizens of South Korea took seriously the second portion of the mandate – namely, that leaders must rule justly. South Korea demonstrates that democratization and human rights can fit with the traditional values of Confucianism.

In the cases of both Argentina and South Korea, threat perceptions played an important role as the chief cause for the military to seize power and subvert human rights. The militaries in both countries believed that the survival of the state was at stake. In Argentina, "reducing the threats" meant that the subversives of the left were virtually wiped out in the "dirty war," although the economic problems remained. In South Korea, authoritarian rule and economic growth created one of the economic powerhouses of East Asia. As the threats lessened, the military felt more assured that they could return to the barracks and allow the democratic transition to begin.

Also important in explaining the movement to democratic rule and greater respect for human rights is the role played by civil society and the pressure it brought to bear on the respective regimes. In Argentina, waning support for the junta's economic policies followed by the Malvinas debacle saw the military beat a hasty retreat in the face of growing public criticism. Numerous segments of Argentine society initially supported the military coup for many of the same reasons espoused by the military – democracy had failed to bring peace, order, and prosperity. Public condemnation, coupled with the military's realization that the forces of communism had been defeated, made it easier for them to relinquish power. In South Korea's case, the prosperity generated under the military rule eliminated one of the threats to South Korea but created seeds for its own demise – a strong, vibrant, middle class that demanded a share of political power to accompany its growing economic clout.[42] In both cases, a growing weariness with authoritarian rule and the suppression of human rights created pressure for a return to civilian government.

Consequences

One of the most interesting consequences of human rights abuses in these two cases is the dilemma of how to deal with the perpetrators of the abuses during the transition to democracy.[43] This raises a central question: can military regimes that have horrendous human rights records be held accountable for the past without provoking their return to power and disrupting the transition to democracy?[44] This has been an important issue for other regimes making the transition and for the cause of human rights in general. Most of the time, the military negotiated a pact before leaving, to protect themselves from prosecution: on many occasions, the pact was honoured; however, sometimes, civilian authorities revoked the agreement once the military had stepped down. Nevertheless, new civilian governments rarely tried to hold the military accountable for past human rights abuses. The two cases in this chapter are exceptions to this pattern: both Argentina and South Korea attempted to prosecute perpetrators of human rights abuses, with different results.

Argentina

Although President Alfonsín initially intended to conduct limited and carefully controlled prosecutions of only the top-ranking junta officials responsible for human rights violations, the process soon spiralled out of his control:[45] eventually, approximately 3,000 cases were pending in Argentine courts. This appeared to many in the military as a process without end.[46]

For the armed forces, these trials were a travesty. The "dirty war" had been a struggle crucial to the national security of Argentina. Winning that war, despite the brutal tactics, was a necessary and significant achievement. General Roberto Eduardo Viola remarked in 1981: "[A] victorious army is not investigated. If the Reich's troops had won the last world war the tribunal would have been held not in Nuremberg but in Virginia."[47] To be prosecuted for defending the nation was an absurd accusation, in the minds of many soldiers. As Deborah Norden argues, the trials:

... reflected an official condemnation of the military institution, and condemnation on the one front where the armed forces believed they had succeeded. Rather than honoring the military heroes for defending the nation from a dangerous enemy, the trials portrayed them as criminals and the "enemy" as innocent victims.[48]

As a result, it was difficult for the military to remain on the sidelines while their institution was under attack for fulfilling their most noble assignment – safeguarding the nation. The military viewed the prosecutions as persecutions. Although the government did make efforts to condemn the leftist guerrillas for their share of the political violence, the armed forces were not convinced: the trials were a threat to the military as an institution and had to be stopped.[49]

The trials themselves represented an important dimension of the transition to democracy – namely, efforts to reassert civilian control of the military. In addition to the trials, President Alfonsín placed civilians in charge of the Ministry of Defence and reduced the power of the service chiefs.[50] The government also passed two laws that restricted the military's involvement in domestic politics: first, the penalty for leading a coup was increased from 15 to 25 years; second, military intelligence agencies were prohibited from any internal defence missions and confined solely to operations against external enemies.[51] In addition to passing laws, the Argentine Government implemented drastic cuts in the military budget: in 1979, three years into the junta, military expenditures stood at $2.8 billion (6.2 per cent of GDP); by 1986, when the 3,000 cases were pending, military expenditures had shrunk to $1.15 billion (1.7 per cent of GDP).[52]

With the likelihood of ever-expanding prosecutions – which appeared, to military personnel, to be part of a broader government policy to punish, and possibly destroy, the military – something had to be done. To put an end to the trials, in April 1987, soldiers [named *carapintadas* (painted faces) for the battlefield make-up worn on their faces] seized control of an army base near Buenos Aires. President Alfonsín travelled to the base and obtained the rebels' surrender. In return (although this was not made public) Alfonsín agreed to push a law that exempted from prosecution any one below the rank of colonel. The law, *Obendencia Debida* [Due Obedience], returned the trials to Alfonsín's original intention of limiting the prosecutions to only the top-ranking officers.[53] Three more insurrections followed in January 1988, December 1988, and December 1990. The last two rebellions were more an attempt to carve out a niche for themselves in Argentine politics than an action to end the trials; however, few in the military supported these efforts, and the last insurrection was crushed decisively by loyalist troops.[54]

Alfonsín had embarked on a process that he hoped would lead to the prosecution of several top-level junta members, while also keeping the military on the sideline. In the end, he failed: despite his efforts, Alfonsín eventually lost control of the process and led to a situation that threatened not only the fate of individual officers but also that of the military as an institution. For many in the armed forces, this was unacceptable and required intervention to bring the trials to a halt. The public was outraged by the military's actions and massive demonstrations followed. Nevertheless, the military had demonstrated unmistakably that there were limits to what they would tolerate during the transition, and the government was unable to stop them from flexing their muscles. Although some of the highest-ranking officers were convicted, eventually they all received pardons after serving only partial sentences. Thus, the transition to democracy did not include holding the military accountable, and many Argentines still lament the lack of punishment for the atrocities of the past.

South Korea

South Korea also prosecuted former members of its military government, but with different results. In this case, the military stayed on the sidelines and showed little interest in disturbing the judicial proceedings and the transition to democracy. The differences here between South Korea and Argentina provide some guidance about how prosecutions can go forward without provoking military intervention.

In November 1995, South Korean authorities arrested former president Roh Tae Woo on charges of accumulating a massive slush fund from numerous businesses in return for government favours. Chun Doo Hwan was also indicted for similar offences. Later, the charges grew to include mutiny for the 1979–1980 coup and treason stemming from the Kwangju massacre. Fourteen other officers and nine business leaders were added to the list of defendants. When the dust settled, seven months later, Chun and Roh were convicted: as the ringleader, Chun was given a death sentence, while Roh received a sentence of 22.5 years in prison;[55] the sentences were later reduced on appeal to life in prison and 17 years, respectively. In addition, 13 of the 14 officers were found guilty, receiving sentences ranging from 4 to 10 years.

Throughout the trials, many expected President Kim Young Sam to pardon Chun and Roh prior to leaving office. On 18 December 1997, two days after South Koreans had elected Kim Dae Jung – Opposition Party candidate and hated enemy of the former military regime – to be their next president, the two Kims agreed to the pardons. Kim Dae Jung had pledged during his campaign not to seek revenge against these two leaders, who had sought his execution. The two Kims presented the pardons as a gesture of reconciliation to old enemies and a call for unity in the midst of the 1997 economic crisis. However, Chun and Roh were still responsible for $270 million and $350 million, respectively, in fines as punishment for slush fund convictions.[56] Many South Koreans were unhappy with the pardons, but most grudgingly accepted the outcome.

In contrast to the Argentine military, the South Korean armed forces stayed on the sidelines while 16 of their highest-ranking officers were prosecuted. There are several reasons for this course of action. First, in South Korea, the trials were not perceived by the military as an attack on the institution and were limited in scope (as government officials stated from the outset) to the top leaders, namely Chun, Roh, and others. Numerous actions were taken by authorities to establish civilian control of the military, including purging officers, restricting intelligence agencies from domestic surveillance, and banning the formation of private military clubs; nevertheless, the armed forces as a whole did not see these trials as a vendetta against the military as an institution. Second, the new civilian government did not punish the military with drastic cuts in defence spending; instead, throughout the transition and trials, the South Korean government maintained a large military budget that rose from $4.4 billion in 1986 to $15.1 billion in 1996 (a 243 per cent increase);[57] these levels of defence spending were necessary because of the serious security threat that remained to the north. In addition, the continuing threat from Pyongyang helped to keep the military out of domestic politics and occupied with external missions.

Second, South Korean leaders did not prosecute the military early in their transition to democracy. To be sure, this was not intentional: the first post-authoritarian president in South Korea was Roh Tae Woo; he certainly had no desire to initiate prosecutions, since he was high on the list of those to be tried! Furthermore, the next President, Kim Young Sam, had ties to the ruling party of Chun and Roh and had little intention of pushing the prosecutions forward. Once in office, President Kim noted that "... the matter should be left to history. I think our unfortunate past history should not be a road block to the progress of our nation."[58] It was significant that South Korea worked first to bring the military under civilian control before mounting the prosecutions. By following this route, the civilian government had more time to reassert and to institutionalize its hold on the armed forces before testing that control with trials, and thereby provoking a backlash that could derail the transition to democracy.

Finally, the economic successes of the authoritarian period created a relative political consensus on continuing its economic policies. This, in turn, ensured the country's military security. Thus, the South Korean military could feel secure that threats to the nation would not re-emerge if they allowed thorough civilian control over the military to be restored.

Conclusions

Two conclusions seem evident from an examination of these two cases. First, the human rights violations in Argentina and South Korea were primarily a reaction to perceived political and economic threats, not to divisions based on race, ethnicity, or religion. Their legacy of human rights abuses was based primarily on political and economic threats that were less deeply rooted or broad-based. Although there was a strong desire to hold the regime and its leaders accountable, there was less residual animosity between larger segments of society to complicate the transition to democracy. The absence of ethnic divisions should make it easier to build the consensus, unity, and institutions necessary for a functioning democracy. Concerns for power sharing between various groups were not a serious issue in Argentina and South Korea. Also, with the dissipation of the perceived security threats, the military (although still protective of its institutional interests) was more willing to leave the reins of government in the hands of civilians. Trials, or other efforts to deal with the past – such as truth commissions or investigations – complicate any transition to democracy. However, if the proceedings are not made worse by issues of race, ethnicity, or religion, the trials may not be problematic for the transition – as long as they do not become a vendetta against the military as a whole and are not perceived by the military as facilitating the re-emergence of threats to the nation.

The human rights abuses were generated largely by the militaries' perception of what needed to be done to save their countries from disaster. With the military gone and democracy firmly in place, even apparently given Argentina's continued economic woes, respect for human rights has returned. In Argentina and South Korea, human rights and democratization go hand in hand: democracy has led to more respect for human rights, and vice versa. Although some vestiges of the authoritarian past remain, both societies enjoy high degrees of governing by the rule of law, greater press freedom, and tolerance of political opposition. In short, both Argentina and South Korea have been relative success stories for human rights and societies in transition.

The second conclusion is alluded to in *The Third Wave*, where Samuel Huntington asks whether it is better to "prosecute and punish" or "forgive and forget."[59] During the transition, there is often great pressure to hold the offenders in the previous military regime accountable for human rights abuses. As one newspaper reporter noted after covering the trial in Argentina, "[o]ne has to ask oneself how it is possible to live in this country with people who murdered, people who tortured and still walk among us; with fathers who will grow old without their sons, and sons who will have to grow up without their fathers."[60] Holding members of the military, or any authoritarian regime, accountable for human rights abuses is a delicate but crucial undertaking. Democracies are grounded in the rule of law and have an obligation to uphold the law. In addition, many of the human rights abuses of these regimes are violations not only of domestic law but also of numerous international legal agreements. Prosecutions help to demonstrate and build the values and rule of law on which the new democracy is founded. According to Juan E. Méndez, imposing justice "highlights the fundamental character of the new order to be established, an order based on the rule of law and on respect for the dignity and worth of each human person."[61] To let perpetrators go with no consequence is to encourage further egregious behaviour so "that impunity will only encourage new abuses in the new or distant future."[62] Determined judicial proceedings help not only to deter future human rights abuses but also to encourage the military to remain in the barracks all together. To embark on some path to accountability helps to establish respect for the rule of law and human rights while dissuading others from similar violations in the future.

But trials risk provoking the wrath of the military and derailing the transition to democracy. How to accomplish both? There is no simple answer to this dilemma. These two cases point to the possibility that the perpetrators can be held accountable; however, this must be done carefully and, perhaps, in a more limited manner that does not provoke the military. First, efforts to rein in the military need to be taken before the trials begin, allowing civilians the time to establish a firm grip on the armed forces. Second, civilian leaders need to be careful that their actions do not threaten the military as an institution. The scope of prosecutions may need to be more limited than many would like, and other measures – drastic budget cuts, purges, restrictions on military prerogatives – may need to be less severe, or at least not implemented in rapid succession. Third, prosecutions are unlikely to be successful if large proportions of the military believe that these will open the way for fresh threats to the nation. By taking account of these issues, human rights standards can be upheld to some degree without provoking the armed forces to step back into power.

Notes

1. Huntington's study of democratic transitions identified three waves of democratization, with the first two waves occurring from 1828 to 1926 and from 1943 to 1962. The "Third Wave" began in 1974 with Portugal and Greece and concluded in the early 1990s with Paraguay, South Africa, and the Former Soviet States. Samuel P. Huntington, *The Third Wave*, Norman: University of Oklahoma Press, 1991, pp. 13–26.

2. Deborah L. Norden, *Military Rebellion in Argentina: Between Coups and Consolidation*, Lincoln: University of Nebraska Press, 1996, p. 40.
3. Edward C. Epstein, "Democracy in Argentina," in Edward C. Epstein, ed., *The New Argentine Democracy*, Westport: Praeger, 1992, p. 11, and Norden, *Military Rebellion in Argentina*, p. 43.
4. Epstein, "Democracy in Argentina," p. 11.
5. Joseph Page, *Perón: A Biography*, New York: Random House, 1983, pp. 492–493.
6. Norden, *Military Rebellion in Argentina*, p. 46, and Gary Wynia, *Argentina: Illusions and Realities*, 2nd edn, New York: Holmes and Meier, 1992, p. 62.
7. Wynia, *Argentina: Illusions and Realities*, 2nd edn, p. 86.
8. Iain Guest, *Behind the Disappearances: Argentina's Dirty War Against Human Rights and the United Nations*, Philadelphia: University of Pennsylvania Press, 1990, p. 22.
9. Thomas E. Skidmore and Peter H. Smith, *Modern Latin America*, 3rd edn, New York: Oxford University Press, 1992, p. 103.
10. Guest, *Behind the Disappearances*, p. 30.
11. *Nunca Más: The Report of the Argentine National Commission of the Disappeared*, New York: Farrar, Straus and Giroux, 1986, pp. 60–61.
12. Calvin Sims, "Argentine Tells of Dumping 'Dirty War' Captives Into Sea," *New York Times*, March 13, 1995; and "For the First Time, Argentine Army Admits 'Dirty War' Killings," *New York Times*, 26 April 1995.
13. *Nunca Más*, pp. 286–305.
14. Ibid., p. 443.
15. David Pion-Berlin, *Through Corridors of Power: Institutions and Civil–Military Relations in Argentina*, University Park: Pennsylvania State University, 1997, p. 59.
16. Wynia, *Argentina: Illusions and Realities*, 2nd edn, pp. 213–214.
17. General Jorge Videla, one of the convicted junta members, was unrepentant to the end, maintaining he would not accept a presidential pardon since he had done nothing wrong. Ibid., pp. 214–215.
18. John Kie-chiang Oh, *Korean Politics*, Ithaca: Cornell University Press, 1999, p. 40.
19. Bruce Cumings, *Korea's Place in the Sun*, New York: W.W. Norton, 1997, p. 356.
20. Kim Young Sam served as South Korea's President from 1993 to 1998. Kim Dae Jung became President in 1998, with a term ending in 2003.
21. Carter J. Eckert, Ki-baik Lee, Young Ick Lew, Michael Robinson, and Edward W. Wagner, *Korea Old and New: A History*, Cambridge: Harvard University Press, 1990, pp. 363–365.
22. Ibid., p. 369.
23. The coup began in December 1979 with a mutiny within the army, and eventually led to his consolidation of power in August 1980. See Kim Sunhyuk, "State and Civil Society in South Korea's Democratic Consolidation," *Asian Survey*, Vol. XXXVII, No. 12, December 1997, p. 1138.
24. The final results of the 1987 election gave opposition candidates Kim Young Sam and Kim Dae Jung 28 and 27 per cent, respectively, of the vote count, for a total of 55 per cent. Anything close to this combined total would have easily have topped Roh Tae Woo's 37 per cent.
25. Shim Jae Hoon, "No to Roh dynasty," *Far Eastern Economic Review*, 25 April 1991, p. 16; and "Kith and Kim," *Far Eastern Economic Review*, 28 December 1989, p. 8.
26. The National Security Law (NSL), first passed in 1948, banned communism and any activity that showed sympathy or support for the North. The law was used to arrest and jail thousands of political opponents.
27. "Kim Vows to Restore Honor of Kwangju Citizens," *Korea Newsreview*, 22 May 1993, p. 4.

28. Shim Jae Hoon, "Bitter Harvest," *Far Eastern Economic Review*, 27 May 1993, p. 15.
29. José Zalaquett, "From Dictatorship to Democracy," *The New Republic*, Vol. 193, December 1985, pp. 18–19.
30. As quoted in David Pion-Berlin and George A. Lopez, "Of Victims and Executioners: Argentine State Terror, 1975–1979," *International Studies Quarterly*, 35, 1991, p. 71.
31. As quoted in J. Patrice McSherry, *Incomplete Transition: Military Power and Democracy in Argentina*, New York: St. Martin's Press, 1997, p. 78.
32. *Buenos Aires Herald*, 10 October 1976, as quoted in McSherry, *Incomplete Transition*, p. 93.
33. Speech given by General Leopoldo Galtieri, contained in Brian Loveman and Thomas M. Davies, eds, *The Politics of Antipolitics*, 2nd edn, Lincoln: University of Nebraska Press, 1989, p. 202.
34. For more on the National Security Doctrine, see Pion-Berlin and George A. Lopez, "Of Victims and Executioners: Argentine State Terror, 1975–1979," pp. 69–71.
35. Eckert et al., *Korea Old and New*, pp. 356–358.
36. Han Sung-joo, *The Failure of Democracy in South Korea*, Berkeley: University of California Press, 1974, p. 28.
37. Se-jin Kim, *The Politics of Military Revolution*, Chapel Hill: University of North Carolina Press, 1971, p. 30.
38. Gregory Henderson, *The Politics of the Vortex*, Cambridge: Harvard University Press, 1968, p. 179.
39. Oh, *Korean Politics*, p. 31.
40. Seoul: Hyangmunsa, 1963, trans. Leon Sinder, pp. 105–107, as quoted in Oh, *Korean Politics*, pp. 51–52.
41. Eckert et al., *Korea Old and New*, p. 369.
42. For an excellent treatment of South Korean civil society during the transition to democracy, see Sunhyuk Kim, *The Politics of Democratization in Korea: The Role of Civil Society*, Pittsburgh: University of Pittsburgh Press, 2000.
43. A thorough treatment of transitional justice in Argentina, Greece, and South Korea is contained in Terence Roehrig, *The Prosecution of Former Military Leaders in Newly Democratic Nations: The Cases of Argentina, Greece and South Korea*, Jefferson: McFarland Press, 2001.
44. There has been a lively debate among scholars and practitioners concerning the merits of prosecuting human rights violations. The following is a small sample of the vast literature on the subject. Jamal Benomar, "Justice after Transitions," *Journal of Democracy*, Vol. 4, No. 1, June 1993, pp. 3–14; Luc Huyse, "Justice after Transition: On the Choices Successor Elites Make in Dealing with the Past," *Law and Social Inquiry*, Vol. 20, No. 1, Winter 1995, pp. 51–78; Neil J. Kritz, ed., *Transitional Justice: How Emerging Democracies Reckon with Former Regimes*, Volumes I, II, and III, Washington D.C.: United States Institute of Peace Press, 1995; Jaime Malamud-Goti, "Transitional Governments in the Breach: Why Punish State Criminals?" *Human Rights Quarterly*, Vol. 12, February 1990, pp. 1–16; A. James McAdams, ed., *Transitional Justice and the Rule of Law in New Democracies*, Notre Dame: University of Notre Dame Press, 1997; and David Pion-Berlin, "To Prosecute or to Pardon? Human Rights Decisions in the Latin American Southern Cone," *Human Rights Quarterly*, Vol. 16, No. 1, February 1994, pp. 105–130.
45. Despite Alfonsín's hopes, civilian courts bucked efforts by the executive branch to limit the number of prosecutions. When Alfonsín obtained legislative approval in 1986 for *Punto Final* (End Point Law) that imposed a 60-day time limit on initiating new cases against military personnel, judges and prosecutors raced to indict as many as possible before the deadline expired.

46. Pion-Berlin, *Through Corridors of Power*, p. 91.
47. *Clarín* (Buenos Aires), March 22, 1981 as quoted in Guest, *Behind the Disappearances*, p. 277.
48. Norden, *Military Rebellion in Argentina*, p. 126.
49. Ibid., p. 126–127.
50. Robert A. Potash, "The Military under Alfonsín and Menem," in Colin M. Lewis and Nissa Torrents, eds, *Argentina in the Crisis Years (1983–1990)*, London: The Institute of Latin American Studies, University of London, 1993, p. 57, and Norden, *Military Rebellion in Argentina*, p. 96.
51. Norden, *Military Rebellion in Argentina*, p. 97; and Potash, "The Military under Alfonsín and Menem," p. 61.
52. These figures are taken from *The Military Balance*, London: Institute of International Studies, 1980–1981 and 1987–1988 editions. Given the high inflation rates and currency fluctuations present in Argentina at the time, precise numbers are difficult to tabulate.
53. Norden, *Military Rebellion in Argentina*, p. 104.
54. Ibid., pp. 131–138, and Potash, "The Military under Alfonsín and Menem," p. 66.
55. Sheryl WuDunn, "Ex-Leader in Seoul Faces Death Sentence," *New York Times*, 26 August 1996.
56. Andrew Pollack, "New Korean Leader Agrees to Pardon of 2 Ex-Dictators," *New York Times*, 21 December 1997, p. A10 and "S. Korea president to pardon jailed ex-presidents," *CNN Interactive* ⟨http://www.cnn.com/WORLD/9712/20/skorea.pardon⟩.
57. The figures given were taken from *The Military Balance*, London: Institute of International Studies. As a percentage of GDP, these numbers represent a decrease. However, this was due more to the growth of the South Korean economy than to any cuts in military spending.
58. "Controversy over Probing Former Presidents," *Korea Newsreview*, 14 August 1993, p. 8.
59. Huntington, *The Third Wave*, p. 211. In Huntington's view, the most prudent course of action is "do not prosecute, do not punish, do not forgive, and, above all, do not forget." Ibid., p. 231.
60. *Diario del Juicio* 13, 20 August 1985, as quoted in Guest, *Behind the Disappearances*, p. 6.
61. Juan E. Méndez, "In Defense of Transition Justice," in A. James McAdams, ed., *Transitional Justice and the Rule of Law in New Democracies*, Notre Dame: University of Notre Dame Press, 1997, p. 1.
62. Ibid., p. 3.

Conclusion

18

Protecting human rights in transition societies: Lessons and recommendations

Albrecht Schnabel and Shale Horowitz

In order to devise appropriate and effective policies to promote human rights protection in transition societies, international, regional, and local actors must be aware of the causes and consequences of human rights violations. Important causes of violations are repressive political regimes and leaders, self-serving manipulation of local cultures and identities through state-controlled mass media and other cultural institutions, poverty and economic instability, and civil and international conflict. Alleviating or preventing these sources of human rights abuse considerably raises the chances for adequate human rights protection. As the preceding case studies have shown, human rights practices have an important impact on a society's ability to manage its conflicts peacefully, develop economically, and build and strengthen institutions of democratic and good governance. Favourable human rights practices foster peaceful and prosperous futures, whereas negative human rights practices undermine them.

Drawing on the thematic and case studies in this volume, this concluding examination reviews some of the most crucial causes and consequences of human rights violations and protections. It then offers recommendations for national, regional, global, and civil-society actors involved in shaping human rights practices in fragile transition societies.

Reasons for human rights violations and protections

For internal and external actors to prevent human rights violations and instil a pro-rights culture within society and state structures, they have to address the root causes of violations, not just their symptoms. Understanding the reasons for human rights violations is the first step towards effective proaction. As the findings of the various case studies in this volume show, causes for human rights violations vary from region to region and from country to country. Nevertheless, there are a number of overarching root causes that apply in similar fashion in many different societies. Local, national, regional, and global actors must cooperate in designing and implementing the most appropriate response strategies to generic as well as context-specific root causes of human rights violations. Furthermore, some countries develop and implement policies that advance human rights. The reasons for this tell us much about states' motivations for protecting human rights – motivations that need to be fostered from within the region and by the international community. Interestingly, these motivations are often quite similar to those of oppressive states: to strengthen one's hold on power and privilege – now, however, achieved through broad acceptance as a legitimate authority and not through the spread of fear. With the old authoritarian alternatives now more ideologically discredited, élites are forced to pursue their power and wealth interests in more constrained and enlightened ways.

Drawing on the regional and country studies of this volume, the following paragraphs summarize some of the most salient root causes of human rights violations, as well as reasons for policies that promote human rights.

The African continent is plagued by numerous instances of military, one-party, and personal rule of collapsing and weakened states. Encouraged by the legacy of colonialism and Cold War-era superpower rivalry, repressive regimes and leaders have perpetrated violations in efforts to sustain unjust political structures. Political leadership tends to be repressive and corrupt. Nation-building projects place emphasis on citizens' duties to the state, rather than on citizens' rights. Entrenched systems of ethnic stratification, discrimination, domination, and exclusion are maintained and reinforced by state power holders. Indigenous cultures are being destroyed and often replaced by alien values. Consequently, ordinary citizens have lost faith in the state and increasingly view it as an illegitimate perpetrator of abuses, rather than as a protector of their rights.

The state subjugates citizen rights to the supposed imperatives of "development," while grave inequalities between the "haves" and "have-nots" are perpetuated to secure wealth for ruling élites and their political allies. The region is characterized by rigid and discriminatory economic structures. Severe economic crises and poorly implemented structural-adjustment programmes further encourage and justify violations. Moreover, foreign-developed, natural resource-based income streams make repressive leaders less dependent on broader economic development, further insulating them from the need to pursue responsible policies.

There is increased militarization of politics in the region, resulting in the spread of civil war and political violence. This is perpetuated by a culture of impunity and non-accountability on the part of the police and security forces. Civil strife and international interference heighten instability and war. The interests and activities of multinationals and rogue foreign investors arm combatants and help to fuel conflicts and state violence. In this context, not even the most basic human rights can be ensured.

Nevertheless, some states have pursued broader protection of human rights in response to the post-Cold War legitimacy crisis of the authoritarian post-colonial state. This loss of legitimacy was associated with the rise and intervention of pro-democracy, pro-civil liberties, and other politically active civil-society constituents. When governments have become more participatory, the goals of opposition parties and civil society in general – labour, the middle class, students, academics, the media – converge to sustain this new-found freedom and sense of participation and to prevent a return to authoritarianism. This is paralleled by the determination of minorities and other previously marginalized and excluded groups to stop any relapse into a system of unfettered domination. Moreover, previously excluded élites pursue increased inclusion and participation in the political and economic life of the society, thus benefiting the population at large. Governments also pursue pro-human rights policies, not just for ideological reasons but also to appease the citizenry and to maintain legitimacy and power. In the same vein, development and improved distribution of the benefits of increased wealth are seen as a way to cling to power: where old authoritarian regimes are discredited, the relative ideological legitimacy of human rights-oriented regimes is greater. Unfortunately, without significant and parallel improvements in political stability and economic development, such human rights gains often prove fragile.

The Middle East does not fare any better. The region has been cursed with military rule and a praetorian mentality of the élite (e.g. Algeria, Iraq, Libya, Sudan, and Syria). Sometimes authoritarian regimes have used politicized interpretations of Islam to justify internal repression (e.g. Iran, Saudi Arabia, and Sudan). Energy-based *rentier* states make societies dependent on the welfare state and less able to influence rulers (e.g. Algeria, Iraq, Iran, Libya, Saudi Arabia, and the Gulf States). The presence of implacable oppositions engaged in long-term conflict – such as secessionist groups, Islamic opposition, or occupied peoples (e.g. Algeria, Egypt, Iran, Iraq, Israel, Sudan, Syria, Turkey) – feeds chronic warfare and fuels political cultures often defined by Sultanistic rule and a history of civil rights violations. In many cases, such conflicts are cultivated and perpetuated because they provide convenient diversions from internal legitimacy problems. For many years, the international community contributed to great suffering and human rights violations by imposing economic sanctions on Iraq. If the international community was determined to alter Saddam Hussein's behaviour (and thus to forestall a regime change by external, US-led military force), it should have attempted to do so in a manner that influenced him more directly – whether with economic sanctions or by other means.

In some countries of the Middle East, democratic governments have pursued human rights protection as part of their mandate to serve the interests of the populace (e.g. Turkey, Israel). Even limited forms of democracy (e.g. Iran, Jordan, and Lebanon) force authoritarian rulers to devote more of their efforts and resources to goals supported by broad segments of the population. Relatively benevolent élites and constitutional guarantees in some countries also offer some human rights protection (e.g. Jordan, the Gulf Emirates, and Egypt). In other countries, inducements are offered through trade agreements with major trading blocs or individual countries (e.g. the European Union and the United States *vis-à-vis* Turkey, Jordan, and Egypt). However, authoritarian regimes tend to stop short of human rights improvements that are viewed as threats to their power.

In Pakistan, the military has repeatedly intervened in political affairs. This has been justified by reference to chronic internal corruption and inefficiency and the need to combat internal and external threats to national unity. Nevertheless, both military and civil administrations have been repressive, corrupt, and inefficient, and have used Islam and the Kashmir conflict to divert attention from internal divisions and problems. Although democratic institutions and human rights norms have had a favourable influence in India, a variety of factors – traditional norms and social structures, an often corrupt and inefficient administration, and poverty – have contributed to widespread local human rights violations. Women, children, the poor, and various minority groups have suffered most. However, human rights in India have benefited from strong democratic institutions and, in the last decade or so, from a more sustained effort at economic development. Pakistan would have benefited from both of these efforts; however, in the past, Pakistan's greater internal ethnic divisions have made rulers more fearful of the consequences of giving up centralized power and patronage.

Authoritarian regimes in Eastern Europe, the former Yugoslavia, and

the former Soviet Union have used human rights violations as a
retaining power. Civil and international conflicts throughout the
have undermined human rights directly. They have also done so
rectly, by undermining reformist political movements and weakening
society. Some national identities are not oriented strongly enough t
wards a break with the communist past and its poor human rights record.
To a lesser extent, human rights practices suffer from weak economic
development, associated with weaker national identities, lower levels of
education, and stronger economic interest groups opposed to reform.
Throughout the region, states are often plagued by insufficient capacity
to provide adequately for the security and well-being of their citizens.

On the other hand, democratic regimes not only have valued human
rights protection for their own sake but also have used human rights
protection as a means of consolidating democracy and achieving other
reforms. For many governments, particularly those unwilling to use authoritarian methods, enlightened human rights policies help to preserve
legitimacy and popularity. A number of factors influence élite willingness
and ability to embrace democracy and human rights protection. These
include national identities that are strongly oriented towards a break with
the communist past, including a break with its poor human rights record;
an understanding of the need to avoid civil and international conflicts
(or, at least, to end them as quickly as possible); movement towards
integration with the EU; and, to a lesser extent, strong economic development, associated with stronger national identities, higher levels of education, and weaker economic interest groups opposed to reforms.

Human rights violations in the People's Republic of China are driven
by the regime's determination to pre-empt threats to its power, primarily
through laws that suppress civil and political rights. Poverty and corruption also restrict civil and economic rights throughout the country. Some
human rights protections are granted as means to a certain level of political legitimacy, to developing and maintaining a minimum standard of
living and quality of life, and to enhancing national economic and military power. In Taiwan, democratization has brought much greater respect for human rights. This is enhanced by evolving local human rights
norms, as well as pressure from key external actors (particularly the
United States).

In both Argentina and South Korea, the primary cause for human
rights violations has been the military's reaction to perceived threats.
They believed that their countries were experiencing a breakdown in the
economic and social order and were threatened by communism. In Argentina, that threat was primarily internal (communist subversion); in
South Korea, the threat was primarily external (North Korea), with a
more limited danger of internal subversion. Human rights violations oc-

...inate these economic and political threats and, ...ld of the reins of government. Military leaders ...s opposed to a civilian government) could ...easing security and order. In both countries, ...er once perceived threats to the nation re- ...gitimacy because of repression, economic ...ion. This unleashed rights-oriented civil soci- ... helped to restore democracy and facilitated many ...improvements. These transitions were possible, largely be- ...he military rulers did not seek power for its own sake and were willing to cede power to civilian governments possessing broadly similar ideological commitments.

The reasons for human rights violations can be quite diverse: they include external intervention or sanctions, politicization of Islam and other traditional cultures and values, state control of energy resources, military rule, caste structures, and communist or colonial legacies. Nevertheless, some root causes appear to be almost universal: these are the presence of corrupt, unaccountable, and repressive governments that are unable to gain the support of their population by legitimate means; systems of economic privilege perpetuating poverty and inequalities between rich and poor segments of society; and religious or ethnic stratification, exclusion, domination, or repression. These issues need to be tackled to prepare a more fertile ground for state-sponsored human rights improvements. The major reasons for positive developments in the protection of rights include political and economic pressure from external actors (strong states and international organizations), including the prospects of joining promising regional organizations; new ideological standards, usually due to poor performance of old authoritarian systems; pressure from civil society; and the quest of governing élites for at least a modest degree of internal as well as external legitimacy – the latter, in essence, a compromise attempt to maintain one's hold on power.

Human rights violations and protection: Impact on conflict management, economic development, and democratization

Human rights violations have strong negative effects on a society's capacity to manage conflict, to develop economically, and to democratize, whereas protecting and promoting human rights has the opposite effect. These impacts can be seen in every regional and national context.

Throughout much of Africa, human rights violations exacerbate political and social violence, growing out of the suffering of excluded, marginalized, and dominated communities. In some countries – such as Liberia, Sierra Leone, Guinea-Bissau, or Guinea – this has led to full-scale civil war. Human rights violations trigger and increase separatist agitation by minorities: they trigger violence during elections and changes of government; they delegitimize institutions – such as the police and judiciary – that are crucial to the maintenance of law and order. Moreover, in war-torn societies, peace agreements are difficult to implement and sustain in the presence of continued human rights violations. Cyclical wars and conflicts have a negative impact on people's daily lives. Only if leaders and their constituents grow tired of conflict, will they end up negotiating settlements. By doing so, they make it possible to move from violating human rights to reinforcing respect for them. However, conflict-related and post-conflict-related human rights violations highlight persistent injustice, inequality, and bad governance.

Human rights violations hamper economic development and encourage corruption and formal sector inefficiency (which are also causes of human rights violations). They trigger violent opposition to multinational corporations and foreign investors and, thus, stifle development even further. There is general agreement that the economic situation in Africa has favoured those leaders (and their cronies) who violate human rights. Kleptocracies – which loot national resources and monopolize opportunities – worsen societal schisms and deny some (or most) of the population access to public goods and services and larger shares of national wealth. Human rights violations make democratization processes, if existent, highly volatile and more violent. Human rights protection, on the other hand, has given previously excluded and marginalized groups a stake in the democratization process, by ensuring access and participation. It has also gradually restored the credibility of power sharing and has given civil society some freedom to operate. This reduces the likelihood that new civil conflicts will break out, and makes it easier to resolve or damp down existing conflicts. Whereas human rights protections have contributed to democratization and economic development, deep ethnic cleavages and economic difficulties have meant that such advances have been limited and, often, temporary.

In the Middle East, human rights violations by the government of Iraq have exacerbated the Kurdish problem and have led to a virtual division of the country. In addition, the UN Security Council's economic sanctions on Iraq have violated the human rights of ordinary Iraqis and have extended the stalemate rather than contributed to a resolution of the conflict. Violations of Kurdish rights by Turkey have led to domestic divisions and problems with the European Union and have failed to advance a solution to Turkey's Kurdish situation. Israel's violations of the rights of Palestinians draw sharp criticism from the international community and even its closest ally (the United States). At the same time, the decades-long war against Israel conducted by authoritarian regimes and élites has forced Israel to fight a succession of high- and low-intensity conflicts, often amid civilian populations. The conflict has been dramatically worsened by these regimes' needs to divert attention from internal repression and corruption. Violations of civil, economic, social, and cultural rights have been largely responsible for the economic stagnation and decline afflicting the Middle East, and they have severely limited progress towards democratization.

On a more positive note, protection of human rights has promoted conflict prevention between the Jordanian government and its Islamic opposition, and has contributed significantly to democratization (such as a functioning parliament). Improvements in human rights practices in Egypt have not led to real political liberalization but have contributed to conflict management. In Iran, democracy has suffered as a result of the violation of the civil and political rights of the opposition, but a slight easing of repression by hard-liners in the government has reduced confrontation with the opposition. In Israel and Turkey, broader protection of human rights has helped to advance democracy, economic development, and Turkey's prospects of joining the European Union.

In Pakistan, human rights violations have made it more difficult to soften the country's ethnic divisions and to address the Kashmir conflict through non-violent means. They also contribute to keeping the country mired in poverty. In India, ongoing limitations in civil, economic, social, and cultural rights remain important obstacles to a more accountable political system and broader diffusion of economic opportunities. However, recently improved protection of economic rights has improved access to economic opportunities and facilitated faster economic development.

In Eastern Europe, the former Yugoslavia, and the former Soviet Union, human rights violations have had a particularly negative impact on conflict management where demands of groups potentially engaged in conflict were not better accommodated through stronger human rights protections and democratic political compromise. As well, the impact of human rights abuses on economic development has often been damaging, principally by imposing less equal economic opportunities through cronyism and corruption and thereby preventing resources from flowing to their most profitable use. Human rights practices typically evolved along with regime type: effective democratization typically accommodates the basic goals of key groups and thus prevents violent conflict; on the other hand, human rights violations destroy confidence in, and respect for, democracy, and hence delegitimize and undermine democratization processes. In particular, lack of fairness in electoral processes (during election campaigns, voting, and vote-counting) undermines popular trust in democratic institutions and discourages participation in political life and development of effective political parties.

Positive human rights practices have been beneficial where demands of groups that might potentially be engaged in conflict could be accommodated through political compromise. This prevents and minimizes the escalation of differences to violent conflict. The impact on economic development has been beneficial, principally by minimizing cronyism and corruption and providing more equal economic opportunities. Protecting individual security and property rights and developing a fair and just legal system fosters investment and economic development. Human rights practices were typically chosen along with democratization. Where democratization can accommodate the basic goals of key groups, human rights practices help to increase confidence in, and respect for, democracy and hence help to consolidate democracy by increasing its legitimacy. Freedoms of expression and association have been critical for the development of political competition and are crucial for effective and lasting democratization processes.

In the People's Republic of China opposition voices are suppressed, which often makes conflicts more difficult to resolve. Democratization has been extremely slow, largely because of continued oppression of civil society. In the last 20 years, however, greater protection of civil and economic rights has facilitated economic development; on the other hand, cronyism continues to restrict opportunities in many parts of the country. Some protection of civil and political rights is the first step towards economic development and democratization. In Taiwan, earlier and stronger improvements in human rights practices facilitated more rapid economic growth and, eventually, democratization.

In Argentina and South Korea, as often happens, human rights violations and authoritarianism went hand in hand. If anything, the human rights violations in Argentina worsened economic conditions. On the other hand, the South Korean example shows that, if basic civil and economic rights are maintained and other economic policies are favourable, authoritarianism can provide conditions favourable to economic growth. In both countries, human rights protection and democratization are interdependent forces, as democratization has led to human rights protection and vice versa. In neither case is it obvious that economic development has improved with broadened political rights; however, neither has economic performance obviously deteriorated.

Both external and internal actors play critical roles in promoting and supporting societies' efforts to protect human rights and to further stability and development. The subsequent sections suggest some immediate and medium-term actions that should be taken by national governments, regional and sub-regional organizations, the United Nations, and civil-society actors to advance human rights protection in transition societies.

Recommendations for national governments

Governments should seek to implement the Universal Declaration of Human Rights in their national context, i.e. to implement the International Bill of Rights through national bills of rights. Many modern, newly drafted, constitutions should follow the model or standard set by the UDHR, which, because it is not in itself a legal document, floats above national efforts in the hope that they will "copy" it. Societies in transition countries should take heart from the fact that the Declaration includes social, economic, and cultural rights: it can thus be used as a powerful reference tool for measures taken to solve one's own societal problems. Moreover, as the Declaration is based on the premise of international as well as sub-national cooperation, national governments need to address the rights of members of minority groups – often particularly sore points for societies in transition.

Addressing relativist approaches to human rights should be as much a part of the dialogue with traditional and authoritarian societies as are "enforcement" procedures. Serving a multitude of interests and hetero-geneous societies, national governments are often less relativistic than internal subgroups, which should be shown respect and given ownership in the development of national strategies on issues affected by relativism.

Governments should continue to invest in negative rights: these include physical security rights, freedom of speech, association, religion, and due process rights. To the extent of available resources, governments should promote cultural, social, and economic rights in areas such as work, housing, health, or education. Governments need to match resources to rhetoric, by optimizing available resources and attention. They need to embrace long-term perspectives, develop realistic expectations, and ensure that the link between human rights practices and development, good governance (and government legitimacy), and political stability are well understood – by the government and by the society at large.

NGOs play an important role in this task. Unfortunately, some countries are moving to restrict space for human rights NGOs and to increase control over them. On the contrary, however, states must provide space for domestic and international NGOs to lobby, campaign, and stage non-violent protests to improve human rights practices. Thus, in transition societies as well as the donor community, states must educate the public about the benefits of the international promotion and defence of human rights, and about existing frameworks such as the UDHR and other manifestations of human rights law. They must emphasize human rights education in the teaching curriculum at all stages of the educational system. National governments must educate, socialize, and persuade subgroups to share levels of human rights standards that may already be promoted by progressive national élites.

Governments of rights-respecting states should realize that it is in their long-term national interests for other countries to adopt and solidify commitments to human rights norms. Pressure on rights-violating allies will often be muted where political liberalization carries a risk of bringing more threatening regimes to power. Nevertheless, even in such cases, countries should encourage allies to begin by respecting civil, economic, and other rights. Such limited improvements not only are desirable in themselves but also can ease the way for future expansions of rights.

Finally, governments must support the authorization of humanitarian intervention in cases of grave crimes against humanity. They must support the quest for an international consensus on the right and obligation to undertake such interventions on a principled basis. Governments must support international calls for UN-sponsored intervention in failed states, and they need to penalize abuses justified in terms of humanitarian intervention. Although humanitarian intervention will continue to be constrained by limited national interests, governments and their peoples should be better educated about the long-term benefits, as well as the legal and moral responsibilities, of effective human rights protection abroad. As mentioned above, education and awareness-raising are thus as important in the donor community as they are in human rights-challenged transition societies.

Recommendations for regional and sub-regional organizations and the United Nations

Regional and sub-regional organizations need to establish, encourage, and enforce human rights commitments throughout their region. They should establish regional standards for best human rights practices and norms, build security communities, and foster regional trust and balance among states. The European post-World War II experience could serve as a useful reference point for other regional cooperation and integration projects. (Sub)-regional organizations must embrace regional responses to human rights violations – diplomatic, economic, and (if necessary) military – to deal with rule breakers. Given international disagreements over human rights, it may be less difficult to achieve consensus and a willingness to act at the regional level. Regional approaches should serve as bridges to more effective international measures, and as interim steps for increasingly structured and institutionalized global cooperation. Progress in this direction depends on achieving regional critical masses of rights-respecting political regimes. Thus, (sub)-regional organizations need to work more closely with governments to promote best practices in human rights policy.

The United Nations must do more to hold major and great powers responsible to human rights standards, despite their political weight in the Security Council and other UN organs. Although this may be difficult to accomplish politically, yet, as the United Nations is the only organization that is (at least, potentially) in the position to exert such influence, it must at least attempt to live up to this responsibility; this will also improve its legitimacy *vis-à-vis* smaller states. Notably, the United Nations must ensure that major powers do not abuse humanitarian operations to their advantage, as it must also stop coalitions of weaker states from using the norm of non-intervention to excuse or ignore human rights violations. At the same time, it must discourage states from unjustifiably involving themselves in other countries' internal conflicts and rebuke those that support conflict and war in other countries. The United Nations must collaborate more effectively with (sub)-regional organizations in promoting human rights- and human security-driven domestic and foreign policies. It must foster principled responses; act as the champion of regions with weak and ineffective (sub)-regional organizations; and channel funds to regional and (sub)-regional organizations and NGOs to provide early warning, early assistance, and effective involvement in humanitarian emergencies. Again, progress in these directions will probably depend on – and accelerate with – piecemeal expansion of the number of rights-respecting political regimes.

(Sub)-regional organizations and the United Nations should seek to play a mediating role between the UDHR as an abstract statement and the regional efforts already undertaken in Europe, Latin America, and Africa. This would also help the United Nations to address issues of cultural and regional relativism more successfully. All regions should have, or should develop, their regional Charters of Human Rights. An Asian Charter of Human Rights, for example, would force more frank and thorough discussions of similar and divergent human rights norms and practices and on acceptable degrees of diversity.

International organizations should devote greater efforts to building the capacity of domestic NGOs, which need to be provided with opportunities to lobby and influence (sub)-regional organizations and the United Nations. They must be given space and provisions to participate in the official processes of regional IGOs and the United Nations. Once international organizations have emphasized human rights education as a critical task of responsible member states, they should promote NGO–state partnerships as some of the most effective vehicles for improvements in human rights practices.

(Sub)-regional organizations and the United Nations can take leading roles in advancing multifaceted approaches to reconciling relativist and universalist positions in national policies. This would focus on finding joint approaches to specific weak areas of human rights practices. The persuasive powers of IGOs, as well as those of NGOs, need to be augmented, and strategies that have an impact on traditional thought and practice, including economic development, need to receive greater attention as tools to circumvent relativist objections to human rights protection.

Finally, international organizations need to focus more on rights that have yet to be developed. Regional human rights regimes need to be strengthened by establishing more rigorous human rights-reporting requirements. Human rights commissions need to be established that have the authority to investigate human rights abuses, report on them, and advise governments. Human rights educational commissions need to be established to promote human rights education among school children, university students, the media, churches, police, military, and government officials. While an inter-civilizational dialogue is taking place at various levels (facilitated, for instance, by UNESCO), inter-societal dialogues are less evident. Public education that seeks to bring traditional societies and subgroups into greater compliance is weak. Unfortunately – and probably because of political considerations – the approach of the international community to public education often appears to be minimalist and half-hearted.

Recommendations for non-governmental organizations

Non-governmental organizations must seek opportunities to collaborate with (sub)-regional organizations and the United Nations in advocating and promoting good human rights practices and in monitoring human rights improvements. In relations with other NGOs, they need to reduce counter-productive turf fights and, instead, to coordinate efforts. Moreover, international NGOs need to work in a collaborative and supportive manner with domestic NGOs.

NGOs need to strengthen their focus on educating the public to respect and protect rights; they also need to emphasize peace and human rights education inside and outside schools and universities. In turn, schools and universities need to do more to educate citizens on human rights.

Then, in turn, an educated citizenry will probably place greater pressure on their own governments to respect human rights at home and to support efforts abroad to promote human rights and prevent human tragedies. NGOs need to encourage opinion makers, educators, and faith-based organizations and movements to support peaceful conflict resolution rather than to incite hostility. Likewise, in addition to monitoring and evaluating government policies and the field activities of (sub)-regional organizations and the United Nations, they must monitor activities of fellow NGO actors, thus creating much-needed legitimacy and accountability within the NGO community.

Local and international NGOs need to ensure transparency and accountability in their work and procedures, so that accusations of paternalism and corruption do not erode their legitimacy and moral authority. Mutual codes of conduct are crucial in that effort: they need to emphasize professionalism, non-partisanship, and independence. Local NGOs must strive to become less dependent on foreign funding, by establishing membership fees, by engaging in local fund-raising, and by creating a stronger sense of local ownership. Both local and international NGOs need to establish broader bases of membership to enhance their credibility and visibility.

Summing up

Authoritarian regimes that preserve their power through political repression, cultural control and manipulation, economic cronyism, and diversionary civil and international conflict are the most systematic source of human rights violations. Because of the willingness of such regimes to use repression and violence to stay in power, there is no easy way to produce quick improvements across the board. Even in the rare cases where other regimes are willing to use force to dislodge rights-violating regimes, the conflicts have high costs and there is no guarantee that the post-conflict situations will be significantly improved. There are similar limits to the actions and even the ideological efforts of intergovernmental organizations, including the United Nations.

The main recommendations therefore focus on longer-term efforts at ideological persuasion and harmonization. The strength of the international human rights regime – at the national, intergovernmental, and sub-national levels – has always been the creation and advancement of human rights norms. It is this strength that promises the greatest long-term prospects for reform. Such reform can be achieved broadly only through the gradual conversion of mass and élite opinion, above all in the rights-abusing authoritarian states that most strongly resist this message.

This requires a continuous effort to promote broad human rights norms at every level, by national, intergovernmental, and sub-national actors. This effort must be attentive to local traditions and conditions, without compromising its basic principles.

An essential element of this ideological strategy is to emphasize the need for broad economic development and peaceful conflict resolution. This targets the authoritarian practices, observed throughout this volume, of protecting power indirectly through economic cronyism and diversionary conflict. It also offers authoritarian regimes an alternative source of legitimacy. Even if such regimes are unwilling to offer broad political rights in the near term, it is important to encourage them to protect civil, economic, social, and cultural rights in pursuit of harmonious economic development and peaceful conflict resolution. In the future, this also holds out the promise of a more consensual – and hence more peaceful and lasting – transition to democracy. If sustained economic development and peaceful conflict resolution are not achieved, it is questionable whether democratization and other rights improvements can be sustained.

Abbreviations and acronyms

ACUNS	Academic Council on the United States System
ADB	African Development Bank
AHRC	Asian Human Rights Commission
AI	Amnesty International
AKP	Justice and Development Party (Turkish)
ANC	African National Congress
ASEAN	Association of South-East Asian Nations
AU	African Union
BLT&BTF	Bodo Liberation Tiger & Bhindranwale Tigers Force
CAHR	Chinese Association for Human Rights
CCP	Chinese Communist Party
CFA	*Communauté Financière Africaine* (African Financial Community)
CGT	*Confederación General del Trabajo* (General Confederation of Labour)
CIA	Central Intelligence Agency (USA)
CLI	Civil Liberties Index (Freedom House)
Codesa	Convention for a Democratic South Africa
CPI	Corruption Perception Index
DHD	Dima Halim Daogah
DOS	Democratic Opposition of Serbia
DPP	Democratic Progressive Party
DSP	Democratic Left (Turkish)
EBRD	European Bank for Reconstruction and Development
EC	European Community

430

ECOMOG	ECOWAS Military Observer Group
ECOSOC	Economic and Social Council
ECOWAS	Economic Community of West African States
ERP	*Ejército Revolucionario del Pueblo* (Revolutionary Army of the People)
EU	European Union
FAO	Food and Agriculture Organization (of the United Nations)
FGM	female genital mutilation
FRY	Federal Republic of Yugoslavia
GDP	Gross Domestic Product
GNP	Gross National Product
HDZ	Croatian Democratic Union
HIV/AIDS	human immunodeficiency virus/acquired immunodeficiency syndrome
HKHRC	Hong Kong Human Rights Commission
HKHRM	Hong Kong Human Rights Monitor
HKSAR	Hong Kong Special Autonomous Region
ICAC	Independent Commission Against Corruption
ICC	International Criminal Court
ICCPR	International Covenant on Civil and Political Rights
ICESCR	International Covenant on Economic, Social and Cultural Rights
ICISS	International Commission on Intervention and State Sovereignty
ICTR	International Criminal Tribunal for Rwanda
ICTY	International Criminal Tribunal for the former Yugoslavia
IFIs	international financial institutions
IGAD	Intergovernmental Authority on Development
IGO	intergovernmental organization
ILO	International Labour Organization
IMF	International Monetary Fund
IMT	International Military Tribunal
INGOs	international non-governmental organizations
IOs	international organizations
IPC	Indian Penal Code
IRP	Islamic Renaissance Party (Tajikistan)
KCIA	Korean Central Intelligence Agency
KCP	Kangleipak Communist Party
KDP	Kurdish Democratic Party
KFOR	Kosovo Force
KLA	Kosovo Liberation Army
KMT	Kuomintong
KNA	Kuki National Army
KNF	Kuki National Front
KNV	Karbi National Volunteers
MCM	million cubic metres
MHP	National Action Party (Turkish)
MNF	Multinational Force in Haiti

MPF	Multinational Protection Force
NATO	North Atlantic Treaty Organization
NCM	National Commission for Minorities
NCRB	National Crime Records Bureau (India)
NCW	National Commission for Women
NDFB	National Democratic Front of Bodoland
NED	National Endowment for Democracy
NGO	non-governmental organization
NHRC	National Human Rights Commission (India)
NIIA	Nigerian Institute of International Affairs
NPCSC	Standing Committee of the National People's Congress
NSCN/DHD	National Socialist Council of Nagaland/Dima Halong Daga
NSCN–IM	National Socialist Council of Nagaland–Isak-Muivah
NSD	National Security Doctrine
OAS	Organization of American States
OAU	Organization of African Unity
OCHA	Office for the Coordination of Humanitarian Affairs
OECD	Organization for Economic Co-operation and Development
OPEC	Organization of Petroleum-Exporting Countries
OSCE	Organization for Security and Cooperation in Europe
PAC	Pan-Africanist Congress
PCO	Provisional Constitutional Order
PKK	Partiya Karkeren Kurdistan (Kurdish Workers' Party)
PLA	People's Liberation Army
PRC	People's Republic of China
PREPAK	People's Revolutionary Party of Kangleipak
PRGF	Poverty Relief and Growth Facility (of the IMF)
PRI	Political Rights Index (Freedom House)
PUCL	People's Union for Civil Liberties
PUCLDR	People's Union for Civil Liberties and Democratic Rights
PUDR	People's Union for Democratic Rights
PUK	Patriotic Union of Kurds
RCC	Revolutionary Command Council (Iraq)
ROC	Republic of China (Taiwan)
RS	Republika Srpska
SAIR	South Asia Intelligence Review
SAPs	structural adjustment programmes
SC/STs	Scheduled Castes and Scheduled Tribes
SCIRI	Supreme Council of the Islamic Revolution in Iraq
SECI	Southeast European Cooperative Initiative
SFOR	Stabilization Force
SFRY	Socialist Federal Republic of Yugoslavia
SHRC	State Human Rights Commissions
SLORC	State Law and Order Restoration Council (Burma)
SNPC	Somalia National Peace Conference
SPS	Socialist Party of Serbia

SRS	Serb Radical Party
SSJ	Party of Serb Unity
TAHR	Taiwan Association for Human Rights
TNG	Transitional National Government (Somalia)
TRC	Truth and Reconciliation Commission
UDHR	Universal Declaration of Human Rights
ULFA	United Liberation Front of Asom
UMIK	United Nations Interim Administration Mission in Kosovo
UN	United Nations (adj)
UNAMET	UN Mission in East Timor
UNAMIR	UN Assistance Mission for Rwanda
UNAMSIL	UN Mission in Sierra Leone
UNCIO	United Nations Conference on International Organization
UNCU	UN Coordination Unit
UNDP	United Nations Development Programme
UNHCR	United Nations High Commissioner for Refugees
UNICEF	United Nations Children's Fund
UNITAF	Unified Task Force
UNLF	United National Liberation Front
UNMIH	UN Mission in Haiti
UNOMSIL	UN Observer Mission in Sierra Leone
UNOSOM	UN Operation in Somalia
UNTAET	UN Transitional Administration in East Timor
UPDS	United People's Democratic Solidarity
USAID	United States Agency for International Development
USCR	US Committee for Refugees
USIA	United States Information Agency
WFP	World Food Programme
WHO	World Health Organization
WMD	weapons of mass destruction
WTO	World Trade Organization

Contributors

David P. Forsythe is University
Professor and Charles J. Mach
Distinguished Professor of Political
Science at the University of
Nebraska-Lincoln, USA. Educated
at Wake Forest (BA) and Princeton
(MA, PhD) universities, he joined
the faculty at UNL in 1973 and
served as Department Chair from
1993 to 1998. He has held
postdoctoral fellowships at
Princeton and Yale and visiting
professorships at universities in
Denmark, Ireland, the Netherlands,
and Switzerland. He has been a
consultant to the International Red
Cross and to the United Nations
Office of the High Commissioner for
Refugees. He served as President of
the Human Rights Committee of the
International Political Science
Association, Vice-President of the
International Studies Association,
and a member of the Committee
on Scientific Freedom and

Responsibility of the American
Association for the Advancement
of Science. His more than 75
publications on different aspects of
International Relations include:
*Human Rights in International
Relations* (Cambridge University
Press, 2000, translated into Arabic,
Chinese, and Bulgarian), *Human
Rights and Comparative Foreign
Policy* (United Nations University
Press, 2000; edited), *The United
States and Human Rights*
(University of Nebraska Press, 2000;
edited), and *The United Nations and
Changing World Politics* (Westview
Press, 2000; with two other authors,
4th edn in process).

Shale Horowitz is an Associate
Professor of Political Science at the
University of Wisconsin-Milwaukee.
He was educated at the University
of California, Berkeley (BA) and
the University of California, Los

Angeles (MA and PhD). He previously taught at the Central European University (1996–1997). Horowitz is co-editor of *Conflict in Asia: Korea, China–Taiwan, and India–Pakistan* (Praeger, 2002) and *The Political Economy of International Financial Crisis: Interest Groups, Ideologies, and Institutions* (Rowman and Littlefield, 2001). He is the author or co-author of articles in *Communist and Post-Communist Studies, Comparative Political Studies, Comparative Studies in Society and History, East European Politics and Societies, European Journal of International Relations, Journal of Peace Research, Nationalities Papers, Party Politics*, and other journals. He currently co-edits the quarterly publication *Analysis of Current Events*.

D.R. Kaarthikeyan is an Advisor in Law, Human Rights-Corporate Affairs. A trained lawyer, he joined the élite Indian Police Service and in that capacity held several positions including District Superintendent of Police, Director of Police Training Academy, Chief of Intelligence and Security, Director-General of the Central Reserve Police Force, Chief of Investigation of former Prime Minister Rajiv Gandhi's assassination case, Director of the Central Bureau of Investigation of India, Director of Trade Promotion in Australia with headquarters in Sydney, Diplomat and Head of Chancery in Indian Embassy in Moscow (then USSR), and Director-General in National Human Rights Commission. He is currently a Professor Emeritus at various universities; President

of *Life Positive* magazine; and Chairperson/Adviser/Member in several voluntary organizations, such as the World Community Service Centre, National Agriculturist Awareness Movement, Human Rights Organization, National Alliance for Fundamental Right Education, Academy for a Better World, All-India Conference of Intellectuals, World Congress for Peace and Harmony, Indian Council of Arbitration, Association of Asian Union, and the ORG Institute of Polity and Governance.

Man-To Leung is an Assistant Professor at the Department of Political Science, National Cheng Kung University in Taiwan. He received his doctorate in politics from Oxford University. His research interests include theories of democracy and human rights, history of political thought, Enlightenment thinkers, contemporary political philosophy, and public ethics. He has published articles on human rights, theories of social justice, e-democracy, and good governance.

Paul J. Magnarella is Professor of Anthropology, Law and African Studies at the University of Florida and Professor of Peace Studies at Warren Wilson College, Asheville, NC. He holds a PhD (Harvard University) and JD (University of Florida). Magnarella serves as Legal Counsel to the Association of Third World Studies (ATWS) and to the American Anthropological Association's Human Rights Committee. He has served as Expert on Mission with the UN Criminal Tribunal for the Former Yugoslavia. His book, *Justice in Africa:*

Rwanda's Genocide, Its National Courts and the U.N. Criminal Tribunal (2000), won the ATWS annual book award and was nominated for the Raphael Lemkin book award. Ideas expressed in his chapter do not necessarily represent the views of the above organizations.

Mahmood Monshipouri is Professor and Chair of the Political Science Department at Quinnipiac University. He received his PhD from the University of Georgia in 1987. He is co-editor of *Constructing Human Rights in the Age of Globalization* (M.E. Sharpe, 2003), and the author of *Islamism, Secularism, and Human Rights in the Middle East* (Lynne Rienner Publishers, 1998), and *Democratization, Liberalization, and Human Rights in the Third World* (Lynne Rienner Publishers, 1995). His most recent articles have appeared in *Human Rights Quarterly*, *International Peacekeeping*, and *Middle East Policy*. He specializes in human rights, democratization, Middle Eastern Politics, European politics, and globalization and its impacts in the Muslim world. He is the President of the International Studies Association – Northeast Section, the Executive Director of the Center for Iranian Research and Analysis, and Co-chair of the Jewish–Islamic Cultural Studies Program at Quinnipiac University. Mahmood Monshipouri is also a Visiting Fellow at the Yale Center for International and Area Studies.

Johannes Morsink is Professor of Political Philosophy in the Department of Political Science at Drew University, Madison, NJ,

USA. After writing articles on Aristotle's biology, he published essays on the Universal Declaration of Human Rights in the *Human Rights Quarterly*. His most recent work is *The Universal Declaration of Human Rights: Origins, Drafting and Intent* (University of Pennsylvania Press, 1999), for which book he received the 2000 Certificate of Merit from the American Society of International Law.

W. Ofuatey-Kodjoe is a Professor in the Department of Political Science, Queens College and the CUNY Graduate Center, The City University of New York. He received his PhD from Columbia University. He has served as Director of the African Studies and Research Institute at Queens College (1973–1982), Visiting Professor at the University of Ghana-Legon (1977), the University of North Carolina at Chapel Hill (1979), the School of International Service at American University (1982–1983), and the University of Lagos (1986). His major publications include "Regional Organizations and the Resolution of International Conflict: The ECOWAS Intervention in Liberia," in *International Peacekeeping*, Vol. 1, No. 3, (Autumn 1995); "The United Nations and the Protection of Individual and Group Rights," *International Social Science Journal*, No. 144, (1995); "Self-Determination," in Oscar Schachter and Christopher Joyner, eds, *United Nations Legal Order* (Cambridge University Press, 1994); *Pan-Africanism: New Directions in Strategy* (University Press of America, 1986, edited); and *The*

Principle of Self-Determination in International Law (Nellen, 1977).

Wafula Okumu is an Analyst in the Peace and Security Directorate of the African Union. Prior to joining the African Union he served as an Academic Programme Associate in the Peace and Governance Programme at the United Nations University. He has taught Peace Studies, Human Rights, and African Politics courses at Prescott College, Mississippi University for Women, and Chapman University. His undergraduate studies were at the University of Nairobi and his graduate work at Atlanta University, where he received a PhD in Political Science in 1992. He also holds an International Diploma in Humanitarian Assistance from the Center for International Health and Cooperation at Hunter College of the City University of New York. He has conducted research and published in the areas of peace, democracy, and human rights in Africa.

Eghosa E. Osaghae is Professor of Political Science and Director of the Ford Foundation's Programme on Ethnic and Federal Studies at the University of Ibadan, Nigeria. He holds a PhD in Political Science from the same institution. He has held other academic appointments in the United States, South Africa, Liberia, Sweden, and Northern Ireland, and was until 1998 Professor and Head of Political Studies at the University of Transkei in South Africa. His major research interests are in the state in Africa, federalism, and the management of ethnicity. He has published extensively in these areas.

His books include *Between State and Civil Society in Africa* (CODESRIA Books, 1994), *Structural Adjustment and Ethnicity in Nigeria* (Nordiska Afrikainstitutet, 1995), and *Crippled Giant: Nigeria Since Independence* (C. Hurst/Indiana University Press, 1998). Professor Osaghae is currently a MacArthur Fellow, and is completing a book on *The Federal Solution in Africa*.

Aleksandar Resanovic works at the Center for Antiwar Action, where he is a member of the executive board. He previously served as Head of the Legal Affairs Department of the Yugoslav Federation for Sports, as Counsellor of the Minister in the Yugoslav Ministry of Justice, and as the founder and first coordinator of the Yugoslav Campaign to Ban Landmines. He was educated at the Faculty of Law at Belgrade University and has published six books and several expert papers in the field of international public law. He is a member of the Forum for International Relations and the Serbian Bar Association, both in Belgrade.

Barbara Ann J. Rieffer is an Assistant Professor of Political Science at Bethany College. After taking her BA from the State University of New York at Geneseo, she received her Masters in Philosophy from the University of Nebraska-Lincoln, concentrating on moral philosophy and the work of John Rawls. In her doctoral programme at UNL she emphasized the interplay of religion and politics. She is particularly concerned with how religious freedom and religious identity affect both conflict and conflict resolution. Her publications include "Religion and Nationalism: Understanding the Consequences of a Complex Relationship," in *Ethnicities* (Vol. 3, No. 2, June 2003), and "US Foreign Policy and Enlarging the Democratic Community," *Human Rights Quarterly* (Fall, 2000, coauthor).

Terence Roehrig is an Associate Professor of Political Science at Cardinal Stritch University. He received his PhD from the University of Wisconsin-Madison in political science and is the author of *The Prosecution of Former Military Leaders in Newly Democratic Nations: The Cases of Argentina, Greece, and South Korea* (McFarland & Company, 2002). He has published articles on North Korea's nuclear weapons pro-gramme, US–North Korean rela-tions, and Korean security issues.

Albrecht Schnabel is a Senior Research Fellow at swisspeace – Swiss Peace Foundation, Bern, Switzerland. Most recently, he served as Academic Officer in the Peace and Governance Programme of the United Nations University, Tokyo, Japan (1998–2003). He was educated at the University of Munich, the University of Nevada, and Queen's University, Canada, where he received his PhD in Political Studies in 1995. He has taught at Queen's University (1994), the American University in Bulgaria (1995–1996), the Central European University (1996–1998), and Aoyama Gakuin University (2002–2003). He was the 2001–2002 President of the International Association of Peacekeeping Training Centres and currently serves as trainer for the UN

System Staff College course on *Early Warning and Early Response.* His work on ethnic conflict, conflict prevention and management, peacekeeping, peacebuilding, refugees, and humanitarian intervention have appeared in numerous journals, reports, and edited volumes. Recent edited books include *Kosovo and the Challenge of Humanitarian Intervention* (with Ramesh Thakur, United Nations University Press, 2000); *Southeast European Security: Threats, Responses, Challenges* (Nova Science, 2001), *Recovering from Civil Conflict: Reconciliation, Peace and Development* (with Edward Newman, Frank Cass, 2002), *Conflict Prevention: Path to Peace or Grand Illusion?* (with David Carment, United Nations University Press, 2003) and *Democratization in the Middle East* (with Amin Saikal, United Nations University Press, 2003).

Richard Lewis Siegel is Professor of Political Science and Faculty Associate of the Grant Sawyer Center for Justice Studies at the University of Nevada, Reno. He received a BA in Politics from Brandeis University in 1961 and a PhD in Public Law and Government from Columbia University in 1967. Recent publications include *Employment and Human Rights* (University of Pennsylvania Press, 1994); "AIDS and Human Rights," *Human Rights Quarterly*, May 1998; "Transitional Justice: A Decade of Debate and Experience," *Human Rights Quarterly*, May 1998; and "The Right to Work: Core Minimum Obligations," in Audrey Chapman and Sage Russell, eds,

Core Obligations: Building a Framework for Economic, Social and Cultural Rights (Intersentia Publishers, 2002). Siegel has also been a leader of the American Civil Liberties Union, serving on its National Board of Directors from 1975 to 1988 and as President of its Nevada affiliate since 2000.

Geneviève Souillac is a Lecturer in French Studies at the University of Sydney. Previously, she was an Assistant Professor in European Studies in the Government and International Studies Department of the Hong Kong Baptist University, and an Academic Programme Associate in the Peace and Governance Programme at the United Nations University. Educated in France, Australia, and Hong Kong, where she studied with Daniel A. Bell on the subject of universal human rights, Souillac has a forthcoming book with Lexington Books on French political and social theory, entitled *Human Rights in Crisis: Contestation and Reform in Contemporary French Social and Political Thought.*

Jenab Tutunji has been an Assistant Professorial Lecturer in Political Science at George Washington University since 1995. He earned an MA in Philosophy from the American University of Beirut in 1968, and a PhD in Political Science from George Washington University in 1995. He has worked as a journalist and freelance writer for many years. He was managing editor of *The Jordan Times*, Amman, Jordan (1977–1980), and assistant editor, *Journal of Palestine Studies*, Beirut, Lebanon (1975–1976). Tutunji has written on the Lebanese civil war, the Arab–Israeli conflict, Jordan, the United Arab Emirates, and the political economy of the Middle East.

Index